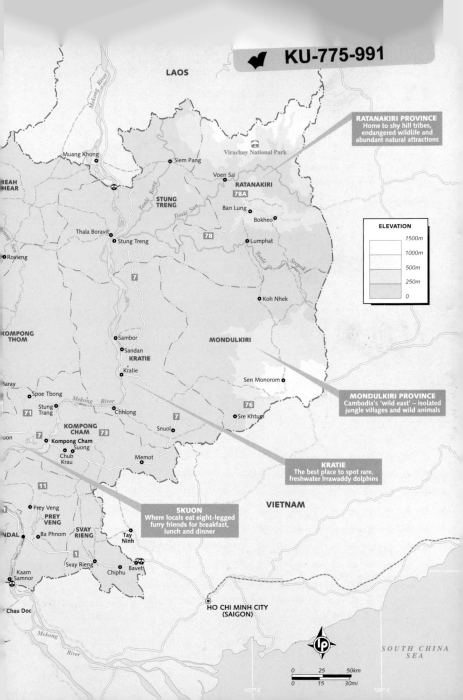

KU-775-991

LAOS

Muang Khong

Siem Pang

Voen Sai

Virachay National Park

RATANAKIRI PROVINCE
Home to shy hill tribes,
endangered wildlife and
abundant natural attractions

RATANAKIRI

78A

Ban Lung

Bokheo

STUNG
TRENG

Thala Boravit

Stung Treng

Lumphat

Rovieng

ELEVATION

| 1500m |
| 1000m |
| 500m |
| 250m |
| 0 |

KOMPONG
THOM

Koh Nhek

Sambor

Sandan

MONDULKIRI

KRATIE

Kratie

Baray

Sen Monorom

Spoe Tbong

MONDULKIRI PROVINCE
Cambodia's 'wild east' – isolated
jungle villages and wild animals

Mekong River

Stung
Trang

Chhlong

76

KOMPONG
CHAM

Snuol

Sre Khtum

Memot

KRATIE
The best place to spot rare,
freshwater Irrawaddy dolphins

Kompong Cham

Suong

Chub
Krau

VIETNAM

11

Prey Veng

SKUON
Where locals eat eight-legged
furry friends for breakfast,
lunch and dinner

PREY
VENG

Ba Phnom

SVAY
RIENG

Tay
Ninh

Svay Rieng

Chiphu

Bavet

Kaam
Samnor

Chau Doc

**HO CHI MINH CITY
(SAIGON)**

Mekong River

SOUTH CHINA
SEA

0   25   50km
0   15   30mi

107° E   108° E

Cambodia
4th edition – August 2002
First published – September 1992

Published by
Lonely Planet Publications Pty Ltd ABN 36 005 607 983
90 Maribyrnong St, Footscray, Victoria 3011, Australia

Lonely Planet offices
Australia Locked Bag 1, Footscray, Victoria 3011
USA 150 Linden St, Oakland, CA 94607
UK 10a Spring Place, London NW5 3BH
France 1 rue du Dahomey, 75011 Paris

Photographs
Many of the images in this guide are available for licensing from
Lonely Planet Images.
www.lonelyplanetimages.com

Front cover photograph
Roots growing over doorway, Ta Prohm temple, Angkor
(Anders Blomqvist)

ISBN 1 74509 111 9

text & maps © Lonely Planet Publications Pty Ltd 2002
photos © photographers as indicated 2002

Printed by Craft Print International Ltd, Singapore

All rights reserved. No part of this publication may be reproduced,
stored in a retrieval system or transmitted in any form by any means,
electronic, mechanical, photocopying, recording or otherwise, except
brief extracts for the purpose of review, without the written permission
of the publisher.

Lonely Planet, the Lonely Planet logo, Lonely Planet Images, CitySync
and eKno are trade marks of Lonely Planet Publications Pty Ltd. Other
trade marks are the property of their respective owners.

Although the authors and Lonely Planet try to make the information as accurate as possible, we accept no responsibility for any loss, injury or inconvenience sustained by anyone using this book.

Cambodia

Nick Ray

LONELY PLANET PUBLICATIONS
Melbourne • Oakland • London • Paris

CAMBODIA

THAILAND

PRASAT PREAH VIHEAR
A dramatic mountaintop temple with breathtaking views

Prasat Preah Vihear

Chuor Phnom Dangkrek
(Dangkrek Mountains)

● Samraong

ODDAR MEANCHEY

Anlong Veng ●

● Choam Ksant

69

ANGKOR
Stunning ruins and religious monuments that once formed the heart of the Khmer empire

● Thmor Pouk

BANTEAY MEANCHEY

SIEM REAP

Kulen ●

Phnom Kulen National Park

● Siyong

Tbeng Meanchey

Aranya Prathet ● ● Poipet

● Kralanh

Svay Leu ●

▲ Phnom Kulen (487m)

Khrau ●

● Ta Seng

5

● Sisophon
● Mongkol Borei

67

6

🏯 *Angkor*

BATTAMBANG

● Kouk Kduoch

Siem Reap ●

● Dam Dek

BATTAMBANG
An elegant riverside town rich in colonial ambience

● Battambang

Tonlé Sap Lake

● Pailin

Kamping Poy

Reang Kesei

● Stoeng

Treng ●

57

Siung

Moung Russei ●

Kompong Thom ●

6

5

Pursat ● Krakor

Kompong Luong ●

▲ Phnom Krapang (1711m)

Stung Pouthisat

● Kompong Chhnang

Trat ●

Phnom Sam Koh ▲ (1717m)

PURSAT

KOMPONG CHHNANG

● Romeas

5

Ko Chang

Chuor Phnom Kravanh (Cardamom Mountains)

Phnom ▲ Knang Trapeang (1213m)

Phnom Aoral (1771m) ▲

Udong ●

12° N

Khlong Yai ●

Hat Lek ●

44

KOMPONG SPEU

PHNOM PENH

Krong Koh Kong ●

Takhmau ●

Ko Kut

PHNOM PENH
Revitalised capital city with wats and French-colonial architecture blended with a cosmopolitan restaurant and nightlife scene

KOH KONG

Kompong Speu ●

Koh Kong ●

48

Kirirom National Park 🏕

46

4

2

Boutum Sakor National Park 🏕

Sre Ambel ●

3

Chuor Phnom Damrei (Elephant Mountains)

Angk Tasaom ●

Takeo ●

Phnom Da

BOKOR NATIONAL PARK
Remote jungle, abandoned hill stations and amazing views of the Gulf of Thailand

Koh Samit ●

4

KAMPOT

Chhuk ●

TAKE

11° N

Gulf of Kompong Som

Bokor National Park

Tani ●

31

Tuk Meas ●

Bokor Hill Station

3

Koh Rong ●

Veal Renh ●

Kampot ●

33

Gulf of Thailand

Koh Rong Samloem ●

Sihanoukville ●

Koh Thmei

Kep National Park 🏕 ● Kep

Ha Tien ●

SIHANOUKVILLE
Empty beaches, tropical islands, fresh seafood and buzzing nightlife

Ream National Park

Koh Tonsay

Phu Quoc Island

102° E

103° E

Contents – Text

Contents – Maps

MAP INDEX

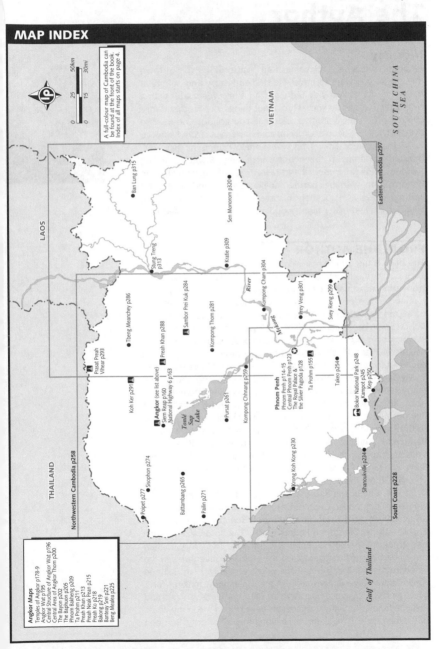

Angkor Maps
Temples of Angkor p178-9
Angkor Wat p195
Central Structure of Angkor Wat p196
Central Area of Angkor Thom p200
The Bayon p202
The Baphuon p205
Phnom Bakheng p209
Ta Prohm p211
Preah Khan p213
Preah Neak Pean p215
Preah Ko p218
Bakong p219
Banteay Srei p221
Beng Mealea p225

A full-colour map of Cambodia can be found at the front of the book. Index of all maps starts on page 4.

Northwestern Cambodia p258

THAILAND

LAOS

VIETNAM

Eastern Cambodia p297

SOUTH CHINA SEA

South Coast p228

Gulf of Thailand

0   25   50km
0   15   30mi

Ban Lung p315

Sen Monorom p320

Stung Treng p313

Kratie p309

Kompong Cham p304

Mekong River

Prey Veng p301

Svey Rieng p299

Tbeng Meanchey p286

Preah Khan p288

Sambor Prei Kuk p284

Prasat Preah Vihear p293

Koh Ker p291

Kompong Thom p281

Siem Reap p160
Angkor (see list above)
National Highway 6 p163

Poipet p277

Sisophon p274

Kompong Chhnang p259

Tonlé Sap Lake

Pursat p261

Phnom Penh p114-15
Central Phnom Penh p123
The Royal Palace & the Silver Pagoda p128

Ta Prohm p155

Takeo p254

Bokor National Park p248

Kep p250

Kampot p245

Battambang p265

Pailin p271

Krong Koh Kong p230

Sihanoukville p234

The Author

Nick Ray

A Londoner of sorts, Nick comes from Watford, the sort of town that makes you want to travel. He studied history and politics at the University of Warwick and emerged a few years later with a certificate that said he knew stuff about things, or was that things about stuff? After a stint as a journalist in London, he headed overseas, leading people astray on adventure tours from Morocco to Vietnam. Since linking up with Lonely Planet, he has contributed to about a dozen titles, including: *Britain; Cycling Vietnam, Laos & Cambodia;* and *East Africa*. He currently lives in Phnom Penh with his partner Kulikar Sotho, and when not writing, works as a location manager and scout for television, commercials and major films, including *Tomb Raider* in 2000.

FROM THE AUTHOR

This book is the sum of many parts. As always, a huge thank you goes out to the people of Cambodia: the Khmers are warm and wonderful with an abundance of strength, spirit and stoicism. One Cambodian in particular helped to make this book possible with her constant love, support and encouragement over the past few years. Kulikar Sotho has shared the highs and lows of life on the road, from staring down across the forests of Cambodia from the dizzying heights of Prasat Preah Vihear, to the true misery of some of the country's most horrible trails. I look forward to our future together.

My parents have been unwavering in their love and support, and many of my friends have made it out here, including, more recently, Andy Richardson on a 'cultural exchange' with his break-dance demonstration at Phnom Penh's Fine Arts School. A big hello also to Chris Johnson, Andrew Dear, Andrew Johnson, Andrew Burke, Paul Ladd, Anthony Euden, Fiona Thompson, Tara Burke, Tam Wiltshire, Dan Prince, Nik Baldwin, Michelle Kirschner, Alan Buxton, Steve and Linda Prince, and Gren and Elaine Kershaw. The rest of you, you know the door is always open.

Back in Cambodia, Sotho Tan (Ma) is a great example to the women of Cambodia. Choulean Ang (Mia) of Apsara Authority is an eminent historian and his assistant Im Sokrithy a good friend. Thanks also to Christophe Poittier at EFEO, who provided much background on remote temples in Cambodia. John McGeoghan has a heart of gold and has joined me on many adventures in the kingdom, as has Ian Felton at the British embassy. Alan Bell and Ambassador Steve Bridges are also great company, making for a lively embassy crowd. A big hello to Paul Im, Lindsay Watt and Philippe Janowski. Many Cambodians have helped me in my work, but some people have gone well beyond the call of duty. Bunthon in Siem Reap has survived some wet-season trips to remote temples in Preah Vihear, while Rith has kept a constant eye on bars and restaurants that are popping up by the week. Thanks to Sun Ming and Nara in Phnom Penh for help with language issues, as well as Heng (Lucky), one of the most clued-up moto drivers in the city. Thanks also to Ministry of Tourism staff who managed to provide new base maps for this edition. HE Veng Sereyvuth, minister of tourism, is committed to bringing Cambodia to the world stage and is a lively ambassador for his country.

Many friends from the world of film and television have shared great experiences with me in Cambodia: Ian Wright, Donal Geraghty, Sam Breckman, Terry Wells, Ian Glen, Lloyd Levin, Jean-Jacques Annaud and Christophe Cheysson. One final thank you to the team at Lonely Planet headquarters who have worked on this edition. They have been a pleasure to work with and have made a significant contribution to what I believe to be a better book in every way. And a big sorry to all those I have missed but there is just no more space…

This Book

From the Publisher

Nick Ray thoroughly revised and expanded this 4th edition of *Cambodia*. His work on the 3rd edition built on the efforts of Chris Taylor, who updated the original guide written by Tony Wheeler & Daniel Robinson.

This edition of *Cambodia* was coordinated in Lonely Planet's Melbourne office by Rebecca Hobbs (editing) and Jacqui Saunders (mapping and design). Jane Thompson, Victoria Harrison and Simone Egger assisted with editing, while Nina Rousseau and Kyla Gillzan helped out with proofing. Chris Love assisted with mapping. Leonie Mugavin checked travel information and Shahara Ahmed cast an eye over all health matters. Quentin Frayne and Emma Koch organised the Language chapter with help from Ta Rath, and Sun Ming in Cambodia was invaluable in providing Khmer script. Mark Germanchis lent Quark support, Maria Vallianos designed the cover and Glenn Beanland from LPI provided the photographs. Meredith Mail and Jack Gavran assisted with layout checks and Nicholas Stebbing helped generate the index. A particularly big thank you to Jane and Chris for their patient guidance and to Bruce Evans for answering a never-ending stream of questions.

THANKS
Many thanks to the travellers who used the last edition and wrote to us with helpful hints, advice and interesting anecdotes. Your names appear in the back of this book.

Foreword

ABOUT LONELY PLANET GUIDEBOOKS

The story begins with a classic travel adventure: Tony and Maureen Wheeler's 1972 journey across Europe and Asia to Australia. There was no useful information about the overland trail then, so Tony and Maureen published the first Lonely Planet guidebook to meet a growing need.

From a kitchen table, Lonely Planet has grown to become the largest independent travel publisher in the world, with offices in Melbourne (Australia), Oakland (USA), London (UK) and Paris (France).

Today Lonely Planet guidebooks cover the globe. There is an ever-growing list of books and information in a variety of media. Some things haven't changed. The main aim is still to make it possible for adventurous travellers to get out there – to explore and better understand the world.

At Lonely Planet we believe travellers can make a positive contribution to the countries they visit – if they respect their host communities and spend their money wisely. Since 1986 a percentage of the income from each book has been donated to aid projects and human rights campaigns, and, more recently, to wildlife conservation.

Although inclusion in a guidebook usually implies a recommendation we cannot list every good place. Exclusion does not necessarily imply criticism. In fact there are a number of reasons why we might exclude a place – sometimes it is simply inappropriate to encourage an influx of travellers.

UPDATES & READER FEEDBACK

Things change – prices go up, schedules change, good places go bad and bad places go bankrupt. Nothing stays the same. So, if you find things better or worse, recently opened or long-since closed, please tell us and help make the next edition even more accurate and useful.

Lonely Planet thoroughly updates each guidebook as often as possible – usually every two years, although for some destinations the gap can be longer. Between editions, up-to-date information is available in our free, quarterly *Planet Talk* newsletter and monthly email bulletin *Comet*. The *Upgrades* section of our website (W www.lonelyplanet.com) is also regularly updated by Lonely Planet authors, and the site's *Scoop* section covers news and current affairs relevant to travellers. Lastly, the *Thorn Tree* bulletin board and *Postcards* section carry unverified, but fascinating, reports from travellers.

Tell us about it! We genuinely value your feedback. A well-travelled team at Lonely Planet reads and acknowledges every email and letter we receive and ensures that every morsel of information finds its way to the relevant authors, editors and cartographers.

Everyone who writes to us will find their name listed in the next edition of the appropriate guidebook, and will receive the latest issue of *Comet* or *Planet Talk*. The very best contributions will be rewarded with a free guidebook.

We may edit, reproduce and incorporate your comments in Lonely Planet products such as guidebooks, websites and digital products, so let us know if you don't want your comments reproduced or your name acknowledged.

How to contact Lonely Planet:
Online: e talk2us@lonelyplanet.com.au, W www.lonelyplanet.com
Australia: Locked Bag 1, Footscray, Victoria 3011
UK: 10a Spring Place, London NW5 3BH
USA: 150 Linden St, Oakland, CA 94607

Introduction

Cambodia is back on the map! The word is out, Cambodia is *the* place to be in Asia right now and no longer a country where visitors need fear tread. Peace has come to this beautiful yet blighted land after three decades of civil war and the Cambodian people are opening their arms to the world. Now is the perfect time to witness this rebirth of a nation before it becomes just another stop on the tourist merry-go-round.

For far too long, war combined with a vast communist-inspired 'experiment' removed Cambodia from the tourist map. The very word Cambodia came to be associated with atrocities, poverty and refugees. The tragedy of it all belonged to the Cambodians themselves, but it was also a great loss to travellers in Asia.

During much of the 1990s Cambodia remained a difficult country in which to travel due to the presence of Khmer Rouge guerrillas in many provinces. If that wasn't enough to scare people away, then the politicians in Phnom Penh usually managed to cook up a crisis that would deter those contemplating a fleeting visit. However, the long and bloody civil war is definitively over and the Khmer Rouge is no longer terrorising the people of Cambodia. This is good news, not just for the country's stoical people, but also for tourists planning a trip to Cambodia, as all of the country is open for exploration, most of which could not be visited just a few years ago.

Cambodia lies at the heart of Indochina, bordered by Thailand to the west, Laos and Thailand to the north and Vietnam to the east. It is a fascinating place that, despite its tiny size and large, powerful neighbours, has managed to remain uniquely Khmer. Its cultural traditions have travelled the passage of time, predating those of Thailand, and unlike Vietnam, which was always influenced by China, its dominant influences stem from the Indian subcontinent.

Modern-day Cambodia is the successor-state to the mighty Khmer empire, which

during the Angkorian period (9th to 14th centuries AD) was the cultural heartland of Southeast Asia. It ruled over much of what is now Vietnam, Laos and Thailand, and its legacy is one of the wonders of the world. The ruins of Angkor are in a class of their own: there is no other historical site in Southeast Asia that matches their grandeur. The traveller's first glimpse of Angkor Wat, which represents the full flowering of Khmer genius, is a breathtaking experience, matched by only a few places on earth such as the Great Pyramid of Giza or Machu Picchu in Peru.

Cambodia has enormous potential as a travel destination, and investors are moving in with an eye to the day when tourists arrive in the numbers that nearby Thailand enjoys. The land borders with Thailand are now open to foreigners and there are direct flights between Siem Reap and many neighbouring capitals. Angkor is once more at the forefront of visitor's minds on a journey to Southeast Asia, as it was before the war cast a shadow over this kingdom. To talk in terms of millions may sound fanciful, but with the temples of Angkor, Cambodia has something unique that none of its neighbours can rival. It also has empty beaches and islands along the south coast, with barely a bungalow in sight, and isolated national parks that are just starting to see the first trickle of visitors. The meandering Mekong River holds the promise of boat trips through Cambodia, north into Laos or south to Vietnam's Mekong Delta. Its mighty waters also provide a habitat for some of the last remaining freshwater dolphins in Asia. In the northeast of the country are wild and mountainous landscapes, home to Cambodia's ethnic minorities and much of the country's diminishing wildlife and forest. Lost in the jungles of the north are countless mysterious temple complexes, forgotten to the world for several long and turbulent decades, offering the visitor the chance to capture the emotions of explorers of old.

Finally there are the people. Cambodians have weathered years of bloodshed, poverty and political instability. Somehow they have come through the experience with smiles still intact. Admittedly Cambodia needs the money that tourism brings, but there is an air of genuine enthusiasm and warmth towards foreign visitors. Nobody comes away from Cambodia without a measure of admiration and affection for the inhabitants of this beautiful yet troubled country.

Facts about Cambodia

HISTORY
Early Beginnings
Cambodia came into being, so the legend goes, through the union of a princess and a foreigner. The foreigner was an Indian Brahman named Kaundinya. The princess was the daughter of a dragon king who ruled over a watery land. One day, as Kaundinya sailed by, the princess paddled out in a boat to greet him. Kaundinya shot an arrow from his magic bow into her boat, causing the princess to fearfully agree to marriage. In need of a dowry, her father drank up the waters of his land and presented them to Kaundinya to rule over. The new kingdom was named Kambuja.

Like many legends, this one is historically opaque, but it does say something about the cultural forces that brought Cambodia into existence; in particular its relationship with its great subcontinental neighbour, India. Cambodia's religious, royal and written traditions stemmed from India and began to coalesce as a cultural entity in their own right between the 1st and 4th centuries AD.

Very little is known about prehistoric Cambodia. A large area of modern-day Cambodia was under water as recently as 6000 years ago. Much of the southeast was a vast, shallow gulf that was progressively silted up by the mouths of the Mekong, leaving pancake-flat, mineral-rich land ideal for farming. Evidence of cave dwellers has been found in the northwest of Cambodia. Carbon dating on ceramic pots found in the area shows that they were made around 4200 BC, but it is difficult to say whether there is a direct relationship between these cave-dwelling pot makers and contemporary Khmers. Examinations of bones dating back to around 1500 BC, however, suggest that the people living in Cambodia at that time resembled the Cambodians of today.

Archaeological evidence shows that prior to 1000 BC Cambodians lived in houses on stilts (as they do today), and subsisted on a diet that included large quantities of fish and cultivated rice. Early Chinese records report that the Cambodians were 'ugly' and 'dark' and went about naked; but a pinch of salt is always required when reading the culturally chauvinistic reports of imperial China concerning its 'barbarian' neighbours.

Indianisation & Funan
The early Indianisation of Cambodia probably occurred via trading settlements that sprang up from the 1st century AD on the coastline of what is now southern Vietnam, but was then inhabited by Cambodians. Such settlements served as ports of call for boats following the trading route from the Bay of Bengal to the southern provinces of China. The largest of these nascent kingdoms was known as Funan by the Chinese, and may have existed across an area between Ba Phnom in Prey Veng Province and Oc-Eo in Kien Giang Province in southern Vietnam. It would have been contemporaneous with Champasak in southern Laos (then known as Kuruksetra) and other lesser fiefdoms in the region.

Funan is a Chinese name, and it may be a transliteration of the ancient Khmer word *bnam* (mountain). Although very little is known about Funan, much has been made of its importance as an early Southeast Asian centre of power despite there being little evidence to support this.

It is most likely that between the 1st and 8th centuries AD Cambodia was a collection of small states, each with its own elites that sometimes strategically intermarried and sometimes went to war with one another. Funan was no doubt one of these states, and as a major sea port was undoubtedly pivotal in the transmission of Indian culture into the interior of Cambodia.

What historians do know about Funan they have mostly gleaned from Chinese sources. These report that Funan-period

Cambodia (1st to 6th centuries AD) embraced the worship of the Hindu deities Shiva and Vishnu and, at the same time, Buddhism. The *linga* (phallic totem) appears to have been the focus of ritual and an emblem of kingly might, a feature that was to evolve further in the Angkorian cult of the god king (see Angkorian Period later). The people practised primitive irrigation, which enabled the cultivation of rice, and traded raw commodities such as spices with China and India.

Chenla Period

From the 6th century the Funan kingdom's importance as a port declined, and Cambodia's population gradually concentrated along the Mekong and Tonlé Sap Rivers (as is the case today). The move may be related to the development of wet-rice agriculture. From the 6th to the 8th centuries it was likely that Cambodia was a collection of competing kingdoms, ruled by autocratic kings who legitimised their absolute rule through hierarchical social concepts borrowed from India.

This era is generally referred to as the Chenla period. Again, as is the case with Funan, it is a Chinese term and there is little to support the idea that the Chenla was a unified kingdom that held sway over all Cambodia. Indeed, the Chinese themselves referred to 'water Chenla' and 'land Chenla'. Water Chenla was located around Angkor Borei, near the present-day provincial capital of Takeo; and land Chenla in the upper reaches of the Mekong River and east of the Tonlé Sap lake, around Sambor Prei Kuk, the region's first temple city.

Still, the people of Cambodia were well known to the Chinese, and gradually the region was becoming more cohesive. Before long the fractured kingdoms of Cambodia would merge to become the greatest empire in Southeast Asia.

Angkorian Period

An inscription at the sacred mountain of Phnom Kulen, northeast of Angkor, reads that in AD 802 Jayavarman II participated in a ritual that proclaimed him a 'universal monarch', or a *devaraja* (god king). Who was Jayavarman II and what was he doing before this? It is thought he may have resided in the Buddhist Shailendras' court in Java as a young man. One of the first things he did when he returned to Cambodia was to hold a ritual to reject Javanese control of the lands of Cambodia. From this point, Jayavarman II brought the lands of Cambodia under his control through alliances and conquests, proclaiming himself king in the process.

Jayavarman II was the first of a long succession of kings who presided over the rise and fall of the Southeast Asian empire that was to leave the stunning legacy of Angkor. The first records of the massive irrigation works that supported the population of Angkor date to the reign of Indravarman I (877–89). His rule also marks the beginning of Angkorian art, with the building of temples in the Roluos area, notably the Bakong. His son Yasovarman I (reigned 889–910) moved the royal court to Angkor proper, establishing a temple mountain on the summit of Phnom Bakheng.

By the turn of the 11th century the kingdom of Angkor was losing control of its territories. Suryavarman I (reigned 1002–49), an usurper, moved into the power vacuum and, like Jayavarman II two centuries before, reunified the kingdom through war and alliances. He annexed the kingdom of Lopburi in Thailand and widened his control of Cambodia, stretching the empire to perhaps its greatest extent. A pattern was beginning to emerge, and can be seen throughout the Angkorian period: dislocation and turmoil, followed by reunification and further expansion under a powerful king. Architecturally, the most productive periods occurred after periods of turmoil, indicating that newly incumbent monarchs felt the need to celebrate and perhaps legitimise their rule with massive building projects.

By 1066 Angkor was again riven by conflict, becoming the focus of rival bids for power. It was not until 1112, with the accession of Suryavarman II, that the kingdom was again unified. Suryavarman II embarked on another phase of expansion, waging wars in Vietnam and the region of southern Vietnam known as Champa. He also established links with China. But Suryavarman II will mostly be remembered as the king who, in his devotion to the Hindu deity Vishnu, commissioned the unrivalled Angkor Wat.

Suryavarman II had brought Champa to heel and reduced it to vassal status. In 1177, however, the Chams struck back with a naval expedition up the Mekong and into Tonlé Sap lake. They took the city of Angkor by surprise and put King Dharanindravarman II to death. A year later a cousin of Suryavarman II gathered forces about him and defeated the Chams in another naval battle. The new leader was crowned in 1181 as Jayavarman VII.

A devout follower of Mahayana Buddhism, Jayavarman VII built the city of Angkor Thom and many other monuments. Indeed, most of the monuments visited by tourists in Angkor today were constructed during Jayavarman VII's reign. He also commissioned a vast array of public works. But as David Chandler points out in his *History of Cambodia,* Jayavarman VII is a figure of many contradictions. The bas-reliefs of the Bayon, for example, depict him presiding over battles of terrible ferocity, while statues of the king show him in a meditative, otherworldly aspect. His programme of temple construction and other public works was carried out in great haste, no doubt bringing enormous hardship to the labourers who provided the muscle, and thus accelerating the decline of the empire. He was partly driven by a desire to legitimise his rule, as there may have been other contenders closer to the royal bloodline, and partly by the need to introduce a new religion to a population predominantly Hindu in faith.

For more on the Angkorian period see the 'Temples of Angkor' special section.

Decline & Fall

Some scholars maintain that decline was hovering in the wings at the time Angkor Wat was built, when the Angkorian empire was at the height of its remarkable productivity. There are indications that the irrigation network was overworked and slowly starting to silt up due to the massive deforestation that had taken place in the heavily populated areas to the north and east of Angkor. Massive construction projects such as Angkor Wat and Angkor Thom no doubt put an enormous strain on the royal coffers and on the common people who subsidised them in taxes and hard work. Certainly, after the reign of Jayavarman VII, temple construction effectively came to a halt, in large part because Jayavarman VII's public works quarried local sandstone into oblivion and the people were exhausted.

Another important aspect of this period was the decline of Cambodian political influence on the peripheries of its empire. The Thai kingdom of Ayuthaya, on the other hand, grew in strength and made repeated incursions into Angkor, sacking the city in 1431. During this period, perhaps drawn by the opportunities for sea trade with China and fearful of the increasingly bellicose Thais, the Khmer elite began to migrate to the Phnom Penh area.

The next 150 years of Khmer history was dominated by dynastic rivalries and almost continuous warfare with the Thais. Although the Khmers once pushed westward all the way to the Thai capital of Ayuthaya (only to find it occupied by the Burmese), the Thais recovered and dealt a crushing blow to the Khmers by capturing their capital of Lovek in 1594.

Shortly before the Khmer defeat, the Cambodian king, Satha, requested the assistance of the Spanish and Portuguese, who had recently become active in the region. In 1596 a Spanish expedition arrived in Cambodia to assist Satha, only to find that he had been deposed by an usurper, Chung Prei. After a series of disagreements and the sacking of the Chinese quarter of Phnom Penh by Spanish forces, the Spanish attacked the palace and killed Chung Prei. The Spanish then decided to return to Manila, but while marching through Laos they changed their minds and returned to Phnom Penh, installing one of Satha's sons on the throne. Resentment of the power wielded by the Spanish grew among court officials until, in 1599, the Spanish garrison at Phnom Penh was massacred. Shortly thereafter, Satha's brother ascended the throne with the help of the Thais.

The Dark Ages

From about 1600 until the arrival of the French in 1863, Cambodia was ruled by a series of weak kings who, because of continual challenges by dissident members of the royal family, were forced to seek the protection – granted, of course, at a price – of either Thailand or Vietnam. In the 17th century, assistance from the Nguyen lords of southern Vietnam was given on the condition that Vietnamese be allowed to settle in what is now the Mekong Delta region of Vietnam, at that time part of Cambodia and today still referred to by the Khmers as Kampuchea Krom (Lower Cambodia). Ho Chi Minh City (Saigon) was then a small Cambodian village known as Prey Nokor.

In the west, the Thais established dominion over the provinces of Battambang and Siem Reap from 1794; by the late 18th century they had firm control of the Cambodian royal family. Indeed, one king was crowned in Bangkok and placed on the throne at Udong with the help of the Thai army. That Cambodia survived through the 18th century as a distinct entity is due to the preoccupations of its neighbours: while the Thais were expending their energy and resources in fighting the Burmese, the Vietnamese were wholly absorbed by internal strife. This pattern of dynastic rivalry and political infighting, a betrayal of the people's trust, continues even today.

French Rule

Cambodia's dual Thai and Vietnamese suzerainty ended in 1864, when French gunboats intimidated King Norodom I (reigned 1860–1904) into signing a treaty of protectorate. French control of Cambodia, which developed as an adjunct to French-colonial interests in Vietnam, at first involved relatively little direct interference in Cambodia's affairs of state. However, the French presence did prevent Cambodia's expansionist neighbours from annexing any more Khmer territory and helped keep Norodom on the throne despite the ambitions of his rebellious half-brothers.

By the 1870s French officials in Cambodia began pressing for greater control over internal affairs. In 1884 Norodom was forced into signing a treaty that turned his country into a virtual colony. This sparked a two-year rebellion that constituted the only major anti-French movement in Cambodia until after WWII. This uprising ended when the king was persuaded to call upon the rebel fighters to lay down their weapons in exchange for a return to the pre-treaty arrangement.

During the next two decades senior Cambodian officials, who saw certain advantages in acquiescing to French power, opened the door to direct French control over the day-to-day administration of the country. At the same time the French maintained Norodom's court in a splendour probably unequalled since the Angkorian period, thereby greatly enhancing the symbolic position of the monarchy. The king's increased stature served to legitimise the Cambodian state, thereby pre-empting the growth of any broad-based nationalist movement, a situation in marked contrast to that in Vietnam. Indeed, the only large-scale popular protest of any kind between the 1880s and the 1940s was an essentially peaceful peasant uprising in 1916, which ended when the king agreed to consider their grievances.

King Norodom I was succeeded by King Sisowath (reigned 1904–27), who was then followed by King Monivong (reigned 1927–41). Upon King Monivong's death, the French governor general of Japanese-occupied Indochina, Admiral Jean Decoux, placed 19-year-old Prince Norodom Sihanouk on the Cambodian throne. The choice was based on the assumption that Sihanouk would prove pliable; this proved to be a major miscalculation.

During WWII, Japanese forces occupied much of Asia, and Cambodia was no exception. However, with many in France collaborating with the occupying forces in mainland Europe, the Japanese were happy to let these French allies control affairs in Cambodia. The price was conceding to Thailand (a Japanese ally of sorts) much of Battambang and Siem Reap Provinces, areas that weren't returned until 1947. However, with the fall of Paris in 1944 and coordinated French policy in disarray, the Japanese were forced to take direct control of the territory by early 1945. After WWII the French returned, making Cambodia an 'autonomous state within the French Union', but retaining de facto control. The years after 1945 were marked by strife among the country's various political groupings, a situation made more unstable by the Franco–Viet Minh War then raging in Vietnam and Laos, which spilled over into parts of Cambodia. The Vietnamese, as they were also to do 20 years later in the war against Lon Nol, trained and fought with bands of Khmer Issarak and Khmer Serei against the French authorities.

Independence & Sihanouk's Rule

In January 1953 King Sihanouk, who had been at odds with the dominant Democratic Party, took decisive action. He dissolved the parliament, declared martial law and embarked on what became known as the 'royal crusade': his travelling campaign to drum up international support for his country's independence.

Independence was proclaimed on 9 November 1953 and recognised by the Geneva Conference of May 1954, which ended French control of Indochina. However, internal political turmoil continued, much of it the result of conflicts between Sihanouk and his domestic opponents. In March 1955 Sihanouk abdicated in favour of his father Norodom Suramarit to pursue a career as a politician. His newly established party, Sangkum Reastr Niyum (People's Socialist Community Party), won every seat in parliament in the September 1955 elections. Sihanouk dominated Cambodian politics for the next 15 years, serving as prime minister until his father's death in 1960 and, when no new king was named, also as head of state.

Although he feared the Vietnamese communists, during the early 1960s Sihanouk considered South Vietnam and Thailand, both allies of the USA (which he mistrusted), the greatest threats to Cambodia's security and even survival. He was particularly shaken by the overthrow and subsequent murder of President Ngo Diem of South Vietnam in an American-backed coup in 1963. Diem had been a staunch ally of Washington, so what hope was there for an unreliable Sihanouk? In an attempt to fend off these many dangers, he declared Cambodia neutral in international affairs and refused to accept any further US aid, which had accounted for a substantial chunk of the country's military budget. He also nationalised many industries, including the rice trade. In May 1965 Sihanouk, convinced that the USA had been plotting against him and his family, broke diplomatic relations with Washington and tilted towards North Vietnam, the Viet Cong and China. In addition, he accepted that the North Vietnamese army and the Viet Cong would use Cambodian territory in their battle against South Vietnam and the USA.

These moves and his socialist economic policies alienated right-leaning elements in Cambodian society, including the officer corps of the army and the urban elite. At the same time, left-wing Cambodians, many of them educated abroad, deeply resented his internal policies, which did not allow for political dissent. Compounding Sihanouk's problems was the fact that all classes were fed up with the pervasive corruption in government ranks, some of it uncomfortably close to the queen's family. Although most peasants – the vast majority of the population – revered Sihanouk as a semidivine figure, in 1967 a rural-based rebellion broke out in Samlot, Battambang, leading him to conclude that the greatest threat to his regime came from the left. Bowing to pressure from the army, he implemented a policy of harsh repression against left-wingers.

By 1969 the conflict between the army and leftist rebels had become more serious, as the Vietnamese sought sanctuary deeper in Cambodia. Sihanouk's political position had also greatly deteriorated – due in no small part to his obsession with filmmaking, which was leading him to neglect affairs of state. In March 1970, while Sihanouk was on a trip to France, General Lon Nol and Prince Sisowath Sirik Matak, Sihanouk's cousin, deposed him as chief of state, apparently with tacit US consent. Sihanouk took up residence in Beijing, where he set up a government-in-exile nominally in control of an indigenous Cambodian revolutionary movement that Sihanouk had nicknamed the Khmer Rouge. This was a definitive moment in contemporary Cambodian history: the Khmer Rouge exploited its partnership with Sihanouk to draw new recruits into their small organisation. Many former Khmer Rouge fighters argue that they 'went

King Sihanouk

Norodom Sihanouk has been a constant presence in the topsy-turvy world of Cambodian politics. A colourful character of many enthusiasms and shifting political positions, his amatory exploits tended to dominate his early reputation. Later he became the prince who stage-managed the close of French colonialism, autocratically led an independent Cambodia, was imprisoned by the Khmer Rouge and, from privileged exile, finally returned triumphant as king. Whatever else he may be, he is certainly a survivor.

Sihanouk was born in 1922, the only son of Prince Norodom Suramarit, grandson of King Norodom (1860–1904), and Princess Sisowath Kossamak, daughter of King Sisowath Monivong (1927–41). He was not an obvious contender for the throne; the French saw the young prince as a pliant monarch. He was crowned in 1941, at just 19 years old, with his education incomplete. And in the four years before the Japanese arrived and presented Cambodia briefly with the gift of liberation, he was all the French had hoped he would be.

With the French-colonial masters removed, however, Sihanouk promptly abolished two French laws: the first was the compulsory Romanisation of the Khmer alphabet; the second was the enforcement of the Gregorian calendar over the traditional lunar one. This was, it must be said, his only act of defiance in five months of de facto independence, but it marks the cautious beginning of Sihanouk's involvement in politics.

Sihanouk acquiesced quietly to the return of French rule in August 1945. But by 1952 he had embarked on his self-styled 'royal crusade' for independence. He began it by dismissing an elected government and appointing himself prime minister, announcing that within three years Cambodia would be independent. He embarked on a lobbying and publicity campaign in France and the USA, a brief defiant exile in Thailand, and sponsored a civil militia that attracted some 100,000 volunteers. The French backed out of Cambodia in late 1953.

A year after achieving independence, Sihanouk made one of his characteristically unpredictable decisions: he would abdicate. Thwarted in his attempts to revise the constitution and provide the throne with far-reaching political powers, he was probably afraid of being marginalised to the pomp of royal ceremony. The 'royal crusader' became 'citizen Sihanouk'. He vowed never again to return to the throne. Meanwhile his father became king. It was a masterstroke that offered Sihanouk both royal authority and supreme political power.

Elections held in 1955 were marred by intimidating violence and voting fraud. Sihanouk's Sangkum Reastr Niyum (People's Socialist Community Party) won 83% of the vote. By this time he was in full political swing and had discovered a passion for rhetoric.

By the mid-1960s Sihanouk had been supreme commander of Cambodia for a decade. After innumerable love affairs, he had finally settled on Monique Izzi, the daughter of a Franco-Italian father and a Cambodian mother, as his consort. As war raged in Vietnam and leftist discontent with right-wing politics blossomed at home, Sihanouk launched his movie career.

The conventional wisdom was that 'Sihanouk is Cambodia' – his leadership was unassailable. But as the cinema took more and more of his time, Cambodia was being drawn inexorably into the

to the hills' (a euphemism for joining the Khmer Rouge) to fight for their king.

Lon Nol Regime

Sihanouk was condemned to death *in absentia,* an excessive move on the part of the new government, and one that effectively ruled out any chance for compromise over the next five years. Lon Nol gave communist Vietnamese forces an ultimatum to withdraw their forces within one week, which amounted to a virtual declaration of war, as no communists wanted to return to Vietnam to face the Americans. Pogroms against ethnic Vietnamese living in Cambodia soon broke out, prompting many to flee.

King Sihanouk

American war in Vietnam. Government troops battled with a leftist insurgency in the countryside, the economy was in tatters, and Sihanouk came to be regarded as a liability. His involvement in the film industry and his announcements that Cambodia was 'an oasis of peace' suggested a man who had not only abdicated from the throne but also from reality.

In early 1970, with forces gathering against him, Sihanouk briefly flirted with the idea of reclaiming the throne. Instead, he departed for France. On 18 March the National Assembly voted to remove Sihanouk from office. Not long after, Cambodia was declared a republic and Sihanouk was sentenced to death *in absentia.*

Sihanouk went into exile in Beijing and threw in his lot with the communists. It was a practical step. The communists aimed to topple the Lon Nol government, and this suited Sihanouk. When the Khmer Rouge marched into Phnom Penh on 17 April 1975, Sihanouk issued a statement in Beijing heralding the event as a great victory against imperialism.

In a deserted Phnom Penh, Sihanouk was confined to the Royal Palace as a prisoner of the Khmer Rouge. He remained there until early 1979 when, on the eve of the Vietnamese invasion, he was flown to Beijing. The Khmer Rouge killed many of Sihanouk's children, grandchildren and relatives, but curiously they spared the patriarch's life, no doubt under Chinese pressure.

It was to be more than a decade before Sihanouk finally returned to Cambodia. Meanwhile, against all odds, he was back at centre stage again, calling the shots, forming alliances with the Khmer Rouge and breaking them off. He clearly hadn't learned much from his first disastrous association with the group. After the May 1993 elections, Sihanouk suddenly announced that he was forming a coalition government with himself starring as president, prime minister and military leader. He failed.

Sihanouk never quite gave up wanting to be everything for Cambodia: international statesman, general, president, film director, man of the people. On 24 September 1993, after 38 years in politics, he settled once again for the role of king.

King Sihanouk remains a popular monarch in the countryside, but many urban Cambodians have less time for him, feeling he has allowed himself to be consistently outwitted, first by the Khmer Rouge and later by Hun Sen and the Cambodian People's Party (CPP). It is hard for him to detach himself from the political arena in Cambodia, as his son Prince Norodom Ranariddh leads the National United Front for an Independent, Peaceful and Cooperative Cambodia (Funcinpec), one of the country's leading parties.

The most important question regarding King Sihanouk, and one that has yet to be answered is: who will succeed him? It has yet to be decided by the heavily politicised committee, and should the king pass away in the meantime, the country could once again be plunged into chaos. One thing is certain: if the monarchy continues to exist in Cambodia, the new monarch, whoever it may be, will never match the presence of Sihanouk – the last in a long line of Angkor's god kings.

On 30 April 1970 US and South Vietnamese forces invaded Cambodia in an effort to rout some 40,000 or more Viet Cong and North Vietnamese troops who were using Cambodian bases in their war to overthrow the South Vietnamese government. As a result of the invasion, the Vietnamese communists withdrew deeper into Cambodia, thus posing an even greater threat to the Lon Nol government. Cambodia's tiny army never stood a chance and within the space of a few months Vietnamese forces and their Khmer Rouge allies controlled almost half the country. The ultimate humiliation came in July 1970 when the Vietnamese seized the temples of Angkor.

In 1969 the USA had begun a secret programme of bombing suspected communist base camps in Cambodia. For the next four years, until bombing was halted by the US Congress in August 1973, huge areas of the eastern half of the country were carpet-bombed by US B-52s, killing uncounted thousands of civilians and turning hundreds of thousands more into refugees. Some historians believe the bombing campaign may have killed as many as 250,000 Cambodians, as many targets were selected from maps drawn in 1970 that took little account of rural displacement created by the first wave of bombs. Undoubtedly, the bombing campaign helped the Khmer Rouge in their recruitment drive, as more and more peasants were losing family members to the aerial assaults. While the final, heaviest bombing in the first half of 1973 may have saved Phnom Penh from a premature fall, its ferocity also helped to harden the attitude of many Khmer Rouge cadres and may have contributed to the later brutality of the regime.

Savage fighting engulfed the entire country, bringing misery to millions of Cambodians; many fled rural areas for the relative safety of Phnom Penh and provincial capitals. Between 1970 and 1975 several hundred thousand people died in the fighting. During these years the Khmer Rouge came to play a dominant role in trying to overthrow the Lon Nol regime. It was strengthened by the support of the Vietnamese, although the Khmer Rouge leadership would vehemently deny this from 1975 onwards. The Vietnamese had much more combat experience than their Khmer Rouge counterparts and it was their forces that took control of much of the north and east after Sihanouk was overthrown.

The leadership of the Khmer Rouge, including Paris-educated Pol Pot (formerly Saloth Sar) and Ieng Sary, had fled into the countryside in the 1960s to escape the summary justice then being meted out to suspected leftists by Sihanouk's security forces. They consolidated control over the movement and began to move against opponents before they took Phnom Penh. Many of the Vietnamese-trained Cambodian communists who had been based in Hanoi since the 1954 Geneva Accords returned down the Ho Chi Minh Trail to join the Khmer Rouge in 1970. Many were dead by 1975, executed on orders of the Pol Pot faction as they were perceived as a threat. Likewise, many moderate Sihanouk supporters who had joined the Khmer Rouge as a show of loyalty to their fallen leader rather than a show of ideology to the radicals were victims of purges before the regime took power. This set a precedent for internal purges and mass executions that was to eventually bring the downfall of the Khmer Rouge.

It didn't take long for the Lon Nol government to become very unpopular as a result of unprecedented greed and corruption in its ranks. As the USA bankrolled the war, government and military personnel found lucrative means to make a fortune, such as inventing 'phantom soldiers' and pocketing their pay, or selling weapons to the enemy. Lon Nol was widely perceived as an ineffectual leader, obsessed by superstition, fortune tellers and mystical crusades. This perception increased with his stroke in March 1971 and for the next four years his grip on reality seemed to weaken as his corrupt brother Lon Non's power grew.

Despite massive US military and economic aid, Lon Nol never succeeded in gaining the initiative against the Khmer Rouge, which pursued a strategy of rural attrition. Large parts of the countryside fell to the rebels and many provincial capitals were cut off from Phnom Penh. Lon Nol fled the country in early April 1975, leaving Sirik Matak in charge, who refused evacuation to the end. 'I cannot alas leave in such a cowardly fashion…I have committed only one mistake, that of believing in you, the Americans' were the words Sirik Matak poignantly penned to US ambassador John Gunther Dean. On 17 April 1975 – two weeks before the fall of Saigon (now Ho Chi Minh City) – Phnom Penh surrendered to the Khmer Rouge.

Khmer Rouge Regime

Upon taking Phnom Penh, the Khmer Rouge implemented one of the most radical and brutal restructurings of a society ever attempted; its goal was to transform Cambodia into a Maoist, peasant-dominated agrarian cooperative. Within two weeks of the Khmer Rouge coming to power the entire population of the capital and provincial towns, including the sick, elderly and infirm, was forced to march out to the countryside and undertake slave labour in mobile work teams – preparing the fields, digging irrigation canals – for 12 to 15 hours a day. Disobedience of any sort often brought immediate execution. The advent of Khmer Rouge rule was proclaimed Year Zero. Currency was abolished and postal services were halted. Except for one fortnightly flight to Beijing (China was providing aid and advisers to the Khmer Rouge), the country was cut off from the outside world.

Sihanouk returned to Phnom Penh in September 1975 as titular chief of state but resigned three months later. He remained in Phnom Penh, imprisoned in his palace and kept alive only at the insistence of the Chinese, who considered him useful. During the Vietnamese invasion of Cambodia in December 1978, Sihanouk was flown to Beijing to prevent him falling into the hands of the new government, as had he cooperated with his old Vietnamese friends it would have brought immediate legitimacy to the government.

In the eyes of Pol Pot the Khmer Rouge was not a unified movement, but a series of factions that needed to be cleansed. This process had begun previously with attacks on Vietnamese-trained Khmer Rouge and Sihanouk's supporters, but Pol Pot's initial fury upon seizing power was directed against the enemies of the former regime. All of the senior government and military figures who had been associated with Lon Nol were executed within days of the takeover. Many executions took place at a provincial level and were simply acts of anger, vengeance and frustration, but these began to peter out by summer 1975. The centre was gearing up for its assault on the outer regions, which had been separated into geographic zones. The loyalist Southwestern Zone forces under the control of Ta Mok were sent into region after region to purify the people, and thousands perished.

Much of the northwest has never been under Khmer Rouge control and many of the early regional leaders were former civil servants with no ideological affinity with the Khmer Rouge. This had made it an easier place to live, but when the purge began it arrived with a vengeance. Soldiers from the southwest would ask the local population to speak out against hardships under the revolution and the local leaders, and the many that did were taken away for execution.

The cleansing reached grotesque heights in the final and bloodiest purge against the powerful and independent Eastern Zone. Generally considered more moderate than other Khmer Rouge factions (although 'moderate' is hardly positive in the context of the regime), the Eastern Zone was closer to Vietnam. The Pol Pot faction consolidated the rest of the country before moving against the east from 1977 onwards. Hundreds of leaders were executed before open rebellion broke out and set the scene for a virtual civil war in the east. Many Eastern Zone leaders fled to Vietnam, forming the nucleus of the government installed by the Vietnamese in January 1979. The population was defenceless and distrusted – 'Cambodian bodies with Vietnamese minds' – and was deported to the northwest with new, blue *krama* (scarves). Had it not been for the Vietnamese invasion, all would have perished,

Blood Brother No 1

Pol Pot, Brother No 1 in the Khmer Rouge regime, is a name that sends shivers down the spines of most Cambodians and foreigners alike. It is Pol Pot who is most associated with the bloody madness of the regime he led between 1975 and 1979, and his policies heaped misery, suffering and death on millions of Cambodians. Even after being overthrown in 1979 he cast a long shadow over the Cambodian people: for many of them, just knowing he was still alive was traumatic and unjust. He died on 15 April 1998.

Pol Pot was born Saloth Sar in a small village near Kompong Thom in 1925. He had a relatively privileged upbringing and his education included, ironically, some time in a wat (Buddhist temple-monastery). As a young man he won a scholarship to study in Paris and spent several years there with Ieng Sary, who would later become foreign minister of Democratic Kampuchea. It is here that he is believed to have developed his radical Marxist thought, later to transform into the politics of extreme Maoist agrarianism. Back in Cambodia, Saloth Sar became a school teacher, entering politics in the late 1950s. Very little is known about his early political career.

During the 1960s Sihanouk switched from friend of the left to foe and back again, but in 1963 his repressive policies sent Saloth Sar and comrades fleeing to the jungles of Ratanakiri. It was from this time that he began to call himself Pol Pot, although it was not for a number of years that anyone would make the connection between the one-time teacher and the leader of Democratic Kampuchea. Once the Khmer Rouge was allied with Sihanouk, following his overthrow by Lon Nol in 1970 and subsequent exile in Beijing, its support soared and the faces of the leadership became familiar. However, Pol Pot remained a shadowy figure in the hierarchy, leaving the public duties to Khieu Samphan and Ieng Sary.

When the Khmer Rouge marched into Phnom Penh on 17 April 1975, few people could have anticipated the hell that was to come. Pol Pot, with the help of others, was the architect of one of the most radical and brutal revolutions in the history of mankind. Proclaimed as Year Zero, Cambodia was on a self-destructive course to sever all ties with the past.

Pol Pot was not to emerge as the public face of the revolution until the end of 1976, after returning from a trip to his mentors in Beijing. During his leadership he spent much of his time living in Phnom Penh, moving from residence to residence, paranoid about his security. He granted almost

as the blue krama was a secret party sign indicating an eastern enemy of the revolution.

It is still not known how many Cambodians died at the hands of the Khmer Rouge during the three years, eight months and 21 days (all Cambodians know this number too well) of its rule. The Vietnamese claimed three million deaths, while foreign experts long considered the number closer to one million. In early 1996 Yale University researchers undertaking ongoing investigations estimated that the figure is at least two million.

Several hundred thousand people were executed by the Khmer Rouge leadership, while hundreds of thousands more died of famine and disease. Meals consisted of little

more than watery rice porridge twice a day, meant to sustain men, women and children through a back-breaking day in the fields. Disease stalked the work camps, malaria and dysentery striking down whole families, death a relief for many from the horrors of life. Some zones were better than others, some leaders fairer than others, but life for the majority was one of unending misery and suffering.

As the centre eliminated more and more moderates, communal eating was introduced and family foraging outlawed as an act of individuals. Angkar (The Organisation) was now the only family people needed and those who did not agree were sought out and destroyed. The Khmer Rouge detached the

Blood Brother No 1

no interviews to foreign media and was seen only on propaganda movies produced by government television and on the occasional broadcast by Yugoslav journalists. Curiously enough, however, those who did meet Pol Pot during this period described him as a genial and charismatic man. Such was his aura and reputation that by the last year of the regime a cult of personality was developing around him and busts were produced.

He was fervently anti-Vietnamese, a sentiment fuelled by the pivotal role the Vietnamese played in arming and advising the Khmer Rouge during its jungle years. It was the Vietnamese that called the shots in the early days of the guerrilla war, something that rankled a fiercely patriotic Pol Pot. He was never to forget that the Vietnamese considered the Cambodian revolution of secondary importance to their own. Ironically, it was the Vietnamese that turned out to be his greatest enemy, invading Cambodia on 25 December 1978 and overthrowing the Khmer Rouge government on 7 January 1979. Pol Pot and his supporters were sent fleeing to the jungle near the Thai border, from where they spent the next decade launching attacks on government positions in Cambodia.

Pol Pot spent much of the 1980s living in an armed compound in Thailand, and with the connivance of both China and the West was able to rebuild his shattered forces and once again threaten the stability of Cambodia. It is thought he stepped down as nominal head of the Khmer Rouge in 1985, but no doubt continued to call the shots from behind the scenes as he had done in the earliest days of the revolution. Throughout the 1980s and 1990s his enigma increased as the international media speculated as to the real fate of Pol Pot. His demise was reported so often that when he finally passed away on 15 April 1998 many Cambodians refused to believe it until they had seen his body on television or in newspapers. Even then many were sceptical.

Pol Pot is a name known throughout the world, yet little is known about the man himself. Even the author of his biography *Brother Number One,* Cambodia expert David Chandler, could not find more than 200 pages to write about the man. He granted an interview to journalist Nate Thayer in 1997, but this was far from revealing as he disclaimed all responsibility for the excesses of his regime. It would be equally misleading to put together a portrait of the man from Khmer Rouge sources now living in Pailin, as it is all too easy to blame a dead man for the horrors of their rule. The truth about many episodes in his life will now never be known: he has carried his secrets to the grave.

Cambodian people from all they held dear: their families, their food, their fields and their faith. Even the peasants who had supported the revolution could no longer maintain their support. Nobody cared for the Khmer Rouge by 1978, but nobody had an ounce of strength to do anything about it...except the neighbourly Vietnamese.

Vietnamese Intervention

From 1976 to 1978, the xenophobic government in Phnom Penh instigated a series of border clashes with Vietnam, and claimed its southern region (once part of the Khmer empire). Khmer Rouge incursions into Vietnamese border provinces left hundreds of Vietnamese civilians dead. On 25 December 1978 Vietnam launched a full-scale invasion of Cambodia, toppling the Pol Pot government two weeks later. As Vietnamese tanks neared Phnom Penh, the Khmer Rouge fled westward with as many civilians as it could seize, taking refuge in the jungles and mountains on both sides of the Thai border. The Vietnamese installed a new government led by several former Khmer Rouge officers, including Hun Sen, who had defected to Vietnam in 1977, and Heng Samrin, who had done the same in 1978. The official version of events is that the Heng Samrin government came to power in a revolutionary uprising against the Pol Pot regime. The Khmer Rouge's patrons, the Chinese communists, launched a massive reprisal raid across Vietnam's northernmost border in early 1979 in an attempt to buy their allies time. It failed, and after 17 days the Chinese withdrew, their fingers badly burnt by their Vietnamese enemies. The Vietnamese then staged a show trial in which Pol Pot and Ieng Sary were condemned to death for their genocidal acts.

The social and economic dislocation that accompanied the Vietnamese invasion – along with the destruction of rice stocks and unharvested fields by both sides (to prevent their use by the enemy) – resulted in a vastly reduced rice harvest in early 1979. The chaotic situation led to very little rice being planted in the summer of 1979. By the middle of that year the country was suffering from a widespread famine.

As hundreds of thousands of Cambodians fled to Thailand, a massive international famine relief effort, sponsored by the United Nations (UN), was launched. The international community wanted to inject aid across a land bridge at Poipet, while the new Phnom Penh government wanted all supplies to come through the capital via Kompong Som (Sihanoukville) or the Mekong River. Both sides had their reasons – the new government did not want aid to fall into the hands of its Khmer Rouge enemies, while the international community didn't believe the new government had the infrastructure to distribute the aid – and both were right.

Some agencies distributed aid the slow way through Phnom Penh, others set up camps in Thailand. The camps became a magnet for half of Cambodia, as many Khmers still feared the return of the Khmer Rouge or were seeking a new life overseas. The Thai military bullied and blackmailed the international community into distributing all aid through their people and used this as a cloak to rebuild the shattered Khmer Rouge forces as an effective resistance against the Vietnamese. In fact, in 1979 Thailand demanded that, as a condition for allowing international food aid for Cambodia to pass through its territory, food had to be supplied to the Khmer Rouge forces encamped in the Thai border region as well. Along with weaponry supplied by China

(and delivered by the Thai army), this international assistance was essential in enabling the Khmer Rouge to rebuild its military strength. The Khmer Rouge regrouped with food and shelter from willing donors and managed to fight on for another 20 years.

In June 1982 Sihanouk agreed, under pressure from China, to head a military and political front opposed to the Phnom Penh government and the 170,000 Vietnamese troops defending it. The Sihanouk-led resistance coalition brought together – on paper, at least – Funcinpec (the French acronym for the National United Front for an Independent, Neutral, Peaceful and Cooperative Cambodia), which comprised a royalist group loyal to Sihanouk; the Khmer People's National Liberation Front, a noncommunist grouping formed by former prime minister and banker Son Sann; and the Khmer Rouge, officially known as the Party of Democratic Kampuchea and by far the largest and most powerful of the three. The undisputed crimes of the Khmer Rouge were conveniently overlooked to ensure a compromise that suited the great powers.

Countries such as Malaysia and Singapore supplied weapons to the two smaller factions of the coalition. During the mid-1980s the British government dispatched the Special Air Service (SAS) to a Malaysian jungle camp to train guerrilla fighters in land mine–laying techniques. Although officially assisting the smaller factions, it is certain the Khmer Rouge benefited from this experience. It then used these new-found skills to intimidate and terrorise the Cambodian people. As part of its campaign to harass and isolate Hanoi, the USA gave more than US$15 million a year in aid to the noncommunist factions of the Khmer Rouge–dominated coalition and helped the group retain its seat at the UN assembly in New York. Those responsible for the genocide were representing their victims on the international stage.

For much of the 1980s Cambodia remained closed to the Western world, save for the presence of some aid groups. Government policy was effectively under the control of the Vietnamese so Cambodia found itself very much in the Eastern-bloc camp. Students were made to learn Russian and many studied in cities like Moscow, Prague and Warsaw. Chinese Khmers found life hard under the Vietnamese occupation, as they were often singled out for ill-treatment, and for a time the Vietnamese had a plan to repatriate them to China. The economy was in tatters for much of this period, as Cambodia, like Vietnam, suffered from the effects of a US-sponsored embargo. However, with the advent of Mikhail Gorbachev in the former USSR, and the Vietnamese embrace of their own form of *perestroika*, known as *doi moi*, Cambodia became something of a laboratory for their economic experiments.

In 1985 the Vietnamese overran all the major rebel camps inside Cambodia, forcing the Khmer Rouge and its allies to retreat into Thailand. From that time the Khmer Rouge – and, to a much more limited extent, the other two factions – engaged in guerrilla warfare aimed at demoralising its opponents. Tactics used by the Khmer Rouge included shelling government-controlled garrison towns, planting thousands of mines along roads and in rice fields, attacking road transport, blowing up bridges, kidnapping village chiefs, and killing local administrators and school teachers. The Khmer Rouge also forced thousands of men, women and children living in the refugee camps it controlled to work as porters, ferrying ammunition and other supplies into Cambodia across heavily mined sections of the border. The Vietnamese for their part laid the world's longest minefield, known as K-5, stretching from the Gulf of Thailand to the Lao border, in an attempt to seal out the guerrillas. They also sent Cambodians into the forests to cut down trees on remote sections of road to prevent ambushes. Hundreds, surely thousands, died of disease and from injuries sustained from land mines.

By the late 1980s the military wing of Funcinpec, the Armée Nationale Sihanoukiste, had 12,000 troops; Son Sann's faction, plagued by internal divisions, could field some 8000 soldiers; and the Khmer Rouge's National Army of Democratic Kampuchea was believed to have 40,000 troops. The army of the Phnom Penh government, the Kampuchean People's Revolutionary Armed Forces, had 50,000 regular soldiers and another 100,000 men and women serving in local militia forces.

Untac at the Helm

In September 1989 Vietnam, suffering from economic woes and eager to end its international isolation, announced that it had withdrawn all of its troops from Cambodia; however, evidence suggests that Vietnamese soldiers wearing Cambodian uniforms remained in the country well into 1990. With most of the Vietnamese gone, the opposition coalition, still dominated by the Khmer Rouge, launched a series of offensives, bringing the number of refugees inside the country to more than 150,000 by the autumn of 1990. In the first eight months of 1990 more than 2000 Cambodians lost their lives in the fighting between the Khmer Rouge–dominated coalition and government forces.

Diplomatic efforts to end the civil war began to bear fruit in September 1990, when a plan agreed upon in Paris by the five permanent members of the UN Security Council (the USA, the former USSR, China, France and Britain) was accepted by both the Phnom Penh government and the three factions of the resistance coalition. According to the plan, the Supreme National Council (SNC), a coalition of all factions, was to be formed under the presidency of Sihanouk. Meanwhile the United Nations Transitional Authority in Cambodia (Untac) was to supervise the administration of the country and to create an atmosphere in which free elections could take place.

Untac was successful in achieving SNC agreement to most international human-rights covenants; a large number of non-governmental organisations (NGOs) were established in Cambodia; and, most importantly, on 25 May 1993, elections were held with a 89.6% turnout. The results were far from decisive, however: Funcinpec, led by Prince Norodom Ranariddh, took 58 seats in the National Assembly; the Cambodian

People's Party (CPP), which represented the previous communist government, took 51 seats; and the Buddhist Liberal Democratic Party (BLDP) took 10 seats. The CPP had lost the election, but some party members threatened a secession of the eastern provinces of the country. As a result, Cambodia ended up with two prime ministers: Norodom Ranariddh as first prime minister, and Hun Sen as second prime minister. Control of the various ministries was also spread among the three contending parties.

Within months of the elections taking place, local diplomats and reporters were complaining that the diffusion of central authority had led to real power lying in the hands of provincial leaders, whose loyalties lay with the CPP and communist-style power structures.

Untac was quick to pack up and go home, patting itself on the back for a job well done. Even today, it is heralded as one of the UN's success stories. The reality is that it was an ill-conceived and poorly executed peace because so many of the powers involved in brokering the deal had their own agendas to advance. It was a travesty that the Khmer Rouge was allowed to play a part in the process after the barbarities it had inflicted on its people; it must have seemed like a cruel joke to the many Cambodians who had lost countless family members under its rule. It rapidly became far more than a cruel joke, as the UN's half-botched disarmament programme took weapons away from rural militias who for so long provided the backbone of the government's provincial defence network against the Khmer Rouge. This left communities throughout the country vulnerable to attack, while the Khmer Rouge used the veil of legitimacy conferred upon it by the peace process to re-establish a guerrilla network throughout the country. It is not an exaggeration to say that by 1994, when it was finally outlawed by the government, the Khmer Rouge was probably a greater threat to the stability of Cambodia than at any time since 1979. Untac's main goals had been to 'restore and maintain peace' and 'promote national reconciliation' and it achieved neither. It did oversee free and fair elections,

however these were later annulled by the actions of Cambodia's politicians. But a lot of people rode the gravy train as it steamed through Cambodia, with an army of highly paid consultants and advisers flying in, 1st and business class of course.

If that wasn't bad enough, the UN presence also kick-started Cambodia's AIDS epidemic, with well-paid overseas soldiers boosting the prostitution industry. Cambodia's AIDS problem is now among the worst in Asia.

Machiavellian Times

As early as 1995 there were two major political incidents that boded ill for democratic politics. The first of these was the ouster of Sam Rainsy, a Paris-educated accountant, from Funcinpec. In mid-1994 Rainsy lost his position as finance minister, a job he had excelled at, largely, it was surmised, because of his outspoken criticisms concerning corruption and government policy. Several Funcinpec politicians, high on ideals during the campaign, soon had their heads in the trough and this wasn't something he would quietly accept. In May 1995 his party membership was rescinded and one month later he was sacked from the National Assembly. He formed the Khmer Nation Party (now called the Sam Rainsy Party) and found himself the country's leading dissident in no time at all. Even his former Funcinpec allies turned against him; First Prime Minister Norodom Prince Ranariddh was famously heard to remark in early 1995 that foremost among the prospects for Rainsy's wife was widowhood.

The other political headline of 1995 was the arrest and exile of Prince Norodom Sirivudh, secretary general of Funcinpec, former foreign minister and half-brother of King Sihanouk. He had allegedly plotted to kill Hun Sen. Prince Sirivudh is well known as a good-humoured man, always quick with an off-the-cuff joke, but the only one laughing at his one-liner about assassinating Hun Sen was Hun Sen himself, who found himself with the perfect excuse to clear another political prominent adversary from his path.

Dealing with the Khmer Rouge

When the Vietnamese toppled the Pol Pot government in 1979, the Khmer Rouge disappeared into the jungle. The regime boycotted the 1993 elections and later rejected peace talks aimed at creating a ceasefire. Although it was a signatory to the Paris Peace Accords, the alliance collapsed over the role the CPP should play in the political process: to the Khmer Rouge it was anathema to deal with anyone so close to the Vietnamese.

The defection of some 2000 troops from the Khmer Rouge army in the months following the elections offered some hope that the long-running insurrection would fizzle out. Government-sponsored amnesty programmes, however, initially turned out to be ill-conceived: the policy of reconscripting Khmer Rouge troops and returning them to fight their former comrades with poor pay and conditions provided little incentive to desert.

The problem was not just the poorly equipped and frequently unpaid Cambodian army. Evidence pointed to military cooperation with the Khmer Rouge. Leaked Khmer Rouge documents in mid-1994 revealed that large quantities of arms were sold to it by the Cambodian military, and that such arms sales were continuing even as those conducting the sales were attacking Khmer Rouge positions.

In 1994 the Khmer Rouge resorted to a new tactic of targeting tourists, with horrendous results for a number of foreigners in Cambodia. During 1994 three people were taken from a taxi on the road to Sihanoukville and subsequently shot. A few months later another three foreigners were seized from a train bound for Sihanoukville and in the ransom drama that followed they were executed, probably some time in September, as the army closed in.

The government changed its course during the middle of the 1990s, opting for more carrot and less stick in a bid to end the war. The defection programme was stepped up a gear and, slowly but surely, isolated Khmer Rouge units began coming over to the government side in return for amnesties and an

army uniform. Another important development was that the Thai government, a longtime supporter of the rebels, finally began to clamp down on Khmer Rouge border movements, an act that theoretically severed the Khmer Rouge lines of revenue: gems and timber transported into Thailand for sale.

The defection programme certainly advanced government control in certain provinces, but countrywide the situation smacked of stalemate, with neither side advancing significantly. The breakthrough came in August 1996 when Ieng Sary, Brother No 3 in the Khmer Rouge hierarchy and foreign minister during its rule, was denounced by Pol Pot for corruption. He subsequently led a mass defection of fighters and their dependants from the Pailin area, and this effectively sealed the fate of the remaining Khmer Rouge. Pailin, rich in gems and timber, had long been the economic springboard from which the Khmer Rouge could launch counter-offensives against the government. The severing of this income, coupled with the fact that government forces now had only one front on which to concentrate their resources, suggested that the days of civil war were numbered.

By 1997 cracks were appearing in the paper-thin coalition and the fledgling democracy once again found itself under siege. On 31 March 1997 a grenade was thrown into a group of Sam Rainsy supporters demonstrating peacefully outside the National Assembly. Many were killed and Sam Rainsy narrowly escaped injury. He fled into self-imposed exile, blaming Hun Sen and the CPP for the attack. However, it was the Khmer Rouge that again grabbed the headlines. As the politicians in Phnom Penh vied to draw the remaining Khmer Rouge out of their northern bases, Pol Pot ordered the execution of Son Sen, defence minister during the Khmer Rouge regime, and many of his family members. This provoked a putsch within the Khmer Rouge leadership, and the one-legged hardline general Ta Mok seized control of the movement and put Pol Pot on 'trial'. This was widely seen as a cosmetic exercise carried out in an attempt to shift the collective responsibility of the mass killings onto the shoulders of one man. Rumours flew about Phnom Penh that Pol Pot would be brought there to face international justice, but it was never to happen. July saw the focus shift back to Phnom Penh as the brittle government coalition fell apart amid scenes of heavy fighting.

The Coup

The events of July 1997, as they are euphemistically referred to in Cambodia, were preceded by a lengthy courting period in which both Funcinpec and the CPP attempted to win the trust of the remaining Khmer Rouge hardliners in northern Cambodia. First Prime Minister Norodom Ranariddh was close to forging a deal with the jungle fighters and was keen to get it sewn up before Cambodia's accession to the Association of Southeast Asian Nations (Asean), as nothing would provide a better entry fanfare than the ending of Cambodia's long civil war. In his haste, he didn't pay enough attention to detail and was outflanked and subsequently outgunned by Second Prime Minister Hun Sen. On 5 July 1997 fighting again erupted on the streets of Phnom Penh as troops loyal to the CPP clashed with those loyal to Funcinpec. The heaviest exchanges were around Pochentong airport and key government buildings, but before long the dust had settled and the CPP once again effectively controlled Cambodia. Hun Sen accused Ranariddh of attempting to illegally ship arms into Cambodia via the port of Sihanoukville and of colluding with the Khmer Rouge. They were pretty spurious charges and they led many in the international community to roundly condemn Hun Sen's actions. The strongman had finally flexed his muscles and there was no doubt as to which party commanded the most support within the military.

The international reaction was swift and decisive. Asean suspended Cambodia's imminent membership, the Cambodian seat at the UN was declared vacant and a freeze was put on all new aid money. This was to have a serious impact on the Cambodian economy over the next two years.

Following the coup, the remnants of Funcinpec forces on the Thai border around O Smach formed an alliance with the last of the Khmer Rouge under Ta Mok's control. The fighting may have ended, but the deaths certainly did not: several prominent Funcinpec politicians and military leaders were subjected to extra-judicial executions, and even today no-one has been brought to justice for these crimes. Many of Funcinpec's leading politicians fled abroad, while the leading generals camped out in the jungle near the Thai border, leading a resistance struggle, together with the Khmer Rouge, against forces loyal to the CPP. Hun Sen quickly appointed Ung Huot, a Funcinpec parliamentarian, as first prime minister, although real power now lay firmly in the hands of the second prime minister.

As 1998 began the CPP announced an all-out offensive against its enemies in the north. By April it was closing in on the Khmer Rouge strongholds of Anlong Veng and Preah Vihear, and amid this heavy fighting Pol Pot unfortunately managed to evade justice by dying a sorry death on 15 April in the Khmer Rouge's captivity. He was cremated on a pyre of burning tyres soon after; an official autopsy was never performed, which bred rumours and gossip in Phnom Penh for a few weeks. The fall of Anlong Veng in April was followed by the fall of Preah Vihear in May; and the big three, Ta Mok, Khieu Samphan and Nuon Chea, were forced to flee into the jungle near the Thai border with their remaining troops. It was around this time that the strategically important Hill 200 fell to government forces; here they found the so-called 'KR papers', all the notes from high-level meetings that had taken place over the preceding year. In them were details of how the organisation planned to betray Ranariddh, after using an alliance with Funcinpec to secure a foothold in Cambodian politics once more. The plan was ambitious, if not absurd, but the papers certainly highlight the risk Ranariddh took in dealing with the devil. Hun Sen was to ably exploit these papers to defend his coup.

Naming Rights

Cambodia has changed its name so many times over the last few decades that there are understandable grounds for confusion. To the Cambodians, their country is Kampuchea. The name is derived from the word Kambu-ja, meaning 'those born of Kambu', the mythical founder of the country. It dates back as far as the 10th century. The Portuguese 'Camboxa' and the French 'Cambodge' (from which the English name 'Cambodia' is derived) are adaptations of 'Kambu-ja'.

Since gaining independence in 1953, the country has been known in English by various names before coming full circle:

- The Kingdom of Cambodia (French: Le Royaume du Cambodge)
- The Khmer Republic (under Lon Nol, who reigned from 1970 to 1975)
- Democratic Kampuchea (under the Khmer Rouge, which controlled the country from 1975 to 1979)
- The People's Republic of Kampuchea (under the Vietnamese-backed Phnom Penh government from 1979 to 1989)
- The State of Cambodia (French: L'État du Cambodge; Khmer: Roët Kampuchea) from mid-1989
- The Kingdom of Cambodia (from May 1993)

It was the Khmer Rouge that insisted the outside world use the name Kampuchea. Changing the country's official English name back to Cambodia (which has been used by the US State Department all along) was intended as a symbolic move to distance the present government in Phnom Penh from the bitter connotations of the name Kampuchea, which Westerners and overseas Khmers alike associate with the murderous Khmer Rouge regime.

Election Time Again

Much of 1998 was dominated by election fever. It was to be the country's second postwar election and many observers were pessimistic about the chances for democracy after the tumultuous events of 1997. At the start of 1998 Funcinpec leader, Prince Norodom Ranariddh, had still not returned to the country, as he faced a variety of charges amounting to treason. Funcinpec's provincial network was also in tatters as many of its representatives had either left the country, been murdered or switched allegiances in a bid for political survival. However, Sam Rainsy was back: he returned to Cambodia at the end of 1997 after many months of self-imposed exile.

Ranariddh was tried *in absentia* during March and found guilty on charges of both arms smuggling and collusion with the Khmer Rouge. On 21 March he received a pardon from King Sihanouk at Hun Sen's request, and returned to Cambodia at the end of the month. The run-up to the election was remarkably quiet by Cambodian standards. To contest the elections the opposition formed an alliance called the National United Front (NUF), which brought together Funcinpec and the Sam Rainsy Party, plus a couple of smaller parties. They were never exactly united, but the alliance gave the parties a stronger voice against the government. The Khmer Rouge was roundly ignored and fortunately its threats to destabilise the election came to a single deadly attack near the polling station in Anlong Veng.

The election took place on 26 July amid opposition charges of voter intimidation. Numerous election observers had flown into Cambodia some months earlier to ensure the process was free and fair, and they hastily declared the ballot a success. The opposition cried foul and the subsequent stand-off again plunged Cambodia into a crisis of confidence. The results gave the CPP 64 seats, Funcinpec 43 seats and the Sam Rainsy Party 15 seats. The CPP was now the dominant force in Cambodian politics, but lacked the two-thirds majority required to govern alone. As the opposition escalated its campaign for democracy in August, mass demonstrations began in the capital, which soon descended into rioting, fighting and repression. The country looked set for yet another period of instability.

King Sihanouk added his voice to the post-electoral debate, offering to act as a mediator in the formation of a coalition. He was able to bring the squabbling leaders to a table at his residence in Siem Reap and, after much posturing on all sides, a coalition was announced on 23 November. It was still business as usual, with a much-weakened Funcinpec agreeing to govern with a now dominant CPP. Part of the coalition deal ensured amnesties for those Funcinpec supporters still facing charges, including exiled princes Sirivudh and Chakrapong, and General Neak Bun Chhay.

The formation of a new coalition government allowed the politicians to once more concentrate on bringing an end to the civil war. In December 1998 almost all the remaining Khmer Rouge guerrillas turned themselves over to government forces in return for amnesty and the Khmer Rouge effectively ceased to exist as a military organisation. However, the big three continued to remain at large with an increasingly small number of soldiers, numbering perhaps only several hundred.

On 25 December Hun Sen received the Christmas present he had been waiting for: telephoning from Pailin, Khieu Samphan requested that he and Nuon Chea be permitted to defect to the government side. Hun Sen had long been an advocate of a trial for these remaining leaders, but he appeared to do an about-turn and treated them to a lavish VIP reception, talking of the need for reconciliation. At a press conference in Phnom Penh, Nuon Chea, former Brother No 2 in the Khmer Rouge hierarchy, made a pathetic apology to the Cambodian people for their suffering; it was so lame that even Ieng Sary (foreign minister during the Khmer Rouge's rule) later rebuked him. The international community began to pile on the pressure for the establishment of some sort of war-crimes tribunal to try the remaining Khmer Rouge leadership, while Hun Sen fired off contradictory salvos about who should be tried and for what.

After lengthy negotiations, agreement was finally reached on the composition of a court to try the surviving leaders of the Khmer Rouge. The CPP was suspicious of a UN-administered trial as the UN had sided with the Khmer Rouge–dominated coalition against the government in Phnom Penh and the ruling party wanted a major say in who was to be tried. The UN for its part rightly doubted that the judiciary in Cambodia was sophisticated or impartial enough to fairly oversee such a major trial. A compromise solution – a mixed tribunal of three international and four Cambodian judges requiring a super majority of two plus three for a verdict – was eventually agreed upon. However, all this was blown apart with the dramatic UN decision to pull out of the process in early 2002. Many member governments were extremely unhappy with the decision and have been pressuring the UN to change its mind. In the meantime, individual countries have offered to provide legal counsel for any local proceedings. With the UN up to its neck in places like Afghanistan, and war-crimes proceedings already underway in Sierra Leone, it seems the Cambodian peoples' search for justice will go on, while former leaders of the Khmer Rouge die in freedom.

Although many Cambodians want to see the Khmer Rouge leadership put on trial for genocide, there are also some politicians, both within Cambodia and abroad, that don't. Many prominent figures within the contemporary Cambodian elite were involved in the Khmer Rouge movement at some stage, and while there is no suggestion of their direct involvement in crimes against humanity, there may be one or two skeletons in the closet. So far there has been no provision to try politicians from the USA for their systematic and illegal bombing campaign, which may have killed as many as 250,000 Cambodians. China has been very wary of the trial, as it was the one government to steadfastly support the

Khmer Rouge throughout. There is also the delicate issue of national reconciliation to consider, as Cambodia is now at peace for the first time in more then 30 years. A trial of senior leaders could cause former Khmer Rouge fighters to wonder if they, too, are vulnerable, and lead to a resumption of unrest.

The Cambodian people deserve justice after so much suffering, but it could be argued that the nation would be better served by a truth commission that cleanses the nation's soul without seeking revenge. For senior leaders, all blame resides with a dead Pol Pot, and dead men tell no tales, but if lower-ranking cadres are encouraged to come forward the full truth may emerge. There is an awful lot of simmering anger and frustration in Cambodia and knowing the truth could prove more cathartic to the average Cambodian than seeing a bunch of pathetic geriatrics on trial, 20 years too late.

GEOGRAPHY & GEOLOGY

Cambodia covers 181,035 sq km (a little over half the size of Vietnam). The country's maximum extent is about 580km east-west and 450km north-south. It is bound on the west by Thailand, on the north by Thailand and Laos, on the east by Vietnam and to the south by the Gulf of Thailand.

Cambodia's two dominant topographical features are the Mekong River, which is almost 5km wide in places, and the Tonlé Sap lake. The Mekong, which rises in Tibet, flows about 486km through Cambodia before continuing, via southern Vietnam, to the South China Sea. At Phnom Penh it splits into the Upper River (called simply the Mekong or, in Vietnamese, the Tien Giang) and the Lower River (Tonlé Bassac; in Vietnamese, the Hau Giang). The rich sediment deposited during the Mekong's annual wet-season flooding has made for very fertile agricultural land. Most of Cambodia's streams and rivers flow into the Mekong–Tonlé Sap basin.

In the centre of Cambodia, around the Tonlé Sap lake and the upper Mekong Delta, is a low-lying alluvial plain where the vast majority of Cambodians live. Extending outward from this plain are thinly forested transitional plains with elevations of no more than about 100m above sea level.

In the southwest, much of the area between the Gulf of Thailand and the Tonlé Sap lake is covered by a highland region formed by two distinct upland blocks: the Chuor Phnom Kravanh (Cardamom Mountains) in southwestern Battambang Province and Pursat Province, and the Chuor Phnom Damrei (Elephant Mountains) in the provinces of Kompong Speu, Koh Kong and Kampot. Along the south coast is a heavily forested lowland strip isolated from the rest of the country by the mountains to the north. Cambodia's highest peak is Phnom Aoral (1813m), in Pursat Province.

Along Cambodia's northern border with Thailand, the plains abut an east-west oriented sandstone escarpment more than 300km long and 180m to 550m in height that marks the southern limit of the Chuor Phnom Dangkrek (Dangkrek Mountains). In the northeastern corner of the country (the provinces of Ratanakiri and Mondulkiri), the transitional plains give way to the Eastern Highlands, a remote region of densely forested mountains and high plateaus that extends eastward into Vietnam's central highlands and northward into Laos.

Cambodia can be neatly divided into two geomorphologic regions: the central plains of the Mekong–Tonlé Sap basin, which formed from an ancient marine gulf and later filled with alluvium and colluvium (rock fragments from the base of cliffs) from the Mekong River; and the basin periphery of mountain ranges, which include a variety of mineral and soil types. Cambodia's main mineral resources include basalt in Kompong Cham Province; granite in Kompong Chhnang Province; limestone in the west and northwest; quartz in Takeo Province; marble in Pursat and Stung Treng Province; and gems in Pailin and, to a lesser extent, Ratanakiri Province. There are thought to be extensive natural gas deposits off the coast of Cambodia and sufficient oil, if recoverable, to make the country energy self-sufficient.

CLIMATE

The climate of Cambodia is governed by two monsoons that set the rhythm of rural life. The cool, dry, northeastern monsoon, which carries little rain, blows from about November to April. From May to October, the southwestern monsoon brings strong winds, high humidity and heavy rains. Even during the wet season, it rarely rains in the morning; most precipitation comes in the afternoon, and even then only sporadically.

Annual rainfall varies considerably from area to area. Whereas the seaward slopes of the southwestern highlands receive more than 5000mm of rain per annum, the central lowlands average only about 1400mm. Between 70% and 80% of the annual rainfall is brought by the southwestern monsoon.

Daily temperatures can reach 40°C in April, the hottest month, and are around 30°C during January, the coolest month. Daily minimum temperatures are usually no more than 10°C below the maximums, but it has been known to drop as low as 14°C at night in late December or early January.

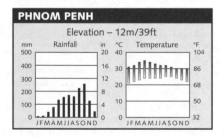

ECOLOGY & ENVIRONMENT
Logging

The biggest threat to the environment in Cambodia is logging. In the mid-1960s Cambodia was reckoned to have around 75% rainforest coverage. Surveys carried out in 1998 concluded that this had been reduced to 30%, around half of which was primary forest. Worse still, the wholesale shift from a command economy to a market economy led to an asset-stripping bonanza by the cash-strapped government and military. Most of Cambodia's primary resources beyond the national parks were signed away to logging companies during the first coalition government, with the acquiescence of both prime ministers. Logging companies set about decimating the forests while the politicians sat back and counted the cash.

International demand for timber is huge, and as neighbouring countries like Thailand and Laos enforce much tougher logging regulations while at the same time helping to flout Cambodia's lax restrictions, it's small wonder that foreign logging companies flocked to Cambodia. By late 1995, 27 companies had licences or applications to log Cambodia's rainforests. By the height of the country's logging epidemic, at the end of 1997, just under 70,000 sq km of the country's land area had been allocated as concessions, amounting to almost all of Cambodia's forest except national parks and protected areas. However, even in these supposed havens, illegal logging continued.

Logging deals are controversial for many reasons, not least the destruction of Cambodia's natural habitat. Confidential, under-the-table deals were cut by the prime ministers without reference to forestry officials, and stipulations on how the logging should be carried out were loose to say the least. In late 1998 British environmental group Global Witness obtained official papers in Laos containing the signatures of both Ung Huot, the former first prime minister, and the current prime minister Hun Sen (who was at that time second prime minister) authorising illegal timber exports. With collusion at the most senior level, what hope is there for Cambodia's disappearing forest and its rare fauna?

The Royal Cambodian Armed Forces (RCAF) has been the driving force behind much of the logging in Cambodia: it assists in logging legal concessions under the guise of providing security, and then logs illegally elsewhere. The proceeds from these operations contribute towards the army's grey (undeclared) budget, with its nominal budget already taking up more than half the government's cash. More recently the Thai military has turned up in Cambodia to build

The Heartbeat of Cambodia

The Tonlé Sap lake is the largest in Southeast Asia, an incredible natural phenomenon that provides fish proteins and irrigation waters for almost half the population of Cambodia.

The lake is linked to the Mekong at Phnom Penh by a 100km-long channel, also known as the Tonlé Sap, tonlé meaning 'river'. From mid-May to early October (the wet season) the level of the Mekong rises, backing up the Tonlé Sap river and causing it to flow northwest into the Tonlé Sap lake. During this period, the lake swells from 2500 sq km to 13,000 sq km or more, its maximum depth increasing from about 2.2m to more than 10m. Around the start of October, as the water level of the Mekong begins to fall, the Tonlé Sap river reverses its flow, draining the waters of the lake back into the Mekong.

This extraordinary process makes the Tonlé Sap lake one of the world's richest sources of freshwater fish, as flooded forest makes for a fertile spawning ground. Experts believe fish migrations from the Tonlé Sap lake help to restock fisheries as far north as China. The fishing industry supports about one million people in Cambodia and a dry-season catch on the great lake can average 100kg to 200kg per day.

This unique ecosystem has helped to earn the Tonlé Sap lake biosphere status, but this may not be enough to protect it from the twin threats of upstream dams and excessive deforestation. The dams hold uncertain consequences for flow patterns of the Mekong and migratory patterns of fish. Illegal logging loosens topsoil in upland Cambodia and this silt is carried down the country's rivers into the lake. The shallowest areas may in time begin to silt up, bringing disastrous consequences not only for Cambodians, but also for neighbouring Vietnam. Hopefully, immediate action will be taken to do all that is possible to protect this unique natural wonder from further harm, but with the Cambodian population growing by 300,000 a year, the task is going to be a far from easy.

For more information about the Tonlé Sap lake and its unique ecosystem, consider visiting the exhibition about the Tonlé Sap, and the Gecko Environment Centre in Siem Reap (see Things to See & Do and Floating Village of Chong Kneas in the Siem Reap chapter).

roads in the west of the country. Many of these roads are being cut through the heart of Cambodia's forests and no doubt many logs are disappearing across the border into Thailand, before resurfacing as garden furniture in Europe.

In the short term, deforestation is contributing to worsening floods along the Mekong, but the long-term implications of logging will be far more damaging. Without trees to cloak the hills, the rains will inevitably carry away large amounts of topsoil during future monsoons. There can be no doubt that in time this will have a catastrophic effect on Tonlé Sap lake, as the shallow waters recede from prolonged siltation – a similar situation to that marking the fall of the Angkorian empire? (See Decline & Fall in the History section earlier for details.) Combined with overfishing and

pollution, these problems may lead to the eventual destruction of the lake – an unmitigated disaster for future generations.

The tragedy is that the money generated from all this illegal activity could easily be raised for the treasury's coffers through controlled and sustainable logging, and with the loss of far fewer trees. Processed tropical hardwoods are extremely valuable, but Cambodia usually sells unprocessed timber at a fraction of its market value, robbing the country of its real assets. In 1997 the government officially made about US$12.8 million from the forests, but illegal operations over the same period generated an estimated US$184.2 million. This is money that such a poor country can ill-afford to lose, but with the endemic culture of corruption in Cambodia it is difficult to be optimistic for the future of the forests, especially when few in the international community are willing or able to do much about it. Every time the subject is brought up at international donor meetings, action against illegal logging is taken until the cheques are signed, and then it is business as usual until the next round of handouts.

More recently there have been some encouraging signs, but once again it is hard to tell if it's showmanship or a genuine change of heart. In 2000 environmental watchdog Global Witness was appointed as the official monitor for logging in Cambodia. There have been several high-profile military operations against small-scale sawmills, although these are soft targets compared with the big international companies. The big news at the end of 2001 was that all logging contracts were effectively frozen, pending further negotiations with the government. This is great news for environmentalists, but what message does it send to investors? These were contracts signed by the prime ministers and if they aren't considered binding, is any contract in Cambodia worth the paper it's written on? It is hoped that ongoing negotiations lead to the creation of a sustainable forestry management plan that protects Cambodia's natural environment while ensuring the country benefits economically. It is not too late for Cambodia's forests, but without sustained action it soon will be.

Pollution

Cambodia has a pollution problem, but it is not of the same nature as the carbon monoxide crises in neighbouring capitals such as Bangkok and Jakarta: Phnom Penh is the only city that suffers from air pollution. The country does, however, suffer the ill-effects of an extremely primitive sanitation system in urban areas, and in rural areas sanitary facilities are nonexistent, with only a tiny percentage of the population having access to proper facilities. These conditions breed and spread disease, with people being forced to defecate on open ground and urinate in rivers. Epidemics of diarrhoea are not uncommon and it is the number-one killer of young children in Cambodia. This type of

biological pollution may not be as immediately apparent as smog over a city, but in the shorter term it is far more hazardous to the average Cambodian.

Damming the Mekong

With a meandering length of around 4200km, the Mekong is the longest river in Southeast Asia, and some 50 million people depend on it for their livelihoods. In terms of fish biodiversity, the Mekong is second only to the Amazon; but with regional energy needs ever spiralling, it is very tempting for a poor country like Cambodia to dam the river and make money from hydroelectric power. Even more tempting for Cambodia is the fact that the United Nations Development Programme (UNDP) and the Asia Development Bank (ADB) would pay much of the construction costs. Environmental groups are already calling foul.

Overseeing development plans for the river is the Mekong River Commission (MRC), formed by the UNDP and comprising Cambodia, Thailand, Laos and Vietnam. The odd one out is China, which has around 20% of the Mekong but feels it can do what it wants with the river. China is already at work on a number of dam projects on the upper reaches of the Mekong, and many environmentalists fear that such projects will have an adverse effect down river.

China's dam projects are shrouded in secrecy, but there are thought to be 15 projects planned, with three operational by the year 2009. Meanwhile, the MRC has plans for 11 dams for the Mekong in Laos and Cambodia. Environmental concerns focus on a number of issues. For a start, even though the MRC dams planned for the Mekong will be small, it is thought they will flood some 1900 sq km and displace around 60,000 people. Secondly, there are worries about how the dams will affect fish migration – some environmentalists claim that the dams might halve the fish population of the Mekong and perhaps even Tonlé Sap lake. Finally, and perhaps of most concern, is the importance of the annual monsoon flooding of the Mekong, which deposits nutrient-rich silt across vast tracts of land used for agriculture.

NICK RAY

BERNARD NAPTHINE

NICK RAY

COREY WISE

Cambodians have managed to weather years of war and instability with smiles still intact

JULIET COOMBE

Locally made sausages hang out to dry

TOM COCKREM

Typical Cambodian grocery shop

JULIET COOMBE

Silver fish make pungent fermented fish sauce

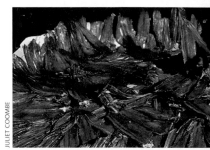
JULIET COOMBE

Dried fish in Psar Leu, Siem Reap

JULIET COOMBE

Fresh pomelos, jackfruit, lychees and longans

NICK RAY

Delicious spiders on the streets of Phnom Penh

JULIET COOMBE

An ice-cream seller prepares his wares

JULIET COOMBE

Hot savoury pancakes

Environmentalists say even a drop of 1m in Mekong water levels would result in around 2000 sq km less flood area around Tonlé Sap lake, a result with potentially disastrous consequences for Cambodia's farmers.

The Mekong is a huge untapped resource. It is probably inevitable that it will be harnessed to make much-needed power for the region. Local environmentalists hope that this can happen in the context of open discussion and with foresight. Many fear, however, that long-term interests will be scrapped in favour of short-term profits.

Dams are planned for a few other rivers around Cambodia, although if you were to believe some of the ministry maps you would think the government was going to dam every bit of water in the country. The most realistic project is the damming of one of the great northeastern rivers that flows into the Mekong at Stung Treng. Tonlé San, Tonlé Sekong and Tonlé Srepok contribute an estimated 10% to 20% of the Mekong's total flow at Kratie. If a dam goes ahead it could be a major earner, with exports of power going to Thailand and Vietnam, or energy used to supply a power-starved population in northern Cambodia. However, the effects on the local indigenous population, Virachay National Park and fish stocks have not been considered in any detail yet – and perhaps never will be.

FLORA

The central lowland consists of rice paddies, fields of dry crops such as corn and tobacco, tracts of reeds and tall grass, and thinly wooded areas. The transitional plains are mostly covered with savanna grasses, which grow to a height of 1.5m.

In the southwest, virgin rainforests grow to heights of 50m or more on the rainy seaward slopes of the mountains. Nearby, higher elevations support pine forests. Vegetation in the coastal strip includes both evergreen and mangrove forests. In the northern mountains there are broadleaf evergreen forests with trees soaring 30m above the thick undergrowth of vines, bamboos, palms and assorted woody and herbaceous ground plants. The Eastern Highlands are covered with grassland and deciduous forests. Forested upland areas support many varieties of orchid. However, in the past two decades, a great deal of deforestation has taken place – see the Logging section in Ecology & Environment earlier for more details.

The symbol of Cambodia is the sugar palm tree, which is used in construction (for roofs and walls) and in the production of medicine, wine and vinegar. Because of the way sugar palms grow (over the years, the tree keeps getting taller but the trunk, which lacks normal bark, does not grow thicker), their trunks retain shrapnel marks from every battle that has ever raged around them. Some sugar palms have been shot right through the trunk.

FAUNA

Cambodia's larger wild animals include bears, elephants, leopards, tigers and oxen. The lion, although often incorporated into Angkorian heraldic devices, has never been seen here. Among the country's more common birds are cormorants, cranes, egrets, grouse, herons, pelicans, pheasants and wild ducks. There is also a great variety of butterflies across the kingdom. Four types of snake are especially dangerous: the cobra, the king cobra, the banded krait and the Russell's viper.

Endangered Species

Cambodia is home to a number of diminishing species and more will no doubt join the list as the country's forest habitat continues to disappear. Very little is known about the remaining numbers of most rare animals because their habitats are extremely remote and few surveys have been undertaken.

Mammals under threat in Cambodia include the Asian elephant, Asian golden cat, Asiatic wild dog, black finless porpoise, black gibbon, brown-antlered deer, Chinese white dolphin, clouded leopard, duoc langur, dugong, fishing cat, gaur, hairy-nosed otter, leopard, mainland serow, marbled cat, Marshall's horseshoe bat, northern smooth-tailed tree shrew, otter civet, pileated gibbon, pygmy loris, stump-tailed macaque, sun bear and wild water buffalo.

Given that much of the country has been off limits for such a long time, some suggest Cambodia harbours animals that have become extinct elsewhere in the region. For the moment it remains conjecture, but as the national park system becomes more effective, hopefully whatever is out there will at least be protected. The *kouprey* (wild ox), adopted by Sihanouk as the national animal in 1963, could possibly remain in very small numbers in the northeast of Cambodia. The kouprey and the Wroughton's free-tailed bat, previously thought to exist in only one part of India, but recently discovered in Preah Vihear Province, are the only Cambodian mammals on the Globally Threatened – Critical list, the last stop before extinction. The discovery of an isolated herd of Javan rhinoceroses, one of the rarest large mammal species in the world, in southwestern Vietnam in 1998 suggests that there could be more in nearby Mondulkiri or Ratanakiri Provinces.

There is a large number of rare bird species in Cambodia, drawn to the area by its rich water resources throughout the year.

Even in areas of dry forest such as Preah Vihear Province, there are small ponds that contain water year-round and attract large birds. Larger birds include: the Asian openbill stork, greater adjutant stork, giant ibis and spot-billed pelican. There are now several sanctuaries in Cambodia where many of these birds can be seen in impressive numbers. See the Around Siem Reap section of the Siem Reap chapter for details on Prek Toal Bird Sanctuary and Ang Trapeng Thmor Reserve, home of the extremely rare sarus crane, as depicted on the bas-reliefs at Angkor. Some other rare birds include the coral-billed ground cuckoo, greater spotted eagle, Siamese fireback and spot-bellied eagle owl. For more about birds in Cambodia, look out for *Cambodia Bird News,* a twice-yearly publication available for US$5 in hotels and bookshops in Phnom Penh and Siem Reap.

Cambodia has some of the last remaining freshwater Irrawaddy dolphins, known as *trey trasak* in Khmer. These inhabit stretches of the Mekong between Kratie and the Lao border. The giant catfish, sometimes reaching

On the Trail of the Tiger

In 1995 the Worldwide Fund for Nature (WWF) announced a fundraising campaign to save the tigers of Indochina. Six international nongovernmental organisations (NGOs) are currently engaged in efforts to protect Cambodia's remaining big cats, although experts fear there may be as few as 150 left in the wild. Millions of dollars have been pumped into studies, surveys and assessments, but the time has come for action, as without a drastic initiative there may soon be no tigers left at all.

Tigers are known to inhabit Virachay National Park in Ratanakiri Province, remote parts of Mondulkiri and Preah Vihear Provinces and in the Chuor Phnom Kravanh (Cardamom Mountains) in the southwest, but they are under serious threat from poachers. The magical powers of potency (mainly sexual) ascribed to tiger parts throughout Asia push up the value of a carcass, and uneducated peasant poachers aren't easily convinced of the argument that you can sell a dead tiger only once, but can sell a live tiger time and time again. Fortunately, some hunters are now employed as rangers, making it easier to educate other hunters about the negative impact of the trade.

The fact that tigers are spread across such geographically diverse areas makes them harder to protect from poachers and so environmental NGOs are having to give serious thought to promoting the establishment of tiger sanctuaries similar to those found in India. This would concentrate the remaining tigers in a secure environment and, in time, generate a vast income for Cambodia from ecotourism. The lessons that African conservationists learnt in the 1970s when battling to protect rhinos and elephants may need to be learnt today by a new generation of Cambodian conservationists. It would be a terrible tragedy if this majestic creature were to disappear from Cambodia's forests forever.

5m in length, is also threatened, due to its popularity on menus from Hong Kong to Tokyo. Other rare fish include the Indochina featherback and silver shark.

The list of endangered reptiles includes the Asian green tortoise, green turtle, hawksbill turtle, impressed tortoise, Indian python and Siamese crocodile.

NATIONAL PARKS

In 1925 Cambodia established the first national park in the region, protecting the forest around the temples of Angkor. By 1969 there were six national parks, together covering 22,000 sq km (around 12% of the country). The long civil war effectively destroyed this system and it wasn't reintroduced until 1993, when a royal decree designated 23 areas as national parks, wildlife sanctuaries, protected landscapes and multiple-use areas. In total these cover 33,000 sq km (around 18% of the country).

Cambodia's most important national parks include: Bokor, which occupies a 1km-high plateau on the south coast overlooking Kampot; Ream, which includes a marine reserve and is just a short distance from Sihanoukville; Kirirom, 675m above sea level in the Chuor Phnom Damrei, 112km southwest of Phnom Penh; and Virachay, the kingdom's largest park, nestled against the Lao and Vietnamese borders in northeastern Cambodia. Bokor is home to wild elephants and has accommodation available at the summit. Ream has a visitor programme, which includes a boat trip and guided walks, while Kirirom has a basic guesthouse and is popular with Khmers at weekends. There is little in the way of facilities at Virachay, but rangers are keen to welcome visitors and have centres in Voen Sai and Siem Pang. Boutum Sokor is a coastal park with endless white-sand beaches; it has much potential for ecotourism, as any casual observer can see on the boat journey between Krong Koh Kong and Sihanoukville.

Other protected areas in the country aren't exactly protected, as there simply aren't the resources available to patrol them. The government has enough trouble finding funds to pay the rangers who patrol the most popular parks, let alone recruiting more staff for the remote sanctuaries.

GOVERNMENT & POLITICS

Following the May 1993 elections, Cambodia became a constitutional monarchy. Prince Sihanouk, who abdicated in 1955, accepted the crown once more and rules as king. Theoretically, the constitution of September 1993 allows for separation of powers between the executive, legislative and judicial branches of government. In practice, however, it rarely works this way. Decades of war and one-party rule have made Cambodia's administrative and legal structures slow to respond to the challenge of neutrality.

Following the turbulent elections of July 1998, Funcinpec and the CPP were again forced to engage in an uneasy political embrace. The CPP came out holding 16 ministries, including finance, commerce and foreign affairs; Funcinpec holds 15, including the poisoned chalice of the social ministries.

Hun Sen is the country's sole prime minister, while Ranariddh has had to settle for the less-influential position of president of the National Assembly. Part of the electoral deal was also the formation of a Senate to check the legislative power of the assembly, but most observers see this as little more than an indulgence for Chea Sim, CPP president and acting head of state in the king's absence. The CPP effectively controls the country because it is in firm control of the Royal Cambodian Armed Forces (RCAF).

Politically, Cambodia is plagued by the divisions of its past. Politicians were either with the Vietnamese or against them, either members of the CPP or of Funcinpec – all of which can have a considerable effect on any Cambodian's career chances. Funcinpec's provincial hierarchy was decimated in the aftermath of July 1997, and the party remains divided over the strategy pursued by its leader Prince Norodom Ranariddh in the months that followed. Although previously popular due to the royal connection, Funcinpec lacks the muscle to seriously challenge the CPP, and Ranariddh has allowed himself to be somewhat sidelined as president of the National Assembly. The return of popular Prince Norodom Sirivudh to the party fold has brought new impetus and he is seen as the one Funcinpec politician the CPP genuinely fears. However, the party has lost support as too many of its politicians have forsaken political principle for personal gain. Funcinpec is also perceived as too close to the CPP for its own good. Despite his popularity among young, educated Cambodians in Phnom Penh and other urban centres, Sam Rainsy and his eponymously named party have no role in the government. He remains the perceived voice of democracy, however, and is the only effective opposition in the country.

The depressing reality of politics in Cambodia is that the political elite within the country have consistently and wholeheartedly betrayed the long-term interests of their people for their own short-term gain. There is very little national interest in politics, but a whole lot of self-interest – entering politics is not about national service, but self-service.

Hun Sen is no one-man show and owes some of his success to figures in the business world and the military: he is only guaranteed to stay in power as long as he showers them with cash or opportunity. However, he does command the respect of the most important elements of the military and this should help satisfy his political ambitions for several years to come.

Hun Sen, the master chess player from Takhmau, has a political guile and cunning unrivalled in Cambodia. Love him or hate him, he does at least offer some sort of stability and is a wily politician who has shown himself consistently able to outflank the opposition. He has proven himself to be a survivor, personally as well as politically, for he lost an eye during the battle for Phnom Penh in 1975. With the opposition under his thumb, a shortage of clean and able politicians in Cambodia and a poorly educated electorate, it appears, for the time at least, that 'in the country of the blind, the one-eyed man is king'.

Hun Sen's biggest challenge is likely to come from a new generation of technocrats within the CPP who believe governing means getting things done, not feathering the nest. Phnom Penh Mayor Chea Sophara is the most prominent of this reform-minded element and is changing the face of the capital daily. Hopefully his example will serve to drag the old guard into the new world and ensure that actions rather than words are the barometer of political success in Cambodia.

Cambodia is divided into 24 provinces, each administered by a politically appointed governor. Under the provincial structure are districts, communes and villages, which until early 2002 were also filled with political appointees. In February 2002 the first free commune elections since before the war were held throughout Cambodia. These elections should have allowed a democratic departure from the CPP-appointed commune chiefs of the past, but the CPP still managed to take an overwhelming majority, the Sam Rainsy Party coming in second and Funcinpec an embarrassing third. Intimidation, vote-buying and rumours about a less-than-secret ballot didn't help the opposition's attempts to make inroads.

Terrorism is high on the international agenda these days and Cambodia has its own ineffectual terrorist organisation called the Cambodian Freedom Fighters (CFF). Formed by Cambodian-Americans who have little understanding of how much the average Cambodian yearns for peace after three decades of war, it promises to liberate Cambodia from the Vietnamese yoke. That the Vietnamese pulled out more than a decade ago and that Cambodia is now much more in the orbit of China appears to have escaped the group's limited attention.

The press continues to enjoy the sort of freedom of speech that is unthinkable in many of the neighbouring Asean countries, but the intimidation and murder of opposition journalists is sadly not uncommon, and state television is now firmly under the control of the CPP – dishing out a daily diet of propaganda between karaoke videos and soap operas.

ECONOMY

Badly traumatised by decades of internal conflict, Cambodia's economy is in terrible shape, a gecko compared with the neighbouring dragons, but things are slowly improving.

For many years rubber was Cambodia's primary export, but the plantations in the north and east of the country produce very little compared with colonial days. In the 1960s many a car in this region had tyres made by Angkor, the leading tyre company in Cambodia, sadly no longer in existence. Tourism was also a major earner before the war: the temples of Angkor were the place to be in Asia, drawing thousands of visitors before anyone knew how to pronounce Phuket. Rice and agricultural products also contributed a significant amount to export earnings.

Rubber has been eclipsed in recent years by tourism, garment manufacturing and timber exports. Timber exports were the big earner of much of the 90s, accounting for nearly half the country's export earnings. Such figures, of course, disguise illegal exports of timber such as those carried out by the military or the Vietnamese.

The garment sector has been growing rapidly in recent years, thanks to a relatively liberal investment code and cheap labour, and now accounts for up to 80% of exports. There are several hundred factories in Phnom Penh and Sihanoukville and many internationally known brands are manufactured here, including Columbia, Gap, Quiksilver and Calvin Klein. A number of television programmes have drawn negative attention to labour conditions in Cambodia and other Asian countries, but many labour observers argue conditions are considerably better in Cambodia than other countries. Cambodia can't hope to compete with producers like China and India on economies of scale, but it can carve a niche for itself as an ethical environment for manufacturing. Wages are low and conditions can be tough, but the alternative is usually the rice fields or the fringes of the entertainment industry, often a rocky road to some form of prostitution, for the poor and uneducated young women who work in the factories.

Tourism is probably Cambodia's biggest industry and is undoubtedly the fastest growing: visitor numbers leap by 30% each year. The tourism industry is a huge employer; many businesses are Cambodian and family-run, generating income to support an extended network of dependants. While salaries are low by Western standards, regular tips guarantee a high income by rural standards. As travellers delve deeper into other provinces, the benefits are starting to spread across the country. The picture at the top end is not quite so pretty, as most of the major hotels are foreign-owned and profits are rapidly repatriated to Singapore, France or wherever the shareholders are eagerly waiting. Visitor numbers look set to reach one million in the near future and this will have a huge impact on the Cambodian economy.

Interestingly, another big export earner in Cambodia is the transhipment of cigarettes and consumer goods from places such as Singapore, Malaysia and China. Cambodia has a customs system willing to 'overlook' taxes, and imports can thus be lucratively shipped on to more restrictive regional markets such as Thailand and Vietnam.

Cambodia is one of the poorest countries in Asia, although you could be forgiven for not realising this should you visit only Phnom Penh and Siem Reap. Cambodia's economic statistics are low by international standards, with average salaries around US$260 a year and about 36% of the population classified as poor. The figures look worse when you consider that some of Cambodia's principal sources of foreign exchange are unsustainable: foreign aid and timber sales. Foreign aid has far and away been Cambodia's chief money-spinner over recent years, contributing to more than half the government's annual budget. It accounts for most of the signs of affluence that the visitor sees in Phnom Penh – foreign cars, European restaurants and mobile phones. It also explains why many government workers were paid late or not at all during 1998; with aid frozen in the aftermath of July

1997's fighting, there simply wasn't enough money left in the coffers.

Out in the countryside, where 85% of the population lives, most people's livelihoods are agriculturally based and reliant on the vagaries of the annual southwestern monsoon. Rain shortages can result in bad harvests, as in 1994 and 1995, while major floods, such as those in 2000 and 2001, can wipe out crops. International relief efforts and government assistance have only narrowly staved off famine in some areas of the country. Most of the rural population is engaged in a subsistence struggle for survival, growing rice and other basic crops or fishing the rivers and lakes. Such lifestyles are often viewed by outsiders as timeless and idyllic, but idealised observations fail to account for the everyday realities of disease, land mines, a military intent on land grabs, and commercial fishing lots that businesspeople will protect at all costs. Despite this, life is good for some in the countryside, and it is generally true that to be poor in the countryside is better that to be poor in the city, but for the majority of Cambodians life remains an ongoing struggle to survive.

The regional economic crisis that engulfed much of Asia in the late 1990s had fewer repercussions for Cambodia than some of its larger neighbours because Cambodia's economy is so undeveloped in the first place. However, investment from countries such as Malaysia, which poured millions of dollars into Cambodia during the 1990s, has nose-dived. Some of the tourism projects being touted were dubious in the extreme (such as Disney-esque light shows at Angkor) and their cancellation can

A Penny More, Not a Penny Less

Cambodians have a proverb for every walk of life and the rampant problem of corruption is no exception. The saying goes, 'Small people take small bribes, big people take big bribes' and this aptly sums up the situation in Cambodia today. *Puk roluy* is Khmer for 'corruption' and translates literally as 'something that is rotten and should be thrown away'. And indeed, in a survey carried out by the Centre for Social Development, the results of which were published in August 1998, 98% of Cambodians questioned said it was very important to end corruption in the country.

Corruption is by no means a new trend in Cambodia – by the 19th century the problem was so widespread that many Cambodians had virtually enslaved themselves to their protectors. Yet another proverb summed up the situation succinctly: 'The rich must protect the poor, just as clothing protects the body'.

Following Cambodia's independence, the word 'government' became synonymous with corruption. It is alleged that in almost any matter that required government involvement, money had to change hands. The situation worsened when the USA moved in to prop up the Lon Nol government; nonexistent soldiers were added to the payroll and deaths and desertions went unreported. It is thought that by 1972 the military was pocketing the pay of about 100,000 of these phantom fighters. More seriously perhaps, many in the military and government sold weapons and supplies to the highest bidder, regardless of which side they fought for.

Corruption faded during the Pol Pot era, but for many Cambodians the stakes were much higher, as often they were buying their lives in gold or jewellery. Following the overthrow of the Khmer Rouge by the Vietnamese, survival was often the daily challenge and there was little or no scope for widespread corruption. However, certain sections of the government managed to accumulate personal fortunes during this period, and in the Thai border camps small-scale corruption was rampant as unscrupulous characters bartered and sold aid supplies.

It was the arrival of the free market and, later, the United Nations (UN) that really sent corruption spiralling out of control. The arrival of the United Nations Transitional Authority in Cambodia be considered extremely good news for Cambodia.

The factional fighting of July 1997 had a much bigger impact on the economy than the regional crisis. Donors suspended lucrative aid packages, leading to a budgetary crisis for much of 1998.

Little or no tax is paid in most parts of the country. A 10% sales tax was introduced at the start of 1999, but this alone is not enough to fund the sorts of social programmes that Cambodia needs. However, many private citizens are understandably unwilling to pay tax while corruption remains pervasive (see the boxed text 'A Penny More, Not a Penny Less'). However, happy days are here again: the international community has disbursed somewhere in the region of US$500 million each year since the Tokyo round of negotiations in early 1999. This subsidises almost half of Cambodia's government spending, some of which is going towards demobilising the vastly inflated armed forces.

Some observers suggest the key to Cambodia's future lies in scaling down aid money to demonstrate clearly to the Cambodian people just who is responsible for their plight and force the government to get its act together. However, it is just as feasible that the country would collapse if aid money was permanently withdrawn.

Membership of Asean is a step forward for the country, both economically and politically. It means that Cambodia's neighbours have a vested interest in peace and prosperity. While membership will no doubt lead to a greater exploitation of Cambodia's economy by some of these partners, it should attract more technical assistance for social welfare, health care and infrastructure

A Penny More, Not a Penny Less

(Untac) heralded the injection of more than US$2 billion into the country's tiny economy and created a bonanza of opportunity. The situation was so bad that by 1995 corruption was costing the government an estimated US$100 million a year in lost revenue. The figure today may be much higher, as the revenue lost to illegal logging alone is more than US$100 million. The saddest part of the saga is that the majority of Cambodians are extremely honest and their struggle to survive is already hard enough without having to contend with widespread corruption.

The average Cambodian encounters corruption from an early age – even some doctors and nurses are known to demand money before administering crucial treatment. It is not uncommon for students to bribe teachers to see exam papers in advance or for well-connected pupils to buy someone else's results after the test, thus depriving an able student of the chance for a scholarship. Teachers have been known to sell text books donated from overseas to make money, and many teachers levy a charge for pupils to attend class, preventing poor families from sending their children to school.

Jobs in the police force and the army can also be particularly lucrative, and for the tourist this is usually the only time you will encounter corruption. Traffic police are visible all over Phnom Penh, but certain areas of the city are considered more desirable than others because they offer the opportunity for a shakedown or two. The military earns a steady income on checkpoints in more remote parts of the country, shaking down truck and taxi drivers before letting the overcrowded vehicles pass.

Corruption needs to be eradicated in Cambodia before the country can realistically travel the road to development. However, with low salaries and little action, it would appear the country is set for many more years of puk roluy. If you are a tourist you'll probably part with only a few thousand riel during your visit, but if you're on business, you'd better come with a briefcase stuffed full of cash – that's dollars, not riel.

projects. It also offers Cambodia the chance to benefit from joint promotions of tourism and culture, funded by Asean.

The challenge for Cambodia is to create an environment where sustainable economic development can take place. At present, the signs indicate that the government is all too willing to encourage foreign investment in projects that generate short-term wealth for a few, but offer few long-term benefits for the many. Deforestation is an obvious example of this, but the endemic culture of corruption means that any investment in Cambodia is likely to do the same. Every country in the world suffers from corruption, but it is the scale in Cambodia that is galling to the average citizen. Most Cambodians are hard-working and honest; it would be good if the same could be said for all of their politicians.

POPULATION & PEOPLE

Cambodia's first census in decades, carried out in 1998, put the country's population at nearly 11.5 million. With an annual growth rate of 2.4%, the population is well on its way to 13 million and is predicted to exceed 20 million by 2020.

Phnom Penh is the largest city, with a population of about one million. Other major population centres include Battambang, Siem Reap and Sihanoukville. The most populous province is Kompong Cham, where 14% of Cambodians live, followed by Kandal, which is also the most densely populated (300 people per sq km). The most sparsely populated is Mondulkiri, which is also the country's largest province. Krong Kep and Krong Pailin have the smallest populations, although these are small autonomous districts rather than provinces.

Cambodia is set for major demographic changes in the next couple of decades. Currently, just 15% of the population lives in urban areas, which contrasts starkly with the country's more-developed neighbours such as Malaysia and Thailand. Increasing numbers of young people in search of opportunity are likely to migrate to the cities, changing forever the face of contemporary Cambodian society.

Infant mortality rates in Cambodia are among the highest in Southeast Asia, at 73 per 1000. Due to poverty, poor sanitation and disease, it is estimated that nearly one child in 10 dies before the age of five. Diarrhoea is the biggest killer of young children. Malnutrition and the effects of a mononutritional (single-staple) diet are also common, with about half the children under five either stunted or underweight. Maternal mortality rates are also high at 650 per 100,000 live births.

Life expectancy is low, at an average of 53.6 years for men and 58.6 years for women. The much discussed imbalance of men to women due to years of conflict is not as serious as it was in 1980, but it is still significant: there are currently 93.1 males to every 100 females, up from 86.1 to 100 in 1980. There is, however, a marked imbalance in age groups: about 50% of the population is under the age of 15.

Women

The status of women in Cambodia is somewhat ambiguous. While up to 20% of women head the household, and in some families women are the sole breadwinners, men have a monopoly on all of the most important positions of power at a governmental level and have a dominant social role at a domestic level.

While Cambodian political and religious policies do not directly discriminate against women, females are rarely afforded the same opportunities as males. In recent years, laws passed on abortion, domestic violence and trafficking have improved the legal position of women, but they have had little effect on the bigger picture.

As young children, females are treated fairly equally, but as they get older their access to education becomes more restricted. This is particularly so in rural areas, where girls are not allowed to live and study in wats (Buddhist temple-monasteries).

Many women set up simple businesses in their towns or villages, but it is not an easy path should they want to progress further. Only two women (both Funcinpec members) hold ministerial rank and there are

Khmer Krom

The Khmer Krom people of southern Vietnam are ethnic Khmers separated from Cambodia by historical deals and Vietnamese encroachment on what was once Cambodian territory. Nobody is sure just how many of them there are – estimates vary from one million to seven million, depending on who is doing the counting; but however many Khmer Krom there are, the issue of their treatment in Vietnam is gaining increasing attention. Local representatives point to Bosnia as an example of how ethnic frustration can erupt into violence if left to simmer for too long.

The history of Vietnamese expansion into Khmer territory has long been a staple of Khmer schoolbooks. King Chey Chetha II of Cambodia, in keeping with the wishes of his Vietnamese queen, first allowed Vietnamese to settle in the Cambodian town of Prey Nokor in 1620. It was obviously the thin edge of the wedge – Prey Nokor is now better known as Ho Chi Minh City (Saigon).

Representatives of the Khmer Krom claim that although they dress as Vietnamese and carry Vietnamese identity cards, they remain culturally Khmer. Vietnamese attempts to quash Khmer Krom language and religion (the Khmers are Theravada Buddhists, while the Vietnamese practise Mahayana Buddhism) have for the most part failed. Even assimilation through intermarriage has failed to take place on a large scale.

Many Khmer Krom would like to see Cambodia act as a mediator in the quest for greater autonomy and ethnic representation in Vietnam. The Cambodian government, for its part, is more concerned with the vast numbers of illegal Vietnamese inside its borders, as well as reports of Vietnamese encroachments on the eastern borders of Cambodia.

---

only seven female legislators in Parliament from a total of 122, even though women make up 56% of the voters. There are no female prosecutors or provincial governors and just eight female judges among 110. Only 13% of administrative and management positions and 28% of professional positions are held by women nationally.

Other issues of concern for women in Cambodia are those of domestic violence, prostitution and the spread of sexually transmitted infections (STIs). Domestic violence is quite widespread but, because of fear and shame, it's not known exactly how serious a problem it is. There is a high incidence of child prostitution and illegal trafficking of prostitutes within Cambodia, Thailand and Vietnam. See the boxed text 'The Abuse of Innocence' in the Facts for the Visitor chapter for more on the scourge of child prostitution in Cambodia.

Cambodia has the highest rate of human immunodeficiency virus (HIV) infection in Southeast Asia. World Health Organization (WHO) figures indicate that 3.2% of Cambodians have HIV/AIDS; 33.2% of sex workers are infected.

Ethnic Khmers

According to official statistics, around 96% of the people who live in Cambodia are ethnic Khmers, making the country the most homogeneous in Southeast Asia. In reality, perhaps 10% of the population is Cham, Chinese or Vietnamese.

The Khmers have inhabited Cambodia since the beginning of recorded history (around the 2nd century AD), many centuries before the Thais and Vietnamese migrated to the region. During the next 600 years, Khmer culture and religion were influenced by contact with the civilisations of India and Java. Over the centuries, the Khmers have mixed with other groups residing in Cambodia, including the Javanese and Malays (8th century), Thais (10th to 15th centuries), Vietnamese (from the early 17th century) and Chinese (since the 18th century).

Ethnic Vietnamese

The Vietnamese are one of the largest non-Khmer groups in Cambodia. According to government figures, Cambodia is host to around 100,000 Vietnamese. Unofficial observers claim that the real figure may be as high as half a million. There is a great deal of dislike and distrust between the Cambodians and the Vietnamese, even among those who have been living in Cambodia for generations. While the Khmers refer to the Vietnamese as *yuon,* a derogatory term that means 'barbarians', the Vietnamese look down on the Khmers and consider them lazy for not farming every available bit of land, an absolute necessity in densely populated Vietnam.

For the Khmers the mistrust of the Vietnamese has a historical basis. The Vietnamese appropriated the lands of the Mekong Delta from the Khmers in the 17th century and now govern the area known as Kampuchea Krom (Lower Cambodia). Vietnamese encroachments on Cambodian territory remain a major concern to the Cambodian government, and with the border between the two countries still not satisfactorily demarcated, it is unlikely that such prejudice will fade any time in the forseeable future (see the boxed text 'Khmer Krom' earlier in this chapter for more details).

Ethnic Chinese

The government claims that there are around 50,000 ethnic Chinese in Cambodia. Other informed observers say there are more likely to be as many as half a million in urban areas. Many Chinese Cambodians have lived in Cambodia for generations and have adopted the Khmer culture, language and identity.

Until 1975, ethnic Chinese controlled the economic life of Cambodia. In recent years the group has re-emerged as a powerful economic force, mainly due to increased investment by overseas Chinese. Many of the illegal Chinese immigrants who have come to Cambodia during the last decade have managed to retain their culture to a significant degree.

Cham Muslims

Cambodia's Cham Muslims (known locally as the Khmer Islam) officially number around 200,000. Unofficial counts put the figure at around 300,000. The Chams live in villages on the banks of the Mekong and the Tonlé Sap Rivers, mostly in Kompong Cham, Kompong Speu and Kompong Chhnang Provinces. They suffered particularly vicious persecution between 1975 and 1979, when a large part of their community was exterminated. Many Cham mosques that were destroyed under the Khmer Rouge have been rebuilt. Not all Cambodian Muslims are of Cham origin; a significant minority are descended from Malay immigrants who have since intermarried with the Chams.

Ethno-Linguistic Minorities

Cambodia's diverse Khmer Loeu (Upper Khmer) or *chunchiet* (minorities), who live in the country's mountainous regions, probably number between 60,000 and 70,000.

The majority of these groups live in the northeast of Cambodia, in the provinces of Ratanakiri, Mondulkiri, Stung Treng and Kratie. The largest group is the Tumpoun (many other spellings are used), who number around 15,000. Other groups include the Pnong, Kreung, Kra Chok, Kavet, Brao and Jarai.

The hill tribes of Cambodia have long been isolated from mainstream Khmer society, and there is little in the way of mutual understanding. They practise shifting cultivation, rarely staying in one place for more than four or five years. Finding a new location for a village requires a village elder to mediate with the spirit world. Very few of the minorities wear the sort of colourful traditional costumes you see in Thailand, Laos and Vietnam. While this may not make for interesting photographs, it takes away that depressing human safari-park feel that surrounds visits to tribal villages in other countries.

Little research has been done on Cambodia's hill tribes, and tourism in the northeast is still in its infancy. There is much to be concerned about regarding the impact of tourism, development and logging on Cambodia's more isolated tribes. Increasing numbers of Khmers are buying up tribal lands in these remote areas, while some foreigners have been buying old totems from sacred burial grounds in Ratanakiri; neither of these actions have the long-term interests of the minorities at heart.

Repatriation Programmes

Since 1992 the United Nations High Commission for Refugees (UNHCR) has repatriated more than 370,000 Cambodians, mostly those who had sought refuge in Thailand. The first returnees crossed the border at Poipet (Poay Pet) on 30 March 1992. The following year, hundreds of thousands more were resettled and able to take part in their country's elections. Dozens of nongovernmental aid agencies provided support for the programme, one of the largest and most complex ever undertaken.

As the civil war dragged on, there remained significant numbers of people who had fled heavy fighting in the north and northwest of the country. During the first half of 1999, many of these internally displaced Cambodians were returned to their areas of origin.

EDUCATION

Under French rule the education of Cambodians was grossly neglected, with only one high school in Phnom Penh before WWII, and no universities. Early in his reign King Sihanouk took a lively interest in education. Between 1953 and 1968 the number of primary students rocketed from 300,000 to one million. Even more spectacularly, the number of secondary students increased from 5000 to around one million. Nine universities were also established in this period. Unfortunately, despite its good intentions, the programme has been widely criticised for creating uniformly poor educational levels and unrealistic employment expectations – there were not enough highly skilled jobs to go around.

The Pol Pot regime put a stop to educational development. Indeed, as far as the Khmer Rouge was concerned, education was an evil. Many qualified teachers perished at this time, and by 1979 Cambodia had only around 3000 secondary school teachers remaining.

Through the 1980s and 1990s the situation gradually improved. Adult literacy rates are currently around 65%, but vary wildly between provinces. It is generally thought that overall education standards are higher than they have ever been. Four technical institutions (including the popular National Institute of Management) and two universities have been established. In Phnom Penh and regional centres, private schools have blossomed.

Sadly, there is a disparity between the number of males and females in the education system. This can be partly accounted for by the opportunity for males to continue their education within the environment of a wat, thus lessening the cost burden on the family, but must also come down to a certain degree of inequality between the sexes (see Women in the Population & People section earlier in this chapter).

ARTS

The Khmer Rouge's assault on the arts was a terrible blow to Cambodian culture. Indeed, for many years the common consensus among Khmers was that their culture had been irrevocably lost. The Khmer Rouge not only did away with living bearers of Khmer culture, it also destroyed cultural artefacts, statues, musical instruments, books and anything else that served as a reminder of a past it was trying to efface. The temples of Angkor were spared as a symbol of Khmer glory and empire, but little else survived. Despite this, Cambodia is witnessing a resurgence of traditional arts and a growing interest in experimentation in modern arts and cross-cultural fusion. A trip to the School of Fine Arts in Phnom Penh is evidence of the extent to which Khmer culture has bounced back.

Dance

More than any of the other traditional arts, Cambodia's royal ballet is a tangible link with the glory of Angkor. Early in his reign, King Sihanouk released the traditional harem of royal *apsara* (heavenly nymphs) that went with the crown. Nevertheless, prior to the Pol Pot regime, classical ballet was still taught at the palace. Its traditions stretched long into the past, when the art of the apsara resounded to the glory of the divine king.

Cambodian court dance is related to the dance of Thailand, Java and India: all share the same cultural sources, and many of the dances enact scenes from the Hindu epic the *Ramayana*. However, the apsara dance is unique to Cambodia, devised by King Sihanouk's mother Kossamak Neariroth as a means of bringing history to life.

Dance fared particularly badly during the Pol Pot years. Very few dancers and teachers survived, including only one old woman who knew how to make the elaborate costumes that are sewn piece by piece onto the dancers before a performance. In 1981, with a handful of teachers, the School of Fine Arts was reopened and the training of dance students resumed. Orphans were given first preference in the initial intake of students.

Much of Cambodian royal dance resembles that of India and Thailand, as the Thais learnt their techniques from the Khmers after sacking Angkor in the 15th century: the same stylised hand movements; the same sequined, lamé costumes; the same opulent stupa-like headwear. Where royal dance was traditionally an all-female affair (with the exception of the role of the monkey), there are now more male dancers featured.

Many of the popular dances staged today incorporate elements of more lively folk dance. Cambodian folk dances such as *robam choon pore* (wishing dance) or *robam rop trey* (fishing dance) often have roots in spirit worship and animist traditions, and represent asking the gods for a good harvest, a good catch or better rainfall.

Another interesting dance tradition is *lkhaon khol,* Cambodia's masked theatre. Traditionally all the roles were played by men, and it was a popular form of entertainment, with troupes touring the country presenting performances of the *Ramayana* over several evenings. A narrator presides over the performance, providing dialogue and instructions to the small accompanying orchestra. Short performances of masked theatre are sometimes included in shows put on for foreign tourists.

Music

The bas-reliefs on some of the monuments in the Angkor region depict musicians and apsara holding instruments similar to the traditional Khmer instruments of today. This demonstrates that Cambodia has a long musical tradition all its own.

Traditionally, music was an accompaniment to a ritual or performance that had religious significance. Musicologists have identified six types of Cambodian musical ensemble, each used in different settings. The most traditional of these is the *areak ka,* an ensemble that performs at weddings. The instruments of the areak ka include a *tro khmae* (three-stringed fiddle), a *khsae muoy* (singled-stringed bowed instrument) and *skor areak* (drums), among others.

Instruments used to accompany dance are more percussive, and are played by a reduced ensemble of musicians. The instruments generally include at least one stringed instrument, a *roneat* (xylophone) and sets of drums and cymbals.

Much of Cambodia's traditional music was lost during the Pol Pot era. The Khmer Rouge targeted famous singers and the great Sin Sisamuth, Cambodia's most famous songwriter and performer, was executed in the first days of the regime. After this time many Khmers settled in the USA, where a lively Khmer pop industry developed. Influenced by US music and later exported back to Cambodia, it has been enormously popular and many of the contemporary karaoke videos originate in Long Beach, California.

A new generation of overseas Khmers growing up with influences from the West is starting to produce its own sound. *The Khmer Rouge* is a rap album produced by a young Cambodian-American. It draws heavily on the sound of Public Enemy and Dr Dre, but with a unique Cambodian twist; it's well worth seeking out in Phnom Penh's markets.

Phnom Penh too has a burgeoning pop industry, many of whose famous stars perform at the huge restaurants located across the Japanese Bridge. It is easy to join in the fun by visiting one of the innumerable karaoke bars around the country.

One form of music unique to Cambodia is *chapaye,* a sort of Cambodian blues sung to the accompaniment of a two-stringed wooden instrument similar in sound to a bass guitar without the amplifier. There are few old masters such as Pra Chouen left alive, but chapaye is still often shown on late-night Cambodian television before transmission ends.

Literature

Cambodia's literary tradition is limited and very much tied in with Buddhism or myth and legend. Sanskrit, and later Pali, came to Cambodia with Hinduism and Buddhism and much of Cambodia's religious scripture exists only in these ancient languages. Legend has been used to expound the core Cambodian values of family and faith, as well as obedience to authority.

One of the most popular stories is *Thum Tio*. Tio, a young girl, falls for Thum, a travelling monk who gives up his robes to become a musician. Tio's mother is unhappy about this young love and sends her daughter to the palace to become a concubine of the king. Tio is very unhappy and tells the king she misses home, so the king arranges for some musicians to come to the palace to play to her. Thum is among them and Tio breaks down, sharing their story with the king. He is touched by this true love and sanctions their marriage, making Thum a court musician. One day, Tio receives a message her mother is ill and returns to visit her. In fact it is a trick, as the mother has arranged for her to marry the son of the Kompong Cham governor. When she fails to return, Thum comes to find her and is murdered by the new husband. Tio finds his body and is heartbroken, killing herself with a dagger on the spot. When the king finds out, he has the governor's family tried and killed.

Many Cambodians believe that this story is true, and it certainly does contain all the elements of a contemporary crisis that might face village girls today, their parents lured by substantial sums of money into organising arranged marriages with no basis in love.

Architecture

Khmer architecture reached its peak during the Angkorian era (the 9th to 14th centuries AD). Some of the finest examples of architecture from this period are Angkor Wat and the structures of Angkor Thom. See the 'Temples of Angkor' special section for more information on the architectural styles of the Angkorian era.

Today, most rural Cambodian houses are built on high wood pilings (if the family can afford it) and have thatch roofs, walls made of palm mats and floors of woven bamboo strips resting on bamboo joists. The shady space underneath is used for storage and for people to relax at midday. Wealthier families have houses with wooden walls and tiled roofs, but the basic design remains the same.

The French left their mark in Cambodia in the form of handsome villas and government buildings built in neoclassical style – Romanesque pillars and all. Some of the best examples are in Phnom Penh, but most provincial capitals have at least one or two examples of architecture from the colonial period. The Russians, fortunately, left few marks, but the Council of Ministers building is a good example of how ugly they could make a building when they tried. Most modern structures are influenced by the wedding-cake school of architecture from Thailand or Vietnam, although a number of buildings are going up in neocolonial style.

Sculpture

Even in the pre-Angkorian era, in the periods generally referred to as Funan and Chenla, the people of Cambodia were producing masterfully sensuous sculpture that was no simple copy of the Indian forms it was modelled on. Some scholars maintain that the Cambodian forms are unrivalled in India itself.

The earliest surviving Cambodian sculpture dates from the 6th century AD. Most of it depicts Vishnu with four or eight arms. Generally Vishnu has acquired Indochinese facial characteristics and is more muscular than similar Indian sculpture, in which divinities tend towards rounded flabbiness. A large eight-armed Vishnu from this period is displayed at the National Museum in Phnom Penh.

Also on display at the National Museum is a statue of Harihara, a divinity who combines aspects of both Vishnu and Shiva. The statue dates from the end of the 7th century, and the sensuous plasticity of the musculature prefigures the technical accomplishment of Angkorian-era art.

The sculpture of the pre-Angkorian period is not restricted to the depiction of Hindu deities. This period also features much Buddhist-inspired sculpture, mainly in the form of Bodhisattva. By the 9th century and the beginning of the Angkorian empire, however, the sculptures are exclusively Hindu-inspired.

Innovations of the early Angkorian era include freestanding sculpture that dispenses with the stone aureole that in earlier works supported the multiple arms of Hindu deities. The faces assume an air of tranquillity, and the overall effect is less animated. In the National Museum, look for the statue of Shiva from the Bakong for an example of early Angkorian sculpture: it depicts a stocky frame and a smiling face that is characteristic of this period.

The Banteay Srei style of the late 10th century is commonly regarded as a high point in the evolution of Southeast Asian art. The National Museum has a splendid piece from this period: a sandstone statue of Shiva holding Uma, his wife, on his knee. The Baphuon style of the 11th century was inspired to a certain extent by the sculpture of Banteay Srei, producing some of the finest works to have survived today. In the National Museum, look for the life-size *Vishnu Reclining,* which is featured in the bronze display hall. Only the head, shoulders and two right arms have survived; it was once inlaid with precious metal and gems that must have brought the statue to life.

The statuary of the Angkor Wat period is felt to be conservative and stilted, lacking the grace of earlier work. The genius of this period manifests itself more clearly in the architecture and fabulous bas-reliefs of Angkor Wat itself.

TRUDI CANAVAN

Head of King Jayavarman VII

The final high point in Angkorian sculpture is the Bayon period from the end of the 12th century to the beginning of the 13th century. In the National Museum in Phnom Penh, look for the superb representation of Jayavarman VII, an image that simultaneously projects great power and sublime tranquillity. Also represented from this period is the simple image of Jayarajadevi from Preah Khan in central Cambodia.

Sculpture in the post-Angkorian period remained highly stylised, as demonstrated by the 16th-century bas-reliefs added to the incomplete lower galleries of Angkor Wat. However, sculptors tended to move away from stone to the carving of wooden Buddhas, many of which are now on display in the National Museum in a permanent collection of post-Angkorian Buddhas.

Handicrafts

With a tradition of craftsmanship that produced the temples of Angkor, it is hardly surprising to find that even today Khmers produce exquisitely carved silver, wood and stone. Many of the designs hark back to those of the Angkorian period and are tasteful objects of art. Pottery is also an industry

Sihanouk & the Silver Screen

Between 1965 and 1969 Sihanouk wrote, directed and produced nine feature films, a figure that would put the average workaholic Hollywood director to shame. Sihanouk took the business of making films very seriously, and family and officials were called upon to do their bit – the minister of foreign affairs played the male lead in Sihanouk's first feature, *Apsara* (Heavenly Nymph). When, in the same movie, a show of military hardware was required, the air force was brought into action, as was the army's fleet of helicopters.

The world premiere of *Apsara* was something of a flop, the foreign community failing to patronise the movie. Although, as Milton Osbourne says in his biography *Sihanouk – Prince of Light, Prince of Darkness,* the Chinese embassy staff did at least have the good manners to excuse themselves on the pretext of pressing business elsewhere – 'because of the Cultural Revolution'.

Not that this put the royal film maker off. On the contrary, Sihanouk continued to make movies, often taking on the leading roles himself. Notable performances saw him as a spirit of the forest and as a victorious general. Perhaps it was no surprise, given the king's apparent addiction to the world of celluloid dreams, that Cambodia should challenge Cannes and Berlin with its Phnom Penh International Film Festival. The festival was held twice, in 1968 and 1969. Sihanouk won the grand prize on both occasions.

with a long history in Cambodia and there are many ancient kiln sites scattered throughout the country. Designs range from the extremely simple, to much more intricate drinking cups carved in the image of elephants, teapots carved in the image of birds and jars carved in the image of gods. The modern pottery industry is based around clay-fired pots produced in Kompong Chhnang, but in time it is likely that older designs will once more be produced for tourist consumption.

Cinema

The film industry in Cambodia was given a new lease of life in 2000 with the release of *Pos Keng Kong* (The Giant Snake). A remake of a 1950s Cambodian classic, it tells the story of a powerful young girl born from a rural relationship between a woman and a snake king. It is an interesting love story, albeit with dodgy special effects, and achieved massive box-office success around the region. Sadly, its success also points to the downfall of the Cambodian industry, as bootleg versions soon appeared all over Asia.

At least one overseas Cambodian director has had success in recent years: Rithy Panh's *People of the Rice Fields* was nominated for the Palme d'Or at the Cannes Film Festival

in May 1995. The film touches only fleetingly on the Khmer Rouge, depicting the lives of a family eking out an arduous existence in the rice fields. Rithy Panh has been active in encouraging other young Cambodians to take up film making, holding screenwriting seminars in Phnom Penh. More recently he released *One Night After the War*.

However, the general picture of cinema in Cambodia is one of decline. In 1989 some 200 film companies were registered with the Cinema Department. These days there are just a handful left, mostly showing karaoke videos. Local directors point to low audience numbers and the popularity of foreign videos as the main problem. It doesn't help that there is only one real cinema left in the country – and it's no multiplex. Even Prime Minister Hun Sen has weighed in on the issue, claiming that local scriptwriters should 'write more happy endings' if they want to revive the industry.

SOCIETY & CONDUCT

Cambodia is a very traditional society that values family structures and the role of religion in regulating life. Like its regional neighbours, it is also a country in the midst of change as a new postwar generation grows up oblivious to the hardships of their parents, who unsurprisingly don't want to dwell on a painful past. Young urban Cambodians have grown up with MTV and Western movies and no longer share the values to which their traditional elders ascribe. Youth rebellion is on the rise and it is likely that some of the trad-itions older Cambodians have clung to in order to rebuild and refocus their lives after the war will fall by the wayside in a rush to modernise. However, for now, Cambodian society is much more traditional than those of Thailand and Vietnam, and the conduct of outsiders needs to be adjusted accordingly.

Greetings

Cambodians traditionally greet each other with the *sompiah,* which involves pressing the hands together in prayer and bowing, similar to the *wai* in Thailand. In general the higher the hands and the lower the bow the more respect is shown. In recent decades this custom has been partially replaced by the Western practice of shaking hands. But, although men tend to shake hands with each other, women usually use the traditional greeting with both men and women. It is considered acceptable (or perhaps excusable) for foreigners to shake hands with Cambodians of both sexes.

Dress

Both men and women often wear sarongs (made of cotton, a cotton-synthetic blend or silk), especially at home. Men who can afford it usually prefer to wear silk sarongs. Most urban Khmer men dress in trousers and many women dress in Western-style clothing.

On formal occasions such as religious festivals and family celebrations, women often wear a *hol* (a type of shirt) during the day. At night they change into single-colour silk dresses called *phamuong,* which are decorated along the hems. If the celebration is a wedding, the colours of such garments are stipulated by the day of the week on which the wedding is held.

The women of Cambodia are generally modest in their dress, although this is changing in Phnom Penh. When eating at home,

they sit on floor mats with their feet to the side rather than in the lotus position, as do the men. As in Thailand, nude bathing is unacceptable.

Travellers crossing the border from liberal Thai islands such as Ko Pha Ngan or Ko Chang, should remember they have crossed back in time as far as traditions are concerned and that wandering around the temples of Angkor bare-chested (men) or scantily clad (women) will not be appreciated by Khmers.

Visiting Khmers

A small token of gratitude in the form of a gift is always appreciated when visiting someone. Gifts should always be offered with the right hand. If you want to be particularly polite, support your right elbow with the fingers of your left hand as you do so. Before entering a Khmer home, always remove your shoes if the homeowners do so. This applies to some guesthouses and restaurants as well – if there is a pile of shoes at the doorway, take yours off as well. When eating a meal with Khmers, be sure not to leave the chopsticks vertically in the bowl, as this symbolises death.

Visiting Pagodas

The Khmers are tolerant and may choose not to point out improper behaviour to their foreign guests, but it is important to dress and act with the utmost respect when visiting wats or other religious sites (such as some of the temples of Angkor). This is all the more important given the vital role Buddhism has played in the lives of many Cambodians in the aftermath of the Khmer Rouge holocaust. Proper etiquette in Cambodian pagodas is mostly a matter of common sense.

Unlike in Thailand, a woman may accept something from a monk, but must be extremely careful not to touch him in the process. A few other tips include:

- Don't wear shorts or tank tops.
- Take off your hat when entering the grounds of a wat.
- Take off your shoes before going into the *vihara* (temple sanctuary).

- If you sit down in front of the dais (the platform on which the Buddhas are placed), sit with your feet to the side rather than in the lotus position.
- Bow slightly in the presence of a monk, particularly an elderly monk. This isn't so important with younger monks who are looking to practise their English, but is always important to Khmers who view monks as temporary incarnations of the Buddha.
- Putting a small sum of money in the donation box will be much appreciated by residents at the temple and visiting Khmers, as it is a mark of respect towards their faith and traditions.
- Never point your finger – or, nirvana forbid, the soles of your feet – towards a monk or a Buddha figure.

Dos & Don'ts
There are some other guidelines that are worth remembering while visiting the country:

- Getting angry and showing it by shouting or becoming abusive is impolite and a poor reflection on you; it is also unlikely to accomplish much. Getting angry means loss of face and makes all Asians uncomfortable – take a deep breath and keep your cool. If things aren't being done as they should, remember that there is a critical shortage of trained people in the country because the majority of educated Cambodians either fled the country or were killed between 1975 and 1979.
- The head is considered holy and so it is improper to pat adults or children on the head.
- If you would like someone to come over to you, motion with your whole hand held palm down – signalling with your index finger and your palm pointed skyward may be interpreted as being sexually suggestive.
- When using a toothpick, it is considered polite to hold it in one hand and to cover your open mouth with the other.
- When handing things to other people, use both hands or your right hand only, never your left hand (reserved for bathroom ablutions).

Treatment of Animals
There's lots of animal cruelty in Cambodia, as to most Cambodians animals are considered little more than a protein source. From live, peeled frogs in the market, to hundreds of chickens bouncing up and down on the back of a *moto* (small motorcycle with driver), everything abhorrent to an animal lover can be found in Cambodia. However, this is hardly cruelty in a vindictive sense of the word – most Khmers are just trying to survive and worrying about the health and comfort of their future food is not a priority. There is no point in getting steamed up about it; just learn to avoid the food sections of markets if this sort of thing is upsetting.

In some restaurants and guesthouses, birds or monkeys are kept as pets. Often the birdcages are pitifully small or the ropes for the monkeys disturbingly short. Some people used to keep bears and other wild creatures in cages in their houses, possibly for medicinal use, but thankfully this is dying out, as new animal trafficking laws impose heavy fines on such individuals, as well as any restaurant that sells bush meats.

RELIGION
Hinduism
Hinduism flourished alongside Buddhism from the 1st century AD until the 14th century. During the pre-Angkorian period, Hinduism was represented by the worship of Harihara (Shiva and Vishnu embodied in a single deity). During the time of Angkor, Shiva was the deity most in favour with the royal family, although in the 12th century he seems to have been superseded by Vishnu. Today some elements of Hinduism are still incorporated into important ceremonies involving birth, marriage and death.

Buddhism
The majority of the people of Cambodia are followers of Theravada Buddhism. Buddhism was introduced to Cambodia between the 13th and 14th centuries and was the state religion until 1975. There are two sects of Buddhism in Cambodia: the Mahanikai and the Thammayut. The Thammayut sect was brought from Thailand into Cambodia by 19th-century Cambodian kings and princes. Thammayut monks wear darker robes than their saffron-clad Mahanikai counterparts.

Archaeologists have determined that before the 9th century, a period during which Sanskrit was used in ritual inscriptions, the

MARTIN HARRIS

Buddhist monk

Theravada school constituted the prevalent form of Buddhism in Cambodia. Inscriptions and images indicate that Mahayana Buddhism was in favour after the 9th century, but was replaced in the 13th century by a form of Theravada Buddhism, which arrived, along with the Pali language, from Sri Lanka via Thailand.

Between 1975 and 1979 the vast majority of Cambodia's Buddhist monks were murdered by the Khmer Rouge and nearly all of the country's wats (more than 3000) were damaged or destroyed. In the late 1980s Buddhism was again made the state religion. At that time, Cambodia had about 6000 monks, who by law had to be at least 60 years old. The age requirements have been relaxed and young monks are once again a common sight throughout the country. Many wats have been rebuilt or rehabilitated in the past decade and visitors will encounter money-raising drives for this work taking place on the roadside in every corner of the country.

The Theravada (Teaching of the Elders) school of Buddhism is an earlier and, according to its followers, less-corrupted form of Buddhism than the Mahayana schools found in eastern Asia or in the Himalayan lands. The Theravada school is also called the 'southern' school, as it took the southern route from India, its place of origin, through Southeast Asia – in this case Myanmar (Burma), Thailand, Laos and Cambodia – while the 'northern' school proceeded north into Nepal, Tibet, China, Korea, Mongolia, Vietnam and Japan. Because the southern school tried to preserve or limit the Buddhist doctrines to only those canons codified in the early Buddhist era, the northern school gave Theravada Buddhism the derogatory name Hinayana, meaning 'Lesser Vehicle'. The northern school considered itself Mahayana (Great Vehicle) because it built upon the earlier teachings, 'expanding' the doctrine to respond more to the needs of lay people, or so it claimed.

Theravada doctrine stresses the three principal aspects of existence: *dukkha* (suffering, unsatisfactoriness, disease), *anicca* (impermanency, transience of all things), and *anatta* (nonsubstantiality or nonessentiality of reality; no permanent 'soul'). These concepts, when 'discovered' by Siddhartha Gautama in the 6th century BC, were in direct contrast to the Hindu belief in an eternal, blissful Self.

Gautama, an Indian prince turned ascetic, subjected himself to many years of severe austerities to arrive at this vision of the world and was given the title Buddha (the Enlightened or the Awakened). Gautama Buddha spoke of four noble truths, which had the power to liberate any human being who could realise them. These four noble truths are:

- The truth of suffering – 'Existence is suffering'
- The truth of the cause of suffering – 'Suffering is caused by desire'

- The truth of the cessation of suffering – 'Eliminate the cause of suffering (desire) and suffering will cease to arise'
- The truth of the path – 'The eightfold path is the way to eliminate desire/extinguish suffering'

The eightfold path *(atthangika-magga)* consists of:

- Right understanding
- Right-mindedness (or 'right thought')
- Right speech
- Right bodily conduct
- Right livelihood
- Right effort
- Right attentiveness
- Right concentration

These eight limbs belong to three different 'pillars' of practice: morality or *sila* (speech, bodily conduct, livelihood), concentration or *samadhi* (effort, attentiveness), and wisdom or *panna* (understanding, thought).

The eightfold path is also known as the Middle Way since it avoids both extreme austerity and extreme sensuality.

The ultimate goal of Theravada Buddhism is *nirvana,* which literally means the 'blowing out' or 'extinction' of all causes of dukkha. Effectively, it means elimination of all desire and suffering, reaching a blessed state – the final stage of reincarnation. In reality, most Buddhists aim for rebirth in a 'better' existence rather than the supramundane goal of nirvana, which is highly misunderstood by Asians as well as Westerners. Many Buddhists express the feeling that they are somehow unworthy of nirvana. By feeding monks, giving donations to temples and performing regular worship at the local wat they hope to improve their lot, acquiring enough merit to prevent, or at least reduce, the number of rebirths. The making of merit is an important social and religious activity. The concept of reincarnation is universally accepted by Cambodian Buddhists, and to some extent even by non-Buddhists.

The Trilatna (Triratna), or Triple Gems of Buddhism, are the Buddha, the Dharma (the Teachings) and the Sangha (the Buddhist Brotherhood). The Buddha in his sculptural form is found on high shelves or altars in homes and shops as well as in temples. The Dharma is chanted morning and evening in every wat. The Sangha is represented by the street presence of orange-robed monks, especially in the early morning hours when they perform their alms rounds, in what has almost become a travel-guide cliche in motion.

Socially, every Buddhist male is expected to become a monk *(lok song)* for a short period in his life, optimally between the time he finishes school and starts a career or marries. Men or boys under 20 years of age may enter the Sangha as novices and this is not unusual since a family earns great merit when one of its sons takes robe and bowl. Traditionally, the time spent in the wat is three months during the Buddhist Lent *(phansaa* or *watsa),* which begins in July and coincides with the wet season. However, nowadays men may spend as little as a week or 15 days to accrue merit as monks. Some younger monks in Cambodia may be petty criminals fresh out of prison and attempting to redress their karmic balance.

Monks must follow 227 vows or precepts and many monks ordain for a lifetime. Of these, a large percentage become scholars and teachers, while some specialise in healing and/or folk magic. There is no similar hermit-like order for nuns, but women are welcome to reside in temples as lay nuns *(doan chee)* with shaved heads and white robes.

The women have to follow only eight precepts. Because discipline for these 'nuns' is much less arduous, they don't attain quite as high a social status as do monks. However, despite not performing ceremonies on behalf of other lay persons, they engage in the same basic religious activities (meditation and study of Dharma) as monks. The reality is that wats that draw sizable contingents of nuns are highly respected because women don't choose temples for reasons of clerical status – when more than a few reside at one temple it's because the teachings there are considered particularly strong.

Animism

Both Hinduism and Buddhism were gradually absorbed from beyond the borders of

Cambodia, fusing with the animist beliefs already present among the Khmers before Indianisation. Local beliefs didn't simply fade away, but were incorporated into the new religions to form something uniquely Cambodian. The concept of Neak Ta is unique to Cambodia and has its foundations in animist beliefs regarding sacred soil and the sacred spirit around us. Neak Ta can be viewed as a Mother Earth concept, an energy force uniting a community with its earth and water. It can be represented in many forms from stone to wood to termite hills, anything that symbolises both a link between the people and the fertility of their land, and a link to their ancestors before them.

The purest form of animism is practised among the Khmer Loeu, or ethnic minorities of the northeast (see Ethno-Linguistic Minorities in the Population & People section earlier in this chapter). Some have converted to Buddhism, but the majority continues to worship spirits of the earth and skies and the spirits of their forefathers. In times of bad harvest or misfortune, a tribe will pray to the spirits of nature to ask for an end to the punishment. Villagers communicate with these spirits through the medium of rice wine, drinking until inebriated and then entering a trance.

Islam

Cambodia's Muslims are descendants of Chams who migrated from what is now central Vietnam after the final defeat of the kingdom of Champa by the Vietnamese in 1471, since intermarried with mercantile immigrants from Malaysia (see Cham Muslims in the People & Population section earlier in this chapter). Whereas their compatriots who remained in Vietnam were only partly Islamicised, the Cambodian Chams adopted a fairly orthodox version of Sunni Islam and maintained links with other Muslim communities in the region. Like

their Buddhist neighbours, however, the Cham Muslims call the faithful to prayer by banging a drum, rather than with the call of the *muezzin* (official who proclaims the call to prayer), as in most Muslim lands. However, modern influences such as loudspeakers have led some mosques to adopt the muezzin call to prayer.

There are very few Muslims in Cambodia fluent in Arabic, the language of the Koran. Halal meat (killed according to Islamic law) is available in Phnom Penh in the Psar O Russei, Psar Tuol Tom Pong and Psar Chaa markets.

A small community known as the Zahidin follows traditions similar to those of the Muslim Chams of Vietnam, praying once a week (on Friday) and observing Ramadan (a month of dawn-to-dusk fasting) only on the first, middle and last days of the month.

The Khmer Rouge made a concerted effort to discriminate against Cambodia's Cham Muslim community. All Muslims were forced to eat pork, even when other Khmers were deprived of meat, and many were systematically singled out for execution for simply refusing to do so.

Christianity

Christianity made limited headway into Cambodia compared with neighbouring Vietnam. There were a number of churches in Cambodia before the war, but many of these were systematically destroyed by the Khmer Rouge, including Notre Dame Cathedral in Phnom Penh, originally located between Hotel Le Royal and the National Institute of Management. Christianity made a comeback of sorts throughout the refugee camps on the Thai border in the 1980s, as a number of food-for-faith type charities set up shop dispensing Jesus with every meal. Many Cambodians changed their public faith for survival, before converting back to Buddhism on their departure from the camps.

Facts for the Visitor

THE BEST & WORST

The best news is undoubtedly that Cambodia is now a *safe,* serene and splendid country in which to travel, inhabited by some of the warmest, most welcoming people in the region. The worst news is that the advent of mass tourism is upon Angkor, and Cambodia is no longer Asia's best-kept secret. However, compared with Thailand, and even Vietnam, tourism is still very much in its infancy, making a visit to Cambodia a rich and rewarding experience.

Until the long civil war ended, Cambodia was a *very* difficult country in which to travel. Security was a perennial concern for visitors and many people found it simpler and safer to restrict their trips to Phnom Penh and Angkor. Those who did venture off the trail, however, found themselves in a beautiful country of friendly people, untainted by mass tourism. Cambodia is set for big changes as word continues to spread that peace has broken out. As long as the politicians can keep their bickering to words, not weapons, the country can expect a vast increase in tourist arrivals.

Cambodia has relied heavily on Angkor when promoting itself as a tourist destination, and not without good reason: it really is one of the most impressive sights on earth. Few can fail to be moved by the sheer grace and majesty of Angkor Wat: the sublime unity of its five towers; the delicate and intricate sculpture that decorates the lower walls; and the sheer size of the temple complex, the world's largest religious building.

Angkor is much more than one temple. There are many religious buildings scattered across a wide area around Siem Reap and visitors will discover a wealth of architecture as they explore: the enigmatic and intimidating faces watching over the Bayon; the devouring might of the jungle eating its way through Ta Prohm; and the demure beauty of Banteay Srei, host to some of the Angkorian period's finest carving.

However, just as Angkor is more than its wat, Cambodia is more than its temples. As the country's roads have opened up, many more places that were long kept off the map by conflict or cost can now be visited. Sihanoukville has long attracted visitors to its tropical beaches, but now the offshore islands are increasingly accessible – although at present there's not a bungalow in sight. Kampot Province has opened its arms to tourism and it's possible to visit the abandoned seaside town of Kep and the wilds of Bokor National Park with its eerie, abandoned mountain-top town that offers beautiful views on a clear day. The northeastern provinces of Ratanakiri and Mondulkiri, some of the most remote areas in the country, are home to all of Cambodia's Khmer Loeu (Upper Khmer), much of its vanishing wildlife and forest, and some landscapes of outstanding natural beauty.

Elsewhere in Cambodia, the numerous sleepy provincial capitals make interesting and economical transit stops as you journey through the country. They all tend to offer the same steady diet of crumbling French architecture, riverside location and some very friendly locals. Perhaps the best of the bunch are: Battambang, with its well-preserved architecture and nearby temples; Kratie, home to rare freshwater dolphins, and an overland stop on the route to Laos or the northeast; and Kompong Thom, conveniently located between Phnom Penh and Siem Reap, and a base from which to explore Sambor Prei Kuk.

There aren't many bad places in Cambodia, as the locals help to make even the most boring town lively. However, there is at least one obvious exception and unfortunately it is the first place many overland travellers see when they arrive in Cambodia: Poipet. It is an unattractive border town, with little history and a lot of casinos, and after too long there you could be forgiven for asking yourself why you have come to Cambodia.

Cambodia's road system is undeniably one of the worst in Asia, but is steadily being upgraded. The words 'national highway' may conjure up dreams of tarmac and top speed, but until recently, most suffered from endless potholes the size of bomb craters. See the Getting Around chapter for more bile on Cambodia's roads.

On a more serious note, Cambodia's political history has been extremely ugly and Cambodia's politicians have a habit of messing things up for their people, so don't assume it is possible to go anywhere and do anything just because you have read about a place in this guide. There is no substitute for checking out the latest situation in Cambodia on the ground, either in local newspapers, from nongovernmental organisations (NGOs) or embassies, or over a beer on a guesthouse veranda.

SUGGESTED ITINERARIES
Cambodia is a relatively small country, but travelling around is complicated by the poor infrastructure in the provinces. Hopefully, once the current round of roadworks are complete in 2004, it will feel like a different country. As in all places, what you see in Cambodia depends mainly on how much time and money you have available and, if travelling by road, having a little bit of luck – breakdowns are pretty common and they can wipe a day or so out of a schedule. Don't forget that the seasons can also have an effect on your mobility. During Cambodia's wet season, many roads become much harder to navigate and this can slow travel considerably – often by several days over the course of a few weeks.

One Week
Visitors with only a few days at their disposal should concentrate on Angkor, as there is nothing else in the world quite like it. Visitors with just a week to spare in the country will realistically find themselves restricted to seeing the temples of Angkor and the capital, Phnom Penh. Those with 10 days might like to spend more time at the temples and include a visit to some of the outlying sites, such as Beng Mealea and Kbal Spean. A trip to the beaches at Sihanoukville, or a boat journey from Phnom Penh up the Mekong River to Kratie or Kompong Cham could also be considered.

Two Weeks
Two weeks allows the visitor to embark on a more ambitious trip into the provinces. It is possible to do a loop around the attractions of the south coast, taking in Sihanoukville, Kampot, Bokor National Park, Kep, the ruined temples around Takeo and the other attractions along National Hwy 2 (NH2), including Phnom Chisor, the wildlife sanctuary at Phnom Tamao, and Tonlé Bati. Another option is to stop in some of the provincial towns around the Tonlé Sap lake between Phnom Penh and Siem Reap or include the pre-Angkorian temples of Sambor Prei Kuk, near Kompong Thom. A side trip to Battambang could also be built into the Angkor experience. Remote sections of the northeast are more difficult to include on an itinerary because transport is not always as reliable as elsewhere in the country. By road, it is relatively straightforward to get from Phnom Penh to Mondulkiri and back in just five days with enough time to get a feel for the lifestyle. However, Ratanakiri can be considered only as part of a two-week trip if you are willing to factor in a return flight, otherwise it is generally a two-day journey in each direction.

Three Weeks
Those with three weeks in Cambodia can see much of the country, including Phnom Penh, Angkor, the south coast and one of the other destinations listed as an option for a two-week trip.

Four Weeks
If you decide to stay for one month, as many travellers end up doing, you can see almost all of the country's attractions, although in the wet season road conditions may limit access to one or two places. It is not unrealistic to include all of the places listed previously, although you may find yourself choosing between Mondulkiri and

Ratanakiri unless you are willing to consider a flight to the latter. The adventurous may want to try an overland trip to one or two of Cambodia's remote jungle temples, such as Koh Ker, Preah Khan or Prasat Preah Vihear, all located in isolated Preah Vihear Province.

More than a month and you are a lucky bugger – there is time to see every corner of this enigmatic and enchanting country.

PLANNING
When to Go

Cambodia can be visited at any time of year. Some visitors like to coordinate their trip, however, with one of the annual festivals, such as Bon Om Tuk, the water festival, in Phnom Penh – see the Public Holidays & Special Events section later in this chapter.

The ideal months to be in Cambodia are December, January and February, when humidity levels are relatively low and there is little likelihood of rain. From early February temperatures start to rise until the hottest month, April, in which temperatures often exceed 40°C. Some time in May the southwestern monsoon brings rain and slightly cooler weather. The wet season, which lasts from May to October, need not be a bad time to visit, as the rain tends to come in short, sharp downpours. Angkor is surrounded by lush foliage and the moats are full of water at this time of year. If you are planning to visit isolated areas, however, the wet season makes travel pretty tough on some of the more remote tracks.

Maps

Lonely Planet's *Thailand, Vietnam, Laos & Cambodia Road Atlas* is the best, most up-to-date source of maps for Cambodia and includes full-colour maps of Phnom Penh, Siem Reap and the temples of Angkor. It also features handy trip maps, distance charts and a comprehensive index.

Tourist maps of Cambodia and Phnom Penh are available in Phnom Penh and Siem Reap, though they are of fairly poor quality. The Karto Atelier *Cambodia Road Map* at 1:750,000 scale is the best foldout map around and is very up to date.

Point Maps & Guides produces some nice 3-D maps of both Phnom Penh and Siem Reap, but they are very dated.

For serious map buffs or cartographers, Psar Thmei (New Market) in Phnom Penh is well stocked with Vietnamese and Khmer-produced maps of towns and provinces, as well as 1970 US military maps at a scale of 1:50,000. Roads have generally deteriorated since the civil war, rather than improved.

What to Bring

Bring as little as possible. Phnom Penh is surprisingly well stocked with travel provisions, so anything that is forgotten or lost can be replaced there, though prices are generally higher than in Bangkok or Ho Chi Minh City (Saigon). Nevertheless, it is always best to be prepared.

A good backpack is one outlay you will never regret. Consider buying a pack that converts into a carry bag – it is less likely to be damaged on airport carousels and is more presentable if you don't want to come across as a backpacker. Cheap backpacks are available in Phnom Penh, made in Vietnam for leading companies such as Lowe Alpine and Jack Wolfskin.

A day-pack is essential and a belt-pack is OK for maps, extra film and other bits and pieces, but don't use it for valuables such as travellers cheques and passport. Again, these packs are cheap to buy in Phnom Penh.

Take few clothes, as Cambodia is blessed with year-round warm to steaming-hot weather. The exception is December, when night temperatures can drop fast and it can be cool in the highlands. No need to pack something warm though, as fleeces and the like are available in the markets of Phnom Penh and Siem Reap. As is the case almost everywhere in Southeast Asia, sleeping bags are unnecessary, as it is so hot. Those staying in guesthouses might like to come prepared with a duvet cover or 'sheet sleeping bag' (two sheets sewn together), but the bedding provided in Cambodia is generally reasonable.

It's absolutely essential to bring a good pair of sunglasses and some sunscreen (UV) lotion, although the latter can be bought at supermarkets in Phnom Penh. An alarm clock is important for getting up on time to catch your flight, bus or whatever – make sure yours is lightweight and reliable, and bring extra batteries or a battery charger (size AA rechargeable batteries can be bought all over Cambodia).

The following is a check list of things you might consider packing:

- Photocopy of passport, documents including vaccination certificate, diplomas, photocopy of marriage licence and student ID card, and visa photos (the more the better for those travelling around the region)
- Money belt or vest, padlock, day-pack
- Long pants, short pants, long-sleeved shirt, T-shirts, nylon jacket, socks, thongs (flip-flops) or sandals, swimwear, comfortable walking shoes or boots
- Umbrella or rain poncho, waterproof cover for backpack
- Sunglasses, sun hat, contact-lens solution
- Deodorant, shampoo, soap, razor, razor blades, shaving cream, sewing kit, tampons, toothbrush, toothpaste, comb, nail clippers, tweezers
- Compass, Swiss army knife, leak-proof water bottle, alarm clock, camera and accessories, short-wave radio, personal music player, address book, pens, notepad, torch (flashlight) with batteries
- Mosquito repellent, sunscreen, vitamins, laxatives, contraceptives, medical kit (see the boxed text 'Medical Kit Check List' later in this chapter)

RESPONSIBLE TOURISM

Cambodia is experiencing unprecedented growth in the tourism sector and this inevitably brings the bad as well as the good. Worst of all has been the paedophile sex tourists who come to Cambodia to abuse young children – for more on this disgrace and what you can do to help prevent it, see the boxed text 'The Abuse of Innocence'.

Looting from the temples of Angkor and other remote sites around Cambodia has been a huge problem over the past couple of decades, most of it driven by demand from Western art markets. Don't contribute to this cultural rape by buying old stone carvings.

Good-quality reproductions are available in Phnom Penh and Siem Reap, complete with export certificates. Anyone seeking to buy old Angkorian pieces will be contributing to an illicit trade that has deprived Cambodia of much of its heritage, and may well be arrested when leaving the country.

Similarly, there are plenty of marine products such as coral and conches for sale in Sihanoukville and other coastal resorts. Do not buy these products, as it will only encourage the further depletion of the sea's natural wonders.

Finally, as tourism takes off, let us not forget what the Cambodians have been through in the protracted years of war, genocide and famine. It's a good idea to support local, Cambodian-owned businesses where the chance arises, because if anyone deserves to profit from the new-found interest in this wonderful country, it is surely the long-suffering Khmers.

TOURIST OFFICES

Cambodia has only a handful of tourist offices, and those encountered by the independent traveller in Phnom Penh and Siem Reap are generally unhelpful unless you look like you're going to spend money. However, in the provinces it is a different story, as the staff are often shocked and excited to see visitors. They may have to drag the director out of a nearby karaoke bar, even at 10am, but once it is made clear that you are a genuine tourist they will usually tell you everything there is to know about places of interest. More and more towns are ambitiously opening tourist offices, but they generally have little in the way of brochures or handouts. You'll find tourist offices listed in the relevant destination sections in this book.

Cambodia has no tourist offices abroad and it is unlikely that Cambodian embassies will be of much assistance in planning a trip, besides providing visas.

VISAS & DOCUMENTS
Passport

Not only is a passport essential but you also need to make sure that it's valid for at least six months beyond the *end* of your trip –

The Abuse of Innocence

The sexual abuse of children by foreign paedophiles is a serious problem in Cambodia. Moral grounds alone should be enough to deter foreigners from seeking under-age sexual partners in Cambodia, but unfortunately basic morality is absent in some individuals. Paedophiles are treated as criminals in Cambodia and several have served or are serving jail sentences as a result. There is no such thing as isolation units for sex offenders in Cambodia. Countries such as Australia, France, Germany, the UK and the USA have also introduced much-needed legislation that sees nationals prosecuted in their home country for having under-age sex abroad.

This abuse of a child's innocence is disgusting and is, slowly but surely, being combated, although in a country as poor as Cambodia, money can tempt people into selling babies for adoption and children for sex. The trafficking of innocent children has many shapes and forms, and the sex trade is just the thin end of the wedge. Poor parents have been known to rent their children out as beggars, labourers or sellers; many child prostitutes in Cambodia are Vietnamese and have been sold into the business by family back in Vietnam. Once in the trade, it is difficult to escape a life of violence and abuse. Gang rapes and beatings are common experiences for many adult prostitutes, and for a child to be subject to this animal behaviour is horrific. Drugs are also being used to keep children dependent on their pimps, with bosses giving out *yama* (a dirty meta-amphetamine) or heroin to dull their senses. All in all, it is the sickest of many sick trades and needs to be stopped immediately.

Visitors can do their bit to fight this menace by keeping an eye out for suspicious behaviour on the part of foreigners. Don't ignore it. Try and pass on any relevant information such as the name and nationality of the individual to the embassy concerned. There is also a Cambodian hotline ☎ 023-720555 and a confidential nongovernmental-organisation (NGO) hotline ☎ 012-888840 for those with information on sexual abuse or exploitation of children. End Child Prostitution and Trafficking (Ecpat; Ⓦ www.ecpat.org) is a global network aimed at stopping child prostitution, child pornography and the traffic of children for sexual purposes, and has affiliates in most Western countries.

most countries will not issue a visa if you have less than six months validity left on your passport.

It's also important to make sure that there is plenty of space left in your passport. Do not set off on a six-month trek across Asia with only two blank pages left – a Cambodian visa alone takes up one page. It is sometimes possible to have extra pages added to your passport, but most people will be required to get a new passport. This is possible for most foreign nationals in Cambodia, but it can be time consuming and costly, as many embassies process new passports in Bangkok.

Losing a passport is not the end of the world, but it is a serious inconvenience. To expedite the issuing of a new passport, make sure that you have the information from your data pages written down somewhere, or better still make a photocopy of these pages, and keep these records separate from your passport. See the Copies section later for details on Lonely Planet's free online Travel Vault.

Visas

Most nationalities receive a one-month visa on arrival at Pochentong and Siem Reap International Airports. The cost is US$20 for a tourist visa and US$25 for a business visa. One passport photo is required. Those seeking work in Cambodia should opt for the business visa as, officially, it is easily extended for long periods and, unofficially, can be extended indefinitely. A tourist visa can be extended only once and only for one month.

Visas are also available at some, though not all, land borders. Entering from Thailand, visas are available on arrival at Poipet and Krong Koh Kong. Those attempting to cross at any of the more remote borders should obtain a visa in advance. Travellers planning a day trip to Prasat Preah Vihear from Thailand do not require visas, but access to the temple from the Thai side was closed at the time of writing.

Travellers arriving overland from Vietnam will have to obtain a visa before they reach the border, and this can be done either at the embassy in Hanoi or the consulate in Ho Chi Minh City.

The land border with Laos opened in the latter half of 2000 and a small number of travellers have crossed this way. It is necessary to arrange a Cambodian visa in advance and this can be done in Bangkok or Vientiane.

Overstaying your visa currently costs a whopping US$5 a day.

Visa Extensions Visa extensions are issued by a new immigration office located directly across the road from Pochentong airport in Phnom Penh. Tourist visas can be extended only once for one month, whereas business visas can be extended indefinitely as long as you come with a bulging wallet. You can probably even arrange citizenship if you bring enough of the old greenbacks.

There are two ways of getting an extension, one official and one unofficial, and unsurprisingly the time and money involved differ greatly. Officially, a one-week extension costs US$20, one month US$30, three months US$60, six months US$100, and one year US$150; using this route they will hold your passport for 25 days and, for a business extension, will require more paperwork than a communist bureaucrat could dream up. This is fine for expatriates with an employer to make the arrangements, but those on their own really need to go unofficial. They don't call it corruption in Cambodia but 'under the table', and you can have your passport back the next day for inflated prices of US$45 for one month, US$80 for three months, US$150 for six months and US$250 for one year. Once you are one of the 'unofficials' it is pretty straightforward to extend the visa ad infinitum.

One passport photograph is required for visa extensions and there is a US$1 charge for the application form.

Onward Tickets

There is no requirement for an onward ticket for overseas nationals visiting Cambodia.

Travel Insurance

A travel insurance policy that covers theft, property loss and medical expenses is more essential for Cambodia than for most other parts of Southeast Asia. Theft is less a problem in Cambodia than some might imagine, but in the event of serious medical problems or an accident it may be necessary to be airlifted to Bangkok, an expense that stretches beyond the average traveller's budget.

There are a wide variety of travel insurance policies available, and it's wise to check with a reliable travel agent as to which is most suitable for Cambodia. The policies handled by STA Travel (which has branches in Bangkok) are usually good value.

When buying your travel insurance *always* check the small print:

- Some policies specifically exclude 'dangerous activities' such as scuba diving and motorcycling. If you are going to be riding a motorbike in Cambodia, check that you will be covered.
- Check whether the medical coverage is on a pay first, claim later basis; if this is the case, keep all documents relating to any medical treatment.

WARNING

Do not visit Cambodia without medical insurance. Hospitals are extremely basic in the provinces and even in Phnom Penh facilities are generally not up to the standards you may be accustomed to. Anyone who has a serious injury or illness while in Cambodia may require emergency evacuation to Bangkok. With an insurance policy costing no more than the equivalent of a bottle of beer a day, this evacuation is free. Without an insurance policy, it will cost between US$10,000 and US$20,000 – somewhat more than the average traveller's budget. Don't gamble with your health in Cambodia or you may end up another statistic!

- In the case of Cambodia, it is essential to check that medical coverage includes the cost of emergency evacuation.

Driving Licence

Self-drive car hire is not available in Cambodia, and in any case, would not be recommended given the abysmal state of many roads and the prominence of the psychopathic driver gene among many Cambodian road users. It is very unlikely that a driving licence will be of any use, save for those coming to work with one of the many foreign organisations in Cambodia.

Motorbikes are available for hire in Phnom Penh, but licences are never requested. If you can drive the bike out of the shop, you can drive it anywhere, or so the logic goes.

Student & Youth Cards

Student and youth cards are all but worthless in Cambodia, though they may be of use in Thailand. In general, the availability of cheap counterfeit student cards in places like Bangkok has done much to rob the student card of whatever value it once had.

Vaccination Certificates

There are no direct flights from areas where infection with yellow fever is a possibility, so, in theory, a certificate should not be required. If you have an International Certificate of Vaccination though, it's best to carry it, just in case. This is particularly so if you are travelling from infected areas of Africa or South America via an Asian gateway to Cambodia. See Immunisations under Predeparture Planning in the Health section later in this chapter for recommended vaccinations.

Copies

All important documents (passport data page and visa page, credit cards, travel insurance policy, air tickets and so on) should be photocopied before departure. Leave one copy with someone at home and keep another with you, separate from the originals.

It's also a good idea to store details of your vital travel documents on Lonely Planet's free online Travel Vault in case you lose the photocopies or can't be bothered with them. Your password-protected Travel Vault is accessible online anywhere in the world – create it at W www.ekno.lonely planet.com.

EMBASSIES & CONSULATES
Cambodian Embassies & Consulates

Cambodian diplomatic representation abroad is still thin on the ground, though the situation is gradually improving. However, as visas are available on arrival at airports and the popular land crossings with Thailand, most visitors don't need to visit a Cambodian embassy in advance.

There are currently no visas issued at land borders with Vietnam, so it is necessary to arrange a visa in Hanoi or Ho Chi Minh City. These visas are usually turned around in just a day or two. Similarly, when crossing overland from Laos to Cambodia, it is essential to arrange a Cambodian visa in Vientiane or Bangkok, as no visas are issued at the border.

Cambodian diplomatic missions abroad include:

Australia (☎ 02-6273 1259, fax 6273 1053) 5 Canterbury Cres, Deakin, ACT 2600
China (☎ 010-6532 1889, fax 6532 3507) 9 Dongzhimenwai Dajie, Beijing 100600
France (☎ 01-45 03 47 20, fax 45 03 47 40) 4 Rue Adolphe Yvon, 75116 Paris
Germany (☎ 30-48 63 79 01) Arnold Zweing Str, 1013189 Berlin
Hong Kong (☎ 2546 0718, fax 2803 0570) Unit 616, 6th floor, 3 Salisbury Rd, Tsim Sha Tsui, Kowloon
India (☎/fax 011-642 3782) B47 Soami Nagar, New Delhi 110017
Indonesia (☎ 021-548 3716, fax 548 3684) 4th floor, Panin Bank Plaza, Jalan 52 Palmerah Utara, Jakarta 11480
Japan (☎ 03-5412 8521, fax 5412 8526) 8-6-9 Akasaka, Minato-ku, Tokyo 1070052
Laos (☎/fax 21-314952) Tha Deau, Bon That Khao, Vientiane
Thailand (☎ 02-254 6630, fax 253 9859) 185 Rajadamri Rd, Bangkok 10330
USA (☎ 202-726 7742, fax 726 8381) 4500 16th St, NW, Washington DC 20011
Vietnam (☎ 04-825 3788, fax 826 5225) 71 Tran Hung Dao St, Hanoi
  Consulate: (☎ 08-829 2751, fax 829 2744) 41 Phung Khac Khoan St, Ho Chi Minh City

Cambodia also has embassies in Bulgaria, Cuba, Russia and North Korea.

Embassies & Consulates in Cambodia

There is quite a number of embassies in Phnom Penh, though some travellers will find that their nearest embassy is in Bangkok. Most will happily provide information to their nationals about the current security situation in Cambodia and can replace a passport in the event that it is lost or stolen. Embassies will not, however, provide funds for onward travel, though some will contact relatives at home and request them to forward money on your behalf.

Those intending to visit Laos should note that Lao visas are available in Phnom Penh for US$35 and take two working days. For Vietnam, one-month, single-entry visas cost US$30 and take just one day, faster still at the Vietnamese consulate in Sihanoukville.

Embassies in Phnom Penh include:

Australia (☎ 213470, fax 213413) 11 Ph 254
Canada (☎ 213470, fax 211389) 11 Ph 254
China (☎ 720920, fax 720922) 256 Mao Tse Toung Blvd
France (☎ 430020, fax 430038) 1 Monivong Blvd
  Consulate: contact Colonel Billaut, PO Box 17, Siem Reap, 20 Wat Bo Village
Germany (☎ 216193, fax 427746) 76–78 Ph 214
India (☎ 210912, fax 213640) 777 Monivong Blvd
Indonesia (☎ 216148, fax 217566) 90 Norodom Blvd
Japan (☎ 217161, fax 216162) 194 Norodom Blvd
Laos (☎ 982632, fax 720907) 15–17 Mao Tse Toung Blvd
Malaysia (☎ 216176, fax 216004) 161 Ph 51
Myanmar (☎ 213664, fax 213665) 181 Norodom Blvd
Philippines (☎ 215145, fax 215143) 33 Ph 294
Thailand (☎ 363869) 196 Norodom Blvd
UK (☎ 427124, fax 427125) 27–29 Ph 75
USA (☎ 216436, fax 216437) 27 Ph 240
Vietnam (☎ 362531, fax 362314) 436 Monivong Blvd
  Consulate: (☎ 012-340495) Ph Ekareach, Sihanoukville

Your Own Embassy

It's important to realise what your own embassy – the embassy of the country of which you are a citizen – can and can't do to help you if you get into trouble.

Generally speaking, it won't be much help in emergencies if the trouble is remotely your own fault. Remember that all foreign nationals are bound by the laws of Cambodia when in Cambodia. Your embassy will not be sympathetic if you end up in jail after committing a crime locally, even if such actions are legal in your own country.

In genuine emergencies an embassy may be of some assistance, but only if other channels have been exhausted. If you need to get home urgently, a free ticket home is exceedingly unlikely – the embassy would expect you to have insurance. If you have all your money and documents stolen, it might assist with getting a new passport, but a loan for onward travel is out of the question.

Some embassies used to keep letters for travellers or have a small reading room with home newspapers, but it doesn't happen much anymore.

CUSTOMS

If Cambodia has customs allowances, it is close-lipped about them. A 'reasonable amount' of duty-free items are allowed into the country. Travellers arriving by air might bear in mind that alcohol and cigarettes sell at duty-free (and lower) prices on the streets of Phnom Penh – a branded box of 200 cigarettes costs just US$8! International spirits start as low as US$7 a litre!

Like any other country, Cambodia does not allow travellers to import weapons, explosives or narcotics – some would say there are enough in the country already.

MONEY
Currency

Cambodia's currency is the riel, abbreviated in this guide by a lower-case 'r' written after the sum.

Cambodia's second currency (some would say its first) is the US dollar, which is accepted everywhere and by everyone, though change may arrive in riel. Dollar bills with a small tear are unlikely to be accepted by Cambodians, so it's worth scrutinising the change you are given to make sure you are not palmed off with bad bills. In the west of the country, the Thai baht (B) is also commonplace. If three currencies seem a little excessive, perhaps it's because the Cambodians are making up for lost time: during the Pol Pot era, the country had *no* currency. The Khmer Rouge abolished money and blew up the National Bank building in Phnom Penh.

The sinking fortunes of the riel meant that, until recently, it was hardly worth the paper it was printed on. The government has responded by creating new higher-value denominations, although notes of 20,000r and higher are still a fairly rare sight. The riel comes in notes of the following denominations: 100, 200, 500, 1000, 2000, 5000, 10,000, 20,000, 50,000 and 100,000.

Throughout this book, prices are in the currency quoted to the average punter. This is usually US dollars or riel, but in the west it is often baht.

Exchange Rates

country	unit		riel
Australia	A$1	=	2201r
Canada	C$1	=	2580r
euro zone	€1	=	3657r
Hong Kong	HK$1	=	514r
Japan	¥100	=	3131r
Laos	1000 kip	=	553r
New Zealand	NZ$1	=	1849r
Singapore	S$1	=	2221r
Thailand	10B	=	936r
UK	UK£1	=	5841r
USA	US$1	=	4010r
Vietnam	10,000d	=	2764r

Exchanging Money

Cash Cambodia is one country where US dollars are extremely useful. Indeed, if you have enough cash you won't need to use the bank because it is possible to change small amounts of dollars for riel at hotels, restaurants and markets. Hardened travellers argue that your trip ends up being slightly more expensive if you rely on US dollars rather than riel, but in reality there's very little in it. However, it never hurts to support the local

currency against the greenback. It is always handy to have about US$10 worth of riel kicking around, as it is good for *motos* (small motorcycles with drivers) and markets. Pay for something cheap in US dollars and the change comes in riel; gradually enough riel will accumulate in your wallet to pay for small items anyway. In remote areas of the north and northeast, locals often prefer riel.

The only other cash currency that can be useful is Thai baht (in the west of the country). Prices in towns such as Krong Koh Kong, Poipet and Sisophon are often quoted in baht, and even in Battambang it is as common as the dollar.

In the interests of making life as simple as possible, organise a supply of US dollars before arriving in Cambodia. Cash in other major currencies can be changed at banks or markets in Phnom Penh or Siem Reap. However, most banks tend to offer a miserable rate for any non-dollar transaction so it can be better to use moneychangers, which are found in and around every major market. Even at markets, the rate for other currencies is relatively poor compared with the US dollar.

Travellers Cheques Travellers cheques can be changed at only a limited number of banks in Phnom Penh, Siem Reap, Sihanoukville, Battambang and Kompong Cham. If you are travelling upcountry, you should change enough money before you go. It is best to have cheques in US dollars, though it is also possible to change most major currencies at branches of Canadia Bank. Generally, you will pay a minimum of 2% commission to change travellers cheques, although the Foreign Trade Bank on Norodom Blvd in Phnom Penh charges only 1% for US-dollar cheques.

Credit Cards Except for top-end hotels and major purchases such as air tickets, credit cards are not particularly worthwhile, as there are currently no automated teller machines (ATMs) in Cambodia.

Cash advances on credit cards are available in Phnom Penh, Siem Reap, Sihanoukville and Battambang, but usually attract charges. Most banks advertise a minimum charge of US$5 and often a percentage charge on top of that. Canadia Bank offers MasterCard cash advances at no charge.

Several travel agents and hotels near Psar Thmei arrange cash advances for about 5% commission; this can be particularly useful if you get caught short at the weekend.

International Transfers The Foreign Trade Bank can arrange transfers and has correspondent banks in the USA, Europe, Asia and Australia, with relevant addresses and account details helpfully listed on a free handout. Western Union and Moneygram are both now represented in Cambodia for fast, if more expensive, money transfers. Western Union is represented by Acleda Bank and Canadia Bank represents Moneygram.

Black Market The black market hardly exists in Cambodia when it comes to changing money. Exchange rates on the street are the same as those offered by the banks, just without the queues and paperwork.

Security

A lightweight money belt that can be worn comfortably and discreetly inside your clothes is the best bet for carrying the bulk of your travel savings. A pair of nylon stockings with one leg folded inside the other can hold a lot of travellers cheques and other documents. It can be tied inconspicuously around your waist under your clothes without any discomfort. Some travellers wear a pouch around the neck that rests inside their shirts, though this is usually fairly conspicuous. Belt packs (bum-bags to Brits, fanny packs to Americans) are not advisable, as they say 'steal me, steal me' to any would-be thief.

Costs

For the most part, Cambodia is an inexpensive country in which to travel when compared to the Western world. However, it is a little more expensive than its three neighbours, thanks to the prolonged presence of the United Nations (UN) and other development agencies. Prices for food and entertainment are higher in Phnom Penh and

Siem Reap than elsewhere in the country, as increasing numbers of tourists replace the departing aid workers.

Budget travellers can probably manage Phnom Penh on around US$10 a day, though there's not a great deal to be said for travelling this way – there is much that you will have to miss out on. Accommodation can be as cheap as US$2 to US$3 in popular destinations (elsewhere, you will be looking at a minimum of US$5). It is generally possible to eat fairly well for US$2 to US$3, less if you go native and live off inexpensive soups and noodles from local markets.

Transportation used to be a major expense, but with the opening of land borders with Thailand, and the advent of safe and secure roads throughout the country, it is now a lot cheaper to get around by road than by plane or boat. Travelling by train went from free to foreigner price, but is still cheap at 45r per kilometre. It is painfully slow, however. From Phnom Penh there are regular, cheap bus services to Sihanoukville and provincial towns around the capital, and daily buses to Ho Chi Minh City.

Mid-range travellers are probably the best-served in Cambodia. In Phnom Penh and Siem Reap there is an excellent range of accommodation for US$15 to US$25, and if you are happy spending up to US$5 a meal, Phnom Penh in particular can be quite a gourmet experience. Having a little extra money also allows for the luxury of flying one-way or return to Siem Reap, and perhaps renting a taxi to visit sights around Phnom Penh.

At the top end of the scale, Cambodia has several international-standard hotels to make one's stay more than comfortable, although prices in Siem Reap are high by regional standards. Visitors straying beyond Phnom Penh and Siem Reap are not going to find anything other than budget and midrange places.

Visitors to Angkor (surely everybody coming to Cambodia) will have to factor in the cost of entrance fees, which have settled down to US$20 for one day, US$40 for three days and US$60 for one week. An additional expense is transport to get around the ruins, ranging from US$2 for a bicycle through US$6 for a moto to US$20 or more for a car. Those wanting the services of an official guide need to budget for an additional US$20 a day.

Tipping & Bargaining

Tipping is not expected in Cambodia but, as is the case anywhere, if you meet with exceptional service or kindness, a tip is always greatly appreciated. Salaries remain extremely low in Cambodia and service is often superb thanks to a Khmer commitment to hospitality.

Bargaining is the rule in markets, when hiring vehicles and in some guesthouses. The Khmers are not ruthless hagglers, so care should be taken to not come on too strong. A persuasive smile and a little friendly quibbling is usually enough to get a good price. Try to remember that the aim is not to get the lowest possible price, but a price that is acceptable to both you and the seller. Back home, we pay astronomical sums for items, especially clothes, that have been made in poorer countries for next to nothing, and don't even get the chance to bargain for them, just the opportunity to contribute to a corporate director's retirement fund. At least you get to barter in Cambodia, so try not to abuse it. And remember, in many cases a few hundred riel is more important to a Cambodian with a family to support than to a traveller on an extended vacation.

POST & COMMUNICATIONS

Post is now routed by air through Bangkok and other regional centres, which makes Cambodia a faster, though by no means more reliable, place from which to send mail and parcels. Telephone connections with the outside world have improved immensely, though standard international calls are expensive.

Postal Rates

The postal service is very unreliable from Cambodia; send anything valuable by courier or from another country. Make sure postcards and letters are franked before they vanish from your sight.

Postal rates are listed in the Phnom Penh General Post Office (GPO). Postcards cost 1500r to 2100r to send internationally. A 10g airmail letter to anywhere in the world costs 2000r to 2500r, while a 100g letter costs 12,100r to anywhere in Asia, 13,400r to Australia or Europe, and 15,900r to the USA.

Parcel rates are 25,800r for 500g within Asia, 31,500r to Australia and Europe, and 42,800r to the USA. There is a 9000r fee for registered mail, but for valuable items it is worth it.

Letters and parcels sent farther afield than Asia can take up to two or three weeks to reach their destination.

Receiving Mail

The Phnom Penh GPO has a poste restante box at the far-left end of the post counter. Basically anybody can pick up your mail, so it's not a good idea to have anything valuable sent there. It costs 100r per item received. Long-term travellers are better off getting stuff sent to Bangkok.

Telephone

Domestic Local calls are usually pretty cheap, even from hotel rooms. Calling from province to province is considerably more expensive by fixed lines. The easiest way to call in most urban areas is to head to one of the many small private booths plastered with numbers. Operators have a selection of mobile phones and leased lines to ensure that any domestic number you want to call is cheap. Local phone calls can also be made on the Ministry of Post & Telecommunications (MPTC) and Camintel public payphones, which are common in Phnom Penh, Siem Reap, Sihanoukville and Kompong Cham. It can sometimes be difficult to get through to numbers outside Phnom Penh, and there is no directory inquiries service. Some hotels have telephone directories for the capital if you need to track down a number. Try to find a copy of the *Yellow Pages* produced by Interquess, which has a pretty comprehensive coverage of business, services and government offices.

Mobiles Telephone numbers starting with 011, 012, 015, 016 or 018 are mobile phone numbers. If you are travelling with a mobile phone on international roaming, just select a network on arrival, dial away and await a hefty phone bill once you return home. Cambodian roaming charges are very high.

Those who are planning on spending longer in Cambodia will want to hook up with a local network. A wide range of telephones are available cheaply in Cambodia, while those with their own phone need only purchase a SIM card for one of the local operators. Most of the local companies offer fixed-contract deals with monthly bills or pay-as-you-go cards for those who want flexibility. All offer regular promotions, so it is worth shopping around. Local companies based in Phnom Penh include:

Mobitel (☎ 012-801801) 33 Sihanouk Blvd
Samart (☎ 016-810035) 2 Ph 120
Shinawatra (☎ 011-360001) 66 Mao Tse Toung Blvd

Domestic Telephone Codes

Banteay Meanchey	☎ 054
Battambang	☎ 053
Kampot	☎ 033
Kandal	☎ 024
Kep	☎ 036
Koh Kong	☎ 035
Kompong Cham	☎ 042
Kompong Chhnang	☎ 026
Kompong Speu	☎ 025
Kompong Thom	☎ 062
Kratie	☎ 072
Mondulkiri	☎ 073
Oddar Meanchey	☎ 065
Phnom Penh	☎ 023
Preah Vihear	☎ 064
Prey Veng	☎ 043
Pursat	☎ 052
Ratanakiri	☎ 075
Siem Reap	☎ 063
Sihanoukville	☎ 034
Stung Treng	☎ 074
Svay Rieng	☎ 044
Takeo	☎ 032

International There are two international dial-out codes in Cambodia, ☎ 001 and ☎ 007. To call Cambodia from outside the country, the country code is ☎ 855.

There is now a whole lot more choice when it comes to calling overseas than in the bad old days of all calls going via Moscow. There are several telephone cards available for cardphones, several prepaid calling cards for use from any telephone, private booths run from mobile phones and the growing world of Internet phone calls. Calling from hotels attracts a surcharge and the more expensive the hotel, the heftier the hit. As a general rule, whichever way you choose to ring, it is a little cheaper to make a call at weekends.

The cheapest way to call internationally is via Internet phone. Most of the shops and cafes around the country providing email and Internet services also offer Internet calls. Calls usually cost between 1000r and 2000r per minute, depending on the destination. Calling the USA is generally the cheapest. While the price is undoubtedly right, the major drawback is that there is often a significant delay on the phone, making for a conversation of 'hello?' and 'pardon?'.

It is easy to place an international call from MPTC or Camintel phone booths. Purchase a phonecard, which in larger cities can be bought at hotels, restaurants, the post office and many shops. Phonecards come in denominations of US$2, US$5, US$10, US$20, US$50 and US$100.

Before inserting the card into a public phone, always check that there is a readout on the liquid crystal display (LCD) unit. If there isn't, it probably means the phone is broken or there is a power cut – inserting the card at these times can wipe the value off the card. Rather than use the original international access code of ☎ 001, try ☎ 007, which works out considerably cheaper. The name is not Bond, but Tele2, a private operator that has recently set up shop in Cambodia.

Telephoning from Battambang and the west of Cambodia is cheaper and the lines are clearer than in other parts of the country,

Small shrine with incense

Apsara bas-relief, Angkor

Memorial procession in Phnom Penh

Resting in front of a Hindu shrine at Banteay Srei

Monks line up for alms

French colonial architecture, Phnom Penh

Phnom Penh train station

A child and his buddy Ganesh, Phnom Penh

The National Museum, Phnom Penh

Pnong hill-tribe villagers

The Independence Monument, Phnom Penh

as the lines are plugged into the Thailand network. Calls to Thailand are only 10B a minute and calls to the rest of the world work out at about US$2 a minute or less.

Calling by reverse charge is no longer possible.

Fax
Sending faxes is getting cheaper as telephone charges drop. The cheapest fax services are those via the Internet; these can be arranged at Internet cafes in Phnom Penh and Siem Reap for around US$1 to US$2 a page. Some of the more popular mid-range hotels in Phnom Penh have reliable business centres that can send and receive faxes. Cambodia's top-end hotels all have expensive business centres where sending a fax will cost three times the price charged elsewhere.

Email & Internet Access
Internet access is now available in towns throughout the country, thanks to Mobitel establishing the first broadband mobile-based connection in Cambodia, and Telstra Bigpond and Camintel branching out into the provinces. In Phnom Penh prices just keep dropping, thankfully, and now average US$1 to US$1.50 per hour. Siem Reap is a little more expensive at US$2 per hour, while in other provinces it can range from US$5 an hour to as much as US$20 an hour, thanks to expensive domestic phone calls.

Internet cafes in Phnom Penh and Siem Reap offer monthly email-only accounts with unlimited usage for about US$6 to US$12. This is good value if you are intending to stay in the country for a long period.

Visitors carrying a portable computer who are looking for a direct connection to a server have several choices. The easiest way is to pick up one of the prepaid Internet cards offered by Bigpond, Everyday or Mobitel. They come in a range of values from US$10 to US$50 and can be purchased from shops, hotels and petrol stations. Those who like contracts and paperwork can try Bigpond (☎ 430000) at 56 Norodom Blvd, Camintel (☎ 981234) at 1 Sisowath Quay or Mobitel (☎ 012-801801) at 33 Sihanouk Blvd, all in Phnom Penh. Prices are a little expensive by international standards and if you are using a mobile phone from remote areas the connection is poor.

INTERNET RESOURCES
The World Wide Web (WWW) is a rich resource for travellers. You can research your trip, hunt down bargain air fares, book hotels, check on weather conditions or chat with locals and other travellers about the best places to visit (or avoid!).

There's no better place to start your Web explorations than the Lonely Planet website (W www.lonelyplanet.com). Here you'll find succinct summaries on travelling to most places on earth, postcards from other travellers and the Thorn Tree bulletin board, where you can ask questions before you go or dispense advice when you get back. You can also find travel news, and the subWWWay section that links you to the most useful travel resources elsewhere on the Web.

Some useful websites include:

Andy Brouwer's Cambodia Tales This very useful gateway to all things Cambodian includes comprehensive links to other sites and regular travel articles from veteran Cambodian adventurers.
W www.btinternet.com/~andy.brouwer/index.htm

Beauty and Darkness: Cambodia, the Odyssey of the Khmer People This well-produced website concentrates on the turbulent Khmer Rouge period and the years of recovery.
W www.mekong.net/cambodia

Biking Asia with Mr Pumpy The definitive website for cyclists passing through Cambodia and the region. Written with candour and humour by Mr Pumpy's best friend Felix Hude, it is well worth checking out.
W www.mrpumpy.net

The Cambodian Information Center This website lives up to its name, with a comprehensive list of sites relating to the country.
W www.cambodia.org

Cambodian Ministry of Tourism The Cambodian government's official tourism website, this has a lot of useful information on attractions around the country.
W www.mot.gov.kh

Canby Publications: Cambodia Guides Put together by the people that produce the free visitors guides for Phnom Penh, Siem Reap and Sihanoukville, this site has comprehensive information on these cities and other aspects of Cambodia.

W www.canbypublications.com

The Internet Travel Guide This long-running site provides a good introduction to Cambodia.
W www.pmgeiser.ch/cambodia

BOOKS

There has been a lot of ink spilled over Cambodia, particularly on the wonderful temples of Angkor and the horrendous events of the 1970s, but some of the books are quite hard to get hold of outside the region. Phnom Penh's bookshops and markets are the best places for picking up books. See the Information section in the Phnom Penh chapter for details. Siem Reap has an ever-improving selection of bookshops. Bangkok and Ho Chi Minh City bookshops are also worth checking out if you are passing through.

Most books are published in different editions by different publishers in different countries. As a result, a book might be a hardcover rarity in one country while it's readily available in paperback in another. Fortunately, bookshops and libraries search by title or author, making them the best places to advise you on the availability of the following recommendations.

Lonely Planet

Lonely Planet publishes *South-East Asia on a shoestring,* an overall guide to travel on the Southeast Asian trail; the *South-East Asia phrasebook,* with a significant section on the Khmer language; and *Read This First: Asia & India,* aimed at first-time travellers. For those planning to cycle through Cambodia, Lonely Planet publishes *Cycling Vietnam, Laos & Cambodia,* the most comprehensive guidebook available on biking in this region. Also check out *Lonely Planet Unpacked,* a collection of travel disaster stories, for some of the author's misadventures in Cambodia in years gone by.

Other Guidebooks

One of the most interesting guidebooks for the visitor wanting to find some quiet corners of the country is *The Cambodia Less Travelled* by Ray Zepp. He taught for a time at Phnom Penh University and spent his weekends and holidays travelling Cambodia to produce this book, which is part guide, part travel diary. He also produced a series of supplements on other parts of the country not fully covered in *The Cambodia Less Travelled.* These include *The Northwest* (Battambang, Sisophon and Pursat), *The Northeast* (Ratanakiri and Mondulkiri) and *The South Coast* (Kampot, Kep, Bokor and Svay Rieng).

In a similar vein is *The Coast of Cambodia* by Robert Philpotts, a slice of travel literature and guidebook interwoven. It covers Krong Koh Kong to Kompong Trach and has some nice moments.

Another useful book, especially for anyone planning to spend a length of time in Phnom Penh, is the *Guide to Phnom Penh,* compiled by the Women's International Group. All proceeds from the book are donated to Cambodian charities, and it is packed with useful tips on living in Phnom Penh.

Angkor

Countless books on Angkor and Cambodia's temples have been produced over the years, but many of the older titles are either out of print or available only in French. However, as international interest in Angkor reaches fever pitch once more, no doubt many older titles will be reissued.

The definitive guidebook to Angkor has been *Les Monuments du Groupe d'Angkor* by Maurice Glaize, first published in the 1940s and available in English as *A Guide to the Angkor Monuments.* It is getting hard to find in English, but can be freely downloaded from the Internet at **W** www.the angkorguide.com.

Another old classic is *Henri Parmentier's Guide to Angkor,* a pocket volume published in 1959 by one of the elder statesmen of Khmer culture and heritage.

Among the modern titles, *Angkor – An Introduction to the Temples* by Dawn Rooney is probably the most popular, complete with illustrations and photographs; it's a useful companion during a visit to Angkor. Another popular title is the pocket-size *Angkor – Heart of an Asian Empire* by

Bruno Dagens. The emphasis in this book is more on the discovery and restoration of the ruins of Angkor, but it is lavishly illustrated and dripping with interesting asides.

Other older titles that are worth seeking out include *Angkor: An Introduction* by George Coedes, with excellent background information on Angkorian Khmer civilisation from one of the foremost scholars on Cambodian civilisation, and *Arts & Civilization of Angkor* by Bernard Groslier & Jacques Arthaud. Groslier was the head of Ecole Francaise d'Extreme Orient before and during the civil war. For more on the history of the period, look for *History of Angkor* by Madeleine Giteau, a professor at the Royal University of Fine Arts in Phnom Penh before the war, and Malcolm Mac-Donald's *Angkor & the Khmers*.

For a feel of Angkor during its heyday, try *The Customs of Cambodia*, written by a Chinese emissary Chou Ta Kuan (Zhou Daguan) at the end of the 13th century. It is available cheaply in Phnom Penh and has recently been reprinted by a Thai publisher, complete with lavish photographs.

Several books by French explorers and adventurers contain early accounts of Angkor. *Travels in Siam, Cambodia, Laos and Annam* by Henri Mouhot has been reprinted in English by White Lotus and is an interesting account by the man who 'discovered' Angkor.

Khmer Heritage in the Old Siamese Provinces of Cambodia by Etienne Aymonier has also been reprinted recently and covers the author's trips around Cambodia's more remote temples of the northwest in 1901. *A Pilgrimage to Angkor* by Pierre Loti describes a turn-of-the-century visit to Angkor and is credited by many as including some of the best prose ever penned on Angkor, even though he spent only a day and a half there.

When it comes to photographic books, the choice is growing fast, but many are quite expensive if purchased in Cambodia. *Passage Through Angkor* by Mark Standen includes some of the most striking images of Angkor ever produced. *Angkor* by Michael Freeman is possibly the cheapest photographic book for bargain souvenir hunters. Michael Freeman's photographs, together with text by Claudes Jacques, feature in *Angkor Cities and Temples,* another nice souvenir.

There are several beautiful books on the sculpture and art of Khmer civilisation. *Sculpture of Angkor and Ancient Cambodia,* edited by Helen Ibbitson-Jessup & Thierry Zephir, was produced to accompany an exhibition in New York and has incredible photos. *L'Art Khmer* by Madelaine Giteau & Danielle Guiret is a similarly attractive publication in French.

Travel

There are not a lot of travel books about Cambodia. The classic is Norman Lewis' *A Dragon Apparent,* an account of a 1950 foray into an Indochina that was soon to disappear. In the course of his travels, Lewis makes a circuit from Phnom Penh around the Tonlé Sap lake, with a pause in Angkor. The book has been reissued as part of *The Norman Lewis Omnibus.* If Lewis' account is just a little outdated for you, then Lucretia Stewart's *Tiger Balm* covers similar territory 40 years later, at the start of the 1990s.

Gecko Tails by Carol Livingstone, which offers lightweight coverage of travels in the country during and after the United Nations Transitional Authority in Cambodia (Untac) period. It is an easy-going read that introduces some interesting characters the author encountered while living in Cambodia.

Off the Rails in Phnom Penh – Guns, Girls and Ganja by Amit Gilboa is a repellent but popular book dealing with such murky subjects as prostitution and drugs. It feels like he got too close to his subject at times and it's not really a side of Cambodia about which Khmers are proud.

History & Politics

The best widely available history of Cambodia is David Chandler's *History of Cambodia.* Chandler has also documented recent Cambodian history in two more excellent titles: *The Tragedy of Cambodian History – Politics, War & Revolution since*

1945 and *Brother Number One – A Political Biography of Pol Pot*. His latest work is the deeply disturbing yet compelling *Voices from S-21,* which covers the routine of torture and execution established by the Khmer Rouge in Phnom Penh and the stories of individuals incarcerated there.

Also look out for Milton Osbourne's *Sihanouk – Prince of Light, Prince of Darkness*. This superbly written book provides a no-holds-barred look at the man who has played such a crucial role in the shifting fortunes of Cambodia's modern history.

The expansion of the Vietnam War into Cambodian territory and events through the mid-1970s are superbly documented by William Shawcross in his award-winning book *Sideshow: Kissinger, Nixon & the Destruction of Cambodia*. Shawcross' *The Quality of Mercy: Cambodia, Holocaust and Modern Conscience* looks at the contradictions inherent in the massive international famine-relief operation mounted in 1979 and 1980. This title is still highly relevant and is available in Thailand in a paperback edition.

Cambodia: Year Zero by François Ponchaud (originally published in French as *Cambodge: Année Zéro*) is an account of life in Cambodia under the Khmer Rouge, compiled from refugee sources. Another interesting account of the Khmer Rouge period is *When the War Was Over* by Elizabeth Becker, one of a select group of journalists who were invited to visit Democratic Kampuchea in December 1978.

The Pol Pot Regime, by leading Khmer Rouge expert Ben Kiernan, is the most dramatic insight into policy and purges during the time of Democratic Kampuchea.

Brother Enemy by Nayan Chanda is an excellent work and offers an incredible insight into how former allies Cambodia and Vietnam descended into war with a little help from their 'friends' in China, the former USSR and the USA.

Australian journalist Jon Pilger has written many articles on the tragedy of Cambodia and most have been published in collected works, including *Heroes, Distant Voices* and *Hidden Agendas*.

Cambodia: Report from a Troubled Land is a lively account of Cambodia's highs and lows between 1960 and the present day, written by veteran journalist Henry Kamm, a Pulitzer Prize winner.

Survivors' Accounts

There are several poignant accounts of life under the Khmer Rouge, most written by Cambodians who have since settled overseas. One of the first was *The Stones Cry Out: A Cambodian Childhood, 1975-1980* by Molyda Szymusiak, originally published in French as *Les Pierres Crieront: Une Enfance Cambodgienne, 1975-1980*. Another of the first-generation books is *Stay Alive My Son* by Pin Yathay, a distressing account of disease, death and escape.

More recently, *First They Killed My Father* by Luong Ung has won much critical acclaim and covers the steady destruction through execution and disease of an urban Cambodian family in Democratic Kampuchea. *When Broken Glass Floats* by Chanrithy Him is another excellent account by a young survivor of dark years. Both are well written and painfully sad to read.

Correspondents' Memoirs

The wars in Indochina produced a generation of gung-ho war correspondents, the likes of whom will never be seen again. Many have released autobiographies of sorts or had biographies penned about them.

Jon Swain's *River of Time* takes the reader back to an old Indochina, partly lost to the madness of war, and includes firsthand accounts of the French embassy standoff in the first days of the Khmer Rouge takeover.

Tim Page's *Derailed in Uncle Ho's Victory Garden* covers this infamous photographer's quest for the truth behind the disappearance of photojournalist Sean Flynn (son of Errol) in Cambodia in 1970. Tim Page has also produced a photographic testament to the horrors of war called *Requiem*. It is dedicated to correspondents of all sides who died covering the Indochina conflict and includes many images from Cambodia. Page's autobiography *Page by Page* is worth reading, but is hard to find beyond Ho Chi Minh City.

An equally legendary news cameraman, Australian Neil Davies, is the subject of Tim Bowden's book *One Crowded Hour*. Davies fell in love with Cambodia and there is much coverage of his time covering the war in the early 1970s. He died covering a coup in Bangkok in 1985.

FILMS

There have been a couple of definitive films made by Hollywood that deal with the conflict in Cambodia. *The Killing Fields* tells the story of American journalist Sydney Schanberg and his Cambodian assistant Dith Pran during and after the war. As the Khmer Rouge closes in on Phnom Penh, Dith Pran decides to stay and help Schanberg cover the takeover. As the new regime clears out Phnom Penh, most journalists seek refuge in the French embassy. Eventually, Dith Pran is forced to join the rest of Phnom Penh's citizens on the long march into the countryside. The remainder of the film deals with his attempts to survive the horror that engulfs the country. Most of the footage was actually shot in Thailand: it was filmed in 1984 when Cambodia was effectively closed to the West, particularly filmmakers.

The other definitive movie about Cambodia is Francis Ford Coppola's *Apocalypse Now*, which tells the story of a renegade colonel, played by Marlon Brando, who goes AWOL upstream in Cambodia. Martin Sheen plays a young soldier sent to bring him back, and the ensuing encounter makes for one of the most powerful indictments of war ever made. Although no single soldier or story forms the basis of the film, the plot does have some base in historical fact: a number of soldiers did disappear into the bush to train hill tribes in the art of war, including one notorious case in northern Laos. The storyline also draws heavily from the novel set in Africa *Heart of Darkness* by Joseph Conrad and the exploits of famous Vietnam-era soldiers such as Colonel John Paul Vann and Lieutenant-Colonel David Hackett. The film was shot in the Philippines, but the river depicted is thought to be the Tonlé Srepok in Ratanakiri Province, northeastern Cambodia.

Hollywood first came to Cambodia in 1964 to film *Lord Jim*, starring Peter O'Toole, and this was widely credited with kick-starting then-Prince Sihanouk's prolific filmmaking career. It wasn't until 2000 that Hollywood made the return trip when the cast and crew of *Tomb Raider* descended on Siem Reap. The film was far from spectacular, but the temples of Angkor made for some of the most captivating scenes; star Angelina Jolie and many of the crew fell in love with the country. The *Tomb Raider* DVD includes a more in-depth, behind-the-scenes look at the filming in Cambodia.

In early 2001, Matt Dillon rolled into town for the shooting of *Beneath the Banyan Tree*, his directorial debut. Other stars included James Caan and Gerard Depardieu on location in Phnom Penh, Kampot and Bokor. Cambodia looks set to emerge as a hot place for Hollywood to shoot in the coming years.

For information about the Cambodian film industry, see the Arts section in the Facts about Cambodia chapter.

NEWSPAPERS & MAGAZINES

Despite occasional tirades by the government about foreign press interference in the country's 'internal affairs', Cambodia has a lively local English-language press. Bookshops in Phnom Penh have a wide range of English- and French-language newspapers and magazines.

Local Publications

The *Cambodia Daily* nearly lives up to its name, appearing at newsstands and restaurants daily from Monday to Friday. It also has a weekend issue that usually includes a special feature report. It is an excellent overview of international agency stories with some local input, and also has Khmer and Japanese supplements. It costs just 1200r. The Friday edition has a useful 'This Week's Calendar' section.

The *Cambodge Soir* is a French paper that comes out on weekday evenings. It is available in bookshops and most of the restaurants frequented by French patrons around Phnom Penh.

The *Phnom Penh Post* provides a very good overview of events in Cambodia. As well as informative feature stories, it has a lift-out map of Phnom Penh with restaurants and business services. It costs 3500r and is well worth it for its detail.

For the lighter side of life in Cambodia, the free monthly *Bayon Pearnik* combines humorous stories with human-interest features from around the country.

International Publications

The *Bangkok Post* and the *Nation* are Thai English-language dailies that are widely available in Phnom Penh and Siem Reap, usually by mid-morning on the day of publication. Hotels and some cafes and restaurants stock copies you can read free-of-charge if you pop in for a coffee, a snack or a meal.

Monument Books has international magazines in English and French at its outlets at Phnom Penh and Siem Reap airports, while the bookshops in five-star hotels are the best when it comes to newspapers; the French newspaper sections are especially comprehensive. English-language newspapers on sale include the *International Herald Tribune,* the *Guardian Weekly,* and the *Australian*.

On the magazine front, the aforementioned bookshops have current copies of the *Economist, Far Eastern Economic Review, Asiaweek, Time, Newsweek* and a host of European titles in French, German and Italian.

RADIO & TV

The British Broadcasting Corporation (BBC) has broadcasts in Khmer and English at 100MHz FM in the capital. There is also a popular English-language station called Love FM playing tunes in the evening at 98.7MHz FM. The Cambodian radio station in Phnom Penh has an English-language news broadcast at 9pm every evening. French speakers should tune in to Radio France International, which is relayed from Paris.

If you have a short-wave radio, it is possible to pick up the BBC World Service, Radio Australia and so on.

Most of the hotels throughout Cambodia have satellite TV reception, which offers access to BBC World, Cable News Network (CNN), Star TV, MTV, Cartoon Network, TV5 and the Australian Broadcasting Corporation (ABC). Without satellite reception, you are restricted to TV5 (which is French).

Khmer television has a couple of channels, including state-run TVK and the private channels Apsara and Bayon, but most of the time the programmes seem to involve forlorn people singing to each other, or savage gunfight dramas imported from Hong Kong and China. They're the good parts – the rest is transparent political propaganda showing politicians engaging in good deeds across the country.

PHOTOGRAPHY & VIDEO
Film & Equipment

Print film and processing is reasonably cheap in Cambodia. A roll of Kodak or Fuji film (36 exposures) costs US$2 for ASA 100, or US$3.50 for ASA 400. Konica film is cheaper again. Printing is also cheap with most laboratories charging about US$4 for a roll. The Fuji labs are generally the best quality, but the Konica ones are sometimes a little cheaper.

Slide film is also available at competitive prices in Phnom Penh. It costs US$5 for a roll of Kodak Elite or Fuji Sensia and US$6 for Fuji's Velvia or Provia range. Purchase as much as you need in Phnom Penh, as it is pretty hard to come by elsewhere in the country. Do not have slide film processed in Cambodia unless it is really urgent. Many shops claim to be able to process slide film, but you'll more than likely end up with black and white X-ray–style shots. City Colour Photo on Monivong Blvd, just north of Psar Thmei, is the best place in the capital.

General camera-supply needs can be satisfied in Phnom Penh. Camera batteries are easy to replace, providing you don't require anything too obscure, but don't forget to carry a spare if you are heading off the trail. There is a good range of new cameras in the capital at affordable prices, including all the leading brands.

If you take a video camera, make sure you have the necessary charger, plugs and transformer for Cambodia (see Electricity later). Take care with some of the electrical wiring in guesthouses around the country, as it can be pretty amateurish. In Phnom Penh and Siem Reap, it is possible to obtain video tapes for most formats, but elsewhere around the country you are unlikely to find much of use. It is often worth buying a few tapes duty-free before you start your trip.

Technical Tips

The best light conditions in Cambodia begin around 20 minutes after sunrise and last for just one to two hours, roughly corresponding to 6am to 8am. The same applies for the late afternoon light, which begins to assume a radiant warm quality around an hour before sunset. From 10am to around 3.30pm you can expect the light to be harsh and bleaching – there's not much you can do with it unless you have a polariser. Bear in mind that you have much more leeway with exposures in print film than you do in slide film. Snaps taken in poor light conditions often turn out OK in the printing process; with slides you either get it right or you don't.

Restrictions

Although the Cambodian armed forces don't seem too concerned about foreigners photographing bridges and so on (most of these were built by foreigners using foreign aid anyway), it would still be sensible to exercise some restraint. Charging up an armed convoy and snapping away might result in unpleasant consequences.

Photographing People

The usual rules apply: be polite about photographing and video taping people; don't push cameras into their faces; and have some respect for monks and people at prayer. It shouldn't be necessary to say this, but unfortunately there are a lot of amateur photographers out there who think that they're on assignment for *National Geographic*. In general, the Khmers are remarkably courteous people and if you ask nicely they'll agree to have their photograph taken. The same goes for video taping – ask permission first, although in rural areas you will often find children desperate to get in front of the lens and astonished to see themselves played back on a LCD screen. It is the closest most of them will get to being on television.

Airport Security

The X-ray machines at Pochentong airport are safe to put film through. If you are carrying 1000 ASA or higher film, you should store it separately and ask to have it inspected by hand. Some professional photographers refuse to put any film through an X-ray machine. This is an unnecessary precaution but, then again, it is their livelihood.

TIME

Cambodia, like Vietnam, Thailand and Laos, is seven hours ahead of Greenwich Mean Time or Universal Time Coordinated (GMT/UTC). When it is midday in Cambodia it is 10pm the previous evening in San Francisco, 1am in New York, 5am in London, 6am in Paris and 3pm in Sydney.

ELECTRICITY

Electricity in Phnom Penh and most of Cambodia is 220V, 50Hz. Power is in short supply in provincial Cambodia and power cuts are frequent. Most hotels and restaurants have their own generators, but in rural areas expect to be without electricity for long periods each day.

Electric power sockets are generally of the round, two-pin variety. Multiple adaptors can be bought cheaply at markets around the country.

WEIGHTS & MEASURES

Cambodia uses the metric system. For those unaccustomed to this system, there is a metric-imperial conversion chart on the inside back cover of this guide.

LAUNDRY

Laundry is never a problem in Cambodia. All guesthouses and hotels provide a laundry service, but it varies from reasonably cheap at budget places to outrageously expensive at the plushest hotels. In every town there are cheap local laundries that undercut even guesthouses and can do a whole bagful for less than the price of washing a single pair of undies in a posh hotel.

TOILETS

Although the occasional squat toilet turns up here and there, particularly in the most budget of budget guesthouses, in general (particularly in hotels), toilets are of the sit-down variety. If you get out into the sticks, you will find that hygiene conditions deteriorate somewhat, but Cambodia is still a cleaner country than, say, China or India.

Public toilets are rare indeed, the only ones in the country being along Phnom Penh's riverfront and near some of Angkor's more important temples. The charge is usually 500r. Should you find nature calling in rural areas, don't let modesty drive you into the bushes: *there may be land mines not far from the road or track*. Stay on the side of the road or grin and bear it.

HEALTH

Your health is more at risk in Cambodia than most other parts of Southeast Asia, due to poor sanitation and a lack of effective medical treatment facilities. Once you venture into rural areas you should consider yourself very much on your own, as even where pharmacies and hospitals are available you may have trouble making yourself understood.

If you feel particularly unwell try to see a doctor rather than visit a hospital; hospitals are pretty primitive and diagnosis can be erratic. If you fall seriously ill in Cambodia you should return to Phnom Penh, as it is the only place in the country with decent emergency treatment. Pharmacies in the larger towns are remarkably well stocked and you don't need a prescription to get your hands on anything from antibiotics to antimalarials. Prices are very reasonable, but do check the expiry date, as some medicine may have been on the shelves for a long time.

Don't let this make you paranoid. Travel health depends on your degree of predeparture preparation, your daily health care while travelling and how you handle any medical problem that may develop. While the potential dangers can seem quite frightening, in reality few travellers experience anything more than upset stomachs.

Predeparture Planning

Immunisations Plan ahead for getting your vaccinations: some of them require more than one injection over a period of time, while others should not be given together. Note that some vaccinations should not be given during pregnancy or to people with allergies – discuss these issues with your doctor.

It is recommended you seek medical advice at least six weeks before travel. Be aware that there is often a greater risk of disease among children and during pregnancy.

Record all vaccinations on an International Certificate of Vaccination, available from your doctor or government health department. It is also a good idea to carry proof of your vaccinations when travelling in Cambodia.

Vaccinations you may want to consider for a trip to Cambodia are listed here, but it is imperative that you discuss your needs with your doctor. For more details about the diseases themselves, see the individual entries later in this section.

Diphtheria & Tetanus Vaccinations for these two diseases are usually combined. After an initial course of three injections (usually given in childhood), boosters are necessary every 10 years.

Hepatitis A This vaccine provides long-term immunity after an initial injection and a booster at six to 12 months. Alternatively, an injection of gamma globulin can provide short-term protection against hepatitis A – two to six months, depending on the dose. It is reasonably effective and, unlike the vaccine, is protective immediately, but because it is a blood product, there are current concerns about its long-term safety. Hepatitis A vaccine is also available in a combined form with hepatitis B vaccine. Three injections over a six-month period are required.

Hepatitis B Travellers who should consider vaccination against hepatitis B include those on a long trip, as well as those visiting countries where there are high levels of hepatitis B infection (such as Cambodia), where blood transfusions may not be adequately screened or where sexual contact or needle sharing is a possibility. Vaccination involves three injections, with a booster at 12 months. More rapid courses are available if necessary.

Japanese B Encephalitis Consider vaccination against this disease if spending a month or longer in Cambodia, when making repeated trips or if visiting during an epidemic. It involves three injections over 30 days.

Polio Everyone should keep up to date with this vaccination, normally given in childhood. A booster every 10 years maintains immunity.

Rabies Vaccination should be considered by those spending a month or longer in Cambodia, especially if they are cycling, handling animals, caving or travelling to remote areas, and for children (who may not report a bite). Vaccination involves having three injections over 21 to 28 days. Vaccinated people who are bitten or scratched by an animal will require two booster injections of vaccine; those not vaccinated require more.

Tuberculosis The risk of travellers contracting TB is usually very low, unless you will be living with or closely associated with local people. Vaccination against TB (BCG) is recommended for children and young adults living in high-risk areas, including Asia, for three months or more.

Typhoid Vaccination against typhoid may be required if you are travelling for more than a couple of weeks in Cambodia.

Yellow Fever A yellow fever vaccine is now the only vaccine that is a legal requirement for entry into Cambodia when coming from an infected area, but this means direct from an infected area and there are no direct flights from Cambodia to Africa or South America.

Malaria Medication Antimalarial drugs do not prevent you from being infected but kill the malaria parasites during their developmental stage, significantly reducing the risk of becoming very ill or dying. Expert advice on medication should be sought, as there are many factors to consider, including the area to be visited, the risk of exposure to malaria-carrying mosquitoes, the side effects of medication, your medical history and whether you are a child or an adult or pregnant. Travellers heading to isolated areas in Cambodia should carry a treatment dose of medication for use if symptoms occur. A new drug called Malarine, supplied and subsidised by the European Union (EU) and World Health Organization (WHO), is available in pharmacies throughout Cambodia for just 7900r, and is undoubtedly the most effective malaria killer available in Cambodia today. See a doctor for advice about the dosage appropriate for you.

Health Insurance Make sure that you have adequate health insurance. See Travel Insurance in the Visas & Documents section earlier in this chapter for details.

Travel Health Guides If you are planning to be travelling in remote areas for a long period of time, you may consider taking a more detailed health guide. Lonely Planet's *Healthy Travel: Asia & India* is a handy pocket-size guide that's packed with useful information including pretrip planning, emergency first aid, immunisation and disease information, and what to do if you get sick on the road. *Where There Is No Doctor,* by David Werner, is a very detailed guide intended for those going to work in an underdeveloped country.

Travel with Children, by Cathy Lanigan, includes advice on travel health for younger children.

There are a number of excellent travel health sites on the Internet. From the Lonely Planet home page there are links at W www.lonelyplanet.com/weblinks/wlheal.htm to the WHO and the US Centers for Disease Control & Prevention.

Other Preparations Make sure you're healthy before you start travelling. If you're going on a long trip make a visit to a dentist before you depart. If you wear glasses take a spare pair and your prescription.

If you require a particular medication take an adequate supply, as it may not be available locally. Take part of the packaging showing the generic name rather than the brand, which will make getting replacements easier. To avoid any problems, it's a good idea to have a legible prescription or letter from your doctor to show that you legally use the medication.

Basic Rules

Food There is a colonial adage that says 'If you can cook it, boil it or peel it you can eat it…otherwise forget it'. Vegetables and fruit should be washed with purified water or peeled where possible. Beware of ice cream that is sold in the street or anywhere it might have been melted and refrozen; if there's any doubt (eg, a power cut in the last day or two), steer well clear. Shellfish such as mussels, oysters and clams should be avoided as well as undercooked meat, particularly in the form of mince. Steaming does not make shellfish safe for eating.

If a place looks clean and well run and the vendor also looks clean and healthy, then the food is probably safe. In general, places that are packed with travellers or locals will be fine, while empty restaurants might be empty for a reason. The food in busy restaurants is cooked and eaten quite quickly with little standing around and is probably not reheated.

Water The number one rule is *be careful of the water and ice,* although the latter is almost always factory-produced, a legacy of the French. If you don't know for certain that the water is safe, assume the worst. Reputable brands of bottled water or soft drinks are generally fine, but you can't safely drink tap water. Only use water from containers with a serrated seal. Take care with fruit juice, particularly if water may have been added. Milk should be treated with suspicion, as it is often unpasteurised, though boiled milk is fine if it is kept hygienically. Tea and coffee should be OK, since the water should have been boiled.

Water Purification The simplest way of purifying water is to boil it thoroughly. Vigorous boiling should be satisfactory; however, at high altitude water boils at a lower temperature, so germs are less likely to be killed. Make sure you boil it for longer in these environments.

Consider purchasing a water filter for a long trip. There are two main kinds of filter. Total filters take out all parasites, bacteria and viruses and make water safe to drink. They are often expensive, but they can be more cost effective than buying bottled water. Simple filters (which can even be a nylon mesh bag) take out dirt and larger foreign bodies from the water so that chemical solutions work much more effectively; if water is dirty, chemical solutions may not work at all. It's very important when buying a filter to read the specifications, so that you know exactly what it removes from the water and what it doesn't. Simple filtering will not remove all dangerous organisms, so if you cannot boil water it should be treated chemically. Chlorine tablets (Puritabs, Steritabs or

Nutrition

If your diet is poor or limited in variety, if you're travelling hard and fast and therefore missing meals or if you simply lose your appetite, you can soon start to lose weight and place your health at risk.

Make sure your diet is well balanced. Cooked eggs, tofu, beans, lentils and nuts are all safe ways to get protein. Fruit you can peel (bananas, oranges or mandarins, for example) is usually safe and a good source of vitamins. Melons can harbour bacteria in their flesh and are best avoided. Try to eat plenty of grains (including rice) and bread. Remember that although food is generally safer if it is well cooked, overcooked food loses much of its nutritional value. If your diet isn't well balanced or if your food intake is insufficient, it's a good idea to take vitamin and iron pills.

In hot climates make sure you drink enough – don't rely on feeling thirsty to indicate when you should drink. Not needing to urinate or voiding small amounts of very dark yellow urine is a danger sign. Always carry a water bottle with you on long trips. Excessive sweating can lead to loss of salt and therefore muscle cramping. Salt tablets are not a good idea as a preventative, but in places where salt is not used much, adding salt to food can help.

Everyday Health

Normal body temperature is up to 37°C (98.6°F); more than 2°C (4°F) higher indicates a high fever. The normal adult pulse rate is 60 to 100 beats per minute (children 80 to 100, babies 100 to 140). As a general rule, the pulse increases about 20 beats per minute for each 1°C (2°F) rise in fever.

Respiration (breathing) rate is also an indicator of illness. Count the number of breaths per minute: between 12 and 20 is normal for adults and older children (up to 30 for younger children, 40 for babies). People with a high fever or serious respiratory illness breathe more quickly than normal. More than 40 shallow breaths a minute may indicate pneumonia.

other brands) will kill many pathogens, but not some parasites like giardia and amoebic cysts. Iodine is more effective in purifying water and is available in tablet form (such as Potable Aqua). Follow the directions carefully and remember that too much iodine can be harmful.

Medical Problems & Treatment

Self-diagnosis and treatment of health problems can be risky, so you should always seek professional medical help. Although we do give drug dosages in this section, they are for emergency use only. Correct diagnosis is vital.

An embassy, consulate or five-star hotel can usually recommend a local doctor or clinic. Antibiotics should ideally be administered only under medical supervision. Take only the recommended dose at the prescribed intervals and use the whole course,

Not a Good Place for Contacts

People wearing contact lenses should be aware that Cambodia is an extremely dusty country and this can cause much irritation when travelling. It is generally bearable in cars, but when travelling by motorbike or pick-up, it is most definitely not. Pack a pair of glasses.

even if the illness seems to be cured earlier. Stop immediately if there are any serious reactions and don't use the antibiotic at all if you are unsure that you have the correct one. Some people are allergic to commonly prescribed antibiotics such as penicillin or sulpha drugs; carry this information (eg, on a bracelet) when travelling.

Environmental Hazards

Heat Exhaustion Dehydration and salt deficiency can cause heat exhaustion. Take time to acclimatise to high temperatures, drink sufficient liquids and do not do anything too physically demanding.

Salt deficiency is characterised by fatigue, lethargy, headaches, giddiness and muscle cramps; salt tablets may help, but adding extra salt to your food is better.

Anhidrotic heat exhaustion is a rare form of heat exhaustion that is caused by an inability to sweat. It tends to affect people who have been in a hot climate for some time, rather than newcomers. It can progress to heatstroke. Treatment involves removal to a cooler climate or immediate cold showers and wet sheets.

Heatstroke This serious, occasionally fatal condition can occur if the body's heat-regulating mechanism breaks down and the body temperature rises to dangerous levels. Long, continuous periods of exposure to high temperatures and insufficient fluids can leave you vulnerable to heatstroke.

The symptoms are feeling unwell, not sweating very much (or at all) and a high body temperature (39°C to 41°C, or 102°F to 106°F). Where sweating has ceased, the skin becomes flushed and red. Severe, throbbing headaches and lack of coordination will also occur, and the sufferer may be confused or aggressive. Eventually the victim will become delirious or convulse. Hospitalisation is essential, but in the interim get victims out of the sun, remove their clothing, cover them with a wet sheet or towel and then fan continually. Give fluids if they are conscious.

Jet Lag Jet lag is experienced when a person travels by air across more than three time zones (each time zone usually represents a one-hour time difference). It occurs because many of the functions of the human body (such as temperature, pulse rate and emptying of the bladder and bowels) are regulated by internal 24-hour cycles. When we travel long distances rapidly, our bodies take time to adjust to the 'new time' of our destination, and we may experience fatigue, disorientation, insomnia, anxiety, impaired concentration and loss of appetite. These effects will usually be gone within three days of arrival, but to minimise the impact of jet lag:

- Rest for a couple of days prior to departure.
- Try to select flight schedules that minimise sleep deprivation; arriving late in the day means you can go to sleep soon after you arrive. For very long flights, try to organise a stopover.
- Avoid excessive eating (which bloats the stomach) and alcohol intake (which causes dehydration) during the flight. Instead, drink plenty of noncarbonated, nonalcoholic drinks such as fruit juice or water.
- Avoid smoking.
- Make yourself comfortable by wearing loose-fitting clothes and perhaps bringing an eye mask and earplugs to help you sleep.
- Try to sleep at the appropriate time for the time zone you are travelling to.

Motion Sickness Eating lightly before and during a trip will reduce the chances of motion sickness. If you are prone to motion sickness try to find a place that minimises movement – near the wing on aircraft, close to midships on boats, near the centre on buses. Fresh air usually helps; reading and cigarette smoke don't. Commercial motion-sickness preparations, which can cause drowsiness, have to be taken before the trip commences. Ginger (available in capsule form) and peppermint (including mint-flavoured sweets) are natural preventatives of motion sickness.

Prickly Heat Prickly heat is an itchy rash caused by excessive perspiration trapped under the skin. It usually strikes people who have just arrived in a hot climate. Keeping cool, bathing often, drying the skin and

using a mild talcum or prickly heat powder, or resorting to the use of air-conditioning may help.

Sunburn You can get sunburnt surprisingly quickly, even through cloud. Use a sunscreen, a hat, and a barrier cream for your nose and lips. Calamine lotion or Stingose are good for mild sunburn. Protect your eyes with good quality sunglasses.

Infectious Diseases

Diarrhoea Simple things like a change of water, food or climate can all cause a mild bout of diarrhoea, but a few rushed toilet trips with no other symptoms are not indicative of a major problem. Almost everyone gets a mild bout of the runs on a longer visit to Cambodia.

Dehydration is the main danger with diarrhoea, particularly in children or the elderly as dehydration can occur quite quickly. Under all circumstances *fluid replacement* (at least equal to the volume being lost) is the most important thing to remember. Weak black tea with a little sugar, soda water, or soft drinks allowed to go flat and diluted 50% with clean water are all good. You need to drink at least the same volume of fluid that you are losing in bowel movements and vomiting. Urine is the best guide to the adequacy of replacement – if you have small amounts of concentrated urine, you need to drink more. Keep drinking small amounts often. Stick to a bland diet as you recover.

With severe diarrhoea, a rehydrating solution is preferable to replace minerals and salts lost. Commercially available oral rehydration salts are very useful; add them to boiled or bottled water. In an emergency you can make up a solution of six teaspoons of sugar and a half-teaspoon of salt to a litre of boiled or bottled water.

Gut-paralysing drugs such as Lomotil or Imodium can be used to bring relief from the symptoms of diarrhoea, although they do not actually cure the problem. Only use these drugs if you do not have access to toilets, eg, if you *must* travel. For children under 12 years the use of Lomotil and

Imodium is not recommended. Do not use these drugs if the person has a high fever or is severely dehydrated.

In certain situations antibiotics may be required: diarrhoea with blood or mucus (dysentery), any diarrhoea with fever, profuse watery diarrhoea, persistent diarrhoea not improving after 48 hours and severe diarrhoea. These suggest a more serious cause of diarrhoea and in these situations gut-paralysing drugs should be avoided.

In these situations, a stool test may be necessary to diagnose what bug is causing your diarrhoea, so you should seek medical help urgently. Where this is not possible the recommended drugs for bacterial diarrhoea (the most likely cause of severe diarrhoea in travellers) are norfloxacin 400mg twice daily for three days, or ciprofloxacin 500mg twice daily for five days. These are not recommended for children or pregnant women. The drug of choice for children would be co-trimoxazole (Bactrim, Septrin or Resprim) with dosage dependent on weight. A five-day course is given. Ampicillin or amoxycillin may be given in pregnancy, but medical care is necessary.

Two other causes of persistent diarrhoea in travellers are giardiasis and amoebic dysentery.

Giardiasis is caused by a common parasite, *Giardia lamblia*. Symptoms include stomach cramps, nausea, a bloated stomach, watery, foul-smelling diarrhoea and frequent gas. Giardiasis can appear several weeks after you have been exposed to the parasite. The symptoms may disappear for a few days and then return; this can go on for several weeks.

Amoebic dysentery, caused by the protozoan *Entamoeba histolytica,* is characterised by a gradual onset of low-grade diarrhoea, often with blood and mucus. Cramping abdominal pain and vomiting are less likely than in other types of diarrhoea, and fever may not be present. Amoebic dysentery will persist until treated and can recur and cause other health problems.

You should seek medical advice if you think you have giardiasis or amoebic dysentery, but where this is not possible, Tinidazole (Fasigyn) or metronidazole (Flagyl) are the recommended drugs, although the side effects of Flagyl are severe. Treatment is a 2g single dose of Fasigyn or 250mg of Flagyl three times daily for five to 10 days.

Fungal Infections Fungal infections occur more commonly in hot weather and are usually on the scalp, between the toes (athlete's foot) or fingers, in the groin and on the body (ringworm). You get ringworm (which is a fungal infection, not a worm) from infected animals or other people. Moisture encourages these infections.

To prevent fungal infections wear loose, comfortable clothes, avoid artificial fibres, wash frequently and dry yourself carefully. If you do get an infection, wash the infected area at least daily with a disinfectant or medicated soap and water, and rinse and dry well. Apply an antifungal cream or powder like tolnaftate (Tinaderm). Try to expose the infected area to air or sunlight as much as possible and wash all towels and underwear in hot water, change them often and let them dry in the sun.

Hepatitis Hepatitis is a general term for inflammation of the liver. It is a common disease worldwide. There are several different viruses that cause hepatitis, and they differ in the way that they are transmitted. The symptoms are similar in all forms of the illness, and include fever, chills, headache, fatigue, feelings of weakness and aches and pains, followed by loss of appetite, nausea, vomiting, abdominal pain, dark urine, light-coloured faeces, jaundiced (yellow) skin and yellowing of the whites of the eyes. People who have had hepatitis should avoid alcohol for some time after the illness, as the liver needs time to recover.

Hepatitis A is transmitted by ingesting contaminated food or water. You should seek medical advice, but there is not much you can do apart from resting, drinking lots of fluids, eating lightly and avoiding fatty foods. Hepatitis E is transmitted in the same way as hepatitis A; it can be particularly serious in pregnant women.

There are almost 300 million chronic carriers of Hepatitis B in the world. It is spread through contact with infected blood, blood products or body fluids, for example, through sexual contact, unsterilised needles and blood transfusions, or contact with blood via small breaks in the skin. Other risk situations include shaving, tattooing or body piercing with contaminated equipment. The symptoms of hepatitis B may be more severe than type A and the disease can lead to long-term problems such as chronic liver damage, liver cancer or a long-term carrier state. Hepatitis C and D are spread in the same way as hepatitis B and can also lead to long term complications.

There are vaccines against hepatitis A and B, but there are currently no vaccines against the other types of hepatitis. Following the basic rules about food and water (hepatitis A and E) and avoiding risk situations (hepatitis B, C and D) are important preventative measures.

HIV/AIDS Infection with the human immunodeficiency virus (HIV) may lead to acquired immune deficiency syndrome (AIDS), which is a fatal disease. Any exposure to blood, blood products or body fluids may put the individual at risk.

The disease is often transmitted through sexual contact or dirty needles – vaccinations, acupuncture, tattooing and body piercing can be potentially as dangerous as intravenous drug use. HIV/AIDS can also be spread through infected-blood transfusions; although the blood centre in Phnom Penh does screen blood used for transfusions, it is unlikely to be done in many of the provinces.

If you do need an injection, ask to see the syringe unwrapped in front of you, or take a needle and syringe pack with you. Fear of HIV infection should never preclude any treatment for serious medical conditions.

According to WHO figures, Cambodian rates of infection are highest among sex workers. The group's HIV prevalence increased from 10% in 1992 to over 40% in 1996. Another group with a high prevalence rate is the military.

Intestinal Worms These parasites are most common in rural, tropical Cambodia. The various worms have different ways of infecting people. Some may be ingested in food such as undercooked meat (eg, tapeworms) and some enter through your skin (eg, hookworms). Infestations may not show up for some time, and although they are generally not serious, if left untreated may cause severe health problems later. Consider having a stool test when you return home to check for worms and determine the appropriate treatment.

Schistosomiasis Also known as bilharzia, this disease is transmitted by minute worms. They infect certain varieties of freshwater snails found in rivers, streams, lakes and particularly dams. The worms multiply and are eventually discharged into the water.

The worm enters through the skin and attaches itself to the intestines or bladder. The first symptom may be feeling generally unwell, or a tingling and sometimes a light rash around the area where the worm entered. Weeks later a high fever may develop. Once the disease is established abdominal pain and blood in the urine are other signs. The infection often causes no symptoms until the disease is well established (several months to years after exposure), when damage to internal organs is irreversible.

Avoiding swimming or bathing in fresh water where bilharzia is present is the main method of preventing the disease. Even deep water can be infected. If you do get wet, dry off quickly and dry your clothes as well.

A blood test is the most reliable way to diagnose the disease, but the test will not show positive until a number of weeks after exposure.

Sexually Transmitted Infections (STIs) Gonorrhoea, herpes and syphilis are among these infections. Sores, blisters or a rash around the genitals and discharges or pain when urinating are common symptoms. With some STIs, such as wart virus or chlamydia, symptoms may be less marked or not observed at all, especially in women. Syphilis symptoms eventually disappear completely, but the disease continues and can cause severe problems in later years. While abstinence from sexual contact is the only 100% effective prevention, using condoms is also effective. Condoms are widely available throughout urban areas of Cambodia. Different STIs each require specific antibiotics. The treatment of gonorrhoea and syphilis is with antibiotics. There is no cure for herpes or AIDS.

Typhoid Typhoid fever is a dangerous gut infection caused by contaminated water and food. Medical help must be sought.

In its initial stages sufferers may feel they have a bad cold or flu on the way, as early symptoms are a headache, body aches and a fever that rises a little each day until it is around 40°C (104°F) or higher. The victim's pulse is often slow relative to the degree of fever present – unlike a normal fever where the pulse increases. There may also be vomiting, abdominal pain, diarrhoea or constipation.

In the second week the high fever and slow pulse continue, and a few pink spots may appear on the body; trembling, delirium, weakness, weight loss and dehydration may occur. Complications such as pneumonia, perforated bowel or meningitis may also present.

Insect-Borne Diseases

Malaria This serious and potentially fatal disease is spread by mosquitoes. If you are travelling in endemic areas it is extremely important to avoid mosquito bites and to take tablets to prevent this disease. There is no malaria in Phnom Penh, Siem Reap and most other major urban areas in Cambodia, so visitors on short trips to the most popular places do not need to take medication. Malaria self-test kits are now available in Cambodia for just 1300r. Pick one up if you are heading to remote areas for a long period.

Symptoms of malaria include fever, chills and sweating, headache, aching joints, diarrhoea and abdominal pains, usually preceded by a vague feeling of ill-health. Seek medical help immediately if malaria is suspected, as without treatment,

the disease can rapidly become more serious or even fatal.

If medical care is not available, malaria tablets can be used for treatment. You need to use a different malaria tablet to the one you were taking when you contracted the disease, as obviously the first type didn't work. If travelling widely in rural areas of Cambodia, it is worth visiting a pharmacy to purchase a treatment dose to save yourself complications in the event of an emergency. Antimalarials are available cheaply throughout Cambodia, although buy them from a clinic to be sure they are not fakes.

Travellers are advised to prevent mosquito bites at all times. The main messages are:

- Wear light-coloured clothing.
- Wear long trousers and long-sleeved shirts.
- Use mosquito repellents containing the compound DEET on exposed areas (prolonged overuse of DEET may be harmful, especially to children, but its use is considered preferable to being bitten by disease-transmitting mosquitoes).
- Avoid perfumes or aftershave.
- Use a mosquito net impregnated with mosquito repellent (permethrin) – it may be worth taking your own.
- Impregnate clothes with permethrin to effectively deter mosquitoes and other insects.

Dengue Fever This viral disease is transmitted by mosquitoes and occurs mainly in tropical and subtropical areas of the world. Generally, there is only a small risk to travellers except during epidemics, which are usually seasonal (during and just after the wet season). With unstable weather patterns thought to be responsible for large outbreaks of dengue fever in Southeast Asia, travellers to Cambodia may be especially at risk of infection.

Unlike the malaria mosquito, the *Aedes aegypti* mosquito, which transmits the dengue virus, is most active during the day and is found mainly in urban areas.

Signs and symptoms of dengue fever include a sudden onset of high fever, headache, joint and muscle pains (hence its old name, 'breakbone fever') and nausea and vomiting. A rash of small red spots appears three to four days after the onset of fever. Dengue is commonly mistaken for other infectious diseases, including influenza.

You should seek medical attention if you think you may be infected. Infection can be diagnosed by a blood test, although there is no specific treatment for the disease. Aspirin should be avoided, as it increases the risk of haemorrhaging. Recovery may be prolonged, with tiredness lasting for several weeks. Severe complications are rare in travellers but include dengue haemorrhagic fever (DHF), which can be fatal without prompt medical treatment. DHF is thought to be a result of secondary infection due to a different strain (there are four major strains) and usually affects residents of the country rather than travellers.

There is no vaccine against dengue fever. The best prevention is to avoid mosquito bites at all times – see the Malaria entry earlier for more details.

Japanese B Encephalitis This viral infection of the brain is transmitted by mosquitoes. Most cases occur in rural areas, as the virus exists in pigs and wading birds. Symptoms include fever, headache and alteration in consciousness. Hospitalisation is needed for correct diagnosis and treatment. There is a high mortality rate among those who have symptoms; of those who survive many are intellectually disabled.

Cuts, Bites & Stings
Cuts & Scratches Wash well and treat any cut with an antiseptic such as povidone-iodine. Apply a breathable waterproof dressing such as Cutifilm or Tegaderm. Coral cuts are notoriously slow to heal and if they are not adequately cleaned, small pieces of coral can remain embedded in the wound. Some wounds just won't heal in the dusty, damp heat of Cambodia and can quickly get worse rather than better. Consider using antibiotics such as Bactrim if a wound appears to be getting infected.

Bedbugs & Lice Bedbugs live in various places, but particularly in dirty mattresses and bedding, evidenced by spots of blood

on bedclothes or on the wall. Bedbugs leave itchy bites in neat rows. Calamine lotion or Stingose spray may help.

All lice cause itching and discomfort. They make themselves at home in your hair (head lice), your clothing (body lice) or in your pubic hair (crabs). You catch lice through direct contact with infected people or by sharing combs, clothing and the like. Powder or shampoo treatment will kill the lice, and infected clothing should be washed in very hot, soapy water and left to dry in the sun.

Bites & Stings Bee and wasp stings are usually painful rather than dangerous. However, in people who are allergic to them severe breathing difficulties may occur and require urgent medical care. Calamine lotion or Stingose spray will relieve itching and ice packs will reduce the pain and swelling.

Jellyfish Avoid contact with these sea creatures, which have stinging tentacles – seek local advice. Dousing in vinegar will deactivate any stingers that have not 'fired'. Calamine lotion, antihistamines and analgesics may reduce the reaction and relieve the pain.

Leeches & Ticks Leeches may be present in damp rainforest conditions; they attach themselves to your skin to suck your blood. Trekkers often get them on their legs or in their boots. Salt or a lighted cigarette end will make them fall off. Do not pull them off, as the bite is then more likely to become infected. Clean and apply pressure if the point of attachment is bleeding. An insect repellent may keep them away, and walkers in tick-infested areas should consider having their boots and trousers impregnated with benzyl benzoate and dibutylphthalate.

You should always check all over your body if you have been walking through a potentially tick-infested area, as ticks can cause skin infections and other more serious diseases. If a tick is found attached, press down around the tick's head with tweezers, grab the head and gently pull upwards. Try to avoid pulling the rear of the body as this may squeeze the tick's gut contents through the attached mouth parts into the skin, increasing the risk of infection and disease. Smearing chemicals on the tick will not make it let go and this is not recommended.

Snakes To minimise your chances of being bitten always wear boots, socks and long trousers when walking through undergrowth where snakes may be present. Don't put your hands into holes and crevices, and be careful if collecting firewood.

Snake bites do not cause instantaneous death and antivenins are usually available. Immediately wrap the bitten limb tightly, as you would for a sprained ankle, and then attach a splint to immobilise it. Keep the victim still and seek medical help, if possible with the dead snake for identification. However, do not attempt to catch the snake if there is any possibility of being bitten. Tourniquets and sucking out the poison are now comprehensively discredited.

Women's Health

Gynaecological Problems Antibiotic use, synthetic underwear, sweating and contraceptive pills can lead to fungal vaginal infections, especially when travelling in hot climates. Thrush (yeast infection or vaginal candidiasis) is characterised by a rash, itching and discharge. Nystatin, miconazole or clotrimazole pessaries or vaginal cream are the usual treatment. Maintaining good personal hygiene and wearing loose-fitting clothes and cotton underwear may help prevent these infections.

STIs are a major cause of vaginal problems. Symptoms include a smelly discharge, painful intercourse and sometimes a burning sensation when urinating. Medical attention should be sought and male sexual partners must also be treated. For more details, see Sexually Transmitted Infections earlier in this section. Besides abstinence, the best thing is to practise safe sex using condoms.

Pregnancy Most miscarriages occur during the first three months of pregnancy. Miscarriage is not uncommon and can occasionally lead to severe bleeding. The last

Medical Kit Check List

Following is a list of items you should consider including in your medical kit – consult your pharmacist for brands available in your country.

☐ **Aspirin** or **paracetamol** (acetaminophen in the USA) – for pain or fever

☐ **Antihistamine** – for allergies, eg, hay fever; to ease the itch from insect bites or stings; and to prevent motion sickness

☐ **Cold** and **flu tablets, throat lozenges** and **nasal decongestant**

☐ **Multivitamins** – consider for long trips, when dietary vitamin intake may be inadequate

☐ **Antibiotics** – consider including these if you're travelling well off the beaten track; see your doctor, as they must be prescribed, and carry the prescription with you

☐ **Loperamide** or **diphenoxylate** –'blockers' for diarrhoea

☐ **Prochlorperazine** or **metaclopramide** – for nausea and vomiting

☐ **Rehydration mixture** – to prevent dehydration, which may occur, for example, during bouts of diarrhoea; particularly important when travelling with children

☐ **Insect repellent, sunscreen, lip balm** and **eye drops**

☐ **Calamine lotion, sting relief spray** or **aloe vera** – to ease irritation from sunburn and insect bites or stings

☐ **Antifungal cream** or **powder** – for fungal skin infections and thrush

☐ **Antiseptic** (such as povidone-iodine) – for cuts and grazes

☐ **Bandages, Band-Aids (plasters)** and other wound dressings

☐ **Water purification tablets** or **iodine**

☐ **Scissors, tweezers** and a **thermometer** – note that mercury thermometers are prohibited by airlines

☐ **Sterile kit (sealed medical kit containing syringes and needles)** – in case you need injections in a country with medical hygiene problems; discuss with your doctor

three months should also be spent within reasonable distance of good medical care. A baby born as early as 24 weeks stands a chance of survival, but only in a good modern hospital. Pregnant women should avoid all unnecessary medication, although vaccinations and malarial prophylactics should still be taken where needed. Additional care should be taken to prevent illness and particular attention should be paid to diet and nutrition. Alcohol and nicotine, for example, should be avoided.

Less Common Diseases
The following diseases pose a small risk to travellers, and so are only mentioned in passing. Seek medical advice if you think you may have any of these diseases.

Cholera This is the worst of the watery diarrhoeas and medical help should be sought. Outbreaks of cholera are generally well reported, so you can avoid such problem areas. *Fluid replacement is the most vital treatment* – the risk of dehydration is severe as you may lose up to 20L a day. If there is a delay in getting to hospital, then begin taking tetracycline. The adult dose is 250mg four times daily. It is not recommended for children under nine years or for pregnant women. Tetracycline may help shorten the illness, but adequate fluids are required to save lives.

Filariasis This is a mosquito-transmitted parasitic infection found in Cambodia. Possible symptoms include fever, pain and swelling of the lymph glands, inflammation of lymph drainage areas, swelling of a limb or the scrotum, skin rashes and blindness. Treatment is available to eliminate the parasites from the body, but some of the damage already caused may not be reversible. Medical advice should be promptly obtained if the infection is suspected.

Rabies This fatal viral infection is found in Cambodia. Many animals can be infected (such as dogs, cats, bats and monkeys) and it is their saliva that is infectious. Any bite, scratch or even lick from an animal should

be cleaned immediately and thoroughly. Scrub with soap and running water, and then apply alcohol or iodine solution. Medical help should be sought promptly if you are bitten by an animal.

Tetanus This disease is caused by a germ that lives in soil and in the faeces of horses and other animals. It enters the body via breaks in the skin. The first symptom may be discomfort in swallowing or stiffening of the jaw and neck; this is followed by painful convulsions of the jaw and whole body. The disease can be fatal. It can be prevented by vaccination.

Tuberculosis TB is a bacterial infection usually transmitted from person to person by coughing, but which may be transmitted through consumption of unpasteurised milk. Milk that has been boiled is safe to drink, and the souring of milk to make yogurt or cheese also kills the bacilli. Travellers are usually not at great risk, as close household contact with the infected person is usually required before the disease is passed on. You may need to have a TB test before you travel, as this can help diagnose the disease if you become ill later.

Typhus This disease is spread by ticks, mites and lice. It begins with fever, chills, headache and muscle pains followed a few days later by a body rash. There is often a large painful sore at the site of the bite and nearby lymph nodes are swollen and painful. Typhus can be treated under medical supervision. See the Leeches & Ticks section in Cuts, Bites & Stings earlier for preventative measures.

WOMEN TRAVELLERS
Women will generally find Cambodia a hassle-free place to travel. Foreign women are unlikely to be targeted by local men, but at the same time it pays to be careful. As is the case anywhere in the world, walking or riding a bike alone late at night is risky, and if you're planning a trip off the beaten trail it would be best to find a travel companion.

Despite the prevalence of sex workers and women's employment as 'beer girls', dancing companions and the like, foreign women will probably find Khmer men to be courteous and polite. It's best to keep things this way by being restrained in your dress. Khmer women dress fairly conservatively, and it's best to follow suit, particularly when visiting wats. In general, long-sleeved shirts and long trousers or skirts are preferred. It is also worth having trousers for heading out at night on motos, as short skirts aren't too practical.

Tampons and sanitary napkins are widely available in the major cities and provincial capitals, but if you are heading into very remote areas for a few days, it is worth having your own supply.

GAY & LESBIAN TRAVELLERS

While Cambodian culture is tolerant of homosexuality, the scene is certainly nothing like that of neighbouring Thailand. Public displays of affection, whether heterosexual or homosexual, are frowned upon.

DISABLED TRAVELLERS

Broken pavements (sidewalks), potholed roads and stairs as steep as ladders at Angkor ensure that for most people with mobility impairments, Cambodia is not going to be an easy country in which to travel. Few buildings in Cambodia have been designed with the disabled in mind, although new projects, such as the international airports at Phnom Penh and Siem Reap, and top-end hotels, include ramps for wheelchair access. Transport in the provinces is usually very overcrowded, but taxi hire from point to point is at least an affordable option.

On the positive side, the Cambodian people are usually very helpful towards all foreigners, and local labour is cheap if you need someone to accompany you at all times. Most guesthouses and small hotels have ground-floor rooms that are reasonably easy to access.

The biggest headache is also the main attraction – the temples of Angkor. Causeways are uneven, obstacles common and

staircases daunting, even for able-bodied people. It is likely to be some years before things improve, although some ramping was introduced at the Bayon in late 2000 for the visit of King Sihanouk and Chinese Premier Jiang Zemin.

Wheelchair travellers will need to undertake a lot of research before visiting Cambodia. There is now a growing network of information sources that can put you in touch with others who have wheeled through Cambodia before. Try contacting the following:

Access Foundation (☎ 516-887-5798) PO Box 356, Malverne, NY 11565, USA
Mobility International (☎ 503-343-1284, W www.miusa.org) PO Box 10767, Eugene, OR 97440, USA
Society for Accessible Travel & Hospitality (SATH; ☎ 212-447-7284, W www.sath.org) 347 Fifth Avenue, Suite 610, New York, NY 10016, USA. SATH publishes a useful magazine called *Open World*.

SENIOR TRAVELLERS

Senior travellers are not eligible for discounts in Cambodia – all foreigners are rich as far as Cambodians are concerned (and they are right, comparatively). Elderly visitors should be realistic about their health and fitness before plunging into an adventure in Cambodia. Cambodia is extremely hot and dehydration and exhaustion are realistic threats, especially for older visitors not used to exerting themselves in such conditions. If you are not that nimble on your feet, it is not recommended that you take adventurous options, such as the boats that travel between Phnom Penh and Siem Reap. It is also important to take great care around the temples of Angkor, as many of the staircases are extremely steep and can be slippery when wet.

Khmer culture shows great respect for elders and this means many Cambodians will go out of their way to help older visitors. In a country where most people don't live much past 50, don't be surprised to be told you are old when in your 50s. Cambodians aren't rude, but they are not always subtle.

TRAVEL WITH CHILDREN

Travellers considering visiting Cambodia with children should pick up a copy of Lonely Planet's *Travel with Children*.

Families planning a visit to Siem Reap and the temples of Angkor should have no problem at all. However, it is worth remembering that young children won't be particularly impressed by the temples and will have more fun playing with local Cambodian children.

The main worry throughout Cambodia is keeping an eye on what strange things infants are putting in their mouths. Their natural curiosity can be a lot more costly in a country where dysentery, typhoid and hepatitis are commonplace. Keeping their hydration levels up and insisting they use sunscreen, despite their protests, is also important.

Phnom Penh, Sihanoukville and other urban areas of Cambodia are also pretty straightforward these days, although be very aware of the chaotic traffic conditions in the capital – better to restrict your child's movements than have them wander into danger. Rural Cambodia is not a good travel destination for children, as there are many land mines littering the countryside. No matter how many warnings a child is given, can you be certain they won't stray from the path?

USEFUL ORGANISATIONS

Cambodia hosts a huge number of NGOs. The best way to find out who exactly is represented in the country is to call in to the Co-operation Committee for Cambodia (CCC; ☎ 214152) at 35 Ph 178, Phnom Penh. This organisation has a handy list of all NGOs, both Cambodian and international, and is extremely helpful.

DANGERS & ANNOYANCES
Security

Cambodia is a relatively safe country in which to travel, a major turnaround from a few years ago. Remembering the golden rule – *stick to marked paths in remote areas* – it is now possible to travel throughout Cambodia with no more difficulty than in neighbouring countries such as Thailand or Vietnam. Politically, Cambodia has proven an unpredictable country and this makes it hard to guarantee safety of travel at any given time. Suffice to say that you are not a target just because you are a tourist.

For many years the security situation was the Achilles heel of Cambodia's tourism industry. Certainly, during Cambodia's civil war, personal security was an issue of greater concern than in neighbouring countries, and for most of the 1990s the Khmer Rouge had a policy of targeting Western tourists. Indeed, a number were killed, and this naturally scared visitors away, while those that came found their movements restricted. The coup of July 1997 and the series of riots and extra-judicial killings that followed the elections of July 1998 further sullied Cambodia's international reputation. This culture of violence persists, but politicians are at last learning that it's not popular with either Western donors or tourists.

Visitors can now travel on all major roads in the country without fear of ambush. Many roads that were off-limits only a few years ago now see regular tourist traffic. These include the road between Poipet and Siem Reap, the road from Siem Reap to Phnom Penh and the road between Phnom Penh and Battambang. The problem of banditry that lingered on into 2000 in certain remote parts of the country seems to have been brought to a halt. The 'bandits' were often soldiers or former Khmer Rouge fighters who did not receive their pay cheques or promised better opportunities.

Cambodia is something of a lawless society in which arms are often preferred to eloquence when settling a dispute. This 'wild west' atmosphere rarely affects tourists, but it is worth knowing about as you can expect to hear gunshots from time to time (usually someone firing into the air when drunk). Phnom Penh is arguably one of the more dangerous places in Cambodia since peace has come to the provinces; it is here that the most guns are concentrated and the most robberies take place. Elsewhere in the provinces you would be very unlucky to have any incident befall you, as the vast majority of Khmers are immensely hospitable, honest and helpful. More importantly perhaps, the majority of Khmers are experiencing peace for the first time in more than 30 years and don't want anything to disturb it.

Trying to pinpoint any lingering areas of concern around the country is always difficult as circumstances change quickly, but the notorious NH7 from Kratie to Stung Treng is now safe for travellers moving between Phnom Penh and Laos or Ratanakiri. Pailin and large parts of Oddar Meanchey and Preah Vihear Provinces were Khmer Rouge controlled until just a few years ago, but are now considered safe. However, if and when a trial for surviving Khmer Rouge leaders moves forward, it may be a different story – just because the former fighters now wear Harry Potter T-shirts instead of Mao caps, it doesn't mean they have forgotten their long struggle.

For the time being, make a point of checking on the latest security situation in the nearest provincial capital before making a trip into very remote areas. Such destinations include the remote temples of Koh Ker, Preah Khan and Prasat Preah Vihear in the north, as well as the tough land routes from Preah Vihear to Stung Treng or from Ratanakiri to Mondulkiri.

Should anyone be unlucky enough to be robbed, it is important to note that the Cambodian police are the best that money can buy. Any help such as a police report is going to cost you. The going rate depends on the size of the claim, but US$20 is a common charge.

Checkpoints

During the long years of civil war there were checkpoints on roads throughout the country. These were supposed to enhance security on provincial roads, but in reality they worsened the situation as the soldiers stationed at checkpoints learned to extort money from every vehicle passing through. However, the situation has improved vastly in recent years and none of the commonly travelled routes have checkpoints today. Where there are checkpoints on major roads, spot checks may be carried out to make sure drivers have paid their road tax or are not carrying illegal guns.

If you are travelling in a taxi or pick-up truck in remote areas of Cambodia and come across a checkpoint, the driver should take care of the payment. If you are on a motorbike you are unlikely to be stopped. However, should you ever find money being demanded of you, try to negotiate the sum to an acceptable level. Do not under any circumstances attempt to take photos of the individuals concerned as things could turn nasty. If the soldiers are adamant that you cannot pass, there may be a genuine security risk so turn back rather than argue.

Undetonated Mines, Mortars & Bombs

Never touch any rockets, artillery shells, mortars, mines, bombs or other war material you may come across. A favourite tactic of the Khmer Rouge was to lay mines along roads and in rice fields in an effort to maim and kill civilians, thus – so the twisted logic concludes – furthering the rebel cause by demoralising the government. The only concrete results of this policy are the many limbless people you see all over Cambodia.

The most heavily mined part of the country is the Battambang and Pailin area, but mines are a problem all over Cambodia. In short: *do not stray from well-marked paths under any circumstances,* even around the monuments of Angkor. If you are planning any walks, even in safer areas such as the remote northeast, it is imperative you take a guide, as there may be unexploded ordnance (UXO) from the American bombing campaign of the early 1970s.

Theft & Street Crime

Given the number of guns in Cambodia, there is less armed-theft than one might expect. Still, hold-ups and motorcycle theft are regular problems in Phnom Penh. See the Dangers & Annoyances section in the Phnom Penh chapter for details. There is no need to be paranoid, just cautious. Walking or riding alone late at night is not ideal, certainly not in rural areas.

Cambodia's Underground War

Cambodia is a country scarred by years of conflict and some of the deepest scars lie just inches beneath the surface. The legacy of land mines in Cambodia is one of the worst anywhere in the world, with an estimated four to six million dotted about the countryside. These insidious inventions are not just weapons of war, but weapons against peace, as they recognise no ceasefire.

As many as 40,000 Cambodians have lost limbs due to mines. Cambodia has one of the world's highest number of amputees per capita – about one in 275 people. After malaria, tuberculosis, diarrhoea and traffic accidents, mines are Cambodia's number-one killer. Land mines litter the country, buried in rice fields and on roadsides and, even after extensive mine-awareness campaigns, they still claim about 40 to 50 victims a month. This is a vast improvement on a decade ago, when the figure was more like 300, but still entirely unacceptable for a country officially at peace. To make matters more complicated, areas that appear safe in the dry season become unsafe in the wet season as the earth softens. It is not uncommon for Cambodian farmers to settle on land during the dry season, only to have their dreams shattered in the wet season when a family member has a leg blown off by a land mine.

The cost to an extensively mined country is enormous. In a developing country like Cambodia, the United Nations (UN) estimates that the lifetime rehabilitation of a land mine victim costs US$3000. With 40,000 victims, the cost is around US$120 million. Then there are indirect costs, such as those resulting from the deaths of grazing livestock. Mines hamper rural development too. Much of Cambodia's agricultural land is mined, making it impossible to farm and causing shortages of food.

There are a number of groups working in Cambodia to alleviate the problem of mines. The Cambodian Mine Action Centre (CMAC) is an all-Cambodian government agency operating with technical support from overseas governments. Hazardous Areas Life (Support) Organisation (HALO) was one of the pioneers of mine clearing in Cambodia, and now has many teams working in provinces such as Pursat, Banteay Meanchey and Siem Reap. The Mines Advisory Group (MAG) is a British outfit that has been training Cambodians in mine clearance. It has launched programmes to train mine

Pickpocketing and theft by stealth is more a problem in Vietnam and Thailand than in Cambodia, but it pays to be careful. The current hotspots are crowded pick-up trucks on popular tourist routes such as Siem Reap to Poipet or Phnom Penh, and the markets of Phnom Penh. Don't make it any easier for thieves by putting your passport and wads of cash in your back pocket. As a precaution, keep a 'secret' stash of cash separate from the bulk of your funds.

Scams

There are fewer scams in Cambodia than neighbouring countries, but once tourism takes off that may start to change. Most current scams are fairly harmless, involving a bit of commission here and there for taxi or moto drivers, particularly in Siem Reap. More annoying for some are the 'cheap' buses from Bangkok to Siem Reap

– for more on this, see the boxed text in the Land section in the Getting There & Away chapter.

There have been one or two reports of police set-ups in Phnom Penh, involving planted drugs. This seems to be very rare, but if you fall victim to the ploy, it will require patience and persistence to sort out, inevitably involving embassies and the like. It may be best to pay them off before it gets out of the room, as the price will only rise the more people there are to pay off.

Begging

Begging is common throughout Cambodia, although much more evident in Phnom Penh and Siem Reap than elsewhere. There are many reasons for begging in a society as poor as Cambodia; there are, for example, amputees who may have lost their legs in frontline battles during the civil war. It is

Cambodia's Underground War

victims and all-women teams in mine clearance. It has also pioneered mine awareness programmes throughout the country involving puppet shows for children and posters in rural communes.

Most sensible travellers will not be wandering around mined areas while they are in Cambodia. Nevertheless, there are some points worth bearing in mind while you are in the country:

- Always check with locals that paths are not mined.
- Never leave a well-trodden path in remote areas.
- Never touch anything that looks remotely like a mine.
- If you find yourself accidentally in a mined area, retrace your steps only if you can clearly see your footprints; if not, you should stay where you are and call for help – as advisory groups put it, 'better to spend a day standing in a minefield than a lifetime as an amputee'.
- If someone is injured in a minefield, even if they are crying out for help, do not rush in; find someone who knows how to safely enter a mined area.
- Do not leave the roadside in remote areas, even for the call of nature, as your limbs are more important than your modesty.

There have been some notable breakthroughs in the last few years in the campaign to ban land mines. In 1997 more than 100 countries signed a treaty banning the production, stockpiling, sale and use of land mines under any circumstances. Some important international players in land mine production signed the treaty, including Italy, France and the UK. However, the world's major producers refused to sign, including China, Russia and the USA, so even as you read this, land mines continue to be produced.

Cambodia was a signatory to the treaty and while it is commendable that it has signed, the treaty does little to alleviate the everyday nightmare of life in heavily mined rural provinces. Mine clearance in Cambodia is, tragically, too often a step-by-step process. For the majority of Cambodians, the underground war goes on.

---

entirely up to individual visitors to give or not, and to decide how much to offer, but it should be remembered that it is common practice for Buddhists to give to those more needy than themselves.

Big brown eyes, runny noses and grubby hands...the sight of children begging is familiar throughout the developing world and Cambodia is no exception. There are many child beggars around Phnom Penh and the temples of Angkor, and with their angelic faces it is often difficult to resist giving them some money. However, some important issues to bear in mind include: giving to child beggars may create a cycle of dependency, which can continue into adulthood; the children may not benefit directly from the money, as they are often made to beg by a begging 'pimp' or their family; and some child beggars, particularly around central Phnom Penh, may use the money to buy

glue to feed their sniffing habit. One way to help these impoverished children is to buy them some food or drink or give them some of your time and attention – it is amazing how quickly they will forget about begging once they are being taught something simple like a whistle, a trick or a game.

The most common beggars around the country are land mine victims. Many of these victims have sustained these injuries fighting, while others have had their legs blown off while working or playing innocently in the fields. You may tire of their attention after a few days in Cambodia, but try to remember that in a country with no social security network, begging is often all they can do to survive.

When giving to beggars, try to offer smaller denominations to avoid making foreigners more of a target than they already are.

Traffic Accidents

Traffic conditions in Cambodia are chaotic, although no worse than in many other underdeveloped countries. If you are riding a bike in Phnom Penh you should stay very alert and take nothing for granted. Traffic moves in all directions on both sides of the road so don't be surprised to see vehicles bearing down on you. The horn is used to alert other drivers of a vehicle's presence – get out of the way if you hear a car or truck behind you.

None of the moto drivers in Cambodia use or provide safety helmets. Fortunately most of them drive at sensible speeds. If you encounter a reckless driver, ask them to slow down or pay them off and find another moto.

Having a major traffic accident in Phnom Penh would be bad enough, but if you have one in rural Cambodia you are in big trouble. Somehow you will have to get back to Phnom Penh for medical treatment.

The basic rule is to drive carefully – there have already been too many shattered dreams in Cambodia, and there's no need to add to them. See the Car & Motorcycle section in the Getting Around chapter for safety tips.

Snakes

Visitors to Ta Prohm, at Angkor, and other overgrown archaeological sites should beware of snakes, including the small but deadly light-green Haluman snake, which often emerges after rainstorms to hunt for insects. They are very well camouflaged so keep your eyes peeled.

LEGAL MATTERS

Marijuana is not legal in Cambodia and police are beginning to take a harder line, although usually for their own benefit rather than a desire to uphold the law. There have been several busts (and a few set-ups too) of foreigner-owned bars and restaurants where ganja was smoked – the days of free bowls in guesthouses are long gone. Marijuana is traditionally used in some Khmer food, so it will continue to be around for a long time, but if you are a smoker, be very discreet. It's probably only a matter of time before the Cambodian police turn the regular busting of foreigners into a lucrative sideline.

This advice applies equally to other narcotic substances, which are also illegal. And think twice about visiting an opium parlour with an unfamiliar moto driver as it may end with you getting robbed after passing out.

BUSINESS HOURS

Government offices, which are open from Monday to Saturday, theoretically begin the working day at 7am or 7.30am, break for a siesta from 11am or 11.30am to 2pm or 2.30pm and end the day at 5.30pm. However, it is a safe bet that few people will be around early in the morning or after 4pm.

Banking hours tend to vary according to the bank, but reckon on core hours of 8.30am to 3.30pm.

Local markets operate seven days a week and usually open and close with the light, running from 6am to 6pm. Markets close for a few days during the major holidays of Chaul Chnam (Khmer New Year), P'chum Ben (Festival of the Dead) and Chinese New Year.

PUBLIC HOLIDAYS & SPECIAL EVENTS

During public holidays and festivals, banks, ministries and embassies close down, so plan ahead if visiting Cambodia during these times. These institutions also seem to take holidays on Christmas Day, New Year's Day, the Day for Remembering the Victory over the Genocidal Regime (7 January) and Chinese New Year, so all said and done they spend a fair number of days on holiday each year. In fact, it is well known in Phnom Penh that Cambodia has more public holidays than any other nation on earth!

The festivals of Cambodia take place according to the lunar calendar so the dates vary from year to year:

Chaul Chnam Held in mid-April, this is a three-day celebration of Khmer New Year: Khmers make offerings at wats, clean out their homes and exchange gifts of new clothes. It is a lively time to visit the country as, like the Thais, Khmers go wild with water and talcum powder, leaving a lot of bemused tourists looking like plaster-cast figures. It is not the best time to visit the temples of Angkor as half the population turns up, leaving you no peace to explore and reflect.

International Workers' Day 1 May

Chat Preah Nengkal Held in early May, this is the Royal Ploughing ceremony, a ritual agricultural festival led by the royal family. It takes place in front of the National Museum, near the Royal Palace in Phnom Penh.

Visakha Puja Celebrated collectively as Buddha's birth, enlightenment and *parinibbana* (passing away), activities are centred on wats. The festival falls on the 15th day of the sixth lunar month and is best observed at Angkor Wat, where you can see candlelit processions of monks.

P'chum Ben This festival falls between mid-September and early October and is a kind of All Souls' Day, when respects are paid to the dead through offerings made at wats.

HM the King's Birthday 30 October to 1 November

Bon Om Tuk Held in early November, this celebrates the reversal of the current of the Tonlé Sap river (with the onset of the dry season water backed up in the Tonlé Sap lake begins to empty into the Mekong). This is one of the most important festivals in the Khmer calendar and a wonderful, if hectic, time to be in Phnom Penh or Siem Reap, as boat races are held on the Tonlé Sap river and the moat around Angkor Wat.

Independence Day 9 November

The Chinese inhabitants of Cambodia celebrate their New Year somewhere between late January and mid-February – for the Vietnamese, this is Tet. As many of Phnom Penh's businesses are run by Chinese, commerce grinds to a halt around this time.

WARNING

In the run-up to major festivals such as P'chum Ben or Chaul Chnam, there is a palpable increase in the number of robberies, particularly in Phnom Penh. Cambodians need money to buy gifts for relatives or pay off debts and for some individuals robbing other people is the quick way to get this money. Be more vigilant at night at these times and don't take valuables out with you unnecessarily. See the Dangers & Annoyances section in the Phnom Penh chapter for more on robberies.

ACTIVITIES

Tourism in Cambodia is still in its infancy and as yet there is little in the way of activities. Phnom Penh is one exception, as the large population of foreigners has led to a boom in leisure activities, such as go-carting, jet-skiing, tenpin bowling and a variety of conventional sports like swimming and tennis. See the Phnom Penh chapter for details on some of these.

Diving & Snorkelling

Snorkelling and diving are available off the coast of Sihanoukville, but it is not generally as spectacular as in Thailand or Indonesia. However, farther afield are some good dive sites such as around Koh Tang, and there are many unexplored areas off the coast of Koh Kong that could put Cambodia on the dive map of Asia in the future.

Boat Trips

With so much water around the country, it is hardly surprising that boat trips are popular with tourists. Some of these are functional yet interesting such as travelling up the Tonlé Sap to Siem Reap or up the Mekong to Kratie, but others are the traditional tourist trips, such as are available in Phnom Penh, Siem Reap and Sihanoukville.

All this water looks set to make canoeing a popular activity of the future. There are already two companies offering canoeing trips around Phnom Penh and farther afield. Adventure Canoe Cambodia (☎ 012-965635, [e] adventurecanoe@yahoo.com), run out of the Lazy Gecko Café on Boeng Kak in Phnom Penh, has small inflatable canoes and offers trips to villages near Phnom Penh and longer trips in the northeast around Kratie and the unexplored rivers of Ratanakiri. Canoeing Cambodia (☎ 012-870993, [e] canoeingcambodia @yahoo.com) has larger plastic kayaks and arranges trips around the sights of the Tonlé Sap and beyond.

The country is slowly establishing a network of national parks with visitor facilities. Ream and Bokor, on the south coast, are the most accessible and interesting to visit. See the South Coast chapter and the National

Parks section in the Facts about Cambodia chapter for more details on these places.

Trekking & Walking

Trekking has limited potential in Cambodia due to the presence of land mines, but there are several areas of the country in which it is relatively safe. The northeastern provinces of Ratanakiri and Mondulkiri were never mined and with their wild, natural scenery, abundant waterfalls and ethnic minority populations, they look set to emerge as walking destinations. Always take a guide, however, as there are some unexploded bombs in these areas from the American bombing campaign of the early 1970s. Elephant rides are also possible in Mondulkiri.

Bird-Watching

Bird-watching is set to be another big draw for Cambodia, as it is home to some of the region's rarest large water birds. For more on birds, see the Fauna section in the Facts about Cambodia chapter; for information on bird sanctuaries see the Around Siem Reap section of the Siem Reap chapter.

Dirt Biking

For experienced riders, dirt biking is very popular in Cambodia, as the roads are generally considered some of the worst in Asia – the best in Asia for die-hard biking enthusiasts. There are incredible rides all over the country, but it is best to stay away from the main highways as traffic and dust make it a choking experience. For more on biking, see the Getting Around chapter or for something organised, have a look at the Angkor Dirt Bike Tours website ($\boxed{W}$ www .toursintheextreme.com).

LANGUAGE COURSES

The only courses available in Cambodia at present are in Khmer and are aimed at expat residents of Phnom Penh rather than at travellers. If you are going to be based in Phnom Penh for some time, however, it would be well worth learning basic Khmer. Ring the Cambodia Development Research Institute ($\boxed{\varpi}$ 368053), based at 56 Ph 315, for information about classes – courses run for two months. Also check out the notice board at the Foreign Correspondents' Club (FCC), where one-hour lessons are often advertised.

WORK

Jobs are available throughout Cambodia. The obvious options are English/French teaching work or volunteer work with one of the many NGOs operating in the country. There is a lot of teaching work available for English-language speakers.

For information about work opportunities with NGOs call into the CCC (see the Useful Organisations section earlier in this chapter), which has a notice board for positions vacant and may also be able to give advice on where to look. If you are thinking of applying for work with NGOs, you should bring copies of your education certificates and work references. However, most of the jobs available are likely to be on a voluntary basis, as most recruiting for specialised positions is done in home countries or through international organisations.

Other places to look for work include the classifieds sections of the *Phnom Penh Post* and the *Cambodia Daily,* and on the notice board at the FCC.

Do not expect to make a lot of money working in Cambodia, but if you want to learn more about the country and help the locals improve their standard of living, it can be a very worthwhile experience.

ACCOMMODATION

The accommodation situation in Cambodia has changed immensely over the past decade. In Phnom Penh, Siem Reap and Sihanoukville there are options to suit all budgets. Elsewhere around Cambodia, options are limited to budget and mid-range, but are nearly always good value.

In this guide, budget accommodation refers to guesthouses where the majority of rooms are within the US$2 to US$10 range, mid-range generally runs from US$10 up to US$50 and top end is US$50 and up.

Budget hostels exist only in Phnom Penh, Siem Reap and Sihanoukville. Costs hover around US$3 to US$5 for a bed. In many rural parts of Cambodia, the standard rate for the cheapest hotels is US$5, although occasionally there may be a few starting at 10,000r that make more by the hour as brothels than they do by the night.

In Phnom Penh, Siem Reap and Sihanoukville, which see a steady flow of tourist traffic, hotels improve significantly once you start spending more than US$10. For US$15 or less it is usually possible to find an air-con room with satellite TV and attached bathroom. If you spend between US$20 and US$50 it is possible to arrange something very comfortable.

Top-end accommodation is available only in Phnom Penh and Siem Reap, but represents a significant leap in price for what aren't always significantly better rooms. There are several international-standard hotels in Phnom Penh and Siem Reap operated by familiar international brands such as Raffles and Sofitel.

Most hotels and guesthouses in Cambodia do not have hot water. Smaller places may have bathrooms where a large jar or cement trough is filled with water for bathing purposes, but most have cold showers these days. A plastic or metal bowl is used to sluice the water over the body. Some hotels in the larger cities will offer small electric shower heaters in their more-expensive rooms. Very few boiler-style water heaters are available outside large international-style hotels.

FOOD

Cambodian food is closely related to the cuisine of neighbouring Thailand and Laos and, to a lesser extent, Vietnam, but there are some distinct local dishes. The overall consensus is that Khmer cooking is similar to Thai cooking but with fewer spices.

It is easy to sample inexpensive Khmer cuisine throughout the country at local markets and cheap restaurants. For more refined Khmer dining, the best restaurants are in Phnom Penh and Siem Reap, where there is also the choice of excellent Thai, Vietnamese, Chinese, Indian, French and Mediterranean cooking. Chinese, and to a lesser extent Vietnamese, food is available in towns across the country due to the large urban populations of both these groups.

Rice is the principal staple, and the Battambang region is the country's rice bowl. Most Cambodian dishes are cooked in a wok, known locally as a *chhnang khteak*.

Local Food

When it comes to breakfast, most Cambodians eat *bobor* (rice porridge) and usually add a little fish or pork. Also popular is *kyteow*, a noodle soup similar to Chinese breakfast soups. Chinese and Vietnamese noodle soups are widely available.

A Cambodian meal almost always includes a soup *(samla)* eaten at the same time as the other courses. *Samla machou banle* is a popular fish soup with a sour flavour rather like the hot-and-sour dishes of neighbouring Thailand. Other soups include *samla chapek* (ginger-flavoured pork soup), *samla machou bangkang* (a prawn soup closely related to the popular Thai *tom yam*) and *samla ktis* (a fish soup with coconut and pineapple).

Much of the fish eaten in Cambodia is freshwater, from the Tonlé Sap lake or Mekong River. *Trey aing* (grilled fish) is a Cambodian speciality (*aing* means 'grilled' and can be applied to many dishes). Traditionally, the fish is eaten as pieces wrapped in lettuce or spinach leaves and dipped into a fish sauce known as *tuk trey*, a close relative of Vietnam's *nam pla* or *nuoc mam*, but with the addition of ground peanuts. *Trey noueng phkea* is fish stuffed with small dried prawns, *trey chorm hoy* is steamed whole fish, and *trey chean noeung spei* is fried fish served with vegetables.

Cambodian 'salad' dishes are also popular and delicious although quite different from the Western idea of a cold salad. *Phlea sach ko* is a beef and vegetable salad, flavoured with coriander, mint leaves and lemon grass. These three herbs find their way into many Cambodian dishes.

Khao phoune is one of the most common Cambodian dishes. Closely related to Malaysia's laksa dishes, the fine rice noodles are prepared in a sauce enriched with coconut milk. Another version of this dish *(nam ben chok)* comes with a fish-based sauce and a selection of wild vegetables.

At weddings and other festivities, sweet specialities like *ansam chruk* (sticky rice balls stuffed with banana) are served. *Nom bat* and *nom kom* are sticky rice cakes; *phleay* is a pastry and palm-sugar concoction that is fried and rolled in grated coconut. Jackfruit is used to make a pudding known as *sangkcha khnor*. All these desserts can be sampled cheaply at night markets around the country. One final sweet snack to look out for is the ice-cream sandwich. No kidding, it's popular with the kids and involves putting a slab of home-made ice cream in a piece of sponge or bread. It actually doesn't taste too bad.

Fast Food

There are no Western fast-food chains in Phnom Penh as yet, but there are a few local copycats. The most successful has been Lucky Burger, with three branches. Other flagrant rip-offs such as KFC (Khmer Fried Chicken?), Pizza Hot and Burger Queen have been forced to close.

Vegetarian

Few Cambodians understand the concept of strict vegetarianism and many will say something is vegetarian when in fact it is not. If you are not a strict vegetarian and can deal with fish sauces and the like, you should have few problems ordering meals, and those who eat fish can sample Khmer cooking at its best. In the major tourist centres, many of the international restaurants feature vegetarian meals, though these are not budget options. Cheaper vegetarian options are usually available at guesthouses. In Khmer and Chinese restaurants, stir-fried vegetable dishes are readily available, as are vegetarian fried rice dishes, but it is unlikely these 'vegetarian' dishes have been cooked in separate woks from other fish- and meat-based dishes. Indian restaurants in Phnom Penh, Siem Reap and Sihanoukville usually provide genuine vegetarian food.

Fruits

Cambodia is blessed with many tropical fruits and sampling these is an integral part of a visit to the country. All the common fruits can be found in abundance, including bananas *(chek)*, pineapples *(menoa)* and coconuts *(duong)*.

Among the larger fruit, jackfruit *(khnau)* is very common, often weighing more than 20kg. Beneath the green skin are bright yellow segments, with a distinctive taste and rubbery texture. The durian *(touraine)* usually needs no introduction, as you can smell it from a mile off. The exterior is green with sharp spines – like an oversized horse chestnut – while inside is a milky, soft interior that the Chinese regard as an aphrodisiac. It stinks, although some maintain it is an acquired taste – best acquired with a nose peg.

The fruits most popular with visitors include the mangosteen *(mongkut)* and rambutan *(sao mao)*. The small mangosteen has a purple skin that contains white segments with an incredible flavour. Queen Victoria once offered a reward to anyone able to transport an edible mangosteen back to England. Don't get the purple mess on your clothing as it won't come off. Similarly popular is the rambutan, the interior like a lychee, but the exterior covered in soft red and green spines. Longan *(mien)* is another lychee look-a-like that comes in small bunches – crack open the small green shell and the fruit inside is a great travel snack.

Best of all, although common throughout the world, are the mangoes *(svay)*. Cambodian mango season is from April to May. Other varieties of mango are available year round, but it's the new-year ones that are a taste sensation.

Self-Catering

The French influence is most clearly seen in the delicious bread baked every day and sold in the markets. It is very cheap at around 300r to 500r, depending on size. Phnom Penh's international supermarkets have excellent supplies of goodies such as European cheeses, peanut butter and cold meats. By supplementing these with some vegetables from the markets, you can put together your own meals at a reasonable cost, although it's still not as cheap or as fun as eating at street stalls or markets.

DRINKS
Nonalcoholic Drinks
Drinking tap water *must* be avoided, especially in the provinces, as it is rarely purified and may lead to stomach complications. Locally produced mineral water is about 500r per bottle, though some locals and expats alike doubt the purity of the cheapest stuff. Those with a weak constitution might want to opt for one of the better local brands, such as Ozone.

All the well-known soft drinks are available in Cambodia. Bottled drinks are about 800r, while canned drinks cost about 1500r. There are also a lot of lesser-known drinks for sale, most of them produced in other Asian countries.

Throughout Cambodia, *tuk kak* (ice) is produced with treated water at local ice factories, a legacy of the French. Transporting it often involves dragging huge blocks along the ground, but most people don't worry about this, as it usually gets cleaned off.

Coffee *(caa-fay)* is sold in most restaurants. It is either served black or *café au lait* (with dollops of condensed milk, which makes it very sweet). Chinese-style tea *(tai)* is popular and in many Khmer and Chinese restaurants a pot will automatically appear for no extra charge as soon as you sit down.

Tukalok are popular throughout Cambodia. They are a little like fruit smoothies and are a great way to wash down a big meal in the provinces. Stalls are set up around local night markets some time before dark and the drinks cost from 1000r to 2000r. Watch out for how much sugar goes in if you don't like sweet drinks, and pass on the offer of an egg if you don't want it super frothy.

Alcoholic Drinks
Beer Lao has appeared in Cambodia in the past few years. It's very drinkable and one of the cheapest beers around. The local beer is Angkor, which is produced by a Malaysian joint-venture company based in Sihanoukville. While not quite up to the standards of Beer Lao, it is a pretty good brew and costs US$1.25 to US$2 for a big bottle in most restaurants and bars. Tiger beer is produced locally at a factory near Phnom Penh. Most Khmer restaurants have a bevy of 'beer girls', each of whom represents a beer brand. They are always friendly and will leave you alone if you prefer not to drink. Brands represented include Angkor, Heineken, Tiger, San Miguel, Stella Artois, Carlsberg, VB, Foster's and Grolsch. At some establishments they have the rather enigmatic Alain Delon beer, named in honour of the French actor. Cans of beer sell for around US$1 in restaurants.

In Phnom Penh and Siem Reap, foreign wines and spirits are sold in supermarkets at very reasonable prices. Wines from Europe and Australia start at about US$4, while the famous names of the spirit world cost between US$6 and US$10.

The local spirits are best avoided, though some expats say that Sra Special, a local whiskey-like concoction, is not bad. At around 2000r a bottle it's a cheap route to oblivion. There has also been a surge in the popularity of 'muscle wines', with enticing pictures of strongmen on the labels and names like Hercules, Great Strength and King Kong. They contain enough unknown substances to contravene the Geneva Chemical Weapons Convention and should only be drunk with care.

ENTERTAINMENT
Bars & Clubs
Phnom Penh is the place for pubs and bars. Siem Reap has an increasing number of good options, but elsewhere in Cambodia drinking takes place in market areas, in restaurants and in nightclubs.

Again, Phnom Penh is the place for disco nightlife: there are several nightclubs that see a good mix of locals and expats. Nightlife in Phnom Penh tends not to get going until fairly late – after-midnight sessions are popular at weekends, after a leisurely meal and some drinks at a bar.

Outside Phnom Penh, nightlife is dominated by Khmer nightclubs. These clubs are aimed at men, though foreign women do not have any trouble in these places. However, as a precaution, it is unwise for women to go it alone. Lighting is low to the point of pitch black and the music alternates between a live band and a DJ, playing an eclectic mix of Khmer, Asian and Western music. The pop tunes used to be a depressing combination of Sha La La La La and Aqua, but seem to be improving as the Thai influence becomes apparent. These clubs are a good place to try to learn traditional Khmer dances, as locals are keen to demonstrate the moves. However, be aware that the hostesses charge the men to dance with them, so you might want to wait until the slow music stops if you don't want an inflated bill.

Traditional Dance
Public performances of professional Cambodian classical dance are few and far between, but many hotels and restaurants in Siem Reap now offer nightly dinner shows that are a reasonable introduction to the grace and beauty of this art form. In Phnom Penh, the best place to see regular dance displays is at the Ecole de Beaux Arts, where pupils practice every morning from around 7.30am to 9.30am. It is worthwhile

checking the local English-language newspapers for news of any upcoming events.

Cinemas
See the Entertainment section in the Phnom Penh chapter for information about venues that sometimes screen international films. Cinemas elsewhere in the country are best avoided, as most of them screen pornography to large crowds of Cambodian men.

SHOPPING
There is some excellent shopping to be had in Cambodia, particularly in Phnom Penh and Siem Reap. As well as the inevitable range of souvenirs, there are many high-quality handicrafts made to support disadvantaged groups in Cambodia – for more on these places and other shopping opportunities in Phnom Penh and Siem Reap, see the Shopping sections in those chapters.

It is important to haggle over purchases made in local markets, otherwise the stallholder may 'shave your head', the local vernacular for 'rip you off'. Beyond the tourist centres it is not necessary to haggle hard, as Khmers are very reasonable people.

Silk & Textiles
Cambodia is world renowned for its exquisite silk, much of which is still traditionally hand-woven and dyed using natural colours from plants and minerals. The best silk comes from Kompong Cham and Takeo Provinces, but not all the silk sold in Cambodia originates here (some is imported from China and Vietnam). Concerted efforts are underway to reintroduce mulberry trees and locally cultivated silk across the country. There are silk farms in Siem Reap and Tbeng Meanchey, and the best places to buy silk include Artisans d'Angkor in Siem Reap, recommended shops in Phnom Penh and Siem Reap that support disabled and impoverished Cambodians, and Psar Tuol Tom Pong (Russian Market) in Phnom Penh.

Sculpture
The beauty and intricacy of Cambodian sculpture is evident for all to see around the

---

Karaoke Jihad

Slap-bang in the middle of research for this edition of *Cambodia,* Prime Minister Hun Sen issued a draconian decree closing all karaoke parlours and nightclubs in Cambodia. There were many rumours as to why this happened, including the gunfights of his infamous nephews outside such establishments, the influence of the Thai premier and his clampdown in Bangkok, a crackdown on prostitution, and many more that are unprintable. Whatever the reason, the fun police moved in and shut down places overnight. Many reopened as restaurants with very little food or found other loopholes to keep operating, usually involving pay-offs to the right people, but no doubt some have fallen by the wayside. We have included all places that existed at the time of writing, as this law may not hold indefinitely, but don't be surprised if one or two have closed down. As always in Cambodia, many suffer for the mistakes of a few.

Krama Chameleon

The colourful checked scarf known as the *krama* is almost universally worn by rural Khmers and is still pretty popular in the cities. The scarves are made from cotton or silk and the most famous silk krama come from Kompong Cham and Takeo Provinces.

Krama have a multitude of uses. They are primarily used to protect Cambodians from the sun, the dust and the wind, and it is for this reason many tourists end up investing in one during a visit. However, they are also slung around the waist as mini-sarongs, used as towels for drying the body, knotted at the neck as decorations, tied across the shoulders as baby carries, placed upon chairs or beds as pillow covers, used to tow broken-down motorbikes and stuffed inside motorbike tyres in the advent of remote punctures – the list is endless.

Krama are sold in markets throughout Cambodia and are an essential purchase for travellers using pick-up trucks or taking boat services. They have become very much a symbol of Cambodia and for many Khmers, wearing one is an affirmation of their identity.

temples of Angkor and in the National Museum in Phnom Penh. There are many skilled stone carvers in Cambodia today, and replica sculpture is widely available in Phnom Penh and Siem Reap. Popular items include busts of Jayavarman VII and statues of Hindu deities such as Ganesh and Harihara. Do not attempt to buy ancient stone sculpture in Cambodia – the reasons should be obvious, but see the Responsible Tourism entry earlier if you need the details.

Woodcarving

Woodcarving is a rich tradition in Cambodia and there are many wooden items that make nice decorative pieces. Reproduction Buddhas are very popular with visitors and there is no restriction on taking Buddha images out of the country. There are also wooden copies available of most of the principal Angkorian sculpture, as well as finely carved animals. Weaving wheels are quite popular and are often elaborately decorated, making nice wall mounts. Betel nut boxes are popular, as are jewellery boxes inlaid with metalwork.

Silver

Cambodian silver is valued overseas for the detail of hand-carving on most of the pieces. However, not all silver has that much silver content, so it is important to be careful what you buy. Cambodian silver ranges from copies with no silver, to 50%

silver alloy, right up to pure silver. Reputable establishments will often tell you the purity of their silver, but market sellers might try to pull a fast one.

Antiques

Cambodia has a reasonable range of antiques, although a lot disappeared or was destroyed during the war years. Popular items include textiles, silver, swords, coins, ceramics and furniture, but when buying antiques be very careful of fakes – they are extremely common in this part of the world. If the prices seem too good to be true, then they usually are and you'll end up with a well-aged, modern copy.

Paintings

The choice was, until recently, limited to the poor-quality Angkor paintings seen throughout the country. However, the selection is improving in Phnom Penh and Siem Reap. Psar Chaa (Old Market) in Siem Reap and the art shops on Ph 178 are good hunting grounds, and there are a number of upmarket galleries in hotels in the capital.

Clothing

Many international brands are made in factories around Phnom Penh; there is a lot of leakage, with items turning up in Psar Tuol Tom Pong at very reasonable prices. See Shopping in the Phnom Penh chapter for more details.

Getting There & Away

AIR
Airports & Airlines
Cambodia has two international airports: Phnom Penh's Pochentong International Airport and Siem Reap International Airport, which serves visitors to Angkor. Cambodia announced an open-skies policy in 1999 and this has led to something of a mini-boom in flights to Siem Reap.

Flights to Cambodia are quite limited, and most links are with neighbouring capitals. Bangkok has the most flights to Cambodia, and it is usually possible to get on a flight with any of the airlines at short notice, although flying Bangkok Airways to Siem Reap can get very busy from November to March. If you are heading to Cambodia for a short holiday and want a minimum of fuss, Thai Airways International (THAI) offers the easiest connections from major cities in Europe, the USA and Australia. Singapore Airlines and its regional wing, Silk Air, is another good option, with at least one flight a day connecting Cambodia to Singapore. Other regional centres with flights to Cambodia are Ho Chi Minh City (Saigon), Vientiane, Kuala Lumpur, Hong Kong, Guangzhou and Shanghai.

Airlines in Cambodia have a habit of opening and closing. Former national carrier Royal Air Cambodge has been grounded since the latter half of 2001 but there are plans to relaunch it as Cambodian National Airlines, backed by a Chinese airline. At the time of writing the choices are Royal Phnom Penh Airways, with its ageing Russian fleet, or Siem Reap Airways, little more than an offshoot of Bangkok Airways. There is also talk of two more airlines opening in the near future – Air Cambodia and Mekong Airlines – serving international destinations around the region. The result of this muddled picture, unfortunately for Cambodia, is that those who have the choice should enter the country on an international carrier such as Bangkok Airways, Silk Air, THAI or Vietnam Airlines rather than a local carrier.

WARNING

The information in this chapter is particularly vulnerable to change: prices for international travel are volatile, routes are introduced and cancelled, schedules change, special deals come and go, and rules and visa requirements are amended. You should check directly with the airline or a travel agent to make sure you understand how a fare (and ticket you may buy) works and be aware of the security requirements for international travel.

The upshot of this is that you should get opinions, quotes and advice from as many airlines and travel agents as possible before you part with your hard-earned cash. The details given in this chapter should be regarded as pointers and are not a substitute for your own careful, up-to-date research.

Buying Tickets
When buying airline tickets, it is always worth shopping around as different agents have many deals available with lots of airlines. Quotes for the same flight can differ significantly because one agent imposes a hefty commission while another gets a lower price from the airline. Buying direct from the airline is usually more expensive, unless the airline is advertising special promotions. As a rule, it is better to book as early as possible, as prices only get higher as the seats fill up.

The time of year has a major impact on flight prices. If you are starting out from Europe, North America or Australia, figure on prices rising dramatically over Christmas and during July and August, and dropping significantly during lax periods of business like February, June and October.

Thailand is the most convenient gateway to Cambodia from outside the region. In Bangkok the Banglamphu area, in particular Khao San Rd, is a good place to buy tickets to Cambodia. Those travelling through Vietnam and on into Cambodia by plane can pick up tickets for Phnom Penh or Siem Reap in the Pham Ngu Lao area of Ho Chi Minh City.

Travellers with Special Needs
The disability-friendly website W www .everybody.co.uk has an airline directory that provides information on the facilities offered by various airlines.

Facilities at large regional airports such as Bangkok, Hong Kong and Singapore generally include ramps, lifts and escorts from the check-in area to the plane should they be required. Facilities at airports in Cambodia are generally fairly basic, although those at Phnom Penh and Siem Reap are undergoing massive upgrades. Escorts are available at these international gateways, but at other provincial airports such as Ratanakiri and Battambang, expect minimal facilities.

Departure Tax
There is a departure tax of US$20 on all international flights out of Pochentong airport in Phnom Penh. From Siem Reap, the international departure tax is US$15 and the domestic departure tax is US$5.

The USA
Discount travel agents in the USA are often known as consolidators (although you won't see a sign on the door saying 'Consolidator'). San Francisco is the ticket consolidator capital of America, although some good deals can be found in Los Angeles, New York and other big cities.

Council Travel (☎ 1800-226-8624, W www.counciltravel.com), America's largest student travel organisation, has around 60 offices in the USA. STA Travel (☎ 1800-781-4040, W www.statravel.com) has offices throughout the country.

From the US west coast, fares to Bangkok, Hong Kong or Singapore cost around US$480/820 one way/return. Flights to Phnom Penh via Ho Chi Minh City and Taipei cost around US$1040 return. However, at certain times of year cheaper promotional fares are sometimes available. Flights from the east coast are a little more expensive (from US$540/880). If you're flying out

of New York, it might prove just as cheap to fly via London.

Canada
Canadian discount air-ticket sellers are also known as consolidators and their air fares tend to be about 10% higher than those sold in the USA.

Travel CUTS (☎ 800-667-2887, W www .travelcuts.com) is Canada's national student travel agency and has offices in all major cities. STA Travel (☎ 1888-427-5639, W www.statravel.ca) has offices in Vancouver and Toronto.

Flights from Vancouver to Bangkok start at CA$575/1200 one way/return. Flights to Phnom Penh via Hong Kong and Ho Chi Minh City are around CA$2550 return. The frequency of flights between Hong Kong and Vancouver means it may work out cheaper to go via Hong Kong to Phnom Penh if you're in a rush. Travellers from the eastern side of Canada may want to consider flying to London and then arranging a cheap flight from there to Bangkok.

Australia
STA Travel (☎ 1300 360 960, W www.sta travel.com.au) has offices in all major cities and on many university campuses. Flight Centre (☎ 131 600, W www.flightcentre .com.au) also has dozens of offices throughout Australia.

There are usually peak and off-peak rates for flights from Australia to Southeast Asia. The peak season is the December to January school-holiday period – flights can often be heavily booked at this time as well as more expensive.

Fares from Sydney and Melbourne to Bangkok or Singapore cost from A$520/780 one way/return. Fares from Darwin or Perth to Bangkok start at A$580/800, while tickets to Singapore are around A$560/700. Flights from Sydney to Phnom Penh via Ho Chi Minh City cost around A$1360 return; flights via Hong Kong are around A$1530 return.

New Zealand
Flight Centre (☎ 0800 243 544, W www .flightcentre.co.nz) has branches throughout

the country. STA Travel (☎ 0508 782 872, W www.statravel.co.nz) is another well-known travel agency.

Tickets between Auckland and Bangkok start at NZ$1225 return. Singapore is a cheaper route, thanks to more competition – expect to pay from NZ$845/1165 one way/return. Flights from Auckland to Phnom Penh via Bangkok cost around NZ$1600 return.

The UK

The UK is one of the world's best places for picking up cheap tickets. STA Travel (☎ 0870 160 0599, W www.statravel.co.uk) has branches across the country. The Sunday editions of most of the major daily newspapers have travel sections with advertisements for tickets to Southeast Asia, as do the free magazines widely available in London.

Many budget fares are with airlines that fly via Eastern Europe or the Middle East. Flights from London start as low as UK£200/350 one way/return. A number of cheap airlines offer a free stopover in their home city – Czech Airlines is a good option, as you get the opportunity to visit Prague. One-way flights to Bangkok start at about UK£250. Return flights to other Asian gateways are often a little more expensive, starting at about UK£400, although flight prices to Hong Kong are more reasonable than in the days before the handover. Fares from London to Phnom Penh via Bangkok cost around UK£1130 return. It is also worth keeping an eye out for promotional fares during the slow periods of business in February, June and October.

Continental Europe

The best centres for picking up discount tickets in Europe are Amsterdam, Antwerp and Frankfurt. Check out the local press for travel ads. Bear in mind that with the advent of budget airlines such as Buzz, Go and Ryanair, it may be cheaper to fly to London to buy your onward ticket.

Asia

All travellers heading to Cambodia by air will have to either pass through or fly from one of the regional air centres: Bangkok is the most likely option, but not the only one. If you are looking to arrange tickets in Cambodia for onward travel, it is usually a little cheaper to buy from a travel agent than through the airline. See Information in the Phnom Penh chapter for recommended travel agencies.

Thailand Flights between Phnom Penh and Bangkok are available daily with THAI (US$135/240 one way/return) and Bangkok Airways (US$120/170).

Bangkok Airways also offers daily flights between Siem Reap and Bangkok (US$160/310) and from Siem Reap to Phuket and Ko Samui via Bangkok.

Vietnam Vietnam Airlines does the short hop between Ho Chi Minh City and Phnom Penh (US$75/130 one way/return, 35 minutes). It also offers daily flights from Phnom Penh to Hanoi (US$185/360) via Ho Chi Minh City, and three flights a week via Vientiane.

Vietnam Airlines (US$110/220) and Siem Reap Airways (US$100/200) fly between Siem Reap and Ho Chi Minh City.

Laos Lao Aviation (US$150/250 one way/return, 1½ hours) and Vietnam Airlines (US$155/310, 1½ hours) each fly between Phnom Penh and Vientiane three times a week. Lao Aviation occasionally has flights between Phnom Penh and Pakse (southern Laos).

Lao Aviation also offers flights between Siem Reap and Vientiane (US$130/220). These occasionally go via Pakse.

Singapore Silk Air connects Singapore with Phnom Penh and Siem Reap (US$260/420 one way/return).

Malaysia Malaysia Airlines flies between Kuala Lumpur and Phnom Penh (US$205/330 one way/return).

Hong Kong Dragonair flies between Hong Kong and Phnom Penh (US$240/450 one way/return).

China China Southern Airlines has flights between Phnom Penh and Guangzhou in southern China (US$260/370 one way/return). Shanghai Airlines has flights connecting Phnom Penh with Shanghai twice a week (US$300/ 395).

Taiwan EVA Air (US$232/390 one way/return) and Mandarin Airlines (US$260/405) have flights between Phnom Penh and Taipei.

LAND

For years overland travellers were restricted to entering or exiting Cambodia at one border crossing with Vietnam. However, the last few years have seen several land options between Cambodia and Thailand open up, as well as new, improved options with Vietnam and, at long last, the border with Laos.

Thailand

Cambodia and Thailand share a lengthy border and while there are several crossing points for locals, foreign nationals are essentially restricted to Poipet in the west and Krong Koh Kong in the southwest. Visas are available at both crossings for US$20 or 1000B – it doesn't take a rocket scientist to work out that for as long as the Thai baht stays below an exchange rate of 50B to US$1, dollars is the way to go.

Poipet The land border between Cambodia and Thailand at Poipet was opened to foreigners in early 1998. An increasing number of travellers have come and gone this way since and the good news is the road east to Sisophon and Siem Reap is much improved.

There are two trains a day from Hualamphong train station in Bangkok to the town of Aranya Prathet (48B), but the 5.50am service is the one to go for unless you want to end up spending the night in a border town. There are also regular bus services to Aranya Prathet (175B air-con). From Aranya Prathet take a *songthaew* (pick-up truck) the 4km to the border for about 10B, or take a *tuk-tuk* (motorised three-wheeled pedicab) for 20B. Some travel agencies around Khao San Rd in Bangkok offer minibus services direct to

Siem Reap, but read the boxed text 'Poipet Warning' before taking this 'easy' option. Once over the border in Poipet negotiate hard for a pick-up to Sisophon for about 5000r in the cab or 3000r on the back. From Sisophon, it is possible to make for either Siem Reap or Battambang. It is worth noting that the road between Sisophon and Siem Reap can become very nasty at times during the wet season.

Leaving Cambodia by land there is no departure tax. From Poipet, take a tuk-tuk or songthaew to Aranya Prathet, from where there are two trains a day to Bangkok (6.40am and 1.45am), and buses every hour from 4am until 10pm. Several guesthouses in Siem Reap run minibuses and coasters to the border for around US$8, although this should get cheaper as the road improves.

Krong Koh Kong The coastal border between Krong Koh Kong (Koh Kong town) and Trat Province in Thailand is also a popular crossing for tourists.

Coming from Bangkok take a bus to Trat from platform 10 at the city's Eastern bus station (147B, five to six hours). Buses depart every half an hour from 7am until 11.30pm. The 11.30pm bus arrives in Trat early enough to get to Krong Koh Kong in time to catch the 8am fast boat to Sihanoukville. Another convenient option for travellers staying in the Khao San Rd area is to take one of the Koh Chang minibuses as far as Trat. This might work out to be slightly more expensive than taking a public bus, but it saves the hassle of getting to the Eastern bus station in Bangkok.

From Trat you can either take a minibus straight to the border at Hat Lek for 100B, charter a taxi there for about 400B, or go in stages, first to Khlong Yai and then to the border. Take either a songthaew (50B) or a seat in a share taxi (60B) to Khlong Yai and then another songthaew to Hat Lek for 30B. The border opens at 7am so it is possible to stay the night in Trat and, with an early enough start, still make the boat. Alternatively, cross later in the day and stay the night in Krong Koh Kong and see the waterfalls north of there. Once in Cambodia you can

Poipet Warning

Poipet is a wild west kind of place and has attracted a lot of unsavoury characters in the past few years. Unfortunately, many of these are involved in the travel business and carry on like some sort of mafia that does no favours to Cambodia's emerging tourism industry. Some of the scams involve the Thais in Bangkok and some are down to the Cambodians on their side of the border but, regardless of who is responsible, they all end up with foreign visitors getting ripped off. The latest of many scams involves Thai agencies selling tickets from Bangkok to Siem Reap for just 100B to 150B, but as locals couldn't travel this route for much less than 250B, the alarm bells should start to ring. Once travellers get to the border, they will be cajoled into handing over their passports to some helpful guy who will tell them the visa fee at the border is now 1300B rather than the actual 1000B or US$20 – 300B down and counting.

Once inside Cambodia, a new game begins: this time it's driving as slowly as possible to Siem Reap, stopping along the way for food in Sisophon. The road from Poipet to Siem Reap is good enough to cover in about three hours, but somehow the helpful travel company will ensure you arrive after dark at a guesthouse of their choosing. Any attempt to leave this guesthouse to seek another will result in a lot of pleading on the part of the guesthouse owners and outright hostility on the part of the pick-up driver, who gets paid a large commission for every tourist his company provides. So for the bargain price of 100B, you get ripped off on the visa and compromise your flexibility on where to stay. It is, of course, possible to play them at their own game, paying the right price for the visa directly with immigration, staying just one night in the guesthouse they want before moving, and getting a very cheap ticket to Siem Reap.

We have heard several disturbing reports of aggressive and intimidating behaviour on the part of several companies, and it is hard to recommend any operators in this current climate. Coming independently is the best way to keep your options open, although this still involves running the circus from the Thai border into Poipet, where everyone and anyone will harass you. Once on the Cambodian side, try to hold firm on prices to Sisophon, Siem Reap and Battambang and don't believe a soul who tells you it is necessary to hit Siem Reap before Battambang. All in all, it might be best to go as far as Sisophon, have a bite to eat and start afresh from there, away from the parasites.

There are no such problems leaving Cambodia, as the Poipet mafia have nothing to gain from your departure.

take a *moto* (motorcycle with driver; 50B) or taxi (75B to 100B) to Krong Koh Kong over the new bridge, avoiding the old headache of being ripped off by the speedboat operators. These prices are estimates, as the bridge was yet to open at the time of writing.

Fast boats from Krong Koh Kong to Sihanoukville (600B for tourists, four hours) leave at 8am and depart Sihanoukville at 12pm in the other direction. It is not possible to sit on the roof of these boats, as they move very fast and the sea can be dangerously rough at times. They were designed for river travel, not sailing the open seas! Make sure you don't get on a fast boat going to Sre Ambel or you'll end up in a smugglers' port quite a distance from Sihanoukville. From Sihanoukville there are cheap air-con buses to Phnom Penh; see the Sihanoukville section in the South Coast chapter and the Getting There & Away section in the Phnom Penh chapter for details.

Leaving Cambodia, there is no real reason to stay in Krong Koh Kong. Get off the boat either at the commune of Pak Long, just before Krong Koh Kong, or in the town itself. From Pak Long there are speedboats through the mangroves to the border (100B, 30 minutes) and it is an easy walk from the dock to the immigration post, though the moto drivers will try and convince you otherwise. If you stay on the boat right into Krong Koh Kong, you will have to take either a taxi or moto across the bridge to the border. Once over the border you can take a minibus or songthaew/taxi combination to Trat and from Trat there are regular buses to Bangkok. Alternatively, stay the night in Trat and then head to Ko Chang or the surrounding islands the following day.

Those heading direct from Phnom Penh to Thailand without stopping in Sihanoukville can take a faster route via Sre Ambel. Take a minibus (6000r) or share taxi (8000r, US$15 for the vehicle) from Psar Dangkor to Sre Ambel, departing no later than 7am. Pick up the fast boat from Sre Ambel to Krong Koh Kong (500B, four hours, 11am), which leaves less likelihood of getting stuck in Krong Koh Kong for the night. Sometimes these boats are small and dangerously overcrowded – not much fun. However, large boats, similar to those on the Sihanoukville to Krong Koh Kong run, also make this trip. There are also fishing boats (300B) leaving Sre Ambel for Krong Koh Kong at 4pm daily. This trip takes four hours and passes by some malaria-infested areas, so take a mosquito net if you fancy this adventure.

Other Crossings Other prominent borders between Cambodia and Thailand are either closed to foreigners or are in isolated locations that are inaccessible to most travellers.

The crossing between O Smach (in remote northwestern Cambodia) and Chong Jom in Thailand is currently open for weekend and Monday crossings for Thai nationals visiting the casino in O Smach.

The crossing between Anh Seh (in the extremely remote north of Cambodia) and Anh Mah in Thailand is presently closed to foreigners and this may not be a bad thing, as there is nothing resembling a road on the Cambodian side. It is about 12km south of the Thai town of Nam Yeun and 20km north of the Cambodian town of Choam Ksant, but the border itself is nothing but a jungle market where Thais sell consumer goods to Khmer traders and the Khmers sell their pigs to the Thais. Much of this area is mined and it is unlikely this border will open in the near future.

There is also a closed border called Preah Sra Lie north of Anlong Veng, but this also suffers from bad roads on the Cambodian side and there are land mines in the area.

Local sources are confident that the crossing between Pruhm (in the west of Cambodia near Pailin) and Takra in Thailand will be open by the end of 2002, but ask around in Bangkok or Battambang before trying it; a Cambodian visa is likely to be required for entry here.

There is also a border at Prasat Preah Vihear, the stunning Cambodian temple perched atop Phnom Dangkrek mountain range. This is currently just a day crossing for tourists wanting to visit the temple from the Thai side, the only straightforward way to get there for now. For more on visiting Prasat Preah Vihear and the Thai intrigues at this historically sensitive frontier, see the Northwestern Cambodia chapter later in this book.

Vietnam

Cambodia and Vietnam share a long frontier with plenty of border crossings for locals. Foreigners are currently permitted to cross at only two points, although the border at Ha Tien near the south coast may open in the near future. The borders between Mondulkiri and Ratanakiri and Vietnam's central highlands region are unlikely to open any time soon due to unrest among marginalised ethnic minorities in Vietnam. Stay tuned for forthcoming changes. It is no longer necessary to stipulate your exact point of entry and exit on the Vietnam visa, or the exact date of arrival, making travel much more flexible.

Bavet The original land crossing between Vietnam and Cambodia has seen steady traffic for a decade. The trip by bus or share taxi between Phnom Penh and Ho Chi Minh City should take only seven hours, but often takes about 10 hours in the wet season. NH1 from Phnom Penh to the border is in a pretty terrible state after Neak Luong, but is in the process of being comprehensively overhauled. The road on the Vietnamese side is in great shape.

Most travellers use the minibus services run by Capitol and Narin guesthouses in Phnom Penh, costing just US$6 all the way to Ho Chi Minh City with a change of buses at the border. In Vietnam, transport can be arranged through backpacker travel agencies such as Sinh Café and Kim Café. It is also possible to use share taxis on both sides of the border, usually around US$5 for each leg, making a total of US$10. See the Phnom Penh chapter for more details on these and other services.

Cheaper still, you can take a local bus to Tay Ninh from the Ben Tanh bus station in Ho Chi Minh City for 3000d (dong) and ask to be let off at the turn-off for Moc Bai, on the Vietnamese side of the border with Cambodia. Moto drivers can take you the rest of the way for about 10,000d. On the Cambodian side you can take a share taxi as far as Neak Luong (8000r), cross the Mekong by ferry (100r for foot passengers) and take an air-con bus to Phnom Penh's Psar Thmei (New Market) for 4000r. It ends up just as expensive as the backpacker buses, but might be an option for the more adventurous.

Kaam Samnor Cambodia and Vietnam opened their border on the Mekong at the end of 2000 and it has rapidly grown popular with independent travellers. It is a far more interesting trip than taking the road, as it involves a fast boat on the Mekong in Cambodia and some very picturesque areas of the Mekong Delta in Vietnam.

Some guesthouses in Phnom Penh and backpacker travel agents in Ho Chi Minh City have daily departures right through to Chau Doc for around US$12. It is also possible to book three- or four-day tours between Phnom Penh and Ho Chi Minh City, including a few days in the Mekong Delta. Royal Boats has a daily service leaving from the new boat dock in Phnom Penh at 9.30am for US$15, with a change of boat at the border. For those looking for a lot more comfort, Victoria Hotels ([W] www.victoria hotels-asia.com) has a boat making infrequent runs between Phnom Penh and its luxury property in Chau Doc.

However, some find it more adventurous to do it on their own. Leaving Cambodia, take a Ho Wah Genting bus from Psar Thmei in Phnom Penh to Neak Luong (4000r, regular departures). Jump off the bus on the west bank of the Mekong (don't take the ferry across the river!) and ask around for outboards to Kaam Samnor (one hour). They depart from a small pier about 300m south of the ferry. It costs US$15 to charter the whole boat, but those with a little time on their hands can wait until it fills with locals and pay 10,000r (US$2.50) for a place. The border posts at Kaam Samnor are several kilometres apart so hire a moto (2000r to 3000r) to carry you from building to building to deal with the lengthy bureaucracy. There are separate offices for immigration and customs on both sides of the border, so it can end up taking as much as an hour to navigate. Once officially in Vietnam at the village of Vinh Xuong, take a *xe om* (moto) to Chau Doc (50,000d/US$4, one hour). From Chau Doc, there are frequent buses to Cantho and Ho Chi Minh City, as well as more-expensive boat services.

Those entering Cambodia via Vinh Xuong can just run the aforementioned route in reverse.

Laos

Cambodia and Laos share a remote frontier that includes some of the wildest areas of both countries. There is only one border crossing open to foreigners and given the remoteness of the region, it is unlikely any more will open in the near future.

Koh Chheuteal Thom & Dom Kralor

The border between Cambodia and Laos officially opened to foreigners in 2000. It is not yet the most popular border crossing in the region, but for those also planning to visit northeastern Cambodia and southern Laos, it offers an adventurous and cheap way to combine the two. On the Cambodian side of the border, there are confusingly two possible crossings: one on the river (Koh Chheuteal Thom) and one on the old road from Stung Treng (Dom Kralor). Most travellers cross at Koh Chheuteal Thom.

It is necessary to arrange a Cambodian visa in Bangkok or Vientiane if using this route. Likewise, those exiting Cambodia for Laos should arrange a Lao visa in advance in Phnom Penh. Both sides of the border seem to charge an overtime fee for those crossing at lunch time or after dark, although the exact sum depends on gentle but persuasive bargaining.

Exiting Cambodia, it is first necessary to get to the remote town of Stung Treng; see the Eastern Cambodia chapter for details. Before heading to the border, it is necessary to arrange a *laissez passer* (exit permit) with immigration police in Stung Treng town, as there are no international immigration officials stationed at the border as yet. Many enterprising locals have been making a lot of money from tourists by overcharging to assist in this service. However, the best way is to go direct to the provincial police headquarters and arrange it with the immigration police for the official fee of US$5. Hopefully this idiotic system will soon be scrapped as Phnom Penh authorities bring things under central control.

From Stung Treng there are regular boats heading north up the Mekong to the border. The cheapest option is the scheduled wooden passenger boat leaving Stung Treng some time after 7am (5000r, four hours). Much faster are the outboards (US$30 for the boat, 1½ hours), which can be chartered at any hour and take up to six people.

Cambodian immigration is on the west bank of the Mekong and Lao immigration is on the east bank. Once in Laos, there are outboards running up to the island of Don Khon (US$5, 20 minutes). Those heading farther north can take a motorcycle taxi to Nakasong for about 40,000 kip and arrange a *jamboh* (three-wheeled motorcyle taxi) on to Hat Xai Khun for transport to Pakse or for the boat across to Don Khong. There are also a couple of buses from Nakasong to Pakse (15,000 kip, 3½ hours) leaving at about 6am and 9am. Finally, there is also a cheap but erratic local bus from the border to Hat Xai Khun (4000 kip, 45 minutes) leaving around midday.

Coming to Cambodia from Laos, the options outlined above can be run in reverse, with the exception of the direct bus from Hat Xai Khun, which leaves earlier on the run south. There are always a few Cambodian outboards hanging around the dock at Voen

Kham on the Lao side and the passenger boat chugs back to Stung Treng at about midday.

The old road from the other side of the Tonlé San at Stung Treng to the Lao border is 57km of potholes and not worth considering unless you hear that it has been upgraded.

Car & Motorcycle

Car drivers and motorbike riders will need registration papers, insurance documents and an International Driving Permit to bring vehicles into Cambodia. It is complicated to bring in a car, while relatively straightforward to bring in a motorbike, as long as you have a *carnet de passage* (vehicle passport). This acts as a temporary import-duty waiver and should save a lot of hassles when dealing with Cambodian customs. Increasing numbers of international bikers are crossing into Cambodia, while most of the foreign cars that tend to make it are Thai-registered.

ORGANISED TOURS

In the early days of Cambodian tourism, organised tours were a near necessity. The situation has changed dramatically in the past decade and it is now much easier to organise your own trip. Budget and mid-range travellers in particular are best off going it alone, as arrangements are cheap and easy on the ground. If you are on a tight schedule, you may like to book a flight to Siem Reap before you leave to ensure that you have enough time at Angkor. Once at Angkor, guides and all forms of transport under the sun are plentiful.

Some major overseas operators are listed in this section. It is also possible to book direct with local Cambodian operators, most of which act as ground agents for some of the companies mentioned here. This can save money, but involves the additional hassle of arranging your own flight. Hanuman Tourism-Voyages offers personalised tours with an emphasis on culture and nature. See the travel agencies section in the Phnom Penh chapter for contact details. Other reliable local operators based in Phnom Penh include: Mittapheap Tours (☎ 216666, fax 213331, **e** mtours@cam net.com.kh) at 262 Monivong Blvd, with a range of itineraries to most of the major destinations; and PM Green Travel (☎ 216296) at 118, Ph 163, with an emphasis on ecotourism in the northeast, and cycling.

The USA & Canada

Adventure Center (☎ 1800-228-8747, fax 510-654-4200, W www.adventure-center .com) is a major North American agent selling Cambodia tours on behalf of popular Australian and UK-based adventure travel companies.

Australia

Orbitours (☎ 1300 363 055, fax 02-9956 7707, W www.orbitours.com.au) is a major Sydney-based tour operator for English-speaking visitors. It operates tours out of Bangkok, and can also combine Cambodia with the other countries in Indochina.

Intrepid Travel (☎ 1300 360 667, fax 03-9419 5878, W www.intrepid travel.com), based in Melbourne, has a number of tours to Cambodia and overland trips from Bangkok to Ho Chi Minh City.

The UK

Regent Holidays (☎ 0117-921 1711, fax 0117-925 4866, W www.regent-holidays .co.uk) is a major operator from the UK.

Explore Worldwide (☎ 01252-76 0100, fax 01252-76 0001, W www.exploreworld wide.com) offers a nine-day Cambodian trip, and is planning to offer a two-week Cambodia adventure in the near future.

Symbiosis (☎ 020-7924 5906, fax 020-7924 5907, W www.symbiosis-travel.com) offers a sort of bespoke travel service, carefully tailoring trips to Cambodia and Asia to the needs of individual clients.

France

La Route des Indes (☎ 4260 6090, fax 4261 1170, e indes@easynet.fr) at 7 Rue d'Argenteuil, 75001, Paris, organises a range of tailored cultural itineraries around Cambodia.

Compagnie des Indes & Extreme Orient (☎ 4260 9091, fax 4260 9010) at 19 Rue Moliere, 75001, Paris, is another company arranging a programme of tours throughout the kingdom.

Thailand

Diethelm Travel (☎ 255 9150, fax 256 0248, W www.diethelm-travel.com) is the major operator for tours to Indochina. Diethelm also has offices in Phnom Penh and Siem Reap (see Travel Agencies in the Phnom Penh chapter for details) and is well represented in capitals throughout the region.

Getting Around

AIR
Domestic Air Services
Domestic flights offer a quick, if relatively expensive way to travel around the country. There are currently four domestic airlines operating in Cambodia. Royal Air Cambodge (RAC) was barely surviving and had no planes at the time of writing; Siem Reap Airways serves the Phnom Penh to Siem Reap route with modern ATRs from France; President Airlines and Royal Phnom Penh Airways serve the whole country, but with a fleet of older Russian planes.

There are up to six flights a day between Phnom Penh and Siem Reap and it is usually possible to get on a flight at short notice. However, tickets for Siem Reap Airways (US$65/125 one way/return) book out fast in peak season, as fewer agents will book with President Airlines (US$55/105) and Royal Phnom Penh Airways (US$55/105). During peak season, demand for flights to other destinations around the country – particularly Battambang and Ratanakiri – often exceeds supply. President Airlines and Royal Phnom Penh Airways serve Battambang (US$45/85), Ratanakiri (US$55/105) and Stung Treng (US$55/105).

If the runways are operational, there are also services to Koh Kong and Mondulkiri, but both of these were not available at the time of writing.

The baggage allowance for domestic flights is only 10kg per passenger, but unless you are way over the limit it is unlikely you will have to pay for excess baggage.

Domestic Departure Tax
The airport tax for domestic flights is US$4 from regional airports and a whopping US$10 from Pochentong airport in Phnom Penh.

Helicopter
There used to be a selection of Russian transport helicopters available for charter, but most of these are now grounded. Flights were occasionally advertised between Siem Reap and Phnom Penh. Should any of these choppers get off the ground again, it may be wise to give them a wide berth; they are hardly the best-maintained flying machines in the world.

Helicopters Cambodia (☎ 012-814500, 016-839565, e helicopter.com@bigpond .com.kh) is based in Siem Reap and has a reliable chopper available for rent. It mostly operates scenic flights around Angkor, but can be chartered for any journey. See the 'Getting Around the Temples of Angkor' boxed text in the 'Temples of Angkor' special section for details.

BUS
The range of road transport is extensive in Cambodia. On sealed roads, large air-conditioned buses are the best choice. Elsewhere in the country, a pick-up truck, share taxi or minibus is the way to go.

Bus services have improved immeasurably in the last few years and the situation will get better as more roads are upgraded. The services used most regularly by foreigners are those from Phnom Penh to Sihanoukville and Kompong Cham, and the tourist buses from Siem Reap to Poipet or Phnom Penh.

There is a clean and comfortable bus service to towns and villages in the vicinity of Phnom Penh. Operated by the Ho Wah Genting Bus Company, prices are very cheap and English-speaking staff can help you get on the right bus. See the Phnom Penh chapter for more details on services to attractions such as Udong and Phnom Chisor.

Minibuses serve most provincial routes, but are not widely used by Western visitors. They are very cheap, but often uncomfortably overcrowded and driven by maniacs, like the meanest of *matatus* (minibus taxi) in East Africa. Only really consider them if there is no alternative.

TRAIN

Cambodia's rail system is fairly primitive, to say the least, but is once again open to foreigners. For Khmers it's about 15r a kilometre (less than half a US cent), and although it still works out to be ludicrously cheap, foreigner prices are now levied at three times the Khmer price without three times the level of service.

It is fun to try the trains, but only for shorter sections of the network, the best being between Kampot and Sihanoukville or Pursat and Battambang. Trains travel at an average 20km/h and mechanical problems can mean unscheduled overnight stops. Bridges are not always maintained and the ride is often as bumpy as on some of the roads. That said, the locals who use the trains regularly are particularly welcoming to foreigners who choose to travel this way.

The rail network consists of around 645km of single-track metre-gauge lines. The 382km northwestern line, built before WWII, links Phnom Penh with Pursat (165km), Battambang (274km) and Sisophon (302km). The 263km southwestern line, which was completed in 1969, connects Phnom Penh with Takeo (75km), Kampot (166km), Kep (156km; get off at Damnak Chang Aeu) and the port of Sihanoukville (228km).

The civil war during much of the 1980s and 1990s led to some unique developments in the Cambodian rail system. Each train was equipped with a tin-roofed, armoured carriage sporting a huge machine gun and numerous gun ports in its sides. In addition, the first two flat-bed carriages of the train operated as mine sweepers. Travel on the first carriage was free and on the second carriage half-price and, despite the risks, these options were extremely popular with the locals. Gladly for the Cambodian people, these precautions are no longer necessary.

PICK-UP, TAXI & JEEP

As a basic rule, pick-ups and jeeps are best on bad roads and taxis are best on sealed roads. When using pick-up trucks or taxis, it is an advantage to travel in numbers, as you can buy spare seats to make the journey more comfortable. Double the price for the front seat and quadruple it for the back seats.

Long-distance pick-up trucks take on the traditionally dreadful roads from Phnom Penh to Siem Reap, Battambang and the northwest, and to Kratie, Stung Treng and the northeast. Passengers can sit in the cab or, if money is short and comfort an alien concept, out on the back; trucks depart when seriously full. Passengers sitting on the back should try to get a seat on rice sacks as it is more comfortable, and remember to carry a scarf to protect you from the dust and a hat and sunscreen to protect against the heat. In the wet season a raincoat is as good as compulsory. Arranging pick-ups directly is less expensive than getting a guesthouse to organise it, but involves considerable aggravation. Haggle patiently to ensure a fair price.

Share taxis are widely available for hire in Cambodia and some travellers use them to get around the south coast or to Vietnam. For the major destinations they can be hired individually or you can pay for a seat and wait for other passengers to turn up. Guesthouses are also very helpful when it comes to arranging share taxis.

In the remote northeast of the country, where the roads are so bad they look sculpted, sturdy Russian jeeps and high-clearance pick-ups are the transport of choice. These seem to keep moving in even the most nightmarish conditions.

In very remote areas, particularly in the wet season, when the roads are even more abysmal than usual, huge six-wheel-drive Russian military trucks act as periodic transport. These are known as *lan damrei* (elephant trucks).

CAR & MOTORCYCLE

Drive with due care and attention, as medical facilities are less than adequate in Cambodia and traffic is erratic, particularly in Phnom Penh, where anarchy would be too constructive a word to describe how people drive. If you have never ridden a motorbike before, the capital is not the best place to start, but once out of the city it does get easier. If you're jumping in at the deep end, make sure you are under the supervision of someone who knows how to ride.

The advantage of motorcycle travel is that it allows for complete freedom of movement. You can stop in small villages that Westerners rarely visit (you will be assured of a lively reception) and a motorbike is great for visiting out-of-town attractions in the Phnom Penh area. It is possible to take motorcycles upcountry for tours, but only experienced off-road bikers should take to these roads with a dirt bike. Even riders with more experience should take care if intending to ride to Siem Reap, Battambang and the northeast, as road conditions are appalling and get worse with the rains. Roads in Cambodia are not the same as roads at home! Anyone planning a longer ride should try out the bike around Phnom Penh for a day or so to make sure it is in good health.

For those with experience, Cambodia offers some of the best roads in the world for dirt biking, particularly in Preah Vihear, Mondulkiri and Ratanakiri. For those who don't want to ride that far, the road up to Bokor hill station near Kampot is very exhilarating.

Angkor Dirt Bike Tours (W www.toursin theextreme.com) is a local company specialising in motorbike trips throughout Cambodia. It runs an annual dry-season programme that includes Mondulkiri, Bokor and the remote temples of northern Cambodia.

Road Rules

If there are road rules in Cambodia it is doubtful that anyone is following them. The best advice if you drive a car or ride a motorbike in Cambodia is to take nothing for granted and assume that your fellow motorists are visually challenged psychopaths. Seriously though, in Cambodia traffic drives on the right. There are few traffic lights at junctions in Phnom Penh, so

Road Distances (km)

	Ban Lung	Battambang	Kampot	Kompong Cham	Kompong Chhnang	Kompong Thom	Kratie	Phnom Penh	Poipet	Prey Veng	Pursat	Sen Monorom	Siem Reap	Sihanoukville	Sisophon	Stung Treng	Svay Rieng	Takeo	Tbeng Meanchey
Ban Lung	---																		
Battambang	928	---																	
Kampot	783	441	---																
Kompong Cham	515	413	263	---															
Kompong Chhnang	726	202	239	211	---														
Kompong Thom	654	322	313	139	256	---													
Kratie	287	641	496	228	439	367	---												
Phnom Penh	635	293	148	120	91	165	348	---											
Poipet	957	117	558	442	319	303	670	410	---										
Prey Veng	580	384	239	78	182	217	293	90	520	---									
Pursat	823	105	336	308	97	353	536	188	222	279	---								
Sen Monorom	155	663	518	250	461	389	215	370	692	315	558	---							
Siem Reap	805	171	464	290	373	151	664	317	152	407	276	540	---						
Sihanoukville	865	523	105	350	321	395	578	230	640	321	418	600	546	---					
Sisophon	908	68	509	393	270	254	621	361	49	471	173	643	103	591	---				
Stung Treng	165	782	637	369	580	508	141	489	811	434	677	356	659	719	762	---			
Svay Rieng	675	418	273	173	216	290	388	125	535	95	313	410	441	355	486	529	---		
Takeo	710	368	85	195	166	240	423	75	485	166	263	445	391	190	436	564	200	---	
Tbeng Meanchey	791	459	450	276	393	137	504	302	440	354	490	526	288	532	391	645	467	377	---

Highways from Hell?

Cambodia has long been home to the most miserable road system in Asia, with many of the country's so-called national highways (NH) in a horrendous state of disrepair. Many would argue that Cambodia is up there among the contenders for worst roads in the world, along with the Republic of the Congo and Mozambique. Many of the roads around the country have not been maintained since the 1960s, and in some places the damage from war, weather, and wear and tear has been hideous. However, all this is set to change with the huge rebuilding programme currently underway on Cambodia's highways, including NH1, NH2, NH3, NH5, NH6 and NH7, a miracle funded by international aid.

This is all going to take a couple more years, so for now, travelling around Cambodia remains something like a steeplechase: some fast bits, some bumpy bits, and many vehicles failing far before the final finish line.

Black-cab drivers in London pride themselves on knowing every street in the city; indeed, the only way they get the job is to pass a tough test called 'the knowledge'. But that's nothing compared to the average Cambodian cabbie, who has to know every pothole in the road just to keep his vehicle alive. Experienced drivers can shave an hour or two off longer journeys, while an amateur can break an axle just a few kilometres down the road. Unfortunately, there is no real trick to telling who can drive and who can't before you start the journey. However, the choice of vehicle helps and for the most part you'll find you are better off in a pick-up truck than in a taxi or minibus – pick-ups often have 4WD. That said, if the road is really shocking, it may actually be an advantage to travel by taxi as they are lighter: an overladen pick-up is more likely to come a cropper in the big holes.

While bouncing and bumping their way around Cambodia, many a traveller has engaged in debate as to which is the worst of the many diabolical roads in the country. A Lonely Planet poll has come up with a new 'top five' now our old favourites are all being repaired – Cambodia's highways from hell:

- Kratie to Stung Treng – this is the last section of major highway with no funding, lots of broken rocks and deep sand. It's 141km of pain and anguish.
- Tbeng Meanchey to Choam Ksant – an absolute howler: seas of sand, swamps of mud, bamboo groves and broken bridges. Don't do it.
- Tani to Kompong Trach – just a short, sharp stretch on the back road to Kep, but one that will be remembered by the fools who try.
- Tbeng Meanchey to Preah Khan – more sand than the Sahara, at least that's how it feels after 56km of struggling to keep the vehicle straight. Another one to be studiously avoided.
- Beng Mealea to Koh Ker – even the locals have given up using this route, preferring to take a 150km detour to avoid this 50km of unending misery. Don't even think about it.

The good news is that there are already some impressive highways in the country, including NH4 to Sihanoukville and the road from Phnom Penh to Kompong Cham. The bad news, if you wanted more, is that in the wet season it gets a lot, lot worse, particularly in the remote provinces. Try travelling from Ratanakiri to Mondulkiri in September and you may, in time, come to appreciate Cambodia's other roads.

most traffic turns left into the oncoming traffic, edging along the left-hand side of the road until a gap becomes apparent. For the uninitiated it looks like a disaster waiting to happen, but Cambodians are quite used to the system. Foreigners should stop at crossings and develop a habit of constant vigilance.

Phnom Penh is the one place where, amid all the chaos, traffic police take issue with Westerners breaking even the most trivial road rules. Make sure you don't turn left at a 'no left turn' sign or travel with your headlights on during the day (although strangely, it doesn't seem to be illegal for Cambodians to travel without headlights at night). See Dangers & Annoyances in the Phnom Penh chapter for details of possible fines and how to avoid paying them.

Expatriates working in Phnom Penh may end up driving a 4WD or car, but will certainly need to drive with more care than at home – in Phnom Penh traffic is a law unto itself and in the provinces roads can resemble roller coasters. Residents with their own vehicle should not attempt inter-provincial travel at night.

Security

Travelling and living in Cambodia, it is easy to lull yourself into a false sense of security and assume that down every rural road is yet another friendly village. However, even with the demise of the Khmer Rouge, odd incidents of banditry and robbery occur in rural areas. When travelling in your own vehicle, and particularly by motorcycle in rural areas, make certain you check the latest security information in communities along the way. Many Cambodians do not travel beyond the village or town limits at night for fear of robbery, and it would be advisable to follow suit. The risks may be low for a foreigner on a bike, but there is no sense in courting potential danger.

You may encounter military checkpoints on some of Cambodia's remote roads. For checkpoint security tips see the Dangers & Annoyances section in the Facts for the Visitor chapter.

Other general security suggestions for those travelling by motorbike include:

- Try to get hold of a helmet for long journeys or high-speed riding.
- Carry a basic repair kit, including some tyre levers, a puncture repair kit and a pump.
- Always carry a rope for towing on longer journeys in case you break down. Things like camera straps, sarongs and *krama* (scarves) just aren't strong enough, although a couple of trusty krama are the best if you are really stuck.
- In remote areas always carry several litres of water, as you never know when you will run out.
- Travel in small groups, not alone.

- When in a group, stay close together in case of any incident or accident.
- Don't be a cheapskate with petrol – running out in a rural area could jeopardise your health, especially if water runs out too.
- Do not travel at night.
- Do not smoke marijuana or drink alcohol and drive, as it impairs your skills.
- Keep your eyes firmly fixed on the road; Cambodian potholes eat people for fun.

Rental

Car hire is available only with a driver and is only really useful for sightseeing in Phnom Penh and Angkor. Some tourists with a healthy budget also arrange cars or 4WDs with drivers for touring the south coast. Driving yourself is just about possible but inadvisable due to chaotic road conditions, personal liability in the case of an accident and higher charges. Hiring a car with a driver is about US$20 for a day in and around Cambodia's towns. Heading into the provinces it rises from US$25 to US$40 or more depending on the destination, and for those staying overnight, the driver will also need looking after. 4WDs are around US$60 to US$100 a day, depending on the model and the distance travelled.

Motorcycles are available for rent in Phnom Penh, Sihanoukville and Kampot. In Siem Reap, it is sometimes illegal for foreigners to ride motorbikes, but rules change regularly. In other provincial towns it is usually possible to rent a small motorbike after a bit of negotiation. Costs are US$3 per day for a 100cc motorcycle and US$7 for a 250cc dirt bike in Phnom Penh and Sihanoukville, US$5 for all types of motorbike in Kampot.

Motorcycle Purchase

Buying a motorbike is pretty straightforward in Phnom Penh. A second-hand 100cc Daelim starts at about US$300; better brands like Honda and Suzuki cost more. A 250cc motorbike can be bought for as little as US$800 through private sale, but the motorbike may have been poorly maintained. Private sales are advertised in local English-language newspapers, as well as on notice boards in popular restaurants and bars. It is safer to buy through a shop in the capital, as the motorbikes are overhauled on their arrival from Japan. Places with a good reputation include Lucky! Lucky! 2 on Ph 130, Flying Bikes on Ph 114 and Vay's Motorcycle Shop on Ph 110. Shop around to get the best price. The Honda Baja is the most common model in Cambodia and probably the easiest to maintain. They should cost around US$1500 from these shops. Consider getting a motorbike with a bigger petrol tank if you know you will be travelling in remote areas.

BICYCLE

For the full story on cycle touring in Cambodia, see Lonely Planet's *Cycling Vietnam, Laos & Cambodia,* which has the lowdown on planning a major ride. It includes 14 days' worth of rides in Cambodia, including a five-day ride from Phnom Penh to Ho Chi Minh City via Kompong Cham and Prey Veng.

Cambodia is a great country for adventurous cyclists to tour. Needless to say, a mountain bike is obligatory. The roads are often in bad condition, but there is usually a flat trail along the side. Travelling at such a gentle speed allows for much more interaction with the locals. Although bicycles are common in Cambodian villages, cycling tourists are still very much a novelty and will be wildly welcomed in most small villages. In many parts of the country there are new dirt tracks being laid down for motor-bikes and bicycles and these are a wonderful way to travel into remote parts of Cambodia.

Cycling around Angkor is an awesome experience as it really helps to get a measure of the size and scale of the temple complexes. Mountain biking is likely to take off in Mondulkiri and Ratanakiri over the coming years.

Bicycles are available for rent in Phnom Penh, Siem Reap, Sihanoukville and Krong Koh Kong. Expect more people to get into this game in other provincial cities as tourism takes off. Buying a bicycle in Cambodia is not such a good idea for those planning a tour, as most bikes sold here are poor-quality imports from China. The best place to buy a bike is Ph 182 in Phnom Penh, near the Capitol Guesthouse. Shop around and it is sometimes possible to find a second-hand mountain bike with decent Shimano components for US$50 or so.

HITCHING

Hitching is never entirely safe in any country, and we don't recommend it. Travellers who decide to hitch should understand that they are taking a small but potentially serious risk. People who do choose to hitch will be safer if they travel in pairs and let someone know where they are planning to go.

The only vehicles in which it might be possible to arrange a safe and free lift are those of nongovernmental organisations (NGOs). However, they certainly don't want to be randomly pestered by hordes of travellers passing through the provinces. All's well and good if you meet an expat in a provincial restaurant and they offer you a ride somewhere, but unsolicited approaches won't be popular.

Hitching with truck drivers is another possibility, but it is very uncomfortable and should be considered extremely unsafe for lone women. Expect to pay for the ride.

BOAT

Cambodia's 1900km of navigable waterways are a key element in the country's transportation system, particularly given the state of many roads and the railways. Phnom Penh, some 320km from the mouth of the Mekong River, can be reached by ocean-going vessels with a draft of less than 3.3m. North of the capital, the Mekong is easily navigable by slow or fast boat as far north as Kratie, and from July to January even large boats can make it as far as Stung Treng. There are fast boat services between Siem Reap and Battambang, and the Tonlé Sap lake is also navigable year-round, although only by smaller boats between March and July.

The most popular boat services with foreigners are those that run between Phnom Penh and Siem Reap. The express services do the trip in as little as five hours. The boats between Phnom Penh and Siem Reap are horrendously overcrowded and foreigners are charged almost twice the price of Khmers for the 'privilege' of sitting on the roof. It is not the most interesting boat journey in Cambodia, as the Tonlé Sap lake is like a vast sea, offering little scenery. The boat services up the Mekong from the capital and the small boat between Siem Reap and Battambang are more pleasant. Furthermore, should a breakdown occur, as it often does, it is easier to disembark from a river than from the middle of a lake. Whichever fast-boat journey takes your fancy, you may well end up on the roof so remember to use sun block and wear a head covering.

Slow-boat services run the same routes as many of the fast boats, but often take longer, a day or two longer if you are unlucky, to complete the journey. They are also unstable and have been known to sink. They are best avoided unless time and comfort are of limited importance. Those who try their luck must remember to pack a hammock and mosquito net.

For detailed information on these and other boat journeys, see Getting There & Away in the relevant destination sections.

Many travellers use the fast boat between Sihanoukville and Krong Koh Kong as a way of travelling between Thailand and Cambodia. See the Getting There & Away chapter for details on this journey, and details on the boat journey from Phnom Penh to Chau Doc along the Mekong.

LOCAL TRANSPORT
Taxi
Taxi hire is getting easier in Cambodia, but there are still next to no metered taxis when compared with Bangkok or Ho Chi Minh City. There are many private operators working throughout Cambodia. Guesthouses, hotels and travel agents can arrange them for sightseeing in and around towns. Even in Phnom Penh, however, it can be almost impossible to find a taxi for short hops unless you've booked a car in advance or are leaving popular nightspots late at night.

> ### WARNING
> Moto drivers and cyclo riders with little or no English may not understand where you want them to go even though they nod vigorously. This is a particular headache in a big city like Phnom Penh – see the boxed text 'We're on a Road to Nowhere' in that chapter.

Moto
Motos, also known as *motodops,* are small motorcycle taxis and their drivers almost universally wear a baseball cap. They are a quick way of making short hops around towns and cities. Prices range from 500r to US$1, depending on the distance and town. Most journeys are about 1000r; expect to pay an extra charge late at night. Moto drivers assume you know the cost of a trip and prices are rarely agreed before starting. However, if it's late at night or if you're staying at a fancy hotel it may be worth negotiating the fare to avoid a protracted argument at the journey's end.

Be careful not to put your leg near the exhaust pipe after long journeys; many travellers have received nasty burns, which can take a long time to heal in the sticky weather and often require antibiotics.

Cyclo
As in Vietnam and Laos, the *samlor* or *cyclo* (pedicab) is a cheap way to get around urban areas. In Phnom Penh cyclo drivers can either be flagged down on main roads or found loitering around markets and major hotels. It is necessary to bargain the fare if taking a cyclo from outside an expensive hotel or popular restaurant or bar. Average fares are about the same as those of motos. There are few cyclos in the provinces and in Phnom Penh the cyclo is fast losing ground to the moto.

Remorque-kang
The *remorque-kang* is a trailer pulled by a bicycle, effectively a kind of cyclo with the passenger travelling behind. The coming of the moto has led to a dwindling in numbers, but they are still widely seen in Battambang,

Kampot and Kratie. Fares are about the same as moto rides.

Remorque-moto

The *remorque-moto* is a large trailer hitched to a motorbike and pretty much operates as a low-tech local bus with natural air-conditioning. They are used throughout rural Cambodia to transport people and goods, and are often seen on the edge of towns ready to ferry farmers back to the countryside. Remorque-motos offer a cheap way to sightsee in some of the provinces, as long as you can make the driver understand where you want to get off. Fares are very cheap, at around 100r per kilometre.

Rotei Ses

Rotei means 'cart' or 'carriage' and *ses* is 'horse', but the term is used for any cart pulled by an animal. Ox carts are a common form of transport in remote parts of the country, as they are the only things that can get through thick mud in the height of the wet season. They are usually pulled by water buffalo or cows. Horse-and-carts are commonly seen in rural Cambodia, although very few tourists like the idea of being pulled along by one of these poor horses.

Outboards

Outboards (out-**boor**) are the equivalent of Venice's vaporetto, a sort of local river bus or taxi. Found all over the country, they are small fibreglass boats with 15hp and 40hp engines, and can carry up to six people for local or longer trips. They rarely run to schedules, but locals wait patiently for them to fill up. Those with time on their hands can join the wait, those in a hurry can charter the whole boat and take off. Visitors tend to use them for the journey from Takeo to Phnom Da, or when departing the country via Krong Koh Kong to Thailand or via Stung Treng.

Phnom Penh ភ្នំពេញ

☎ 023 • pop 1 million

At times beautiful and beguiling, at times desperate and distressing, Phnom Penh is a crossroad of Asia's past and present, a city of extremes of poverty and excess, but one that never fails to captivate the visitor.

Phnom Penh sits at the confluence of the Mekong, Tonlé Bassac and Tonlé Sap Rivers. Long considered the loveliest of the French-built cities of Indochina, its charm, while tarnished, has largely managed to survive the violence of its recent history and the present invasion of property speculators and motor vehicles.

Most of Phnom Penh's tourist attractions are low-key, which means that many travellers spend only a short time here. This is a pity; Phnom Penh is a city that is rediscovering itself and, after the obligatory sightseeing circuit is completed, a fascinating place to take in at leisure. The French left a legacy of now-crumbling colonial architecture, some of which is being tastefully renovated; the wats (Buddhist temple-monasteries) have come back to life with a passion – monks in saffron robes can be seen wandering around carrying alms bowls; and sidewalk restaurants have sprung up all over the city, a great prelude to some pretty lively nightlife at weekends.

The riverfront area in Phnom Penh is undoubtedly one of the most splendid in Asia, lined with swaying palms and billowing flags, the mightiest river in Asia converging and diverging as a backdrop. And it is set to get better. The city authorities plan to build a park all the way down the riverfront, and across the river on the Chruoy Changvar peninsula work is already well underway on a city park and the Mekong Conference Centre. After many years of neglect, Phnom Penh at last seems to be on the move and, if it can learn from the mistakes of its larger neighbours, it could once again become the 'Pearl of Asia'.

Highlights

- Check out the 5000 silver floor tiles at the Silver Pagoda in the Royal Palace.
- Explore the National Museum, home to a sublime collection of sculpture from the Angkorian era.
- Pray for luck at Wat Phnom, a place of legends, including one that gave the capital its name.
- Face a darker past at Tuol Sleng Museum, a grisly reminder of Cambodia's recent nightmares that's essential to understanding how far the country has progressed.
- Sample the city's vibrant nightlife by warming up with a happy-hour cocktail or two.

HISTORY

Legend has it that Phnom Penh was founded when an old woman named Penh found four Buddha images that had come to rest on the banks of the Mekong. She housed them on a nearby hill, and the town that emerged around the hill came to be known as Phnom Penh (Hill of Penh).

The story, however, gives no hint as to why, in the 1430s, Angkor was abandoned

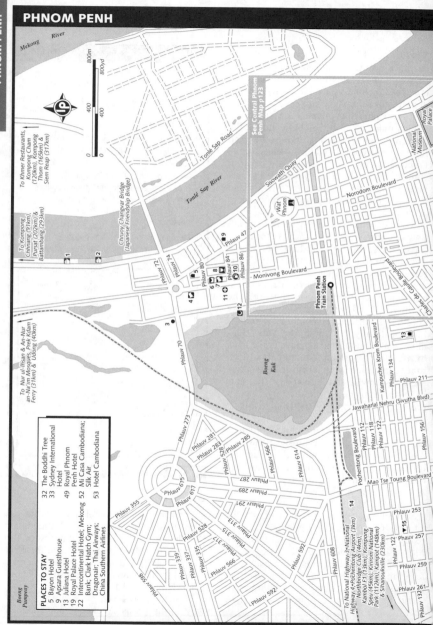

PHNOM PENH

Mekong River

To Kompong
Chhnang (91km),
Pursat (202km) &
Battambang (293km)

To Nur ul-Ihsan & An-Nur
an-Nur Im Mosques; Prek Kdam
Ferry (31km) & Udong (40km)

Tonlé Sap Road

To Khmer Restaurants,
Kompong Cham
(120km), Kompong
Thom (165km) &
Siem Reap (317km)

Chruoy Changvar Bridge
(Japanese Friendship Bridge)

Tonlé Sap River

See Central Phnom
Penh Map p123

Royal
Palace

National
Museum

Sisowath Quay

Wat
Phnom

Norodom Boulevard

Monivong Boulevard

Phnom Penh Train Station

Chararles de Gaulle Boulevard

Phlauv 72
Phlauv 74
Phlauv 70

Phlauv 80
Phlauv 84
Phlauv 86
Phlauv 47

Boeng
Kak

Kampuchea Krom Boulevard

Phlauv 134

Phlauv 211

Jawaharlal Nehru (Sivutha Blvd)

Phlauv 156

Phlauv 273

Phlauv 281
Phlauv 283
Phlauv 285
Phlauv 528
Phlauv 566
Phlauv 614

Pochentong Boulevard

Phlauv 112
Phlauv 118
Phlauv 122

Mao Tse Toung Boulevard

Phlauv 287
Phlauv 289
Phlauv 291
Phlauv 313

Phlauv 615
Phlauv 617

Phlauv 355

Phlauv 339
Phlauv 337
Phlauv 335
Phlauv 528
Phlauv 315
Phlauv 317

Phlauv 566
Phlauv 592

Phlauv 508

Phlauv 608

Phlauv 592

Phlauv 122

Phlauv 253
Phlauv 257
Phlauv 259
Phlauv 261
Phlauv 321

To National Highway 3; National
Highway 4–Pochentong Airport (3km);
Northbridge Club (4km);
Kambol F1 (13km); Kompong
Speu (48km); Kirirom National
Park (112km); Kampot (148km)
& Sihanoukville (230km)

Boeng
Pumpeay

PLACES TO STAY
5   Bayon Hotel
9   Apsara Guesthouse
19 Juliana Hotel
22 Royal Palace Hotel
    Intercontinental Hotel; Mekong
    Bank; Clark Hatch Gym;
    Dragonair; Thai Airways;
    China Southern Airlines
32 The Boddhi Tree
33 Sydney International
    Hotel
49 Royal Phnom
    Penh Hotel
52 Mi Casa Cambodiana;
    Silk Air
53 Hotel Cambodiana

0   400   800m
0   400   800yd

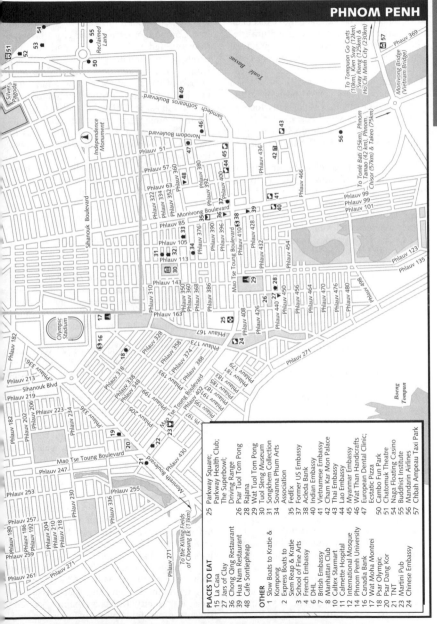

PLACES TO EAT
15 La Casa
27 Jars of Clay
36 Chong Qing Restaurant
39 Hua Nam Restaurant
48 Cafe Sontiepheap

OTHER
1 Slow Boats to Kratie & Kompong
2 Express Boats to Siem Reap & Kratie
3 School of Fine Arts
4 French Embassy
6 DHL
7 British Embassy
8 Manhattan Club
10 Caltex Starmart
11 Calmette Hospital
12 International Mosque
14 Phnom Penh University
16 Canadia Bank
17 Wat Moha Montrei
18 Psar Olympic
20 Psar Dang Kor
21 TNT
23 Martini Pub
24 Chinese Embassy

25 Parkway Square;
   Parkway Health Club;
   The Superbowl;
   Driving Range
26 Psar Tuol Tom Pong
28 Rajana
29 Wat Tuol Tom Pong
30 Tuol Sleng Museum
31 Songkhem Collection
34 Sovanna Phum Arts
   Association
35 FedEx
37 Former US Embassy
38 Acleda Bank
40 Indian Embassy
41 Vietnamese Embassy
42 Cham Kar Mon Palace
43 Thai Embassy
44 Lao Embassy
45 Myanmar Embassy
46 Wat Than Handicrafts
47 European Dental Clinic;
   Ecstatic Pizza
50 Cambo Fun Park
51 Chatomuk Theatre
54 Naga Floating Casino
55 Buddhist Institute
56 Mandarin Airlines
57 Chbah Ampeau Taxi Park

and Phnom Penh chosen as the site of the new Cambodian capital. The move has been much lamented as evidence of cultural decline, but it made a good deal of practical sense. Angkor was poorly situated for trade and subject to attacks from the Siamese (Thai) kingdom of Ayuthaya. Phnom Penh commanded a more central position in the Khmer territories and was perfectly located for riverine trade with Laos and China via the Mekong Delta. The Tonlé Sap river provided access to the rich fishing grounds of the Tonlé Sap lake.

By the mid-16th century, trade had turned Phnom Penh into a regional power. Indonesian and Chinese traders were drawn to the city in large numbers. A century later, however, Vietnamese incursions into Khmer territory had robbed the city of access to sea lanes, and Chinese merchants driven south by the Manchu (Qing) dynasty began to monopolise trade. The landlocked and increasingly isolated kingdom became a buffer between ascendant Thais and Vietnamese. In 1772 the Thais burnt Phnom Penh to the ground. Although the city was rebuilt, Phnom Penh was buffeted by the rival hegemonic interests of the Thai and Vietnamese courts until the French took over in 1863. Its population is thought not to have risen much above 25,000 during this period.

The French protectorate in Cambodia gave Phnom Penh the layout we know today. The city was divided into districts or *quartiers:* the French administrators and European traders inhabiting the area north of Wat Phnom between Monivong Blvd and the Tonlé Sap; the Chinese merchants occupying the riverfront area south of Wat Phnom to the Royal Palace and west as far as Norodom Blvd; and the Cambodians and Vietnamese living around and south of the palace. By the time of their departure, the French had left many important landmarks, including the Royal Palace, National Museum, Psar Thmei (New Market) and impressive government ministries.

The city grew fast in the postindependence peacetime years of Sihanouk's rule. By the time he was overthrown in 1970, the population of Phnom Penh was approximately 500,000. As the Vietnam War spread into Cambodian territory the city's population swelled with refugees, and reached about two million in early 1975. The Khmer Rouge took the city on 17 April 1975 and, as part of its radical social programme, immediately forced the entire population into the countryside. Different factions of the Khmer Rouge were responsible for evacuating different zones of the city; civilians to the east of Norodom Blvd were sent east, those south of the palace to the south, and so on. Whole families were split up on those fateful first days of 'liberation' and for many thousands of Cambodians their experience of the dark days of Khmer Rouge rule depended on which area of the city they had been in that day.

During the time of Democratic Kampuchea, many tens of thousands of former Phnom Penhois – including the vast majority of the capital's educated residents – were killed. The population of Phnom Penh during the Khmer Rouge regime was never more than about 50,000, a figure made up of senior party members, factory workers and trusted military leaders.

Repopulation of the city began when the Vietnamese arrived in 1979, although at first it was strictly controlled by the new government. During much of the 1980s, cows were more common than cars on the streets of the capital, and it was not until the government dispensed with its communist baggage at the end of the decade that Phnom Penh began to develop. The 90s were boom years for some: along with the arrival of the United Nations Transitional Authority in Cambodia (Untac) came US$2 billion, much of it in salaries for expats. Well-connected residents were only too happy to help foreigners part with their money through high rents and hefty price-hikes. Businesses followed hot on the heels of Untac and commercial buildings began to spring up.

The biggest changes to life in the city have come under current Mayor Chea Sophara who has embarked on a one-man mission to clean up the city. Roads are being repaired, sewage pipes laid, parks inaugurated and riverbanks reclaimed – you can't help feeling Phnom Penh is finally on the move.

According to the 1998 census, there are about one million residents in Phnom Penh, although exact numbers fluctuate depending on the season (many suburban squatters return to the countryside to plant rice in the wet season).

ORIENTATION

A minor hurdle to orientation in Phnom Penh is the frequency with which street names and numbers are changed, depending on the prevailing political winds. The current denominations, which date back to 1993, seem to have settled in, but there is still a chance that some of the numbered streets will change again.

The major boulevards of Phnom Penh run north-south, parallel to the banks of the Tonlé Sap and Tonlé Bassac. Monivong Blvd cuts north-south through the centre of town, passing just west of Psar Thmei. Its northern sector is the main shopping strip and is also home to some of the longest-running hotels and travel agents in town. Norodom Blvd runs north-south from Wat Phnom, and is largely lined with administrative buildings; the northern end contains banks, while farther south are government ministries. Samdech Sothearos Blvd runs north-south near the riverfront, past the Royal Palace, Silver Pagoda and National Assembly building. Sisowath Quay hugs the river and is where many of the city's most popular restaurants and bars are located. The major east-west boulevards are Pochentong Blvd in the north of town, Sihanouk Blvd, which passes the Independence Monument and ends just south of Hotel Cambodiana, and Mao Tse Toung Blvd (also known as Issarak Blvd). Mao Tse Toung Blvd, a ring road of sorts, also runs north-south in the west of the city.

Intersecting the main boulevards is a network of hundreds of numbered smaller streets. As a rule of thumb, streets running east-west have even numbers that increase the farther south they are in town, while streets that run north-south have odd numbers that increase the farther west you go.

Most buildings around town have signs with both their building number and *phlauv* (street) number. Finding a building purely by its address, however, is not always easy, as numbers are rarely sequential. See the boxed text 'Knowing When Your Number's Up' and don't forget to pity the postman.

Maps

There are few maps that go into greater detail than those in this guidebook. However, for a handy pocket-size map, look out for a free copy of the *Phnom Penh Map,* which is distributed at Pochentong airport and selected bars and restaurants around the city.

Knowing When Your Number's Up

Navigating the streets of Phnom Penh should be pretty straightforward thanks to the grid system put in place by the French authorities. The total and utter lack of an effective house-numbering system, however, makes some guesthouses, restaurants and offices that bit harder to track down. The long years of war, abandonment and reoccupation destroyed the old system and as residents began to re-populate the city, they seem to have picked numbers out of the air. It is not uncommon to drive past a row of houses numbered 13A, 34, 7, 26. Make sense of that and you might get a job as a code cracker. Worse still, several different houses might use the same number on the same street. The long and the short of it is that when you get to a guesthouse or restaurant recommended in this chapter only to discover it appears to have turned into a *prahoc* (fermented fish paste) shop, don't curse us for the bad smell. Just down the road will be another place with the same number – the guesthouse or restaurant you were looking for...unless, of course, it really has gone into the prahoc business.

Try to get a cross-reference for an address, such as 'close to the intersection of Phlauv (Ph) 107 and Ph 182'. The letters 'EO' after a street address stand for *étage zéro* (ground floor).

Another city map, although dated, is the 3-D map produced by Interquess, which also produces Cambodia's *Yellow Pages*. This map is available in Psar Thmei and at most book and stationery shops.

The local publications *Phnom Penh Post* and *Bayon Pearnik* include maps with regularly updated listings, though entries are sponsored by advertisers and are far from comprehensive. The free *Phnom Penh Visitors Guide* is a useful publication that comes out every few months and includes extensive listings and a map.

INFORMATION
Tourist Offices

Due to lack of government funding, you can forget about useful tourist information in Phnom Penh. The tourist office at Pochentong airport has information on certain hotels around town and can make bookings, but other than this you are effectively on your own.

The head office of Phnom Penh Tourism is across from Wat Ounalom at the oblique intersection of Samdech Sothearos Blvd and Sisowath Quay. However, don't actually expect any information from this organisation, as these days it functions as a private tour operator.

The Ministry of Tourism (☎ 426876) is in a white two-storey building on the western corner of Monivong Blvd and Ph 232. Inside, chaos prevails and unless you have plans to build a large, expensive hotel you will find little assistance here. However, plans are afoot to establish a tourism board and once established, this will be the best bet for dependable information.

Money

Those looking to change cash into riel need look no farther than jewellery stalls around the markets of Phnom Penh – Psar Thmei and Psar Tuol Tom Pong (Russian Market) are the most convenient.

Most banks in Phnom Penh are open from roughly from 8.30am to 3.30pm weekdays and from 8.30am to 11.30am Saturday. The Foreign Trade Bank (☎ 723466) at 3 Ph 114 is a good option, with the longest opening hours of any bank in Phnom Penh (from 7am to 3.45pm weekdays). Cash withdrawal on credit card is available for a hefty 4%, but commission on travellers cheques is only 1% (US dollars only). This is also the most convenient bank at which to arrange an international money transfer.

Canadia Bank (☎ 215286) at 265 Ph 110 will change travellers cheques of many international currencies for a 2% commission, and has a second branch (☎ 214668) at 126 Ph 217, near the Olympic Stadium. It also offers cash advances on MasterCard at no charge!

Cambodian Commercial Bank (CCB; ☎ 426145) at 26 Monivong Blvd offers cash advances on MasterCard, JCB and Visa. There is a minimum charge of US$5 for transactions under US$250, and 2% thereafter. A limit of US$2000 is imposed on cash advances.

Mekong Bank (☎ 217112) at 1 Ph 114 offers efficient cash advances with Visa and JCB for a charge of 2%. It also has a desk at Pochentong airport and a small branch in the Intercontinental Hotel with an after-hours service from 3.30pm to 8pm Monday to Saturday and from 8am to 1pm Sunday. It changes travellers cheques and offers cash advances on credit cards.

A number of upmarket hotels offer money-changing services, although this is usually reserved for guests. Many travel agents can change travellers cheques and offer credit-card advances for at least a 5% fee. These places are usually open on weekends and public holidays (there are many in Cambodia). The Diamond Hotel, near Psar Thmei, and nearby travel agents are probably the most conveniently located.

Those needing to organise an international money transfer can use the Foreign Trade Bank (see earlier in this section for details). However, it may be quicker (and more expensive) to use an international company like MoneyGram or Western Union. MoneyGram is represented by Canadia Bank, while Western Union can be found at the Singapore Banking Corporation (☎ 217771) at 68 Ph 214 or Acleda Bank (☎ 214634) at 28 Mac Tse Toung Blvd.

Post

The main post office is housed in a charming building just east of Wat Phnom on Ph 13. It is open from 7am to 7pm daily and offers postal services as well as telephone and fax links. For postal rates see the Post & Communications section in the Facts for the Visitor chapter.

If you need to get valuables or belongings home in a hurry, there are several international courier companies represented in Phnom Penh including:

DHL (☎ 427726, fax 427680) 28 Monivong Blvd
EMS (☎ 723511, fax 725209) Main Post Office, Ph 13
FedEx (☎ 216712, fax 216721) 701D Monivong Blvd
TNT (☎ 424022, fax 880661) 139 Monireth Blvd
UPS (☎ 724746, fax 366323) 27 Ph 134

Telephone

For information on making domestic and international calls, see the Telephone section under Post & Communications in the Facts for the Visitor chapter.

The cheapest local and domestic calls in Phnom Penh are available from private booths found throughout the city. Whatever the number you are dialling, private booths will have a selection of telephones to make sure you get the best rate. Most local calls are 500r a minute.

There are public phone boxes operated by Camintel and Telstra in many parts of the city. Nearby will be a local shop that sells phonecards.

Many Internet cafes in Phnom Penh offer telephone services at reasonable prices, including Internet phone calls, which are much cheaper than normal international calls, but involve an irritating delay that turns half the conversation into 'hello?' and 'pardon?'.

Guesthouses and hotels have phone services, but at expensive hotels the mark-up is nothing short of daylight robbery.

Fax

Most Internet cafes around the city offer a fax service, either from a fax machine or using e-fax over the Internet. Prices for an international fax are between US$1 and US$2 per page.

Some of the larger hotels have business centres, although prices start at US$5 per page.

Email & Internet Access

Phnom Penh is now well and truly wired, prices dropping from US$10 an hour in 1998, to between US$1 and US$2 per hour today. There are Internet cafes throughout the city, although the most convenient are the dozen or more along the riverfront. Many budget guesthouses also offer some sort of Internet access and in the main backpacker areas there are several Internet cafes. Those in more expensive hotels should venture out to find an online fix, as in-house business centres are overpriced.

With so much competition, it is hardly fair to recommend one Internet cafe above another, but there are a couple of places that stand out.

Netrec, housed within the School of Pedagogy on the corner of Norodom and Sihanouk Blvds, was set up as part of a teacher-training programme and offers one of the best rates in town at US$1 per hour. It also offers monthly email accounts for just US$6.

KIDS (☎ 218452), at 17 Ph 178, is a self-styled cybergarden, and offers one of the calmest places to get online, with bamboo bungalows set around a fountain. There is also an inexpensive cafe and mid-range guesthouse here. Internet access is US$1/2 per hour for guests/non-guests.

Travel Agencies

There are several reasonably priced travel agencies on Monivong Blvd, near Psar Thmei, including PTM Travel & Tours (☎ 364768) at 200 Monivong Blvd and Avia Angkor Travel (☎ 212567) at 192 Monivong Blvd. These places are also open on Sunday.

Diethelm Travel (☎ 426648, fax 219150, W www.diethelm-travel.com), at 65 Ph 240, just off Monivong Blvd, is a reliable company with a second branch in the Foreign Correspondents' Club (FCC).

Hanuman Tourism-Voyages (☎ 218356, fax 218398, W www.hanumantourism .com), at 128 Norodom Blvd, just south of the Independence Monument, is a good place to arrange worldwide flights and regional visas, and is popular with local nongovernmental organisations (NGOs).

Transpeed Travel (☎ 723999), at 19 Ph 106, is well-established locally and offers worldwide ticketing and hotel reservations.

Bookshops

The London Book Centre (☎ 214258), at 51 Ph 240, near Norodom Blvd, is the best place in town for browsing. The shelves are stacked with second-hand stock shipped in from the UK and prices are about US$5 a book, less if you have something to trade.

Monument Books, at 111 Norodom Blvd, is probably the best-stocked bookshop in Phnom Penh, with almost every Cambodia-related book currently in print available. Prices are relatively high, but at least the stock is original. It has small branches in both terminals at Pochentong airport.

The International Stationery & Book Centre (☎ 218352), at 37 Sihanouk Blvd, is devoted mainly to English-language textbooks and dictionaries, but it also stocks many dirt-cheap books on Cambodian history and culture.

The best French-language bookshop in town is Mekong Libris (☎ 722751), located opposite the main post office.

For new books and magazines, the bookshops at Hotel Le Royal and Hotel Cambodiana are some of the best-stocked in town, but prices are also five star. They have a very good selection of French newspapers, magazines and books, as well as an extensive selection of English-language coffeetable publications, novels and weeklies such as the *Far Eastern Economic Review, The Economist, Time, Newsweek* and *Asiaweek*.

Libraries

The National Library (Bibliothèque Nationale), on Ph 92 near Wat Phnom, is in a delightful old building, but has only a small selection of reading material for foreign visitors. Opening hours are from 8am to 11am and from 2pm to 5pm Tuesday to Sunday.

The Khmer Rouge turned this graceful building, constructed in 1924, into a stable and destroyed most of the books. Many were thrown out into the streets, where they were picked up by people, some of whom donated them back to the library after 1979, others who used them as food wrapping.

Today the National Library has about 100,000 volumes, including many crumbling French-language books. Part of the English-language collection consists of books taken from the US embassy when it was sacked after the communist takeover in 1975. Cornell University is assisting the National Library to preserve its collection of palm-leaf manuscripts, which are housed in the new Buddhist Institute near Hotel Cambodiana.

French speakers should call into the French Cultural Centre on Ph 184 (near the corner of Monivong Blvd). It has a good range of reading material.

Clubs & Associations

A good opportunity to meet local expatriates is via the Hash House Harriers, usually referred to simply as 'the Hash'. A weekly run/walk takes place every Sunday. Participants meet in front of the Phnom Penh train station at 2.45pm. The entry fee of US$5 includes refreshments (mainly a lot of beer) at the end.

The Foreign Correspondents' Club (FCC), at 363 Sisowath Quay, is unlike many FCCs around the world in that it is open to everyone. Membership costs US$150 per year for local residents and US$75 for overseas members. Membership provides access to the members' room, business facilities, a 20% discount on food and drinks and, reciprocal rights to other FCCs, such as the impenetrable bastion in Hong Kong.

The Rotary Club of Phnom Penh meets every Wednesday from 12.30pm at the Intercontinental Hotel and guests are welcome.

Have a look in the *Cambodia Daily* and the *Phnom Penh Post* for announcements of upcoming performances by the Phnom Penh Players. The players comprise residents who perform a play every few months.

Laundry

Most guesthouses around town offer reasonably priced laundry services at around 1000r an item. Cheaper still are the local laundries throughout the city and these are a very worthwhile consideration for those staying in expensive hotels. There is a whole row of them on Ph 51 (Rue Pasteur), just south of the Heart of Darkness bar.

Medical Services

The SOS International Medical Centre (☎ 216911, fax 215811), at 161 Ph 51, is one of the best medical services around town. As you might expect, consultation fees are on par with those overseas, so think twice about visiting if you are crazy enough not to have insurance. Office hours are from 8am to 5.30pm Monday to Friday, and from 8am to noon Saturday.

For advice on tropical ailments try the Tropical & Travellers Medical Centre (☎ 366802), at 88 Ph 108. A rather eccentric British doctor runs it in partnership with a Khmer doctor. It is open from 8.30am to noon and from 2pm to 5pm Monday to Friday, and on Saturday morning.

The Calmette Hospital (☎ 725373), on Monivong Blvd, is French administered and the best of the local hospitals.

For dental problems, try the European Dental Clinic (☎ 362656), at 195A Norodom Blvd. Office hours are from 8am to noon and from 2.30pm to 6pm Monday to Friday, and from 8am to 1pm Saturday. SOS International Medical Centre (☎ 216911), at 161 Ph 51, also has a resident foreign dentist.

Naga Pharmacy, in the Hong Kong Centre on Samdech Sothearos Blvd, is open 24 hours.

Emergency

Phnom Penh's general emergency telephone numbers are:

Ambulance	☎ 119
Fire	☎ 118
Police	☎ 117

There are two 24-hour emergency police numbers (☎ 366841, 012-999999) in Phnom Penh that will connect to English-speaking officers.

The emergency numbers for Phnom Penh's ambulance service are ☎ 724891, ☎ 426948 and ☎ 012-808915. In the event of a medical emergency it may be necessary to be flown to Bangkok. The SOS International Medical Centre (☎ 216911), at 161 Ph 51, has a 24-hour emergency service and can also organise evacuation. The European Dental Clinic, at 195A Norodom Blvd, also has an after-hours service (☎ 018-812055).

Dangers & Annoyances

Phnom Penh is not as dangerous as many people imagine, but it is still important to take care. Armed robberies do happen regularly, but statistically you would be very unlucky to be a victim. Guesthouses often make the situation out to be even more dangerous than it is to keep customers in their restaurants.

Should you become the victim of a robbery, do not panic and do not, under any circumstances, struggle. Calmly raise your hands and let them take what they want. *Do not* reach for your pockets as the assailant may think you are reaching for a gun! They will probably be as nervous as you, and you will most likely get any documents back later via your guesthouse or embassy, as the robbers often want only cash and valuables. For the time being, even passports and credit cards seem to be returned. Do not carry a bag at night, as it is more likely to make you a target.

It is not sensible to ride a motorbike alone late at night; and if there is one area to avoid at night, it is Tuol Kauk, to the north of Boeng Kak lake, which is the old brothel quarter and the kind of place where drunk Khmers shoot each other over a karaoke microphone.

If you ride your own motorbike during the day, police will often try to fleece you for the most trivial of offences, such as turning left in violation of a no left-turn sign. At their most audacious, they try to get you for riding with your headlights on during the day, although worryingly, it doesn't seem to be illegal for Cambodians to travel without their headlights on at night. They will most likely demand US$5 and threaten to take you to the police station for an official US$20 fine if you don't pay. If you are patient and smile, you can usually get away with handing over 1000r or a few cigarettes. The trick is not to stop in the first place by not catching their eye.

The riverfront area of Phnom Penh, particularly places with outdoor seating, attracts many beggars, as does Psar Thmei and Psar Tuol Tom Pong. Generally, however, there is little in the way of push and shove. If giving to beggars, do as the locals do and keep the denominations small – this way, hopefully, foreigners will not become permanent targets for their generosity. When giving to children, food is better than money, as money may be passed on to an unscrupulous adult or, in some cases, used to buy glue. See the Dangers & Annoyances section in the Facts for the Visitor chapter for more on this.

NATIONAL MUSEUM
សារមន្ទីរជាតិ

The National Museum of Cambodia (admission $2; open 8am-11.30am & 2pm-5.30pm daily except national holidays), just north of the Royal Palace, is housed in a graceful terracotta structure of traditional design (built 1917–20).

Unfortunately, photography is prohibited inside. English- and French-speaking guides are available, and there is also a useful exhibition booklet, *Khmer Art in Stone*, available at the front desk.

The museum comprises four courtyards, which face a garden. The most significant displays of sculpture are in the courtyards to the left and straight ahead of the entrance. Some highlights include the eight-armed statue of Vishnu from the 6th or 7th century AD, the statue of Shiva (c. 866–77) and the sublime statue of Jayavarman VII seated (c. 1181–1218), his head bowed slightly in a meditative pose. The museum also contains displays of pottery and bronzes dating from the pre-Angkorian periods of Funan and Chenla (4th to 9th centuries), the Indravarman period (9th and 10th centuries), the classical Angkorian period (10th to 14th centuries), as well as more recent works. There is a permanent collection of post-Angkorian Buddhas, many of which were rescued from Angkor Wat when the civil war erupted.

See the Sculpture section in the Facts about Cambodia chapter for more information about the exhibits in the National Museum.

The **School of Fine Arts** (*École des Beaux-Arts*) has its headquarters in a structure behind the main National Museum building.

Bats in the Belfry

The elegant curves of the National Museum make for a picturesque sight when framed against the pink and mauve of a sunset. It's also about this time of day that hundreds of bats stream out from the museum's roof. Most of the bats belong to a recently identified species: the Cambodian freetail.

Some bat experts claim that the National Museum has the largest bat population of any artificial structure in the world. The problem is that bat droppings are corrosive, and until 1994 they were falling through the ceiling, damaging the exhibits. Meanwhile, museum patrons were having to do their sightseeing in a miasma of bat poo.

Fortunately, Australia came to the rescue. In an agreement that saw the 'Treasures of the National Museum of Cambodia' exhibited at the Australian National Gallery, the Australian International Development Assistance Bureau (Aidab) undertook to help maintain the contents of the museum and do something about the bats. It was considered ecologically unsound to remove the bats, so a second artificial ceiling was constructed to stop the droppings falling through. Let's just hope it holds up under the weight.

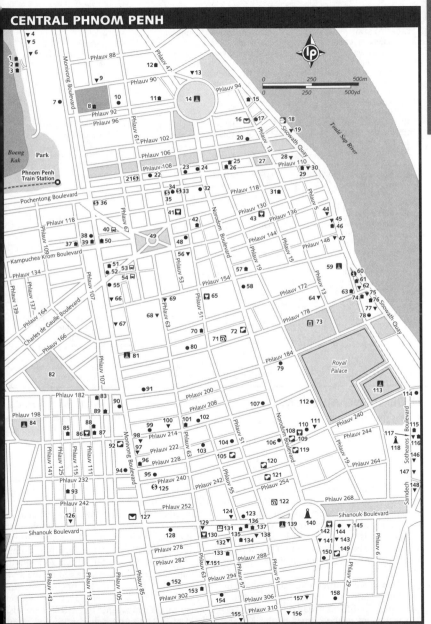

CENTRAL PHNOM PENH

CENTRAL PHNOM PENH

PLACES TO STAY
1 Simon's Guesthouse;
  Happy Guesthouse
2 Same Same But Different;
  Shanti Lodge
3 Number 9 Guesthouse;
  Lakeside Guesthouse
8 Hotel Le Royal
11 Sunway Hotel
12 Sharaton Cambodia Hotel
15 Riverside Hotel
25 The Last Home
26 Cathay Hotel
29 Lyon D'Or
31 Dara Reang Sey Hotel
37 Morakat Hotel
39 Paradise Hotel
42 Hawaii Hotel
46 Hotel Indochine;
  Sunshine Hotel
50 Singapore Hotel
51 Diamond Hotel;
  Malaysia Airlines
57 Royal Guesthouse
61 California Hotel;
  EID Restaurant;
  Ponlok Restaurant
63 Riverview Hotel
70 Walkabout Hotel
74 Dream World
  Guesthouse;
  The Rising Sun
76 Bali Café
83 Capitol Guesthouse;
85 Lucky Guesthouse

87 Seng Sokhom Guesthouse;
  Mama's Restaurant
88 Narin 2 Guesthouse
89 Hello Guesthouse
93 Narin Guesthouse;
  Tat Guesthouse
96 Princess Hotel
101 Queen Hotel
115 Regent Park Hotel;
  Pizza House
116 Okay Guesthouse
133 Goldiana Hotel
134 Golden Gate Hotel Annex
135 Golden Gate Hotel
136 Beauty Inn Hotel
137 Golden Bridge Hotel;
  Golden Sun Hotel
153 Champs Élysées Hotel

PLACES TO EAT
4 Lazy Gecko Café
5 Curry Pot
6 Red Corner
9 Wilhelm Tell
13 Le Deauville; Anthony Pizza
19 Goldfish River Restaurant
28 Chi Cha
30 Riverside Restaurant &
  Lounge
44 Rendez-Vous; Veiyo Tonle
45 La Croisette; Orient
47 Riverside Bistro
56 Psar Ta Pang
62 Happy Herb's; The Pink
  Elephant; Wagon Wheel

64 Friends
66 Christina
67 Lian Rong Dumpling Hall
68 Kiwi Bakery
69 63 Soup
75 Foreign Correspondents'
  Club; Pop Café;
  Made in Cambodia;
  Diethelm Travel
77 The Globe Bar & Restaurant;
  Air France
97 Wah Kee Restaurant
98 Dararasmey Restaurant
100 Lumbini Restaurant
111 The Shop; Wangdome
  Restaurant; Tamarind Bar
117 Le Louisiane
124 Nagasaki
126 Chaay Heng Restaurant
129 Phnom Kiev Restaurant;
  Nike's Pizza House
132 Khmer Surin
138 Amoc Café
141 The Mex
143 Le Bistrot
145 Java Café
146 Topaz
147 Origami; Mondo Burger
148 Chiang Mai Riverside; An
  Nam; Hong Kong Centre;
  Naga Pharmacy
151 Boat Noodle Restaurant
155 Garden Center Café;
  Seeing Hands Massage
156 Le Rit's; Nyemo

TUOL SLENG MUSEUM
សារមន្ទីរទួលស្លែង

In 1975 Tuol Svay Prey High School was taken over by Pol Pot's security forces and turned into a prison known as Security Prison 21 (S-21). It soon became the largest centre of detention and torture in the country. Between 1975 and 1978 more than 17,000 people held at S-21 were taken to the extermination camp at Choeung Ek (see the Killing Fields of Choeung Ek later in this section); detainees who died during torture were buried in mass graves in the prison grounds.

S-21 has been turned into the Tuol Sleng Museum *(admission US$2; open 8am-11.30am & 2pm-5.30pm daily)*, which serves as a testament to the crimes of the Khmer Rouge. It is usually possible to visit any time of day despite the official opening hours. Entry is on the western side of Ph 113, just north of Ph 350. It costs US$5 to take in a video camera.

Like the Nazis, the Khmer Rouge was meticulous in keeping records of its barbarism. Each prisoner who passed through S-21 was photographed, sometimes before and after torture. The museum displays include room after room of photographs covering the walls from floor to ceiling virtually all of the men, women and children pictured were later killed. You can tell which year a picture was taken by the style of number-board that appears on the prisoner's chest. Several foreigners from Australia, France and the USA were also held at S-21 before being murdered. Their

CENTRAL PHNOM PENH

157 Baan Thai

BARS & CLUBS
41 Cathouse Tavern
43 Sharky's
65 Heart of Darkness;
   Howie's Bar
86 Teukai Bar
109 Freebird
130 Celtic Tiger Pub
142 Nexus; Shiva Shakti

OTHER
7 City Hall
10 National Library
14 Wat Phnom
16 Main Post Office; EMS
17 Mekong Libris
18 Tourist Boat Dock
20 Transpeed Travel;
   Shanghai Airlines
21 Canadia Bank
22 Tropical & Travellers
   Medical Centre
23 Vay's Motorcycle Shop
24 NCDP Handicrafts;
   Seeing Hands Massage
27 Psar Chaa
32 National Blood Transfusion
   Centre
33 Mekong Bank
34 Flying Bikes
35 Foreign Trade
   Bank

36 Cambodian Commercial
   Bank
38 Bayon Market;
   City Colour Photo
40 Share Taxis;
   Pick-ups & Minibuses
48 Lucky! Lucky! 2
49 Psar Thmei
52 Aria Angkor Travel
53 Ho Wah Genting Buses
54 GST Buses
55 PTM Travel & Tours
58 President Airlines
59 Wat Ounalom
60 Phnom Penh Tourism
71 KIDS (Internet)
72 Japanese Embassy
73 National Museum;
   School of Fine Arts
78 Unesco
79 Language Schools
80 Cooperation Committee for
   Cambodia
81 Wat Koh
82 Psar O Russei
84 Wat Sampao Meas
90 Lucky! Lucky!; New! New!
91 French Cultural Centre
92 German Embassy
94 Ministry of Tourism
95 Diethelm Travel
99 Bangkok Airways;
   Siem Reap Airways
102 Vietnam Airlines

103 Hanuman Fine Arts Shop
104 SOS International Medical
   Centre
105 US Embassy
106 Monument Books
107 Pencil Supermarket
108 Indonesian Embassy
110 London Book Centre
112 Royal Phnom Penh Airways
113 Silver Pagoda
114 National Assembly Building
118 Cambodia-Vietnam
   Friendship Monument
119 Singaporian Embassy
120 Malaysian Embassy
121 Australian Embassy;
   Canadian Embassy
122 Netrec (Internet)
123 International Stationery &
   Book Centre
125 Singapore Banking
   Corporation
127 Post Office
128 Lucky Supermarket;
   Lucky Burger
131 Movie Street
139 Wat Lang Ka
140 Independence Monument
144 Lao Aviation
149 Philippines Embassy
150 Hanuman Tourism-Voyages
152 Phnom Penh Bowling Club
154 Khemara Handicrafts
158 Prayuvong Buddha Factories

documents are on display. It is worth paying US$2 to have a guide show you around, as they can tell you the stories behind some of the people in the photographs.

As the Khmer Rouge 'revolution' reached ever greater heights of insanity, it began devouring its own children. Generations of torturers and executioners who worked here were in turn killed by those who took their places. During early 1977, when the party purges of Eastern Zone cadres were getting underway, S-21 claimed an average of 100 victims a day.

When the Vietnamese army liberated Phnom Penh in early 1979, it found only seven prisoners alive at S-21. Fourteen others had been tortured to death as Vietnamese forces were closing in on the city. Photographs of their gruesome deaths are on display in the rooms where their decomposing corpses were found. Their graves are nearby in the courtyard.

Altogether, a visit to Tuol Sleng is a profoundly depressing experience. The sheer ordinariness of the place makes it even more horrific: the suburban setting, the plain school buildings, the grassy playing area where children kick around balls, rusted beds, instruments of torture and wall after wall of harrowing black-and-white portraits conjure up images of humanity at its worst. It demonstrates the darkest side of humanity that lurks within us all. Tuol Sleng is not for the squeamish.

For further reading on Tuol Sleng, try David Chandler's *Voices from S-21* or *A Cambodian Prison Portrait* by Vann Nath, one of the seven survivors, whose paintings are on display at the museum. Comrade Deuch (born Kaing Khek Iev) ran the institution and is now in prison in Phnom Penh, awaiting trial on charges of genocide. You can judge the evidence for yourself.

The Documentation Center of Cambodia (DC-Cam) was established in 1995 through Yale University's Cambodian Genocide Program to research and document the crimes of the Khmer Rouge. DC-Cam became an independent organisation in 1997 and researchers have spent years translating confessions and paperwork from Tuol Sleng, mapping mass graves and preserving evidence of Khmer Rouge crimes. Visit **w** www.yale.edu/cgp for more on its crucial work.

KILLING FIELDS OF CHOEUNG EK
វាលពិឃាតជើងឯក

Between 1975 and 1978 about 17,000 men, women, children and infants (including nine Westerners) who had been detained and tortured at S-21 were transported to the extermination camp of Choeung Ek *(admission US$2; open 7am-5.30pm daily)*. They were often bludgeoned to death to avoid wasting precious bullets.

The remains of 8985 people, many of whom were bound and blindfolded, were exhumed in 1980 from mass graves in this one-time longan orchard; 43 of the 129 communal graves here have been left untouched. Fragments of human bone and bits of cloth are scattered around the disinterred pits. More than 8000 skulls, arranged by sex and age, are visible behind the clear glass panels of the Memorial Stupa, which was erected in 1988.

The Killing Fields of Choeung Ek are 15km from central Phnom Penh and well signposted in English. To get here, take Monireth Blvd southwest out of the city. The site is 13km from the bridge near Ph 271. Take the left fork when the road splits and pretty soon you will find yourself in rural surroundings. Look out for an archway on the right and it's another kilometre or so down this track. A memorial ceremony is held annually at Choeung Ek on 9 May.

WAT PHNOM
វត្តភ្នំ

Set on top of a 27m-high tree-covered knoll, Wat Phnom *(admission US$1; open 7am-5.30pm daily)* is the only hill in town. According to legend, the first pagoda on this site was erected in 1373 to house four statues of Buddha deposited here by the waters of the Mekong River and discovered by a woman named Penh. The main entrance to Wat Phnom is via the grand eastern staircase, which is guarded by lions and *naga* (mythical serpent) balustrades.

Today, many people come here to pray for good luck and success in school exams or business affairs. When a petitioner's wish is granted, he or she returns to make the offering promised (such as a garland of jasmine flowers or a bunch of bananas, of which the spirits are said to be especially fond) when the request was made.

The *vihara* (temple sanctuary) was rebuilt in 1434, 1806, 1894 and 1926. West of the vihara is a huge stupa containing the ashes of King Ponhea Yat (reigned 1405–67). In a pavilion on the southern side of the passage between the vihara and the stupa is a statue of a smiling and rather plump Madame Penh.

A bit to the north of and below the vihara is an eclectic shrine dedicated to the genie Preah Chau, who is especially revered by the Vietnamese. On either side of the entrance to the chamber containing a statue of Preah Chau are guardian spirits bearing iron bats. On the tiled table in front of the two guardian spirits are drawings of Confucius, as well as two Chinese-style figures of the sages Thang Cheng (on the right) and Thang Thay (on the left). To the left of the central altar is an eight-armed statue of Vishnu.

Down the hill from the shrine is a royal stupa sprouting full-size trees from its roof. For now, the roots are holding the bricks together in their net-like grip, but when the trees die the tower will slowly crumble. If you can't make it out to Angkor, this stupa will give you a pretty good idea of what the jungle can do (and is doing) to Cambodia's monuments.

[Continued on page 129]

THE ROYAL PALACE & THE SILVER PAGODA
ព្រះបរមរាជវាំង និង វត្តព្រះកែវ

Phnom Penh's Royal Palace *(admission US$3; open 8am-11am & 2pm-5pm daily)*, which stands on the site of the former citadel, Banteay Kev (built in 1813), fronts Samdech Sothearos Blvd between Ph 184 and Ph 240. Since King Sihanouk's return to Cambodia, visitors are only allowed to visit the palace's Silver Pagoda and its surrounding compound. It is an extra US$2 to take in a camera and US$5 for a video camera. However, photography is not permitted inside the pagoda itself.

Chan Chaya Pavilion Performances of classical Cambodian dance were once staged in the Chan Chaya Pavilion, through which guests enter the grounds of the Royal Palace.

Throne Hall The Throne Hall, topped by a 59m-high tower inspired by the Bayon at Angkor, was inaugurated in 1919 by King Sisowath; the present cement building replaced a vast wooden structure that was built on this site in 1869. The Throne Hall was used for coronations and ceremonies such as the presentation of credentials by diplomats. Many of the items once displayed here were destroyed by the Khmer Rouge. In the courtyard is a curious iron house, given to King Norodom by Napoleon III of France.

Silver Pagoda The Silver Pagoda, so named because the floor is covered with over 5000 silver tiles weighing 1kg each, is also known as Wat Preah Keo (Pagoda of the Emerald Buddha). It was constructed of wood in 1892 during the rule of King Norodom, who was apparently inspired by Bangkok's Wat Phra Keo, and was rebuilt in 1962.

The Silver Pagoda was preserved by the Khmer Rouge to demonstrate to the outside world its concern for the conservation of Cambodia's cultural riches. Although some 60% of the pagoda's contents were destroyed under Pol Pot, what remains is spectacular. This is one of the few places in Cambodia where objects embodying some of the brilliance and richness of Khmer civilisation can still be viewed.

The staircase leading to the Silver Pagoda is made of Italian marble. Inside, the Emerald Buddha, said to be made of Baccarat crystal, sits on a gilt pedestal high atop the dais. In front of the dais stands a life-size gold Buddha decorated with 9584 diamonds, the largest of which weighs 25 carats. Created in the palace workshops during 1906 and 1907, the gold Buddha weighs some 90kg. Directly in front of it, in a Formica case, is a miniature silver-and-gold stupa containing a relic of Buddha brought from Sri Lanka. To the left is an 80kg bronze Buddha, and to the right a silver Buddha. On the far right, figurines of solid gold tell the story of the Buddha.

Behind the dais is a standing marble Buddha from Myanmar (Burma) and a litter (portable bed), used by the king on coronation day; designed to be carried by 12 men, its gold parts weigh 23kg. To either side are silver models of King Norodom's stupa and Wat Preah Keo's library. At the back of the hall is a case containing two gold Buddhas, each decorated with diamonds weighing up to 16 carats; the lower figure weighs 4.5kg, the upper 1.5kg.

Along the walls of the pagoda are examples of extraordinary Khmer artisanship, including bejewelled masks used in classical dance and dozens of solid and hollow gold Buddhas. The many precious gifts given to Cambodia's monarchs by foreign heads of state appear rather spiritless when displayed next to such diverse and exuberant Khmer art. The epic of the *Ramayana* (a Sanskrit poem) is depicted on a colossal mural enclosing the pagoda compound, created around 1900; the story begins just south of the east gate.

Other structures in the complex (listed clockwise from the north gate) include the *mondap* (library), which housed richly illuminated sacred texts written on palm leaves; the shrine of King Norodom (reigned 1860–1904); an equestrian statue of King Norodom; the shrine of King Ang Duong (reigned 1845–59); a pavilion housing a huge footprint of the Buddha; Phnom Mondap, an artificial hill with a structure containing a bronze footprint of the Buddha from Sri Lanka; a shrine dedicated to one of Prince Sihanouk's daughters; a pavilion for celebrations held by the royal family; the shrine of Prince Sihanouk's father, King Norodom Suramarit (reigned 1955–60); and a bell tower, whose bell is rung to order the gates to be opened or closed.

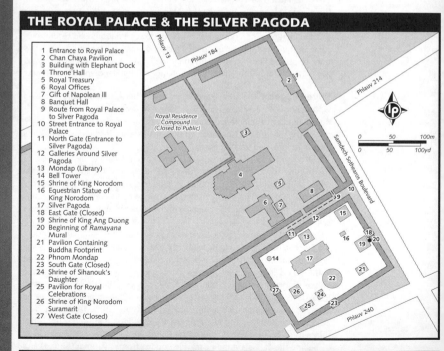

THE ROYAL PALACE & THE SILVER PAGODA

1 Entrance to Royal Palace
2 Chan Chaya Pavilion
3 Building with Elephant Dock
4 Throne Hall
5 Royal Treasury
6 Royal Offices
7 Gift of Napolean III
8 Banquet Hall
9 Route from Royal Palace to Silver Pagoda
10 Street Entrance to Royal Palace
11 North Gate (Entrance to Silver Pagoda)
12 Galleries Around Silver Pagoda
13 Mondap (Library)
14 Bell Tower
15 Shrine of King Norodom
16 Equestrian Statue of King Norodom
17 Silver Pagoda
18 East Gate (Closed)
19 Shrine of King Ang Duong
20 Beginning of *Ramayana* Mural
21 Pavilion Containing Buddha Footprint
22 Phnom Mondap
23 South Gate (Closed)
24 Shrine of Sihanouk's Daughter
25 Pavilion for Royal Celebrations
26 Shrine of King Norodom Suramarit
27 West Gate (Closed)

NICK RAY

JOHN BANAGAN

Top: The ornate roof of the Royal Palace, Phnom Penh. Built in 1866 by King Norodom, the Royal Palace is now home to the king and queen of Cambodia

Bottom: Members of the National Ballet perform an ancient *apsara* (heavenly nymph) dance at the Royal Palace, Phnom Penh

The Royal Palace & the Silver Pagoda

BERNARD NAPTHINE

BERNARD NAPTHINE

BERNARD NAPTHINE

Top: Intricate mural depicting the *Ramayana* in the Silver Pagoda, Phnom Penh

Middle: Buddha image on a glass panel at the Silver Pagoda

Bottom: Another scene from the *Ramayana* mural in the Silver Pagoda

[Continued from page 126]

Wat Phnom can be a bit of a circus. Beggars, street urchins, women selling drinks and children selling birds in cages (you pay to set the bird free – locals claim the birds are trained to return to their cage afterwards) pester everyone who turns up to slog the 27m to the summit. Fortunately it's all high-spirited stuff, and it's difficult to be annoyed by the vendors, who, after all, are only trying to eke out a living. You can also have a short elephant ride around the base of the hill, perfect for those elephant-trekking photos, but without the accompanying sore butt.

It is hardly the most stunning location you are likely to visit in Cambodia, but as a symbol of Phnom Penh it is a popular spot. At night it is lit up like a Christmas tree by fairy lights – far less dignified than a splash of silver plating and some spotlights.

WAT OUNALOM
វត្តឧណ្ណាលោម

Wat Ounalom, across the road from Phnom Penh Tourism, is the headquarters of the Cambodian Buddhist patriarchate. It was founded in 1443 and comprises 44 structures. It received a battering during the Pol Pot era, but today the wat is coming back to life. The head of the country's Buddhist hierarchy lives here, along with an increasing number of monks.

On the 2nd floor of the main building, to the left of the dais, is a statue of Samdech Huot Tat, Fourth Patriarch of Cambodian Buddhism, who was killed by Pol Pot. The statue, made in 1971 when the patriarch was 80, was thrown in the Mekong but retrieved after 1979. To the right of the dais is a statue of a former patriarch of the Thummayuth sect, to which the royal family belongs.

On the 3rd floor of the building is a marble Buddha of Burmese origin broken into pieces by the Khmer Rouge and later re-assembled. On the front right corner of the dais on this floor are the cement remains of a Buddha stripped of its silver covering by the Khmer Rouge. In front of the dais, to either side, are two glass cases containing flags –

each 20m long – used during Buddhist celebrations. The walls are decorated with scenes from the life of Buddha: they were painted when the building was constructed in 1952.

Behind the main building is a stupa containing an eyebrow hair of Buddha. There is an inscription in Pali (an ancient Indian language) over the entrance.

WAT LANG KA
វត្តលង្កា

Wat Lang Ka *(Sihanouk Blvd)*, near the Victory Monument, is a wat enjoying a new lease on life. It is a colourful place with plenty of new paint and young monks in saffron robes. It was the second of Phnom Penh's wats repaired by the post-1979 government (the first was Wat Ounalom). Around the main building are reconstructed stupas. Both the ground- and 2nd-floor chambers of the vihara have been newly painted with colourful scenes from the life of Buddha.

WAT KOH
វត្តកោះ

Wat Koh *(Monivong Blvd)*, between Ph 174 and Ph 178, is one of Phnom Penh's oldest pagodas. It was established hundreds of years ago (around the time when Wat Phnom was founded), but only became popular with the masses after the lake surrounding its very small vihara was filled in during the 1950s.

WAT MOHA MONTREI
វត្តមហាមន្ត្រី

Wat Moha Montrei *(Sihanouk Blvd)* is on the southern side of the boulevard between Ph 163 and Ph 173 (across from the Olympic Stadium). It was named in honour of one of King Monivong's ministers, Chakrue Ponn, who initiated the founding of the pagoda (*moha montrei* means 'the great minister'). The cement vihara, topped with a 35m-high tower, was completed in 1970. Between 1975 and 1979, the building was used by the Khmer Rouge and surrounding villages to store rice and corn.

PHNOM PENH

Note the assorted Cambodian touches incorporated into the wall murals of the vihara, which tell the story of Buddha. The angels accompanying Buddha to heaven are dressed as classical Khmer dancers and the assembled officials wear white military uniforms of the Sihanouk period. Along the wall to the left of the dais is a painted wooden lion from which religious lessons are preached four times a month. The golden wooden throne nearby is used for the same purpose. All the statues of Buddha here were made after 1979.

INTERNATIONAL MOSQUE
វិហារសាសនាអ៊ីស្លាម

This completely rebuilt mosque (beside Boeng Kak) was built with US$350,000 in donations from Saudi Arabia. Prayers are held five times daily.

NUR UL-IHSAN MOSQUE
វិហារសាសនាអ៊ីស្លាម

The Nur ul-Ihsan Mosque (National Hwy 5) in Khet Chraing Chamres is 7km north of central Phnom Penh. It was founded in 1813 and according to local people was used by the Khmer Rouge as a pigsty and reconsecrated in 1979. It now serves a small community of Cham and ethnic Malay Muslims. Next to the mosque is a madrasa (religious school). Visitors must remove their shoes before entering the mosque.

Few moto (small motorcycle) drivers have heard of Nur ul-Ihsan Mosque, so you may need to ask around a bit to get out there. Buses travelling from Psar Thmei towards Udong pass the mosque en route.

AN-NUR AN-NA'IM MOSQUE
វិហារសាសនាអ៊ីស្លាម

The original An-Nur an-Na'im Mosque was built in 1901 and razed by the Khmer Rouge. A new, more modest brick structure topped with a white dome holding a star and crescent aloft – has been constructed about 1km north of Nur ul-Ihsan Mosque by the local Muslim community.

OTHER ATTRACTIONS
The real name of the 700m Japanese Friendship Bridge, which spans the Tonlé Sap river, is the **Chruoy Changvar Bridge**. It was blown up during fighting in 1975. Long a symbol of the devastation visited upon Cambodia, it was repaired in 1993 with US$23.2 million of Japanese funding. Those who have seen the film The Killing Fields may be interested to note that it was near here on the afternoon of 17 April 1975 – the day Phnom Penh fell – that New York Times correspond-ent Sydney Schanberg and four companions were held prisoner by Khmer Rouge fighters and threatened with death.

West of the Chruoy Changvar Bridge is the Ph 70 branch of the **School of Fine Arts**. This is an active school devoted to training students in the arts of music and dance, and is not a tourist attraction. It is possible, however, to call in early in the morning and watch children rehearsing classical Khmer dance on a dais to the rear of the school. Request permission from the teachers to watch the lessons or to take photographs. There is also a circus school here where children learn acrobatics and trapeze, but the thinness of the crash mats makes it painful to observe.

The **French embassy** on the northern end of Monivong Blvd was for many years used as an orphanage and its apparently larcenous residents were blamed by local people for every theft in the neighbourhood. Today the embassy is back and a high wall surrounds the massive complex. The French have returned to Cambodia in a big way, promoting French language and culture in their former colony.

When Phnom Penh fell in 1975, about 800 foreigners and 600 Cambodians took refuge in the embassy. Within 48 hours, the Khmer Rouge informed the French vice-consul that the new government did not recognise diplomatic privileges and that if all the Cambodians in the compound were not handed over, the lives of the foreigners inside would also be forfeited. Cambodian women married to foreigners could stay; Cambodian men married to foreign women could not.

Foreigners wept as servants, colleagues, friends, lovers and husbands were escorted out of the embassy gates. At the end of the month the foreigners were expelled from Cambodia by truck. Many of the Cambodians were never seen again.

There is a cluster of **private language schools** teaching English and French on Ph 184 between Norodom Blvd and the rear of the Royal Palace compound. Between 5pm and 7pm the area is filled with students who see learning English as the key to making it in post-war Cambodia. This is a good place to meet young locals.

Known collectively as the National Sports Complex, the **Olympic Stadium** (near cnr Sihanouk & Monireth Blvds) includes a sports arena (which doubles as the site of government-sponsored political rallies) and facilities for swimming, boxing, gymnastics, volleyball and other sports. It is currently closed for a renovation that doesn't seem to be progressing at all.

Just south of Hotel Cambodiana, the **Cambo Fun Park** (open 5pm-10pm daily) is the only amusement park in Phnom Penh. By 7pm it is usually packed with school children queuing impatiently to risk their lives on what appear to be some very rickety rides – the management boasts that the whole thing was built in just 20 days. The area between here and the Independence Monument gets pretty lively in the evening, with a whole host of *tukalok* (fruit smoothie) sellers and snack stalls. Many young Khmers hang out around the fountains checking each other out.

The **Independence Monument** (cnr Norodom & Sihanouk Blvds) was built in 1958. It is also a memorial to Cambodia's war dead (at least those the current government chooses to remember) and is sometimes known as the Victory Monument. Wreaths are laid here on national holidays. Nearby, beside Samdech Sothearos Blvd, is the **Cambodia-Vietnam Friendship Monument**, built to a Vietnamese design in 1979.

In order to replace the countless Buddhas and ritual objects smashed by the Khmer Rouge, a whole neighbourhood of private workshops producing cement Buddhas, naga and small stupas has grown up on the grounds of Wat Prayuvong. While the graceless cement figures painted in gaudy colours are hardly works of art, they are part of an effort by the Cambodian people to restore Buddhism to a place of honour in their reconstituted society. The **Prayuvong Buddha factories** (between Ph 308 & Ph 310) are about 300m south of the Independence Monument.

The **former US embassy** (cnr Norodom & Mao Tse Toung Blvds) ran much of the US air war in Cambodia (1969–73). The building now houses the Department of Fisheries of the Ministry of Agriculture.

On the morning of 12 April 1975, 360 heavily armed US Marines brought in by helicopter secured a landing zone several hundred metres from the embassy. Within hours, 276 people – Americans, Cambodians and others – were evacuated by helicopter relay to US ships in the Gulf of Thailand. Among the last to leave was US ambassador John Gunther Dean, carrying the embassy's US flag under his arm.

Cham Kar Mon Palace (Norodom Blvd) was once the residence of Prince Sihanouk. The palace, whose name means 'silkworm fields', is on the western side of the boulevard between Ph 436 and Ph 462 and is now used by visiting heads of state.

BOAT CRUISES

Boat trips on the Tonlé Sap river or Mekong are popular with some visitors. Local tourist boats are available for hire on the riverfront in Phnom Penh and can usually be arranged on the spot for between US$10 and US$20 an hour, depending on negotiations and numbers.

Le Deauville II (☎ 012-763907) is a sophisticated boat offering a daily cruise with lunch at US$25 per person for 15 people, and a sunset cruise with aperitif at US$12 per person for 10 people.

The latest boat to hit local waters is the *Mekong Queen* (☎ 214848), a huge converted cargo boat decked out in fairy lights. It has two-hour afternoon (US$8, 3.30pm) and evening (US$10, 6.30pm) cruises, including a sandwich and tea or coffee. It departs from the tourist boat dock.

MASSAGE

There are plenty of massage parlours in Phnom Penh, but most are just fronts for brothels. There are more traditional massage services at most upmarket hotels, but best of all is the **Seeing Hands Massage** *(US$4 per hour),* intended to raise funds to empower disabled Cambodians in the capital. The blind masseurs here have been trained for many years and can sort out those niggling aches and pains. There are two centres in the capital, one at NCDP Handicrafts *(3 Norodom Blvd)* and the second at the Garden Center Café *(23 Ph 57).*

SWIMMING

The Olympic Stadium was closed for renovation in 2000 and it hasn't reopened, so the Olympic-size pool is no more for the time being.

The cheapest swim is at the **Royal Palace Hotel** *(admission US$3),* but the pool is fairly small. **Hotel Cambodiana** charges US$6 during the week, US$8 at the weekend. Both the **Juliana Hotel** *(admission US$8)* and the **Intercontinental Hotel** *(admission US$10)* have larger pools. **Royal Phnom Penh Hotel** and **Mi Casa Cambodiana** charge US$10 and this includes access to their gyms. The best-value pools are **Parkway Health Club** *(Parkway Square; admission US$8),* which has a pool (indoor, unfortunately), steam bath, sauna and gym, and **Northbridge Club** *(admission US$5),* out towards Pochentong airport.

Most of these places offer long-term membership packages, as does the very luxurious Amrita Spa at Hotel Le Royal. Contact the individual places for more details if you are sticking around Phnom Penh.

GYMNASIUMS

There are plenty of backstreet local gyms in Phnom Penh that charge about 1000r per hour and have very basic weights. For something more sophisticated, there is a **Clark Hatch Gym** at the Intercontinental Hotel that charges US$14 a day.

BOWLING

There are two bowling alleys in town. **The Superbowl** *(Mao Tse Toung Blvd)* at Parkway Square charges US$9 per hour for a lane (any number of bowlers), plus US$1 per pair of shoes. Lanes are often discounted during the day. **Phnom Penh Bowling Club** *(34 Ph 294)* charges US$6 during the day and US$10 from 6pm to 1am, plus US$1 for shoes.

GO-CARTING

There are a couple of go-cart tracks in the Phnom Penh area. The track at **Tompuon** *(US$3 per 10 min),* about 10km across the Monivong Bridge, is pretty small and the carts have seen better days. Much more professional is **Kambol F1 Go-carts** *(US$7 per 10 min),* about 10km beyond Pochentong airport, and 2km off the road to Sihanoukville. It organises races on Sundays, so if you fancy yourself as a new Niki Lauda, turn up then. Prices include helmets and racing suits.

GOLF

A round of golf is outrageously expensive by Cambodian standards. Contact **Royal Golf Club** *(☎ 366689)* on National Hwy 4 (NH4) to Sihanoukville, or **Cambodia Golf and Country Club** *(☎ 363666)* also on NH4, if you can't survive without a swing. Cheaper swingers might try the **driving ranges** at the Royal Phnom Penh Hotel or Parkway Square.

PLACES TO STAY

The hotel and guesthouse scene in Phnom Penh has come a long way since the bad old days of a handful of decrepit, government-owned places falling apart around their guests. Today there is an excellent range of guesthouses, hotels and luxury palaces to suit all wallets passing through Cambodia's capital.

Affordable guesthouses are springing up all over the city. Some places charge as little as US$2 a room; US$5 will guarantee a small room with a fan. The best hotel deals in Phnom Penh fall in the mid-range category and for around US$20 it is possible to

Shooting Ranges in the Sights

Anything goes in Cambodia, or so some Westerners seemed to believe during much of the 1990s. Be it sex, drugs or rock and roll, Cambodia's lack of law enforcement and culture of impunity allowed visitors to do pretty much anything they wanted. The Cambodian military weren't blind to the market opportunities this presented, and with a hefty surplus of weapons from a quarter of a century of civil war, they began to offer their own ammunition reduction scheme involving gung-ho foreigners who wanted to do the Rambo thing.

A number of military bases near Phnom Penh were turned into shooting ranges and rapidly became popular places for tourists wanting to try their luck with an AK-47, an M-60 or a B-40 grenade launcher. It wasn't everyone's cup of tea, but it didn't seem that unusual in a poverty-wracked nation – visitors to Vietnam's Cu Chi Tunnels might remember similar 'opportunities' back in the early 1990s. Even today, visitors heading to some of Angkor's more remote sites shouldn't be surprised to be offered the chance to fire off a couple of rounds on a guard's AK-47. In a country where public sector incomes are US$20 a month, it shouldn't come as a shock that soldiers are learning to be creative. Travellers on a low budget would find it hard to last two days in Cambodia on US$20 – and most don't have a family of five to feed!

The military ranges were an anomaly – loved and loathed in equal measure by visitors to Phnom Penh. By the dawn of the millennium, the government decided enough was enough and that shooting ranges no longer enhanced Cambodia's image as a cultural destination. The ranges were closed and forced underground. However, with the ranges going underground, there was nothing to stop sick Westerners and poverty-stricken soldiers from forming an unholy alliance to shoot live animals. Needless to say, anyone who thinks shooting a cow or chicken is fun is one sick puppy and should not be perverting Cambodia's improving image. Cambodians certainly aren't impressed by this kind of behaviour.

Cambodia needs a reduction in weapon numbers to move towards a lasting peace and reconciliation. To this end, the government has instigated periodic crackdowns on privately held weapons and destroyed the confiscated guns in large public ceremonies. Travellers who want to learn more about the campaign to disarm the nation should contact the Working Group on Weapons Reduction (WGWR; ☎ 216400, fax 363242, Ⓦ www.igc.org/nonviolence/wgwr) at 30 Ph 352. Travellers who want to shoot live animals should get on the first plane home and visit a therapist.

get hooked up with air-con, satellite TV and a hot tub. Top-end travellers will find that Phnom Penh's best hotels are expensive by Cambodian standards; there is often far better value for money at the more comfortable mid-range hotels.

PLACES TO STAY – BUDGET

There is no Khao San Rd as in Bangkok, or Pham Ngu Lao as in Ho Chi Minh City (Saigon) just yet, but for many this is no great shame. There are, however, two emerging backpacker strips, one along the eastern shore of Boeng Kak and another around the long-running Capitol Guesthouse along Ph 182 and Ph 111, just west of Monivong Blvd. The area around Boeng Kak has improved somewhat in the past few years, but the rooms in these guesthouses are pretty basic compared with elsewhere in the city. For those who have seen enough of their fellow travellers to last a lifetime, there are several smaller guesthouses spread across the city.

Boeng Kak Area

Most of the lakeside guesthouses are built on wooden platforms over Boeng Kak, a seriously polluted body of water that no-one should swim in, however many beers they have drunk. The guesthouses used to be rickety shacks with dodgy planking, but are now more solidly built, with great communal areas to while away the day. For some it's like experiencing Ko Pha-Ngan in the city, only Boeng Kak isn't quite the Gulf of Thailand.

Number 9 Guesthouse (e *number9 _guesthouse@hotmail.com, 9 Ph 93*) Singles/ doubles with bathroom US$3/4, without bathroom US$2/3. The longest-running of the lakeside pads is bigger than ever, offering around 50 basic rooms. It used to be a dive, but has come a fair way, adding such simple things as lino flooring to keep the bugs at bay. The restaurant and chill-out area has been spruced up and the management offers safety lockers for valuables.

Lakeside Guesthouse (e *number10 _Lakeside@hotmail.com, 10 Ph 93*) Singles/ doubles with bathroom US$4/5, without bathroom US$3/4, triples with bathroom US$6. This old favourite has added a building with smarter rooms than the rest of the competition. It is worth getting one of the newer rooms for extra comfort. The drinking and dining area stretches out into the lake and makes a nice place to hang out. There are also safety lockers.

Same Same But Different (e *samesame _gh@yahoo.com, Ph 93*) Singles/doubles/ triples without bathroom US$2/3/4. This place has an inspirational name, but otherwise it's same same and the same. The TV has been banished to a separate room, making the restaurant area more sociable. Pizzas are also on offer.

Shanti Lodge (*Ph 93*) Rooms with/ without bathroom US$3/2. This is a friendly little guesthouse offering basic rooms with bed and fan. The restaurant area has no TV, which may appeal to those looking for conversation.

Simon's Guesthouse Rooms with bathroom US$5, rooms without bathroom US$3-4. Definitely not an inspirational name, but the rooms are well-tended here.

Happy Guesthouse (e *ngacafe@hotmail .com, 11 Ph 93*) Rooms with/without bathroom US$4/3. Currently the last of the lakeside strip, this place has compact rooms and a small restaurant.

Psar O Russei Area

The other budget centre starts near Psar O Russei and heads south along the back streets.

Capitol Guesthouse (☎ *364104, fax 21 4014,* e *capitol@bigpond.com.kh, 14 Ph 182*) Singles/doubles with bathroom US$4/5, without bathroom US$3/4, rooms with air-con & hot water US$10. This guesthouse is the longest-running budget guesthouse in Phnom Penh and offers rooms, rooms and more rooms. Try to take a room on the outside of the building with a window. The restaurant downstairs is always a lively, cheap place to eat. The Capitol is the best budget centre from which to arrange travel from Phnom Penh, as the friendly management is the most experienced in the business.

Narin Guesthouse (☎ *982554,* e *touch narin@hotmail.com, 50 Ph 125*) Singles/ doubles with windows US$3/5, doubles with bathroom US$5-6, triples with bathroom US$7. This very popular, family-run place offers hot showers throughout. It's clean and friendly and has a good restaurant.

Narin 2 Guesthouse (☎ *986131, Ph 111*) Singles/doubles with bathroom from US$5/6, rooms with TV & bathroom US$7, with air-con & hot water US$10. This huge place with clean rooms only recently opened its doors. The original guesthouse has more atmosphere, while the new one offers high-speed Internet access.

Tat Guesthouse (☎ *214966, 52 Ph 125*) Doubles/triples with bathroom US$5/6, doubles/twins without bathroom US$3/4. This is a popular new spot next door to Narin, with a rooftop restaurant and fun-loving owners.

Seng Sokhom Guesthouse (e *seng sokhom@hotmail.com, 22 Ph 111*) Singles/ doubles without bathroom US$2/3. This friendly, family-run place is immensely popular with long-termers in Phnom Penh. Its cheap deals make it a good idea to book ahead, as it is often full.

Hello Guesthouse (*242 Ph 107*) Rooms with fan/air-con & bathroom US$4/8, triples without bathroom US$5. This is another small guesthouse that may appeal to those wanting to get away from the crowds at the nearby backpacker 'hotels'.

Lucky Guesthouse (☎ *218910, 99 Ph 214*) Singles with fan US$6, doubles with fan/ air-con US$7/10. This comfortable place is currently overlooked by many travellers, but could come in use if the surrounding guesthouses are full. All rooms here have TV and bathroom.

Around the City
Other guesthouses are evenly spread across the city.

The Last Home (☎ 724917, fax 981166, e sakith@forum.org.kh, 47 Ph 108) Rooms with/without bathroom US$4/3, doubles with TV & bathroom US$5, with air-con US$8. This likeable guesthouse has a reasonable selection of rooms and a good location near Wat Phnom and the riverfront. There is a restaurant and book exchange downstairs.

Okay Guesthouse (Ph 258) Singles/doubles with bathroom US$3/4, without bathroom US$2/3. Located down a side street near Hotel Cambodiana, this fast-expanding place has good-value rooms for those on a tight budget. It also has a cafe downstairs with a teach-yourself board of Khmer phrases.

Riverview Hotel (☎/fax 361814, e sunny dhaka@hotmail.com, 33 Samdech Sothearos Blvd) Singles/doubles with air-con, TV & bathroom US$8/12. For those willing to spend a few more dollars for the chilled air, this place has a very central location near the riverfront and National Museum.

Royal Guesthouse (☎ 218026, e houleng @forum.org.kh, 91 Ph 154) Singles/doubles with fan US$5/7, with air-con US$10/12. Just off Norodom Blvd, the Royal is another option for those seeking to spend a little more for the extra comfort. It has basic rooms with TV and bathroom, and a good selection of air-con rooms that are popular with long-stayers.

Dara Reang Sey Hotel (☎ 428181, e sok srun@camnet.com.kh, 45 Ph 13) Rooms with fan US$6, with air-con US$10-16. Rooms here include bathrooms; an extra US$2 guarantees hot water. The restaurant downstairs has Khmer-priced food and drink.

Apsara Guesthouse (☎ 426698, 24 Ph 47) Rooms with bathroom from US$5, doubles with fan/air-con & hot water US$7/12. This rambling guesthouse, based around a French villa, has a serious selection of rooms. It's a little out of town, but could be considered a quieter option.

The Boddhi Tree (e boddhitree_pp @hotmail.com, 50 Ph 113) Singles US$7-8, doubles US$9-10. The location is not ideal (bang opposite Tuol Sleng Museum) but for those who don't get nightmares, this guesthouse has lots of charm. It is a wooden villa with tastefully decorated rooms, shared bathrooms and an excellent restaurant set in a verdant garden. Stay three nights and save a buck a night.

PLACES TO STAY – MID-RANGE
For those looking to spend between US$15 and US$50 for a room in Phnom Penh, there are some excellent deals to be had around town. The average price for a double with air-con, bathroom, satellite TV and laundry service is US$15 to US$20. Some of the fancier mid-range places are not that far behind the top-range hotels in comfort, but are pleasingly far behind on price, at US$30 to US$50.

As with the budget guesthouses, there is no single mid-range hotel area. The area to the southwest of the Independence Monument has the greatest concentration of mid-range deals, while the riverfront is a popular area for its views and breezes. The stretch of Monivong Blvd between Pochentong and Sihanouk Blvds is the old hotel district, but this is not the most charming area of town.

Riverfront Area
California Hotel (☎ 982182, e cambodia _hotel_california@hotmail.com, 317 Sisowath Quay) Singles/doubles with air-con, TV, fridge & hot water US$15/20. This clean and compact guesthouse has nice rooms at an appealing price given the location. Pay a little extra for a room at the front and catch the river breeze. Prices include breakfast.

Hotel Indochine (☎ 724239, fax 427292, 251 Sisowath Quay) Singles US$10-12, doubles US$15-17, triples US$18-20. Some of the smaller rooms here aren't much of a deal, but those with a view over the river are a worthwhile choice. Rooms include air-con, TV and bathroom, although hot water comes at a US$2 premium.

Sunshine Hotel (☎ 725684, fax 218256, 253 Sisowath Quay) Singles/doubles US$15/20, doubles with river view US$25.

Next door to Hotel Indochine, this is a slightly more sophisticated place, providing value for money. Rooms include air-con, TV, fridge and hot water and the river-view rooms include a hot tub for anyone missing a soak.

Bali Café (☎ 982211, e royalalita @camintel.com, 379 Sisowath Quay) Singles/doubles with bathroom US$15/20. The rooms here are a little plain, with no TV, hot water or view, but are otherwise comfortable. Breakfast is included in the price. It also has a good Indonesian restaurant.

Dream World Guesthouse (☎ 427708, fax 982113, 22 Ph 178) Rooms with air-con & TV US$10, rooms with fan/air-con & bathroom US$10/15. This new place has a desirable location, opposite the National Museum and a stone's throw from the river (don't test this, it might hurt someone!), and offers reasonable value for money.

Lyon D'Or (☎/fax 217710, e lyondor @bigpond.com.kh, 12 Ph 110) Rooms US$5, with air-con, TV & bathroom from US$10, with hot water US$15, large rooms US$20. This place has a range of good-value rooms.

Riverside Hotel (☎ 723318, fax 723428, e riverside-hotel@camnet.com.kh, cnr Sisowath Quay & Ph 94) Singles/twins at the rear US$25/30, at the front US$30/35. This place is definitely a class apart for this sort of money. Despite the ugly exterior, the rooms are of a three-star standard and it has a fine location overlooking the Tonlé Sap to the front and Wat Phnom at the back. Rooms include minibar, safety box, hot tub and breakfast.

Foreign Correspondents' Club (☎ 210142, fax 427758, e fcc@cafeasia.net, 363 Sisowath Quay) Rooms US$45-65. This club offers three elegant rooms in a stylish location. Two of the rooms have breezy balconies overlooking the Tonlé Sap and all include a minibar clearly aimed at the journalists who pass through town – the spirits come in 1L bottles rather than miniatures. Prices include breakfast. Definitely book ahead.

Central Phnom Penh

Golden Gate Hotel (☎/fax 721161, e golden gatehtls@hotmail.com, 6 Ph 278) Singles/

doubles US$15/20, larger deluxe rooms with hot tub US$30. This is a justly popular hotel with NGOs, offering great value for money. Rooms include air-con, TV, minibar, bathroom and generous free laundry service; the deluxe rooms include breakfast. There's also a restaurant downstairs and inexpensive Internet access. It's a good idea to email ahead and book. The nearby annexe rooms are less impressive than those in the main building.

Golden Bridge Hotel (☎ 721396, fax 721395, 6 Ph 278) Rooms with air-con, TV, fridge & hot water US$15. Right next door to the Golden Gate, this place offers clean and comfortable rooms that are good value. There is a free laundry service.

Another door down, the **Golden Sun Hotel** (☎ 721317, fax 216303, e goldensun @bigpond.com.kh, 6B Ph 278) has exactly the same deal as the Golden Bridge Hotel, although some rooms (such as minisuite 14) are better than others.

Goldiana Hotel (☎ 218490, fax 217558, e goldiana.ht@bigpond.com.kh, 10 Ph 282) Standard singles/doubles US$25/35, deluxe singles/doubles US$35/45, suites US$85. This huge hotel has 157 rooms and offers a great deal considering facilities include a swimming pool and fitness centre. Rooms come with all the trimmings, but deluxe rooms are bigger and brighter and include breakfast. The price includes a free transfer from Pochentong airport, effectively making rooms US$7 cheaper, as you save the taxi fare.

Beauty Inn Hotel (☎ 722676, fax 722677, e bti@bigpond.com.kh, 100 Sihanouk Blvd) Singles/doubles US$13/18. This place is real value for money, as rooms include air-con, TV, minibar and hot water. Doubles include a hot tub and there is a travel agency in the lobby.

Champs Élysées Hotel (☎ 721080, fax 724153, 185 Ph 63) Singles US$15, doubles US$20-22. This place offers comfortable enough rooms and promises the receptionists will 'serve you without displeased'.

Walkabout Hotel (☎ 211715, e walk about@bigpond.com.kh, cnr Ph 51 & Ph 174) Rooms with air-con US$12-25. This place started as a budget hotel, but has steadily upped its rooms and prices. Unfortunately, its standards have slipped in other ways and it has a reputation for a surfeit of local ladies on short stays. The new rooms priced from US$18 are looking quite nice, but are not too couple-friendly thanks to the late-night bar downstairs.

Cathay Hotel (☎ 427178, fax 426303, e cathay_hotel@hotmail.com, 123 Ph 110) Large rooms with air-con, TV, fridge & hot tub US$15. The Cathay used to be popular with resident journalists and photographers, but it is pretty quiet these days with no war to attract them. The rooms are a reasonable deal for the location, but a little aged.

Singapore Hotel (☎ 725552, fax 426570, 62 Monivong Blvd) Rooms with fan & bathroom from US$5, singles/doubles with air-con, TV & hot water US$10/15. This is an uninspiring kind of place, a little like Singapore, some cynics might say, but the rooms are cheap enough.

Morakat Hotel (☎ 880180, 33 Ph 107) Rooms with air-con, TV, fridge & hot water US$20, minisuites US$25. This hotel has no lift so it offers 3rd- and 4th-floor rooms for just US$15 – something of a steal for those who don't mind the climb.

Paradise Hotel (☎ 880539, fax 427280, 213 Monivong Blvd) Singles/doubles with bathroom US$20/25. Paradise may be stretching the truth a little, but the rooms are reasonable enough in this centrally located place.

Queen Hotel (☎ 213001, fax 213002, Ph 214) Singles/twins with air-con, TV, minibar & bathroom US$25/30. This popular hotel offers clean and comfortable rooms that draw in small tour groups.

Princess Hotel (☎ 801809, fax 801217, e princess@camnet.com.kh, 302 Ph 228) Rooms US$30-35. This hotel offers smart rooms for the money, including satellite TV, minibar and a hot tub.

Hawaii Hotel (☎ 426747, fax 427251, e hawaiihotel@bigpond.com.kh, 18 Ph 130) Singles/doubles/junior suites US$22/33/44. For something comfortable and central, the Hawaii, near Psar Thmei, remains a good option. The double rooms include air-con,

while the suites are nicely decorated in wooden furnishings.

Diamond Hotel (☎ 217328, fax 216637, e diamondhotel@bigpond.com.kh, 172 Monivong Blvd) Singles/doubles US$35/45. These prices are half what they used to be and make this place a very attractive option with its wooden floors, comprehensive trimmings and in-room safes. Prices include breakfast.

Regent Park Hotel (☎ 427131, fax 361999, e regentpark@bigpond.com.kh, 58 Samdech Sothearos Blvd) Singles/doubles US$45/50. Housed in a rather ugly building near the National Assembly building, this hotel has smart rooms and is good value for the extra level of comfort.

Beyond the City Centre

Bayon Hotel (☎ 430158, fax 427378, e bayon@bigpond.com.kh, 2 Ph 75) Singles/doubles/deluxe rooms US$25/35/45 plus 15% tax & service. This French-run hotel has 30 well-presented rooms and offers video players and access to a huge in-house library of films. Downstairs is a well-regarded restaurant.

Sydney International Hotel (☎ 428312, fax 427907, 360 Ph 360) Rooms with/without balcony US$25/20. This place is good value thanks to its inconvenient location. Rooms include air-con, TV, fridge, hot tub and breakfast.

Royal Palace Hotel (☎ 884823, fax 884825, e royalpalacehotel@bigpond.com.kh, 93 Monireth Blvd) Rooms/suites US$35/60. The rooms here are a bit of a bargain thanks to the poor location, and three-star touches for a two-star price. Facilities include a swimming pool, and breakfast is included in the price.

PLACES TO STAY – TOP END

Walk-in rates at many of Phnom Penh's luxury hotels are high by regional standards. Consider booking through a local travel agent for a better deal.

Hotel Le Royal (☎ 981888, fax 981168, w www.raffles.com, cnr Monivong Blvd & Ph 92) Singles/doubles from US$260/290, personality suites/royal suite US$360/2000. This historic hotel opened its doors once more at the end of 1997. It is Phnom Penh's finest hotel, with a heritage to match its comfort and class. Those who are really flush can opt for the royal suite, but given this sum of money could support several Cambodian families for a year, it would be a little over the top. The hotel has a swimming pool, a gym, a spa, a business centre, and bars and restaurants with lavish food and drink.

Between 1970 and 1975 most journalists working in Phnom Penh stayed here, and part of the film *The Killing Fields* was set in the hotel (though filmed in Hua Hin, Thailand). When foreign-aid workers set up shop in the country after the Vietnamese takeover, this is where they stayed.

Intercontinental Hotel (☎ 424888, fax 424885, ⓦ www.interconti.com, cnr Mao Tse Toung & Monireth Blvds) Singles/doubles from US$170/200. The city's first five-star hotel, the Intercontinental is Phnom Penh's tallest building, at about 15 floors. It has a Clark Hatch fitness centre, a swimming pool, a business centre, conference facilities, live music in the lobby bar and the best pillows in Cambodia, but the location is a little out of the way.

Hotel Cambodiana (☎ 426288, fax 426290, ⓦ www.hotelcambodiana.com.kh, 313 Sisowath Quay) Singles/doubles from US$102/114. Despite parting company with the Sofitel chain in 2001, this four-star pad remains one of the best options in Phnom Penh, thanks primarily to its excellent location on the banks of the Mekong. Begun in 1967, the unfinished structure and its grounds were used as a military base by the Lon Nol government, and by 1975 thousands of refugees from the countryside sheltered under its concrete roof. It finally opened its doors in 1991. It has restaurants, bars, a small swimming pool, tennis courts, a health centre, a business centre and shops.

Mi Casa Cambodiana (☎ 214555, fax 213071, ⓔ reservation@micasa.com.kh, 313 Sisowath Quay) Singles/doubles US$90/97. This new hotel and apartment block overlooks the Mekong and has smart, well-equipped rooms. Facilities include tennis courts and a pool.

Sunway Hotel (☎ 430333, fax 430339, ⓔ asunway@bigpond.com.kh, 1 Ph 92) Singles/doubles US$65/75. The Sunway has a good location overlooking Wat Phnom, but a less-than-sympathetic exterior. The comfort is of a high standard for the money and facilities include restaurants, a business centre and conference rooms.

Royal Phnom Penh Hotel (☎ 982673, fax 360036, ⓔ royalphnompenh@bigpond.com .kh, 26 Samdech Sothearos Blvd) Singles/doubles US$85/95. This Thai-run hotel is due for a renovation, but is cheaper than it used to be. It has a swimming pool and golf driving range, all set in spacious gardens.

Juliana Hotel (☎ 366070, fax 366072, ⓔ juliana@camnet.com.kh, Ph 152) Singles/twins/deluxe rooms US$55/65/80. The Juliana, northwest of Psar O Russei, is a nice top-end option. It features a garden setting with a large swimming pool, and has a fitness centre, a sauna, a bar and restaurants. Room rates are half the price of a few years ago.

Sharaton Cambodia Hotel (☎/fax 361199, Ph 47) Rooms from US$50. The Sharaton (no, not *Sheraton*) is just north of Wat Phnom and is popular with Chinese tourists. There is a noisy nightclub downstairs.

PLACES TO EAT

The increasing affluence of some urban Phnom Penhois and the large NGO population of the city has helped foster a healthy selection of international cuisines. Visitors to Phnom Penh are quite literally spoilt for choice.

Most of the foreign restaurants around town (and there are a lot of them) are expensive by local standards, but it's worth splashing out at least once on a good French or Italian meal, or at least a pizza.

Many of the guesthouses around town have reasonably priced restaurants and some tasty food, but with so much great grub available in Phnom Penh it seems a shame to get into the habit of chowing down at the nearest terrace. Guesthouse restaurants are a good place for trading tales about the latest situation upcountry, but you won't meet many locals dining in these places. Service can also be pretty slow at these places, but that's no problem for those chilling out at the lake.

Dining for a Cause

There are several restaurants around town that are run by aid organisations to help fund their social programmes in Cambodia. These are worth seeking out, as the proceeds of a hearty meal go towards helping Cambodia's recovery and allow restaurant staff to gain valuable work experience.

Friends (☎ 426748, 215 Ph 13) Tapas US$1, specials US$2-3. Open Mon-Sat. Located near the National Museum, the menu includes more than 20 light dishes ranging from Cambodian chicken curry to a crunchy salad with a dressing to make your eyes twitch. A couple of dishes washed down with a shake is as good as any meal in town. The bill is better still, as is the cause – namely helping street children in Phnom Penh.

Le Rit's (☎ 213160, 14 Ph 310) Breakfast from US$3, set lunch US$5. Open breakfast & lunch Mon-Sat, dinner Wed-Sun. Lunch here is a three-course affair and is a pleasant experience in the well-groomed garden. The food comes with a French flourish, while the set dinner is Thai-style. Proceeds assist disadvantaged women re-enter the workplace.

La Casa (Ph 257) Open Tues-Sun. This place offers a limited menu of French and Khmer dishes, as well as some pastas. Unfortunately, it's a long hike out of the city, just off Kampuchea Krom Blvd. Proceeds go to Krousar Thmey (New Family), an NGO helping impoverished and unprotected children.

Cambodian

The best bet for budget dining in Phnom Penh is to head to one of the city's many markets. The dining areas may not be the most sophisticated in the world, but the food is tasty and cheap. Contrary to the opinion of certain expats, dining in these places is no more likely to consign you to the toilet for a week than other eateries around Phnom Penh, as much of the food is fresh and prepared in front of you.

The best markets for dining are **Psar Thmei**, **Psar Tuol Tom Pong** and **Psar O Russei**, which is pretty handy given that these are also the best bets for shopping. There are also several areas around the city with open-air food stalls during the early evening – try **Psar Ta Pang** (cnr Ph 51 & Ph 126) for excellent *bobor* (rice porridge) and tasty desserts.

If the markets are just too hot or claustrophobic for your taste, then look out for the mobile street sellers carrying their wares on their shoulders or wheeling it around in small carts. Almost anything from fried noodles to Cambodian sandwiches is available and the prices are even lower than in the markets.

Scattered around town are numerous Khmer restaurants that set up outdoor tables and chairs in the evenings. These places rarely have English signs and are as much about drinking beer as about eating, but they're lively places for an inexpensive meal and the food is usually very good.

Cook-your-own soup (soup chhnang dei) restaurants are very popular with Khmers and are great fun if you go in a group. Other diners will often help with protocol, as it is important to cook things in the right order so as not to overcook half the ingredients and eat the rest raw. These places also offer *phnom pleung* (hill of fire), which amounts to cook-your-own beef, shrimp, squid (or anything else that takes your fancy) over a personal barbecue.

Dararasmey Restaurant (292 Ph 214) Phnom pleung US$3, soup chhnang dei US$5, other dishes US$2. Just off Monivong Blvd, this is the most popular do-it-yourself restaurant, heaving with Khmers every night, and a lively spot to pass an evening as an amateur chef.

63 Soup (cnr Ph 63 & Ph 154) Phnom pleung 10,000r, soup chnnang dei 15,000r. This place is a little raw, but attracts a crowd each night to sit in the large outdoor area.

Chaay Heng Restaurant (cnr Ph 125 & Sihanouk Blvd) Mains 6000r including rice, beer US$1 per can. This popular Cambodian diner offers a good selection of classic Cambodian cuisine and appears to have almost as many 'beer girls' as dishes on the menu.

Goldfish River Restaurant (Riverbank of Sisowath Quay, opposite Ph 106) Meals from

8000r. Built on stilts over the Tonlé Sap, this is one of the best Cambodian restaurants in the city. Crab with black pepper is excellent here, as are the fish and frog dishes. Save some space for the tasty banana flambees.

Ponlok Restaurant *(☎ 212025, 319 Sisowath Quay)* This place has good views of the river from its upstairs dining area, and the English-language menu takes visitors on a guided tour of standard local cuisine. Prices are slightly higher than many local restaurants.

Khmer Surin *(☎ 363050, 9 Ph 57)* Dishes US$3-4. The Cambodian and Thai food here is popular with overseas residents of Phnom Penh, thanks in part to the charming setting in an old wooden house. The menu is extensive and the atmosphere alluring.

Amoc Café *(2 Ph 278)* Mains US$3-4. Named in honour of one of Cambodia's national dishes, this place serves delicious *amoc* (fish coconut curry in a banana leaf), as well as a maze of Khmer and Thai favourites.

Phnom Kiev Restaurant *(☎ 721387, 138 Sihanouk Blvd)* Dishes US$2-5. For inexpensive Khmer food with a Gallic touch, try the Phnom Kiev. It has a small garden area out front and does a good range of Franco-Khmer food.

Chinese

There are numerous Chinese restaurants around Phnom Penh. Many offer an authentic taste of the Middle Kingdom. There are several real-deal Chinese restaurants along Ph 136, opposite the Ho Wah Genting bus station, with names like Peking and Shanghai. These are the perfect place for a meal before or after a long bus ride.

Wah Kee Restaurant *(296 Monivong Blvd)* Dishes from US$1. This late-night canteen is the place to go if you get struck with a

---

Over the Bridge

The reconstruction of the Chruoy Changvar Bridge spanning the Tonlé Sap river created a restaurant boom on the river's east bank. There are dozens of restaurants lining the highway – from the decidedly downmarket to the obviously over-the-top – but most are interesting places for a very Cambodian night out. These are places frequented by well-to-do Khmers, and on the weekend are packed with literally thousands of people on a big night out. Most charge from US$3 a dish (with around 300 dishes to choose from) and about US$2 for a big bottle of beer. Heading north, the restaurants start to appear about 1km from the east bank. They range from small, family-run places to enormous fairy-light festooned complexes with fountains and neon signs. Many of the larger places include a resident band and the amps are often cranked up pretty high – remember to sit a fair distance from the stage.

Places come in and out of favour, but following are some of the most consistently popular. All are well signposted from the main road. A moto should cost about US$1 each way from the city centre.

Heng Lay Restaurant This is one of the largest places. It hosts leading comedians every night and is popular with Cambodians. It's very slapstick, but the food is well-regarded, if relatively expensive.

Hang Neak Restaurant Another colossus, this restaurant has a large wall mount of Angkor Wat, popular with Chinese gamblers who can't be bothered visiting the real thing. It has good food and a massive seating area that allows visitors to get away from the loud music.

Rum Chang Restaurant Currently in favour as the best place for Khmer food, there is no band here and the location overlooking the Mekong is very pleasant.

Boeng Bopha Restaurant The food here is nothing out of the ordinary, but this is currently an 'in place' for a younger crowd out drinking and listening to the band.

Ta Oeu Restaurant This simple place is popular for its value-for-money food, which has a reputation as being authentic and tasty.

Boeng Kak Restaurant This was one of the first restaurants in Phnom Penh, originally located at Boeng Kak and still going strong this side of the river.

hunger after midnight. Tasty noodle dishes are just US$1 and a lot of Chinese call in here for the freshly cooked food.

Lian Rong Dumpling Hall *(246 Monivong Blvd)* Meals US$3-5. This is an inconspicuous little place that turns out a selection of flavoursome food.

Chong Qing Restaurant *(727 Monivong Blvd)* Soup US$5. This restaurant is popular with Chinese residents in Phnom Penh – always a good sign – and specialises in Sichuan soup cooked at your table. To the uninitiated, the dining table has built-in pots shaped like Yin and Yang; one side is fiery chilli soup, the other a light stock flavour. The ingredients can be dunked in either side to cook.

Hua Nam Restaurant *(☎ 364005, 753 Monivong Blvd)* Mains from US$5. This place is a heavyweight Chinese dining experience, including delicacies such as goose webs, but meals here are very expensive by local standards.

Thai

Boat Noodle Restaurant *(Ph 63)* Dishes 2500-10,000r. This is currently the cheapest Thai restaurant in town, knocking together flavoursome food at low prices, but service can be slow.

Wangdome Restaurant *(35 Ph 240)* Dishes US$4-6. Located in an elegant French house from bygone days, the food here is well-presented and worth checking out for those craving a genuine Thai fix. Fishcakes, *laap* (spicy meat salad with mint) and curries are all delicious.

Baan Thai *(☎ 362991, 2 Ph 306)* Dishes US$3-5. Set within a classic Khmer wooden house, Baan Thai (Thai House) doesn't rate highly for an original name. It offers a choice of traditional floor seating or tables and chairs, and the menu includes the full array of Thai notables.

Chiang Mai Riverside *(227 Sisowath Quay)* Dishes US$2.50-5. This riverfront restaurant has been around for a while and has a reputation for authentic Thai cuisine at sensible prices.

EID Restaurant *(☎ 367614, 327 Sisowath Quay)* Dishes US$2-4. This is a small, basic

place with value-for-money Thai food, including a healthy *pad thai* (fried rice-noodle dish) for just US$1.50.

Vietnamese

For cheap and delicious *pho bo* (Vietnamese noodle soup), try the hole in the wall just 50m east of the Independence Monument on Sihanouk Blvd. A bowl costs around 3000r.

Christina *(☎ 723487, 226 Monivong Blvd)* Meals US$2-5. This place has some fine fare in dull surroundings. Vietnamese pancakes are good, as are the soups.

An Nam *(☎ 212460, 118 Samdech Sothearos Blvd)* Mains US$4-6. The food here may be good, but it is overpriced compared with nearby Ho Chi Minh City. US$5 would buy you a meal at the best restaurant in town across the border.

Indonesian

Bali Café *(☎ 982211, 379 Sisowath Quay)* Dishes US$2-4. This restaurant and guesthouse has a great riverfront location, but tends to be overshadowed by the Foreign Correspondents' Club. All the favourites are found here from *nasi goreng* (fried rice) to *gado gado* (vegetable salad with peanut sauce), and at affordable prices.

Indian & Nepalese

Chi Cha *(☎ 366065, 27 Ph 110)* Set lunch US$2. This Bangladeshi curry house has some of the cheapest subcontinent selections in town.

Curry Pot *(Boeng Kak)* Curries US$2. Located in the heart of backpackersville, this place is rated by some as home of the best curries in town, but wear your patient head, as service can be rather slow. Pop down the road for a beer after ordering!

Lumbini Restaurant *(☎ 212544, 51 Ph 214)* Meals US$5. This Nepalese-run restaurant offers a good selection of Indian and Nepalese food, including delicious dhal and cheap thali (rice and assorted dishes).

Shiva Shakti *(70 Sihanouk Blvd)* Dishes from US$5. This extravagant food palace has a refined menu of quality Indian food, but at prices that are rather excessive, even for little old Phnom Penh. It's US$15 for a full spread.

French

Le Louisiane *(76 Samdech Sothearos Blvd)* Dishes US$4-5, 3-course set lunch US$6. This place is not a Cajun restaurant as the name might suggest, but has a predominantly French menu with some of the best-value, sauciest steaks in town and a selection of original fish dishes. The set lunch is shockingly good value.

Le Deauville *(Wat Phnom)* Mains around US$5. Justly popular for its French menu, this place on the northern side of the city landmark is often packed with well-heeled expats. It also has live music on Friday evening.

Italian

Happy Herb's *(☎ 362349, 345 Sisowath Quay)* Pizzas from US$4. This place is something of a Phnom Penh institution, famous for its special pizzas. Those wanting to pass an evening in a bemused haze can ask the waiter for a 'happy' pizza, while those with nothing pressing on the agenda for a couple of days might request 'very happy'. The non-marijuana pizzas are equally good and don't alter the mind.

Veiyo Tonle *(237 Sisowath Quay)* Pizzas US$5, Khmer dishes US$3-4. This riverfront restaurant has good pizzas, pastas and salads, as well as a fair selection of Asian favourites.

Nike's Pizza House *(160 Ph 63)* Pizzas from US$4. This unassuming pizza house has probably the best pizzas in town, with almost 50 to choose from. The menu includes pastas, side salads and gnocchi.

Another decent pizza place is **Ecstatic Pizza** *(☎ 365089, 193 Norodom Blvd)* – don't get the wrong idea just because of Happy Herb's – south of the Independence Monument.

Pop Café *(371 Sisowath Quay)* This tiny slither of a cafe offers traditional Italian cooking in an informal environment. Soups, pastas and regional dishes make up the small menu.

Anthony Pizza *(Wat Phnom)* The US$5 lunch deal here of a pizza, salad and drink is enticing.

Japanese

As is the case almost everywhere, Japanese food in Phnom Penh is expensive.

Origami *(88 Samdech Sothearos Blvd)* Set meals US$10, Kyoto boxes US$7. This tiny restaurant is full of character and is the best-value Japanese restaurant in town. Sets include beautifully presented sushi, sashimi and tempura, and there is a small Japanese-style dining area.

Nagasaki *(☎ 218394, 39 Sihanouk Blvd)* Full meals US$20. This restaurant is reasonably authentic and has pleasant rooms with *tatami* (woven matting) for group dining. There's something galling about paying Tokyo prices for a meal in Phnom Penh, however.

International

There is now a plethora of foreign restaurants offering a dazzling array of cuisines.

Foreign Correspondents' Club *(FCC; ☎ 724014, 363 Sisowath Quay)* Mains US$5-10, set menu US$10. FCC has a restaurant and bar on its 3rd floor with fabulous views of the Tonlé Sap river on one side and the National Museum on the other. The food here is very good and there is a daily set menu.

The Globe Bar & Restaurant *(☎ 215923, 389 Sisowath Quay)* Mains US$5-8. Set in perhaps the most handsome building in the city, this place has a menu offering a range of European and Asian dishes for discerning diners. Prices are at the high end of the Phnom Penh scale, but the ambience might justify the splash.

Heading north along the riverfront, there is a glut of pleasant European restaurants.

Wagon Wheel *(☎ 363601, 353 Sisowath Quay)* Meals from US$4. This place has long been popular for its big breakfasts, but also offers a healthy range of Euro-steaks, Asian food and a splash of fast food.

Riverside Bistro *(☎ 213898, 373 Sisowath Quay)* Meals US$3-6. Occupying another of the classic French villas still standing in Phnom Penh, Riverside offers an eclectic mix of healthy portions from around the world, particularly Central Europe.

La Croisette *(241 Sisowath Quay)* Mains around US$5. This French-style bistro specialises in unique *brochettes* (kebabs) as well as a good selection of steaks and fresh-water fish.

Rendez-Vous *(239 Sisowath Quay)* Dishes US$3-5. This popular riverfront restaurant has a large menu of salads, soups and pizzas, with a range of international offerings to complete the picture. The filet mignon is wholesome.

Riverhouse Restaurant & Lounge *(☎ 212302, cnr Ph 110 & Sisowath Quay)* Asian dishes US$3-5, European mains US$5-8. This classy restaurant on the river is very popular with overseas residents, with a menu ranging from Marrakech to Milan and a slice of Bangkok for good measure.

Topaz *(☎ 211054, 100 Samdech Sothearos Blvd)* Thai dishes US$4-6, European dishes US$6-15, set menu around US$9. This upmarket restaurant is popular with busi-nesspeople and diplomats. It has a sophisti-cated ambience, and while the food is certainly good, the European dishes are ex-pensive in their context. The daily set menus are good value.

Le Bistrot *(4 Ph 29)* Pastas US$4-5, Khmer dishes US$3. The leafy garden here is pleas-ant for lunch, and the home-made pastas are popular at any time. The menu includes some mouthwatering desserts like home-made lemon tart.

Wilhelm Tell *(☎ 430650, 13 Ph 90)* Mains from US$6. Tucked away behind Hotel Le Royal, this Swiss and German restaurant offers huge portions of well-presented Central European classics – a revelation for those who thought it was all bratwurst and sauerkraut.

The Boddhi Tree *(Ph 113)* Dishes US$2-4. Located opposite Tuol Sleng, this is one place that is definitely worth a stop. The menu has a mixture of Asian dishes, sand-wiches, salads and desserts, all freshly prepared and packed full of flavour.

Fast Food

There are a few places around town that do burgers, french fries and the sort. The good news is that at present none of the big fast-food chains grace Phnom Penh, just a few copycats including **Pizza House**, in the Regent Park Hotel, and **Lucky Burger**, part of Lucky Supermarket.

More popular than these copycats are the Khmer burger joints opening around town that pull in students between and after classes. There is a whole strip on Samdech Sothearos Blvd south of the Royal Palace, including **Mondo Burger**. Don't expect Mc Donalds, but at least the food has flavour.

California Hotel *(317 Sisowath Quay)* California Hotel has an American-style diner with a menu of burgers and beef.

The Mex *(☎ 360535, 116 Norodom Blvd)* Dishes US$2-4. This place has takeaway and inexpensive sit-down meals, but it is hardly the most authentic Mexican food this side of Mexico City.

Backpacker Cafes

There are few backpacker cafes of the sort so popular in nearby Vietnam, with the exception of the restaurants in the popular guesthouses.

Mama's Restaurant *(Ph 111)* Dishes around US$1. The food at this little restaur-ant is some of the best value in town and includes unlikely surprises such as stuffed tomatoes and couscous.

Red Corner *(Boeng Kak)* Meals US$2-3. This ramshackle restaurant-bar has one of the tastiest chicken curries in town – a blend of Thai and Sri Lankan – as well as large por-tions of Western food like fried chicken and steaks. It throws in a drink for free and on that note, is not a bad place for a beer either.

Lazy Gecko Café *(Boeng Kak)* This little place has regular barbies for those missing an institution from back home.

Pub Grub & Bar Food

Several of the bars around town offer good pub-style grub, large portions and all, in-cluding the excellent **Cafe Sontiepheap**, **The Pink Elephant**, and **The Rising Sun**. **Teukai Bar** has very good European food at un-European prices. For more on these places, see Bars & Clubs later in this chapter.

Cafes

Garden Center Café *(☎ 363002, 23 Ph 57)* Breakfast US$2-6, lunch US$3-6. This place is outrageously popular with expats for its massive breakfasts and range of lunches. The menu includes a lot of Western food, a selection of Thai and some great desserts such as apple cobbler (crumble) and cream.

Jars of Clay (☎ 300281, 39 Ph 155) Cakes US$1, meals US$2-3. Open Tues-Sat. This little cafe is a great escape from the rigours of the Russian Market. It offers home-made cakes and ice-cream sundaes, as well as light bites like Ploughman's lunches and filled potatoes. If you're not hungry, there is a wide range of teas and coffees.

Java Café (56 Sihanouk Blvd) Open Tues-Sun. This is the place for a coffee fix – it's this cafe's speciality. There is also a menu of light and tasty bites like wraps and salads.

The Shop (39 Ph 40) Salads & sandwiches US$2.50-3.50. This place is not a shop, but more of a cafe or sandwich bar like you'd find back home. The meals are excellent here, as are the adventurous shakes such as banana and date, or mint and cucumber.

Bakeries
Kiwi Bakery (☎ 215784, 83 Ph 63) This is the best-value place in Phnom Penh for fresh breads and cakes, established by a Khmer family returning home after years of running a bakery in New Zealand. It has everything from jam tarts and gingerbread men to cheesecakes and eclairs.

Most of the city's finest hotels also operate bakery outlets with extravagant patisseries, but prices are higher than elsewhere. Try visiting after 6pm when they offer a 50% discount. The larger supermarkets also stock their own range of breads and cakes, freshly baked on the premises.

Self-Catering
Self-catering is easy enough in Phnom Penh, but it often works out considerably more expensive than eating at food stalls in the local markets. The markets are well stocked with fruit and vegetables, fish and meat, all at reasonable prices if you are prepared to bargain a little. Baguettes are widely available around town, and usually cost from 300r to 500r. For something to eat with them, Phnom Penh's supermarkets are remarkably well stocked. Naturally, imported items tend to be expensive, but for around US$2 to US$4 there are treats such as German meats, French cheeses and American snacks.

The best known of the Phnom Penh supermarkets is **Lucky Supermarket** (160 Sihanouk Blvd) with a serious range of products. **Pencil Supermarket** (Ph 214) is a newer Thai-run place, perhaps the largest in town right now, while **Bayon Market** (133 Monivong Blvd) is smaller, but with some nice surprises that don't turn up elsewhere in the city. Many petrol stations include shops with a good selection of imported products; most **Starmart** shops at Caltex petrol stations on major junctions in the city are now open 24 hours.

ENTERTAINMENT
For news of what's happening where while you are in town, check the back page of the Friday edition of *The Cambodia Daily,* the latest issue of the *Phnom Penh Post* or the *Bayon Pearnik.*

Bars & Clubs
Phnom Penh has some great bars and it's definitely worth at least one night on the town when staying here. Many are clustered along the riverfront, but one or two of the best are tucked away in the back streets. Many of the wooden guesthouse platforms built over Boeng Kak double as great sunset bars with cheap drinks and offer much more atmosphere than other guesthouse bars around town. Keep an eye out for happy hours around town as these include two-for-the-price-of-one offers and the like that can save quite a bit of cash. One of the best-known happy hours is at the **Elephant Bar** in Hotel Le Royal from 4pm to 7pm. Drinks are two for one and this includes cocktails like Singapore Slings. Cambodians don't tend to drink in bars, preferring restaurants, karaoke parlours or nightclubs.

Foreign Correspondents' Club (363 Sisowath Quay) This is a definitive drinking hole for tourists and expats alike. There's a touch of colonial about the ambience, but the views are contemporary. Happy hour is from 5.30pm to 7.30pm.

A magnificent travellers palm in front of historic Wat Ounalom, Phnom Penh

Cyclo transport in Phnom Penh

Children preparing for a traditional folk dance

Antiques for sale at Psar Tuol Tom Pong

A woman sells birds captured for religious purposes, on the Phnom Penh waterfront

JULIET COOMBE

A 'petrol station' in Phnom Penh

JULIET COOMBE

Passengers travelling on the roof of the Battambang–Phnom Penh train

ANDREW BURKE

The Pink Elephant (343 Sisowath Quay) This riverfront pub draws a healthy crowd for a middle-of-the-evening session, with good tunes, cheap beer and free pool. The only drawback is the hordes of 'soo-sine, Bangkok Poh, you wan buy flower, one doll-aah' kids passing by all night. Enter the spirit (or consume the spirit) and it's all good fun.

The Rising Sun (20 Ph 178) Bringing a blend of English pub and backpacker cafe to the riverfront area, this bar has professional pub grub, including hearty portions, and a crowd of regulars.

Café Sonteipheap (W www.sonteipheap .com, 234 Ph 63) Also known as Sokha's Peace Café, this friendly bar-cafe has one of the nicer ambiences in Phnom Penh. Warm service, chilled decor and some good tunes make it worth the trek south. It has a great menu of bar food from around the world, including a large selection of sandwiches, and hosts a Brit-style pub quiz every Monday.

Teukei Bar (23 Ph 111) This is one of the coolest bars in town, pumping out a steady flow of ambient sounds and inexpensive drinks. The food here is also excellent, including some of the finest fish in Phnom Penh. Potent rum punches are a speciality at US$1.50 and luckily it is just stumbling distance from several popular guesthouses.

Celtic Tiger Pub (170 Ph 63) Just south of Sihanouk Blvd, this Irish bar has a loyal following among the NGO crowd and cheap drinks.

Freebird (69 Ph 240) This American-style bar is rich on patriotic fervour and popular among some expats. It is a friendly spot for an early evening drink.

Tamarind Bar (31 Ph 240) Farther east on the same road as Freebird is this atmospheric, pricey place rich on decoration and specialising in tapas and North African food.

Heart of Darkness (26 Ph 51) The most popular late-night haunt in Phnom Penh, The Heart, as locals call it, just keeps on growing. It's generally deserted before 10pm but often packed from midnight and the music can be great. There is also a pool table out back, but get your name up early as it is a popular institution. Heart of Darkness usually stays open until the last person leaves.

Howie's Bar (30 Ph 51) Just a couple of doors down from the Heart, this little bar is popular with expats and is a nice bolthole if the Heart is too packed.

Walkabout Hotel (cnr Ph 51 & Ph 174) Open 24 hrs. This bar seems to have changed its image as it has expanded, with working girls outnumbering the customers during the long night shift.

Cathouse Tavern (cnr Ph 51 & Ph 118) Around since the early 90s, this is a pub crossed with a bamboo beach bar, which has its regulars.

Sharky's (Ph 130) This pool bar has the most tables in town. However, there are a lot of young sex workers hanging around, attracting older Western men, which gives it a sleazy edge.

Nexus (68 Sihanouk Blvd) This is a happening little bar-club located near the Independence Monument. Regular DJs, thumping tunes and speciality cocktails make this a popular place at weekends.

Many of the city's nightclubs were closed following a draconian directive by Hun Sen. The dust had yet to settle at the time of writing and so the following long-running places may look slightly different by the time you read this.

Manhattan Club Admission free. Open until daylight. The Manhattan is the closest thing Cambodia has to a full-on club with banging tunes, and is usually heaving most nights. Don't get too excited though, as the music is generally mainstream techno. Drinks are overpriced (US$5 a beer), so if you are feeling thirsty, pop across the road to the drink stalls where beer is available for just US$1 a can.

Martini Pub (402 Mao Tse Toung Blvd) Admission free. Around for years, Martini has both a beer garden showing movies and a dark dance space. Slowly but surely, the drinkers have been outnumbered by the working girls and it can be an intimidating, hard-sell for the uninitiated. Some of the sex workers look disturbingly young.

Live Music

Live music is pretty limited in Phnom Penh. On Saturdays, **The Globe Bar & Restaurant**

Flower Power

Anyone who spends a night or two on the town in Phnom Penh will soon be familiar with young girls and boys entering popular bars and restaurants to sell decorative flowers. The kids are incredibly sweet and most people succumb to their charms and buy a flower or two. All these late nights for young children might not be so bad if they were benefiting from their hard-earned cash, but usually they are not. Look down the road and there will be a *moto* (small motorcycle) driver with an ice bucket full of these flowers waiting to ferry the children to another popular spot. Yet again, the charms of children are exploited for the benefit of adults who should know better but are too poor to worry about it. By all means buy, but bear in mind the child may not reap the reward.

hosts an informal jam session from 9pm – anyone is welcome to join in as long as they can play. Duncan, the owner, was formerly a member of the Psychedelic Furs. There is live music at **Le Deauville** every Saturday at 9pm.

Several of the larger hotels have lobby bands from the Philippines, including the **Intercontinental Hotel** and **Hotel Cambodiana**.

Classical Dance & Arts
Check the latest information on performances at the **Chatomuk Theatre**, just north of Hotel Cambodiana. Officially, it has been turned into a government conference centre, but it is occasionally the venue for displays of traditional dance, as is the **School of Fine Arts** branch in the north of the city.

Apsara Arts Association *(71 Ph 598)* Alternate performances of classical dance and folk dance are held here every Saturday at 7pm (admission US$3). Visitors are also welcome from 7.30am to 10.30am and from 2pm to 5pm Monday to Saturday to watch the students in training (admission by donation).

Sovanna Phum Arts Association *(111 Ph 360)* Impressive traditional shadow puppet performances are held here at 7.30pm on Friday night. Tickets start at about US$3 depending on the story being told. On alternate Fridays there are classical dance performances costing US$5.

It is also possible to watch students training at the **School of Fine Arts** *(Ph 70)*. However, it is important to remember that this is a school of learning – noise and flash photography should be kept to a minimum.

Cinemas
Even if you understand Khmer, Phnom Penh's cinemas are probably best avoided. The patrons are crowded into poorly ventilated halls with no fire escapes, and often it's only pornographic films being screened. However, the king has made an appeal for the reopening of certain historic cinemas dating from the 1950s and 1960s and renovation work has begun.

Movie Street *(Sihanouk Blvd)* This video shop near the Independence Monument offers private rooms with large TVs for that personal cinema experience. It pretty much has all the latest titles from Hollywood, the UK and Europe, and charges about US$10 to US$12 per film.

The French Cultural Centre *(Ph 184)* The FCC has frequent movie screenings – generally at 6pm several times a week. Check at the centre, where a monthly programme is available.

Nexus *(68 Sihanouk Blvd)* Nexus screens one or two free movies every Sunday evening. Double bills kick off at 6pm, single screenings at 7pm. It is a very civilised experience, relaxing in comfy chairs, complete with gin and tonic in hand.

Casinos
The few casinos in Phnom Penh that used to exist were big-buck establishments popular with Asian business travellers, but these were all shut down during 1999 after a spate of kidnappings of prominent Chinese gamblers. No casinos are allowed to be located within 200km of Phnom Penh, except the **Naga Floating Casino**, moored behind Hotel Cambodiana.

SHOPPING

There is some great shopping to be had in Phnom Penh, but don't forget to bargain in the markets or you'll have your 'head shaved'. Most markets are open from around 6.30am to 5.30pm. Shops keep shorter hours. Apart from the well-stocked Psar Tuol Tom Pong and Psar Thmei, there are a host of tasteful shops selling handicrafts and textiles to raise money for projects to assist disadvantaged Cambodians. These are a good place to spend some dollars, as it helps to put a little bit back into the country.

Psar Thmei
ផ្សារថ្មី

The dark-yellow Art Deco Psar Thmei *(New Market; open early morning-early evening)* is also referred to as the Central Market, a reference to its location and size. The central domed hall resembles a Babylonian ziggurat and some claim it ranks as one of the largest domes in the world. It has four wings filled with stalls selling gold and silver jewellery, antique coins, fake name-brand watches, clothing and other such items. Around the main building are stalls offering *krama* (scarves), stationery, household items, cloth for sarongs, flowers and second-hand clothes, usually from Europe and the USA. For photographers, the fresh-food section affords many opportunities. There are a host of good-value food stalls on the structure's western side, which faces Monivong Blvd.

Psar Thmei is undoubtedly the best of Phnom Penh's markets for browsing. It is also the cleanest and has the widest range of products for sale. However, it is definitely not the best place to buy things at because it has a local reputation among Cambodians for head-shaving or overcharging on everything.

Psar Tuol Tom Pong
ផ្សារទួលទំពូង

More commonly referred to by foreigners as the Russian Market (this is where the Russians shopped during the 1980s) this market *(cnr Ph 440 & Ph 163)*, south of Mao Tse Toung Blvd, is the best place in town for souvenir and clothes shopping. It has a large range of real and fake antiquities, including miniature Buddhas, wood carvings, betel nut boxes, silk, silver jewellery, jewellery cases, musical instruments and so on. Much of the stuff is modern and artificially aged, but there are old items in and among the new stuff. Bargain hard as thousands of tourists pass through here each month.

This is also the market where all the Western clothing made in garment factories around Phnom Penh turns up. There is a good range of trousers, skirts, shirts, T-shirts, boxer shorts and shoes, all at just 10% of the price paid back home. Popular brands include Gap, Colombia, Calvin Klein, Quiksilver, Aigle and Next, but more are coming to Cambodia all the time. Double-check Gap stuff, as some of the shirts and T-shirts are just locally made with labels sewn in.

Also available are inexpensive DVDs, CDs and computer programmes, as well as a host of other goodies. This is the one market all visitors should come to at least once during a trip to Phnom Penh.

Psar O Russei
ផ្សារអូរុស្សី

Not to be confused with the aforementioned Psar Tuol Tom Pong, Psar O Russei *(Ph 182)* sells luxury foodstuffs, costume jewellery, imported toiletries, second-hand clothes and everything else you can imagine from hundreds of stalls. The market is housed in a huge new building and is a real labyrinth of a place.

Psar Olympic
ផ្សារអូឡាំពិក

A great deal of wholesaling is done at Psar Olympic, which is near the Olympic Stadium and Wat Moha Montrei. Items for sale include bicycle parts, clothes, electronics and assorted edibles. This is quite a modern market set in a covered location.

Psar Dang Kor
ផ្សារដងកោរ

Psar Dang Kor (cnr Mao Tse Toung & Monireth Blvds) is just north of this intersection. Taxis for the south coast leave from here.

Psar Chaa
ផ្សារចាស់

Psar Chaa (Old Market; Ph 110) lives up to its name. It's a scruffy place that deals in household goods, clothes and jewellery. Small restaurants, food vendors and jewellery stalls are scattered throughout the area, as well as some good fresh-fruit stalls outside.

Shopping For a Cause
These are just some of the best-known shops that assist disadvantaged Cambodians.

NCDP Handicrafts (3 Norodom Blvd) This shop was set up by the National Centre for Disabled Persons (NCDP). Articles on sale include silk and leather bags, slippers, krama, shirts, wallets and purses, and notebooks and greeting cards. Part of the building is an inexpensive cafe where staff serve a variety of food.

Wat Than Handicrafts (Norodom Blvd) The handicrafts shop here is along similar lines to NCDP Handicrafts. Proceeds go to help land-mine and polio victims. The emphasis here is on products made from Khmer silk.

Khemara Handicrafts (18 Ph 302) Run by a local NGO and women's self-help groups, this place has a nice garden setting. Downstairs is a cafe, while the shop upstairs is a relaxing place for some hassle-free browsing through the silk collection and other handicrafts.

Made in Cambodia (373 Sisowath Quay) Tucked away underneath FCC, this is another good gift shop helping disabled people in Cambodia. It specialises in silk products, but also offers wood carvings and jewellery.

Rajana (170 Ph 450; in Psar Tuol Tom Pong) There are two convenient branches of Rajana, aimed at promoting fair wages and training. They have a beautiful selection of cards, some quirky metalware products, quality jewellery, bamboo crafts and a range of condiments from Cambodia.

Songkhem Collection (118 Ph 113) Opposite Tuol Sleng, this shop has the inevitable silk, as well as some delightful handmade cards and coconut shell utensils, although some might be a little taken aback by all the Christian religious carvings in a Buddhist country.

Nyemo (33 Ph 310) Helping disadvantaged women back into the workplace, Nyemo focuses on quality silk.

Art & Antiques
There are plenty of shops selling locally produced paintings along Ph 178 opposite the National Museum. It used to be a pretty sorry selection of the amateurish Angkor paintings seen all over the country, but now with a new generation of artists coming up, the selection is much better. It is necessary to bargain vigorously.

There are several boutiques and antique shops around the city, including some very expensive ones in the city's luxury hotels. When it comes to genuine antiques, **Hanuman Fine Arts Shop** (34 Ph 222) has a large collection of classic Buddhas, old silverware and ancient textiles, while **Orient** (Sisowath Quay), near La Croisette, has a range of expensive Asian furniture and pottery from China and the region.

Postcards
Postcards are widely available in Phnom Penh. The easiest places to find them are Psar Thmei or Psar Tuol Tom Pong, where books of 10 cost around US$1 depending on your negotiating skills. Better quality, but more expensive postcards are available at bookshops and hotels in town.

Film
Camera film is available all over the city – just pick your brand and there will be a shop within a few hundred metres. The best place for developing photos is **City Colour Photo** (123 Monivong Blvd).

GETTING THERE & AWAY
Air
For information on international and domestic air services to and from Phnom Penh, see the Getting There & Away and Getting Around chapters earlier in this book.

Airline offices around town include:

Air France (☎ 219220, W www.airfrance.com) 389 Sisowath Quay
Bangkok Airways (☎ 722545, W www.bangkok air.com) 61 Ph 214
China Southern Airlines (☎ 424588, W www.cs -air.com) A3 Regency Square, Intercontinental Hotel
Dragonair (☎ 424300, W www.dragonair.com) A4 Regency Square, Intercontinental Hotel
Lao Aviation (☎ 216563, W www.lao-aviation .com) 58 Sihanouk Blvd
Malaysia Airlines (☎ 426688, W www.malaysia airlines.com.my) Diamond Hotel, 172 Monivong Blvd
Mandarin Airlines (☎ 216601, W www.man darin-airlines.com) 281 Norodom Blvd
President Airlines (☎ 212887) 50 Norodom Blvd
Royal Phnom Penh Airways (☎ 217419, W www.royalpnhair.com) 209 Ph 19
Shanghai Airlines (☎ 723999, W www.shanghai -air.com) 19 Ph 106
Siem Reap Airways (☎ 426707, W www.siem reapairways.com) 61 Ph 214
Silk Air (☎ 426808, W www.silkair.net) Mi Casa Cambodiana, 313 Sisowath Quay
Thai Airways International (☎ 214359, W www.thaiair.com) A15 Regency Square, Intercontinental Hotel
Vietnam Airlines (☎ 363396, W www.vietnam air.com.vn) 41 Ph 214

Bus
There are increasing numbers of bus services opening as roads are steadily rebuilt. By 2004, there should be comfortable bus services to most parts of the country. The information here is brief; for more details, see Getting There & Away in the relevant destination section. For Sihanoukville (12,000r, three to four hours), GST and Ho Wah Genting both have large, comfortable air-con buses offering kung fu videos and complimentary water. Buses depart from the ticket offices, located southwest of Psar Thmei. Capitol tours also operate buses on this route. For departure and arrival times,

see the Sihanoukville section in the South Coast chapter.

Ho Wah Genting also runs regular services to Kompong Cham (7000r, two hours, six daily), Kompong Chhnang (4500r, two hours, 11 daily), Udong (3000r, one hour, 13 daily), and Takeo (4500r, two hours, 10 daily), Tonlé Bati (3000r, one hour, 10 daily) and Phnom Chisor (4000r, 1½ hours), which makes sightseeing around the capital much cheaper than it used to be. The buses are clean, comfortable and cheap. Buses to Neak Luong (4000r) via Kien Svay (1500r) every hour. GST also run services to Kompong Cham (7000r, two hours, twice daily).

The bigger guesthouses such as Capitol are now running bus services between Phnom Penh and Siem Reap, departing 7.30am and costing US$10, but it's slow-going compared with pick-ups while the road remains bad.

Ho Chi Minh City Several guesthouses such as Capitol (US$6, departs 6.45am) and Narin (US$6, departs 6.45am) have daily bus services between Phnom Penh and Ho Chi Minh City, with a change of bus on the border. For more details on the road run, as well as the boat run, see the Getting There & Away chapter earlier in this book.

Train
Train travel may be pretty cheap, even with the foreigner price of three times the Khmer price, but it is generally not the most time-effective way to travel, as trains are extremely slow (they travel at about 20km/h). Yes, for a few minutes you can outrun the train! There is one train a day on both the line south and the line west. If the trains leave Phnom Penh Monday, they return Tuesday and so on, so always check the latest schedule at the station a couple of days ahead.

Trains to Takeo (3400r, three hours, 75km), Kampot (7500r, six hours, 166km) and Sihanoukville (12,300r, 12 hours, 270km) leave at 6.20am every other day.

Trains to Battambang (12,400r, 14 to 16 hours, 274km), and Pursat (7500r, eight hours, 165km) depart from the Phnom Penh train station at 6.20am every other day.

Taxi, Pick-up & Minibus

Taxis, pick-ups and minibuses leave Phnom Penh for destinations all over the country. Vehicles for the south coast leave from Psar Dang Kor in the southwest of the city, those for Svay Rieng and Vietnam leave from Chbah Ampeau taxi park on the eastern side of Monivong Bridge in the south of town, while those for most other destinations leave from around Psar Thmei. Different vehicles run different routes depending on the quality of the road. The following prices are those quoted for the most commonly used vehicle on that particular route. For more information on journeys to specific destinations, see Getting There & Away in the relevant destination sections.

Share-taxis (10,000r, three hours) and minibuses (7000r, four hours) run to Sihanoukville, but it's not a pleasant way to travel when compared with the bus services. Taxis go to Kampot (8000r, three hours), but the minibuses are cheaper (6000r). To travel as far as Takeo costs just 6000r in a taxi and only 3000r in a minibus.

Taxis go to the Vietnam border (US$25 to charter or US$5 per person, four hours). Minibuses also make the journey and are cheaper (8000r). From Moc Bai it costs about US$5 per person to downtown Ho Chi Minh City (two hours). Taxis and minibuses leave from Chbah Ampeau.

It is also possible to hire taxis on a per-day basis. Rates start at US$25 for around Phnom Penh and nearby destinations, and then go up according to distance and the language skills of the driver.

Pick-up trucks are the best bet for tackling most of the country's harsher roads, including the journey to Siem Reap (25,000/10,000r inside/on the back, eight to 10 hours), Battambang (20,000/8000r, seven hours) and Pursat (10,000/4000r, four hours).

Minibuses run to Skuon (3000r), Kompong Cham (5000r) and Kompong Thom (6000r). For Kompong Cham, the large aircon buses are safer, while for Kompong Thom the share taxis (10,000r) are more comfortable. From Kompong Cham, there is transport to the northeast of the country, while from Kompong Thom, there are links to Siem Reap and Tbeng Meanchey in Preah Vihear Province.

Boat

There are numerous ferry operators that used to be located north of the Chruoy Changvar Bridge, but are steadily relocating to the new tourist boat dock on Sisowath Quay, at the eastern end of Ph 106. Boats go to Siem Reap up the Tonlé Sap and to Kompong Cham, Chhlong, Kratie and Stung Treng on the Mekong.

Siem Reap The most popular boat services are those to Siem Reap (US$25, five hours), but this popularity is based on expensive domestic flights and bad roads, rather than the particular merits of the journey itself. Several companies have daily services departing at 7am from a dock north of Chruoy Changvar Bridge and usually take it in turns to make the run. The first stretch of the journey along the river is scenic, but once the boat hits the lake, the fun is over as it is a vast inland sea with not a village in sight.

Express services serving Siem Reap are overcrowded, and often appear to have nothing in the way of safety gear. Most tourists prefer to sit on the roof of the express boats, but don't forget a head covering and sunscreen as thick as paint. However, less-nimble travellers or fair-skinned folk might prefer to be inside. Unfortunately, not everyone can sit inside, as companies sell twice as many tickets as there are seats! The one exception is Channa boat in the wet season, which operates a huge hydrofoil and no-one is allowed on the roof. In the dry season, the boats are very small and dangerously overcrowded to the point that they have sunk, as in April 2000.

Guesthouses can save you anything from US$2 to US$4 on the price. US$25 is an unofficial foreigner price (locals pay 50,000r), which has to come down once the road is upgraded all the way to Siem Reap. The boat operators and accommodation owners probably split the difference between them, but there is little anyone can do about it apart from voting with the feet and travelling by another means.

Slow boats to Siem Reap (25,000r, 24 to 36 hours) leave on an irregular basis, so it is important to ask ahead about the next departure. They are not the most stable of boats if the winds pick up across the Tonlé Sap lake. If you really want to travel this way, buy a hammock at Psar Thmei and stock up on food and drinks for the trip.

For details on the boat dock in Siem Reap, see the Siem Reap chapter later in the book.

Up the Mekong Possible stops on the Mekong River are Kompong Cham, Kratie, Chhlong and Stung Treng. There are no foreigner prices on these routes, making them much better value and generally less overcrowded.

There are daily express boats from Phnom Penh to Kompong Cham (10,000r, 2½ hours) and Kratie (30,000r, five hours). Boats leave at 7am and also stop at Chhlong (25,000r, 4½ hours), the start of the new logging road to Mondulkiri. The bus is more sensible for Kompong Cham, the boat much more so for Kratie. Express services from Phnom Penh to Stung Treng operate from July through November, as the river level drops in the dry season, and the 10-hour run costs 60,000r. This is far too long on a boat and it is much more pleasant to break the journey in Kratie, see the dolphins and continue the journey the next day.

There are also slow cargo boats running up the Mekong, but slow is the operative word. From Phnom Penh to Kompong Cham takes one day and to Kratie two days and one night.

For more details on boat services up the Mekong, see the Kompong Cham and Kratie and Stung Treng sections in the Eastern Cambodia chapter.

GETTING AROUND

Phnom Penh is not too bad to get around, as traffic is lighter than in neighbouring cities such as Bangkok, hardly surprising really. The worst time for bottlenecks is the early evening from 5pm to 7pm, particularly around Monivong and Norodom Blvds.

To/From the Airport

Pochentong International Airport is 7km west of central Phnom Penh, via Pochentong Blvd. Official taxis from the airport to the city centre cost US$7 and unofficial taxes are no longer allowed to wait at the terminal. Taxi drivers will take you to only one destination for this price, so make sure that they take you to where you want to go, not where they want you to go. A moto into town should cost between US$1 and US$1.50 depending on bargaining skills. The journey usually takes 30 minutes or less.

Heading to the airport from central Phnom Penh, a taxi should cost no more than US$5.

Bus

Local buses don't really exist in Phnom Penh. Most Cambodians use motos or cyclos to get around the city. A pilot scheme was set up in summer 2001 for a month, but most city residents have become just too used to the convenience of travelling door to door to take to it yet. Give it five years and worse traffic jams.

Car & Motorcycle

Car hire is available through travel agencies, guesthouses and hotels in Phnom Penh. Everything from cars (US$25) to 4WDs (US$50 and up) are available for travelling around the city. Prices rise the greater the distance travelled.

There are numerous motorbike hire places around town. Bear in mind that motorbike theft is a problem in Phnom Penh, and if the bike gets stolen you will be liable. Ask for a lock and use it, plus keep the bike in guarded parking areas when possible, such as outside markets (300r). The best places for motorbike hire are Lucky! Lucky! and New! New! on Monivong Blvd next to the Hong Kong Hotel. A 100cc Honda costs US$3 to US$4 per day or US$20 per week and 250cc dirt bikes cost US$7 per day or US$40 a week. For details on buying a motorbike in Phnom Penh, see the Getting Around chapter earlier in the book.

Taxi

Phnom Penh has no metered taxis of the sort seen in Vietnam. Bailey's Taxis (☎ 012-890000) and Taxi Vantha (☎ 012-855000) offer taxis 24 hours a day, but have a limited number of cars. They do the airport run for US$5 and charge about US$1 per kilometre elsewhere.

Private taxis tend to wait outside popular nightspots, but it is important to agree on a price in advance.

Bicycle

It is possible to hire bicycles at the Capitol Guesthouse for 4000r a day, but take a look at the anarchic traffic conditions before venturing forth. Once you get used to the chaos, it can be a pleasant way to get around, if a little dusty.

Moto

Motos are easily recognisable by the baseball caps favoured by the drivers. In areas frequented by foreigners, moto drivers generally speak English and sometimes a little French. Elsewhere around town it can be difficult to find anyone who understands where you want to go – see the 'We're on a Road to Nowhere' boxed text for ways to survive. Most trips are about 1000r and more again at night, although if you want to get from one end of the city to the other you have to pay more. Prices are rarely negotiated in advance when taking rides. However, those staying in a luxury hotel must negotiate before they hop

on or they will find themselves well and truly ripped off. Likewise, night owls taking a moto home from popular drinking holes should consider negotiating to avoid an expensive surprise.

Many of the moto drivers who wait outside the popular guesthouses and hotels have good English and are able to act as guides for a daily rate of about US$6 to US$8 depending on the destinations.

Cyclo

Cyclos are still common on the streets of Phnom Penh, but have lost a lot of business to the moto drivers. It is a more relaxing way to see the sights in the centre of town, but they are just too slow for going from one end of the city to another. For a day of sightseeing, think around US$5 to US$7 depending on exactly where you go and how many hours pedalling it includes. Late at night, they would have to be considered a security hazard for all but the shortest of journeys, but most drivers are asleep in their cyclos at this time anyway. Costs are generally similar to moto fares.

Around Phnom Penh

There are several attractions around Phnom Penh that make good day trips out of the capital, although they are quite low key when compared with what's on offer in other parts of the country. The Angkorian temple

---

We're on a Road to Nowhere

Taking a ride on a *moto* (small motorcycle with driver) or *cyclo* (pedicab) is not quite as easy it looks. Drivers who loiter around guesthouses, hotels, restaurants and bars may speak streetwise English and know the city well, but elsewhere the knowledge and understanding required to get you to your destination dries up fast. Flag a moto or cyclo down on the street or grab one from outside the market and you could end up pretty much anywhere in the city. You name your destination, and they nod confidently, eager for the extra money a foreigner may bring, but not having the first clue of where you want to go. They start driving or pedalling furiously down the road and await your instructions. You don't give them any instructions, as you think they know where they are going. Before you realise it, you are halfway to Thailand or Vietnam. The moral of the story is always carry a map of Phnom Penh and keep a close eye on the driver unless he speaks enough English to understand where the hell you want to go.

of Tonlé Bati and the hilltop pagoda of Phnom Chisor are best visited in one trip, and can be incorporated into a southward journey to either Takeo or Kampot, both covered in the South Coast chapter. Phnom Udong, once the capital of Cambodia, is also a pleasant day trip and can be combined with a visit to Kompong Chhnang, a 'genuine' Cambodian town, covered in the Northwestern Cambodia chapter.

There is now a clean, comfortable and cheap bus network operated by the Ho Wah Genting Bus Company covering most of the places in this chapter. For experienced riders, motorcycles are another interesting way to visit these attractions, as there are plenty of small villages along the way. See the Getting Around section earlier in this chapter for details on motorbike rentals. If time is more important than money, you can rent a taxi to whisk you around for between US$25 and US$30 a day, depending on the destination. Capitol Guesthouse offer inexpensive tours with or without a guide to most of the places covered here.

KIEN SVAY
កៀនស្វាយ

Kien Svay is a very popular picnic area on a small tributary of the Mekong. Hundreds of bamboo huts have been built over the water and Khmers love to come here and sit around gossiping and munching at the weekend.

Kien Svay is a peculiarly Cambodian institution, a mixture of the universal love of picnicking by the water, and the unique Khmer fondness for lounging about on mats. It works like this: for 1500r or so an hour, picnickers rent an area on a raised open hut covered with reed mats. Be sure to agree on the price *before* you rent a space. The tiny boat trip to the huts should be included in the price.

All sorts of food is sold at Kien Svay, although it is necessary to bargain to ensure a fair price. Prices generally seem reasonable thanks to the massive competition – there are perhaps 50 or more sellers here. Popular dishes include grilled chicken and fish, river lobster and fresh fruit. The area

is pretty deserted during the week, but this can make it a calmer time to picnic.

Getting There & Away
Kien Svay is a district in Kandal Province and the actual picnic spot is just before the small town of Koki, about 15km east of Phnom Penh. To get here from Phnom Penh, turn left off NH1, which links Phnom Penh with Ho Chi Minh City, through a wat-style gate at a point 15km east of the Monivong Bridge. You will know you are on the right track if you see plenty of beggars and hundreds of cars. Buses regularly depart from Psar Thmei for Kien Svay and cost just 1500r. The local way to get there would be to take a *remorque-moto* (trailer pulled by a motorcycle) from the Chbah Ampeau taxi and minibus station, just east of the Monivong Bridge. This would cost around 1000r, but the trip is very slow, if somewhat amusing. A round-trip moto should cost about US$4.

PHNOM UDONG
ភ្នំឧត្តុង្គ

Udong (the Victorious) served as the capital of Cambodia under several sovereigns between 1618 and 1866. A number of kings, including King Norodom, were crowned here. The main attractions these days are the two humps of Phnom Udong, which have several stupas on them. Both ends of the ridge have good views of the Cambodian countryside dotted with innumerable sugar-palm trees. From Phnom Penh's taller buildings (weather permitting) the bluffs of Udong appear as two symmetrical hills – one of which is topped with spires – in the middle of the plains stretching northward from the city.

Udong is not a major attraction, but for those with the time it's worth seeing. It's generally very quiet, though picnickers tend to arrive from Phnom Penh on the weekends. The Ministries of Culture and Tourism have big plans for the place and there is a lot of work underway on upgrading stairways and stupas.

The smaller ridge has two structures – both heavily damaged – and several stupas on top. **Ta San Mosque** faces westward towards Mecca. Only the bullet- and shrapnel-pocked walls survived the years of Khmer Rouge rule, though there are said to be plans to rebuild the entire structure. Across the plains to the south of the mosque you can see **Phnom Vihear Leu**, a small hill on which a vihara stands between two white poles. To the right of the vihara is a building used as a prison under Pol Pot's rule. To the left of the vihara and below it is a pagoda known as **Arey Ka Sap**.

The larger ridge, Phnom Preah Reach Throap (Hill of the Royal Fortune), is so named because a 16th-century Khmer king is said to have hidden the national treasury here during a war with the Thais. The most impressive structure on Phnom Preah Reach Throap is **Vihear Preah Ath Roes** (Vihara of the 18 Cubit Buddha). The vihara and the Buddha, dedicated in 1911 by King Sisowath, were blown up by the Khmer Rouge in 1977; only sections of the walls, the bases of eight enormous columns and the right arm and part of the right side of the Buddha remain.

About 120m northwest of Vihear Preah Ath Roes is a line of small viharas. The first is **Vihear Preah Ko**, a brick-roofed structure that contains a statue of Preah Ko, the sacred bull; the original statue was carried away by the Thais long ago. The second structure, which has a seated Buddha inside, is **Vihear Preah Keo**. The third is **Vihear Prak Neak**, its cracked walls topped with a temporary thatch roof. Inside is a seated Buddha who is guarded by a naga (*prak neak* means 'protected by a naga').

At the northwestern extremity of the ridge stand three large stupas. The first is the cement **Chet Dey Mak Proum**, the final resting place of King Monivong (reigned 1927–41). Decorated with *garuda* (half-man, half-bird creatures), floral designs and elephants, it has four faces on top. The middle stupa, **Tray Troeng**, is decorated with coloured tiles; it was built in 1891 by King Norodom for the ashes of his father, King Ang Duong (reigned 1845–59). But some say King Ang Duong was buried next to the Silver Pagoda in Phnom Penh. The third stupa, **Damrei Sam**

Poan, was built by King Chey Chethar II (reigned 1618–26) for the ashes of his predecessor, King Soriyopor.

An eastward-oriented staircase leads down the hillside from the stupa of King Monivong. Just north of its base is a pavilion decorated with graphic murals depicting Khmer Rouge atrocities.

At the base of the ridge, close to the path, is a **memorial** to the victims of Pol Pot that contains the bones of some of the people who were buried in approximately 100 mass graves, each containing about a dozen bodies. Instruments of torture were unearthed along with the bones when a number of the 2m by 2.5m pits were disinterred in 1981 and 1982.

Places to Eat

There are plenty of **Cambodian snack stalls** around the base of the hill, as well as some **small restaurants** back at the turnoff from NH5. For a good view of Phnom Udong, there are several **restaurants** opposite the Prek Kdam ferry about 9km back towards Phnom Penh. They are built on wooden platforms over the wet-season flood plains, but are only really convenient for those with their own transport.

Getting There & Away

Udong is 41km from the capital. To get there, head north out of Phnom Penh on NH5. Continue past Prek Kdam ferry for 4.5km and turn left (south) at the archway. Udong is 3.5km south of the turn-off; the access road goes through the village of Psar Dek Krom, and passes by a memorial to Pol Pot's victims and a structure known as the Blue Stupa, before arriving at a short staircase.

A cheap and convenient way to get to Udong is by air-con local bus (3000r, one hour) from Phnom Penh. Buses depart from near Psar Thmei and run regularly throughout the day. The bus drivers can drop you at the access road to Udong, from where you can arrange a moto to the base of the hill for about 1500r. Buses to/from Kompong Chhnang also stop here, so you can combine your visit to the temples with a visit to a Cambodian town that sees few tourists.

A taxi from Phnom Penh to Phnom Udong and back will cost around US$25. It might be a good idea to hire the car for the day and include another destination such as Kompong Chhnang. Moto drivers also run people to Udong for about US$6 for the day, but when compared with the bus this isn't the most pleasant way to go, as the road is pretty busy and very dusty.

TONLÉ BATI
ទន្លេបាទី

Ta Prohm
តាព្រហ្ម

The laterite temple of Ta Prohm *(admission US$2)* was built by King Jayavarman VII (reigned 1181–1219) on the site of an ancient 6th-century Khmer shrine. A stele found here dates from 1574.

The main sanctuary consists of five chambers; in each is a *linga* (phallic symbol), all of which show signs of the destruction wrought by the Khmer Rouge.

Entering the sanctuary from the east gate, 15m ahead on the right is a bas-relief depicting a woman and a man who is bowing

to another, larger woman. The smaller woman has just given birth and failed to show proper respect for the midwife (the larger woman). The new mother has been condemned to carry the afterbirth on her head in a box for the rest of her life. The husband is asking that his wife be forgiven.

Around the corner to the right of the north gate is a bas-relief in which a king sits to the right of his wife. Because she has been unfaithful, a servant in the scene below is shown trampling her to death with a horse.

Inside the north gate is a damaged statue of the Hindu god Preah Noreay. Women come here to pray for the birth of children.

Yeay Peau
យាយពៅ

Yeay Peau temple, named after King Ta Prohm's mother, is 150m north of Ta Prohm. Legend has it that Peau gave birth to a son, Prohm. When Prohm discovered his father was King Preah Ket Mealea, he set off to live with the king. After a few years, he returned to his mother but did not recognise her and, taken by her beauty, asked her to become his wife. He refused to believe Peau's protests that she was his mother.

To settle the matter, Peau suggested that she and Prohm build a temple; whoever finished first would get their way. The contest was held at night, with the women helping Peau and the men helping Prohm. After many hours, Peau sent aloft an artificial morning star. The men, thinking it was dawn, went to sleep. Meanwhile Peau's temple was completed, and Prohm, defeated, recognised Peau as his mother.

Nearby is Wat Tonlé Bati, a modern cement structure heavily damaged by the Khmer Rouge. The only remnant of the pagoda's pre-1975 complement of statues is an 80cm-high metal Buddha's head.

The Lakefront
About 300m northwest of Ta Prohm, a long, narrow peninsula juts into Tonlé Bati. It used to be packed on Sunday with vendors selling food, drink and fruit, but their high prices have led most Phnom Penh residents to give

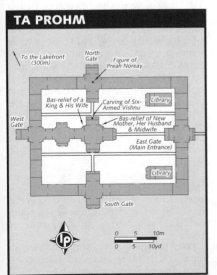

TA PROHM

To the Lakefront (300m)

North Gate

Figure of Preah Noreay

Bas-relief of a King & His Wife

Carving of Six-Armed Vishnu

Library

West Gate

Bas-relief of New Mother, Her Husband & Midwife

East Gate (Main Entrance)

Library

South Gate

0   5   10m
0   5   10yd

the place a miss or bring picnics. You are best to do likewise.

Getting There & Away

The access road to Ta Prohm intersects NH2 at a point 31km south of Phnom Penh, 19km north of the access road to Phnom Chisor and 46km north of Takeo town. The temple is 2.5km from the highway.

Buses leave for Takeo at fairly regular intervals throughout the day and can drop passengers at the access road. The fare is 3000r. The first bus from Phnom Penh leaves at 7am and there are hourly services until 4pm. Buses returning from Takeo in the afternoon leave hourly from 12pm to 4pm and take about one hour to get to Tonlé Bati. If you are heading to the zoo at Phnom Tamao (see the following entry) these services also apply.

PHNOM TAMAO WILDLIFE SANCTUARY
ភ្នំតាម៉ៅ

Phnom Tamao is the site of Cambodia's leading wildlife sanctuary *(admission 1000r)*, a home for animals confiscated from traffickers or saved from poachers traps. It occupies a vast site south of the capital and its animals are kept in varying conditions that are rapidly improving. Spread out as it is, it feels like a zoo crossed with a safari park, and gradually some of this space is being used to provide a better habitat for the larger animals. The flagship enclosure is that of the sun bears, funded by an Australian NGO, and a young cub was recently born in captivity – a first here. The tigers have been given a large, new enclosure, but the solitary lion still looks pretty lost, lonely and miserable. If you don't like zoos you probably won't like this one, but it is certainly far better than many of the animal prisons you see elsewhere in the developing world. At the rate it is improving, Phnom Tamao could be one of the best animal sanctuaries in the region in a couple of years.

Getting There & Away

Phnom Tamao is about 44km from Phnom Penh down NH2. Take a left turn after the sign for the zoo (36km), and it is 6km farther down a sandy track. On weekends, you can combine an air-con bus ride with a remorque-moto, but on weekdays it may be easier to rent a motorbike if you are used to riding. See the previous Tonlé Bati section for details on bus times and prices.

PHNOM CHISOR
ភ្នំជីស៊ូ

Phnom Chisor is an Angkorian-era temple set upon a solitary hill in Takeo Province. Try to get to Phnom Chisor early in the morning or late in the afternoon, as it is a very uncomfortable climb in the heat of the midday sun.

The main temple stands at the eastern side of the hilltop. Constructed of laterite and brick with carved lintels of sandstone, the complex is surrounded by the partially ruined walls of a 2.5m-wide gallery with windows.

Inscriptions found here date from the 11th century, when this site was known as Suryagiri. The wooden doors to the sanctuary in the centre of the complex, which open to the east, are decorated with carvings of figures standing on pigs. Inside the sanctuary are statues of the Buddha.

On the plain to the east of Phnom Chisor are the sanctuaries of **Sen Thmol** (at the bottom of Phnom Chisor) and **Sen Ravang** (farther east), and the former sacred pond of **Tonlé Om**. All three of these features form a straight line from Phnom Chisor in the direction of Angkor. During rituals held here 900 years ago, the king, his Brahmans and their entourage would climb a monumental 400 steps to Suryagiri from this direction.

There is a spectacular view of the temples and plains from the roofless gallery opposite the wooden doors to the central shrine. Near the main temple is a modern Buddhist vihara that is used by resident monks.

There are two paths up the 100m-high ridge, which takes about 15 minutes to climb. The northern path, which has a mild gradient, begins at a cement pavilion with windows shaped like the squared-off silhouette of a bell. The building is topped with a miniature replica of an Angkorian-style tower. The steeper southern route, which begins 600m south of the northern path, consists of a long stairway. A good way to see the view in all directions is to go up the northern path and come down the southern stairway.

Getting There & Away
The intersection of NH2 and the east-bound access road to Phnom Chisor is marked by the two brick towers of Prasat Neang Khmau (Temple of the Black Virgin), an 11th-century temple that may have once served as a sanctuary to Kali, the dark goddess of destruction. These towers are located 50km south of central Phnom Penh and 27km north of Takeo town. It's about 4km from the highway to the base of the hill.

The cheapest way to get to Phnom Chisor is to take a Takeo bus from Phnom Penh and ask to be let off at Prasat Neang Khmau. This costs 4000r and from here you can take a moto to the bottom of the hill for about 1500r. See Getting There & Away in the Tonlé Bati section earlier for details on times. Alternatively, you can charter a taxi for about US$25 to visit both Phnom Chisor and Tonlé Bati, or there is the option of hiring a motorcycle in Phnom Penh.

KIRIROM NATIONAL PARK
ឧទ្យានជាតិគីរីរម្យ
The hill station of Kirirom, set amid pine forests 675m above sea level, has been established as a national park. It is 112km southwest of Phnom Penh in **Chuor Phnom Damrei** (Elephant Mountains) to the west of NH4. It is popular with Khmers at weekends, although this has led to something of a litter problem, which blights parts of the park. It is not the most interesting of Cambodia's national parks, but it is the most accessible from the capital and the scenery is notably different from the flat agricultural land that surrounds Phnom Penh, and the climate is also noticeably cooler. There is a small **guesthouse** in the park with rooms for US$10.

Getting There & Away
Unless you have your own transport it is not that easy to get to Kirirom National Park because it is about 25km east of NH4. You could catch a bus going to Sihanoukville and ask to be let off at Kirirom or Preah Suramarit Kossomak National Park (the full name in Khmer). However, you would still have to hire a moto to drive you around the park itself. The best way to visit is to hire a motorcycle in Phnom Penh or get a group together and charter a taxi for about US$40. Coming under your own steam, the turn-off for the park is about 85km from Phnom Penh, and is marked by a sign on the right.

Siem Reap សៀមរាប

☎ 063 • pop 85,000

Siem Reap is the gateway to the temples of Angkor, Cambodia's spiritual and cultural heartland. It was a quiet, sleepy backwater until a few years ago and even now, in the midst of a tourism boom, it remains a charming town with rural qualities. Old French shophouses, shady tree-lined boulevards and a gentle winding river are remnants of the past, while five-star hotels, air-conditioned buses and international restaurants are pointers to the future. There is a gold rush in Siem Reap: hotels going up every month, guesthouses and restaurants every week. Siem Reapolinos it is thankfully not, but if developers have their way it will certainly be a very different town in years to come. Tourism is the lifeblood of Siem Reap. The world has finally woken up to Angkor and this little town is set for big, big changes.

Siem Reap (see-**em** ree-**ep**) is just north of the western extent of the Tonlé Sap lake. The name Siem Reap means 'Siamese Defeated', hardly the most subtle name for a major city near Thailand and a touch ironic given that Thailand ultimately defeated Cambodia, and controlled Siem Reap and Angkor from 1794 to 1907.

Siem Reap is a great place to relax for several days and many visitors end up staying a week, thanks to a good range of facilities and the world's most magnificent temples slapbang on the doorstep. Angkor is a place to be savoured, not rushed, and Siem Reap is the perfect place from which to plan your adventures.

ORIENTATION

It is possible to walk around most of Siem Reap in just an hour or so; there is little risk of getting lost. National Hwy 6 (NH6) cuts through the northern part of the town, past Psar Leu (Central Market), the Royal Residence and the Grand Hotel d'Angkor, and then heads out to the airport and beyond. Stung Siem Reap flows north-south through the centre of town, and has enough bridges

Highlights

- Explore the bird-lovers paradise Prek Toal, home to rare storks and pelicans.
- View outstanding sunsets at the Vietnamese floating village of Chong Kneas.
- Indulge in a massage – the right medicine for weary bodies.
- Learn some groovy moves at the town's dark and noisy nightclubs.

that you won't have to worry too much about being on the wrong side.

Angkor Wat and Angkor Thom are only 6km and 8km north of town respectively, while the Roluos group of temples is 13km east of town along NH6 – see the Temples of Angkor map in the 'Temples of Angkor' special section for the location of these and other places out of the city centre.

INFORMATION
Tourist Offices

Angkor Tourism is in a white building opposite the Grand Hotel d'Angkor. There's a sign saying 'Tourist Information', but this is a little optimistic unless you come as a paid-up client on one of their private tours. Khmer Angkor Tour Guides Association is also based here, and is the best place to arrange an official guide for Angkor – see the 'Temples of Angkor' special section for more details.

There are now a couple of free guides produced on Siem Reap and the Angkor area. The *Siem Reap Angkor Visitors Guide* comes out four times a year, and focuses mainly on businesses around town.

Money

There are several banks in Siem Reap. The Cambodian Commercial Bank (CCB; ☎ 380154), at 130 Phlauv (Ph) Sivatha, is open weekdays from 8am to 3.30pm and changes travellers cheques for a 2% commission. Cash advances (with a limit of US$2000) are available on major credit cards for a flat fee of US$5 for advances up to US$250, and 2% thereafter. The bank has a very useful exchange booth, open daily from 9am to 5pm, in the eastern corner of Psar Chaa (Old Market) that offers the same services as the main branch.

Canadia Bank (☎ 964808), opposite Psar Chaa, offers free cash advances on Master-Card and can change travellers cheques in most major currencies.

Mekong Bank (☎ 964417), at 43 Ph Sivatha, can arrange cash advances on Visa cards for a charge of US$5. It also has an after-hours booth here, open Monday to Saturday from 3.30pm to 8pm and Sunday from 8am to 1pm.

The National Bank of Cambodia (☎ 963534), near Psar Chaa, is open weekdays from 7.30am to 4pm. It also charges a 2% commission for changing travellers cheques, but doesn't provide cash advances.

Post & Communications

The post office is along the river, 400m south of the Grand Hotel d'Angkor. It is probably best to save any post for Phnom Penh or Bangkok, where services are more reliable; many people have reported mail going astray.

Making international calls from Siem Reap is as simple as from Phnom Penh. The cheapest way is to use the services offered by the major Internet cafes, at around US$0.50

per minute, but there can be a lot of echo and delay. The cheapest unblemished calls can be arranged through one of the many private booths advertising telephone services. There are a few Ministry of Post and Telecommunications (MPTC) and Camintel public phone booths around town, including several around Psar Chaa. Phonecards are sold at shops and hotels around town. For domestic calls, it is cheaper to call from a private booth. Hotels impose hefty surcharges on calls.

If you need to send or receive faxes and are not based in a hotel that offers this service, try one of the many reasonably priced Internet cafes in the Psar Chaa area.

Emergency

There is a tourist police office (☎ 012-969991) in Siem Reap's central police station.

Anyone who has a major injury or falls seriously ill in Siem Reap is best to seek treatment in Bangkok. Siem Reap's best clinic is the Naga Medical Centre (☎ 380344) at 593 NH6 west. It's open 24 hours.

Dangers & Annoyances

There are a lot of commission scams in Siem Reap involving certain guesthouses and small hotels as well as *moto* (small motorcycle) and taxi drivers. This is hardly unique to Cambodia, but worth knowing about in advance. Ways to avoid the scam include booking ahead via email and arranging a pick-up, or sticking with a partner guesthouse if you are coming from Phnom Penh. Alternatively, just go with the flow and negotiate with the hotel or guesthouse on arrival.

For more on the commission scams facing those travelling to Siem Reap by land from Thailand, see the boxed text 'Poipet Warning' in the Getting There & Away chapter.

There are a lot of beggars around town and some visitors quickly develop beggar fatigue. However, try and remember that with no social security network and no government support, life is pretty tough for the poorest of the poor in Cambodia. There is no need to give to everybody, but there is also no need to blank them as if they don't exist. In the case of children, it is often better to

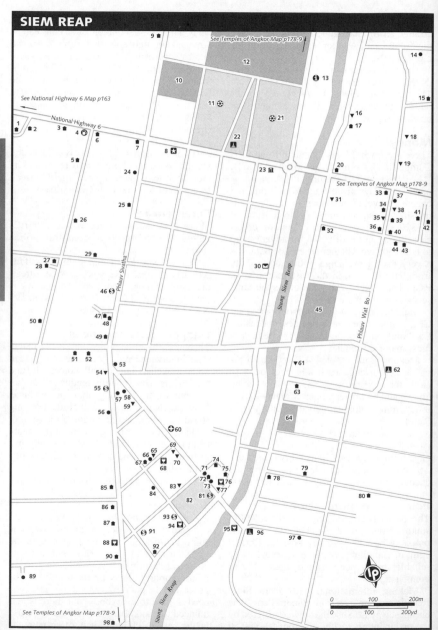

SIEM REAP

SIEM REAP

SIEM REAP

PLACES TO STAY
1 Victory Guesthouse
2 Apsara Angkor Guesthouse
3 Ta Som Guesthouse
5 Paris D'Angkor Hotel
6 Chenla Guesthouse
7 Golden Angkor Hotel
9 Angkor Century Hotel
10 Victoria Siem Reap Hotel
    (under construction)
12 Grand Hotel D'Angkor;
    Elephant Bar
15 Borann L'Auberge des
    Temples
17 La Noria Guesthouse
    & Restaurant
20 Angkor Saphir Hotel
25 Neak Pean Hotel
26 Angkor Wat Guesthouse
27 Mith La Or Guesthouse
28 Smiley Guesthouse
29 Green Garden
    Guesthouse
32 Angkor Temple Hotel
33 Koh Ker Hotel
34 Garden House
36 Mini Hotel
39 Mom's Guesthouse
40 Mahogany Guesthouse
41 Happy Guesthouse
42 European Guesthouse
43 Saron's Guesthouse
44 Siem Reap Angkor
    Guesthouse
45 Pan Sea Hotel
47 Family Guesthouse
48 Dara Guesthouse
49 Rosa Guesthouse
50 Auberge Mont Royal
51 Naga Guesthouse
52 Orchidae Guesthouse
63 Big Lyna Villa

64 Bopha Angkor Hotel;
    Bopha Angkor Restaurant
67 Red Piano Guesthouse
72 Chao Say Guesthouse
    & Restaurant; Lotus
74 Stung Siem Reap Hotel
75 Rasmei Angkor
    Guesthouse;
    Continental Café
78 Bayon Hotel
79 Ivy Annexe
80 Angkor Village
85 Royal Hotel
86 Vimean Thmei Hotel
87 Reaksmey Chanreas Hotel
90 Villa Bakong
92 Ta Prohm Hotel
98 Popular Guesthouse;
    New Millenium Guesthouse

PLACES TO EAT
16 Arun Restaurant
18 Sawasdee Restaurant;
    Yak Lom
19 Bayon II Restaurant
31 Samapheap Restaurant
35 Chivit Thai
38 Bayon Restaurant
54 Angkor Green Restaurant;
    Seeing Hands III
59 Blue Pumpkin;
    Le Gecko Mayonnaise
61 Angkor Borey Restaurant
65 Dead Fish Phuket; Rajana
69 Soup Dragon
70 Little India Restaurant
77 Kampuccino Pizza;
    Tooi Tooi Bar
83 Taj Mahal

BARS & CLUBS
68 The Angkor Wat?

76 Liquid
88 Zanzybar
94 Ivy Bar & Guesthouse
95 Martini

OTHER
4 Caltex Starmart
8 Central Police Station
11 Lotus Gardens
13 Angkor Tourism;
    Khmer Angkor Tour
    Guides Association
14 Angkor Wat & Banteay
    Srei Miniature Replicas
21 Royal Gardens
22 Prasat Preah Ang Charm
23 Royal Residence
24 President Airlines
30 Post Office
37 Siem Reap Thmei Photo
46 Mekong Bank
53 New Market Building
55 Cambodian Commercial
    Bank
56 Royal Motorbikes
57 Siem Reap Moto Club
58 Lao Aviation
60 Hospital
62 Wat Bo
66 Rajana
71 Lotus Supermarket;
    Senteurs D'Angkor
73 Made in Cambodia
81 CCB Exchange
82 Psar Chaa
84 Helicopters Cambodia
89 Les Chantiers Ecoles;
    Artisans D'Angkor
91 National Bank of Cambodia
93 Canadia Bank
96 Wat Dam Nak
97 French Cultural Centre

SIEM REAP

offer food, as money usually ends up being passed on to someone else. For more on beggars, sellers and the general jamboree at the temples, see the 'Temples of Angkor' special section.

Out at the remote temple sites beyond Angkor, stick to clearly marked trails. There are still land mines at locations such as Phnom Kulen and Kbal Spean. See Dangers & Annoyances in the Facts for the Visitor chapter for more information about Cambodia's land mines.

THINGS TO SEE & DO

Most people are in Siem Reap to see Angkor. The sights in and around the town generally pale in comparison, but they make interesting options for those who find themselves templed out after a few days.

Modern temples around Siem Reap offer an interesting contrast to the ancient sandstone structures of Angkor. **Wat Bo** is one of the town's oldest temples and has a collection of well-preserved wall paintings from around the turn of the 19th century depicting the life of Buddha. Another wat to consider visiting while in town is **Preah Inkosei**, built on the site of an early Angkorian brick temple north of town, which still stands today.

Nearby is a workshop called the **House of Peace Association**, where leather shadow puppets are made, including characters from Hindu mythology. Small puppets cost about US$10 while larger pieces can be as much as US$150. They are also sold in a second workshop, just before the airport turn-off on NH6 west.

Wat Athvea is another interesting pagoda on the site of an ancient temple south of the city centre. The old temple is still in very good condition and sees far fewer visitors than the main temples in the Angkor area, making it a peaceful spot in the late afternoon. **Wat Thmei**, on the left fork of the road to Angkor Wat, has a small memorial stupa containing the skulls and bones of victims of the Khmer Rouge. **Wat Dam Nak** was formerly a royal palace during the reign of King Sisowath, hence the name *dam nak* (palace). Today it houses the Centre for Khmer Studies, an independent institution promoting a greater understanding of Khmer culture.

Siem Reap has become something of a force in the drive to revitalise Khmer cultural skills, which were dealt such a harsh blow by the Khmer Rouge and the years of instability that followed its rule. **Les Chantiers Ecoles** (☎ 380187, e artcefp@rep .forum.org.kh) is a school specialising in

teaching wood- and stone-carving techniques to young people from impoverished backgrounds. Staff are quite willing to show genuinely interested individuals or small groups around. It has a beautiful shop on the premises, called **Artisans d'Angkor**, that sells everything from beautiful stone and wood reproductions of Angkorian-era statues to household furniture. Tucked down a side road, the school can be quite hard to find. Look out for a large sign on the left side of the road heading west from Villa Bakong. The sign reads 'Direction Provinciale: Education, jeunesse et sports', and underneath it, a smaller sign reads 'Chantiers Ecoles de Formation Professionelle'.

The school also maintains a **Silk Farm** about 16km west of Siem Reap, just off the road to Sisophon in the village of Puok. All stages of the production process can be seen here, from the cultivation of mulberry trees to the dyeing and weaving of silk. The work produced and sold here is some of the best in the country; many of the patterns are ancient royal Cambodian designs rediscovered with assistance from Khmer Surin (Thai Cambodians), experts in neighbouring Thailand.

One of the more quirky sights in town are the **miniature replicas** (admission US$1) of Angkor Wat and Banteay Srei that the town's master sculptor has constructed in his garden. It is a bluffer's way to get that

---

War of the War Museums

Set up by local deminer Aki Ra, the **Land Mine Museum** (donations accepted) was very popular with travellers during 1999 and 2000. The museum included extensive information about the types of mines used during the civil war in Cambodia, but critics claimed it was dangerous, as some live weapons were kept at the site. Local authorities persistently harassed Aki Ra, citing that his museum portrayed a negative image of the country, and he ended up behind bars on more than one occasion. The reasons soon became clear: in 2001 the **War Museum** (admission US$3; open 8am-5.30pm daily), run by a local military commander, opened near the airport. Clearly, Siem Reap wasn't big enough for two war museums and Aki Ra lost the civil war.

Technically, it is still possible to visit the Land Mine Museum: there is no charge so it is not operating as a museum. It can be found by following Stung Siem Reap about 1km north of Angkor Conservation. The new War Museum is heavily signposted on the road to the airport; and is overpriced for an uninspiring collection of old military equipment hauled out of former Khmer Rouge areas.

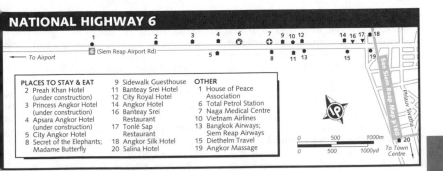

NATIONAL HIGHWAY 6

← To Airport   ⑥ (Siem Reap Airport Rd)

PLACES TO STAY & EAT	9 Sidewalk Guesthouse	OTHER
2 Preah Khan Hotel	11 Banteay Srei Hotel	1 House of Peace
(under construction)	12 City Royal Hotel	Association
3 Princess Angkor Hotel	14 Angkor Hotel	6 Total Petrol Station
(under construction)	16 Banteay Srei	7 Naga Medical Centre
4 Apsara Angkor Hotel	Restaurant	10 Vietnam Airlines
(under construction)	17 Tonlé Sap	13 Bangkok Airways;
5 City Angkor Hotel	Restaurant	Siem Reap Airways
8 Secret of the Elephants;	18 Angkor Silk Hotel	15 Diethelm Travel
Madame Butterfly	20 Salina Hotel	19 Angkor Massage

aerial shot of Angkor without chartering a helicopter, although the astute might question the presence of oversized insects in the shot. Work is currently underway on a miniature Bayon.

About 1.5km south of the town centre is a **crocodile farm** *(admission US$1)*, which is pretty stinky, but is worth considering for those who have never been to this kind of place. Other small animals and birds are kept in pathetic conditions and it's not a nice sight.

Krousar Thmey, a nongovernmental organisation (NGO) supporting orphans has an interesting **exhibition about the Tonlé Sap lake** *(admission free; open daily)*. The exhibition contains photos, models and fishing equipment from around the lake as well as an informative video.

The covered **Psar Leu**, 1.6km east of Stung Siem Reap, is currently under reconstruction and may be an interesting alternative to the tourist market of Psar Chaa once it reopens.

ACTIVITIES
Swimming
There are no public swimming pools in Siem Reap, but locals like to swim in the waters of the Western Baray at the weekend – see the 'Temples of Angkor' special section for more details. There are fairly small swimming pools at the **Angkor Hotel**, **Angkor Village** and **City Angkor Hotel**; each charges US$5 per day. The incredible **lagoon pool** *(admission US$24)* and gym at the Sofitel Royal Angkor, to the north of the city centre, are open to all.

Massage
Deserving of support are **Angkor Massage** and **Seeing Hands Massage III** *(both $4 per hour)*, training blind people in the art of massage. Some of the money raised assists blind people in Siem Reap Province. It is very reasonably priced, and you will certainly need a massage if you have arrived by road from Phnom Penh or Poipet.

Krousar Thmey also has massage (US$5) by the blind, at its interesting exhibition about the Tonlé Sap lake.

For something more indulgent, **Chai Massage** *(opposite Sofitel Royal Angkor; US$20 per hour)*, north of the city centre, is popular for shiatsu (Japanese massage). The Sofitel also has a lavish **spa** *(services from US$50)* and offers a range of massage, facials and other health treatments.

PLACES TO STAY
The hotel scene in Siem Reap has changed immensely from the early 1990s, when travellers were essentially restricted to the venerable Grand Hotel d'Angkor (then in terminal decline). A vast number of family-run guesthouses charging less than US$5 a room have sprung up for budget travellers, while those looking for mid-range accommodation can choose upmarket guesthouses from US$10 to US$15, or small hotels, which cost from around US$15 per room. Those wanting air-con at a budget price may find better value at cheap hotels and upmarket guesthouses than in the budget guesthouses offering only a few air-con rooms. There are now plenty of mid-range

to top-end hotels around town and, as the construction boom continues unabated, these will soon be supplemented by further arrivals. In fact, it wouldn't be an exaggeration to say that there are now more places to stay in Siem Reap than there are temples at Angkor. And new guesthouses and hotels are opening literally every month, so dozens more new places will open during the lifetime of this book.

Another thing to bear in mind is that a number of guesthouse and small-hotel owners have pushed their prices up following positive reviews in the past. The price is an integral part of the assessment, so if prices have gone up, vote with your feet and head elsewhere. With so much competition, the only excuse for a price rise is a wholehearted renovation.

In the low season (April to September), it may be possible to negotiate discounts at some of these places.

PLACES TO STAY – BUDGET

Touts for budget guesthouses wait at Phnom Krom (where the fast boat from Phnom Penh docks) and at the airport. Even if you have not decided where to stay in Siem Reap, do not be surprised to see a noticeboard displaying your name, as most guesthouses in the capital either have partners up here or sell your name on to another guesthouse! This system usually involves a free ride into town. There is no obligation to stay at their guesthouse if you don't like the look of the place, but the 'free lift' might suddenly cost US$1.

Apart from the guesthouses listed here, there are lots of other places around town with rooms ranging from US$3 to US$5. Many places offer small discounts for those staying for five days to a week.

Psar Chaa Area

Popular Guesthouse (☎ 012-916165, e chom@camnet.com.kh) Doubles with bathroom US$5-7, singles without bathroom US$2-3, doubles without bathroom US$4. In the southern part of town, near the river, this friendly guesthouse, as its name suggests, is pretty popular with backpackers.

There is a pleasant rooftop restaurant, with an extensive menu that includes good salad and pastas, as well as Khmer and backpacker favourites.

New Millennium Guesthouse (☎ 012 939871, e garden@camintel.com) Twins, doubles with bathroom US$5/6. The name may be a hangover from those heady days when millennium fever came to Cambodia but the place is pleasant enough. Strange logic to the prices though, it's cheaper for two beds than one.

Rasmei Angkor Guesthouse (☎ 015-834264) Rooms with fan US$5, rooms with/without hot water & air-con US$15/12. The only budget guesthouse with a riverside view, this place is in a pleasant, breezy building dating from French colonial days. The owners have recently renovated the place, making it an excellent choice for location and atmosphere at this price, particularly the clean, fan rooms.

Ivy Guesthouse (☎ 012-800860) Doubles with bathroom US$8-10, singles/doubles without bathroom US$5/6. This small pad above the Ivy Bar offers a homely environment in the centre of town. There is a pleasant chill-out area upstairs and it's not far to the bar. There is also a nice **annexe** across the river, near the Bayon Hotel, which offers dorm beds for US$2 and clean double rooms with bathroom for US$6.

Fresh Air Guesthouse (☎ 012-980453, e wabsreap@hotmail.com, just south of city centre) Singles/doubles with bathroom US$3/6, without bathroom US$2/4, rooms with bathroom & air-con US$8. Rooms at this new place are competitively priced, including a tempting free laundry service, although it's a little way south of town.

Beng Mealea Villa (☎ 963476, fax 380025, e 012630559@mobitel.com.kh, road to Phnom Krom) Rooms with/without bathroom US$5/4, with TV US$6, with air-con US$12. Including this in the Psar Chaa area is a bit of a liberty, as this place is inconveniently about 1.5km along the road to the fast boat. However, the large, cheap fan rooms here might make it an option for those who don't mind being a little way out of town.

Phlauv Sivatha Area

Family Guesthouse (☎ 760077, e familygh @everyday.com.kh) Doubles with bathroom US$6, singles/doubles without bathroom US$3/4, in the new wing US$8/10. In a nice wooden house that once upon a time was Smiley's, this family-run guesthouse (no surprises given the name) is a relaxing place to stay.

Dara Guesthouse (☎ 012-630448, 10 Ph Sivatha) Rooms US$4, rooms with fan/air-con, TV & fridge US$8/13. All rooms include bathroom.

Rosa Guesthouse (☎ 012-921986, 6 Ph Sivatha) Rooms with fan US$5-7, with air-con US$13. This townhouse stretches back a fair way, offering average kind of rooms at an average kind of price.

Naga Guesthouse (☎ 963439, 100m west of Ph Sivatha) Singles/doubles with bathroom US$3/4, without bathroom US$2/3. This place has been around for years and is still one of the cheapest guesthouses in town. It's a big place with basic rooms, and between the early-morning sunrise seekers and the late-night drinking crowd it tends to be bustling at all times.

Orchidae Guesthouse (☎ 012-849716, e kongheng_luy@yahoo.com, 50m west of Ph Sivatha) Singles/twins with bathroom US$4/5, rooms with air-con US$10. The card at this small wooden guesthouse says 'we are looking for word to your visit'. 'Hello' or 'welcome' should do it.

Angkor Wat Guesthouse (☎ 963531) Twins with fan/air-con & bathroom US$6/10. While nowhere near as grand as its namesake, it does offer clean rooms with satellite TV.

Mith La Or Guesthouse (☎/fax 964387, e nfesr@camintel.com) Singles/doubles/triples with bathroom US$4/5/6. With a name meaning 'best friend guesthouse', this little place offers well-kept rooms.

Smiley Guesthouse (☎ 012-852955) Singles US$6-8, doubles US$7-9. The Smiley family has moved into a smart new building (really a backpacker hotel), offering clean, bright rooms, some of which include hot water. It has a good restaurant set around a garden courtyard.

National Highway 6 West Area

Sidewalk Guesthouse (☎ 012-893468, e meanchanthon@bigpond.com.kh) Singles/doubles without bathroom US$2/3. The location, on the road to the airport, is not ideal but the staff more than make up for it by offering free bicycle hire and lifts into town. The rooms are clean and include tea and coffee, making this a real bargain.

Apsara Angkor Guesthouse (☎ 963476, fax 380025) Doubles with bathroom US$5-7, singles/doubles without bathroom US$3/4, rooms with air-con, TV & hot water US$12. This pad is usually busy thanks to a healthy selection of rooms. The garden diner has meals priced in riel.

Victory Guesthouse (☎ 012-940539, e sambosay@yahoo.com, south of NH6 west) Twins/triples with fan & bathroom US$5/7. This guesthouse has a nice local feel, as the extended family that owns it live together in a big compound. The rooms are clean and new, making it a sound choice.

Ta Som Guesthouse Singles/doubles US$4/5, rooms with air-con US$12. This small guesthouse is popular with Japanese travellers and has clean, basic rooms with bathroom.

Chenla Guesthouse (☎ 963233, e 012 835488@mobitel.com.kh) Singles/doubles with bathroom US$5/6, with air-con, TV & hot water US$12/15. This family-run guesthouse has been completely rebuilt over the past few years and offers well-tended rooms.

East Bank of the River

East of Stung Siem Reap, just south of NH6, is a ghetto of long-running guesthouses.

Garden House (☎ 963523, 129 Ph Wat Bo) Rooms with/without bathroom US$6/4. Garden House is an old-style wooden guesthouse with very basic lodgings.

Mom's Guesthouse (☎/fax 964037, e moms@bigpond.com.kh, 99 Ph Wat Bo) Rooms with fan/air-con & bathroom US$10/15, rooms without bathroom US$5. This place doesn't seem such good value compared with the competition these days – rooms have been upgraded, but not as much as the prices.

SIEM REAP

Mahogany Guesthouse (☎ *963417, fax 380025,* e *proeun@bigpond.com.kh)* Doubles with fan/air-con & bathroom US$8/13, doubles/twins without bathroom US$5/6. This popular place has reasonable rooms, although the shared bathroom options are overpriced compared with places nearby. It's a large two-storey building with a veranda area for hanging out.

Mini Hotel (☎ *012-842145, 711 Ph Wat Bo)* Twins with fan/air-con & bathroom US$5/10. This looks very good value compared with the more-established competition, and offers clean comfort at a sensible price.

Heading farther away from the river are a couple of cheaper guesthouses.

Siem Reap Angkor Guesthouse (☎ *012-933161,* e *siemreapagh@yahoo.com)* Singles with/without bathroom US$3/2, doubles with bathroom US$4. This place has a small garden cafe. Almost next door is **Saron's Guesthouse** (☎ *012-630297),* with basic rooms US$3-5, and some with air-con for US$10.

Happy Guesthouse (☎ *012-937071,* e *johnny@free.iside.net)* Rooms with/without bathroom US$7/5, with air-con & bathroom US$12. This lively little guesthouse has another of the garden restaurants so popular in this area, and a fair selection of rooms.

European Guesthouse (☎ *012-890917,* e *jhoekstra@angkorhospital.org)* Rooms without bathroom US$4-6. This place has clean, neat rooms.

PLACES TO STAY – MID-RANGE

As with the budget scene, there has been a mid-range guesthouse and hotel boom in Siem Reap, and there are some very good deals around.

Psar Chaa Area

The Red Piano (☎ *963240,* e *redpiano@rep.forum.org.kh)* Rooms US$14-24. This Siem Reap landmark offers thoughtfully decorated rooms, all of which include TV, hot water and customised Red Piano beds. The higher-priced rooms are larger and some include a hot tub.

Villa Bakong (☎ *380126, fax 963419,* e *bakong@rep.forum.org.kh, 1 Ph Sivatha)*

Singles/doubles with air-con & hot water US$15/20. This upmarket guesthouse offers comfortable and clean modern rooms in a contemporary villa and is always busy.

At the southern end of Ph Sivatha is a string of minihotels offering the same kind of deal. **Vimean Thmei Hotel** (☎ *963494, 12 Ph Sivatha)* has singles/doubles with air-con, TV & hot water from US$12/15. **Reaksmey Chanreas Hotel** (☎ *963557, 330 Ph Sivatha)* is pretty much identical, but has a couple of larger rooms, almost like minisuites, that are reasonable value for US$15. **Royal Hotel** (☎ *012-630278, 441 Ph Sivatha)* has rooms with air-con, TV, fridge & hot water for US$15 that look like good value for money.

Chao Say Guesthouse (☎/fax *380065,* e *lotustempletours@hotmail.com)* Singles/doubles with fan US$8/12, with air-con US$12/16. Well located in an old French town house overlooking Psar Chaa, this guesthouse has a reasonable range of small rooms, all with bathroom.

Stung Siem Reap Hotel (☎/fax *380139)* Rooms with air-con, TV & fridge US$20. This is a well-located alternative to the string of hotels on the east bank and has helpful and friendly management. The new, lower prices make it an attractive deal, but watch out for the nearby red-light district.

Auberge Mont Royal (☎ *964044,* e *mont-royal@mobitel.com.kh)* Standard singles/doubles US$25/30, deluxe rooms with hot tub US$45/50. Tucked away on a dirt road to the west of Ph Sivatha is this attractive villa offering well-presented air-con rooms with minibar and bathroom. There is a nice ambience here, but don't forget to add 10% tax and US$2.50 for breakfast.

National Highway 6 West Area

Paris d'Angkor Hotel (☎ *963303, south of NH6 west)* Rooms with air-con, TV, fridge & hot water US$15. This is one of the best deals around at the cheaper end of the scale.

Golden Angkor Hotel (☎/fax *964039,* e *012893272@mobitel.com.kh, cnr Ph Sivatha & NH6 west)* Rooms with fan US$12, with air-con, TV, fridge & bathroom US$15. This place is an older option, with less inspiring rooms, but is reasonable value.

Green Garden Guesthouse (☎ 963342, e 012890363@mobitel.com.kh, just off Ph Sivatha) Doubles with fan US$10, rooms with air-con US$17, rooms with air-con, TV & fridge US$20. This guesthouse has been upgrading in recent years and rooms include a bathroom. The old fan and air-con rooms are poor value, but the new air-con rooms are looking nice with some thought given to the decoration. There is, as you might imagine, an attractive communal area set in a lush garden.

Banteay Srei Hotel (☎/fax 964353) Singles/doubles US$30/35. Out towards the airport, this used to be one of the more expensive places in Siem Reap, but with no new investment, it now offers rooms at competitive rates. Rooms come with all the usual amenities, and breakfast is included.

Secret of the Elephants (☎ 964328, e info@angkor-travel.com) Singles/doubles with fan US$25/30, with air-con US$35/40. This place has much character and is popular with French visitors, but the price is more about ambience than value-for-money comfort. The carefully decorated rooms include hot showers, while those upstairs have individual bathrooms outside. It is better value for couples than solo tourists. Prices include breakfast.

Salina Hotel (☎ 380221, fax 380035, e salina@camintel.com) Singles/doubles/ suites US$45/55/70. This Thai-run hotel is the cheapest in its range. The location is poor, but the rooms are well finished.

Angkor Silk Hotel (☎ 963241, fax 963373) Singles/doubles US$40/45. The owners of Salina Hotel recently opened this pleasant place, which offers a more tasteful decor, but no pool. Prices include breakfast.

East Bank of the River

Many of the hotels here are on or near the riverfront, a pleasant, shaded area of town.

Big Lyna Villa (☎ 964807, fax 963476, e aic@mobitel.com.kh) Twins with fan/air-con, TV & bathroom US$10/20. This traditional wooden house offers spacious rooms with some nice touches. It is in a quiet part of town near the river.

Koh Ker Hotel (☎/fax 963234, e kohker @camintel.com) Singles/twins US$20/25. At these prices, this new hotel looks like a very attractive deal with smart rooms including TV, minibar, hot tub, and curtains and bedding finished in silk.

Bayon Hotel (☎/fax 963993) Rooms US$25. Prices have continued to tumble at this riverfront hotel, making it a pretty sensible deal considering all rooms have hot tubs and the usual gadgets. Prices include breakfast.

La Noria Guesthouse (☎ 964242, fax 964243, e lanoria@bigpond.com.kh) Singles/doubles with fan US$31/34, with air-con US$42/45. La Noria is a tasteful villa complex, but prices have crept up, making the rooms a touch overpriced. The small rooms are thoughtfully decorated and include their own veranda, but no TV or fridge. Prices include breakfast and tax.

Borann L'Auberge des Temples (☎ 964740, e borann@bigpond.com.kh) Singles/doubles US$33/44. Very similar to its sister La Noria, this auberge has attractive rooms set around a garden and swimming pool, each room with its own balcony.

Yak Lom Angkor Lodge (☎ 964456, e yaklom@camintel.com) Singles/doubles with air-con US$25/35. The individual bungalows in this place near Sawasdee Restaurant are rather small and a little close together, but are well decorated and have balconies. Prices include breakfast.

Bopha Angkor Hotel (☎ 964928, fax 964446, e hba@rep.forum.org.kh, Pokambor Blvd) Singles/doubles US$48/52. This hotel has recently undergone a pleasing renovation and all rooms are decorated with local touches. The standards are of a high level, with a turn-down service to make you feel cared for. The Khmer restaurant here has some of the best food in town.

Angkor Temple Hotel (☎ 380038, fax 964449, e angtempl@camintel.com, Pokambor Blvd) Singles/doubles/triples US$40/45/ 55. Popular with tour groups, the choice of colour for the renovation here was particularly poor. The Thai-style rooms are nicer than before, but not to the tune of US$40 and up.

Angkor Saphir Hotel (☎ 963566, fax 380213, e saphir@mobitel.com.kh, NH6 east) Rooms US$25-40. This somewhat faceless hotel offers a pretty good deal for its rooms, all equipped with hot tub, air-con, TV and minibar.

There are several hotels strung out along NH6 to the east of the city centre, and while they are comfortable, their location isn't ideal and their prices are relatively high.

Freedom Hotel (☎ 963473, fax 964274, e freedom@bigpond.com.kh) Singles/doubles/triples US$30/45/55. Prices have shot up here, as it has become popular with adventure-tour groups and the rooms have all the trimmings. The manager knows the Siem Reap area well, but might need to check out the competition more carefully.

Borei Angkor Hotel (☎ 964406, fax 963436, e boreiaca@camintel.com) Singles/doubles US$35/40. Near the Freedom Hotel, the rooms here are newer and more slick, although it is still a little far from the action.

Rama Hotel (☎ 760024, fax 760020, e ramahotel@bigpond.com.kh) Singles/doubles US$35/40. The rooms here are smart, with some obvious Thai touches, and include the usual TV, fridge and air-con. Prices include breakfast.

The Road to Angkor

Pavillon Indochine (☎ 012-849681, w www.pavillon-indochine.com) Rooms US$20-30, bungalows US$25. This charming guesthouse has tasteful rooms with individual furnishings and a pleasant ambience. Near Wat Thmei, it is the closest place to the temples of Angkor and includes an atmospheric bar and restaurant area.

Hanuman Alaya (☎ 023-218356, fax 023-218398, w www.hanumantourism.com) Rooms US$25. This traditional wooden home is near the river just south of Angkor Conservation. The three rooms are lovingly decorated and include air-con, satellite TV, minibar and hot water. Prices include continental breakfast.

PLACES TO STAY – TOP END

Most of the hotels in this range levy an additional 10% charge for service and 10% government tax, so don't forget to factor it in as an extra cost. Breakfast is included though, so there is no need to head off to the market for a baguette. Competition in this sector is starting to bring prices down, although booking through a local agent can save considerable money on the walk-in rate.

Grand Hotel d'Angkor (☎ 963888, fax 963168, w www.raffles.com) Singles/doubles/personality suites US$310/360/460. If money is no obstacle, then this historic hotel, which has been fully renovated and extended by the Raffles group, is the most luxurious in town. It is in these sorts of opulent surroundings that you can imagine what it was like to be a tourist in colonial days, and the original 1929 lift still carries guests between floors. The rooms are the most comfortable in town, but service can be a little formal and austere.

Sofitel Royal Angkor (☎ 964600, fax 964610, w www.sofitel.com, Vithei Charles de Gaulle) Singles/doubles US$280/320. This was the first five-star resort hotel to open its doors in Siem Reap and brings a touch of the Thai islands to the north of town. The rooms are very comfortable and exceptional features include one of the finest swimming pools in the region and a luxury spa with massage and health treatments. It also offers a swim-up bar, several restaurants, a video room and library.

Pan Sea Hotel (☎ 963390, fax 963391, w www.pansea-angkor.com, Pokambor Blvd) Rooms US$280. This charming wooden resort-hotel offers well-designed, open-plan rooms with the best hot tubs in town. It is luxurious while modest throughout, including a minimalist reception, a restaurant, bar and a large central swimming pool.

Angkor Century Hotel (☎ 963777, fax 963123, w www.angkorcentury.com, Ph Sivatha) Singles/doubles US$250/270. This is a four-star version of the Sofitel, somewhat less sophisticated but popular with tour groups. The rooms, like the exterior, are businesslike, but the swimming pool and courtyard garden are impressive. It also has a humidor for serious cigar smokers.

Angkor Village (☎ 963563, fax 380104, w www.angkorvillage.com) Standard rooms with air-con & hot water US$70, deluxe rooms with hot tub US$105, suites US$125. Designed by its eccentric owner, a French architect, the wooden bungalows are set around a recessed restaurant and ornately sculpted water gardens. Although pricey, it is regularly full due to its sophisticated ambience, so book ahead. Prices do not include breakfast.

Neak Pean Hotel (☎ 964429, fax 380073, 53 Ph Sivatha) Singles/twins/suites US$80/90/120. Formerly a non-descript town hotel, the owners have added an Angkor Village –style annexe finished in wood, around the swimming pool. Pleasant enough, but it needs to be a little cheaper to dent the business of the established competition.

Ta Prohm Hotel (☎ 380117, fax 380116, e taprohm@camintel.com, near Psar Chaa) Singles/doubles US$60/70, suite singles/doubles US$100/110. This hotel has a great location overlooking Stung Siem Reap and is popular with European tour groups. Reasonable comfort at a reasonable price.

There is a cluster of somewhat characterless upmarket hotels along NH6 west, the road to the airport.

City Angkor Hotel (☎ 380200, fax 380022, e ctangkor@camintel.com) Singles/doubles/suites US$100/120/168. Until 1997, this three-star hotel was the best in Siem Reap. It lacks character, but is popular with tour groups and includes a swimming pool. The same owners operate the cheaper **City Royal Hotel** (☎ 380320, fax 380325, e ctroyal@camintel.com) with similar single/doubles from US$80/90.

Angkor Hotel (☎ 964301, fax 964302, w www.angkor-hotel-cambodia.com) Singles/doubles from US$100/125, Angkor suite US$210. Along the same strip, this place is similar to the competition, but has an attractive wood finish throughout. The hotel also has business facilities, a swimming pool and a health club.

Other top-end hotels due to open include: the **Victoria Siem Reap Hotel**, built in neo-colonial style right next to the venerable Grand; and the **Preah Khan Hotel** and the **Princess Angkor Hotel**, farther out towards the airport.

PLACES TO EAT

The restaurant scene in Siem Reap has taken great leaps forward in the past couple of years and there is now a wide range of international flavours available. Several of the older local restaurants have been overrun by tour groups in recent years, making dining quite an impersonal experience, but the food remains good.

Many of the budget guesthouses have good menus offering a selection of local dishes and Western meals; while it's all too easy to get into the habit of ordering in-house, it hardly counts as the full Siem Reap experience.

Several of the mid-range hotels and all the top-end places have restaurants, some of which warrant an individual listing in this section. When it comes to the luxury palaces and their gastronomic (by Cambodian standards astronomic) buffets, the Sofitel Royal Angkor leads the pack, as you might expect from a French-run chain. For details on dinner and a performance of classical dance, as offered at several hotels and restaurants around town, see the Entertainment section later.

For more on the lunch options available in and around Angkor, see the boxed text 'Out to Lunch' in the 'Temples of Angkor' special section.

Khmer

Psar Chaa has plenty of cheap food stalls with signs and menus in English and these are becoming increasingly lively, atmospheric places for a local meal at very reasonable prices. Some dishes are on display, others are cooked to order, but nothing costs much more than US$1.

Arun Restaurant (☎ 964227, north of NH6 east) Dishes US$2-3. One of the oldest restaurants in town, Arun hasn't been inundated by tour groups, probably because of its small size. It serves wholesome local dishes at an affordable price.

Bayon Restaurant (Ph Wat Bo) Dishes US$2-4. Another golden oldie, this place was being completely rebuilt at the time of writing. The food was always good, but expect something bigger and brasher once it reopens. The same owners operate **Bayon II Restaurant**, on the other side of NH6, another outdoor restaurant with a car park full of coaches. It serves good food though.

Samapheap Restaurant *(Pokambor Blvd)* Meals US$2.50-5. This huge garden restaurant is popular with Khmers for its tasty food and fast service. Tour groups have taken over of late, and it's not uncommon for 200 people to be dining under the fairy lights at night.

Angkor Borey Restaurant *(Pokambor Blvd)* Dishes US$2-4. On the eastern side of the river, this is an interesting place for an evening meal if you can take the background music. There is a huge choice of Khmer dishes and other Asian classics. The place is not short on 'beer girls' and often draws a healthy-sized local crowd.

Banteay Srei Restaurant *(NH6 west)* This place has a pleasant garden to dine in and is popular with Khmers rather than tourists. The Khmer cuisine is pretty authentic here.

Bopha Angkor Restaurant *(Pokambor Blvd)* Mains US$3-5, set meals from US$6. Part of the Bopha Angkor Hotel, this restaurant sets a high standard of taste and ambience. The menu is extensive, including a full complement of traditional Cambodian food, and at a price that is affordable to all.

Madame Butterfly *(NH6 west)* Mains US$5, set meals from US$10. Next door to Secret of the Elephants guesthouse, this restaurant is full of character and offers a fusion of Asian cuisines in exotic surroundings, with slightly exotic prices to match.

Thai

Chivit Thai *(Ph Wat Bo)* Dishes US$2-4. This is arguably the most atmospheric restaurant in town for Thai cuisine. The setting is delightfully traditional with raised eating platforms, and the large menu offers the best of Thai cooking. Unless you are a fire-eater don't ask for anything extra spicy.

Sawasdee Restaurant *(Ph Wat Bo)* Sawasdee offers a similar selection of dishes to Chivit Thai, including excellent fish cakes, but in a less attractive environment.

Dead Fish Phuket *(north of Psar Chaa)* Dishes US$2-4. This Thai pub-restaurant

promises to 'be sure we don't serve dog, cat, rat or worm'. The food is good and the atmosphere can be lively at night.

Vietnamese

Soup Dragon *(north of Psar Chaa)* Vietnamese dishes US$2-3, Western dishes US$4-6. This restaurant has perhaps the best *pho* (Vietnamese rice-noodle soup) in Cambodia, making the perfect breakfast at just 2500r. The spicy clay pots with fish are delicious, served with fried morning-glory so you can get your greens too.

Indian

Taj Mahal *(Psar Chaa)* Mains US$3-5. This is currently the best Indian restaurant in town, with a full range of well-prepared food to please even the most seasoned curry lovers or curry-craving Brits. The vegetarian thali is excellent value at US$3.

Little India Restaurant Mains US$2-5. The oldest subcontinental restaurant in town offers a good selection of vegetarian options.

International

Dining near the riverfront is popular in Siem Reap. An old favourite is **Kampuccino Pizza**, with a well-travelled menu and prices from US$3 to US$5. There is something from every corner of the globe and the portions are generous. Fish of the day is always a winner.

Continental Café *(northeast of Psar Chaa)* Dishes US$3-6. In a handsome building near Rasmei Angkor Guesthouse, this restaurant-bar has a wide range of Asian and Western food, including a selection from Cambodia, Thailand and Indonesia, as well as imported steaks from Australia.

Blue Pumpkin *(northwest of Psar Chaa)* Sandwiches & salads US$2-3. This pleasant little cafe offers some of the tastiest light bites in town, including a small selection of Thai food and some wholesome pastries. The fruit shakes served here are up there with the best of them. Almost next door is **Le Gecko Mayonnaise**, a new French cafe with an emphasis on crepes.

The Red Piano *(northwest of Psar Chaa)* Meals US$3-5. When it comes to ambience, this restaurant and bar (in the same building as the guesthouse) has it in abundance and is usually very busy. The menu is by no means unique for Siem Reap, but the food is generally good and filling.

Angkor Green Restaurant *(Ph Sivatha)* Dishes US$3-5. This small restaurant serves an eclectic mix of Western, Thai and Khmer food and remains popular.

Lotus Restaurant Dishes US$3-6. Near the Chao Say Guesthouse, this long-running restaurant has one area serving Khmer and Asian cuisine and another serving well-prepared European cuisine, including some of the best steaks in town.

The elevated, all-wood restaurant at **La Noria** offers an attractive combination of Khmer and French cuisine, including tasty fish and beef brochettes. The restaurant offers a *sbei tuoi* (shadow puppet) show on Wednesday evenings and most of the $12 set-dinner fee goes to a charity supporting local children.

Self-Catering

The **markets** are well stocked with fruit and fresh bread. **Starmart** *(Caltex Petrol Station, NH6 west)* and **Lotus Supermarket** *(opposite Psar Chaa)* both stock imports such as cheese. Eating in the market usually works out cheaper than self-catering, but some folks like to make up a picnic for longer days on the road.

ENTERTAINMENT
Bars

The nightlife in Siem Reap has really started to pick up with the influx of tourists, although it is still pretty quiet compared with Bangkok or even Phnom Penh. It is definitely worth checking out the bars in town at least once, as each has its own character.

Travellers tend to congregate early in the evening on guesthouse verandas to drink cheap beer, then venture out later. Many of the mid-range hotels don't have bars, while those at top-end joints tend to be expensive, with drinks starting from US$4.

Elephant Bar, in the bowels of the Grand Hotel d'Angkor, has a happy hour (or four) from 4pm to 8pm, when most drinks are two for one. This is a cheap way to seek out the

ambience that Siem Reap must have had in the 1930s, when Charlie Chaplin stayed at the hotel here.

The Angkor What?, probably the most popular bar in town, is a hole in the wall that heaves from 9pm most nights and stays open into the early hours. It has cheap drinks, cool tunes and the bar supports a local children's hospital, so drinking here is actually helping someone's liver if not your own.

Ivy Bar has a lot of atmosphere and offers some of the best bar food in town. There is a pool table and the place is usually jumping until midnight or so.

Liquid is down on the riverfront and looks like a slice of designer Singapore or Kuala Lumpur that has been dropped on Siem Reap. The prices are thankfully more Cambodia than the big Asian neighbours, and the Malaysian food here is good.

Tooi Tooi Bar is definitely the smallest bar in town. Near Kampuccino Pizza, it is popular with local French expats.

Zanzybar *(Ph Sivatha)* is one of the oldest bars in town and attracts a mostly male crowd later in the evening, thanks to the presence of local ladies around the bar.

Martini has nothing to do with its namesake in Phnom Penh, and used to be the most popular nightclub in town, with a large beer garden and a dark, dark disco. However, it was closed for refurbishing after the nightclub ban and will no doubt resurface as a 'music restaurant'.

Classical Dance

Several restaurants and hotels offer cultural performances during the evening and for many visitors such shows offer the only opportunity to see Cambodian classical dance. They are very much geared to the tourist and while not quite as sophisticated as a performance of the Royal Ballet in Phnom Penh, to the untrained eye it is nonetheless graceful and alluring. All prices include a buffet meal.

Among the hotels, the **Ta Prohm Hotel** and the **City Angkor Hotel** are the cheapest at US$10, but the buffet food is not that great. **Grand Hotel d'Angkor** and **Angkor Village** are the most expensive in town at US$22. The Grand has a performance house on the banks of Stung Siem Reap, opposite the hotel.

Under the same ownership, **Tonlé Sap Restaurant** (☎ 963388, NH6 west) and **Chao Praya** (☎ 964666, Vithei Charles de Gaulle) both offer large, impersonal shows for US$12 that pull in the big tour groups. Chao Praya focuses on Thai cuisine, while Tonlé Sap on Khmer and sukiyaki, but both include Malay, Japanese and European dishes as well. Shows start at 7.30pm, and aren't such a bad deal if you can put up with the hordes.

There is also a weekly performance of shadow puppetry at **La Noria** – see the restaurant review earlier for more details.

Beatocello (Jayavarman VII Children's Hospital), better known as Dr Beat Richner, performs original music for cello and Bach compositions on Saturday at 7.15pm. Entry is free, but donations are welcome to assist the hospital in its mission to give free medical treatment to the children of Siem Reap.

Cinema

There is no cinema as such in Siem Reap, but several of the **guesthouses**, predictably enough, show movies. French films are shown every Sunday at the **French Cultural Centre**.

SHOPPING

Much of what is seen on sale in the markets of Siem Reap can also be purchased from children and vendors throughout the temple area. Some people get fed up with the endless sales pitches as they navigate the ancient wonders, while others enjoy the banter and a chance to interact with Cambodian people. Whatever your view, it may be an idea to buy at least some items out at the temples as many of the families there are descendants of the original inhabitants of Angkor and arguably have more right than anyone to make a living from these spectacular monuments.

Some visitors will argue that the children should be at school rather than selling, but most do attend at least half of the time, if their families can afford it. It is also quite probable that they are getting a better education interacting with foreigners than they might get in an under-funded, under-staffed village school.

Items touted include postcards, T-shirts, temple bas-relief rubbings, curious musical instruments, ornamental knives and crossbows – the latter might raise a few eyebrows with customs should you try to take one home!

When it comes to shopping in town, **Psar Chaa** is well stocked with anything you may want to buy in Cambodia, and lots you don't. Silverware, silk, wood carvings, stone carvings, Buddhas, paintings, rubbings, notes and coins, T-shirts, table mats...the list goes on and on. There are bargains to be had if you haggle patiently and humorously. Do not buy old stone carvings that vendors claim are from Angkor. Whether they are real or not, buying these artefacts serves only to encourage their plunder and they will usually be confiscated by customs. Buy modern replicas and bury them in the garden for a few months – they will soon look the same. Psar Chaa is in the process of being relocated to a new market building on Ph Sivatha and authorities have yet to decide how to redevelop the old market area.

Artisans d'Angkor sells high-quality souvenirs and its profits go to a cultural rehabilitation project. For further information, see the Things to See & Do section earlier in this chapter.

Another shop with a higher purpose is **Made in Cambodia** (opposite Psar Chaa), which specialises in quality silk products such as wallets, handbags, photo albums and the like. All profits are ploughed back into training and employment for members of Cambodia's disabled community. Nearby, **Senteurs d'Angkor** is a pleasant shop with a good range of local handicrafts.

There is also a branch of **Rajana** in Siem Reap, which produces quirky wooden and metalware objects, well-designed silver jewellery and handmade cards, as well as selling local condiments such as lemongrass, pepper and coffee. The organisation promotes fair trade and employment opportunities for Cambodians.

Photos can be printed in Siem Reap quickly and cheaply. Most of the photo shops are on NH6, just east of the river, and charge about US$4 to process 36 prints. The best is probably **Siem Reap Thmei Photo**, a large Fuji lab opposite the Koh Ker Hotel.

GETTING THERE & AWAY
Air
There are direct international flights to Bangkok, Phuket and Ko Samui in Thailand; Vientiane and occasionally Pakse in Laos; Ho Chi Minh City (Saigon) in Vietnam; and Singapore. For information on international flights to and from Siem Reap, see the Getting There & Away chapter.

Domestic links are limited to Phnom Penh, which is served by Siem Reap Airways (US$65/130 one way/return), Royal Phnom Penh Airways (US$55/110) and President Airlines (US$60/115). With the demise of Royal Air Cambodge, demand for the limited number of flights is high, especially on Siem Reap Airways, so it is sensible to book as far in advance as possible.

Airline offices around town include:

Bangkok Airways (☎ 380191) 571 NH6 west
Lao Aviation (☎ 963283) 73 Psar Chaa
President Airlines (☎ 964338) Ph Sivatha
Royal Phnom Penh Airways (☎ 012-825754) near Psar Chaa
Siem Reap Airways (☎ 380192) NH6 west
Vietnam Airlines (☎ 964488) NH6 west

Bus & Pick-up
Overland travel throughout Cambodia is secure but a little bumpy. You can now come overland from Bangkok (see the Land entry in the Getting There & Away chapter for more details), Battambang and Phnom Penh.

As the security situation has improved, travel by road between Phnom Penh and Siem Reap is becoming increasingly popular among backpackers. Sections of the road are far from pretty, but pick-up trucks complete the journey in about eight to 10 hours. Basically, the road is brilliant until just beyond the temples of Roluos, in a total mess as far as Kompong Thom and then pretty good from there to Phnom Penh. It is earmarked for overhaul, but work had not yet started at the time of writing.

When travelling between Siem Reap and Phnom Penh by road, consider making a stop in Kompong Thom for a night in order to visit the pre-Angkorian temples at Sambor Prei Kuk. See Around Kompong Thom in the Northwestern Cambodia chapter for details. It costs about 25,000/10,000r inside/on the back of a pick-up truck between Siem Reap and Phnom Penh. Guesthouses can help you arrange this, but you will likely have to pay a bit more for the privilege.

There is also a daily bus service (US$10) operated by Capitol Guesthouse in Phnom Penh and Popular Guesthouse in Siem Reap. More guesthouses will no doubt get into this business once the road is rebuilt. The minibus is not such a comfortable means of transport on the hideous stretches of road.

The 152km road to Thailand is also open and is much improved from the bad old days, when half the time was spent driving in the paddy fields to avoid potholes and downed bridges. The run can now take as little as three hours, although in the wet season double that and add some more on an off day. Pick-ups run to Poipet (15,000/8000r) and to Sisophon (10,000/5000r), where it is necessary to change for Battambang. Negotiate hard to get these sorts of prices. Several guesthouses also run buses all the way through to Bangkok (US$9).

Pick-ups and other vehicles used to leave from the dirty and overcrowded Psar Leu. As Psar Leu is under reconstruction, the vehicles have been moved to a new taxi park, a little farther out of town on NH6 towards Phnom Penh. Hopefully the government will open a taxi park in the west of town for vehicles to Sisophon and Poipet, so they won't jam the town any more.

Boat
For those on a tighter budget it is possible to take a fast boat from Siem Reap to Phnom Penh or Battambang (US$21 to US$25, five hours). See Getting There & Away in the Phnom Penh chapter for more information.

Boats from Siem Reap to Phnom Penh leave from Phnom Krom, 11km south of Siem Reap. The boats dock in different places at different times of the year, eg, the

MARTIN HARRIS

Traditional river transport

SIEM REAP

worst time to arrive is May. When the lake recedes in the dry season, both the port and floating village move with it. The lake is extremely low at this time of year and exposes its clay base, which turns as slippery as ice once the rain starts. Cars and motorbikes can't get in or out and passengers end up walking a couple of kilometres in the rain, which isn't that much fun.

Most of the guesthouses in town sell boat tickets, and the companies tend to take it in turns to make the run so don't be surprised to end up on a different boat in each direction. Buying the ticket from your guesthouse usually includes a moto or minibus ride to the port. Otherwise, a moto out here costs about US$1. A taxi is more like US$5.

There are also boats travelling between Siem Reap and Battambang along Stung Sangker; see Getting There & Away in the Battambang section of the Northwestern Cambodia chapter.

GETTING AROUND
For more on transport around Angkor, see the boxed text 'Getting Around the Temples of Angkor' in the 'Temples of Angkor' special section. Following are details on the most common forms of transport used for getting around Siem Reap.

To/From the Airport
Siem Reap International Airport is 7km from the town centre. Many of the hotels and

guesthouses in Siem Reap have a free airport pick-up service if you have booked in advance. Official taxis are available outside the terminal for US$5. A trip to the city centre on the back of a moto will cost US$1.

Car & Motorcycle
Most of the hotels and guesthouses can organise car hire for the day, with a going rate of US$20 to US$25.

The rules on rented motorbikes swing back and forth each year. For many years it was forbidden for foreigners to ride motorbikes around the town and temples. These restrictions were eased at the end of the 1990s, but the situation changes frequently. Ask around at guesthouses and hotels. Guesthouses can supply small bikes for US$5 to US$8 per day. Siem Reap Moto Club at 145 Ph Sivatha, and Royal Motorbikes at 22 Ph Sivatha hire out big bikes for US$12 to US$15. Ask for a lock and keep the bike in guarded parking where possible, as theft is common.

Bicycle
Some of the guesthouses around town hire out bicycles, as do a few shops around Psar Chaa, usually for US$2 a day.

Moto
Motos are available at daily rates of US$6 to US$8. The average cost for a short trip within town is 500r to 1000r. It is not normally necessary to negotiate in advance, but

t can be wise at night or for those staying at luxury hotels. It should be around 2000r to places out on the road to Angkor or to the airport – again, negotiate at night.

Remorque-kang

You can get around Siem Reap in the town's unique and rather uncomfortable *cyclos* (pedicabs), which are essentially standard bicycles with a two-seat trailer in hitch. Trips around the town centre cost about 1000r.

Remorque-moto

These sweet little motorbikes with carriages are a nice way for couples to get about Siem Reap, although drivers like to inflate the prices. Try for US$1 on trips around town, although to the edges of town by night, drivers may charge US$1.50.

Around Siem Reap

BIRD SANCTUARY & BIOSPHERE OF PREK TOAL

ដីរកបក្សីប្រែកទួល

Prek Toal is one of three biospheres on Tonlé Sap lake, and the establishment of the bird sanctuary makes it the most worthwhile and straightforward to visit. It is an ornithologist's fantasy, with a significant number of rare breeds gathered in one small area, including the huge lesser and greater adjutant storks, the milky stork and the spot-billed pelican.

Visitors during the dry season (December to May) will find the concentration of birds like something out of a Hitchcock film. As water starts to dry up elsewhere, the birds congregate here. Serious twitchers know that the best time to see birds is early morning or late afternoon and this requires an overnight at the **environment office**, where there are basic beds for US$7.

Getting there under your own steam requires taking a moto (US$1) or taxi (US$5) to the floating village of Chong Kneas. At the village, arrange a boat to the environment office (around US$80 return; 1 hour

each way), from where rowing boats with guides take you into the sanctuary (US$15), half an hour beyond the office.

Binoculars are available for those who don't carry their own, and sunscreen and head protection are essential, as it can get very hot in the dry season. For real enthusiasts, it may be best to head out of Siem Reap after lunch, to get to the sanctuary at around 4pm for an afternoon viewing. Stay overnight at the environment office, and view the birds in the morning before returning to Siem Reap for lunch.

One company in Siem Reap offers organised tours for day-trippers to help promote the benefits of responsible tourism to the Cambodian people and financially contribute to the conservation of the area. **Osmose** (☎ 012-832812, e *osmose@bigpond .com.kh*) runs day trips that cost US$60 per person with a minimum group of four. Tours offered by this nonprofit agency include transportation, entrance fees, guides, breakfast, lunch and water, making it a very reasonable deal. **Terre Cambodge** (☎ 964391, w *www.terrecambodge.com*) offers trips to the flooded forest of Kompong Phluk, near the bird sanctuary.

There is another bird sanctuary, **Ang Trapeng Thmor Reserve** just across the border in Banteay Meanchey Province in the Phnom Srok region, about 100km from Siem Reap. It's one of only two places in the world where it is possible to see the extremely rare sarus crane, as depicted on bas-reliefs at Angkor. Take the road to Sisophon for about 72km before turning north. The reserve is based around a reservoir created by forced labour during the Khmer Rouge regime.

FLOATING VILLAGE OF CHONG KNEAS

ភូមិបណ្តែតចុងគ្នាស

A trip to this floating village has become a popular excursion for visitors wanting a break from the temples, and is easy enough to arrange yourself. Visitors arriving by fast boat get a preview, as the floating village is near Phnom Krom where the boat docks. It is very scenic in the warm light of early morning or late afternoon and can be combined with a view of the sunset from the hilltop temple of Phnom Krom (see the 'Temples of Angkor' special section for more details). Visitors should also check out the **Gecko Environment Centre** *(open 8.30am-5.30pm daily)*, part of the floating village. It has displays on flora and fauna of the area, as well as information on communities living around the lake.

The village moves depending on the season and you will need to rent a boat to get around properly. This costs from US$8 to US$10 per hour, regardless of the number of people, and regardless of safety too, so make sure you don't overfill it. It might also be possible to rent a smaller rowing boat or dugout for just a couple of dollars.

To get to the floating village from Siem Reap costs US$1 by moto each way (more if the driver waits) or US$5 by taxi.

ANDERS BLOMQVIST

BILL WASSMAN

Title Page: Saffron-robe
Vishnu with offerings at
awe-inspiring Angkor
Wat (Photograph by
Frank Carter)

Top: Western side of on
of Angkor's most
beautiful, treasured and
best-preserved temples,
Angkor Wat

Bottom: Guardian
statues in a shrine at
Wat Phnom

The temples of Angkor are the heart and soul of the Kingdom of Cambodia, a source of inspiration and national pride to all Khmers as they struggle to rebuild their lives after the years of terror and trauma. Today, they are a point of pilgrimage for all Cambodians and no tourist will want to miss their extravagant beauty when passing through the region.

The temples of Angkor were built between the 9th and 14th centuries AD, when Khmer civilisation was at the height of its extraordinary creativity. Unparalleled in Southeast Asia – though the temples of Bagan in Myanmar (Burma) are a close runner-up – Angkor rates among the foremost architectural wonders of the world.

From Angkor the kings of the mighty Khmer empire ruled over a vast territory that extended from the tip of what is now southern Vietnam, north to Yunnan in China, and from Vietnam west to the Bay of Bengal. Angkor's 100 or so temples constitute the sacred skeleton of a spectacular administrative and religious centre. Its houses, public buildings and palaces were constructed of wood – now long decayed – because the right to dwell in structures of brick or stone was reserved for the gods.

It is easy to spend as long as a week at Angkor, seeing the temples at a leisurely pace, returning to the principal attractions several times to see them at different times of day, and taking in newly emerging sites farther afield. Many travellers feel that four or five days is the optimum length of time to spend at Angkor. This is just about long enough to fit in all the highlights of the Angkor area without feeling saturated. However, even with only two days at your disposal you can get a lot of sightseeing done providing you make some early starts. If your time is limited and you have only one day to tour the Angkor complex, it is probably best to organise a tour guide and an itinerary to get the most out of the day.

HISTORY
Early Years

The Angkorian period, in which the temples of Angkor were built and the Khmer empire consolidated its position as one of the great powers of Southeast Asia, covers more than 600 years from AD 802 to 1432. This broad sweep of history encompasses periods of decline and revival, and wars with rival powers in Vietnam, Thailand and Myanmar. This brief history deals only with the periods that produced the temples of Angkor.

The Angkorian period begins with the rule of Jayavarman II (reigned 802–50). Little is known of this king. It is thought that he spent his early years in Java, where he was resident at the Shailendras' court. He returned to Cambodia in the late 8th century and established himself as head of an independent Khmer kingdom. His court was variously sited in four different locations: first at Phnom Kulen, 40km northeast of

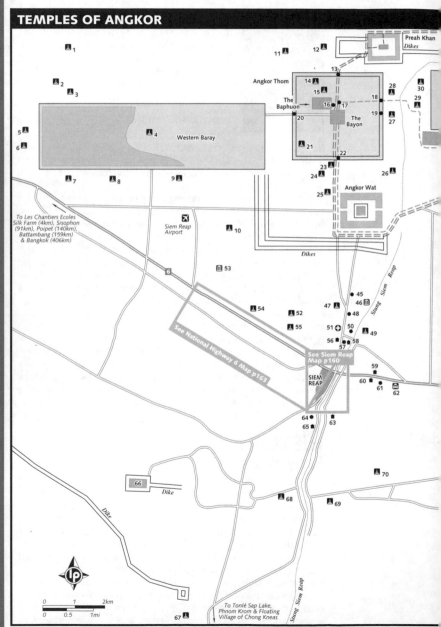

TEMPLES OF ANGKOR

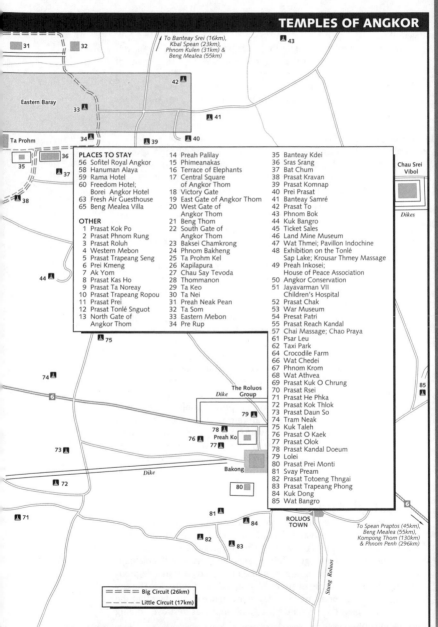

TEMPLES OF ANGKOR

Eastern Baray

Ta Prohm

Chau Srei Vibol

Dikes

The Roluos Group

Preah Ko

Bakong

ROLUOS TOWN

To Banteay Srei (16km), Kbal Spean (23km), Phnom Kulen (31km) & Beng Mealea (55km)

To Spean Praptos (45km), Beng Mealea (55km), Kompong Thom (130km) & Phnom Penh (296km)

Stung Roluos

Dike

PLACES TO STAY
56 Sofitel Royal Angkor
58 Hanuman Alaya
59 Rama Hotel
60 Freedom Hotel; Borei Angkor Hotel
63 Fresh Air Guesthouse
65 Beng Mealea Villa

OTHER
1 Prasat Kok Po
2 Prasat Phnom Rung
3 Prasat Roluh
4 Western Mebon
5 Prasat Trapeang Seng
6 Prei Kmeng
7 Ak Yom
8 Prasat Kas Ho
9 Prasat Ta Noreay
10 Prasat Trapeang Ropou
11 Prasat Prei
12 Prasat Tonlé Snguot
13 North Gate of Angkor Thom

14 Preah Palilay
15 Phimeanakas
16 Terrace of Elephants
17 Central Square of Angkor Thom
18 Victory Gate
19 East Gate of Angkor Thom
20 West Gate of Angkor Thom
21 Beng Thom
22 South Gate of Angkor Thom
23 Baksei Chamkrong
24 Phnom Bakheng
25 Ta Prohm Kel
26 Kapilapura
27 Chau Say Tevoda
28 Thommanon
29 Ta Keo
30 Ta Nei
31 Preah Neak Pean
32 Ta Som
33 Eastern Mebon
34 Pre Rup

35 Banteay Kdei
36 Sras Srang
37 Bat Chum
38 Prasat Kravan
39 Prasat Komnap
40 Prei Prasat
41 Banteay Samré
42 Prasat To
43 Phnom Bok
44 Kuk Bangro
45 Ticket Sales
46 Land Mine Museum
47 Wat Thmei; Pavillon Indochine
48 Exhibition on the Tonlé Sap Lake; Krousar Thmey Massage
49 Preah Inkosei; House of Peace Association
50 Angkor Conservation
51 Jayavarman VII Children's Hospital
52 Prasat Chak
53 War Museum
54 Presat Patri
55 Prasat Reach Kandal
57 Chai Massage; Chao Praya
61 Psar Leu
62 Taxi Park
64 Crocodile Farm
66 Wat Chedei
67 Phnom Krom
68 Wat Athvea
69 Prasat Kuk O Chrung
70 Prasat Rsei
71 Prasat He Phka
72 Prasat Kok Thlok
73 Prasat Daun So
74 Tram Neak
75 Kuk Taleh
76 Prasat O Kaek
77 Prasat Olok
78 Prasat Kandal Doeum
79 Lolei
80 Prasat Prei Monti
81 Svay Pream
82 Prasat Totoeng Thngai
83 Prasat Trapeang Phong
84 Kuk Dong
85 Wat Bangro

==== Big Circuit (26km)
---- Little Circuit (17km)

Angkor; and later at Roluos (known then as Haliharalaya) 13km east of Siem Reap.

Jayavarman II set a precedent that became a feature of the Angkorian period and accounts for the staggering architectural productivity of the Khmers at this time. He established himself as a 'god king' or 'universal king' whose all-reaching power expressed the god-like qualities of Shiva. Shiva's dwelling place is the mythical Mt Meru, and consequently Jayavarman built a 'temple mountain' at Phnom Kulen, which symbolised the holy mountain at the centre of the universe. This cult of the god king is known as *devaraja*.

Indravarman I (reigned 877–89) is believed to have been a usurper, and probably inherited the mantle of god king through conquest. He built a 6.5 sq km *baray* (reservoir) at Roluos and established the temple Preah Ko. The baray marked the first stage of a massive irrigation system that, eventually, was to extensively water the lands around Angkor. But the baray also had religious significance in that according to legend Mt Meru is flanked by lakes. As is often the case, necessity and symbolism dovetail nicely. Indravarman's final work was Bakong, a pyramidal representation of Mt Meru.

For some reason, Indravarman I's son Yasovarman I (reigned 889–910) looked farther afield when it came time to celebrate his divinity and glory in a temple mountain of his own. After building Lolei on an artificial island in the baray established by his father, he began work on the Bakheng, siting it on the hill known today as Phnom Bakheng (a favoured spot for sunset photographs of Angkor Wat). A raised highway was constructed to connect Phnom Bakheng with Roluos, 16km to the southeast, and a large baray was formed to the east of Phnom Bakheng – it is now known as the Eastern Baray and has entirely silted up. Yasovarman also established the temple mountains of Phnom Krom and Phnom Bok.

Following the death of Yasovarman I, power briefly shifted away from the Angkor region to Koh Ker, around 80km to the northeast of Angkor, under another usurper Jayavarman IV. In 944 power returned again to Angkor under the leadership of Rajendravarman II (reigned 944–68), who built the Eastern Mebon and Pre Rup. The rule of his son Jayavarman V (reigned 968–1001) produced the temples Ta Keo and Banteay Srei.

Classical Age

The temples that are now the highlights of any tour of Angkor – Angkor Wat and those in and around the walled city of Angkor Thom – were built during the classical age. The classical appellation conjures up images of a golden age of abundance and leisurely temple construction, but while this period is marked by fits of remarkable productivity, it was also a time of turmoil, conquests and setbacks. The city of Angkor Thom, for example, owes its existence to the fact that the old city of Angkor that stood on the same spot was destroyed during a Cham invasion.

There is much debate as to the origins of Suryavarman I (reigned 1002–49) – he may have been of Malay origin, but is more likely to have hailed from a noble family in the northeast of Cambodia. He was a usurper to the throne who won the day through strategic alliances and military conquests. Although he adopted the Hindu cult of the god king, he is thought to have come from a Mahayana Buddhist background and may even have sponsored the growth of Buddhism in Cambodia. Certainly, Buddhist sculpture became more commonplace in the Angkor region during his time.

Little physical evidence of Suryavarman I's reign remains at Angkor, but his military exploits brought much of southern Thailand and southern Laos into the ambit of Angkorian control. His son Udayadityavarman II (reigned 1049–65) embarked on further military expeditions, extending the empire still further. He built the Baphuon and the Western Mebon.

From 1065 until the end of the century, Angkor was again divided by various contenders for the throne. The first important monarch of the new regime, when it came to be founded, was Suryavarman II (reigned 1112–52). Suryavarman II unified Cambodia and led campaigns against Vietnam, extending Khmer influence to Malaya, Myanmar and Siam. He also set himself apart religiously from earlier kings through his devotion to the Hindu deity Vishnu, to whom he consecrated the largest and arguably the most magnificent of all the Angkorian temples, Angkor Wat.

The reign of Suryavarman II and the construction of Angkor Wat marks one of the high-water marks of Khmer civilisation. But if decline was not inevitable, there were signs that it was waiting in the wings. It is thought that the hydraulic system of reservoirs and canals that supported the agriculture of Angkor had by this time probably been pushed beyond capacity and was slowly starting to silt up. The construction of Angkor was a major strain on resources, and on top of this Suryavarman II led a disastrous campaign against Vietnam late in his reign.

In 1177 the Chams of southern Vietnam (then the Kingdom of Champa and long annexed by the Khmer empire) rose up and sacked Angkor. They burned the wooden city and carried off its accumulated wealth. Four years later Jayavarman VII (reigned 1181–1219) struck back, driving the Chams out of Cambodia and reclaiming Angkor.

Jayavarman VII's reign has given scholars much to debate. It represents a radical departure from those of his predecessors. For centuries the fount of royal divinity had reposed in the Hindu deity Shiva and, occasionally, Vishnu. Jayavarman VII, however, adopted Mahayana Buddhism and looked to Avalokiteshvara, the Buddha of Compassion, for sponsorship of his reign. In doing so he may very likely have been converting to a religion that already enjoyed wide popular support among his subjects. It may also be that the destruction of Angkor was such a blow to royal divinity that a new religious foundation was thought to be needed.

In his reign Jayavarman VII embarked on a dizzying catalogue of temple projects centred on the Baphuon, which was the site of the city destroyed by the Chams. Angkor Thom, Jayavarman VII's new city, was surrounded by walls and a moat (which became another component of Angkor's complex irrigation system). The centrepiece of Angkor Thom was the Bayon, the temple mountain studded with faces that, along with Angkor Wat, is the most famous of the temples of Angkor. Other temples built during the reign of Jayavarman VII include Ta Prohm, Banteay Kdei and Preah Khan. Farther afield he rebuilt vast temple complexes such as Banteay Chhmar and Preah Khan, making him by far the most prolific builder of Angkor's many kings.

He also embarked on a major public-works programme, building roads, schools and hospitals across the empire. Remains of many of these roads and their magnificent bridges can still be seen across Cambodia today. Spean Praptos at Kompong Kdei, 60km southeast of Siem Reap on National Hwy 6 (NH6) is the most famous, but there are many more lost in the forest on the old Angkorian road from Beng Mealea to the great Preah Khan.

After the death of Jayavarman VII around 1219, the Khmer empire went into decline. The state religion reverted to Hinduism for a century or more and much Buddhist sculpture adorning Jayavarman's many temples was vandalised or altered. The Thais sacked Angkor in 1351 and again in 1431. The Khmer court moved to Phnom Penh, only to return fleetingly to Angkor in the 16th century; in the meantime it was abandoned to pilgrims, holy men and the elements.

Angkor Rediscovered

The French 'discovery' of Angkor in the 1860s made an international splash and created a great deal of interest in Cambodia. But 'discovery', with all the romance it implied, was something of a misnomer. For a start, as historian David Chandler points out, when French explorer Henri Mouhot first stumbled across Angkor Wat it was found to contain a 'prosperous monastery…tended by more than 1000 hereditary slaves'. What's more, Portuguese travellers in the 16th century seem to have come across Angkor, referring to it as the Walled City. A 17th-century Japanese pilgrim even drew a detailed plan of Angkor Wat, though he mistakenly concluded he had seen it in India.

Still, it was the publication of *Voyage à Siam et dans le Cambodge* by Mouhot in 1868 that first brought Angkor to the public eye. Although the explorer himself made no such claims, by the 1870s he was being posthumously celebrated as the discoverer of the lost temple city of Cambodia. The fact is, a French missionary known as Charles-Emile Bouillevaux had visited Angkor 10 years before Mouhot and had published his own account of his findings. It was roundly ignored. It was Mouhot's account, with its rich descriptions and tantalising pen-and-ink, colour sketches of the temples, that turned the ruins into an international obsession.

Angkorian Monarchs

A mind-numbing array of kings ruled the Khmer empire from the 9th century to the 14th century. The following list includes the dates they reigned and the more significant monuments built during their reign.

king	dates of reign	temples built
Jayavarman II	802–850	
Jayavarman III	850–877	
Indravarman I	877–889	Preah Ko, Bakong (Roluos)
Yasovarman I	889–910	Lolei (Roluos), Phnom Bakheng
Harshavarman I	910–928	
Jayavarman IV	928–942	
Harshavarman II	942–944	
Rajendravarman II	944–968	Eastern Mebon, Pre Rup, Phimeanakas
Jayavarman V	968–1001	Ta Keo, Banteay Srei
Udayadityavarman I	1001–1002	
Suryavarman I	1002–1049	
Udayadityavarman II	1049–1065	The Baphuon, Western Mebon
Harshavarman III	1065–1090	
Jayavarman VI	1090–1108	
Dharanindravarman I	1108–1112	
Suryavarman II	1112–1152	Angkor Wat, Banteay Samré
Harshavarman IV	1152	
Dharanindravarman II	1152–1177	
Angkor occupied by the Chams		
Jayavarman VII	1181–1219	Angkor Thom, Ta Nei, Preah Khan, Preah Palilay, Ta Prohm, Banteay Kdei
Indravarman II	1219–1243	
Jayavarman VIII	1243–1295	
Sri-Indravarman	1295–1307	
Sri-Indrajayavarman	1307	
Jayavarman Paramesvara	mid-1300s	

From the time of Mouhot, Angkor became the target of financed French expeditions. A few individuals, such as John Thomson (a Scottish photographer who took the first photographs of the temples and was the first to posit the idea that the temples were symbolic representations of the mythical Mt Meru), managed to make their way to the region, but for the most part it was to be the preserve of French archaeological teams.

The first of these expeditions was led by Ernest Doudart de Lagrée, and its principal mission was to determine whether the Mekong River was navigable into China. Doudart de Lagrée died upstream in Yunnan, but not before taking his team on a detour to the Temples of Angkor. The team assembled its findings at Angkor into *Voyage d'exploration en Indo-Chine,* which contained valuable archaeological details concerning Angkor.

Louis Delaporte, who had joined Doudart de Lagrée on the first mission, led the second expedition to Angkor. The aim was to produce plans of the monuments and return to France with examples of Angkorian art. Delaporte brought back some 70 pieces, and his sketches aroused the interest of some Parisian architects, who saw in the monuments of Angkor a bold clash of form and function. Lucien Fournereau, an architect, travelled to Angkor in 1887 and produced plans and meticulously executed cross-sections that were to stand as the best available until the 1960s.

In 1901 the École Française d'Extrême Orient (EFEO) began a long association with Angkor by funding an expedition to the Bayon. In 1907 Angkor, which had been under Thai control, was returned to Cambodia and the EFEO took responsibility for clearing and restoring the whole site. In the same year, the first tourists arrived in Angkor – an unprecedented 200 of them in three months. Angkor had been 'rescued' from the jungle and was assuming its place in the modern world.

ARCHAEOLOGY OF ANGKOR
Angkor Restored

With the exception of Angkor Wat, which was restored for use as a Buddhist shrine in the 16th century by the Khmer royalty, the monuments of Angkor were left to the jungle for many centuries. A large number of the monuments are made of sandstone, which tends to dissolve when in prolonged contact with dampness. Bat droppings took their toll, as did sporadic pilfering of sculptures and cut stones. In the cases of some monuments, such as Ta Prohm, the jungle had stealthily waged an all-out invasion, and plant-life could only be removed at great risk to the structures it now supported in its web of roots.

Initial attempts to clear Angkor under the aegis of the EFEO were fraught with technical difficulties and theoretical disputes. On the technical front, the jungle tended to grow back as soon as it was cleared, and on a theoretical front scholars debated the extent to which temples should be restored and whether later additions (such as Buddha images in Hindu temples) should be removed.

Angkor Conservation

Apsara Authority (Authority for the Protection and Management of Angkor and the region of Siem Reap) is responsible for the research, protection and conservation of cultural heritage around Angkor, as well as urban planning in Siem Reap and tourism development in the region. Quite a mandate, quite a challenge. For more on their work visit w www.autoriteapsara.org. The Siem Reap office is housed within the Angkor Conservation compound.

Angkor Conservation is a Ministry of Culture compound housing more than 5000 statues, *linga* (phallic symbols) and inscribed steles, stored here to protect them from the wanton looting that has blighted hundreds of nearby sites around Angkor. Angkor's finest statuary is hidden away inside Angkor Conservation's warehouses, meticulously numbered and catalogued. Unfortunately, without the right contacts, getting a peek at the statues is a lost cause. Hopefully, some of the statuary will eventually go on public display in some sort of Angkor Museum.

It was not until the late 1920s that a solution came along. It was the method the Dutch had used to restore Borobudur in Java and it was called anastylosis. Put simply, it was a method of reconstructing monuments with the original materials used and in keeping with the original form of the structure. New materials were permitted only where the originals could not be found, and were to be used discreetly. An example of this method can be seen on the right side of the causeway leading to the entrance of Angkor Wat – it is largely the result of French restoration work.

The first major restoration job was carried out on Banteay Srei in the early 1930s. It was deemed such a success that many more extensive restoration projects were undertaken elsewhere around Angkor, a project that culminated in the massive Angkor Wat restoration in the 1960s. Large cranes and earth-moving machines were brought to bear, and the operation was backed by a veritable army of surveying equipment.

The Khmer Rouge victory and Cambodia's subsequent slide into an intractable civil war resulted in far less damage to Angkor than many had assumed, as EFEO and the Ministry of Culture had removed many of the statues from the temple sites for protection. Nevertheless, turmoil in Cambodia resulted in a long interruption of restoration work, allowing the jungle to grow back and once again resume its assault on the monuments. The illegal trade of *objets d'art* on the world art market has also been a major threat to Angkor, although it is the more remote sites that have been targeted recently. Angkor has been under the jurisdiction of the United Nations Educational Scientific and Cultural Organisation (Unesco) since 1992 as a World Heritage site, and international and local efforts continue to preserve and reconstruct the monuments.

ARCHITECTURAL STYLES

From the time of the earliest Angkorian monuments at Roluos, Khmer architecture was continually evolving, often from the rule of one king to the next. Archaeologists therefore divide the monuments of Angkor into nine separate periods, each named after the foremost example of the art style in question.

To a certain extent, however, the evolution of Khmer architecture was the elaboration of a central theme: the idea of the temple mountain. The earlier a temple was constructed the closer it adheres to this fundamental idea. Essentially the mountain was represented by a blunt-topped tower mounted on a tiered base. At the summit was the central sanctuary, usually with an open door to the east, and three false doors at the remaining cardinal points of the compass.

By the time of the Bakheng period, this layout was being embellished. The summit of the central tower, for example, was crowned with five 'peaks', in a quincuncial arrangement – four cells at the points of the compass and one in the centre. Even Angkor Wat features this layout, though on a grand scale. Other features that came to be favoured included an entry tower and a causeway lined with *naga* (mythical serpent) balustrades or sculpture leading up to the temple.

As the temples grew in ambition, the central tower became a less-prominent feature, although it remained the focus of the temple. Courtyards enclosed by colonnaded galleries, with the galleries themselves richly decorated, came to surround the central tower. Smaller towers were placed on gates and on the corners of walls, their overall number generally having a religious or astrological significance.

These refinements and additions culminated in Angkor Wat, which effectively showcases the evolution of Angkorian architecture. The architecture of the Bayon period breaks with tradition to a certain extent in temples such as Ta Prohm and Preah Khan, in which the horizontal layout of galleries, corridors and courtyards seems to completely eclipse the central tower.

The curious narrowness of the corridors and doorways in these structures can be explained by the fact that Angkorian architects engineered

Periods of Angkorian Architecture

style	date
Preah Ko	875–893
The Bakheng	893–925
Koh Ker	921–945
Pre Rup	947–965
Banteay Srei	967–1000
Kleang	965–1010
The Baphuon	1010–1080
Angkor Wat	1100–1175
Bayon	1177–1230

TRUDI CANAVAN

Vishnu reclining on the serpent Anata

arches by laying blocks on top of each other, until they met at a central point. These are known as false arches – they can support only very short spans.

ORIENTATION

Angkor's monuments are spread throughout the forest. Heading north from Siem Reap, you first come to Angkor Wat, then the walled city of Angkor Thom. To the east and west of this city are two vast reservoirs, which helped to feed the Angkor Thom population. Farther east are temples including Ta Prohm, Banteay Kdei and Pre Rup. North of Angkor Thom is Preah Kahn and way beyond in the northeast, Banteay Srei and Phnom Kulen. To the east of Siem Reap is the Roluos group of early Angkorian temples.

Maps

There have been quite a number of excellent maps of the Angkor area published over the years, many of which appear in the books on Angkor recommended in the Books section of the Facts for the Visitor chapter. The free *Siem Reap Visitor's Map*, the *Siem Reap Visitors Guide* and the *Free Complete Angkor Guide* all include an overview of the temples of Angkor and are available at certain hotels, guesthouses and restaurants in town. The May 1982 issue of *National Geographic* magazine has an excellent map that shows Angkor in its prime.

INFORMATION
Visitor Fees

Entrance fees to Angkor have settled to affordable levels, and while relatively expensive by Cambodian standards, they still represent excellent value. Visitors have a choice of a one-day pass (US$20), a three-day pass (US$40) or a one-week pass (US$60). Passes can no longer be extended, so plan your visit in advance. Purchase the entry pass from the large official entrance booth on the road to Angkor Wat. One photo is required for multi-day passes – there are instant cameras at the entrance booth. Visitors entering the monuments after 4pm effectively get a free sunset, as the ticket starts from the following day. This fee includes access to all the monuments of Angkor in the Siem Reap area, but does not currently include the sacred mountain of Phnom Kulen, effectively run as a private enterprise by a local businessman.

Entry tickets to the temples of Angkor are under the control of a local petroleum company called Sokimex, which in return for administrating the site takes the lion's share of the money. A smaller sum goes to the authorities responsible for protecting and conserving the temples. This is a rather ridiculous scenario that will hopefully be scrapped in the coming years, allowing all funds from visitor fees to benefit the preservation of this unique place. Ironically, the situation is better than a few

Out to Lunch

Most of the tour groups around Angkor head back to Siem Reap for lunch. This is as good a reason as any to stick around the temples, taking advantage of the lack of crowds to explore some popular sites and enjoying a local lunch at one of the many stalls. Almost all of the major temples have some sort of nourishment available beyond the walls. The most extensive selection is lined up opposite the entrance to Angkor Wat, including several cheap and cheerful local restaurants, as well as the sophisticated Angkor Café, with refined Khmer food and a pleasant ambience. Chez Sophea offers barbecued fish and home-made salads.

There are dozens of local noodle stalls just north of the Bayon, which are a good spot for a quick bite to eat. Other central temples with food available include Ta Prohm, Preah Khan and Ta Keo. Farther afield, Banteay Srei has several small restaurants, complete with ornate wood furnishings fresh out of Cambodia's forests. Farther north at Kbal Spean, the pickings are more basic, but they can cook up fried rice or a noodle soup.

Water and soft drinks are available throughout the temple area, and many sellers are lurking in hidden corners of the temples, ready to pounce with offers of 'you wanna buy cold drink?'. Sometimes it's at just the right moment, on other occasions it is the 27th time in an hour and you are ready to scream. Try not to – you'll scare your fellow travellers and lose face with the locals.

years ago, when ticket scams abounded and almost nothing of the entry fee filtered through to the temples themselves. Most of the major temples now have uniformed guards to check the tickets, which has reduced the opportunity for scams, although many would argue that the current arrangement with Sokimex is the biggest scam of all! Visitors found inside central temples without a ticket are fined US$30. An Angkor pass is not required for excursions to Kbal Spean, Phnom Kulen, Beng Mealea or villages beyond the Angkor area.

Suggested Itineraries

The chief attractions of Angkor can be summed up in Angkor Wat; the walled city of Angkor Thom (principally the Bayon); and Ta Prohm, which famously has been left to the jungle. However, these are also the most popular and can be very busy at certain times of the day. On a day trip to Angkor, you might restrict your sightseeing to these three attractions – attempting too much is likely to reduce the whole experience to a whirl of impressions. Other spectacular temples that should not be missed include Preah Khan, with its incredible cruciform corridors, and Banteay Srei, home to the most exquisite carving produced in the Angkorian period.

A curious lore of itineraries and times for visiting the monuments has coalesced around Angkor since tourism first started in the 1920s. It is received wisdom that as Angkor Wat faces west, one should be there

When Nature Calls

There are very few toilets in and around the temples of Angkor, so for those with a weak bladder it pays to plan ahead. There are toilet facilities both inside (in the grounds of the southern pagoda) and outside Angkor Wat, on the eastern side of the Bayon, on the western side of Ta Prohm, at Banteay Srei, Kbal Spean and Phnom Kulen. That is pretty much it for now, although the authorities have plans for many more. A trip costs 500r and it might be worth carrying some paper just in case. Remember, in remote areas, don't stray off the path – being seen in a compromising position is infinitely better than stepping on a land mine.

for the sunset, and in the case of the Bayon, which faces east, at sunrise. Ta Prohm, most people seem to agree, can be visited in the middle of the day because of its umbrella of foliage. This is all well and good: Angkor Wat is indeed stunning at sunset and the Bayon is a good place to be for sunrise if you can get out of bed on time. If you reverse the order, however, the temples will still look good – and you can avoid the crowds. For more on keeping away from the crowds, see the 'Avoiding the Hordes' boxed text later.

Back in the early days of tourism, the problem of what to see and in what order was left to two basic temple courses: the Little (Petit) Circuit and the Big (Grand) Circuit. It's difficult to imagine that anyone follows these to the letter any more, but in their time they were often undertaken on the back of an elephant.

The circuits provide a useful guide on breaking a trip into bite-sized chunks. Angkor Wat, Ta Prohm and the principal monuments of Angkor Thom are impressive enough to warrant a morning or afternoon each, as are the remote sites of Kbal Spean or Beng Mealea, best combined in a long day trip with Banteay Srei. Banteay Srei can also be visited in a trip including Banteay Samré and a possible aside to the little-visited hilltop temple of Phnom Bok. Other temples that can be easily grouped together include Preah Khan, Preah Neak Pean, Ta Som, East Mebon and Pre Rup; Chau Sey Tevoda, Thommanon, Ta Keo, Banteay Kdei and Sras Srang; and the Roluos group to the east of Siem Reap.

Little Circuit The 17km Little Circuit begins at Angkor Wat, heads north to Phnom Bakheng, Baksei Chamkrong and Angkor Thom (in which one visits the city wall and gates, the Bayon, the Baphuon, the Royal Enclosure, Phimeanakas, Preah Palilay, Tep Pranam, the Preah Pithu group, the Terrace of the Leper King, the Terrace of Elephants, the Central Square, the North Kleang, the South Kleang and the 12 Towers of Prasat), exits from Angkor Thom via Victory Gate (in the eastern wall), continues to Chau Say Tevoda, Thommanon, Spean Thma and Ta Keo, heads northeast of the road to Ta Nei, turns south to Ta Prohm, continues east to Banteay Kdei and Sras Srang, and finally returns to Angkor Wat via Prasat Kravan.

Big Circuit The 26km Big Circuit is an extension of the Little Circuit: where the latter exits at the east gate of the walled city of Angkor Thom, the Big Circuit exits at the north gate and continues to Preah Khan and Preah Neak Pean, east to Ta Som then south via the Eastern Mebon to Pre Rup. From there it heads west and then southwest on its return to Angkor Wat.

One Day If you have only one day to visit Angkor a good itinerary would be the Bayon for sunrise (or early morning after a quick sunrise at Angkor Wat) and a tour of the other attractions of Angkor Thom, before heading over to Preah Khan late in the morning or early in the afternoon. From here you might visit Ta Prohm and then the Victory Gate of Angkor Thom en route to Angkor Wat for the last couple of hours before sunset on the busy hill of Phnom Bakheng.

Two Days A two-day itinerary might be very similar to the one above, but with more time to explore the temples. Now that the road is surfaced, an important addition is petite Banteay Srei with its fabulous carvings. Finally, on the back circuit to Preah Khan it is worth visiting Preah Neak Pean and Ta Som – small temples with plenty of character.

Three to Five Days If you have three to five days to explore Angkor, it is possible to see most of the important sites described in this chapter. One way to approach a three- to four-day tour of Angkor is to see as much as possible on the first day or two (as covered above) and then spend the final days combining visits to other sites such as Roluos and Banteay Samré, and revisiting the places you liked best on the first day. Others prefer a gradual build up to the most spectacular monuments, progressing through more minor temples first. Another interesting option is to approach it chronologically, starting with the earliest Angkorian temples and working steadily forwards in time to Angkor Thom, taking stock of the evolution of Khmer architecture and artistry along the way.

It is also worth considering a visit to the River of a Thousand Lingas at Kbal Spean, offering the chance to stretch your legs amid natural and manmade splendour, or making a trip to the remote, vast and overgrown temple of Beng Mealea. However, these are easier to accomplish with four days or more, as both require one full day to visit.

One Week Those with the time to spend a week at Angkor will be richly rewarded. Not only is it possible to fit all the temples of the region into an itinerary, but it is possible to take an odd day off for shopping or exploring around Siem Reap. Check out the aforementioned itineraries for some ideas on approach but relax in the knowledge that you'll see it all.

Avoiding the Hordes

The days of serene and spiritual moments within the confines of empty temples are very much coming to an end. Angkor is back on the tourist trail and is destined to get much, much busier. But it's not all bad news, as with a little planning it is still possible to escape from the hordes. However, one important thing to remember, particularly on the subject of sunrise and sunset, is that places are popular for a reason, and it is worth going with the flow at least once.

The most popular place for sunrise is Angkor Wat and particularly the area around the royal ponds. The Bayon is also popular, but definitely sees fewer visitors than Angkor Wat in the early hours. Sras Srang is usually pretty quiet and a good sunrise here can be spectacular thanks to reflections in the extensive waters. Phnom Bakheng could be an attractive option, as the sun comes up behind Angkor Wat and there aren't the madding crowds found at sunset. Phnom Krom is also impressive, but getting out here so early is a real pain.

The definitive sunset spot is the hilltop temple of Phnom Bakheng, but this has been getting well out of control of late, with 500 or more tourists clambering around the small structure. Better to check it out for sunrise or early morning and miss the crowds. Staying within the confines of Angkor Wat can be a rewarding option as most of the package tourists head off to Phnom Bakheng around 5pm or so and it can be pretty peaceful. Its immense upper terraces also offer a good view across the forest canopy as the light shifts. Pre Rup is popular with some for an authentic rural sunset over the surrounding rice fields, but this is starting to get busier. Better is the hilltop temple of Phnom Krom, which offers commanding views across the Tonlé Sap lake, but involves a long drive back to town in the dark. The Western Baray is generally a quiet option, taking the sunset in across its vast waters from the eastern end.

When it comes to the most popular temples, the middle of the day is consistently the quietest time (the large groups head back to town for lunch) but its also the hottest. This makes it tough going around relatively open temples such as Banteay Srei and the Bayon, but fine at well-covered temples such as Ta Prohm, Preah Khan and Beng Mealea, or even the bas-reliefs at Angkor Wat. The busiest times at Angkor Wat are from 6am to 7am and 3pm to 5pm, at the Bayon from 7.30am to 9.30am, at Banteay Srei mid-morning and mid-afternoon, while at other popular temples such as Ta Prohm and Preah Khan, it is hard to predict. At most other temples, it's just a case of pot luck. If you pull up outside and see a car park full of tour buses, move on to somewhere quieter. The wonderful thing about Angkor is that there is always another temple to see.

Organised Tours & Tour Guides

Those on package tours or tailor-made trips will have their Angkor itinerary organised, while most budget and mid-range travellers prefer to take in the temples at their own pace. However, visitors with a

Getting Around the Temples of Angkor

Visitors heading to the temples of Angkor, in other words pretty much everybody coming to Cambodia, need to consider the most suitable way to travel between the temples. Many of the best-known temples are no more than a few kilometres from the walled city of Angkor Thom, just 10km from Siem Reap, and can be visited using anything from a car or motorbike to a sturdy pair of walking boots. Tourists on organised trips are likely to travel around the area by coach, minibus or car, but for the independent traveller there is a daunting range of alternatives to consider. For the ultimate Angkor experience, try a pick and mix, with a *moto* (small motorcycle with driver) one day to cover the more remote sites, a bicycle for a couple of days to get around the central temples, and an exploration on foot for a spot of peace and serenity. All this could one day become irrelevant as there have been persistent and well-founded rumours of a Korean company winning a contract to provide electric cars to get around the site. Disneyland Cambodia? For now the outcry among local moto drivers and transport companies has done enough to keep them at bay.

Car Cars are popular with some for getting about the temples. The obvious advantage is protection from the elements, be it rain in the wet season or punishing sun in the heat of the dry season. Shared between several travellers, they can also be an economical way to explore. The downside is that visitors are a little more isolated from the sights, sounds and smells (good news for some) as they travel between temples. A car for the day around the main temples is US$20 to US$25 and can be arranged with hotels, guesthouses and agencies in town.

Minibus Minibuses are available from various travel agents around town. A 12-seat minibus costs US$40 per day, a 25- or 30-seat minibus US$80 to US$100 per day, depending on the time of year.

4WD Vehicles with 4WD aren't necessary for the vast majority of Angkor's temples. However, people planning adventures farther afield to Preah Khan, Koh Ker or other remote sites in Preah Vihear Province (see the Northwestern Cambodia chapter) will need to arrange a 4WD if they don't want to be on a motorcycle for several long days. Rates are higher the farther you plan to go and the fancier the vehicle. Think US$80 and up per day.

Motorbike Most independent travellers end up visiting the temples by motorbike. Moto drivers accost visitors from the moment they set foot in Siem Reap, but often end up being knowledgeable and friendly, and good companions for a tour around the temples. They can drop you off and pick you up at allotted times and places and even tell you a bit of background about the temples as you zip around. Those on a really tight budget can just take individual moto rides from temple to temple and this may end up cheaper than the US$6 a day most drivers charge. Self-drive is currently prohibited, although there are periodic changes in the regulations. If self-drive is permitted once more, remember to observe the speed restrictions around Angkor as this is a protected area.

Getting Around the Temples of Angkor

It is also important to leave the bike at a guarded parking area or with a stallholder outside each temple, otherwise it might well get stolen.

Remorque-moto Siem Reap now has a new type of *remorque-moto* – a motorbike with a hooded carriage towed behind. These are becoming a very popular way to get around Angkor as travelling partners can still talk to each other as they explore, unlike on the back of a moto. They also offer limited protection from the rain. They are increasingly common around Siem Reap so prices have come down. US$10 to US$12 per day is about the range, depending on the season.

Bicycle Bicycles are a great way to get around the temples. They are environmentally friendly and are used by most locals living around the temples. There are few hills and the roads are in good condition, so there's no need for much cycling experience. Moving about at a slower speed, you soon find that you take in more than out of a car window or on the back of a speeding moto. Some guesthouses and hotels in town rent bikes for around US$1 to US$2 per day.

Cyclo Some companies have introduced *cyclos* (pedicabs) for transporting tour groups around the temples. This might be a good option for those who like the idea of a bicycle, but not the pedalling in the sun part. Rent a local *remorque-kang* (trailer pulled by a bicycle) for the day and the locals will sure get a surprise.

Elephant This was the traditional way to see the temples way back in the early days of tourism at Angkor, at the start of the 20th century. It is once again possible to take an elephant ride between the south gate of Angkor Thom and the Bayon (US$10), or up to the summit of Phnom Bakheng for sunset (US$15). It is hardly reliving the days of the explorers, but some tourists like to get that elephant-at-Angkor photo to show the folks back home. It can't be much fun for the elephants hauling tourists up and down the steep path each day.

Walking Why not forget these fancy-pants methods altogether and explore on foot. There are obvious limitations to what can be seen on foot, as some temples are just too far from Siem Reap. However, it is easy enough to walk to Angkor Wat and the temples of Angkor Thom, and this is a great way to meet up with villagers in the area. Walkers who want to get away from the roads should try the peaceful walk along the walls of Angkor Thom. It is about 13km in total, and offers access to several small, remote temples and a lot of birdlife.

Helicopter Finally, for those with lots of holiday money, there are tourist flights around Angkor Wat (US$68) and the temples outside Angkor Thom (US$120) with Helicopters Cambodia (☎ 012-814500, 016-839565), which has an office near the Psar Chaa in Siem Reap. The company also offers charters to remote temples such as Prasat Preah Vihear and Koh Ker, prices starting at US$1200 per hour plus 10% sales tax. Call the bank manager first.

flexible budget who have only a day or two at this incredible site may prefer something organised locally.

It is possible to link up with an official tour guide in Siem Reap. The Khmer Angkor Tour Guides Association (☎ 964347, e khmerang @camintel.com) in the Angkor Tourism Office is home to all of Angkor's authorised guides. Guides can be booked from US$20 a day for English and French speakers. Other languages such as Italian, German, Spanish, Japanese and Chinese are available, but at a higher charge as there are fewer speakers.

One-day tours to Angkor do not give you very long to explore the ruins. They can be booked through tour agencies in Phnom Penh starting from around US$200; this includes the return flight, entry fees, a guide, transport and lunch. Two-day, one-night tours cost from US$300 depending on accommodation; three days and two nights cost US$350 and up. The prices for overnight tours are based on one person; it gets considerably cheaper for couples or small groups, as transport, guide and room charges are shared.

For something just a little bit different, Terre Cambodge (e tercamb @hotmail.com), run from Tooi Tooi Bar in Siem Reap, offers trips to a variety of remote sites around Angkor.

ANGKOR WAT
អង្គរវត្ត

Angkor Wat is simply unique, a stunning blend of spirituality and symmetry, an enduring example of man's devotion to his gods. Relish the first approach, as that spine-tickling moment when you emerge on the inner causeway will rarely be felt again. It is the largest and undoubtedly the most breathtaking of the monuments of Angkor, widely believed to be the largest religious structure in the world. It is also the best-preserved temple at Angkor, as it was never abandoned to the elements, and repeated visits are always rewarded with previously unnoticed details. Most probably it was constructed as a funerary temple for Suryavarman II (reigned 1112–52) to honour Vishnu, the Hindu deity with whom the king identified.

There is much about Angkor Wat that is unique among the temples of Angkor. The most significant point is that the temple is oriented towards the west. West is symbolically the direction of death, which once led a large number of scholars to conclude that Angkor Wat must have existed primarily as a tomb. This idea was supported by the fact that the magnificent bas-reliefs of the temple were designed to be viewed in an anticlockwise direction, a practice which has antecedents in ancient Hindu funerary rites. Vishnu, however, is also frequently associated with the west, and it is now commonly accepted that Angkor Wat most likely served as both a temple and a mausoleum for Suryavarman II.

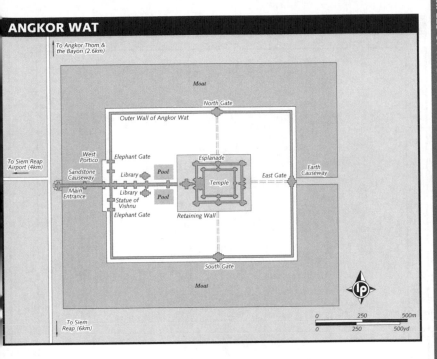

ANGKOR WAT

To Angkor Thom &
the Bayon (2.6km)

Moat

North Gate

Outer Wall of Angkor Wat

To Siem Reap
Airport (4km)

West
Portico

Elephant Gate

Esplanade

Earth
Causeway

Sandstone
Causeway

Library

Pool

East Gate

Main
Entrance

Temple

Library
Statue of
Vishnu

Pool

Elephant Gate

Retaining Wall

South Gate

Moat

To Siem
Reap (6km)

0   250   500m
0   250   500yd

Symbolism

The casual visitor to Angkor Wat is struck by its imposing grandeur
and, at close quarters, its fascinating decorative flourishes and extensive bas-reliefs; but a scholar at the time of its construction would have
revelled in its multilayered levels of meaning in much the same way as
a contemporary literary scholar might delight in James Joyce's Ulysses.

David Chandler, drawing on the research of Eleanor Moron, points
out in his book *History of Cambodia* that the spatial dimensions of
Angkor Wat parallel the lengths of the four ages (Yuga) of classical
Hindu thought. Thus the visitor to Angkor Wat who walks the causeway to the main entrance and through into the courtyards to the final
main tower, which once contained a statue of Vishnu, is metaphoric-
ally travelling back to the first age of the creation of the universe.

Of course, like the other temple mountains of Angkor, Angkor Wat
also replicates the spatial universe in miniature. The central tower is Mt
Meru, with its surrounding smaller peaks, surrounded in turn by continents (the lower courtyards) and the oceans (the moat). In the central
tower, the king prefigures the heaven that awaits him after death, the
lofty peak where *apsara* (heavenly nymphs) frolic with boundless
amorous desire.

TEMPLES OF ANGKOR

CENTRAL STRUCTURE OF ANGKOR WAT

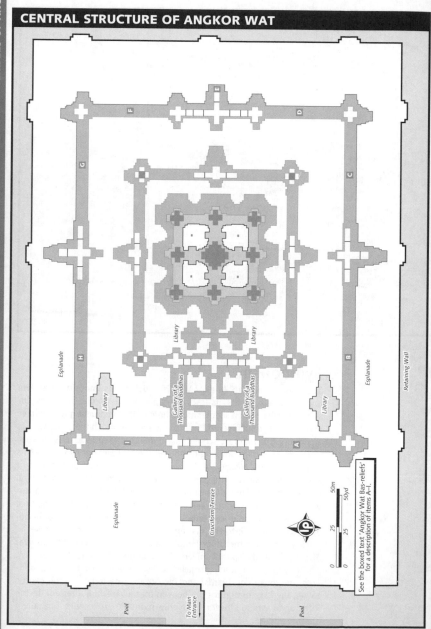

Esplanade

Library

Gallery of a Thousand Buddhas

Gallery of a Thousand Buddhas

Library

Library

Esplanade

Library

Library

Retaining Wall

Esplanade

Cruciform Terrace

Esplanade

Pool

Pool

To Main Entrance

See the boxed text 'Angkor Wat Bas-reliefs' for a description of items A–I.

0   25   50m
0   25   50yd

Angkor Wat Bas-reliefs

Stretching around the outside of the central temple complex, which is enclosed by an esplanade framed by a *naga* (mythical serpent) balustrade, is an 800m-long series of extraordinary bas-reliefs. The carvings were once sheltered by the cloister's wooden roof, which long ago rotted away (except for one original beam in the western half of the north gallery; the other roofed sections are reconstructions). The following is a brief description of the epic events depicted on the panels in the Gallery of Bas-reliefs. They are described in the order in which you'll come to them if you begin on the western side and keep the bas-reliefs to your left.

(A) Battle of Kurukshetra The southern portion of the west gallery depicts a battle scene from the Hindu *Mahabarata* epic, in which the Kauravas (coming from the north) and the Pandavas (coming from the south) advance in serried ranks towards each other, meeting in furious battle. Infantry are shown on the lowest tier, officers on elephant-back and chiefs on the second and third tiers. Among the more interesting details (from left to right): a dead chief lying on a pile of arrows and surrounded by his grieving parents and troops; a warrior on an elephant who, by putting down his weapon, has accepted defeat; and a mortally wounded officer, falling from the conveyance in which he is riding into the arms of his soldiers. Over the centuries, some sections have been polished to look like black marble by the millions of hands that fall upon them. The portico at the southwestern corner is decorated with sculptures representing subjects taken from the *Ramayana*.

(B) Army of Suryavarman II The remarkable western section of the south gallery depicts a triumphal battle-march of Suryavarman II's army. In the southwestern corner about 2m from the floor is Suryavarman II on an elephant, wearing the royal tiara and armed with a battle-axe; he is shaded by 15 umbrellas and fanned by legions of servants. Farther on is a procession of well-armed soldiers and officers on horseback; among them are bold and warlike chiefs on elephants. Just west of the vestibule is the rather disorderly Thai mercenary army, at that time allied with the Khmers in their conflict with the Chams. The Khmer troops have square breastplates and are armed with spears, the Thais wear headdresses and skirts and carry tridents.

The rectangular holes were created when, long ago, pieces of the scene – reputed to possess magical powers – were removed. Part of this panel was damaged by an artillery shell in 1971.

(C) Heaven & Hell The eastern half of the south gallery, the ceiling of which was restored in the 1930s, depicts the punishments and rewards of the 37 heavens and 32 hells. On the left, the upper and middle tiers show fine gentlemen and ladies proceeding towards 18-armed Yama (judge of the dead) seated on a bull; below him are his assistants, Dharma and Sitragupta. On the lower tier is the road to hell,

Angkor Wat Bas-reliefs (continued)

along which the wicked are dragged by devils. To Yama's right, the tableau is divided into two parts separated by a horizontal line of *garuda* (half-man, half-bird creatures): above, the elect dwell in beautiful mansions, served by women, children and attendants; below, the condemned suffer horrible tortures.

(D) Churning of the Ocean of Milk The southern section of the east gallery is decorated by the most famous of the bas-relief scenes at Angkor Wat, the Churning of the Ocean of Milk. This brilliantly executed carving depicts 88 *asura* (devils; on the left) and 92 *deva* (gods) with crested helmets, churning up the sea to extract the elixir of immortality, which both groups covet. The demons hold the head of the serpent and the gods hold its tail. At the centre of the sea, the serpent is coiled around Mt Mandala, which in the tug of war between the demons and the gods turns and churns up the water. Vishnu, incarnated as a huge turtle, lends his shell to serve as the base and pivot of Mt Mandala. Brahma, Shiva, Hanuman (the monkey god) and Lakshmi (the goddess of beauty), all make appearances, while overhead a host of heavenly female spirits sing and dance in encouragement.

(E) Elephant Gate This gate, which has no stairs leading to it, was used by the king and others for mounting and dismounting elephants directly from the gallery. North of the gate is a Khmer inscription recording the erection of a nearby stupa in the 18th century.

(F) Vishnu Conquers the Demons The northern section of the east gallery shows a furious and desperate encounter between Vishnu, riding on a garuda, and innumerable *danava* (demons). Needless to say, he slays all comers. Scholars conjecture that this gallery was executed at a later date, perhaps in the 15th or 16th century.

(G) Krishna & the Demon King The eastern section of the north gallery shows Vishnu incarnated as Krishna riding a garuda. He confronts a burning walled city, the residence of Bana, the demon king. The garuda puts out the fire and Bana is captured. In the final scene Krishna kneels before Shiva and asks that Bana's life be spared.

(H) Battle of the Gods & the Demons The western section of the north gallery depicts the battle between the 21 gods of the Brahmanic pantheon with various demons. The gods are featured with their traditional attributes and mounts. Vishnu, for example has four arms and is seated on a garuda, while Shiva rides a sacred goose.

(I) Battle of Lanka The northern half of the west gallery shows scenes from the *Ramayana*. In the Battle of Lanka, Rama (on the shoulders of Hanuman), along with his army of monkeys, battles 10-headed Ravana, seducer of Rama's beautiful wife Sita. Ravana rides a chariot drawn by monsters and commands an army of giants.

Architectural Layout

Angkor Wat is surrounded by a moat, 190m wide, that forms a giant rectangle measuring 1.5km by 1.3km. It makes the moats around European castles look like kid's play. From the west, a sandstone causeway crosses the moat; the holes in the paving stones held wooden pegs that were used to lift and position the stones during construction, after which the pegs were sawn off. The sandstone blocks from which Angkor Wat was built were apparently quarried more than 50km away (from the district of Svay Leu at the eastern foot of Phnom Kulen) and floated down the Siem Reap River on rafts. The logistics of such an operation must have been incredible, consuming the labour of thousands – an unbelievable feat given the lack of cranes and trucks that we take for granted in contemporary construction projects.

The rectangular outer wall, which measures 1025m by 800m, has a gate on each side, but the main entrance, a 235m-wide porch richly decorated with carvings and sculptures, is on the western side. In the gate tower to the right as you approach is a statue of Vishnu, 3.25m in height and hewn from a single block of sandstone. Vishnu's eight arms hold a mace, a spear, a disk, a conch and other items. You may even see locks of hair lying about. These are an offering by both young women and men preparing to get married or by people who seek to give thanks for their good fortune (such as successful recovery from an illness).

An avenue, 475m long and 9.5m wide and lined with naga balustrades, leads from the main entrance to the central temple, passing between two graceful libraries, the northern one currently under restoration by a Japanese team, and then two pools, the northern one a popular spot from which to watch sunrise.

The central temple complex consists of three storeys, each made of laterite, which enclose a square surrounded by intricately interlinked galleries.

The corners of the second and third storeys are marked by towers, each topped with pointed cupolas (domed structures). Rising 31m above the third level and 55m above the ground is the central tower, which gives the whole ensemble its sublime unity. At one time, the central sanctuary of Angkor Wat held a gold statue of Vishnu mounted on a *garuda* (half-man, half-bird creature) that represented

Right: Awe-inspiring Angkor Wat

KELLI HAMBLET

the deified god king Suryavarman II. The stairs to the upper level are immensely steep, as to reach the kingdom of the gods was no easy task; modern-day visitors should exercise due care and caution when clambering up or down, as they have claimed victims before.

ANGKOR THOM
អង្គរធំ

The fortified city of Angkor Thom (Great Angkor, or Great City), some 10 sq km in extent, was built by Angkor's greatest king, Jayavarman VII (reigned 1181–1219), who came to power just after the disastrous

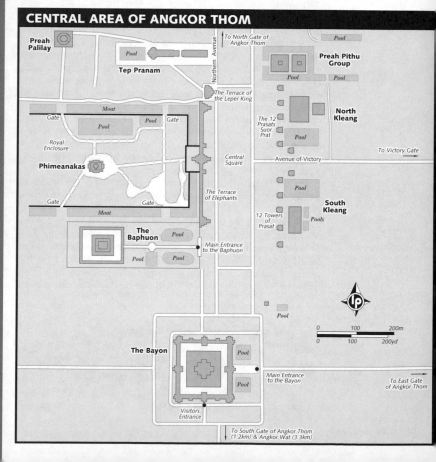

CENTRAL AREA OF ANGKOR THOM

Preah Palilay

To North Gate of Angkor Thom

Pool

Preah Pithu Group

Tep Pranam

Pool

Northern Avenue

The Terrace of the Leper King

Pool

Pool

Moat

Gate

Pool

Pool

Gate

The 12 Prasats Suor Prat

North Kleang

Pool

Royal Enclosure

Phimeanakas

Central Square

Avenue of Victory

To Victory Gate

Gate

Gate

Pool

South Kleang

Moat

The Terrace of Elephants

12 Towers of Prasat

Pools

The Baphuon

Pool

Pool

Pool

Main Entrance to the Baphuon

Pool

0   100   200m
0   100   200yd

The Bayon

Pool

Pool

Main Entrance to the Bayon

To East Gate of Angkor Thom

Visitors Entrance

To South Gate of Angkor Thom (1.2km) & Angkor Wat (3.3km)

sacking of the previous Khmer capital by the Chams. At its height, it may have supported a population of one million people in the surrounding region – at this time the inhabitants of London would have numbered about 50,000. Centred on the Bayon, Angkor Thom is enclosed by a *jayagiri* (square wall) 8m high and 12km in length and encircled by a *jayasindhu* (moat) 100m wide, said to have been inhabited by fierce crocodiles. This is yet another monumental expression of Mt Meru surrounded by the oceans, both the city and the symbolic universe recreated by Jayavarman VII after the sacking of Angkor by the Chams.

The city has five monumental gates, one each in the northern, western and southern walls and two in the eastern wall. The gates, which are 20m in height, are decorated with stone elephant trunks and crowned by four gargantuan faces of the Bodhisattva Avalokiteshvara facing the cardinal directions. In front of each gate stand giant statues of 54 gods (to the left of the causeway) and 54 demons (to the right of the causeway), a motif taken from the story of the Churning of the Ocean of Milk illustrated in the famous bas-relief at Angkor Wat. The south gate is most popular with visitors, as it has been fully restored and many of the heads (usually copies) remain in place. However, this is on the main road into Angkor Thom from Angkor Wat and gets very busy. More peaceful are the east and west gates at the end of uneven trails. The east gate was most recently used as a location on *Tomb Raider* where the bad guys broke into the 'tomb' by pulling down a giant (polystyrene!) apsara.

In the centre of the walled enclosure are the city's most important monuments, including the Bayon, the Baphuon, the Royal Enclosure, Phimeanakas and the Terrace of Elephants.

The Bayon
ប្រាយ័ន

The Bayon takes an easy second place after Angkor Wat as the most popular of Angkor's many temples. It's a place of stooped corridors, precipitous flights of stairs and, best of all, a collection of 54 gothic towers decorated with 216 coldly smiling, gargantuan faces of Avalokiteshvara. Some scholars suggest they may also contain a representation of Jayavarman VII, the Mahayana Buddhist king continuing the devaraja cult of his Hindu predecessors. As you walk around, a dozen or more of the visages are visible at any one time – full-face or in profile, almost level with your eyes or peering down from on high.

The Bayon is now known to have been built by Jayavarman VII, though for many years its origins were obscure. Shrouded in dense jungle, it also took researchers some time to realise that it stands in the exact centre of the city of Angkor Thom. There is still much mystery associated with the Bayon – its exact function and symbolism – and this seems only appropriate for a monument whose signature is an enigmatically smiling face.

A number of locals suggest that the Khmer empire was divided into 54 provinces at the time of the Bayon's construction, hence the all-seeing eyes of Avalokiteshvara (or Jayavarman VII) were keeping watch on the kingdom's far-flung subjects.

The eastward orientation of the Bayon leads most people to visit it early in the morning, preferably just after sunrise, when the sun inches upwards, lighting face after face with warmth. The Bayon, however, looks equally good in the late afternoon, and if you stay for the sunset you get the same effect as at sunrise, in reverse. A Japanese team is restoring several outer areas of the temple.

Architectural Layout Unlike Angkor Wat, which looks impressive from all angles, the Bayon looks like a pile of rubble from a distance. It's only when you enter the temple and make your way up to the third level that its magic becomes apparent.

The basic structure of the Bayon is a simple three levels, which correspond more or less to three distinct phases of building. The first two levels are square and adorned with bas-reliefs. They lead up to a third, circular level, where you will find the towers and the faces. The central sanctuary of the third level is a cave-like cell in a massive, round mass of intricately embellished rock.

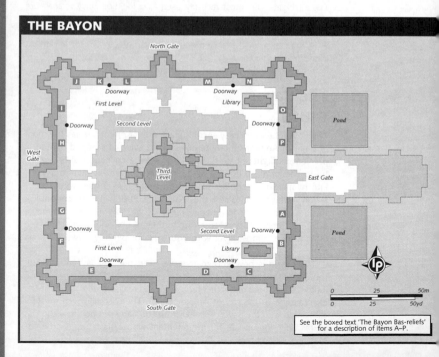

THE BAYON

North Gate

West Gate

East Gate

South Gate

First Level
Second Level
Third Level
Second Level
First Level

Doorway
Doorway
Library
Doorway
Doorway
Doorway
Doorway
Library
Doorway
Doorway

Pond
Pond

0   25   50m
0   25   50yd

See the boxed text 'The Bayon Bas-reliefs' for a description of items A–P.

The Bayon Bas-reliefs

The Bayon is decorated with 1.2km of extraordinary bas-reliefs incorporating over 11,000 figures. The famous carvings on the outer wall of the first level depict vivid scenes of everyday life in 12th-century Cambodia. The bas-reliefs on the second level do not have the epic proportions of those on the first level or the ones at Angkor, and tend to be fragmented. The reliefs described in this section are those

TRUDI CANAVAN

on the first level. The sequence assumes that you will enter the Bayon by the east gate and view the reliefs in a clockwise direction.

(A) Just south of the east gate is a three-level panorama. On the first tier, Khmer soldiers march off to battle; notice the elephants and the ox carts, which are almost exactly like those used in Cambodia today. The second tier depicts the coffins being carried from the battlefield. In the centre of the third tier, Jayavarman VII, shaded by parasols, is shown on horseback followed by legions of concubines (to the left).

(B) The first panel north of the southeastern corner shows Hindus praying to a *linga* (phallic symbol). This image was probably originally a Buddha, later modified by a Hindu king.

(C) The next panel has some of the best-carved reliefs. The scenes are combinations of naval battles between the Khmers and the Chams (with head coverings) and pictures of everyday life by the shores of the Tonlé Sap lake, where the battle was fought. Look out for images of people picking lice from each other's hair, of hunters and, towards the western end of the panel, a woman giving birth.

(D) In the next panel scenes from daily life continue and the naval battle shifts to the shore – the Chams are thrashed by the Khmers. Scenes include two people playing chess (or a similar board game), a cockfight and women selling fish in the market. The scenes of meals being prepared and served are in celebration of the Khmer victory.

(E, F) The last section of the south gallery, depicting a military procession, is unfinished, as is the panel showing elephants being led in from the mountains. Brahmans have been chased up two trees by tigers.

(G) This panel depicts scenes that some scholars maintain is a civil war. Groups of people, some armed, confront each other, and the violence escalates until elephants and warriors join the melee.

bove Right: A bas-relief at the Bayon depicts a cockfight in the 12th century

The Bayon Bas-reliefs (continued)

(H) The fighting continues on a smaller scale in the next panel. An antelope is being swallowed by a gargantuan fish; among the smaller fish is a prawn, under which an inscription proclaims that the king will seek out those in hiding.

(I) This panel depicts a procession that includes the king (carrying a bow). Presumably it is a celebration of his victory.

(J) At the western corner of the northern wall is a Khmer circus. A strong man holds three dwarfs and a man on his back is spinning a wheel with his feet; above, is a group of tightrope walkers. To the right of the circus, the royal court watches from a terrace, below which is a procession of animals. Some of the reliefs in this section remain unfinished.

(K) The two rivers, one next to the doorpost and the other 3m to the right, are teeming with fish.

(L, M, N) On the lowest level of this unfinished three-tiered scene, the Cham armies are being defeated and expelled from the Khmer kingdom. The next panel depicts the Cham armies advancing, and the badly deteriorated panel shows the Chams (on the left) chasing the Khmers.

(O) This panel shows the war of 1177, when the Khmers were defeated by the Chams and Angkor was pillaged. The wounded Khmer king is being lowered from the back of an elephant and a wounded Khmer general is being carried on a hammock suspended from a pole. Directly above, despairing Khmers are getting drunk. The Chams (on the right) are in hot pursuit of their vanquished enemy.

(P) This panel depicts another meeting of the two armies. Notice the flag bearers among the Cham troops (on the right). The Chams were defeated in the war, which ended in 1181, as depicted on panel A.

The Baphuon
បាពួន

The Baphuon, a pyramidal representation of mythical Mt Meru, is 200m northwest of the Bayon, and would have been one of the most spectacular of Angkor's temples in its heyday. Construction probably began under Suryavarman I and was later completed by Udaya-dityavarman II (reigned 1049–65). It marked the centre of the city that existed before the construction of Angkor Thom. The Baphuon was the centre of EFEO restoration efforts as the Cambodian civil war erupted and work was interrupted for a quarter of a century. The EFEO resumed its work in 1995 and much of the temple is currently off-limits, as archaeologists attempt to secure the structure's foundations with concrete supports. The Baphuon is approached by a 200m elevated walkway made of sandstone. The central structure is 43m high, but unfortunately its summit has collapsed, but will be partially restored.

On the western side of the temple, the retaining wall of the second level was fashioned – apparently in the 15th or 16th century – into a reclining Buddha 40m in length. The unfinished figure is difficult to make out, but the head is on the northern side of the wall and the gate is where the hips should be; to the left of the gate protrudes an arm. When it comes to the legs and feet – the latter are entirely gone – imagination must suffice. This huge project undertaken by the Buddhist faithful 500 years ago demonstrates that Angkor was never entirely abandoned in the total sense of the word.

Royal Enclosure & Phimeanakas
ភិមានអាកាស

Phimeanakas stands close to the centre of a walled area that once housed the royal palace, not that there's anything much left of it today except two sandstone pools near the northern wall. Once the site of royal ablutions, these are now used as swimming holes by local children. It is fronted to the east by the Terrace of Elephants. The palace was used by Jayavarman V and Udayadityavarman I, but was later added to and embellished by Jayavarman VII (who else?) and his successors.

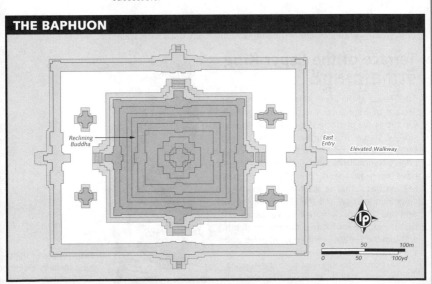

THE BAPHUON

Reclining Buddha

East Entry

Elevated Walkway

0   50   100m
0   50   100yd

Phimeanakas means 'Celestial Palace', and some scholars contend that it was once topped by a golden spire. Today it only hints at its former splendour and looks a little the worse for wear. The temple is another pyramidal representation of Mt Meru with three levels. Most of the decorative features of the temple are broken or have disappeared. Still, it is worth trudging up to the second and third levels (the stairs to the third level are steep) for good views of the Baphuon.

Preah Palilay
ព្រះបាលិទ្បៃ

Preah Palilay, a rather deteriorated temple 200m north of the Royal Enclosure's northern wall, was erected during the rule of Jayavarman VII (reigned 1181–1219). The temple originally housed a Buddha, which has long since disappeared.

Tep Pranam
ទេព្យប្រណាម្យ

Tep Pranam, an 82m by 34m cruciform Buddhist terrace 150m east of Preah Palilay, was once the base of a pagoda of lightweight construction. Nearby is a Buddha 4.5m high – it is a reconstruction of the original. A group of Buddhist nuns live in a wooden structure close by.

Preah Pithu Group
ព្រះពិធូ

Preah Pithu, which is across Northern Ave from Tep Pranam, is a group of five 12th-century Hindu and Buddhist temples enclosed by a wall.

Terrace of the Leper King
ទីលានព្រះគម្លង់

The Terrace of the Leper King, just north of the Terrace of Elephants, is a platform 7m high. On top of the platform stands a nude, though sexless, statue. It is another of Angkor's mysteries. The original of the statue is in Phnom Penh's National Museum, and various theories have been advanced to explain its meaning. Legend has it that at least two of the Angkor kings had leprosy, and the statue may represent one of them. A more likely explanation is that the statue is of Yama, the god of death, and that the Terrace of the Leper King housed the royal crematorium.

The front retaining walls of the terrace are decorated with at least five tiers of

TRUDI CANAVAN

Left: Terrace of the Leper King features exceptional 12th-century carvings

meticulously executed carvings of seated apsara; other figures include kings wearing pointed diadems, armed with short double-edged swords and accompanied by the court and princesses, who are adorned with beautiful rows of pearls. The terrace, built in the late 12th century, between the construction of Angkor Wat and the Bayon, once supported a pavilion made of lightweight materials.

On the southern side of the Terrace of the Leper King (facing the Terrace of Elephants), there is access to the front wall of a hidden terrace that was covered up when the outer structure was built – a terrace within a terrace. The four tiers of apsara and other figures, including naga, look as fresh as if they had been carved yesterday, and some of the figures carry fearsome expressions.

Terrace of Elephants
ទីលានជល់ដំរី

The 350m-long Terrace of Elephants was used as a giant reviewing stand for public ceremonies and served as a base for the king's grand audience hall. As you stand here, try to imagine the pomp and grandeur of the Khmer empire at its height, with infantry, cavalry, horse-drawn chariots and elephants parading across the Central Square in a colourful procession, pennants and standards aloft. Looking on is the god king, crowned with a gold diadem, shaded by multitiered parasols and attended by mandarins and handmaidens bearing gold and silver utensils.

The Terrace of Elephants has five outworks extending towards the Central Square – three in the centre and one at each end. The middle section of the retaining wall is decorated with life-size garuda and lions; towards either end are the two parts of the famous parade of elephants complete with their Khmer mahouts.

Kleangs & 12 Towers of Prasat
ឃ្លាំង / ប្រាសាទសួរព្រាត

Along the east side of Central Square are two groups of buildings, the North Kleang and the South Kleang, that may at one time have been palaces. The North Kleang dates from the period of Jayavarman V (reigned 968–1001).

Along the Central Square in front of the two Kleangs are 12 laterite towers – 10 in a row and two more at right angles facing the Avenue of Victory – known as the 12 Towers of Prasat, Prasat Suor Prat or Temple of the Tightrope Dancers. Archaeologists believe the towers, which form an honour guard along Central Square, were constructed by Jayavarman VII (reigned 1181–1219). It is likely that each one ori-ginally contained either a linga or a statue. It is said artists performed for the king on tightropes or rope-bridges strung between these towers. It is also rumoured they were used for public trials of sorts – during a dispute the two parties would be made to sit inside two prasat, one party eventually succumbing to disease and hence proven guilty.

AROUND ANGKOR THOM
Baksei Chamkrong
បក្សីចាំក្រុង

Located southwest of the south gate of Angkor Thom, Baksei Chamkrong is one of the few brick edifices in the immediate vicinity of Angkor. A well-proportioned though small temple, it was once decorated with a covering of lime mortar. Like virtually all of the structures of Angkor, it opens to the east. In the early 10th century, Harshavarman I erected five statues in this temple: two of Shiva, one of Vishnu and two of Devi.

Phnom Bakheng
ភ្នំបាក់ខែង

Around 400m south of Angkor Thom, the main attraction of Phnom Bakheng is the sunset view of Angkor Wat. Unfortunately, and inevitably, the whole affair has turned into something of a circus, with crowds of tourists gasping up the steep slope of the hill, pestered all the way by nimble-footed soft-drink vendors. Coming down can be even worse as there is nothing at all in the way of lighting. Still, the sunset over the Tonlé Sap lake is very impressive from the hill. To get a decent picture of Angkor Wat in the warm glow of the late afternoon sun you will need at least a 300mm lens, as the temple is 1.3km away.

Phnom Bakheng is also home to the first of the temple mountains built in the vicinity of Angkor. Yasovarman I (reigned 889–910) chose Phnom Bakheng over the Roluos area, where previous temples had been built.

Phnom Bakheng is a five-tiered temple mountain with seven levels, including the base and the summit. At the base are (or were) 44 towers. Each of the five tiers had 12 towers. The summit of the temple has four towers at the cardinal points of the compass as well as a Central Sanctuary. All of these numbers are of symbolic significance. The seven levels, for example, represent the seven Hindu heavens, while the total number of towers, excluding the Central Sanctuary, is 108, a particularly auspicious number and one that correlates to the lunar calendar.

It is now possible to arrange an elephant ride up the hill and the location certainly makes for one of the more memorable journeys you will make, if you can stomach the idea of the elephants hauling themselves up the steep hill day after day.

MICK ELMORE

Top: *Apsara* recently performed at Angkor Wat for the princess of Thailand

Bottom: Young monk at Banteay Srei

KRAIG LIEB

Temples of Angkor

GLENN BEANLAND

COREY WISE

KRAIG LIEB

Top: Beautifully crafted lichen-covered carvings surround the doorways and the corridors at Ta Prohm

Middle: Carved in exquisite detail, mythological figures cover Banteay Srei

Bottom: The 9th-centu Roluos group of temple

PHNOM BAKHENG

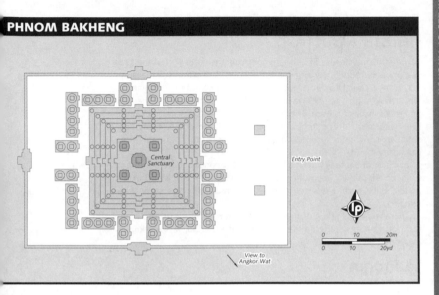

Central
Sanctuary

Entry Point

0   10   20m
0   10   20yd

View to
Angkor Wat

Prasat Kravan
ប្រាសាទក្រវ៉ាន់

The five brick towers of Prasat Kravan, which are arranged in a north-south line and oriented to the east, were built for Hindu worship in 921. The structure is unusual in that it was not constructed by royalty; this accounts for its slightly remote location, away from the centre of the capital. Prasat Kravan is just south of the road between Angkor Wat and Banteay Kdei.

The Prasat Kravan group was partially restored in 1968 and is particularly notable for the bas-reliefs cut into the bricks on the interior walls. The images of Vishnu in the largest central tower show eight-armed Vishnu on the back wall, taking the three gigantic steps with which he reclaimed the world on the left wall, and riding a garuda on the right wall. The northernmost tower displays bas-reliefs of Vishnu's consort, Lakshmi.

One of Vishnu's best-loved incarnations was when he appeared as the dwarf Vamana, and proceeded to reclaim the world from the evil demon king Bali. The dwarf politely asked the demon king for a comfortable patch of ground upon which to meditate, saying that the patch need only be big enough so that he could easily walk across it in three paces. The demon agreed, only to see the dwarf swell into a mighty giant who strode across the universe in three enormous steps. From this legend Vishnu is sometimes known as the 'long strider'.

Banteay Kdei & Sras Srang
ពន្លាយក្ដី / ស្រះស្រង់

Banteay Kdei, a massive Buddhist temple from the latter part of the 12th century, is surrounded by four concentric walls. The outer wall measures 500m by 700m. Each of its four entrances is decorated with garuda, which hold aloft one of Jayavarman VII's favourite themes: the four visages of Avalokiteshvara. The inside of the central tower was never finished and much of the temple is in a ruinous state due to hasty construction. It is considerably less busy than nearby Ta Prohm and this alone can justify a visit.

Just east of Banteay Kdei is a basin of earlier construction, Sras Srang (Pool of Ablutions), measuring 800m by 400m. A tiny island in the middle once bore a wooden temple, of which only the stone base remains.

There is a mass grave of hundreds of victims of the Khmer Rouge, just north of Sras Srang on the other side of the road. It is marked by a wooden memorial.

Ta Prohm
តាព្រហ្ម

Ta Prohm is undoubtedly the most atmospheric ruin at Angkor and should be high on the hit list of every visitor. Its appeal lies in the fact that, unlike the other monuments of Angkor, it has been left to be swallowed by the jungle, and looks very much the way most of the monuments of Angkor appeared when European explorers first stumbled upon them. A visit to Ta Prohm is a unique, other-world experience. The temple is cloaked in dappled shadow, its crumbling towers and walls locked in the slow muscular embrace of vast root systems. If Angkor Wat, the Bayon and other temples are testimony to the genius of the ancient Khmers, Ta Prohm reminds us equally of the awesome fecundity and power of the jungle.

Built around 1186, Ta Prohm was a Buddhist temple dedicated to the mother of Jayavarman VII. It is one of the few temples in the Angkor region where an inscription provides information about the temple's dependents and inhabitants. The numbers quoted really are staggering, although possibly include an element of exaggeration to glorify the king: close to 80,000 people were required to maintain or attend at the temple, among them more than 2700 officials and 615 dancers.

Ta Prohm is a temple of towers, close courtyards and narrow corridors. Many of the corridors are impassable, clogged with jumbled piles of delicately carved stone blocks dislodged by the roots of long-decayed trees. Bas-reliefs on bulging walls are carpeted by lichen, moss and creeping plants, and shrubs sprout from the roofs of monumental porches. Trees, hundreds of years old – some supported by flying buttresses – tower overhead, their leaves filtering the sunlight

TA PROHM

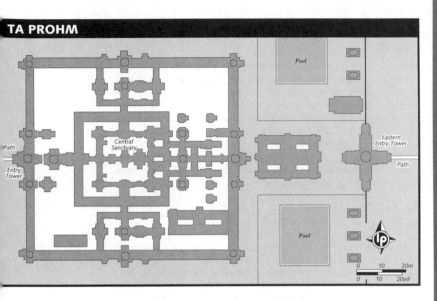

and casting a greenish pall over the whole scene. The most popular of the many strangulating root formations is that on the inside of the easternmost *gopura* (entrance pavilion) of the central enclosure, but there are several other astounding growths. It used to be possible to climb onto the damaged galleries, but this is now prohibited to protect both the temple and visitor. Many of these precariously balancing stones weigh a tonne or more and would do some serious damage if they came down.

Being such a maze of rubble and vegetation, there are predictably plenty of children willing to guide you through the temple. Some readers don't like this idea, some do. Either way, the fact of the matter is that these are mostly poor kids from poor families looking for the chance to make some money. It is easy to say it is somehow wrong and that they should be a school or doing a traditional job, but most Westerners have never experienced poverty in a Cambodian sense and the desperation it breeds. Some of the kids will probably get a better education in this 'university of life' than at rural schools and will certainly make more money than their parents ever did, struggling in the rice fields under the shadow of land mines. Who are we to say this is wrong? Put yourself in their position and imagine what you would do. Probably the same. If you don't want them to follow you around, politely tell them so, but try not to be rude or aggressive, as they are only young. If you want help to find some photo spots and the like, try and agree on a price (1000r or so) in advance. Throwing around dollar bills is not such a good idea, as it breeds expectancy and contempt.

Ta Keo
តាកែវ

Ta Keo is a stark, undecorated temple that undoubtedly would have been one of the finest of all Angkor's structures had it been finished. Built by Jayavarman V (reigned 968–1001), it was dedicated to Shiva and was the first Angkorian monument built entirely of sandstone. The summit of the central tower, which is surrounded by four lower towers, is almost 50m high. This quincuncial arrangement with four towers at the corners of a square and a fifth tower in the centre is typical of many Angkorian temple mountains.

No-one is certain why work was never completed, but a likely cause may have been the death of Jayavarman V.

Ta Nei
តានី

Ta Nei, 800m north of Ta Keo, was built by Jayavarman VII (reigned 1181–1219). There is something of the spirit of Ta Prohm here, albeit on a lesser scale, with moss and tentacle-like roots covering many outer areas of this small temple. It now houses the Apsara Authority's training unit and can be accessed only by walking across the French-built dam. To get to the dam, take the long track on the left, just after the Spean Thmor bridge when coming from Siem Reap.

Spean Thmor
ស្ពានថ្ម

Spean Thmor (Stone Bridge), of which an arch and several piers remain, is 200m east of Thommanon. Jayavarman VII, the last great builder of Angkor, constructed many roads with these immense stone bridges spanning watercourses, but this is the only large bridge remaining in the immediate vicinity of Angkor. The bridge vividly highlights how the water level has dropped over the subsequent centuries and may offer another clue to the collapse of Angkor's extensive irrigation system. Just north of Spean Thmor is a large and surprisingly elegant water wheel.

There are more spectacular examples elsewhere in Siem Reap Province, including Spean Praptos (19 arches) in Kompong Kdei on NH6 from Phnom Penh, and Spean Ta Ong, a 77m bridge complete with a beautiful naga, forgotten in the forest about 25km east of Beng Mealea.

Chau Say Tevoda
ថៅសាយទេវតា

Just east of Angkor Thom's east gate is Chau Say Tevoda. It was probably built during the second quarter of the 12th century and dedicated to Shiva and Vishnu. It is currently under renovation to bring it up to the condition of its twin temple, Thommanon.

Thommanon
ធម្មនន្ទ

Thommanon is just north of Chau Say Tevoda. Although unique, the temple complements its neighbour, as it was built around the same time to a similar design. It was also dedicated to Shiva and Vishnu. Thommanon is in much better condition than the rather ruinous Chau Say Tevoda thanks to extensive work by the EFEO in the 1960s.

Preah Khan
ព្រះខន្ធ

The temple of Preah Khan (Sacred Sword) is one of the largest complexes at Angkor – a maze of vaulted corridors, fine carvings and lichen-clad stonework. It is a good counterpoint to Ta Prohm, although it generally gets fewer visitors. Preah Khan was built by Jayavarman VII (it may have served as his temporary residence while Angkor Thom was being built), and like Ta Prohm it is a place of towered enclosures and shoulder-hugging corridors. Unlike Ta Prohm, however, the temple of Preah Khan is in a reasonable state of preservation and ongoing restoration efforts by the World Monument Fund should improve the picture.

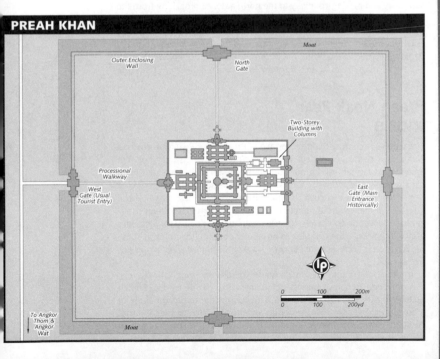

PREAH KHAN

The central sanctuary of the temple was dedicated in 1191 and a large stone stele, originally located within the first eastern enclosure, but now housed safely at Angkor Conservation (see the boxed text 'Angkor Conservation' earlier), says much about Preah Khan's role as a centre for worship and learning. The temple was dedicated to 515 divinities and during the course of a year 18 major festivals took place here, requiring a team of thousands just to maintain the place.

Preah Khan covers a very large area, but the temple itself is within a rectangular enclosing wall of around 700m by 800m. Four processional walkways approach the gates of the temple, and these are bordered by another stunning depiction of the Churning of the Ocean of Milk, as in the approach to Angkor Thom, although most of the heads have disappeared. From the central sanctuary, four long vaulted galleries extend in the cardinal directions. Many of the interior walls of Preah Khan were once coated with plaster held in place by holes in the stone. Today many delicate carvings remain, including *essai* (wise men) and apsara.

The main entrance to Preah Khan is, as with most of the other Angkorian temples, in the east, but the standard practice is to enter at the west gate and walk from here to the north gate (your driver will usually offer to go to the north gate to wait for you). Make sure that you walk the length of the temple to the east gate before doubling back to the central sanctuary and making your way to the north gate. Approaching from the west, there is little clue to nature's genius, but on the outer retaining wall of the east gate, a pair of trees with monstrous roots embrace as they reach for the sky. There is also a curious Mediterranean-style two-storey structure inside the east gate, the purpose of which is unknown.

Just north of Preah Khan is Banteay Prei, which dates from the same period.

Preah Neak Pean
 នាគពន្ធ

The late-12th-century Buddhist temple of Preah Neak Pean (Intertwined Naga) is a petite yet perfect temple constructed by...surely not him again...Jayavarman VII. Pronounced 'neek po-an', it consists of a large square pool surrounded by four smaller square pools. In the centre of the central pool is a circular 'island' encircled by the two naga whose intertwined tails give the temple its name. Although it has been many centuries since the pools were last filled with water, it's easy for a modern visitor to envisage the complex as an opulent bathing complex at some fantasy hotel. Look out for 'Encore Angkor Casino' appearing in Las Vegas soon!

In the pool around the central island there were once four statues, but only one remains, reconstructed from the debris by the French archaeologists who cleared the site. The curious figure has the body of a horse supported by a tangle of human legs. It relates to a legend that Avalokiteshvara once saved a group of shipwrecked followers from an island of ghouls by transforming himself into a flying horse.

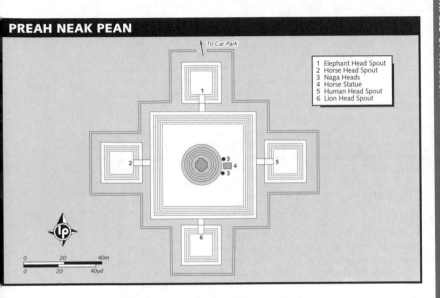

PREAH NEAK PEAN

To Car Park

1 Elephant Head Spout
2 Horse Head Spout
3 Naga Heads
4 Horse Statue
5 Human Head Spout
6 Lion Head Spout

Water once flowed from the central pool into the four peripheral pools via ornamental spouts, which can still be seen in the pavilions at each axis of the pool. The spouts are in the form of an elephant's head, a horse's head, a lion's head and a human's head. The pool was used for ritual purification rites and the complex was originally in the centre of a huge 3km-by-900m baray serving Preah Khan, now dried up and overgrown.

Ta Som
តាសោម

Ta Som, which stands to the east of Preah Neak Pean, is yet another of the late-12th-century Buddhist temples of Jayavarman VII, the Donald Trump of ancient Cambodia. The central area of Ta Som is in a ruined state, but is currently under restoration by the World Monument Fund. The most impressive feature at Ta Som is the huge tree completely overwhelming the eastern gopura, one of the most popular photo opportunities in the Angkor area.

Eastern Baray & Eastern Mebon
បារាយខាងកើត / មេបុណ្យខាងកើត

The enormous one-time reservoir known as the Eastern Baray was excavated by Yasovarman I (reigned 889–910), who marked its four corners with steles. This basin, now entirely dried up, was the most important of the public works of Yasodharapura, Yasovarman I's capital, and is 7km by 1.8km. It was originally fed by Stung Siem Reap.

The Hindu temple known as the Eastern Mebon, erected by Rajend-ravarman II (reigned 944–68), would have been on an islet in the centre of the Eastern Baray, but is now very much on dry land. This temple is like a smaller version of Pre Rup, which was built 15 to 20 years later and lies immediately to the south. The temple mountain form is surmounted by the now familiar quincunx of towers. The elaborate brick shrines are dotted with neatly arranged holes, which have given some observers the idea that they were once covered in metal plates. In fact, the towers were covered in plaster. The base of the temple is guarded at its corners by perfectly carved stone figures of harnessed elephants, many of which are still in a very good state of preservation.

Pre Rup
ប្រែរូប

Pre Rup, built by Rajendravarman II, is about 1.5km south of the Eastern Mebon. Like its nearby predecessor, the temple consists of a pyramid-shaped temple mountain with the uppermost of the three tiers carrying five square shrines arranged as a quincunx. The brick sanctuaries were also once decorated with a plaster coating, fragments of which still remain on the southwestern tower; there are some amazingly detailed lintel carvings here. Several of the outermost eastern towers are perilously close to collapse and are propped up by armies of wooden supports.

Pre Rup means 'Turning the Body' and refers to a traditional method of cremation in which a corpse's outline is traced in the cinders, first in one direction and then in the other; this suggests that the temple may have served as an early royal crematorium.

Banteay Samré
បន្ទាយសំរែ

Banteay Samré dates from around the same period as Angkor Wat and was built by Suryavarman II (reigned 1112–52). The temple is in a fairly healthy state of preservation due to some extensive renovation work, although its isolation has resulted in some devastating looting over the past two decades. The area consists of a central temple with four wings preceded by a hall and also accompanied by two libraries, the southern of which is remarkably well preserved. The whole ensemble is enclosed by two large concentric walls around what would have been the unique feature of an inner moat, sadly now dried up.

Banteay Samré is located 400m east of the Eastern Baray, which in practical terms means following the road to Banteay Srei until the village of Pradek and continuing straight ahead on a dirt road rather than following the tarmac to the right. A visit here can be combined with a trip to Banteay Srei or Phnom Bok.

The Western Baray
បារាយណ៍ខាងលិច

The Western Baray (Baray Occidental), measuring an incredible 8km by 2.3km, was excavated by hand to provide water for the intensive cultivation of lands around Angkor. In the centre of the basin is the Western Mebon, where the giant bronze statue of Vishnu, now in the National Museum in Phnom Penh, was found. The Western Baray is accessible by boat from the dam on the southern shore, but is a total ruin. The baray is also the leading local swimming pool around Siem Reap. There is a small beach of sorts at the western extreme, complete with picnic huts and inner tubes for rent, which attracts plenty of Khmers at weekends.

ROLUOS GROUP
រលួស

The monuments of Roluos, which served as Indravarman I's (reigned 877–89) capital, Haliharalaya, are among the earliest large, permanent temples built by the Khmers and mark the beginning of the age of Khmer classical art. Before the construction of Roluos, generally only lighter (and less-durable) construction materials such as brick were employed.

The temples can be found 13km east of Siem Reap along NH6 near the modern-day town of Roluos: Preah Ko is 600m south of NH6, while Bakong is 1.5km south of the highway. There are contemporary Buddhist monasteries at both Bakong and Lolei. For those who aren't travelling much beyond Siem Reap and Phnom Penh, it might be worth venturing into the genuine Cambodian town of Roluos for a refreshing drink.

Preah Ko
ព្រះគោ

Preah Ko was erected by Indravarman I in the late 9th century. The six *prasat* (stone halls), aligned in two rows and decorated with carved sandstone and plaster reliefs, face east; the central tower of the front row is a great deal larger than the other towers. There are elaborate inscriptions in the ancient Hindu language of Sanskrit on the doorposts of each temple.

The temples of Preah Ko (Sacred Ox) feature three *nandi* (sacred oxen) in front of the first row of temples, all in poor condition. Preah Ko was dedicated by Indravarman I to his deified ancestors in 880AD. The front towers relate to male ancestors or gods, the rear towers to female ancestors or goddesses. A series of lions guard the steps up to the temple platform.

PREAH KO

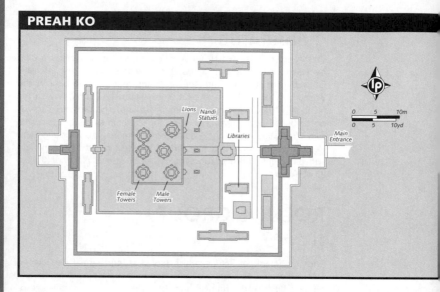

Bakong
ប្រាគង

Bakong is the largest and most interesting of the Roluos group temples, and has an active Buddhist monastery just to the north of the east entrance. It was built and dedicated to Shiva by Indravarman I. Built as a representation of Mt Meru, it served as the city's central temple. The east-facing complex consists of a five-tier central pyramid of sandstone, 60m square at the base, flanked by eight towers (or what's left of them) of brick and sandstone and by other minor sanctuaries. Several of the eight towers down below are still partly covered by their original plasterwork.

The complex is enclosed by three concentric walls and a broad moat. There are well-preserved statues of stone elephants on each corner of the first three levels of the central temple. There are 12 stupas – four to a side – on the third tier. The sanctuary on the fifth level was a later addition.

Lolei
លលៃ

The four brick towers of Lolei, an almost exact replica of the towers of Preah Ko (although in much worse shape) were built on an islet in the centre of a large reservoir – now rice fields – by Yasovarman I (reigned 889–910), the founder of the first city at Angkor. The sandstone carvings in the niches of the temples are worth a look and there are

BAKONG

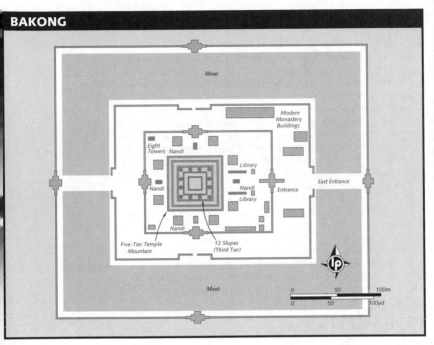

Sanskrit inscriptions on the doorposts. According to one of the inscriptions, the four towers were dedicated by Yasovarman I to his mother, his father and his maternal grandparents on 12 July 893.

AROUND ANGKOR
Phnom Krom
ភ្នំក្រោម

The temple of Phnom Krom, 12km south of Siem Reap on a hill overlooking the Tonlé Sap lake, dates from the reign of Yasovarman I in the late 9th or early 10th century. The name means 'lower hill' and is a reference to its geographic location in relation to its sister temples of Phnom Bakheng and Phnom Bok. The three towers, dedicated (from north to south) to Vishnu, Shiva and Brahma, are in a ruined state, but this remains one of the more tranquil spots from which to view sunset, complete with an active wat. The fast boats from Phnom Penh dock near here, but it is not possible to see the temple from beneath the hill. Visitors arriving by plane usually get an aerial glimpse just before landing.

Phnom Bok
ភ្នំបូក

Making up the triplicate of temple mountains built by Yasovarman I in the late 9th or early 10th century, this peaceful but remote location sees few visitors. The small temple is in reasonable shape and includes two frangipani trees growing out of a pair of ruinous towers – they look like some sort of extravagant haircut when in full flower. However, it is the views of Phnom Kulen to the north and the plains of Angkor to the south from this 212m hill that make it well worth the trip. The remains of a 5m linga are also visible at the opposite end of the hill and there were believed to have been similar lingas at Phnom Bakheng and Phnom Krom. Unfortunately it is not a sensible place for sunrise or sunset, as it would require a long journey in the dark to get here or get back.

Phnom Bok is about 25km from Siem Reap and is clearly visible from the road to Banteay Srei. It is accessible by continuing east on the road to Banteay Samré for another 6km. It is possible to loop back to Siem Reap via the temples of Roluos by heading south instead of west on the return journey, offering some pleasant glimpses of rural life. There is a long, winding trail snaking up the hill, not suitable for bikes, that takes about 20 minutes to climb. Avoid the heat of the middle of the day and carry plenty of water, which can be purchased near the base of the mountain.

Chau Srei Vibol
ចៅស្រីវិបុល

This petite hilltop temple sees few visitors, as it is really only accessible by motorbike. The central hilltop sanctuary is in a ruined state, but is nicely complemented by the construction of a modern wat nearby. Surrounding the base of the hill are laterite walls, each with a small entrance hall in reasonable condition. To get here turn east off the reasonable dirt road between Phnom Bok and Roluos at a point about 8km north of NH6, or 5km south of Phnom Bok. From here, the trail deteriorates and crosses several small, rickety bridges, helping to explain why tour buses don't make it here. The path also crosses a small Angkorian bridge, built at the end of the 12th century, complete with naga balustrades. The route is easy to lose along this way, so keep asking locals for directions at junctions and eventually you will find yourself in a monastic compound at the base of the small hill.

Banteay Srei
បន្ទាយស្រី

Banteay Srei is a Hindu temple dedicated to Shiva. Considered by many to be the jewel in the crown of Angkorian art, the temple is cut from stone of a pinkish hue and includes some of the finest stone carving seen anywhere on the planet. It is not a particularly extensive temple site, but

Right: Classical Khmer
art at Banteay Srei

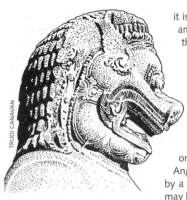

TRUDI CANAVAN

it is wonderfully well preserved
and many of its carvings are
three-dimensional.   Banteay
Srei means 'Citadel of the
Women' and it is said that it
must have been built by a
woman, as the elaborate
carvings are too fine for the
touch of a man.

Construction on Banteay
Srei began in 967 and it is
one of the few temples around
Angkor not to be commissioned
by a king, but by a Brahmin who
may have been a tutor to Jayavar-
man V. The temple is square and has entrances at the east and west, the
east approached by a causeway. Of interest are the lavishly decorated
libraries and the three central towers, which are decorated with male and
female divinities and beautiful filigree relief work.

Classic carvings at Banteay Srei include delicate women with lotus
flowers in hand and traditional skirts clearly visible, as well as breathtaking re-creations of scenes from the epic *Ramayana* adorning the
library frontons (carved inlays above a lintel). However, the sum of the
parts is no greater than the whole – almost every inch of these interior
buildings is covered in decoration. Standing watch over such perfect cre-
ations are the mythical guardians, all of which are copies of originals
stored in the National Museum.

Banteay Srei was the first major temple-restoration undertaken by the
EFEO in 1930 using the anastylosis method. The project, as evidenced
today, was a major success and soon led to other larger projects such as
the restoration of the Bayon. However, it was not the first time the
temple had hit the headlines, as in 1923 Frenchman André Malraux was
arrested in Phnom Penh for attempting to steal several major statues and
pieces of sculpture. Ironically, Malraux was later appointed minister of
culture under Charles de Gaulle.

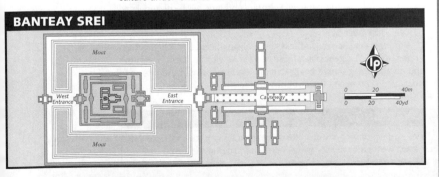

BANTEAY SREI

Banteay Srei is 21km northeast of the Bayon or about 32km from Siem Reap. It is well signposted and the road is now surfaced all the way – a trip from Siem Reap should take just 45 minutes. It is possible to combine a visit here with a trip to the River of a Thousand Lingas at Kbal Spean or to Banteay Samré and Phnom Bok. It can be very busy out here in the morning; lunch time is quiet, but very hot.

Kbal Spean
ក្បាលស្ពាន

Kbal Spean is a spectacularly carved riverbed, set deep in the jungle to the northeast of Angkor. More commonly referred to in English as the 'River of a Thousand Lingas', the name actually means 'bridgehead', a reference to the natural rock bridge at the site. Lingas have been elaborately carved into the riverbed, and images of Hindu deities are dotted about the area. Kbal Spean was 'discovered' in 1969, when EFEO ethnologist Jean Boulbet was shown the area by an essai; the area was soon off-limits due to the civil war, only becoming safe again in 1998.

It is about a half-hour walk to where the carvings begin along a pleasant path that winds its way up into the jungle, passing by some interesting boulder formations along the way. Carry plenty of water up the hill, as there is none available beyond the parking area. The path eventually splits to the waterfall or the river carvings. It is best to start with the river carvings and work your way back down to the waterfall. There is an impressive carving of Vishnu on the upper section of the river, followed by a series of carvings at the bridgehead itself (including Shiva's mount Nandi), many of which have tragically been hacked off in the past few years. This whole area is now roped off to protect the carvings from further damage.

Following the river down, there are several more impressive carvings of Vishnu, and Shiva with his consort Uma, and farther downstream hundreds of lingas appear on the riverbed. At the top of the waterfall, there are many animal images, including a cow and a frog, and a path winds around the boulders to a wooden staircase leading down to the base of the falls. Visitors between February and June will be disappointed to see very little water here. The best time to visit is between September and December.

Although Kbal Spean is of less spiritual significance to Khmers than Phnom Kulen, it is generally a more rewarding visit, as there is less litter and no whopping charge going to a private businessman. Admission to Kbal Spean is free and the last entry to the site is at 3.30pm.

WARNING

At no point during a visit to Kbal Spean or Phnom Kulen should you leave well-trodden paths as there are land mines in the area.

Kbal Spean is about 50km northeast of Siem Reap or about 18km beyond the temple of Banteay Srei on a fairly reasonable dirt road in the dry season that's somewhat unreasonable in the wet season. It is usually a 30-minute drive from Banteay Srei if you stick to the main trail until the large wooden sign on the left. This road continues north to Anlong Veng, formerly a stronghold of the Khmer Rouge.

Moto (small motorcycle) drivers will no doubt want a bit of extra money to take you here – a few extra dollars should do, or US$10 for the day maximum, including a trip to Banteay Srei. A surcharge is also charged to come out here by car.

Phnom Kulen
ភ្នំគូលែន

Phnom Kulen is considered by Khmers to be the most sacred mountain in Cambodia and is a popular place of pilgrimage during weekends and festivals. It played a significant role in the history of the Khmer empire, as it was from here in 802 that Jayavarman II proclaimed independence from Java, giving birth to modern-day Cambodia. There is a small wat at the summit of the mountain, which houses a large reclining Buddha carved into the sandstone boulder upon which it is built. Nearby is a large waterfall and above it are smaller bathing areas and a number of carvings in the riverbed, including numerous lingas. The bad news is that a private businessman bulldozed a road up here in 1999 and now charges a US$20 toll per foreign visitor, an outrageous fee compared with what you get for your money at Angkor. None of the toll goes towards preserving the site.

The new road winds its way through some spectacular jungle scenery, emerging on the plateau after a 45-minute ascent. The road eventually splits, the left fork leading to the picnic spot, waterfalls and ruins of a 9th-century temple, the right fork continuing over a bridge and some riverbed carvings to the reclining Buddha. This is the focal point of a pilgrimage here for Khmer people, so it is important to take off your shoes and any head coverings before climbing the stairs to the sanctuary. The views from the 487m peak are tremendous, as you can see right across the forested plateau.

The waterfall is an attractive spot, but could be much more beautiful were it not for all the litter left here by families picnicking at the weekend. You can cool off here if you like and, if you have a bit of time to kill, it's worthwhile clearing up some of the mess and burning it. If people can be shown how much more pristine the area is without their leftovers then they might start disposing of things better themselves. Near the waterfall is a jungle-clad temple known as Prasat Krau Romeas, dating from the 9th century – but explore it with care, as there are land mines around Phnom Kulen.

There are plenty of other Angkorian sites on Phnom Kulen, including as many as 20 minor temples around the plateau, the most important of which is Prasat Rong Chen, the first pyramid or temple mountain to be constructed in the Angkor area. Most impressive of all are the giant stone animals or guardians of the mountain, known as Sra Damrei (Elephant Pond). These are very difficult to get to, the route passing through mined sections of the mountain and the trail impossible in the wet season. The few who make it, however, are rewarded with a life-size replica of a stone elephant, a full 4m long and 3m tall, and smaller statues of lions, a frog and a cow. These were constructed on the southern face of the mountain and from here there are spectacular views across the plains below. Getting here requires taking a moto from Wat Pre Ang Thom for about one hour on very rough trails through thick forest before arriving at a sheer rock face. From here it is a 20-minute walk to the animals through the forest. Don't try and find it on your own; expect to pay the moto driver about 20,000r with some hard negotiating and carry plenty of water, as none is available.

Before the construction of the private road up Phnom Kulen, visitors had to scale the mountain and then walk across the top of the plateau to the reclining Buddha. This route takes more than two hours and is still an option. About 15km east of the new road up Kulen, the sandy trail winds its way to a small pagoda called Wat Chou, set into the cliff face from which a *tuk chou* (spring) emerges. The water is considered holy and Khmers like to bottle it up to take home with them. This water source eventually flows into the Tonlé Sap lake and is thought to bring a blessing to the waterways of Cambodia.

Phnom Kulen mountain is a huge plateau around 50km from Siem Reap and about 15km from Banteay Srei. To get here on the new toll road, take the well-signposted right fork just before Banteay Srei village and follow this, going straight ahead at the crossroads. Just before the road starts to climb the mountain, there is a barrier and it is here that the US$20 charge is levied.

To walk to the site, head east along the base of the mountain instead of going straight ahead at the major crossroads after the right fork. After about 15km, there is a wat-style gate on the left and a sandy trail. Follow this to a small community from where the climb begins. It is about a 30-minute climb, including a new staircase up the final cliffs, and then an hour or more in a westerly direction along the top of the plateau. This route of the pilgrims of old should cost nothing, although it takes considerably longer.

Moto drivers are likely to want about US$10 to bring you out here and rented cars will cost even more.

Beng Mealea
បឹងមាលា

Beng Mealea is a spectacular sight to behold, one of the most mysterious temples at Angkor, as nature has well and truly run riot here. This 12th-century temple, built under Suryavarman II (reigned 1112–52), is very similar in design to Angkor Wat, although only on a single level and not multilayered.

Beng Mealea is enclosed by a massive moat measuring 1200m by 900m, most of which has dried up today. The temple has been utterly subsumed by jungle, and standing just a few metres away from the trees it is hard to tell what lies beneath. Entering from the south, visitors wend their way over piles of masonry, through long dark chambers and between hanging vines to arrive at the central tower, which has completely collapsed. Hidden away among the rubble and foliage are several impressive carvings, as well as a well-preserved library in the northeastern quadrant. It is a special place and it is worth taking the time to explore thoroughly.

Beng Mealea lies at the centre of an ancient Angkorian road connecting Angkor Thom and Preah Khan in Preah Vihear Province. A small Angkorian bridge just west of Chau Srei Vibol temple is the only remaining trace of the old Angkorian road between Beng Mealea and Angkor Thom; between Beng Mealea and Preah Khan there are at least 10 bridges abandoned in the forest. This is one way to get to Preah Khan temple for extreme adventurers – see the Northwestern Cambodia chapter and don't undertake the journey lightly.

There is no charge to visit Beng Mealea. It is best to undertake a long day trip combining Beng Mealea, Kbal Spean and Banteay Srei. At the very least include Banteay Srei, as you almost pass it on the way.

Beng Mealea is about 40km east of the Bayon (as the crow flies) and 6.5km southeast of Phnom Kulen. By road it is about 60km or more from Siem Reap and is at least a two-hour trip.

There are two routes to Beng Mealea: the most popular along the base of Phnom Kulen and the other going via the small town of Dam Dek on

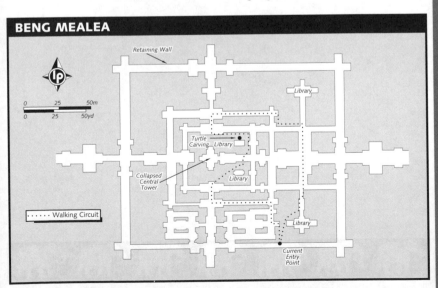

BENG MEALEA

Retaining Wall

Library

0   25   50m
0   25   50yd

Turtle Carving Library

Collapsed Central Tower

Library

...... Walking Circuit

Library

Current Entry Point

NH6 towards Phnom Penh. For the more popular route, take the road towards Banteay Srei and follow the right fork to Phnom Kulen, continuing right at the major crossroads along the base of the holy mountain. Follow this route for about 25km until you leave Kulen behind and veer left at the T-junction. Another 10km or so northeast of here is the village of Beng Mealea and the temple is to the left at the main junction in town.

The second route is less complicated, but road conditions are worse. Follow NH6 east to Dam Dek, before turning north immediately after the market. Continue on this road for 20km or so and then straight ahead when the main road bears left towards Phnom Kulen – this is where the two routes meet. The final 10km or so used to be a mess of miserable sand and mud, but it's being upgraded by the same entrepreneur who hijacked Phnom Kulen. While the road will get better, a hefty fee will no doubt be introduced and none of it will go towards the temple's protection.

Remote Angkorian Sites

For information on the remote Angkorian sites of Banteay Chhmar, Koh Ker, Preah Khan and Prasat Preah Vihear, see the Northwestern Cambodia chapter.

South Coast

The south coast of Cambodia is home to tropical beaches, unspoilt islands, abandoned colonial resorts and several of Cambodia's nascent national parks. It also includes a cradle of ancient Cambodian civilisation in the Angkor Borei region near Takeo, dating from the 6th century. The area is becoming increasingly popular with visitors and offers a number of diverse attractions that, with a little planning, can be seen in less than a week.

Much of the coastline is dotted with small fishing communities making their living from the sea. The western portion of this region is wild and remote and includes the uninhabited uplands of Chuor Phnom Kravanh (Cardamom Mountains), while the area to the east is generally heavily settled, with the forest yielding to farmland long ago. Tourism looks set to be the big growth industry of the future, as many of the islands in this region are lined with perfect palm-fringed beaches and covered in a blanket of forest. They easily rival some of Thailand's finest, but as yet there is not a beach bungalow in sight beyond the shores of Sihanoukville.

Historically, the towns of Kampot and Kep were the most important centres in the region – Kampot as Cambodia's principal port and Kep the leading beach town. Kampot was eclipsed following the founding of Sihanoukville port in 1959, and with the steady destruction of Kep during and after the civil war, Sihanoukville was soon to claim the mantle as the most popular beach town in Cambodia. Today, it remains the commercial and entertainment centre of the south coast. Krong Koh Kong is an up-and-coming commercial centre benefiting from its close proximity to Thailand and the construction of a new road and bridge, plugging it into the world from both the east and west.

For travellers arriving in Sihanoukville from Krong Koh Kong by boat, there is the option of continuing along the coast to Kampot. This sleepy riverside town makes a good

Highlights

- Relax in Sihanoukville, where empty beaches, tropical islands, fresh seafood and a buzzing nightlife make the city as good as an essential stop on a trip south.

- Take in the breathtaking views across the Gulf of Thailand from abandoned Bokor hill station.

- Check out Kampot, a city with some of the best-preserved colonial architecture in the country and a low-key, laid-back feel.

- Explore abandoned villas and remote islands in the beachside ghost town of Kep, a town that's slowly coming back to life.

- Soak up the atmosphere of Phnom Da, an ancient hill temple set among lush paddy fields.

SOUTH COAST

base from which to explore the abandoned seaside resort of Kep and the beautiful Bokor National Park. From Kampot there is a direct road back to Phnom Penh, or you can amble back slowly via Takeo and the nearby ruined temples around Angkor Borei. The road from Takeo to Phnom Penh includes a number of popular destinations such as the hilltop temple of Phnom Chisor, the wildlife

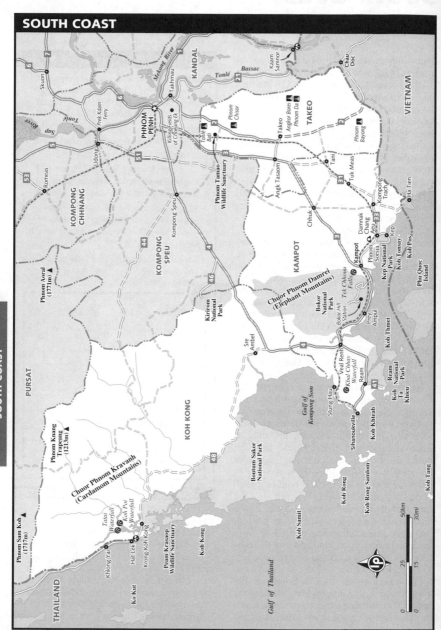

sanctuary at Phnom Tamao and the Angkorian temple of Tonlé Bati. See Around Phnom Penh in the Phnom Penh chapter for details on these three places.

Visitors starting in Phnom Penh would be wiser to run the route in reverse, packing in all the sightseeing first before chillin' out on the beaches at Sihanoukville. All the hot spots covered on the south-coast loop can be reached by public transport or *moto* (small motorcycle with driver), but those on a healthier budget might like to rent a car. The circuit should be pretty straightforward for experienced bikers.

Koh Kong Province
ខេត្តកោះកុង

Koh Kong is a vast but sparsely populated province in Cambodia's southwest, where the overwhelming majority of the population live along the coastline and where the mountains remain untamed. Not surprisingly, fishing is the main source of income for most residents. The shrimp farming industry introduced from Thailand died a quick death, leaving many Cambodian entrepreneurs penniless – see the boxed text 'Prawn Crackers' later for more on this sorry tale. Tourism is tiny, as most people are transiting from Thailand to Sihanoukville only, but there is great potential for future growth thanks to the incredible beaches lining Boutum Sakor National Park and nearby islands like Koh Kong – yes, confusingly enough, the province and island share the same name. Diving off the coast and ecotourism in the upcountry jungle will take off, but for now, you are effectively on your own.

Getting around the province is limited to boat travel, as there are no roads linking Krong Koh Kong to the rest of Cambodia. This is fast-changing, as the Thai military is bulldozing a road from the Thai border all the way through the jungle to join National Hwy 4 (NH4) near Sre Ambel. Soon Krong Koh Kong will be just five hours from Phnom Penh by road, revolutionising life for the residents of the town. Thailand is not well-known for magnanimous gestures towards its smaller, 'inferior' neighbours. This road construction has a hidden price, namely the destruction of much of Cambodia's pristine forest remaining in this wilderness region. The cost could end up being bigger still for Cambodia, as the road cuts through Chuor Phnom Kravanh – a unique ecosystem believed to be home to many endangered species.

KRONG KOH KONG
កោះកុង

☎ 035 • pop 29,500

Krong Koh Kong is not Cambodia's most interesting town, but increasing numbers of travellers are staying here when journeying between Cambodia and Thailand by land and sea. It is something of a boom town for trade (both legal and illegal) attracting migrants from other parts of the country who are seeking opportunities in this fast-growing frontier area. The border area is popular with Thais, as casinos are a legal and thriving business in Cambodia, unlike in Thailand.

In time, Krong Koh Kong may become a base from which to explore Cambodia's nearby islands, but for now it remains primarily a transit stop. Those who hang around can choose from a scruffy but quiet beach to the east of town, and two attractive waterfalls upstream to pass the time.

The big news for the town is the new bridge crossing Stung Koh Poi. Built by the Thai military, it is 1.9km in length and should be open by the time you read this. It is great news for tourists as well as locals, as boat drivers were robbing visitors blind on this crossing. No more hassles with the boats now the bridge is open – that just leaves the taxi and moto drivers!

Information
Both US dollars and Thai baht (B) can be used around Krong Koh Kong. Changing either currency into riel is easy at Psar Leu (Central Market) or at most guesthouses. The nearest banks that deal with travellers cheques and credit cards are in Sihanoukville or Thailand.

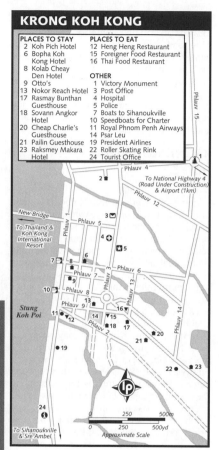

KRONG KOH KONG

PLACES TO STAY	PLACES TO EAT
2 Koh Pich Hotel	12 Heng Heng Restaurant
6 Bopha Koh	15 Foreigner Food Restaurant
Kong Hotel	16 Thai Food Restaurant
8 Kolab Cheay	
Den Hotel	OTHER
9 Otto's	1 Victory Monument
13 Nokor Reach Hotel	3 Post Office
17 Rasmay Bunthan	4 Hospital
Guesthouse	5 Police
18 Sovann Angkor	7 Boats to Sihanoukville
Hotel	10 Speedboats for Charter
20 Cheap Charlie's	11 Royal Phnom Penh Airways
Guesthouse	14 Psar Leu
21 Pailin Guesthouse	19 President Airlines
23 Raksmey Makara	22 Roller Skating Rink
Hotel	24 Tourist Office

There is a post office in town, but it is better to send mail from Thailand before crossing into Cambodia, or wait until Phnom Penh. There are plenty of private phone booths around town from where reasonably priced local calls can be made. International calls are expensive, but no doubt someone will set up an Internet call service in the near future. Email services are available at Otto's.

There is a tourist office on the waterfront about 1km south of the boat dock, but often guesthouses, such as Cheap Charlie's and Otto's, prove more useful.

Things to See & Do

Krong Koh Kong has several **beaches** in the vicinity. There is a beach (of sorts) a few kilometres south of town where the river estuary meets the sea. Locals like it and there are pedalos and jet skis for rent. Anyone who has been unnerved by Cambodian driving will be twice as terrified to see how they manage a jet ski. Keep a safe distance away. This beach is also just downstream from town and there are no prizes for guessing where the town's effluent goes. Farther afield are countless beaches that can be accessed by moto or boat. There are some fantastic beaches on the western side of the **island of Koh Kong**, but these aren't so cheap to get to, particularly now that boat drivers have become accustomed to the idea of ripping off tourists. Try to pay around 800B per boat for a round-trip charter.

There are some scenic waterfalls upriver from Krong Koh Kong, although in the dry season they are less impressive, as the water level drops. The water is fairly pure, as it comes down from Chuor Phnom Kravanh, where there are almost no human settlements. The most spectacular is **Tatai Waterfall**, located nearly an hour upstream from Krong Koh Kong. Set in a lush jungle gorge, it is a thundering set of rapids in the wet season, plunging over a 4m rock shelf. In the dry season, visitors can walk across much of the ledge, rather like at the famous Victoria Falls on the Zimbabwe-Zambia border. The wet season is more spectacular, but the dry season is more fun, as it is possible to take a dip in the gentle-flowing river. Tatai waterfall can be reached on the road to Sre Ambel, with a little directional help from the Thai military, although once the roadworks are finished it will probably be signposted. There is a second waterfall or set of rapids, known as the **Koh Poi Waterfall**, on another tributary of the river. It's great to clamber about here in the dry season, as there are immense boulders to use as stepping stones. It is possible to visit both these waterfalls in one boat trip. Negotiate hard with the driver and aim to pay around 800B.

SOUTH COAST

Places to Stay

Being Cambodia's original 'wild west', long before Pailin and Poipet started to muscle in on the gambling and prostitution business, several of the town's guesthouses double as brothels. Some places offer moto drivers a commission for bringing customers, which has led to some unscrupulous drivers telling lies. If they say somewhere is closed, check it out first, as it's more likely that the guesthouse is one that won't pay them a commission.

Cheap Charlie's Guesthouse (☎ 016-853450) Doubles with fan 50B. These basic rooms without bathroom are easily the cheapest in town and there is little room for complaint at this price. Cheap Charlie's is also a good source of traveller info on the area.

Otto's (☎ 012-924249, e 012924249@ mobitel.com.kh) Rooms without bathroom 80-100B. This small wooden guesthouse has reasonably priced basic rooms; it tends to attract the Pattaya crowd coming here on visa runs.

Pailin Guesthouse Rooms with fan/air-con & squat loo 100/200B. These rooms are basic but cheap; 200B is pretty damn reasonable for air-con.

Kolab Cheay Den Hotel (☎ 016-887680) Rooms with fan/air-con, TV & bathroom 150/300B. This clean, friendly mini-hotel offers a good deal and is very close to the boat dock.

Rasmay Bunthan Guesthouse (☎ 936070) Rooms with fan/air-con, TV & bathroom 150/300B. The rooms here are very clean but come with squat loo only for the time being.

Sovann Angkor Hotel Rooms with fan/air-con & bathroom 150/250B. The rooms here are fairly basic, but there is a nice upstairs veranda area.

Nokor Reach Hotel (☎ 016-863207, e maosopheap@yahoo.com) Rooms with fan/air-con & TV 200/350B, without TV 150/300B. Overlooking the market, this place is little different from the competition and all rooms have a bathroom.

Koh Pich Hotel (☎ 936114, fax 936113) Rooms with fan 150B, doubles with air-con, TV & bathroom 300B, doubles with fridge & hot water 400B. This is the biggest hotel in town and has some well-appointed doubles at a fair price. There are some cheaper, basic rooms behind the main building.

Raksmey Makara Hotel (☎ 936058) Singles/doubles with air-con, TV & bathroom US$8/10, VIP rooms with fridge & hot water US$13. This upmarket place is a long way out of town, but has smart rooms. VIP rooms are hardly that, and it's probably better value at the Koh Pich for now.

Bopha Koh Kong Hotel is undergoing reconstruction from the ground up, but should be the fanciest place in town once completed. There is another smart-looking **hotel** under construction on the riverfront, which should prove the best location in town.

Koh Kong International Resort Rooms from 900B. Beyond town, on the border with Thailand, this resort turns out pretty fancy rooms, including the only beach bungalows this side of the border.

Places to Eat

Dining options are limited. As always, the best bets for a budget meal are the stalls found in and around Psar Leu. There are also cheap stalls near the boat dock that turn out basic, cheap food.

Thai Food Restaurant Dishes 25B. Opposite the Rasmay Bunthan Guesthouse, this place does exactly what the sign says. There is a limited range of tasty Thai food at bargain prices.

Foreigner Food Restaurant Opposite Psar Leu, this restaurant turns out popular traveller food, such as pancakes and omelettes, at low prices.

Heng Heng Restaurant This is a popular Khmer restaurant for tasty Chinese and Cambodian breakfasts of noodle soup and porridge.

Otto's This Western-style restaurant makes a convenient stop for a quick breakfast before taking the boat to Sihanoukville. The menu also includes Thai food and one of the best bratwurst in Cambodia. It's calmer after 8pm when the Pattaya crowd heads out on the town.

Entertainment

There used to be more to do by night in Krong Koh Kong than during daylight hours. However, pretty much all the nightclubs have closed and entertainment is hard to find. With the new bridge, it may be that people flock to the border area to frequent the bars and restaurants at the border casino, as tends to happen in Pailin these days. The **roller skating rink** is something of a draw for the younger folk in town, with roller-boots you haven't seen since the 1970s and some pumping Asian techno.

Getting There & Away

President Airlines (US$45/90 one way/ return) and Royal Phnom Penh Airways (US$45/85) sometimes operate flights between Phnom Penh and Krong Koh Kong. However, these were suspended at the time of writing.

Construction of the road from Krong Koh Kong to Sre Ambel is well underway. Share taxis take as little as six hours to make the run to the capital, but there are still up to four ferry crossings to slow things up.

There is also a new route through the mountains of Koh Kong to Pailin or Battambang, passing through a wild and remote area formerly controlled by the Khmer Rouge. There is no such thing as regular public transport. This route should be attempted in the dry season only by dirt bikers with plenty of off-road experience.

Otherwise, all transport goes by sea. Boats leave daily for Sihanoukville (600B, four hours, 8am) and Sre Ambel (500B, four hours, 7am).

For more details on travel to Thailand or Sihanoukville, see the Getting There & Away chapter.

Getting Around

Motos are the most popular form of transport around town and most short-hop fares cost 5B; towards the edge of town costs 10B. Bicycles are another option and can be rented at Cheap Charlie's Guesthouse for 50B per day.

With so much water around, boats are a crucial part of the transport network. Boats across the river should cost 20B per person, or 40B for the boat. Boats can also be chartered for trips to nearby islands, beaches and waterfalls. Negotiate hard to get a fair price. With the opening of the bridge, it

Prawn Crackers

Mangroves make ideal grounds for commercial farming of the tiger prawn, a seafood with phenomenal money-making powers throughout Asia. To farm tiger prawns, however, it is necessary to clear the mangroves and create artificial ponds. Fertilisers and chemical feeds are required, and it is necessary to pump out polluted water and replenish it with clean water, which damages the surrounding environment. Within two or three years a pool will have to be abandoned and the farming relocated, leaving a trail of environmental destruction.

There is very little in shrimp farming for Cambodia. Generally, the farms are established with big-business bucks, unskilled Khmer labour is used for the menial work and 90% of the product is shipped to Thailand. The further pity of it is that mangroves foster remarkably diverse ecosystems and have an integral relationship with oceanic fish populations, serving as spawning grounds for many species that are commercially fished. The government is looking at ways to regulate commercial shrimp farming in its mangroves, but underfunding and lack of understanding on the part of the locals living in mangrove areas is making the job difficult.

All in all, the shrimp-farming saga has been a pretty sorry one for Cambodia. Most of the farms have failed, with shrimps dying from disease and a poorly maintained habitat. This has resulted in many Cambodians, who were encouraged to invest in shrimp farms as a lucrative money earner, becoming financially ruined. The mangrove swamps are unlikely to return soon, as many people in the province are now chopping them down for charcoal production.

should be possible to take a moto (50B) or taxi (75B to 100B) the 7km to the border.

SRE AMBEL
ស្រែអំបិល

Located up a river estuary in eastern Koh Kong Province, Sre Amble is something of a smugglers' port. There is little to see or do here, but travellers heading from Phnom Penh direct to Thailand without visiting Sihanoukville can catch fast boats from here to Krong Koh Kong. These leave at 11am, one hour earlier than the Sihanoukville boats, and this greatly reduces the chances of reaching the border late and having to spend a night in Krong Koh Kong. See the Getting There & Away chapter for more on this option. A minibus to Sre Ambel from Psar Dang Kor in Phnom Penh is 6000r, chartering a whole share taxi is US$15. There are also fishing boats leaving Sre Ambel for Krong Koh Kong (300B, 12 hours, 4pm), but carry a mosquito net, as some of the coastal areas are prone to malaria.

Sihanoukville
ក្រុងព្រះសីហនុ

☎ 034 • pop 155,000
Sihanoukville is Cambodia's leading beach resort, a sprawling modern town surrounded by palm-fringed, squeaky white-sand beaches and undeveloped tropical islands. Tourist numbers have taken off in the past few years and the area looks set for big things, although it still has a long way to go to catch up with Thailand. For many this is a great relief and good reason to come.

Named in honour of the king, the town was hacked out of the jungle in the late 1950s to create the country's first and only deepwater port; the USA provided the money for NH4 linking Sihanoukville to Phnom Penh. During the 1960s, it experienced a mini tourism boom and some large hotels were constructed, but Kep remained the most popular beach resort. With the

overthrow of Sihanouk in 19' name was changed to Kompong Sc. didn't revert back to Sihanoukville until 1993. Cambodians refer to the town interchangeably, royalists preferring to use Sihanoukville, old-guard former communists choosing Kompong Som.

Its principal attractions are the four beaches that ring the headland. While none of them qualify as the region's finest, on weekdays it is still possible to have stretches of beach to yourself, although as traveller numbers soar it might involve a concerted hike. Sihanoukville is extremely popular on weekends with well-to-do Khmers who flock south from Phnom Penh. Beyond the immediate beaches surrounding the town are the empty beaches of Otres and Ream National Park, and a dozen more islands that see less than 0.1% of the visitors their counterparts in Thailand receive. Forget about the ideal of *The Beach* in Thailand, it doesn't exist, but it just might in Cambodia.

There is a battle going on for the heart and soul of Sihanoukville. Some Cambodian businessmen and their shadowy associates from neighbouring countries want to turn the town into a concrete casino town of mega-resorts, while expats from nearby Pattaya want to turn it into some sort of sex, sea and sun go-go resort. On the other side, younger expats are hoping to make a new Ko Pha-Ngan on Cambodia's southern coast with the birth of Serendipity Beach, while other investors rub their hands and hope for a Ko Samui gold rush and pleasant garden bungalows set among swaying palms. Whoever wins out in the end, it's certain that Sihanoukville is changing fast. Like Siem Reap, this is another place in Cambodia that doesn't stay still – ask around guesthouses and bars for the latest on what's in and out.

Orientation
The headland of Sihanoukville is spread over several kilometres. The centre of Sihanoukville is the long-popular backpacker hang-out along Phlauv (Ph) Ekareach, which doubles as the main street in town.

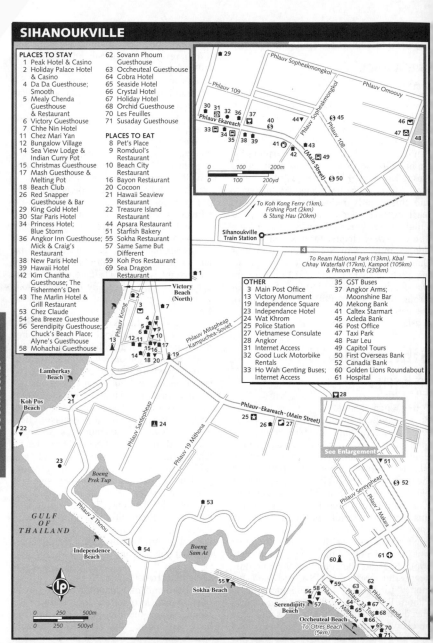

SIHANOUKVILLE

PLACES TO STAY
1 Peak Hotel & Casino
2 Holiday Palace Hotel & Casino
4 Da Da Guesthouse; Smooth
5 Mealy Chenda Guesthouse & Restaurant
6 Victory Guesthouse
7 Chhe Nin Hotel
11 Chez Mari Yan
12 Bungalow Village
14 Sea View Lodge & Indian Curry Pot
15 Christmas Guesthouse
17 Mash Guesthouse & Melting Pot
18 Beach Club
26 Red Snapper Guesthouse & Bar
29 King Gold Hotel
30 Star Paris Hotel
34 Princess Hotel; Blue Storm
36 Angkor Inn Guesthouse; Mick & Craig's Restaurant
38 New Paris Hotel
39 Hawaii Hotel
42 Kim Chantha Guesthouse; The Fishermen's Den
43 The Marlin Hotel & Grill Restaurant
53 Chez Claude
54 Sea Breeze Guesthouse
56 Serendipity Guesthouse; Chuck's Beach Place; Alyne's Guesthouse
58 Mohachai Guesthouse

62 Sovann Phoum Guesthouse
63 Occheuteal Guesthouse
64 Cobra Hotel
65 Seaside Hotel
66 Crystal Hotel
67 Holiday Hotel
68 Orchid Guesthouse
70 Les Feuilles
71 Susaday Guesthouse

PLACES TO EAT
8 Pet's Place
9 Romduol's Restaurant
10 Beach City Restaurant
16 Bayon Restaurant
20 Cocoon
21 Hawaii Seaview Restaurant
22 Treasure Island Restaurant
44 Apsara Restaurant
51 Starfish Bakery
55 Sokha Restaurant
57 Same Same But Different
59 Koh Pos Restaurant
69 Sea Dragon Restaurant

OTHER
3 Main Post Office
13 Victory Monument
19 Independence Square
23 Independence Hotel
24 Wat Khrom
25 Police Station
27 Vietnamese Consulate
28 Angkor
31 Internet Access
32 Good Luck Motorbike Rentals
33 Ho Wah Genting Buses; Internet Access
35 GST Buses
37 Angkor Arms; Moonshine Bar
40 Mekong Bank
41 Caltex Starmart
45 Acleda Bank
46 Post Office
47 Taxi Park
48 Psar Leu
49 Capitol Tours
50 First Overseas Bank
52 Canadia Bank
60 Golden Lions Roundabout
61 Hospital

Phlauv Sopheakmongkol
Phlauv 109
Phlauv Omoouy
Phlauv Ekareach
Phlauv 108
Phlauv Sopheakmongkol
(Main Street)

To Koh Kong Ferry (1km), Fishing Port (2km) & Stung Hau (20km)

Sihanoukville Train Station

To Ream National Park (13km), Kbal Chhay Waterfall (17km), Kampot (105km) & Phnom Penh (230km)

Victory Beach (North)

Phlauv Krong
Phlauv Mitapheap Kampuchea-soviet

Lamherkay Beach

Koh Pos Beach

Phlauv Santepheap

Phlauv 19 Mithona

Phlauv Ekareach (Main Street)

See Enlargement

GULF OF THAILAND

Phlauv 2 Thnou

Boeng Prek Tup

Boeng Sam At

Independence Beach

Phlauv Sereypheap
Phlauv 7 Makara

Sokha Beach

Serendipity Beach

Occheuteal Beach
To Otres Beach (5km)

Phlauv 14 Mithona
Phlauv 23 Tola
Phlauv 1 Kanda

SOUTH COAST

Mid-range Occheuteal Beach and the new backpacker haunt of Serendipity Beach are to the south of the city centre. West of town is tiny Koh Pos Beach and the larger Independence Beach, which is home to the decaying and empty Independence Hotel. Buses from Phnom Penh arrive in the centre of town, while boats from Krong Koh Kong arrive about 3km north of town.

Information

Sihanoukville is evolving fast, so it's important to keep up to date. Grab a copy of *The Sihanoukville Visitors Guide,* a pocket-sized directory that comes out twice a year and can be found at local hotels, guesthouses, restaurants and bars. There is a tourist office in the centre of town, but guesthouses and bars are generally a better source of information.

There are several banks in town. Canadia Bank (☎ 933490) on Ph Ekareach is a useful option for people carrying non–US dollar travellers cheques, as it changes most currencies for a 2% commission. It also offers free cash advances for MasterCard holders and represents Moneygram. Mekong Bank (☎ 933867) on Ph Ekareach offers cash advances on Visa for a minimum charge of US$5 per transaction, or 2% above US$250. Both First Overseas Bank (☎ 320032), Ph Ekareach, and Acleda Bank (☎ 320232), Ph 108, can arrange Western Union transfers for those needing cash in a hurry.

The main post office is near the port, and there is a small branch near Psar Leu (Central Market) but reliability is not something for which either is known. Telephone calls can be made easily from small private booths around town, as well as through guesthouses and hotels.

Email and Internet access is available in Sihanoukville but, with no local provider, prices remain considerably high at US$5 per hour. There are several convenient places to get online around the bus stations in the centre of town.

There is a Vietnamese consulate in Sihanoukville, which offers probably the fastest Vietnamese visas available anywhere in the world. They can normally turn one around in 15 minutes and charge US$30.

Dangers & Annoyances Yaba, the 'crazy' drug from Thailand, is known as yama in Cambodia. It's not just any old diet pill from the pharmacist, but home-made meta-amphetamines produced in labs in Cambodia and the region beyond. The pills are often laced with toxic substances, such as mercury, lithium or whatever else the manufacturer can find. Yama is a dirty drug and more addictive than users would like to admit. Steer clear of the stuff unless you plan on an indefinite extension on your trip to Cambodia.

Night robberies have been occurring in Sihanoukville in recent years, particularly around the red-light district near the port. There are many poorly lit areas around the sprawling town, making late-night revellers easy prey. It shouldn't stop people going out – try to hook up with a reliable moto driver for the evening when heading out on the town.

There have also been numerous incidences of theft from the various beaches around Sihanoukville while people are out swimming. Don't take anything valuable to the beach, unless you have someone to keep an eye on it all the time.

Motorbike theft is also a popular pastime in Sihanoukville. Anyone who rents a motorbike should make sure it comes with a separate padlock. Try not to leave it untended and out of sight, and where there is guarded parking, such as at Psar Leu in the centre of town, use it.

Beaches

All the beaches at Sihanoukville look set for major facelifts, as developers move in to construct resorts. The best all-rounder is **Occheuteal Beach**; the northern end has emerged as a popular traveller hangout nicknamed **Serendipity Beach**, while farther south is popular with Khmers and mid-range tourists staying in the nearby hotels. Serendipity Beach is a cool place to chill out with a drink, but is pretty crowded these days and has rocky waters. It hosts occasional full-moon parties. Lining the back of

Occheuteal are pine trees, which provide useful shade in the heat of the day. The sand stretches on southwards for a couple of kilometres and it's worth trekking down here if you want a bit of privacy. A new resort is under construction in the central part of the beach.

Just around a small headland at the southern end of Occheuteal Beach is **Otres Beach**, a seemingly infinite strip of empty white sand. Government officials are eagerly parcelling up land behind the beach, but for now fewer visitors make it here than other beaches around town. To get to Otres Beach, follow the road behind Occheuteal Beach before branching left then right around a small headland, or follow Ph Omoouy east out of town from Psar Leu for about 7km; both are rough tracks.

Sokha Beach is perhaps the prettiest and most popular beach at Sihanoukville, but a massive resort is under construction at the back of the beach that will change it forever. It is still popular with Khmers, but draws fewer Westerners. It remains to be seen how much public access there will be to the beach once the resort opens.

Victory Beach was the original backpacker beach and remains popular with budget travellers due to its proximity to Sihanoukville's most popular guesthouses. It's arguably the least appealing of all the beaches, as the port is located at the northern end of the beach, hardly making for the perfect tropical moment, and the beach is narrow and scruffy. South around a small headland is another small stretch of sand, usually known as Victory Beach, but also signposted as **Lamherkay Beach**, after the old hotel near here.

Farther south on the western tip of Sihanoukville's headland is tiny **Koh Pos Beach**, which also looks set to be controlled by a developer, as Treasure Island Resort. This is a nice, shady beach, but with rocky waters. Finally, there is **Independence Beach** running southeast from here, a good stretch of clean sand, but lacking shade and facilities. Above the northern end of the beach is the old **Independance Hotel** (sic). Some locals claim the hotel is haunted, and it does

indeed have an eerie look about it. At night it seems to function as some sort of brothel, so if you hear some groaning and moaning, don't worry, it's probably not the ghosts. Canadia Bank investment group has plans for a massive renovation to turn it into a four-star hotel, complete with a Stratosphere-style tower, similar to the one at Vegas but a whole lot smaller.

Islands

There are more than a dozen islands off the coast of Sihanoukville; all are extremely undeveloped by the standards of neighbouring Thailand. There is no accommodation on the islands, but many of the guesthouses, restaurants and cafes around town arrange day trips to the most popular islands, including a spot of snorkelling and lunch.

Most of the islands nearer town are small, rocky and far from ideal for anything but limited snorkelling. Farther afield are the large islands of **Koh Rong** and **Koh Rong Samlon**. Both are surrounded by blissfully empty, beautiful beaches and have freshwater sources, suggesting they will be a major focus for future development. Koh Rong Samlon includes a large heart-shaped bay with some shellfish cultivation, as well as some good beaches on the north coast towards Koh Rong. Koh Rong has a fantastic beach on the southwestern coast, stretching for 5km or more and there's not a beach hut in sight. There are other good beaches around this huge island and a bustling fishing community on the southeast with basic supplies available, plus fresh fish and crab. If one place is set to become the Ko Samui of Cambodia, this is it – don't worry though, it won't be for a decade or more!

Nearer the coast and to the south of Sihanoukville are several smaller islands that are an option if the open waters to Koh Rong are too choppy. **Koh Khteah** is the nearest, but very small; **Koh Ta Khieu** has the better beaches, but is near Cambodia's navy headquarters.

Diving

The marine life near Sihanoukville isn't as impressive as Thailand's or Indonesia's, thanks in part to earlier dynamite fishing. However, farther afield around the island of **Koh Tang** and its nearby reefs, there are some interesting dive sites, although most remain relatively unexplored. Unfortunately, this area can't be reached in a day using the slow fishing boats and so requires an overnight trip, pushing up the costs.

There is currently only one dive operation in town, run by **Claude** (☎ 012-824870) from Chez Claude. He has been in Sihanoukville almost a decade and knows the waters better than anyone. He can arrange day trips to areas around Koh Rong Samlon, as well as longer multi-day trips to the area around Koh Tang. Telephone or climb the hill to Chez Claude's to arrange a trip.

Other Attractions

Kbal Chhay Waterfall is a popular excursion for Khmers visiting Sihanoukville, as it was used as a major location for the filming of the hit movie *Pos Keng Kong* (The Giant Snake), the most successful Cambodian-made film in the post–civil war era. The small falls are attractive, but not as spectacular or isolated as those near Krong Koh Kong. There is also a litter problem here that rather detracts from the natural beauty. Anyone who has seen or is planning to see the falls at Krong Koh Kong can probably give Kbal Chhay a miss. For anyone who has seen *Pos Keng Kong,* it's a must. The falls are located about 17km from the centre of Sihanoukville. The turnoff is signposted on the left from NH4, about 9km out of town. It costs around US$4 for a return trip on a moto, but is easy enough to get to on a rented motorbike.

Just 2km north of the main port is a **fishing port**, which offers some good photo opportunities at sunrise or sunset. Another 20km up the coast is the small fishing town of **Stung Hau**, where the rusting remains of Cambodia's communist navy lie abandoned.

Catching a sunset by the coast is always a popular activity and Sihanoukville is no exception. Most of the beaches have only a partial view of the sunset, as juts of land or small islands obscure the view. A lot of travellers end up hanging out at Serendipity Beach just because it's a chilled-out place to be, but it's not great for catching a sunset. Victory Beach offers the best view, but the port on the horizon somewhat kills the romance. It's often better to get a bit of altitude. The Mealy Chenda Restaurant has great views from its upper balcony, while Chez Claude offers a huge panorama in almost every direction from its hilltop location.

Sihanoukville is also the base from which to organise a visit to **Ream National Park**, a protected area that is home to dolphins, myriad bird species and a number of isolated beaches. See the Ream National Park section under Around Sihanoukville later for more details.

Places to Stay

For the budget traveller there's a wide range of inexpensive rooms in Sihanoukville, from US$3 with a bed and fan to US$10 with air-con, TV and hot-water bathroom. There is also a good selection for mid-range visitors looking to spend between US$15 and US$30, as the arrival of some major casinos with cheap rooms has kept prices down. Beach addicts will no doubt want to stay as close to the beach as possible and this is now an option at several beaches in town. For those who are all beached out, seeking value for money, or prefer a spot of nightlife, try the town centre, but otherwise it is not the most charming area to stay.

Places to Stay – Budget

There are three main areas for budget accommodation in Sihanoukville: the long-running area around Victory Beach, the port area a couple of kilometres west of town, and the up-and-coming Serendipity Beach at the northern end of Occheuteal Beach south of town.

Victory Beach This was the original backpacker area and there are more than 20 guesthouses on the hill above the beach, many with barely a sign and offering just a few basic rooms.

Mealy Chenda Guesthouse (☎ 933472) Rooms with bathroom from US$4. This was the area's original guesthouse and is still going strong. It has been completely rebuilt over the years and now looks more like a hotel than a guesthouse, but still offers good-value rooms at budget prices. More expensive rooms include a balcony or sea view, while cheaper rooms are in the older building.

Victory Guesthouse (☎ 016-886570) Twins with bathroom US$5, rooms without bathroom US$3. Rooms are basic, but then so is the price.

Da Da Guesthouse (☎ 012-879527) Doubles with bathroom US$6, singles without bathroom from US$2, rooms with aircon, TV & bathroom US$8. This small place offers a good deal.

Smooth (☎ 012-859214) Rooms with/without bathroom US$5/3. This small guesthouse has simple rooms with the occasional touch of thoughtful decoration.

Christmas Guesthouse (☎ 012-915498) Rooms with bathroom from US$4. Strategically straddling the corner on the trail towards the beach, all rooms in this friendly place are clean and tidy.

Mash Guesthouse (☎ 012-913714) Rooms with bathroom from US$3. Merged with Melting Pot, this place offers a good range of rooms, some with individual paint schemes.

Beach Club (☎ 012-808813) Singles with/without bathroom US$4/3, doubles/triples with bathroom US$5/6. Set around an old wooden house, this guesthouse has a range of basic rooms similar to elsewhere, but with a better vibe than some. It also offers spa-style treatments for those looking for a lift.

Sea View Lodge (☎ 934040) Dorm beds US$1, simple rooms US$3. The rooms here don't have bathrooms but they're cheap.

Bungalow Village (☎ 933875) Bungalows with bathroom US$5. This place has a collection of basic bamboo huts set around a garden and bar – useful for those seeking a bit more privacy.

Chhe Nin Hotel (☎ 933611) Singles/doubles with fan & bathroom US$5/7, rooms with air-con & hot water US$10. This flash-looking place is actually not as expensive as it looks, offering cheap rooms at the front and hotel-style rooms at the rear.

There are plenty more **guesthouses** in the area, most advertising rates for US$3 or US$4 a night for a small room, sometimes with a squat toilet and a shower. The upshot is that you should always be able to find a bed.

Serendipity Beach All these places are built on land leased from the police and may not be around indefinitely.

Serendipity Guesthouse Rooms without bathroom US$5. This guesthouse comprises a series of basic wooden longhouses divided into small rooms. It's basic but on the beach.

Alyne's Guesthouse Singles/doubles without bathroom US$3/5. Right next door to Serendipity, this newer place has wafer-thin walls between very basic rooms, but is near the water.

Mohachai Guesthouse (☎ 933586) Singles/twins with fan & bathroom US$5/7. Set about 100m back from the beach, this looks more permanent than the others, and offers a better level of comfort at a slightly higher price.

Occheuteal Beach This has traditionally been the turf of mid-range overseas tourists and Khmers, but budget places are making inroads.

Sovann Phoum Guesthouse (☎ 016-864975, Ph 1 Kanda) Rooms with fan, TV & bathroom US$6. Located a couple of blocks back from the beach, the rooms here are clean, comfortable and a good deal.

Cobra Hotel (☎ 933643, Ph 14 Milthona) Bungalows with air-con, TV, fridge & bathroom US$8. This place has always looked a touch dodgy, with karaoke and girls lurking upstairs, but the five Sumatran-style bungalows at the front are pretty good value given that the beach is just across the road.

Occheuteal Guesthouse (☎ 016-821292, Ph 23 Tola) Rooms with fan/air-con, TV & bathroom US$8/10. This is an unassuming guesthouse a block behind the beach, and the rooms are in reasonable shape.

Susaday Guesthouse (☎ 933907, e susa day@camintel.com, Ph 14 Milthona) Doubles with fan & bathroom US$10. The location is good, right across from the beach, but the rooms are pretty simple for the money.

Les Feuilles *(☎ 320156, Ph 23 Tola)* Rooms per person US$4. The rooms here are basic in the extreme (like bed, fan and no window) and should be considered only as a last resort.

Town Centre There are a number of good places around the town centre.

Angkor Inn Guesthouse *(☎ 933615)* Rooms with fan & bathroom US$4-5. This is probably the best value in the area, turning out clean and functional rooms at low prices.

Kim Chantha Guesthouse *(☎ 933680, Ph Sopheakmongkol)* Singles/doubles with fan, TV & bathroom US$5/6. This is similar to the Angkor Inn, but offers TV for those who want to catch up on news, tunes or movies.

Red Snapper Guesthouse *(☎ 012-952486)* Doubles with bathroom US$4. Once a bar, now a guesthouse too, the Snapper has clean rooms at a sensible price. The bar is set in the garden, and it's a short stroll to the town centre.

Star Paris Hotel *(☎ 933609, Ph Ekareach)* Rooms/triples with air-con, TV, fridge & hot water US$10/15. These rooms are heavily armed with trimmings for those who want a little more comfort and have the dollars to spare.

The Marlin Hotel *(☎ 320169, Ph Ekareach)* Rooms with air-con, TV, fridge & hot water US$10. This central hotel is well kitted out for the money and offers travel information for guests.

Places to Stay – Mid-Range

With the exception of weekends, when Khmers pile down from Phnom Penh, there is generally a glut of mid-range rooms available in Sihanoukville. This, coupled with the big casinos slashing their rates dramatically, means there are good deals to be had.

Occheuteal Beach This is the most popular part of town for bigger spenders, thanks to its location – a short stroll to the beach.

Crystal Hotel *(☎ 933880, fax 933881, [e] crystal@camintel.com, Ph 14 Milthona)* Rooms with TV, minibar & hot tub US$25-45. This is a strange-looking kind of hotel,

but the rooms are pretty comfortable, and many offer a sea view of sorts, thanks to the design.

Seaside Hotel *(☎ 933662, fax 933640, Ph 14 Milthona)* Rooms with TV, fridge & hot water US$25-50. This place looks like a junior version of the Cambodiana in Phnom Penh. It offers a variety of well-appointed rooms, but has recently lost its most famous customer, Prime Minister Hun Sen, as he has built a swanky villa almost next door.

Holiday Hotel *(☎ 933658, fax 320113, [e] hotelhld@camintel.com, Ph 23 Tola)* Rooms US$15-25. This place is good value, as it is a block back from the beach. The smart rooms include much the same kit as the aforementioned places, but no sea view.

Orchid Guesthouse *(☎ 933639, Ph 23 Tola)* Rooms with hot water US$15-20. Also back from the beach, this place is popular with small tour groups. The rooms are smart and the owners are building a major annexe on the beach, currently offering budget rooms from US$6 to US$8, but soon to have hotel standards.

Other Beaches There are fewer options to be found on other beaches around town.

Chez Claude *(☎ 012-824870)* Bungalows US$20. This place has views of several of the town's beaches, perched on a hilltop above Sokha Beach. There are several bungalows ranging from a Cambodian-style house to an African *banda* (mud hut with thatch roof). All have atmosphere, air-con and hot water. There are a lot of stairs to climb each day, however.

Chez Mari Yan *(☎ 933709)* Small rooms with fan & bathroom US$10, larger bungalows with bathroom US$15. The setting is pleasant amid a lush garden overlooking Victory Beach, but the rooms are simple for the money. There is definitely a pleasant ambience about the place and an expansion is underway.

Sea Breeze Guesthouse *(☎ 320217)* Singles/doubles/triples with air-con, TV, fridge & hot tub US$15/20/30. This place near Independence Beach has large, clean rooms but it's a long, dark road to town for those who like to go out at night.

Holiday Palace Hotel *(☎ 933808, fax 933809, Ph Krong)* Rooms US$15-45. This massive casino complex, overshadowing Victory Beach, has recently halved its rates to draw in guests. US$15 gets a three-star room that is noticeably plusher than elsewhere in town and is certainly worth considering. Ring ahead to check that rates are still discounted.

Peak Hotel *(☎ 320301, fax 320300)* Standard/superior rooms US$20/30. Another big casino occupying a hill above the port, this place has also cut rates to stimulate demand. It is the only place in town with a swimming pool and tennis courts.

Town Centre The centre of town has a wide range of smart places, with little to distinguish them.

Princess Hotel *(☎ 934789, Ph Ekareach)* Singles/doubles/triples US$13/15/20. This new pad has sparkling bathrooms and tasteful decor, making it an attractive option.

King Gold Hotel *(☎/fax 933829, Ph Boray Kamakor)* Doubles/twins US$10/15. Another new hotel, this is also pretty spotless, with good-value rooms with all amenities.

New Paris Hotel *(☎ 933750, Ph Ekareach)* Doubles/twins with hot tub US$12/15. A relative veteran for this part of town, it has recently added another floor. All rooms are spacious and clean.

Hawaii Hotel *(☎ 933447, Ph Ekareach)* Rooms US$15. Next door to the New Paris, this hotel has decent enough rooms with bathroom, including little touches like a hairdryer for those who like that sort of thing.

Places to Eat

There is now a wide selection of restaurants and cafes in Sihanoukville. The backpacker area above Victory Beach claims a dozen or more restaurants, plus decent food at many of the guesthouses. Other beaches around town have a couple of local restaurants, while Serendipity Beach is a good spot for beachside barbecues. The centre of town has a few places to eat that can be useful before or after the bus or during a night on the town. Most beaches attract vendors selling everything from pineapple and quail eggs to freshly grilled prawns and fish. There is not much hard sell and provided you bargain, this can be an inexpensive way to snack your way through the day.

Victory Beach This is the budget-dining centre of town, with a good range of tasty and inexpensive cuisines available, served out of basic wooden shacks.

Mealy Chenda Restaurant The popular restaurant at Mealy Chenda Guesthouse draws a mixed crowd at night. The menu includes an evening seafood barbecue as well as backpacker breakfasts, but service is slow if it's busy.

Romduol's Restaurant Meals 3000-5000r. With a very similar menu to Mealy Chenda, and just across the road, this is competitively priced in riel rather than US dollars. It is very popular and full to bursting most nights.

Pet's Place Next door to Romduol's, this place has a mix of Western and Asian dishes at very reasonable prices. It also offers dangerously cheap Angkor draft beer at US$0.40 a mug.

Beach City Restaurant The restaurant at the Beach City Guesthouse occupies a strategic location that most people walk past on the way to the beach, and is always packed with satisfied punters.

Melting Pot Part of Mash Guesthouse, this place has a good selection of Western food, with a number of dishes that don't turn up on other menus in town.

Bayon Restaurant Dishes 3000-5000r. This restaurant is next door to the Melting Pot, and is earning rave reviews for cheap, no-frills Western food.

Indian Curry Pot Dishes US$2-4. Part of Sea View Lodge, the Curry Pot offers a pleasant garden for outdoor dining and has the best curries south of Phnom Penh.

Cocoon This place has the only wood-fired pizzas in this part of town and also turns out a selection of tasty pastas.

Other Beaches There are several seafood restaurants located on the beaches around Sihanoukville, including **Sokha Restaurant**

(Sokha Beach) and **Hawaii Seaview Restaurant** *(Lamherkay Beach)*, but it is worth checking the price as you go, as much of the seafood is by the kilo and the bill can mount quickly. There are also several large outdoor restaurants around golden lions roundabout that offer shark's fin soup, popular with visiting Khmers.

Several small restaurants and bars on Serendipity Beach offer meals. **Same Same But Different** has barbecued fish and seafood most nights at reasonable prices. **Chuck's Beach Place** does fast food like burgers and dogs (hot, rather than Vietnamese style) and regular barbies.

There are a few more restaurants just off nearby Occheuteal Beach.

Les Feuilles Steak US$5-6, pasta US$4. The restaurant at this guesthouse has a very provincial-French look to it, probably because it has been around since the early 1990s. It also has a pool table.

Sea Dragon Restaurant Mains US$3-5. One of the more extensive menus in town, this place offers just about every combination of food and flavours imaginable.

Treasure Island Restaurant *(Koh Pos Beach)* On an isolated beach, this is a big seafood restaurant popular with Khmers. Prices are generally reasonable, although shellfish go by the kilo, so check the weight. One litre bottles of Jim Beam are US$13 here, Gordon's Gin US$12 and Smirnoff Vodka just US$8! Not a good idea to drive here if you like your spirits.

Koh Pos Restaurant Previously occupying Koh Pos Beach, but now condemned to the less-memorable golden lions roundabout, this is a local institution among Khmers. The wok-fried curried whole crab is delicious.

Chez Claude Seafood dishes US$5-8. Part of Claude's hilltop empire, the predominantly seafood menu is one of the best in Cambodia, including claypot fish dishes with a French accent and local shellfish such as clams and crab. Prices are above average compared to elsewhere in town, but so is the food. There is a healthy wine cellar and it's a commanding spot for a sunset beer.

Town Centre There are a number of good places in the town centre.

Apsara Restaurant Dishes US$2-5. Right in the centre of town, this is a long-running local restaurant with a selection of Asian cuisine from Cambodia, Vietnam, Thailand and China.

Starfish Bakery Tucked down a little side street is this garden cafe providing filling breakfasts and light lunches in the name of a good cause. The Starfish Project supports local disadvantaged Cambodians who have fallen upon hard times.

Mick & Craig's Restaurant *(Ph Sopheakmongkol)* Mains US$3-4. No prizes for guessing the names of the owners. This little restaurant has a good selection of breakfasts, including hearty vegetarian options, as well as a changing selection of daily lunch and dinner specials of good Western grub. Craig also offers guided walks around the Sihanoukville area.

Marlin Grill Restaurant *(Ekareach St)* Part of the Marlin Hotel, this bar-restaurant offers fast food, such as burgers and steaks.

Entertainment

Nightlife in Sihanoukville has picked up a lot in the past couple of years with the influx of travellers from Thailand. There are abundant drinking holes around Victory Beach, but the late-opening spots are all in the centre of town or at Serendipity Beach. There are no more classic Khmer nightclubs of the dark 'Sha La La La' variety, as Hun Sen's fun police closed them all. There are, however, several 'music restaurants', which amount to Khmer nightclubs in a different form. With the Angkor Brewery located on the outskirts of town, draught beer is very cheap at some places, starting at US$0.40 at some of the budget restaurants above Victory Beach. Nothing stays open late here, but **Melting Pot**, **Romduol's Restaurant**, **Pet's Place** and **Beach City Restaurant** all pull a drinking crowd into the evening.

Angkor Arms *(Ph Ekareach)* Probably the oldest bar in town, this place aims to offer the atmosphere of a British pub with darts and draught. It is much more welcoming than in the old days, with an outdoor seating area for those who want a drink with a breeze.

Moonshine Bar *(Ph Sopheakmongkol)* Next door to Angkor Arms, this place is located on the rooftop of a townhouse, up a rickety staircase. It is usually the last place in town to close.

The Fishermen's Den Above Kim Chantha Guesthouse, this bar is owned by a guy who runs a place in Pattaya, and it has the predictable collection of young, bored-looking local women hanging out here.

Chuck's Beach Place *(Serendipity Beach)* This is a 24-hour beach bar that is hard to beat for location. There are usually one or two souls here until the small hours of the morning. The nearby guesthouses also have bars of their own, but they don't go on all night.

Among the nightclubs to have reopened as 'music restaurants' are **Blue Storm** *(Ph Ekareach)*, a lavish-looking place next to Princess Hotel, and **Angkor** *(Ph Boray-Kamakor)*, which is more popular with locals.

Getting There & Away

Air Sihanoukville airport, 13km out of town near Ream, is currently closed. Once more resorts open up for business, it may reopen for flights between Siem Reap and here for a temples-beach combo, but this is unlikely for a few years yet.

Bus NH4, the 230km road between Sihanoukville and Phnom Penh, is in excellent condition for its whole length. Ho Wah Genting, GST and Capitol Tours operate large, comfortable, air-conditioned buses between Sihanoukville and the capital (12,000r, three to four hours) and their offices are located on Ph Ekareach in the centre of town. Heading to Sihanoukville, Ho Wah Genting departs from Phnom Penh at 6.55am, 7.30am, 8.30am, 12.30pm and 1.30pm, and leaves for the capital from Sihanoukville at 7.10am, 8am, 12.15pm, 1.10pm and 2pm. GST departs at 7.15am, 8.15am, 12.30pm, 1.30pm and 2pm in both directions. Capitol has services at 8am and 12.30pm in both directions.

Train The train service to Sihanoukville is extraordinarily slow when compared with the bus service, and with the advent of foreigner prices is no longer cheap. Anyone really wanting to try the trains is better off using the train for the shorter journey between Sihanoukville and Kampot (4800r, six hours).

Taxi & Minibus Taxis between Phnom Penh and Sihanoukville leave from the southwest of the capital near Psar Dang Kor (Dang Kor Market), and from Sihanoukville opposite Psar Leu. Taxis are worth considering only if you have somehow missed the bus, or are in a real rush. Prices have dropped in the last few years, as the checkpoints on the road (numbering more than 100 once upon a time), have been dismantled. Prices are negotiable, but you can expect to pay about US$20 a vehicle, 10,000r a head in cramped conditions or 15,000r each with just three in the back. Most drivers seem to think they are Michael Schumacher, so if you don't like blind overtaking you may want to sit in the back with some Valium. Travelling by minibus is cheaper at 8000r, but they are very overcrowded and the driving can be erratic.

From Sihanoukville to Kampot (8000r, two hours) is a distance of 105km and the road is excellent while following NH4 to Veal Renh, but deteriorates thereafter. It was getting dreadful after a few years of official neglect, but has recently been flattened, improving journey times again. Taxis to Kampot also depart from opposite Psar Leu. Pick-ups (7000/3000r inside/on the back) also run this route.

Motorcycle Some travellers with biking experience will use motorbikes rented in Phnom Penh to get to Sihanoukville. However, while NH4 is an easy run, it's relatively dull by Cambodian standards, and quite dangerous due to the prevalence of high-speed overtaking on blind corners. A motorbike is useful for exploring areas along the south coast and it is becoming increasingly popular to do a circuit that takes in Kampot, Kep and Bokor hill station. However, it's probably safer and more straightforward to just rent one in Sihanoukville – see the following Getting Around section for details. If you are adamant about riding from the capital, see the Getting Around section in the Phnom Penh chapter for rental details.

Boat There are daily boats departing Sihanoukville (500B, four hours, 12 noon) for Krong Koh Kong. For more details on this boat service, see the Getting There & Away chapter.

Getting Around

Motorcycle Motorbike rental is available all over Sihanoukville. The cheapest rentals are 100cc motos that cost US$3 per day from places above Victory Beach, and you can rent slightly newer bikes for US$4. In the town centre, many bus companies rent out bikes for US$4 per day. Some bike shops also rent larger 250cc trail bikes for US$7 to US$8 per day, depending on the model.

Bicycle Bicycle is a pleasant and environmentally friendly way to get around Sihanoukville. Some of the guesthouses offer rental services in the backpacker area above Victory Beach. Ask around and expect to pay US$1 to US$2 for the day.

Moto There are plenty of motos for hire in Sihanoukville. Moto drivers may try to rip people off, so unfortunately it is necessary to haggle over the price of most journeys. From the guesthouse area to the market is about 1500r, to Sokha and Occheuteal Beaches around 2500r; more might be requested late at night. From the centre of town to any of the beaches should set you back only about 1000r. From the backpacker area to the fast-boat dock is about 1500r, and around 3000r from elsewhere in town.

AROUND SIHANOUKVILLE

For the lowdown on what to see and do in Kirirom National Park, located midway between Sihanoukville and the capital, check out the Around Phnom Penh section in the Phnom Penh chapter.

Ream National Park
ឧទ្យានជាតិរាម

Also known as Preah Sihanouk National Park, Ream National Park was established as a 210 sq km protected area in 1993 and is home to a variety of animal and bird species and an expanse of mangrove swamp and forests.

The park has boats to transport visitors along the river to untouched beaches. Along the estuary you may see monkeys, eagles and even dolphins, and from the empty sands on the coast it is possible to explore some nearby creeks that disappear into the forest.

The programme is very much in its infancy but certainly deserves support, as the boat trip can be both an adventurous and educational ride and the income generated will ensure that the rangers protect the park instead of selling its firewood or poaching its wildlife to make a living. The boat trip costs about US$5 per person, although this depends on numbers; you will need to bring your lunch unless you can arrange something with the rangers. There is also some basic beachfront accommodation available in the Keng Kong Recreation Area near Ream Naval Base, from where rangers may be able to take you on walks into the park.

Getting There & Away Ream National Park is located about 13km east of the centre of Sihanoukville. The park's headquarters is a short distance down a turnoff from the naga statue in Ream. Look out for the Preah Sihanouk National Park sign carved in stone. The building (white with a green roof) is located right next to the little-used airport. Contact the rangers to help organise a trip or try setting one up through a guesthouse in town. To get to the park headquarters, take a moto from Sihanoukville for about US$2, or squeeze in a share taxi to Ream.

Kampot Province

ខេត្តកំពត

This is fast emerging as one of the most popular provinces in Cambodia, thanks to an alluring combination of abandoned colonial towns, abundant natural attractions and easy access from both Phnom Penh and Sihanoukville.

The province's economy never really recovered from the loss of its south coast port status to Sihanoukville in 1959, and was in slow decline until the civil war. With Chinese trading hubs, such as Tani and Tuk Meas, cut off from their former suppliers, agriculture gradually regained supremacy over trade in the province; a wide range of fruit and vege-tables, herbs and spices is cultivated. Durian haters beware: Kampot is Cambodia's leading producer of this spiky, stinky fruit.

Most of the attractions in Kampot can be absorbed in just a few days, including Bokor National Park and its abandoned hill station, the dilapidated seaside resort of Kep and the caves around Kompong Trach. However, this sleepy, atmospheric town often holds people longer than expected.

It wasn't always this way. Kampot remained a dangerous province to visit until the mid-1990s due to the presence of Khmer Rouge units in the surrounding hills. A train travelling between Phnom Penh and Sihanoukville was ambushed in July 1994. Three foreigners and a large number of Khmers were kidnapped. The three Westerners were subsequently executed by the Khmer Rouge, as government forces closed in on Phnom Voal where they were being held. Justice comes slowly and only one man is currently behind bars for this crime – Nuon Paet, the local Khmer Rouge leader at the time. Others involved, such as ambush commander Chhouk Rin, remain free.

NH3 is generally kept in reasonable condition within Kampot, but other roads have tended to be ignored for long periods. The road to Kep is very good, but soon deteriorates farther east towards Kompong Trach. Heading west to Sihanoukville, the road has recently been repaired and the increase in visitor numbers should help to keep it in reasonable shape. The Phnom Penh–Sihanoukville railway line runs right across the province, with the most scenic stretches found here. It is a long journey right through, but taking short sections – such as between Kampot and Takeo or Kampot and Veal Renh – is a nice way to get a taste of life on the rails without the hardships.

KAMPOT

កំពត

☎ 033 • pop 33,000

The somnolent riverside town of Kampot is beginning to attract the visitors it deserves. It is a charming place with a rich French architectural legacy and a relaxed atmosphere. Despite experiencing a commercial decline since the birth of Sihanoukville in 1959, Kampot is well known for producing some of the best pepper in the region. In the years before war took its toll, no self-respecting French restaurant in Paris would be without Kampot pepper on the table. The town is the perfect base to explore the nearby crumbling beach resort of Kep, the abandoned hill station of Bokor and the caves around Kompong Trach.

Orientation

Kampot is bordered to the west by the river, beyond which looms the massive shadow of Phnom Bokor. The centre of town is marked by a large roundabout. To the northwest is the market and to the north is the road to Phnom Penh. To the southeast is the road to Kep and Kompong Trach.

Information

There is nowhere to change travellers cheques in Kampot so carry cash. For quick transfers, Acleda Bank (☎ 932880) represents Western Union. The main post office is on the river to the south of the city centre. There are plenty of telephone booths around town where you can make international calls.

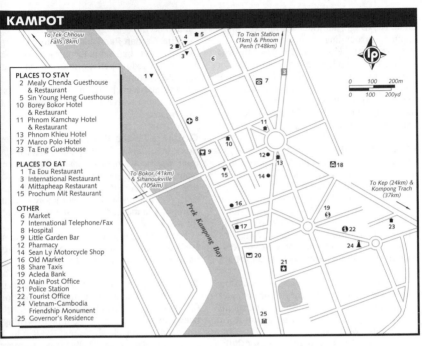

KAMPOT

To Tek Chhouu Falls (8km)

To Train Station (1km) & Phnom Penh (148km)

To Bokor (41km) & Sihanoukville (105km)

To Kep (24km) & Kompong Trach (37km)

Prek Kampong Bay

0   100   200m
0   100   200yd

PLACES TO STAY
2 Mealy Chenda Guesthouse
   & Restaurant
5 Sin Young Heng Guesthouse
10 Borey Bokor Hotel
   & Restaurant
11 Phnom Kamchay Hotel
   & Restaurant
13 Phnom Khieu Hotel
17 Marco Polo Hotel
23 Ta Eng Guesthouse

PLACES TO EAT
1 Ta Eou Restaurant
3 International Restaurant
4 Mittapheap Restaurant
15 Prochum Mit Restaurant

OTHER
6 Market
7 International Telephone/Fax
8 Hospital
9 Little Garden Bar
12 Pharmacy
14 Sean Ly Motorcycle Shop
16 Old Market
18 Share Taxis
19 Acleda Bank
20 Main Post Office
21 Police Station
22 Tourist Office
24 Vietnam-Cambodia
   Friendship Monument
25 Governor's Residence

Boat Trips

Kampot's riverside location makes it a good place to organise a short boat trip upstream. Ask around among local boat owners and you should be able to arrange something for about US$5 an hour. Several of the guesthouses and hotels around town can arrange something a little more organised – try the **Marco Polo Hotel** or **Mealy Chenda Guesthouse**.

Places to Stay

The guesthouse and hotel scene is improving. One thing worth bearing in mind is that after a wet or cloudy day trip up to Bokor hill station, a hot shower might be in order.

Phnom Khieu Hotel (☎ 012-820923) Doubles and twins from US$5, with air-con US$10. The large rooms here are arguably the best bet in town for those seeking comfort and value for money. Rooms include bathroom, TV and fridge.

Mealy Chenda Guesthouse (☎ 012-831559) Singles/doubles with bathroom US$4/6, without bathroom US$3/5. Run by the same family as Mealy Chenda in Sihanoukville, this friendly, modern guesthouse has a small restaurant and the best range of information on attractions in the surrounding area.

Ta Eng Guesthouse (☎ 012-330058) Rooms with/without bathroom US$5/3. This is the longest-running basic backpacker place in town and recently added a new wing. The friendly owner speaks French and English.

Sin Young Heng Guesthouse Rooms with fan/air-con & bathroom US$5/10. This guesthouse has plain rooms and a noisy location next to the market.

Phnom Kamchay Hotel (☎ 932916) Singles/doubles/triples with air-con, fridge & hot water US$12/15/15. This place is looking a little worn these days and is really not great value.

Borey Bokor Hotel (☎ 932826, fax 932555) Singles/doubles US$10/15. This hotel has

SOUTH COAST

some of the best rooms in town, which include TV, fridge, hot water and air-con, all in spotless surroundings.

Marco Polo Hotel (☎ 932314) Rooms without bathroom US$15-20, rooms with hot tub US$25. Set in one of the most venerable buildings overlooking the river, this is a good place to stay for those who want to capture the bygone atmosphere of Kampot. Rooms include air-con and TV.

Places to Eat

There is a good range of dining opportunities in town, although you may have trouble making yourself understood at the hole-in-the-wall establishments. Several hotel restaurants have English menus and offer a fairly standard selection of dishes. **Mealy Chenda Restaurant** has a good range of Western dishes, while the **Borey Bokor Restaurant** and **Phnom Kamchay Restaurant** are popular for breakfast.

Ta Eou Restaurant Dishes 4000-6000r. This place has the best location for a sunset meal, with views across to Bokor. The menu is extensive and includes a good range of seafood and local fish.

Prochum Mit Restaurant Mains 6000r. This place has been going for years, but recently moved location. The Cambodian food is good and often attracts a Khmer crowd. Come the evening, the street plays host to a large number of *tukalok* (fruit smoothie) sellers.

Mittapheap Restaurant Dishes 4000-8000r. This is a favourite with officials from the French embassy, and who is to question the French when it comes to food? Great soups and fair prices.

International Restaurant Dishes US$1.50-3. Near the market, this place has long been popular with the small expat community in Kampot. It serves breakfast, lunch and dinner, and has a mixed menu of Khmer, Chinese and Western dishes.

Entertainment

There are no longer any nightclubs in Kampot; the last two were killed off by the marauding hordes of karaoke parlours. All in all, it's a good place to recharge the batteries before hitting the town in Phnom Penh or Sihanoukville.

Little Garden Bar This is the town's first Western-style bar. Set in the garden of an old French-owned property, drinks are very reasonable, including cocktails and shooters at 12,000r and wine by the glass. There is also a basic menu with salads and sandwiches at low prices.

Getting There & Away

Some travellers with riding experience make their way to Kampot on 250cc motorbikes from the capital; see the Getting Around section in the Phnom Penh chapter for rental details. It is also possible to rent motorcycles in Kampot; see the Getting Around section later for details.

For details on getting to Bokor National Park, Kep and Kompong Trach, see the relevant sections later in this chapter.

Taxi, Pick-up & Minibus Kampot is 148km from Phnom Penh and the condition of NH3 varies depending on how long it's been between repairs. At the time of writing, it was in reasonable shape and the trip took 2½ hours. Share taxis (8000r) leave Kampot from a station just southeast of the roundabout; minibuses cost 5000r; on the back of a pick-up it costs 3000r.

There is also the same selection of vehicles making the 105km journey to Sihanoukville. The prices are pretty much the same as for Phnom Penh, as the road is in terrible condition for long stretches. For more details, see the Sihanoukville section earlier in this chapter.

From Kampot to Takeo is not so straightforward, as there are rarely any direct services. Jump in a vehicle going to Phnom Penh and ask to get off at Angk Tasaom, the turn-off for Takeo, which should cost about 5000r in a share taxi, and less in a minibus or a pick-up. From here, take a moto (US$1) or a cheaper *remorque-moto* (trailer pulled by a motorcycle) for the 13km trip to Takeo.

Train Then there is the train, which in terms of time is the least sensible option, but time is something many travellers have to spare.

It takes about six hours to Phnom Penh or Sihanoukville and even with foreigner prices is still pretty cheap. Coming from Phnom Penh, the section between Takeo and Kampot is the most scenic, as the route passes near some interesting karst formations. Continuing on to Sihanoukville, it follows the base of Phnom Bokor before looping around a quiet, unexplored region of Cambodia's coast. It is possible to ride on the roof, but it's definitely a good idea to apply some war paint, otherwise known as total sun block.

The train runs between Phnom Penh and Sihanoukville on alternate days. The schedule is random, but if it leaves Phnom Penh on Monday, it will leave Sihanoukville on Tuesday. Check at the railway station a couple of days before travelling.

Getting Around

The average fare for a moto ride is 1000r, or 500r for short hops. Expect to pay a little extra at night.

It is possible to rent motorcycles in Kampot. Sean Ly Motorcycle Shop rents 125cc to 250cc trail bikes and 100cc motos for US$5 a bike. Discounts are available for half-day (12-hour) hire.

Kampot has many *remorque-kang* (trailers pulled by bicycles) and the average fare is similar to that of motos.

AROUND KAMPOT
Tek Chhouu Falls
ទឹកឈ្លូរ

Waterfall enthusiasts should prepare themselves for a disappointment, as these falls 8km northwest of town are really just a series of small rapids. It is, however, a pleasant bathing spot and is very popular with locals.

There is a proper waterfall 18km farther up a dirt track from Tek Chhouu, but access is not straightforward, as the trail is pretty bad. Ask about trail conditions before heading up there and take a guide.

Plage de la Reine

This spot was named 'Queen's Beach' in honour of King Sihanouk's mother, Kossamak Nearireath, who had a house here.

It is not as nice as the beaches around Sihanoukville, however there will be no need to reserve your spot on the beach at 6am, as it won't be crowded. Plage de la Reine is 2km south of Prey Ampul, a small fishing village 32km west of Kampot.

BOKOR NATIONAL PARK
ឧទ្យានជាតិបូកគោ

Officially known as Preah Monivong National Park *(admission US$5)*, but more commonly referred to as Bokor, Bokor National Park is one of the country's largest protected areas. It has been open to visitors for several years, having long been kept off the map due to Khmer Rouge activity and more recently the presence of illegal loggers. A decade ago, there was talk of making this vast tropical forest a World Heritage site, but sadly, extensive illegal logging put an end to this initiative.

Within the park boundaries are the nascent tourist attractions of an abandoned French hill station and the Popokvil Falls, a two-tiered waterfall where you can swim. The park is home to significant numbers of birds and mammals, including elephants. However, most of the animals are nocturnal and inhabit the more remote areas of the park, so don't expect to see much wildlife. The park has a ranger post at the foot of Phnom Bokor and a ranger station with accommodation at the Bokor hill station. The entry fee will hopefully provide the rangers with much needed revenue to combat illegal logging.

Both the national park and the hill station are believed to be free of land mines, but as always in Cambodia, do the sensible thing and stick to well-worn paths.

It is easiest to visit the park as a day trip from Kampot, but should you want to visit on the way to or from Sihanoukville, it is best to overnight at Bokor or in Kampot, as it is a lot of ground to cover in one day.

Bokor Hill Station
ស្ថានីយន៍ភ្នំបូកគោ

The old French hill station of Bokor (1080m) is known for its cool climate,

SOUTH COAST

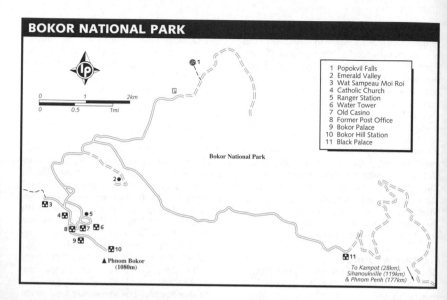

BOKOR NATIONAL PARK

0   1   2km
0   0.5   1mi

Bokor National Park

1 Popokvil Falls
2 Emerald Valley
3 Wat Sampeau Moi Roi
4 Catholic Church
5 Ranger Station
6 Water Tower
7 Old Casino
8 Former Post Office
9 Bokor Palace
10 Bokor Hill Station
11 Black Palace

▲ Phnom Bokor
(1080m)

To Kampot (28km),
Sihanoukville (119km)
& Phnom Penh (177km)

secluded waterfalls and jungle vistas. The French authorities decided to construct a road to Bokor in 1917; the project took several years to complete and many Cambodian indentured labourers perished in the process. With the completion of the road, a small community was established that included a grand colonial hotel, the Bokor Palace, inaugurated in 1925.

The hill station was twice abandoned: first when Vietnamese and Khmer Issarak (Free Khmer) forces overran it in the late 1940s while fighting for independence against the French, and again in 1970 when the Lon Nol regime left it to Khmer Rouge forces that were steadily taking over the countryside. It has since remained uninhabited, save for the presence of either Vietnamese troops or Khmer Rouge guerrillas during much of the past two decades. Its altitude and commanding views made it a place of strategic importance to all sides during the long years of conflict in Cambodia, and it was one location the Vietnamese really had to fight for during their invasion in 1979. The Khmer Rouge held out for several months; one unit was ironically holed up in the Catholic church while the Vietnamese shot at them from the Bokor Palace only 500m away.

The place has a genuine ghost-town feel, and the old **Catholic church** looks like it was locked up only yesterday. Inside, the altar remains intact and drawings of what look like Khmer Rouge fighters adorn the wall.

The old hotel, the **Bokor Palace**, is straight out of the film *The Shining*. At the edge of what was once an outdoor terrace there is a magnificent view over lush, dense jungle stretching almost to the sea. Inside the hotel it is possible to wander up and down the corridors from the kitchens below, through the ballroom to the suites above, imagining what it was like during its heyday. On a cold and foggy day it can get pretty creepy up there, as visibility drops to nothing and the wind howls through the building. Try not to think of Jack Nicholson wielding an axe, screaming 'Here's Johnny!'.

The ruin of **Wat Sampeau Moi Roi** is known locally as Five Boats Wat due to the five large rocks, which some say resemble boats. It was built in 1924 and, like Bokor Palace, affords tremendous views over the jungle to the coastline below. Other buildings dotted around include an old **casino** just opposite the ranger station, an abandoned **post office**, which looks like it has taken a mortar at some stage in its history, and an old **water tower** that looks like something out of *Close Encounters of the Third Kind*.

Debate rages over whether to redevelop the town. Environmentalists say it should be left untouched, while entrepreneurs eye its tried and tested potential. Surely a compromise is in the offing that allows a limited redevelopment of the old town area, thus generating much-needed funds to help protect the actual national park, much of which remains remote and defenceless. After all, it has come back from the dead once before, why not third time lucky?

Places to Stay It is possible to stay up at Bokor hill station in the **ranger station**. There are three dormitories with six bunks (US$5 a person) in each, and one room with a double and single bed for US$20. Bathroom facilities are shared and there is a basic communal kitchen for use by guests and rangers. Don't forget to bring some food from Kampot, as nothing is available here. Running water and electricity keep going until about 9pm, sometimes longer if there is a full house. It can get very cold at night so take some extra layers. If the wind is blowing hard, it might be wise to prop a spare mattress up against the windows, as they are not very well sealed. If the ranger station is full, as sometimes happens during the weekend, rangers can offer camp beds and a blanket for US$2.

Popokvil Falls
ពពកវិល

This two-tiered waterfall is a fine place to bathe on a sunny day. The upper falls are 14m high and are the best place to swim. The lower falls are 18m high, but getting to the bottom is a major challenge. The name translates as 'Swirling Clouds' and for much of the time there do indeed appear to be swirling clouds just above the falls. The falls are located about 15 minutes by road from the hill station, followed by a half-hour walk.

The road to the falls is 37km from Kampot. The road forks – left goes to the hill station, right to the falls. Follow the right road for almost 3km before parking and continuing on foot. Cross a rickety bridge, follow the path straight until you reach the small wooden sign indicating a narrow path on the left. This leads directly to the falls.

Adventure Canoe Cambodia (☎ 965635, ℮ adventurecanoe@yahoo.com), based in Phnom Penh, offers wet-season canoeing trips from the bottom of the falls all the way down to Kampot, currently the closest thing to white-water rafting in Cambodia.

Getting There & Away
Bokor National Park is 41km from Kampot, 132km from Sihanoukville and 190km from Phnom Penh. The access road is 7km west of Kampot, marked by an elaborate interchange system that must have seen its fair share of Peugeots and Citroëns in the resort's heyday. There is a ranger post and a ticket booth 1km beyond this interchange.

The road up to Bokor is one of Cambodia's most stunning, but in terrible condition for the first 25km and best covered on a motorbike or in a sturdy 4WD vehicle. Cars and minibuses can also make it, but it's a bad ride. The road winds its way up through thick jungle and in places the foliage is trying to reclaim the road. Trees do get blown across the road from time to time. The poor surface ends on the top of the plateau, where the first buildings appear and you catch your first glimpse of the wonderful view over the coast.

These first buildings made up Sihanouk's villa complex at Bokor, known as the Black Palace. From here the final 10km of road to the hill station is reasonable, and the scenery is decidedly different with scrub and lichen everywhere. Check out the lush Emerald Valley visible from the main road.

Moto drivers in Kampot take visitors up to Bokor for about US$10. Guesthouses and hotels can set you up with a driver who has a little local knowledge, or you can find English-speaking drivers in the area around the central roundabout.

SOUTH COAST

Many experienced riders like to hire a motorbike and take on the road themselves. The word 'experienced' should be stressed, as the road is not for beginners. Anyone riding the hill on the weekend should be very careful on the myriad hairpin bends, as there is a hell of a lot of traffic going up and down. Motorbikes can be hired in Kampot; see Getting Around in the Kampot section earlier for more details.

Small groups of visitors will find it cheaper to rent a car or pick-up to get up here. Sean Ly Motorcycle Shop in Kampot can hook people up with a vehicle for just US$25, damn good value if you fill it with five people. It might also be possible to charter a car from Kampot's share taxi station – some drivers may take on the road for US$25. Guesthouses and hotels also offer transport services, but they are generally more expensive.

Mountain biking is a final hardcore option. There are no decent bikes to rent as yet, but they may come. If the hill appears too ugly, it is possible to put the bike in the back of a pick-up, cut out the hard part and enjoy an adrenaline-fuelled descent, taking serious care on the corners.

KEP
កែប

☎ 036 • pop 4000

Kep is a permanent and poignant reminder of the devastation and destruction wrought on Cambodia during the long years of civil war. The seaside resort of Kep-sur-Mer was founded as a colonial retreat for the French elite in 1908. Cambodian high rollers continued the tradition, flocking here to enjoy gambling and water sports, and during the 1960s it was home to Cambodia's leading zoo. The war was not kind to Kep and little remains except skeletons of buildings. What wasn't dismantled by Khmer Rouge soldiers was looted by locals for materials to sell to the Vietnamese in order to survive the famine of 1979–80.

On top of the hill near the beach is one of King Sihanouk's many palaces constructed in the early 1990s. Before his overthrow in 1970, Kep was one of Sihanouk's favourite spots in Cambodia; he used to entertain visiting foreign dignitaries on an outlying island nicknamed Ile des Ambassadeurs. He perhaps harboured thoughts of retirement here, but his poor

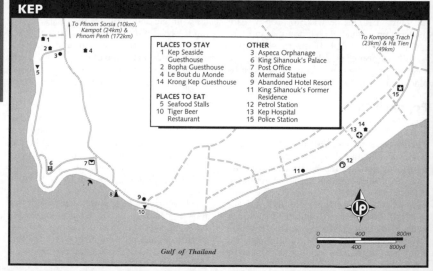

KEP

To Phnom Sorsia (10km),
Kampot (24km) &
Phnom Penh (172km)

To Kompong Trach
(23km) & Ha Tien
(49km)

PLACES TO STAY
1 Kep Seaside Guesthouse
2 Bopha Guesthouse
4 Le Bout du Monde
14 Krong Kep Guesthouse

PLACES TO EAT
5 Seafood Stalls
10 Tiger Beer Restaurant

OTHER
3 Aspeca Orphanage
6 King Sihanouk's Palace
7 Post Office
8 Mermaid Statue
9 Abandoned Hotel Resort
11 King Sihanouk's Former Residence
12 Petrol Station
13 Kep Hospital
15 Police Station

0   400   800m
0   400   800yd

Gulf of Thailand

health and political instability in the country has meant that he has never actually stayed at the palace, which remains unfurnished.

Kep is on a small headland and has a 6km palm-fringed road extending along the coastline. There are regular rumours of redevelopment plans, although there are only a few new villas in town. The beach is rather scruffy, as it was never a natural sandy bay. Before the war, white sand was shipped in from Sihanoukville to keep up appearances. Thirty years on, it needs a clean. Kep may be little more than a shadow of its former self, nonetheless there is a certain atmosphere about the place that draws Cambodians back again and again.

Places to Stay

There are several places to stay in town, although facilities are much more basic than at nearby Kampot, where most choose to stay.

Le Bout du Monde (☎ 012-955670) Singles/doubles with fan & bathroom 15,000/20,000r. This French-run guesthouse is currently the best choice in town. It's a fair way from the beach, up a small track opposite the French nongovernmental organisation's Aspeca orphanage, but is secluded and has a seafood restaurant.

Kep Seaside Guesthouse (☎ 012-897792) Rooms with fan & bathroom US$4-5. This place is far and away the best of the beachside accommodation. A large extension is underway and some rooms include a balcony and sea view. The garden has some thatched pavilions with hammocks, but there is no sandy beach in this part of town.

Bopha Guesthouse (☎ 012-820831) Rooms with fan & bathroom with squat toilet US$5. This is looking a bit worn these days and seems to prefer the karaoke trade to the hotel business.

Krong Kep Guesthouse (☎ 012-872689) Rooms with fan & bathroom US$5. This used to be the only guesthouse in town, but it has not kept up with the competition. It is about 3km past the mermaid statue.

Places to Eat

Lunch in Kep is easy, as there are numerous **bamboo shacks** along the waterfront offering fresh seafood. At about 5000r a kilo, it is one of the cheapest places in the country to gorge on fresh crab, but locals point out that the scales have been tweaked to register 1kg for every 600g. Definitely agree on a price in advance and make sure the seafood is freshly cooked.

Le Bout du Monde has a seafood restaurant, offering a little more sophistication than the stalls by the sea.

There are also a few **restaurants** appearing in small wooden properties along the coast road, including one with a Tiger Beer sign opposite the abandoned hotel resort.

Getting There & Away

Kep is 24km from Kampot, 172km from Phnom Penh and 49km from the Vietnamese town of Ha Tien. From Kampot it is possible to arrange a moto for about US$6 to US$8 per day, or rent a motorbike for US$5. Cheaper by a long way is to go by remorque-moto, but this will involve changing at the statue of the white horse. However, not having transport makes exploration of the surrounding area more difficult. It could be an idea to charter a share taxi from the centre of Kampot, but they are likely to charge US$20 for the day.

To get to Kompong Trach from Kep, turn right at the main junction in Damnak Chang Aeu, home to Kep's train station.

Speaking of railways, it is possible to get to Kep by train. Coming from Kampot it is not really worth it, as the journey is slow and there is only one train every two days (a little constricting for a journey of 24km). However, coming from Phnom Penh, it is quite possible to get off at Damnak Chang Aeu, take a moto into Kep and then continue to Kampot.

AROUND KEP
Koh Tonsay
កោះទន្សាយ

Koh Tonsay (Rabbit Island) is a short boat ride off the coast of Kep and is so named because locals say it resembles a rabbit – another example of what too much local brew can do to your imagination. It has several beaches – all considerably nicer than those at Kep – and it is possible to stay with local families, as long as you can agree on a price for food and lodging. Malaria is prevalent on most islands off Cambodia's coast, so come prepared with a bucket of repellent and a mosquito net. **Boats** can be arranged at the first cluster of food stalls on the coast road. Expect to pay about US$20 a day for the boat, or about US$10 one way, although the price may depend on numbers.

There are several other small islands beyond Koh Tonsay, including **Koh Pos** (Snake Island), but locals won't take foreigners much beyond here, as it's very close to the sea border with Vietnam. As this border is still a contentious issue between the two countries, don't expect a friendly welcome should you stray into Vietnamese waters; locals say machine-gun fire is more likely.

Most of the guesthouses in Kep can also arrange boat trips to the nearby islands.

Caves of Phnom Sorsia
ភ្នំសសៀ

Phnom Sorsia are the most convenient caves to visit from Kampot. It is considered a holy place and there is a small wat at the bottom of the hill. Concrete steps wind their way past altars and statues on a circuit that takes you to several major caves.

The biggest cave is called **Rung Damrey Saa** (White Elephant Cave) because of a stalactite formation thought to resemble a white elephant head. Further on the right is a sign pointing to **100 Rice Fields Cave**. By following a precarious path to a small hole in the cave wall, you are rewarded with a peep show of terraced paddy fields. The final cave is home to many bats that you can hear squeaking before you descend. It is quite spectacular to see them streaming out at sunset. The circuit ends near a small **stupa** from where there are impressive views.

The caves at Phnom Sorsia are worth a stop when travelling between Kep and Kampot. They may not be as spectacular as caves beyond Cambodia, but they have few visitors, which gives them a peace and serenity unmatched by larger tourist attractions. Coming from Kep or Kompong Trach turn left 2.5km after the statue of the white horse. To get here from Kampot, turn right off the main road after 13.5km.

KOMPONG TRACH
កំពង់ត្រាច

Kompong Trach effectively disappeared from the map of Cambodia during the early 1990s, as Khmer Rouge forces were in control of the hills that surround the town. The end of the civil war brought it back to life and it is now drawing a small number of visitors to its caves and wats. The town itself has little to attract the visitor, but may grow in stature with the opening of the border with Vietnam at Ha Tien.

Things to See & Do

The main reason to come to Kompong Trach is to visit **Wat Kirisan**, a modern temple built at the foot of a karst formation called Phnom Sor (White Mountain) that is riddled with caves and passages. From the wat there is an underground passage to the hollow centre of the karst formation, where there is another shrine. From here, other caves lead through the hill. It is easy enough to explore the basic passages unaided, provided you carry a torch, but anyone planning on delving deeper into the network of caves should find a local guide. To get to Wat Kirisan from Kompong Trach, take the dirt road opposite Acleda Bank for 2km to the foot of the karst formation. Follow the road to the right and the wat is just a few hundred metres ahead on the left. Continue on this road a little farther and there is another large cave located halfway up the hillside with an old iron ladder descending into the darkness. This is hard to find without local help, but once inside it leads to the **Cave of a Thousand Rice Fields**, so named because the limestone formations resemble the tiered paddy fields seen in Bali and the Philippines. A moto out here, plus the driver's assistance in exploring the caves, should cost about US$2.

Places to Stay & Eat

Given that it is little more than one hour to Kampot, there is no reason to stay here. Visitors who find themselves stuck, however, can stay at:

Phnom Sor Guesthouse Singles/doubles with bathroom 10,000/15,000r. This unmarked guesthouse, located above Acleda Bank on the main street, offers basic rooms.

There are **food stalls** in the market with basic local food, as well as a few hole-in-the-wall **restaurants** with inexpensive Khmer dishes.

Getting There & Away

Kompong Trach is 37km east of Kampot. 23km of the road is smooth and surfaced, 14km is definitely not. Leaving Kampot, there is a statue of a white horse after 16km, the left fork goes to Kompong Trach and the right to Kep. Most visitors make their way here from Kampot on rented motorcycles. Travellers heading south from Phnom Penh can get to Kompong Trach, before Kampot and Kep, by jumping out at the town of Chhuk on NH3 and taking the excellent 32km laterite road that runs here. A place in a share taxi from Chhuk should cost no more than 4000r. It is also possible to get here by train, as the Phnom Penh-Kampot-Sihanoukville line passes through town.

TUK MEAS
ទុកម៉ាស់

Tuk Meas means 'Golden Water', but it is more usual to encounter green-and-brown stinking puddles in this town, as the roads are almost swamps. This small town is very rarely visited by foreigners, but may draw some spelunkers in future years thanks to being located near some of the most extensive **caves** in Cambodia. There is a major cave with an underwater lake, near the phosphate plant about 5km west of town, but this should be visited only with a knowledgeable local.

There is one **guesthouse** (rooms with bathroom 15,000r) in town on the main strip, located in an unmarked white building. It was originally home to Korean workers running the phosphate plant, but will now take the very occasional tourist.

Getting to Tuk Meas may be more fun than actually being here. Only very experienced off-road bikers should attempt to get to Tuk Meas by road. The roads north to Tani and south to Kompong Trach are so messy that most locals choose to travel by lorry. Chartering a lorry from Kompong Trach to Tuk Meas costs about 20,000r and takes about one hour. Alternatively, wait for the vehicle to fill up and pay only 3000r. It is definitely one of the most amusing ways to get around Cambodia.

The railway line passes west of Tuk Meas, crossing the road to the phosphate mine.

Takeo Province
ខេត្តតាកែវ

Often referred to as 'the cradle of Cambodian civilisation', Takeo Province includes several important pre-Angkorian sites built during the 5th to 8th centuries. This whole area was part of what Chinese annals called 'water Chenla', no doubt a reference to the extensive annual floods that still blanket much of the province. It would have been an important kingdom among several smaller states that existed at that time; its principal centre was at Angkor Borei, with other smaller religious centres at both Phnom Chisor and Phnom Bayong. Places such as Phnom Chisor continued to exact a tight hold on the kings of Angkor and many came to pay tribute to their ancestors in elaborate ceremonies.

Today Takeo is primarily a province of farming and fishing that sees a healthy number of tourists visiting the temples of Tonlé Bati and Phnom Chisor near Phnom Penh, but has few visitors staying overnight in the provincial capital of Takeo. While the town is nothing particularly spectacular, it is the closest provincial town to the capital, and it's easy to score a slice of real Cambodian life here.

NH2 runs south through the province and is in fairly good condition. Elsewhere, roads are poor due to heavy flooding in the wet season, and boats are almost as popular a form of transport as cars.

TAKEO
តាកែវ

☎ 032 • pop 39,000

Takeo, the eponymous provincial capital, is best used as a base to visit the old temples in the Angkor Borei area, although given that they can be seen in a day trip from Phnom Penh, there is no compelling reason to stay here. Takeo lacks the charm of some of the other provincial capitals, as it has less of a French legacy than elsewhere around the country, but it is a convenient stop when travelling between Phnom Penh and Kampot. During the wet season, it becomes a pleasant lakeside town, as much of the surrounding countryside yields to water.

Information

Come with cash, as there is nowhere to change travellers cheques in Takeo. For quick money transfers, Acleda Bank (☎ 932880) on Ph 10 represents Western Union. Telephone calls can be made from booths throughout town.

Takeo Tourism (☎ 931323) has helpful staff and is located opposite Psar Nat (Meeting Market), although the office lacks any information to take away.

Ta Mok's House
ផ្ទះតាម៉ុក

Commander of the Southwestern Zone during Khmer Rouge rule and, until his capture in 1999, military supremo of the ragged guerrilla movement, Ta Mok was born in Takeo Province. He built a large and elaborate house on an island in the lake north of town. He was extremely paranoid about security and was said to have had

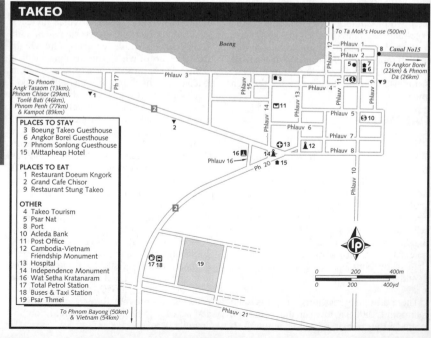

TAKEO

Boeng

To Ta Mok's House (500m)

To Phnom
Angk Tasaom (13km),
Phnom Chisor (29km),
Tonlé Bati (46km),
Phnom Penh (77km)
& Kampot (89km)

To Angkor Borei
(22km) & Phnom
Da (26km)

Phlauv 1
Phlauv 2
8   Canal No15

Phlauv 3

PLACES TO STAY
3   Boeung Takeo Guesthouse
6   Angkor Borei Guesthouse
7   Phnom Sonlong Guesthouse
15 Mittapheap Hotel

PLACES TO EAT
1   Restaurant Doeum Kngork
2   Grand Cafe Chisor
9   Restaurant Stung Takeo

OTHER
4   Takeo Tourism
5   Psar Nat
8   Port
10 Acleda Bank
11 Post Office
12 Cambodia-Vietnam
    Friendship Monument
13 Hospital
14 Independence Monument
16 Wat Setha Kratanaram
17 Total Petrol Station
18 Buses & Taxi Station
19 Psar Thmei

Phlauv 16
Ph 20

0   200   400m
0   200   400yd

To Phnom Bayong (50km)
& Vietnam (54km)

Phlauv 21

architects and builders executed upon completion of each floor, which included hidden rooms and escape passages. It was used as a government hotel during the 1980s, but is occupied by local police today. It is possible to look at the exterior, but not possible to go inside. Ta Mok is currently being held in T-3 prison in Phnom Penh, awaiting trial for crimes against humanity.

Places to Stay
Most of the guesthouses in Takeo are clones so it makes sense to opt for one of the places near the lake.

Boeung Takeo Guesthouse (☎ 931306) Rooms with fan/air-con, TV & bathroom US$5/10. This guesthouse has the best location in town, overlooking the lake. Ask for a room with a view, as it is no more expensive.

Phnom Sonlong Guesthouse Rooms with fan, TV & bathroom US$5. Overlooking Psar Nat, this friendly guesthouse has English-speaking staff. Room 4 offers fine views of the lake.

Angkor Borei Guesthouse (☎ 931340) Rooms with fan & bathroom US$4-5. This place offers the same kind of rooms as the Phnom Sonlong Guesthouse, minus the TV.

Mittapheap Hotel (☎ 931205) Rooms with fan/air-con, TV & bathroom US$5/10. This place might be an option for those who have a particular attraction to Cambodian Independence Monuments, as it overlooks Takeo's.

Places to Eat
There are plenty of inexpensive **food stalls** in the area around the Independence Monument. By night, this is also the place to snack on Cambodian desserts or enjoy a tukalok.

Restaurant Stung Takeo Overlooking the canal to Angkor Borei, this place is built on stilts, as the whole area is a giant lake during the wet season. It's one of the most popular lunch stops in town and a good place to eat before making a trip to Angkor Borei and Phnom Da.

Restaurant Doeum Kngork (☎ 931387) Dishes 6000-8000r. This is a lively spot for a good Cambodian meal; it has an English-language menu and some tasty soups.

Grand Cafe Chisor Dishes US$2-4. This charming garden restaurant brings a sophisticated touch to Takeo, offering local and Western dishes at reasonable prices. It is part of a training initiative to offer new skills to locals.

Getting There & Away
NH2, which links Phnom Penh with Takeo (77km), has deteriorated considerably in the past few years, but will no doubt be overhauled in time. Ho Wah Genting air-con buses run between Phnom Penh and Takeo (4500r, two hours) on the hour from 7am to 4pm in both directions. They leave from Psar Thmei (New Market) in Phnom Penh and from Takeo they depart from in front of Psar Leu. These buses also go past Tonlé Bati and Phnom Chisor.

The price from Phnom Penh by share taxi is 6000r, by minibus 3000r. Travellers continuing by road to Kampot should take a remorque-moto (1000r) or moto (US$1) for the 13km journey to Angk Tasaom and then arrange a seat in a minibus or share taxi on to Kampot.

There are also train services linking Takeo to Phnom Penh, Kampot and Sihanoukville. Trains from Phnom Penh pass through Takeo at around 9.30am on the way to Kampot (4100r, three hours, 89km). Coming from Kampot, they depart for Takeo at around 12pm every second day, depending on what time the train arrives from Sihanoukville.

AROUND TAKEO
For information on the Angkorian temples around Phnom Chisor and Tonlé Bati, both in Takeo Province, see the Around Phnom Penh section in the Phnom Penh chapter.

Angkor Borei & Phnom Da
អង្គរបូរី / ភ្នំដា

Angkor Borei was known as Vyadhapura when it served as the capital of water Chenla in the 8th century, one of many competing kingdoms in the pre-Angkorian era. It is one of the earliest pre-Angkorian sites in Cambodia, dating back to the 5th century. Angkor Borei is actually a small modern town, but in

SOUTH COAST

this instance it is used to refer to the remains of an ancient walled city in the vicinity. The town has a small **museum** *(admission US$1; open 8.30am-noon & 2pm-4.30pm daily),* set up with assistance from the European Union (EU) in 1997. The museum houses a decent collection of Funan- and Chenla-era artefacts, although most pieces are copies of those housed in the National Museum in Phnom Penh.

A few kilometres south of Angkor Borei is the hill of Phnom Da. Four artificial caves, built as shrines, are carved into the northeastern wall of the hill. On top of Phnom Da is a square **laterite temple** open to the north, dating from the 8th century. In the wet season, it is possible to reach Phnom Da by water only, as the hill becomes an island spectacularly isolated by annual floods. During the dry season, it is possible to make it there by road from Phnom Chisor, but it is more atmospheric by boat, as the boats speed along ancient canals through a sea of green rice fields.

Getting There & Away Angkor Borei and Phnom Da are about 20km east of Takeo town along Canal No 15, which is visible in the dry season only and flooded over the rest of the year. Most visitors charter an outboard from Takeo, which costs about US$15, taking around 35 minutes to Angkor Borei and another 15 minutes to Phnom Da. Alternatively, wait around the dock until locals gather to travel, and take a berth for 8000r. There are also slower, larger wooden boats to Angkor Borei that leave at 9am and 1pm and cost 1500r, taking almost two hours.

In the dry season it is also possible to visit by road, taking a route that passes south of Phnom Chisor. Expect to pay about 4000r in a share taxi or about US$5 for a round trip by moto. By boat is definitely the better option, as it is much more atmospheric and road conditions are not so good.

Phnom Bayong
ភ្នំបាយ៉ុង

Phnom Bayong is home to a small Chenla temple, built on the summit of a small hill in Kirivong district near the Vietnamese border. The laterite temple is on the summit of the taller of two hills, and while the temple itself doesn't justify a visit, the views across Vietnam's pancake-flat Mekong Delta just might. NH2, which runs from Takeo to the Vietnamese border, is in a pretty appalling state these days and the 50km journey from Takeo, to the right of the highway, takes about two hours. Due to the bad conditions, motos cost about US$8 to make the journey here. Taking a share taxi towards Vietnam and arranging a local moto to the summit of the hill is a lot cheaper.

Northwestern Cambodia

Northwestern Cambodia covers a broad swathe of the country running right around Tonlé Sap, extending west and north right up to the border with Thailand. It includes some of the most fertile land in the country – the rice bowl of Cambodia – as well as some of the most inhospitable mountain ranges found in the country – Chuor Phnom Kravanh (Cardamom Mountains) and Chuor Phnom Dangkrek (Dangkrek Mountains).

Among the provincial towns, Battambang is attracting the most visitors as there is plenty to see in the surrounding area. However, other pleasant towns include Pursat, once you venture off the main road; Kompong Thom, nestled on Stung Sen and a base for ancient temples; and Pailin, a former Khmer Rouge stronghold of verdant mountains. Beyond the towns lie a number of Cambodia's most remote temples, although these are only for individuals with a serious thirst for adventure and an ability to take the very rough with the rarely smooth. Those with limitless funds can avoid the rough and ensure the smooth by chartering a chopper to these places for about US$1500! See the 'Getting Around Angkor' boxed text in the 'Temples of Angkor' special section for contact details. This region is also home to some amazing natural wilderness, including the brooding Cardamom Mountains, home to rare wildlife, and the dry forests of northern Cambodia, home to rare birdlife.

Much of this region was plagued by war for considerably longer than other parts of the country; the northwest is a long way from Vietnam and very remote in places, both factors that suited the Khmer Rouge.

Beyond National Hwy 5 (NH5) and NH6, both of which are being completely upgraded, much of this area remains extremely remote and getting about can be tough. NH5 connects Phnom Penh, Kompong Chhnang, Pursat, Battambang and Sisophon to the south and west of the Tonlé Sap lake, while NH6 connects Siem Reap, Kompong Thom and Phnom Penh.

Highlights

- Check out the French architectural legacy around Battambang, one of Cambodia's most laid-back towns.
- Explore the pre-Angkorian ruins of Sambor Prei Kuk, near Kompong Thom, Southeast Asia's first temple city.
- Sniff around Banteay Chhmar, a vast temple complex overlooked by most visitors on their rush through Cambodia.
- Catch the glint of gemstones amid the fresh air of Pailin, until recently a bastion of the Khmer Rouge.
- Take on the ultimate adventure in an overland pilgrimage to the mountaintop temple of Prasat Preah Vihear.

Transport between the main towns is straightforward, but anywhere else can take a little more patience. There is one international border crossing in this region at the western end of NH5 at Poipet, and several local crossings that could be upgraded during the lifetime of this book.

All areas of Cambodia are considered secure these days, but it pays to travel with company in remote areas just to be safe. It never hurts to check on the latest security

257

conditions before heading down a little-travelled road.

Kompong Chhnang Province

ខេត្តកំពង់ឆ្នាំង

Kompong Chhnang is a relatively wealthy province thanks to its close proximity to the capital and its extensive fishing and agricultural industries supported by abundant water resources. There aren't a whole lot of places to visit, which has kept visitors to a minimum, although many pass through on their way to Battambang by road or Siem Reap by boat.

KOMPONG CHHNANG

កំពង់ឆ្នាំង

☎ 026 • pop 42,000

Kompong Chhnang is a tale of two cities: the bustling dockside seen by those travelling to Siem Reap by fast boat, and the old French quarter with its pleasant parks and handsome

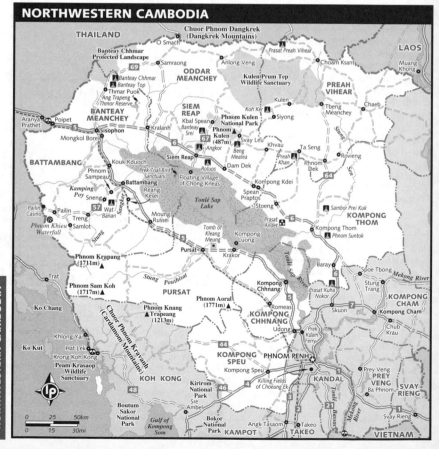

NORTHWESTERN CAMBODIA

buildings. Connecting these very different parts is a long road lined with stilt houses and a maze of narrow walkways. The name Kompong Chhnang comes from the local claypots *(chhnang)* made in villages around the town and sold throughout Cambodia, and from *kompong* meaning 'port' (thanks to its location on the Tonlé Sap river). The town has nothing beyond atmosphere to offer the cas-ual visitor, but for those with limited time who want a feel of provincial Cambodia, it makes for a pleasant transit stop between Phnom Penh and Battambang or an easy day trip from the capital, stopping at Udong along the way.

During much of the 1990s, plans were afoot to redevelop the old Chinese-built runway, constructed during the Khmer Rouge regime to fly in supplies from China for their 'self-sufficient' paradise. The massive runway was never fully operational, but may well have been planned with an attack on Vietnam in mind, as the complex seems too sophisticated for cargo alone. Thousands are believed to have died during construction, as the ultra-paranoid Khmer Rouge leadership was said to have had all workers on the project executed to keep its existence a secret. An investment consortium planned to turn this area into a free-trade zone and had hoped it would eventually rival Hong Kong and Dubai – a project that has never materialised.

Information

Acleda Bank (☎ 988748), located on NH5 towards Phnom Penh, is the only bank in town. It represents Western Union for cash transfers, but can't change travellers cheques.

Telephone and fax services are available at the post office in the old French quarter, but phone calls are more straightforward to arrange from the private telephone booths around town. Odec Email is located on NH5 towards Phnom Penh.

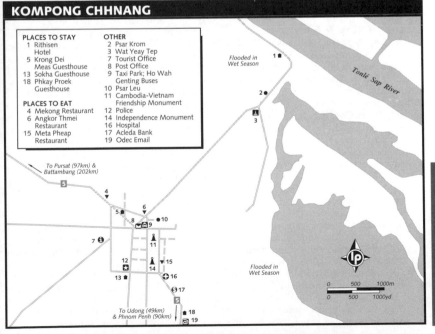

KOMPONG CHHNANG

PLACES TO STAY
1 Rithisen Hotel
5 Krong Dei Meas Guesthouse
13 Sokha Guesthouse
18 Phkay Proek Guesthouse

PLACES TO EAT
4 Mekong Restaurant
6 Angkor Thmei Restaurant
15 Meta Pheap Restaurant

OTHER
2 Psar Krom
3 Wat Yeay Tep
7 Tourist Office
8 Post Office
9 Taxi Park; Ho Wah Genting Buses
10 Psar Leu
11 Cambodia-Vietnam Friendship Monument
12 Police
14 Independence Monument
16 Hospital
17 Acleda Bank
19 Odec Email

Tonlé Sap River
To Pursat (97km) & Battambang (202km)
To Udong (49km) & Phnom Penh (90km)
Flooded in Wet Season

There is a tourist office of sorts in town, located in a rundown portacabin, but it doesn't seem to keep regular hours.

Things to See & Do

Kompong Chhnang has nothing essential to check out, but the riverfront area is interesting to explore. The town is surrounded by water for much of the year and there are a lot of floating communities and fisher folk living on the river. Arranging some sort of **boat trip** might be a nice way to take it all in.

Across the river are several **old temples** dating from the Chenla period, including **Prasat Srei**, but these are only worth considering as the focus of a rural adventure, as they are very dilapidated. You can arrange a *moto* (small motorcycle) driver in town for the day.

Given Kompong Chhnang's claypot connection, it is hardly surprising to hear that the town is well known for its undecorated but intricate **pottery**. There are several stalls selling pots, vases and more on the road to Phnom Penh.

Places to Stay & Eat

Krong Dei Meas Guesthouse Singles/doubles with bathroom US$3/5. This is the cheapest deal in town and offers basic rooms. It is only worth considering for solo travellers, as there are better-value doubles at the other guesthouses.

Phkay Proek Guesthouse Twins with TV & bathroom US$5. Located on the road coming from the capital, this clean, new guesthouse is good value.

Sokha Guesthouse (☎ 988622) Doubles with fan, TV & bathroom US$5, with fan/air-con, fridge & hot water US$8/15. This is the most popular guesthouse in town with visiting nongovernmental organisation (NGO) workers. It occupies several buildings in a sprawling, scenic garden in the south of town and has comfortable rooms.

Rithisen Hotel (☎ 988632) Rooms with fan/air-con & bathroom US$7/10. This is the only pad in town overlooking the Tonlé Sap river. The rooms are clean and some include TV. There are some nice verandas for watching river life go by, but in the dry season the

aromas beneath can get pretty strong when the river is low.

There are plenty of food stalls at the markets in town. **Psar Krom** is on the riverfront, while **Psar Leu** is in the town centre.

Angkor Thmei Restaurant Mains 3000r. This unassuming little place has tasty soups and popular Khmer dishes at budget prices. There is currently no sign in English, but the menu is translated.

Mekong Restaurant Meals 4000-8000r. This restaurant has a small menu, including a good interpretation of a French beefsteak and all the Cambodian greatest hits.

A popular spot for breakfast is the **Meta Pheap Restaurant**, just across the road from the Independence Monument.

Getting There & Away

Kompong Chhnang is 91km north of Phnom Penh on NH5. The section of road to Phnom Penh has generally been maintained in good condition, although the section between Prek Kdam and Phnom Penh was starting to get messy. However, it is being overhauled and should be in fine condition by the time you read this. Ho Wah Genting buses have 11 services in either direction between Kompong Chhnang and Phnom Penh (4500r), generally departing on or close to the hour from 6.15am onwards. Minibuses cost just 3000r, but are much more cramped.

Heading west toward Pursat (minibuses 5000r, pick-ups 6000/3000r inside/on the back, two to three hours) and Battambang (pick-ups 15000/8000r, four to five hours), the road is hideous, but is undergoing a complete reconstruction. Journey times will drop dramatically as the finished road is going to be nothing short of a motorway.

Technically, Kompong Chhnang is on the railway, but the station is at Romeas, about 20km south of town on a good road. This can be a good place to kiss the slowest train in Asia goodbye when coming from Battambang. Staying on the train means a 10pm arrival in Phnom Penh, but jumping off here offers the chance to get to the capital earlier or to stay the night in Kompong Chhnang and see another provincial town.

Pursat Province
ខេត្តពោធិ៍សាត់

Pursat is Cambodia's fourth-largest province, stretching from the Thai border eastwards to the Tonlé Sap lake. It encompasses Chuor Phnom Kravanh (Cardamom Mountains), one of the most remote areas of the country. Small-scale industries in Pursat include fishing and farming in the north of the province; marble quarrying, as some of Cambodia's only marble is found here; and the harvesting of sandalwood oil, which fetches huge prices elsewhere in Asia, but is disappearing fast in Cambodia. Illegal logging and poaching remain a serious problem in remote areas. Few travellers ever see much more than the provincial capital, but getting around the province should soon become easier with the complete overhaul of NH5.

PURSAT
ពោធិ៍សាត់

☎ 052 • pop 57,000

Pursat sees very few tourists beyond those stopping for lunch on the road between Phnom Penh and Battambang. It appears to be a dull kind of town from NH5, but is actually quite pleasant away from the main road, along the banks of the river towards the older part of town. Pursat is also the base for those wanting to explore the floating town of Kompong Luong on the Tonlé Sap lake, or the lush forests in the nearby Chuor Phnom Kravanh.

Information

Carry cash, as there is nowhere to change travellers cheques here. Acleda Bank (☎ 951434), just west of the river on NH5, is a small bank representing Western Union for easy money transfers.

There are several phone and fax outlets near Psar Leu (Central Market) and a post office on the riverbank. Internet access (500r per minute) and cheap Internet telephone calls (1500r per minute to Europe, the USA and Australia) are available at the Lao

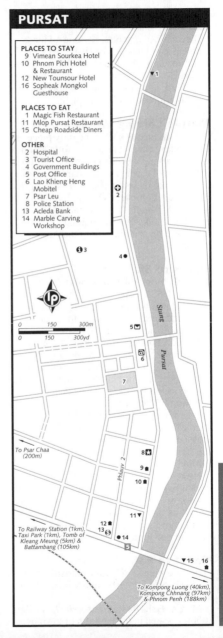

PURSAT

PLACES TO STAY
9 Vimean Sourkea Hotel
10 Phnom Pich Hotel & Restaurant
12 New Tounsour Hotel
16 Sopheak Mongkol Guesthouse

PLACES TO EAT
1 Magic Fish Restaurant
11 Mlop Pursat Restaurant
15 Cheap Roadside Diners

OTHER
2 Hospital
3 Tourist Office
4 Government Buildings
5 Post Office
6 Lao Khieng Heng Mobitel
7 Psar Leu
8 Police Station
13 Acleda Bank
14 Marble Carving Workshop

0   150   300m
0   150   300yd

To Psar Chaa (200m)

Stung

Pursat

Phlauv 2

To Railway Station (1km), Taxi Park (1km), Tomb of Kleang Meung (5km) & Battambang (105km)

To Kompong Luong (40km), Kompong Chhnang (97km) & Phnom Penh (188km)

Khieng Heng Mobitel telephone shop, just north of the market on Ph 1.

There is a tourist office behind all the government buildings on the river's west bank. The director is a helpful chap who knows the province well and has even written his own guidebook in Khmer called *Pursat and Picnics,* as Khmers just love to picnic.

Marble Carving Workshop

Pursat Province is one of the only places in Cambodia where marble is found and a marble carving workshop has been set up in the centre of town. The standard of carving is high, but in some cases so is the price when you compare what is available at Marble Mountains in Vietnam. However, many of the designs are unique to Cambodia, based on sculpture from the Angkorian period.

Places to Stay

Sopheak Mongkol Guesthouse *(NH5 east)* Rooms US$3. The rooms here are the cheapest in town, but are pretty dingy when compared to what's available for a couple of bucks more at the hotels in town.

Vimean Sourkea Hotel (☎ 951466, Ph 1) Rooms with fan/air-con & hot water US$5/8. This hotel may not look much from the outside, but once inside it improves – the air-con rooms are the cheapest deal in town.

Phnom Pich Hotel (☎ 951515, Ph 1) Rooms with fan & bathroom US$5, singles/doubles with air-con & hot water US$10/15. This large pad is the newest place in town and has spick and span rooms with satellite TV and fridge.

New Tounsour Hotel (☎ 951506, Ph 2) Rooms with fan, TV & fridge US$5, with air-con & hot water US$10. This friendly, long-running hotel offers a similar deal to the Phnom Pich Hotel – toss a coin, if you can find one in this coinless country.

Places to Eat

There are plenty of cheap **roadside diners** on NH5, offering tasty, quick meals for as little as 2000r.

Magic Fish Restaurant *(Ph 1)* Dishes 3000r. Located in the far north of town over-

looking the river this place does pretty good food. It is in a yellow building, but has no sign in English.

Mlop Pursat Restaurant *(Ph 1)* Just north of the main bridge, Mlop Pursat has a nice garden setting, but strangely doesn't seem to open at night.

Phnom Pich Restaurant Located in the Phnom Pick Hotel, this place is a popular spot for breakfast.

Getting There & Away

The road between Phnom Penh and Battambang is being comprehensively rebuilt and when completed (late 2003) it will have a big impact on Pursat, which is currently bang in the middle of the worst stretches. Minibuses (8000r) and pick-ups (10,000/4000r inside/on the back) go to Phnom Penh (188km, four hours); share taxis (10,000r) and pick-ups (10,000/4000r) go to Battambang (105km, three hours). Expect journey times to drop dramatically when the road is finished.

One train per day comes through Pursat, heading to Phnom Penh or Battambang on alternate days. It is only really worth considering from Battambang (4900r for foreigners) to avoid the bad road, at least until the overhaul is complete. It is not such a good idea heading to Battambang, as the train doesn't arrive until around 10pm. The longer stretch to Phnom Penh (7500r) is easier by road as the surface is in a reasonable state. The train to Battambang comes through Pursat any time after about 12.30pm (usually later!), while the train from Battambang leaves at 6am, usually arriving at Pursat around midday, but never earlier. Once the road is complete, the train will be a masochistic option.

AROUND PURSAT
Tomb of Kleang Meung
ផ្នូរឃ្លាំងមឿង

Oknha Kleang Meung was a Khmer national hero who defeated the Thais in a celebrated battle in 1482. The old statue of Kleang Meung now sits redundant in a shed; the new shiny gold one was donated by Prince Ranariddh.

NORTHWESTERN CAMBODIA

Kleang Meung's tomb is about 5km out of town in the direction of Battambang, down a little road on the left after the bridge that marks the end of the tarmac. A round trip by moto should cost about 5000r.

Kompong Luong
កំពង់លួង

The floating town of Kompong Luong on the Tonlé Sap lake is arguably one of the most interesting places to visit in Pursat Province. It is a town of as many as 10,000 inhabitants who live permanently afloat on the lake. The town moves with the level of water in the lake, as recognised by a faded signpost on NH5 to Krakor, which states that the distance to Kompong Luong is maximum 7km, minimum 2km. Not much fun for the postman!

The town boasts pretty much all the facilities found in other Cambodian towns except the ubiquitous cars and motorbikes, which comes as something of a relief. There are floating restaurants, schools, medical clinics and karaoke bars and, unlike Venice, the residents here don't have to worry about sinking, as everything has a boat as its base. There are plenty of places to stop for an iced coffee or a beer and just soak up the atmosphere of life on the water. There is not really anywhere to stay, although if you want to get some photographs early in the morning or late in the afternoon it should be possible to negotiate a bed in the nearby town of Krakor.

The population of Kompong Luong is almost predominantly Vietnamese, so you may find the welcome slightly more subdued than in most rural Cambodian towns. This isn't so much a reflection of any latent hostility on the part of the Vietnamese, but rather a reflection of their ambiguous status in Cambodian society, which has taught them to be wary of outsiders. Khmer Rouge massacres of Vietnamese villagers living around the Tonlé Sap lake were commonplace during the first half of the 1990s, and even as late as 1998 more than 20 Vietnamese were killed in a village near Kompong Chhnang.

Expect to pay about US$5 to charter a motorboat around Kompong Luong for an hour, significantly less for a paddle-powered boat.

Getting There & Away Kompong Luong is between 39km and 44km east of Pursat depending on the time of year. The easiest way to get here is to take a taxi or pick-up to Krakor (37km) for a couple of thousand riel and a moto from there for about the same price. Alternately, engage the services of a moto driver in Pursat for about 25,000r for the day. It takes about 1½ hours each way.

From April to June, when the Tonlé Sap lake is very low, the small fast boats ferrying tourists between Phnom Penh and Siem Reap occasionally stop at Kompong Luong for refuelling…at the floating petrol station, of course!

Battambang Province
ខេត្តបាត់ដំបង

This province has changed hands between Thailand and Cambodia on several occasions in the past few centuries. It was only returned to Cambodian control in 1907 and as recently as WWII the Thais cut a deal with the Japanese to take control again for several years. Before Cambodia's civil war Battambang was the largest and richest province in Cambodia, but ceded a large chunk of its territory to Banteay Meanchey for the creation of the new province. It shares a long border with Thailand and a short border with the Tonlé Sap lake and is the fifth-largest province in the country.

Battambang was untouched for much of the early 1970s, as fighting raged elsewhere around the country. For this reason the whole area was viewed with much suspicion by Khmer Rouge leaders and was the victim of successive central purges. Life was little better after the war, as the ongoing guerrilla war and the proliferation of thousands of land mines devastated the agricultural industry that had built the economy. However, the province is slowly recovering as demining groups free up land for agriculture and the many refugees who returned here during the 1990s are permanently settled. Tourism has a lot of potential, as not only is the provincial capital a popular stop, but there are extensive examples of Angkorian heritage in the surrounding countryside.

Travel around the province has traditionally been slow due to disastrous roads, but both NH5, passing through the heart of the province, and NH57 to Pailin are undergoing comprehensive renovations.

BATTAMBANG
បាត់ដំបង

☎ 053 • pop 140,000

Cambodia's second-largest city is an elegant riverside town, home of some of the best-preserved French period architecture in the country and warm and friendly inhabitants. The advent of peace has opened Battambang to overland traffic and it makes a great base from which to explore nearby temples and scenic villages. There is a very popular boat service running between Battambang and Siem Reap, probably the most scenic river trip in the country.

Orientation

Although it is a major city, Battambang is fairly compact and easily negotiable on foot. The centre of town is Psar Nat (Meeting Market) and all commercial activity and most of the city's hotels are located within a few blocks of here. This central area is bordered to the west by the railway line and to the east by Stung Sangker. Across the river are several large properties serving as administrative centres for the large numbers of NGOs represented in the province.

Information

Tourist Offices There is a small provincial tourist office near the Governor's Mansion, which has little to offer in the way of handouts, but staff can tell you quite a lot of information about places of interest near Battambang.

Many of the moto drivers who hang out at the Chhaya Hotel speak excellent English and have a good knowledge of the province. They can take you beyond the tourist sites to experience a slice of local life in the farming communities around the town.

Veteran Cambodia adventurer Ray Zepp has produced a new guidebook to the Battambang region called *Around Battambang*, which continues the philosophy of *The Cambodia Less Travelled*, his first treatise on spending quality time in quieter parts of the country. The new book has a lot of detail on local wats, as well as the major Angkorian temples in Battambang and is a useful companion for a longer stay in the area. The cause is very worthwhile as all proceeds go to the Monks HIV project, which trains monks to spread the message of compassion towards HIV/AIDS sufferers and promotes education and awareness about prevention. *Around Battambang* costs US$5 and is available at selected hotels and restaurants in town.

Money There are several banks in town. Cambodian Commercial Bank, near the train station, does the usual credit-card cash advances for US$5, and changes travellers cheques at 2%. Canadia Bank (☎ 952267) is north of the market and changes travellers cheques in most major currencies for 2% commission, offers MasterCard cash advances at no charge and represents Moneygram. For quick money transfers, Acleda Bank (☎ 370122), located on the east bank of Stung Sangker, represents Western Union.

Post & Communications The main post office is on the riverfront, but for international telephone calls you're best to use an Internet telephone service or visit one of Battambang's numerous Interphone offices. Interphone calls are very clear and are routed via Thailand so it's only 10B a minute to Bangkok or US$2 a minute to Europe, Australia and the USA. Cheaper still are the Internet phone places springing up along the river, which charge around 15B a minute to the USA and 30B a minute to

BATTAMBANG

To Sisophon (68km),
Poipet (117km) &
Siem Reap (171km)

To Wat
Ek Phnom
(13km)

Stung Sangker

Phlauv 1

Phlauv 3

Phlauv 2

Battambang Train Station

Stung Sangker

To Airport (2km), Pursat (105km),
Kompong Chhnang (202km)
& Phnom Penh (293km)

To Phnom Sampeau (18km),
Sneng (26km), Kamping Poy
(36km) & Pailin (83km)

To Wat
Banan (25km)

0   200   400m
0   200   400yd

PLACES TO STAY
2 7 Makara Hotel
6 Royal Hotel
7 Golden Parrot
  Guesthouse
8 Monorom Guesthouse
11 International Hotel
13 Chhaya Hotel
14 Paris Hotel
18 Angkor Hotel
21 Golden River Hotel
30 Teo Hotel

PLACES TO EAT
15 Heng Lim Restaurant
16 White Rose
19 Uy Thean Restaurant
27 Food Stalls
32 Restaurant Neak Poan
34 Cold Night Restaurant
38 Phkay Preuk Restaurant
41 Tarareas Restaurant

OTHER
1 Long-Distance Taxis,
  Minibuses & Pick-ups
3 Hospital
4 Fast Boats to
  Siem Reap
5 Wat Phiphetaram
9 Canadia Bank
10 Psar Nat
12 Royal Phnom
  Penh Airways
17 ABC Computer
20 Than Sour Nightclub
22 Cambodian Commercial
  Bank
23 President Airlines
24 Police Station
25 Wat Kandal
26 Acleda Bank
28 Battambang Museum
29 Wat Damrey Sar
31 Main Post Office
33 Wat Sangker
35 Statue of Dom
  Boeng Kraw Ngum
36 Tourist Office
37 Governor's Residence
39 Wat Kampheng
40 Riverside Balcony Bar

most other countries, but be prepared for an annoying delay. Straightforward Internet access is available at the same places for US$1 for 10 minutes, although the price may drop if a local provider sets up shop.

Things to See & Do

It languished behind closed doors for many years due to a lack of visitors, but the **Battambang Museum** *(admission US$1; open Mon-Fri 8am-11am & 2pm-5pm)* is once again open for business. It houses an attractive collection of fine-carved lintels and statuary from all over Battambang Province, including pieces from Wat Banan and Sneng. Staff at the museum claim it will also open weekends starting some time in 2002.

Much of Battambang's charm lies in the network of old **French shop houses** nestled on the riverbank. The **Governor's Residence** is also a handsome legacy of the French presence in Cambodia.

There are a huge number of wats around town, including **Wat Phiphetaram**, north of the market, and **Wat Kampheng**, south of the Teo Hotel, where a number of the monks speak English and are glad for the chance to practise their conversation. Beyond the town are a number of attractions including hilltop temples, Angkorian-era wats and a large lake.

Places to Stay

Battambang's hotels provide some of the best value in the country as many were built to house UN personnel in the early 1990s and are now suffering a long hangover, with fewer guests to patronise them. Prices are fairly uniform so expect to pay US$5 for a spacious double with bathroom, TV and fridge, and US$10 for the added luxuries of air-con and hot water.

There isn't the vast selection of cheap guesthouse-karaoke-brothels you find in cities like Kompong Cham and Kratie, so basement bargains are limited.

7 Makara Hotel *(NH5 west)* Rooms with/without bathroom 12,000/7,000r. This place is pretty run-down compared with the competition, but offers a wide selection of rooms. Rates are for tiny rooms with fan.

The larger fan or air-con rooms are not really worth considering given what is available elsewhere.

Golden Parrot Guesthouse *(Ph 3)* Top-floor singles/doubles US$2/3, larger lower-floor rooms with TV US$5. Rooms here include a bathroom and are pretty good value for money.

Angkor Hotel *(☎ 952310, Ph 1)* Rooms with air-con & bathroom US$11, with hot water US$13. This hotel is a modern affair, incongruously clinging to the end of some fine old buildings, but possibly the best situated in town.

Monorom Guesthouse *(Ph 1)* Singles/doubles/triples with fan & bathroom US$4/5/6. This place is very good value for such a prime location, particularly for triples.

Chhaya Hotel *(☎ 952170, 118 Ph 3)* Rooms with fan & bathroom US$5, with air-con & hot water US$10. This hotel has emerged as the leading backpacker choice in the centre of town and has just added a mammoth wing at the back with 44 more rooms. Rooms include TV. This is also a sound place to link up with English-speaking moto drivers to explore the province.

Royal Hotel Rooms with fan & bathroom US$4-5, with air-con & hot water US$10-13. Formerly known as the 23 Tola Hotel, the Royal has been fully renovated in the past couple of years and offers clean beds with reasonable amenities.

Golden River Hotel *(☎ 730165, 234 Ph 3)* Singles/doubles with fan & bathroom US$5/6, with air-con & hot water US$8/10. This friendly establishment has good-value rooms and is generally a comfortable place to stay.

Other hotels around town include the **Paris Hotel** *(Ph 3)* and the **International Hotel** *(☎ 952444, opposite Psar Nat)*, but these don't offer hot water.

Teo Hotel *(☎ 952288, Ph 3)* Singles/doubles US$11/13. The exterior of this pad is pretty extravagant, but the rooms are similar to, if a little larger than, other establishments around town and include all the trimmings. It is arguably the most comfortable hotel in town and is often crawling with government delegations and NGOs.

Places to Eat

Like the city's hotels, restaurants in Battambang offer good value for money. Cheap dining is also available in and around **Psar Nat**, although the places inside the main building seem to specialise in what can only be described as 'unusable bits' soup.

White Rose Dishes 1000-3000r. For inexpensive food and fine *tukalok* (fruit smoothies), try this place, known as Colap So in Khmer. The menu includes tasty Khmer dishes, good Vietnamese food, and the Cambodian sandwiches sold throughout the day can make useful picnic food for trips around the province.

Just across the road is the **Uy Thean Restaurant**, with a similar formula that draws the locals.

Heng Lim Restaurant (Ph 3) Dishes 4000-6000r. This place has a healthy menu of mixed Asian cuisine and some of the staff speak English. It is good value for money and centrally located.

Cold Night Restaurant Dishes US$2-4. Those who venture a bit farther afield will find this restaurant has a massive menu comprising around 300 dishes. There is a wide selection of Asian food and a surprising amount of Western food, including burgers and pastas for about US$2 and pizzas from US$3.

Restaurant Neak Poan (Ph 1) If you want to eat by the river, this restaurant has a beer garden and is popular with locals in the evening. Nearby are a host of **food stalls** that set up for business in the late afternoon and make a good place to observe life in this pleasant city.

Tarareas Restaurant (Ph 3) Meals US$1.50-3. Also named Darareas inside, this is one of the best restaurants in town and serves a wide range of Thai and Khmer dishes. 'Four comrades to play fire with shrimp' includes mushrooms, baby corn and other vegetables playing the part of comrades. For something more spicy try the drunken version and wash it all down with a Walls ice-cream sundae.

Phkay Preuk Restaurant (Ph 3) Dishes US$2-3. This Thai restaurant is part of an extended western Cambodian empire that has branches in Sisophon and Poipet. Set in a large garden, it is quite popular by night.

Entertainment

For such a large city, Battambang's nightlife is somewhat limited.

Riverside Balcony Bar (Ph 1) Set in an old wooden house high above the southern section of the riverfront, this place is the recent revelation for the lackadaisical night scene. So far it only tends to open from Thursday to Sunday, but with recent patrons including Angelina Jolie and Billy Bob Thornton its popularity is set to soar. It has a wonderful atmosphere and serves basic Western food, as well as inexpensive drinks.

Elsewhere the **Cold Night Restaurant** is very popular with certain expats, as it shows Western movies regularly. The restaurant at the **Teo Hotel** also draws a small mixed crowd for an occasional beer.

The cheap riverside **food stalls** opposite Battambang Museum attract a good Khmer crowd, with their cheap prices.

Khmer nightclubs are a vanishing species in this town. The **Than Sour Nightclub**, somewhat optimistically meaning 'Paradise', is just about the only one left and has been forced to brighten its lights so nothing dodgy goes on in the dark. Be prepared to be attacked by the myriad 'beer girls' using their charms to encourage you to drink their particular brand – it is something akin to a minor riot.

Getting There & Away

Air There are daily morning flights between Battambang and Phnom Penh with President Airlines and Royal Phnom Penh Airways for US$45/85 one way/return. Departure tax from Battambang is US$4.

Airline offices in town are:

President Airlines (☎ 952915) 225 Ph 3
Royal Phnom Penh Airways (☎ 952794) 72 Ph 3

Train It is a harsh 274km journey to Phnom Penh of at least 15 hours, assuming the train encounters no problems on the way. The train leaves at 6am, running up one day and down another day, and the foreigner price is 12,400r. Check the schedule a day or two in advance. Until work on NH5 is completed, it's best to take the train as far as Pursat (this avoids the worst stretch of road) and then continue to Phnom Penh by taxi. This isn't such a good idea coming from Phnom Penh to Battambang, as the train does not get in until 10pm or so. There is also a train to Sisophon (4000r, four hours), which departs at 7am. This journey is pretty slow when compared with the road, but less bumpy.

Taxi, Pick-up & Minibus The 293km road to Phnom Penh used to be a case of the good, the bad and the ugly. It was plain ugly between the towns of Muong Russei and Pursat, bad from Pursat to Kompong Chhnang and good into Phnom Penh. However, the road is currently being turned into something of a motorway and should be incredible by late 2003. Share taxis (30,000r, six hours) and pick-ups (20,000/8,000r inside/on the back) leave Battambang for Phnom Penh from a station northwest of the town centre. Until the road is finished, many will prefer to break the journey in Pursat (10,000/4000r, three hours).

Sisophon (5000/3000r, two hours) is 80km northwest of Battambang on a road that has deteriorated badly in the past few years. It is due for an overhaul. Pick-ups also run direct to Poipet (10,000/6000r, three hours), but only a seasoned haggler will get the price we've quoted.

For details on the much-improved road to Pailin, see that entry later in this chapter.

Boat There is a fast-boat service between Battambang and Siem Reap along Stung Sangker, which is a good way to avoid the misery of the roads. This journey is arguably the most spectacular in Cambodia, as the boat passes through protected wetlands and narrow waterways. Express boats make the run when the water is high enough between the months of August and January (US$15, three hours). However, if a smaller boat is available, opt for that, as the big boats are extremely unpopular with local communities along the river. Drivers snag fishing nets,

send large waves over small boats and, in the worst case, have been know to cause deaths by capsizing small craft. From February to June, when the water level is too low for bigger boats, six-person speedboats travel this route for the same price, but navigating the shallow waters can take several hours longer. Even these boats can disrupt local fishermen, so try and convey the need for speed is less pressing than the need not to upset the locals.

Getting Around

To/From the Airport The airport is about 2km east of the centre of town. It should cost between 2000r and US$1 by moto. A taxi should cost no more than US$3.

Motorcycle There are no official rental shops as such, but guesthouses can often set visitors up with a bike for US$6 to US$7. Car rental is available from Chhaya Hotel for US$25 a day through Mr Leang Lee.

Moto Battambang is compact enough to explore on foot. That said, motos are cheap and plentiful. Short rides are 500r, longer rides are 1000r, and it costs a little more at night. Taking a driver for the day starts at US$6 and up, depending on the distance covered.

Remorque-kang Instead of *cyclos* (pedicabs) Battambang has *remorque-kang* (trailers pulled by bicycles). Aim to pay about the same as motos.

Norry These are a larger equivalent of what is called the lorry on the south coast railway, a sort of local train built from wood and powered by an electric motor. These can be used for short hops up and down the lines between Battambang and Pursat or Sisophon, and are a fun experience providing you don't run into a train!

AROUND BATTAMBANG

Before setting out on trips around Battambang, try to link up with an English-speaking moto driver, as it improves the experience. The following prices are indicative only, as settling on a price is all about the specific itinerary and your negotiating skills. Moto excursions that include jaunts through the countryside will cost a little more than prices quoted here. Several places can be combined in a day trip, such as Phnom Sampeau, Kamping Poy and Sneng, or Phnom Sampeau and Wat Banan.

NH10 (the road from Battambang to Pailin along which many of the attractions are located) was recently renumbered NH57, but many locals still refer to it as NH10. If you are heading to Pailin in a group of two or more, it could work out reasonable value to charter a taxi there for around US$25 to US$30 and include Phnom Sampeau and Sneng along the way.

Wat Ek Phnom
វត្តឯកភ្នំ

Wat Ek Phnom is a rather dilapidated 11th-century temple dating from the reign of Suryavarman I. It is something of a disappointment after Angkor, but the attractive ride out here on a winding road following the banks of Stung Sangker makes the trip worth the time. It is a very popular picnic and pilgrimage spot for Khmers during festival times. Take a moto (US$2 to US$3) for the 25km round trip. Some drivers will take you on a loop through the countryside on the way back and then link up with NH5.

Phnom Sampeau
ភ្នំសំពៅ

The hilltop temple of Wat Phnom Sampeau is located on top of a striking limestone hill 18km southwest of Battambang. It was formerly the front line in the government's defence of Battambang.

There is a long, hot climb to reach the summit, which is topped by both a small wat and a stupa. Nearby are a couple of large field guns, a hangover from the long civil war. Unless you are on a fitness drive, it may be better to take the winding road up the left side of the mountain and come down the main stairs. The gentler, winding road comes out at a grisly killing field located in a couple of caves. A small staircase leads down to a platform covered in the skulls and bones of victims. Look up to the right and there is a skylight hole where victims were bludgeoned before being thrown into the cave beneath.

There is another mountain nearby, called Crocodile Mountain, which was often occupied by the Khmer Rouge during the civil war and used to lob shells at government troops guarding Phnom Sampeau.

A moto to Phnom Sampeau costs US$3 to US$4, depending on wait time.

Wat Banan
វត្តបាណន់

Wat Banan has five towers pointing skyward and is like a smaller version of the rather more illustrious Angkor Wat. Locals claim it was in fact the inspiration for Angkor Wat, but this should be construed as wishful thinking as there are considerable differences in size and scale. Built in the 11th century by Udayadityavarman II, son of Suryavarman I, it is in a considerably better state of repair than Wat Ek Phnom and its hillside location offers incredible views across the surrounding countryside. There are several impressive carved lintels above the doorways to each tower, although most are now housed in Battambang Museum. There is also a large field gun, dating back to the bad old days when the government had to defend this hill from the Khmer Rouge.

Wat Banan is 25km south of Battambang and the round trip out here costs US$3 to US$4. A visit to Wat Banan can be combined in a loop with Phnom Sampeau, as there is a pleasant country road a few kilometres north of Wat Banan that leads west across to NH57.

Kamping Poy
កំពីងពួយ

Kamping Poy is the site of both a recreational lake and one of the Khmer Rouge's grander schemes – a massive hand-built dam stretching for about 8km between two hillsides. Some locals claim the dam was intended as a sort of final solution for enemies of the revolution, who were to be invited to witness its inauguration but would instead be drowned following the detonation of dynamite charges. It was more likely another step on the road to re-creating the complex irrigation network that Cambodia enjoyed under the kings of Angkor. Whatever the truth, as many as 10,000 Cambodians are thought to have perished during its construction, worked to death under the shadow of executions, malnutrition and disease. Today the lake is a popular swimming spot for locals at the weekend. It is possible to rent a local boat for a short trip around the lake. You should be able to negotiate a price of something like 4000r per hour.

Kamping Poy is 36km southwest of Battambang down a rough road that starts on the right just beyond Phnom Sampeau. It is best combined with a visit to Wat Banan. A moto for a full day here should be about US$7.

Sneng
ស្នឹង

This is a small, nondescript town on NH57 to Pailin, but is home to two small yet interesting temples. **Prasat Yeay Ten** dates from the end of the 10th century and although little more than a pile of blocks, it has three elaborately carved lintels above the doorways that have somehow survived the ravages of time and war. The temple clings to the left-hand side of the highway, so close to the road it could pass as an Angkorian-era tollbooth.

Behind Prasat Yeay Ten is a contemporary wat, and tucked away at the back of this compound are three **brick sanctuaries** with a small amount of reproduction carving adorning the entrances. The sanctuaries look like pre-Angkorian Chenla temples, but given the lack of Chenla presence in western Cambodia, it is possible they date from the same period as Prasat Kravan at Angkor, around the early part of the 10th century.

Sneng is about 26km southwest of Battambang. By moto it can be combined with Phnom Sampeau and Kamping Poy in a long and bumpy day trip. A cheaper option would be to jump in a Pailin pick-up as far as Sneng (35/25B inside/on the back).

Don't Stray From the Path

The area around Pailin and Samlot is one of the most heavily mined in Cambodia. Much of the region between Pailin and Battambang was the frontline in the government's war on the Khmer Rouge, and districts such as Treng and Ratanak Mondul were mined year after year. Similarly, the border with Thailand is riddled with mines. The upshot of this is that you should stick to roads and paths where others have travelled and do not stray from them for any reason. Ignoring this rule could cost you a leg or your life in this part of the country.

PAILIN
ប៉ៃលិន

☎ 053 • pop 22,000

Pailin has an attractive location amid the foothills of Chuor Phnom Kravanh, but the town itself lacks major attractions unless you know a bit about gemstones or like hanging out with geriatrics responsible for mass murder.

This small town near the Thai border has bountiful gem and timber resources, long the economic crutch that kept the Khmer Rouge hobbling along. It was used as a base from which to launch regular dry-season offensives against government positions in and around the province of Battambang. Government forces managed to take Pailin in the summer of 1994, but the Khmer Rouge massed for a counter attack and chased the army all the way up to Phnom Sampeau. However, in August 1996, Ieng Sary, former brother No 3 during the Khmer Rouge regime and Khmer Rouge supremo in these parts, defected to the government side, bringing with him up to 3000 fighters and their dependants. This was critical in bringing about the eventual demise of the Khmer Rouge, as it cut off much-needed sources of revenue for fighters in the north and allowed the Royal Cambodian Armed Forces (RCAF) to concentrate its resources on one front.

Pailin's fortunes rose dramatically in the late 1990s as gem dealers flocked into town

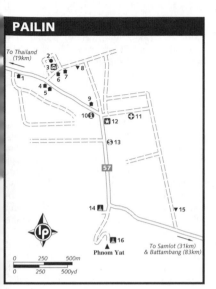

and casinos opened to milk cash from Thai gamblers. However, much of this free-wheelin' activity has moved back to the border area where large casinos like the Caesar International are more convenient for the Thais. Today Pailin is a subdued wild west town in which former leaders of the Khmer Rouge seek haven, avoiding the long arm of international law.

Information
There is a branch of Canadia Bank on NH57 but it does not change travellers cheques.

There are several telephone kiosks around Psar Pailin (Pailin Market).

Things to See & Do
The small hillock of **Phnom Yat** marks the gateway to town, and atop the summit is the eponymous **Wat Phnom Yat**. The wat is nothing to write home about, but there is an attractive old and ornate stupa here dating back to the early part of the 20th century. There are clear views across Pailin from here and it's a top spot for sunrise or sunset. At the base of the hill is **Wat Khaong Kang**, an important centre for Buddhist teaching before the war, which has reopened for business.

The **Phnom Khieu Waterfall** is in the lower reaches of Chuor Phnom Kravanh on Phnom Khieu (Blue Mountain), and draws Khmers at holiday time. It is about 20km southwest of town, and requires the service of a moto driver, as the road disappears into a path up into the forest. The trip out here involves a round-trip hike of about 10km and takes a total of around five or six hours. There are other **swimming holes** around the Pailin area that might make worthwhile excursions during a longer visit to this region.

Down on the Thai border are a couple of major casinos, the **Caesar International Resort** and the **Pailin Casino**, where well-to-do Pailin residents like to be seen at night. They are only really worth considering for those spending more than a couple of nights in town.

Places to Stay
Quite a few of the guesthouse brothels that you see in frontier towns throughout Cambodia have sprung up in Pailin. However, as the casinos and associated mischief have shifted back to the Thai border, rooms have gone to ruin in several places.

Guesthouse Ponleu Pich Pailin Rooms with fan & bathroom 100B. This is by far the best of the cheap deals in town, as the rooms are very clean and brightly lit. It may not sound spectacular, but when you have seen some of the other cells around town, it stands out.

Vimean Srey Sur Guesthouse Rooms 50B. The cheapest place in town is only for those on skid row, as it offers one bed, no window and a share bathroom, in dark and dingy surroundings.

Meas Sam Oeun Guesthouse Rooms with bathroom 100B. This place is unmemorable to say the least, with small cubicles and no charm.

Hotel Lao Lao Kaing Rooms with bathroom 100B. This place has a neglected feel and is really no more of a hotel than the neighbouring guesthouses.

Cheng Leang Guesthouse Rooms with bathroom 150B. This place is a little overpriced compared to the guesthouses around the market, but is in a quieter part of town.

Hang Meas Pailin Hotel (*☎ 012-936746*) Singles/doubles with TV, fridge, air-con & hot water US$11/17. This is undoubtedly the most sophisticated place in town. There is an attached restaurant with pretty good food where live bands and comedians perform most nights. There's also karaoke, making it a veritable entertainment mecca in this part of the world.

Places to Eat

Dining opportunities are fairly limited in Pailin. Apart from the fancy surroundings of the Hang Meas Pailin Hotel and the rather less-fancy surroundings of the local market, there are only a smattering of restaurants in town.

Reaksmey Phnom Yat Restaurant Dishes 40-60B. This is one of the largest diners in town, set a short distance off the main highway back to Battambang. The food is certainly tasty, but there is little in the way of atmosphere.

The no-name **soup restaurant** east of the market is a popular spot for breakfast and offers the full range of Khmer and Chinese soups. Later in the day it offers *soup chhnang dei* (cook-your-own soup).

Getting There & Away

Pailin lies 83km southwest of Battambang and only about 20km from Thailand. The border here is not presently open to foreigners, but may be opened sometime during the lifetime of this book – check for confirmation in either Battambang, Phnom Penh or Bangkok.

The road between Pailin and Battambang has been completely overhauled, a blessing for those who remember how it used to be. Share taxis (200B, 1½ hours) and pick-ups (100/80B inside/on the back) make the journey between Battambang and Pailin. These prices are a little higher than elsewhere in Cambodia, but until recently Cambodian cabbies considered the trip to Pailin as the equivalent of driving to Hades itself!

For hardcore motorbikers with plenty of off-road experience, there is a new logging road running from the Pailin area south to Krong Koh Kong. It starts in the Treng district, about 25km east of Pailin, and runs through former Khmer Rouge strongholds such as Samlot and Veal Veng. It's a dawn-to-dusk day ride in the dry season and shouldn't be attempted in the wet season. There is not yet any public transport on this run.

Pailin's airstrip is slowly being redeveloped and once reopened, sporadic commercial flights may commence.

AROUND PAILIN
Samlot
សំឡូត

Famous for a 1967 peasant rebellion that marked the first major skirmish of the long civil war, Samlot was also one of the last areas to succumb to government control in this part of Cambodia. The Sangkum government did not take kindly to such a wanton act of disobedience and local authorities massacred hundreds of peasants in reprisal. To be fair to Sihanouk, it was likely a local army initiative, but it did much to dent his image in these parts and helped to ensure peasant support for the Khmer Rouge here for three decades. It also kick-started a purge of leftist teachers that was conducted with the knowledge of Sihanouk, pushing remaining urban leftists in Phnom Penh, such as Khieu Samphan, Hou Youn and Hu Nim, into the jungle.

Today Samlot is little more than a small village with a small set of rapids, known locally as a **waterfall**, that locals head to for picnics. It's a scenic spot, but hardly in the A-list of worldwide waterfalls. It is a couple of kilometres from town off the road back to Treng and NH57.

The future may be bright, however, as actor Angelina Jolie has decided to give the village considerable financial support in its fight for recovery. Expect some changes in the near future.

Banteay Meanchey Province

ខេត្តបន្ទាយមានជ័យ

This is one of Cambodia's newest provinces, created in the 1980s from the northern chunk of Battambang. The name means 'Fortress of Victory' and may refer to the fact that it was one area of Battambang Province that the government was able to control during the long civil war, as there are few mountains in the province. Traditionally, rice and staple fruit and vegetables have been grown in Banteay Meanchey. However, thanks to a shared border with Thailand, new opportunities are emerging for trade and several locals-only borders are fast developing as centres of commerce. Poipet has found the best niche of all as the gambling centre of Cambodia and there are now six major casinos and counting.

Travel in the province is improving fast. The nightmare road from Poipet through Sisophon to Siem Reap has been rebuilt, while NH5 south to Battambang is in reasonable shape within the provincial borders, but not thereafter. Several secondary roads have been upgraded, including the one from Sisophon north to the massive Angkorian-era complex of Banteay Chhmar, Banteay Meanchey's leading attraction.

SISOPHON
ស៊ីសុផុន

☎ 054 ● pop 98,000

Sisophon is not one of Cambodia's more inspiring towns, and few visitors linger longer than for lunch on the journey between Thailand and the temples of Angkor. However, a number of travellers do find themselves having to spend the night here, particularly in the wet season when the roads can be unholy. Sisophon also provides a useful base for visits to the Angkorian temples of Banteay Chhmar and Banteay Top, about 50km north of here. Thai baht is the currency of choice here, but as in the rest of Cambodia, US dollars will never be sniffed at.

Information
There is nowhere to change travellers cheques in Sisophon, so come armed with cash. There is a branch of Acleda Bank (☎ 958821) if a Western Union money transfer is required. Telephone services can be arranged at kiosks throughout town. There is a tourist office in town that never seems to be open and is cunningly designed with the entrance at the rear so nobody notices.

Shadow Puppet Theatre
In the centre of Sisophon near the hospital is a workshop run by the NGO Krousar Thmey (New Family), which teaches disadvantaged children the art of shadow puppetry and leatherwork techniques for making the puppets. Shows take place on an irregular basis, but if you can muster a group together Krousar Thmey may be able to arrange a one-off performance in return for a donation.

Places to Stay
There are quite a lot of guesthouses and hotels in Sisophon. The cheapest places are the unnamed guesthouses on the road to Siem Reap, which offer simple fan rooms, but there are also a number of good-value hotels offering air-con and satellite TV.

Sara Torn Guesthouse Singles/doubles with bathroom 100/150B. This is the best of the budget deals, with spacious fan-cooled

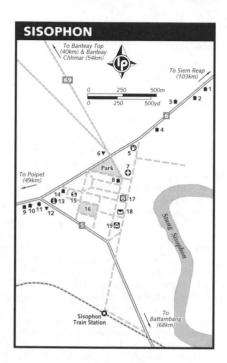

SISOPHON

PLACES TO STAY
1 Che Mongkol Guesthouse
2 Than Suor Guesthouse
3 Sara Torn Guesthouse
4 Prum Mean Rith Guesthouse
8 Proum Meanchey Hotel
9 Sourkear Hotel
10 Roeung Rong Hotel
11 Phnom Svay Hotel; Apsara Restaurant
14 Neak Meas Hotel

PLACES TO EAT
6 Penn Cheth Restaurant
12 Phkay Preuk Restaurant

OTHER
5 Sokimex Petrol Station
7 Hospital
13 Tourist Office
15 Acleda Bank
16 Psar Sisophon
17 Shadow Puppet Theatre
18 Post Office
19 Taxi Park; Food Stalls

rooms and a pleasant veranda area to while away an evening.

Along the same stretch are several other places, including **Che Mongkol Guesthouse** with bland rooms with fan for 100B. The almost identical **Than Suor Guesthouse** also charges 100B. The **Prum Mean Rith Guesthouse** looks far too much like a prison to consider parting with 100B.

Sourkear Hotel (☎ 958810) Rooms with fan & bathroom US$5. Moving up a touch, this hotel is on the road to Poipet.

Roeung Rong Hotel (☎ 958823, NH5 west) Singles/doubles with fan & bathroom US$6/7, rooms with air-con US$10. Located next door to the Sourkear Hotel, this friendly place has clean rooms and large communal areas.

Phnom Svay Hotel (☎ 012-916995) Rooms with TV, fan & bathroom US$5, with air-con & hot water US$10. Also on the road to Poipet, this well-kept place offers good value for money. This is the hotel of

choice with visiting United Nations (UN) or NGO workers and is affectionately known as 'The Birthday Cake' thanks to its extravagant exterior.

Proum Meanchey Hotel (☎ 958925) Rooms with TV, air-con, fridge & hot water US$10. Near the market, this is another modern, clean hotel with reasonable rooms. The owners plan to expand and offer rooms without bathroom for US$5.

Neak Meas Hotel (☎ 012-937215) Singles/doubles with TV, air-con, fridge & hot water US$10/13. This hotel has the best rooms in town. The bad news for light sleepers is that it also has a karaoke bar and disco, although these may not have survived the clampdown.

Places to Eat
The choice of restaurants in Sisophon is not as good as the choice of hotels, but there are a few places to refuel. Those on a tight budget can chow down at inexpensive **food stalls** found all over town, particularly in the area around the taxi park.

Apsara Restaurant Mains 50B. Located right next door to the Phnom Svay Hotel, this friendly little eatery has an English-language menu with a fair selection of cheap and tasty food.

Phkay Preuk Restaurant Dishes 70-100B. Phkay Preuk is becoming something of an empire, with branches in Siem Reap, Battambang and Poipet. Just next door to Apsara Restaurant, it offers a range of Thai dishes, as well as familiar Khmer favourites.

Penn Cheth Restaurant One more option is this huge diner that used to do a roaring trade with soldiers stationed here, but is as quiet as the rest of Sisophon these days.

Entertainment
Peace has not been so kind to the night scene in Sisophon, and without the soldiers to fill them most of the nightclubs have closed down. However, the **Neak Meas Hotel** offers karaoke rooms for those who dare, as well as a small beer garden of sorts. There is also a raging disco, but this doesn't seem to attract the punters like the karaoke.

Getting There & Away
The roads to Siem Reap and Poipet have finally been improved, changing journey times dramatically. Pick-ups travel from Sisophon to Poipet (5000/3000r inside/on the back, one hour), to Siem Reap (15,000/8000r, two hours) and to Battambang (5000/3000r, two hours).

There are also small trains to Battambang (4000r, four hours) leaving some time after 1pm each day. There are no trains to Poipet as the Khmer Rouge ripped up the tracks long ago.

BANTEAY CHHMAR
បន្ទាយឆ្មារ

Vast and remote, Banteay Chhmar (Narrow Fortress) has been repeatedly looted over the years and many of its treasures carted off to private collections around the world. The massive temple complex is yet another that was constructed by Cambodia's most prolific builder, Jayavarman VII (reigned 1181–1201), on the site of an earlier 9th-century temple. Built at the height of the Khmer empire's indulgence, this area would have been one of the most important in Cambodia after Angkor Thom and Preah Khan. There is some debate over its origins, some scholars suggesting it was built in tribute to Jayavarman VII's son Indravarman and the leading Cambodian generals responsible for the defeat of the Chams. Other sources suggest it may have been built as a funerary temple for the grandmother of the king.

Originally enclosed by a 9km-long wall, it housed one of the largest and most impressive Buddhist monasteries of the Angkorian period. This is one of the few temples in Cambodia to feature the faces of Avalokiteshvara as seen at the Bayon in Angkor Thom. However, many of the towers have collapsed over the centuries and it is now only possible to make out three towers with their enigmatic expressions.

The temple was deservedly renowned for its intricate carvings, including scenes of daily life in the Angkorian period similar to those at the Bayon. Unique to Banteay Chhmar was a sequence of eight multi-armed Avalokiteshvara adorning an outer gallery, but six of these were hacked up and trucked into Thailand in a brazen act of looting in 1998. The two that remain are spectacular and offer a glimpse of how this temple must have looked before it was pillaged. Fortunately, Cambodian and Thai authorities have begun to clamp down on the illicit trade in Cambodian antiquities and many of the items plundered in 1998 were intercepted on the road to Bangkok and have since been returned to Cambodia. Unfortunately, it's too late for Banteay Chhmar.

This temple was pretty much off-limits until the end of the civil war in 1999. Like Beng Mealea, 60km east of Angkor, the romantic image of the all-powerful jungle slowly consuming the ancient buildings pointed to massive potential for visitors. However, the authorities decided to clear away the jungle encroaching on the stonework and while this has undoubtedly made exploring the temple a safer experience, it has taken away much of the magic. Tourists with a genuine interest in Cambodia's temples will enjoy a visit here, as will travellers who want to see more of real Cambodia than Siem Reap has to offer. However, don't expect anything quite as spectacular as the principal temples at Angkor.

There are as many as a dozen smaller temples in the vicinity of Banteay Chhmar, all in a ruinous state. These include **Prasat Mebon, Prasat Ta Prohm, Prasat Prom Muk Buon, Prasat Yeay Choun, Prasat Pranang Ta Sok** and **Prasat Chiem Trey**.

Banteay Top
បន្ទាយទព

Banteay Top (Fortress of the Army) may only be a small temple, but there is something special about the atmosphere here. The temple was constructed around the time of Banteay Chhmar, quite possibly as a tribute to the army of Jayavarman VII, who had reaffirmed Cambodian dominance over the region in a comprehensive defeat of the Chams.

Set among the rice paddies, one of the damaged towers almost appears to have been partially rebuilt and looks decidedly precarious, a bony finger pointing skyward. This temple is about 14km southeast of Banteay Chhmar on a poor dirt road. The turn-off from NH69 is marked by a stone plinth with gold inscription, about 9km south of Banteay Chhmar.

Places to Stay & Eat
The small number of visitors coming to Banteay Chhmar usually stay in Sisophon or Siem Reap. The nearest accommodation to Banteay Chhmar is to be found in Thmar Puok, 15km south of the temple. The **Ly Hour Guesthouse** offers basic twins for 180B. This small town has power from 6pm to 11pm only and there is no generator, so sleep can get sticky. The owner plans to build a new guesthouse in the village of Banteay Chhmar overlooking the temple moat.

There are a few **food stalls** clustered around the bedraggled market in the village of Banteay Chhmar. No doubt an entrepreneur will open up a restaurant in the near future, but in the meantime, those who are squeamish about food hygiene should consider a picnic.

Getting There & Away
NH69 from Sisophon to Banteay Chhmar has recently been overhauled with assistance from USAID. The 39km section to Thmar Puok is in very good condition, while the last 15km to Banteay Chhmar is a little bit messy in places. All said it takes just over an hour on a trail bike and 1½ hours by moto or car. Arranging a moto to come here for the day is about US$8 to US$10. Try the hotels in Sisophon if you want to rent a motorbike. It is also possible to get to Banteay Chhmar by taking a pick-up from Sisophon to Thmar Puok (5000/3000r inside/on the back) and arranging a moto for the round trip from there (US$4). Some pick-ups may even carry on to Samraong, passing through Banteay Chhmar village (10,000/6000r), but this is rare.

It is also possible to get here in a long day trip from Siem Reap by motorbike or car. It's too far to be sensible by moto. For details of vehicle hire in Siem Reap, see the Siem Reap chapter. All said, it takes around four hours or so to Banteay Chhmar, so leave Siem Reap very early.

POIPET
ប៉ោយប៉ែត

Viva Poipet! Long the armpit of Cambodia, famous for nothing but mud and mess, Poipet is reinventing itself as the Las Vegas of Cambodia, home to six major casino resorts and counting. With gambling illegal in Thailand, Poipet has emerged as the most popular border destination for neighbourly flutters, eclipsing Krong Koh Kong and Pailin. Names such as Star Vegas and Tropicana don't make it quite as sophisticated as the US desert metropolis just yet, but it is growing fast.

As recently as 1996, the town was under intermittent mortar fire from the Khmer Rouge and so was always a transient place with a transient look. Town roadworks aren't proceeding as fast as resort building, so during the wet season the roads become rivers of mud and detritus. There is

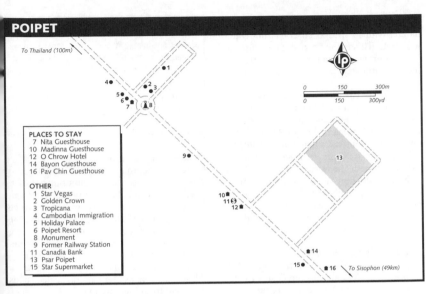

POIPET

To Thailand (100m)

PLACES TO STAY
7 Nita Guesthouse
10 Madinna Guesthouse
12 O Chrow Hotel
14 Bayon Guesthouse
16 Pav Chin Guesthouse

OTHER
1 Star Vegas
2 Golden Crown
3 Tropicana
4 Cambodian Immigration
5 Holiday Palace
6 Poipet Resort
8 Monument
9 Former Railway Station
11 Canadia Bank
13 Psar Poipet
15 Star Supermarket

To Sisophon (49km)

absolutely no reason to spend any time here unless you have a particular urge to part with large amounts of money.

Poipet is also emerging as scam central and many tourists are being ripped off on overland travel to Siem Reap and Battambang. For more on this, see the boxed text 'Poipet Warning' in the Getting There & Away chapter. Hopefully, the good folk of Poipet will realise the bad folk are doing their community and reputation no favours through such behaviour.

Information

There is a handy branch of Canadia Bank (☎ 967107), on NH5 not far from the border post, for changing travellers cheques. Changing cash is faster at shops or restaurants.

Places to Stay & Eat

Many of the cheaper hotels in Poipet have been hijacked by the casinos to house their large staff, so the places covered here include only those with rooms actually available. With all these fancy-pants casino resorts erupting near the border, it should be easy to get an upmarket room in Poipet. However, unlike Las Vegas, hotels don't rent

out rooms to non-gamblers, and most have a minimum stake of 50,000B to 100,000B (about US$1000 to US$2000), a tad expensive for a sorry town like this.

Should you, for some masochistic reason, feel inclined to stay in Poipet, there are a few cheaper guesthouses around town. Note that room rates can rise at weekends, as Thai gamblers flood the town. All the guesthouses covered here are located on NH5.

Bayon Guesthouse Rooms with fan/air-con 100/300B. All rooms here come with bathroom and are good value. About 1.5km east of the border, this hotel also has a small restaurant.

Pav Chin Guesthouse (*opposite Poipet Fish Stall*) Singles/doubles with fan 200/250B, with air-con 300/400B. Rooms here are clean and include satellite TV and bathroom, making this a fair deal.

O Chrow Hotel Rooms with fan/air-con 150/300B. One of the first hotels in town, this place still offers reasonable value for money.

Madinna Guesthouse Rooms with fan/air-con 100/300B. A short distance from the O Chrow Hotel is this place, a badly spelt tribute to the legend herself.

NORTHWESTERN CAMBODIA

Nita Guesthouse (☎ 710004) Singles/doubles with TV, fridge, air-con & hot water 500/800B. This is the nearest guesthouse to the border and offers smart rooms, but may be a little expensive compared with the competition.

As for the casinos, well they are pretty much off-limits to all but those intent on shortening their holiday, but for the record, they include **Tropicana**, **Poipet Resort**, **Holiday Palace**, **Golden Crown** and **Star Vegas**.

There are a couple of **hole-in-the-wall restaurants** near the border area and plenty of **street stalls** here. It is also the last place to find cheap goodies and drinks from Thailand for the journey into Cambodia, as eastward from here the price goes up and the selection goes down.

Getting There & Away

Poipet is connected by road to Thailand to the west and Sisophon to the east. For details of travelling between Thailand and Cambodia via Poipet, see the Land section in the Getting There & Away chapter. With some dedicated negotiating, pick-ups are available to Sisophon (5000/3000r inside/on the back, one hour), direct to Siem Reap (15,000/8000r, three to four hours) or direct to Battambang (10,000/6000r, three hours). These times are all during the dry season – it can take much, much longer in the wet season.

Oddar Meanchey Province

ខេត្តឧត្តរមានជ័យ

This is the newest of Cambodia's provinces, carved out of the sections of Siem Reap Province that the government did not control for much of the 1980s and 1990s. The name means 'Victory Province', a little optimistic for much of that period, but suitable enough by 1999. This is a dirt-poor province thanks to the sorrow of war, and produces very little apart from opportunity for aid organisations. Sharing a lengthy border with Thailand

NORTHWESTERN CAMBODIA

WARNING

Oddar Meanchey is one of the most heavily mined provinces in Cambodia and most of the mines were laid in the past decade. Do not, under any circumstances, stray from previously trodden paths. Those with their own transport should travel only on roads or trails regularly used by locals.

could eventually prove a road to riches for some local entrepreneurs. Illegal logging was rampant for a few years but seems to have stopped for the time being. There are few attractions for tourists in this province, although some visitors are drawn to the former Khmer Rouge town of Anlong Veng, with its many associations with Pol Pot and other leading figures from the movement.

Getting around the province is tough in the wet season, as there are no sealed roads. The road from Siem Reap to Anlong Veng is generally good in the dry season, but it is new roads the locals are eagerly anticipating. The Thai military is building a road from O Smach to Siem Reap and the Cambodian government is building a road from Anlong Veng to Prasat Preah Vihear, both of which could help put this province on the tourist map, at least for transiting, and that's better than nothing.

SAMRAONG
សំរោង

There are Samraongs throughout Cambodia, as the name means 'Dense Jungle', sadly something no longer extensive in this area. Samraong is the provincial capital of Oddar Meanchey Province and is slowly re-emerging after decades of isolation as a result of its frontline position in the long civil war. There is nothing to see or do up here for foreigners, unless they happen to be in development work – something much in demand around here.

There are several guesthouses near the scruffy little market, which is conveniently located right next to the taxi park. The **Stang Tuk Guesthouse** is cheapest, with basic, clean rooms with fan and bathroom for US$5. On the other side of the road is the **Meanchey Guesthouse**, which has rooms with fan from US$6 and a few air-con rooms from US$12, but often fills up with NGOs.

There are several **food stalls** around the market offering saucepans of pre-cooked food for 2000r a plate. Poke your head in and see what takes you fancy. For something more sophisticated, try the **Reaksmey Angkor Meanchey Restaurant**, overlooking the market, which has a good range of provincial Khmer food.

Most visitors make it to Samraong from Kralanh, a small town on NH6 midway between Siem Reap and Sisophon. Getting to Kralanh from either Siem Reap or Sisophon is about 5000/3000r inside/on the back of a pick-up. From Kralanh it is another 65km north to Samraong (8000/5000r) on a bone-shaking road that is gradually improving. It is also sometimes possible to travel between Banteay Chhmar and Samraong, but few trucks go this way. It is unwise to travel to Anlong Veng from Samraong, as the trail is mined in many places, but the road to O Smach (4000/2000r) is safe. The Thai military is scheduled to construct a new road from O Smach to Siem Reap via Samraong, which could dramatically alter the face of this forgotten town in a few years.

O SMACH
អូរស្មាច់

O Smach shot to fame in July 1997 as remnants of the Funcinpec forces regrouped here after the coup. Perched on the mountain, soldiers under the command of General Neak Bun Chhay were able to hold out against the superior forces of the CPP until a peace agreement was brokered allowing the 1998 elections to go ahead.

With the advent of peace, the military moved in and cleared locals off safe land to sell it to a casino developer. The casino attracts thousands of Thais each year to gamble in this remote outpost of Cambodia. Meanwhile, the locals who were evicted were forced to relocate to mined land that the military claimed to have cleared. All too often in Cambodia, the strong exploit the weak, but this episode was particularly heartless and brought to international attention the issue of military land grabs in 'peacetime' Cambodia.

Only hardcore gamblers will consider a visit now, but in the coming years this will be upgraded to a full international border once the surfaced road to Siem Reap is built.

ANLONG VENG
អន្លង់វែង

For almost a decade, this was the ultimate of Khmer Rouge strongholds – home to Pol Pot, Nuon Chea, Khieu Samphan and Ta Mok, the most notorious leaders of Democratic Kampuchea. Anlong Veng fell to government forces in April 1998, at the same time that Pol Pot mysteriously died near the Thai border, and soon after Prime Minister Hun Sen ordered that a major road be bulldozed through the jungle to ensure the population didn't have second thoughts about ending the war.

Today Anlong Veng is a safe, dusty, poor town in Cambodia's far north that has begun to attract some visitors thanks to the macabre lure of all things associated with the Khmer Rouge. The average visitor will find little of interest here compared with what's on offer around Angkor, but for those with a keen interest in contemporary Cambodian history it is an important part of the picture. North of town along the ridge of Chuor Phnom Dangkrek are the houses of several former leaders of the Khmer Rouge, as well as some dense jungle and compelling views.

Things to See & Do
The one-legged military chief of the Khmer Rouge, Ta Mok, ruled the movement in its final years, and his **residence** (admission US$1) is open to visitors. He doesn't need it just now, as he is a guest of the Cambodian government in T-3, a Phnom Penh prison, awaiting trial for genocide. His residence is a large pad, but little remains of the original furnishings, as it was badly looted by government soldiers. There are several evocative Angkorian paintings adorning the upper

walls, as well as some seriously large log supports, reminding visitors how the Khmer Rouge raised revenue in these parts. Downstairs is a large garage, which used to house his luxury Toyota Landcruiser, a suitably simple car for such a simple man.

Some of the guards around the house are former Khmer Rouge soldiers and have an alternative story to tell about Ta Mok. To them, he was harsh but fair, a builder of orphanages and schools, and a leader who kept order, in stark contrast to the anarchic atmosphere that prevailed once the government took over. However, there may be a hefty bias among his former followers, as to most Cambodians Ta Mok is known as 'The Butcher' and was widely known to have been Pol Pot's military enforcer, responsible for thousands of deaths in successive purges during the terrible years of Democratic Kampuchea.

Looking across the swamp in front of the house is a small island with the remains of a toilet outhouse. This is all that remains of **Pol Pot's residence** in Anlong Veng.

There used to be a dilapidated **Angkorian temple** behind the high school in Anlong Veng, but this was destroyed by Ta Mok and his army in their search for ancient statues to sell to the Thais. Sadly, this is not an isolated case and many a small temple that survived the centuries has succumbed to modern greed in the past couple of decades.

Otherwise, the 'attractions' of Anlong Veng are all found in the north of town along the Thai border. The road north begins to climb the escarpment about 8km out of town and deteriorates rapidly. Look out for the intricate **carvings of Khmer Rouge soldiers** cut from a huge boulder in the middle of the trail. The images have been decapitated by government forces, but remain striking for their detail and the fact that they have been hewn entirely from the surrounding rock. It is ironic to see that those responsible for such destruction were capable of such creativity with the right motivation.

Once at the top of the plateau, it is possible to visit the **cremation site of Pol Pot**. He was hastily burned on a pyre of old tyres and rubbish, satisfyingly apt given the suffering he inflicted on millions of Cambodians. But, unfortunately, an autopsy was never carried out, fuelling rumours about his demise that persist today.

Strung out along the border itself are the **safehouses of Pol Pot, Khieu Samphan and Son Sen**, located close enough to Thailand so they could flee like rabbits if the government attacked. As always, the Khmer Rouge was often its own worst enemy, and in 1997 Pol Pot ordered former defence minister Son Sen and all of his family be murdered and their bodies run over by trucks. This incident led to Pol Pot's overthrow by Ta Mok, and his Khmer Rouge show trial. All the remaining houses are shells, as everything of value was long ago looted by soldiers.

Anyone interested in visiting these bizarre sites should link up with a moto driver or guard at Ta Mok's residence in town, as much of the border area is heavily mined.

Places to Stay & Eat
Given the range of options available in Siem Reap, it is not worth staying in Anlong Veng in the dry season. In the wet season, it can become necessary, as road conditions deteriorate significantly. There are only very basic guesthouses available, including the **Reaksmey Angkor Guesthouse**, which has rooms with fan and bathroom for 10,000r.

The restaurant scene is similarly limited. There are several local joints around the central roundabout that can cook up local dishes at low prices.

Getting There & Away
Anlong Veng lies about 115km north of Siem Reap on NH67, a dirt road that is straightforward in the dry season (around two hours), but tough in the wet season (up to five hours). Pick-ups do the run for 10,000/6000r inside/on the back. Coming by motorbike, follow the surfaced road to Banteay Srei temple before continuing north past Kbal Spean. Much of the scenery is monotonous dry forest, but midway through the journey there is a verdant section of jungle to divert the mind.

Anlong Veng is also connected by roads of sorts to Samraong in the west and Prasat

Preah Vihear to the east, but there are many land mines along these stretches making them unsafe options for the time being.

Kompong Thom Province

ខេត្តកំពង់ធំ

The second largest province in Cambodia, Kompong Thom is starting to draw more visitors thanks to the pre-Angkorian temples of Sambor Prei Kuk and other lesser-known Angkorian sites. During the time of the French, it was home to a large minority group called the Stieng, but they have long been assimilated into Cambodian society. Farming and fishing are the mainstay of the population, Stung Sen winding its way through the province and into the Tonlé Sap river in western Kompong Thom.

The province was hard hit by the long civil war and came under particularly fierce US bombardment in the early 1970s in an effort to reopen the severed road between Phnom Penh and Siem Reap.

There are only two roads that visitors tend to use in Kompong Thom Province: NH6, which links Phnom Penh and Siem Reap; and NH64 north to Tbeng Meanchey and Preah Vihear Province. NH6 towards Phnom Penh is in good shape, but west towards Siem Reap is very unpleasant. NH64 is good in the dry season, messy in the wet season, but in line for an all-weather renovation.

KOMPONG THOM
កំពង់ធំ

☎ 062 • pop 66,000

Kompong Thom is a bustling commercial centre on the banks of Stung Sen, strategically located on NH6 midway between Phnom Penh and Siem Reap. It is another one of those towns in which overland travellers stop for a bite to eat, but rarely hang around long enough to get a feel for the place. As long as the road between the capital and the temples of Angkor remains in poor condition, it makes a convenient place

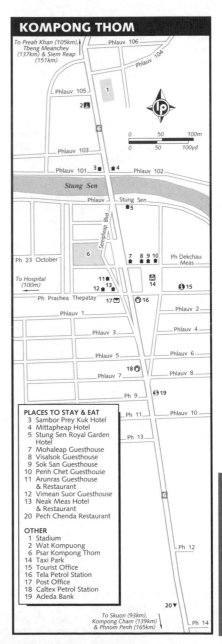

KOMPONG THOM

To Preah Khan (105km), Tbeng Meanchey (137km) & Siem Reap (151km)

Phlauv 106
Phlauv 104
Phlauv 105
Phlauv 103
Phlauv 101
Phlauv 102

Stung Sen
Stung Sen

Phlauv

Serephenp Blvd

Ph 23 October

To Hospital (100km)

Ph Prachea Thepatay

Ph Dekchau Meas

Phlauv 1
Phlauv 2
Phlauv 3
Phlauv 4
Phlauv 5
Phlauv 6
Phlauv 7
Phlauv 8
Ph 9
Ph 11
Phlauv 10
Ph 13
Ph 12
Ph 14

PLACES TO STAY & EAT
3 Sambor Prey Kuk Hotel
4 Mittapheap Hotel
5 Stung Sen Royal Garden Hotel
7 Mohaleap Guesthouse
8 Visalsok Guesthouse
9 Sok San Guesthouse
10 Penh Chet Guesthouse
11 Arunras Guesthouse & Restaurant
12 Vimean Suor Guesthouse
13 Neak Meas Hotel & Restaurant
20 Pech Chenda Restaurant

OTHER
1 Stadium
2 Wat Kompuong
6 Psar Kompong Thom
14 Taxi Park
15 Tourist Office
16 Tela Petrol Station
17 Post Office
18 Caltex Petrol Station
19 Acleda Bank

To Skuon (93km), Kompong Cham (139km) & Phnom Penh (165km)

to break the journey for a night. It is also the ideal base from which to explore the pre-Angkorian Chenla capital of Sambor Prei Kuk and a gateway to the incredible remote temples of Preah Khan, Koh Ker and Prasat Preah Vihear.

Information

There is nowhere to change travellers cheques in Kompong Thom, so bring plenty of cash. Acleda Bank (☎ 961243) on NH6 east can arrange Western Union money transfers.

There are telephone kiosks all around the market, offering national and international calls. There is also a post office opposite the Neak Meas Hotel on Ph Prachea Thepatay.

There is a tourist office on the eastern side of Ph Prachea Thepatay. It is upstairs in an old wooden building and the staff here speak a little English and better French.

Places to Stay

There is a wide range of accommodation available in Kompong Thom to suit every budget, owing to its central location on NH6.

At the budget end there are several cheap guesthouses on Ph Dekchau Meas running east from the market, some of which make more money as brothels.

Penh Chet Guesthouse (9 Ph Dekchau Meas) Doubles with fan 5000r. This place is pretty run down and judging by the posters slapped on the wall, short-term guests are more common here.

Sok San Guesthouse (8 Ph Dekchau Meas) Rooms with/without bathroom & fan 10,000/6000r. Don't be put off by the old cow shed rooms on the right, as there is a new block at the back with spotless comfortable rooms that offer very good value for money. Don't even think about the cow shed just to save 4000r!

Visalsok Guesthouse (7 Ph Dekchau Meas) Rooms with TV & bathroom 12,000r. This is a slightly more upmarket place aiming at the one-hour trade.

Mohaleap Guesthouse (1 Ph Dekchau Meas) Doubles/twins with fan & bathroom 10,000/15,000r. The first place on this strip,

just off the main road, this guesthouse offers good-value, clean rooms, and is run by friendly owners.

Arunras Guesthouse (☎ 961238, 46 Sereipheap Blvd) Singles/twins with fan, 12,000/17,000r, twins with air-con US$8. This pad is probably the most popular with budget travellers. Rooms include TV and bathroom and are a good deal. However, smarter air-con rooms are available at the town's hotels.

Neak Meas Hotel (☎ 961294, Ph Prachea Thepatay) Singles/doubles with air-con & hot water US$10/12. The corridors here are a bit dark and dingy, but the rooms are smart enough. If you are prepared to walk to the top floor of this place, rooms with cold-water bathroom are only US$8.

Vimean Suor Guesthouse (☎ 961294, Ph Prachea Thepatay) Singles/twins with fan US$3/5, twins with air-con US$10. Next door to, and run by the same folks as, the Neak Meas Hotel, this guesthouse has good-value large twins with satellite TV, bathroom and fan. The air-con rooms are not as smart as those in the hotels in town.

Mittapheap Hotel (☎ 961213, NH6 north) Rooms with fan/air-con & hot water US$5/10. This is the newest place in town and possibly the best deal today.

Sambor Prey Kuk Hotel (☎ 961359, NH6 north) Singles/doubles with fan US$5/8, with air-con US$8/10. Another newcomer, rooms in this comfortable hotel have bathrooms and it offers the best-value air-con singles in town.

Stung Sen Royal Garden Hotel (☎ 961228, Ph Stung Sen) Rooms with air-con US$20-25. This is the most expensive hotel in town and has fully furnished rooms and gargantuan suites for an extra five bucks. It is popular with package groups passing through town on a trip to Sambor Prei Kuk.

Places to Eat

There aren't a whole lot of restaurants in town and at some of those claiming to be actually geared up for the karaoke trade there are lots of songs but little food gets served. There are a whole series of **snack stalls** and **tukalok sellers** in front of the market and these are the cheapest places to pick up light bites.

Arunras Restaurant Dishes 3000-5000r. Located underneath the Arunras Guesthouse, this is the most popular restaurant in town, turning out cheap and tasty food for itinerant travellers. The large menu includes the full range of Cambodian cuisine, plus a few dishes of Chinese and Western influence for good measure.

There is a string of restaurants found about 1km out of town on the road to Phnom Penh. Most of these are karaoke pads, but can cook up a meal as well. The **Pech Chenda Restaurant** is the most elaborate of these, with some attractive bamboo pavilions for small groups.

Entertainment

It's all but over for Kompong Thom, as both the traditional nightclubs at the Neak Meas and Sambor Prey Kuk hotels have closed down. This is a real pity, as the clubs offered a great slice of nightlife in the provinces. Learn to love karaoke or learn to love your bed.

Getting There & Away

Strategically located on NH6, Kompong Thom is 165km north of Phnom Penh and 150km southeast of Siem Reap. Share taxis (10,000r, 2½ hours) and minibuses (6000r, three hours) make the run from Phnom Penh.

Between Kompong Thom and Siem Reap the road degenerates into some sort of pothole epidemic. Pick-ups (15,000/7000r inside/on the back, four hours) are the most sturdy for dealing with the terrible conditions, while share taxis are more expensive (20,000r, four hours). The road to Siem Reap can take a whole lot longer in the wet season, but is scheduled for a thorough overhaul.

Heading north to Tbeng Meanchey, often referred to as Preah Vihear by locals, pick-ups (15,000/7000r, three to four hours) are the most common form of transport, but share taxis also do occasional runs (20,000r). For road conditions see the Tbeng Meanchey section later.

AROUND KOMPONG THOM
Sambor Prei Kuk
សំបូរព្រៃគុក

Sambor Prei Kuk is home to the most impressive group of pre-Angkorian monuments anywhere in Cambodia and there are more than 100 small temples scattered through the forest. They are some of the oldest structures in the country. Originally called Ishanapura, Sambor Prei Kuk was the capital of Chenla during the reign of the early-7th-century king Isanavarman, and continued to be an important centre of scholarship during the Angkorian period.

The central complex of temples consists of four groups of edifices, most of which are made of brick, and whose design prefigures a number of later developments in Khmer art. Years of monsoon rains have not been kind to the delicate brick carvings on the exterior, but it is somehow more reassuring to know they have been assailed by the elements rather than the malice of man as seen at later, looted Angkorian sites.

The principle group, known as **Prasat Sambor** and visible from the road, is dedicated to Gambhireshvara, one of Shiva's many forms. The other groups are all dedicated to Shiva himself. Several towers here retain carvings in a reasonable condition and there is a series of large *linga* (phallic symbols) around the central tower that appear to date from a later period, demonstrating the continuity between pre-Angkorian and Angkorian culture.

Prasat Tao boasts the largest of the structures at Sambor Prei Kuk. The name means 'Lion Temple' and there are two excellent examples of Chenla carving in the form of two large and elaborately coiffured lions.

The last major group is **Prasat Yeay Peau**. This is arguably the most atmospheric complex, as it feels more lost in the forest than the others. The eastern gateway stands precariously under the weight of a massive tree, its ancient bricks interwoven with the tree's probing and extensive roots.

In the future, generations of Cambodian brochure writers will no doubt attempt to draw comparison with Bagan in Myanmar

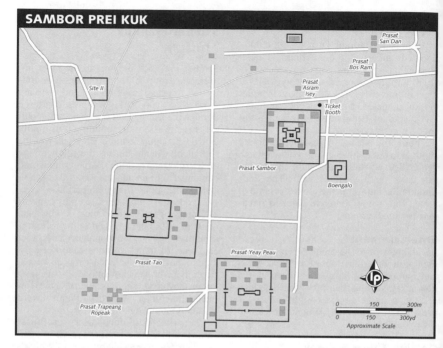

SAMBOR PREI KUK

(Burma), but this is a fanciful description to say the least. However, there is a serene and soothing atmosphere about the place.

Sambor Prei Kuk is best visited on the way to Siem Reap as it offers a chronological insight into the development of temple architecture in Cambodia. Coming from Siem Reap, you might have seen enough temples to last a lifetime, but Sambor Prei Kuk is sufficiently different from Angkor to warrant a visit for those interested in Cambodia's rich architectural legacy.

At the time of writing, there is no entrance charge, but visitor details are taken down in a small notebook and a US$2 'donation' requested at the small booth on the main road near Prasat Sambor. An official charge will no doubt be instituted sometime during the lifetime of this book.

Getting There & Away A new road has recently been completed that links Sambor Prei Kuk to NH64, one of the best roads in the country for its short length. To get here from Kompong Thom, follow NH6 north in the direction of Siem Reap for 5km before continuing straight on NH64 towards Tbeng Meanchey when the main road veers west. The new road to Sambor Prei Kuk starts on the right after a further 11km and is marked by an elaborate laterite sign. The next 14km are bliss.

Visitors without transport can arrange a moto out here; the round trip should cost about US$5, or US$8 for the whole day.

Prasat Andet
ប្រាសាទអណ្ដែត

Dating from the same period as Sambor Prei Kuk (7th century), this small, ruinous brick temple is set amid the grounds of a modern wat. Prasat Andet would have been the focal point of an important commercial centre trading on the Tonlé Sap and some researchers believe it continued to play such a

NORTHWESTERN CAMBODIA

role during the time of Angkor. Today very little remains and it is only worth the visit for dedicated temple-trackers with time on their hands. It is 29km west of Kompong Thom, about 2km south of NH6.

Phnom Suntok
ភ្នំសន្តុក

Phnom Suntok is the most important holy mountain in this region and the hillside is venerated with images of Buddha and a series of pagodas. It is an attractive location, set high above the surrounding countryside, but this means there are a lot of stairs to climb – 980 in fact. They wind their way up through a forest and emerge at a colourful pagoda with many small shrines, quite unlike others seen around Cambodia. There are a number of interesting sandstone boulders balanced around the wat, into which have been carved images of Buddha. Just beneath the southern summit of the mountain are several large reclining Buddhas – some modern incarnations cast in cement, others carved into the mountain itself centuries ago. There is an active wat on the mountain and the local monks are always interested in receiving foreign tourists. For travellers spending the night in Kompong Thom, Phnom Suntok could be a good place from which to catch a magnificent sunset, but this means coming down the mountain in the dark.

Getting There & Away Phnom Suntok is 20km from Kompong Thom. Follow NH6 for 18km in the direction of Phnom Penh and turn left down a sandy trail leading to the mountain. Those coming from Phnom Penh in their own transport should try to fit it in on the way to Kompong Thom so that there is no need for backtracking. A round trip by moto costs from US$3 to US$4, depending on how long the drivers have to wait. Those with trail bikes and a healthy dose of experience can ride up the hill by following the trail to the left of the stairs and veering right when the trail goes up what looks like a rocky dried-out streambed.

Prasat Kuha Nokor
ប្រាសាទគុហានគរ

This 11th-century temple constructed during the reign of Suryavarman I is in extremely good condition thanks to a lengthy renovation before the war. It is set in the grounds of a modern wat and is an easy enough stop for those with their own transport, although a headache for those travelling by pick-up truck or minibus. It is signposted from NH6, about 22km north of Skuon, and is 2km from the main road. Once the road from Phnom Penh to Siem Reap is upgraded, it will no doubt become a morning stop for overland tourist buses.

Preah Vihear Province
ខេត្តព្រះវិហារ

Vast Preah Vihear Province shares borders with Thailand and Laos to the north, as well as Siem Reap, Oddar Meanchey, Stung Treng and Kompong Thom within Cambodia. Much of the province is extremely remote and heavily forested, although large logging concessions are doing their best to change this, carving huge tracts of pristine tropical hardwoods out of the landscape. The province remains desperately poor, thanks in part to a disastrous infrastructure with no major roads in existence. The 'road' linking the provincial capital Tbeng Meanchey to Choam Ksant is only passable for half the year, and that's stretching the definition of passable.

However, the future may be brighter, as within the province's lengthy boundaries are three of the most impressive legacies from the Angkorian era: the mountain temple of Prasat Preah Vihear, the 10th-century capital of Koh Ker and the mighty Preah Khan. These temples are all extremely difficult to visit, requiring long and tough overland journeys and the distinct possibility of a night in the forest. In the wet season, they are simply unreachable. However, there are

WARNING

Preah Vihear Province is one of the most heavily mined provinces in Cambodia and most of the mines were laid in the past decade. Do not, under any circumstances, stray from previously trodden paths. Those with their own transport should travel only on roads or trails regularly used by locals.

various plans to upgrade the roads leading to each of these incredible locations, which in time could ensure the temples of Preah Vihear Province become one of the most important stops on a visit to Cambodia.

However, for now, travel around the province is only for the most resilient of souls. The road south to Kompong Thom is pretty good, as a logging company maintains it to facilitate the rape of the forest. Elsewhere in the province, there are no roads, just some very ugly sandy trails that pretend to be half decent.

TBENG MEANCHEY
ត្បែងមានជ័យ

☎ 064 • pop 22,000

Tbeng Meanchey is one of the more out-of-the-way provincial capitals in Cambodia and this has kept visitors to a minimum. Locals refer to the town as Preah Vihear, a fact that has confused many a foreigner attempting the arduous overland journey to Prasat Preah Vihear, the famous temple 100km farther north on miserable excuses for roads. Foreigners often refer to it as TBY.

Tbeng Meanchey is a sprawling dusty town that basically consists of little more than two major dirt roads running north to south. There is not much to draw the visitor to the town itself, but it is emerging as a gateway to Koh Ker and a staging post on the long haul to the mountaintop temple of Prasat Preah Vihear. This emergence may not last long if planned roads from Siem Reap to Koh Ker and from Anlong Veng to Preah Vihear are completed in the next few years – it could become forgottensville once more!

TBENG MEANCHEY

To Choam Ksant (65km) & Prasat Preah Vihear (105km)

Stung Sen

0   75   150m
0   75   150yd

PLACES TO STAY & EAT
3 New Hotel
4 Mlob Trosek Guesthouse
8 27 May Guesthouse
9 Mlop Dong Restaurant
10 Moha Sombat Guesthouse
11 Bakan Guesthouse

OTHER
1 Motorbike Ferry
2 Post Office
5 Psar Kompong Pranak
6 Taxi Park
7 Police Station
12 Hospital
13 Tourist Office
14 Naga Fountain

To Koh Ker (60km)

To Preah Khan (93km), Kompong Thom (137km) & Phnom Penh (302km)

Information

Bring US dollars as there is nothing in the way of financial institutions in this town. There is mobile phone coverage even this far north and calls can be arranged from booths near the market. There is a small tourist office in the south of town that has a willing director, although he speaks no English.

Joom Noon Silk Project

This silk-weaving centre was established by Veterans International as a training school for amputees. The artificial limb is step one in the rehabilitation process, step two is offering these individuals the chance to make a living. The centre produces fine hand-woven silk scarves and sarongs for export to Australia, Japan and the USA. It is possible to visit the silk-weaving centre, located about 1km east of the naga fountain in the south of town.

Places to Stay & Eat

Tbeng Meanchey has electricity from 6pm to 10pm only, but guesthouses can run their generators all night for an extra charge.

Mlob Trosek Guesthouse (☎ 012-952035) Rooms with fan 15,000r, with all-night electricity 20,000r. This is the currently the best of TBY's places to stay, with a pleasant garden, clean enough rooms with bathroom and the opportunity to have a fan that works all night. The new rooms at the rear are brighter than those on the right-hand side and also have genuine lino floors.

27 May Guesthouse Rooms with bathroom 15,000r. This place has power only until midnight and can get noisy from the early hours with both the market and taxi park nearby.

Moha Sombat Guesthouse Rooms without bathroom 8000r. The rooms here are pretty small, but at US$2 it is hard to complain. Power goes on until midnight if the guesthouse is full.

Bakan Guesthouse Rooms without bathroom 8000r. This attractive looking place has no sign in English, but a lot of potential, as it is an older wooden house with a large shaded garden.

With the exception of the run-down market and a couple of street stalls, there is really only one eatery in town, the **Mlop Dong Restaurant**. The food is cheap and the range of dishes heartening for this part of the world. It is a focal point for the small population of expats living in TBY and after dinner is just about the closest thing to a pub this town boasts.

Getting There & Away

Tbeng Meanchey is 137km north of Kompong Thom on NH64. Pick-ups (15,000/7,000r inside/on the back, three to four hours) run the route daily, while share taxis (20,000r) are less frequent. Share taxis (30,000r) and a luxury pick-up (35,000/25,000r) also run direct through to Phnom Penh, although it's easy to stop for a bite to eat in Kompong Thom and change vehicles. The road is in very good condition for most of its length, due to the pernicious presence of loggers in Preah Vihear Province. However, the final 30km stretch to Tbeng Meanchey climbs over a series of hills, which can get a little ugly in the wet season with minor rivers to ford.

Heading north to Choam Ksant and Prasat Preah Vihear is not for the faint-hearted. The road is without doubt one of the most appalling Cambodia has to offer. It is completely impassable from around June to November as much of the area is lowland swamp, although boats make the run up Stung Sen to Choam Ksant. From December to May it is a motorbiker's nightmare, a heinous mix of deep sand, thick mud, multiple trails, lacerating bamboo and land mines in the bush. It is actually easier in a 4WD and high-clearance pick-ups (15,000/7000r depending on road conditions, three to four hours) do the run from the opposite bank of Stung Sen. Russian jeeps also take on this cruel imitation of a road. For details of continuing from Choam Ksant to Prasat Preah Vihear, see their individual sections later in the chapter.

For details on the remote trail east to Stung Treng via Chaeb, see the Stung Treng section in the Eastern Cambodia chapter.

NORTHWESTERN CAMBODIA

PREAH KHAN

ព្រះខ័ន្ធ

The vast laterite and sandstone temple of Preah Khan is the largest temple enclosure ever constructed during the Angkorian period. Originally dedicated to Hindu deities, it was reconsecrated to Mahayana Buddhist worship during a monumental reconstruction undertaken by Jayavarman VII in the late 12th and early 13th centuries.

Its history is shrouded in mystery, but it was long an important religious site and some of the structures here date back to the 9th century. Both Suryavarman II, builder of Angkor Wat, and Jayavarman VII lived here at times during their lives. This suggests Preah Khan was something of a second city in the Angkorian empire, supporting a large rural population as well as the royal court's urban elite. Jayavarman VII was likely to have been based here during the disastrous occupation of Angkor by the Chams from 1177 and may have already commanded significant regional support among the population in this area, helping him to later consolidate control of Angkor.

Preah Khan was connected to the temples of Angkor by a 100km laterite highway, complete with ornate *naga* (mythical serpent) bridges, many examples of which remain today, forgotten in the forests of northwestern Cambodia. Some scholars suggest it was also linked by an ancient road to the pre-Angkorian centre of Sambor Prei Kuk, which continued as a centre of learning throughout the Angkorian-era. This indicates Preah Khan was of significant importance throughout the period of the Khmer empire.

The complex covers a total area of almost 5 sq km, and includes a massive *baray* (reservoir), which is 3km long. At the eastern end of the baray is a small pyramid temple called **Prasat Damrei** (Temple of the Elephants). Much of the outer structure is

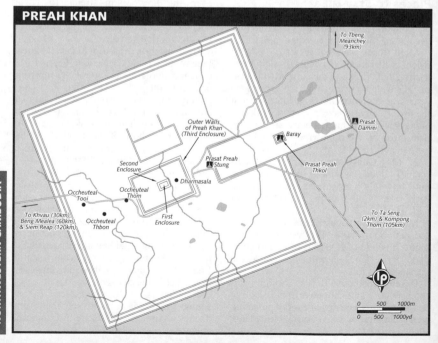

PREAH KHAN

To Tbeng
Meanchey
(93km)

Outer Walls
of Preah Khan
(Third Enclosure)

Prasat
Damrei

Baray

Second
Enclosure

Prasat Preah
Stung

Prasat Preah
Thkol

Occheuteal
Thom

Dharmasala

Occheuteal
Tooi

To Khvau (30km),
Beng Mealea (60km)
& Siem Reap (120km)

Occheuteal
Thbon

First
Enclosure

To Ta Seng
(2km) & Kompong
Thom (105km)

0   500   1000m
0   500   1000yd

no longer standing, but there are several impressive carvings of *devedas* (goddesses) on the remaining entrance wall. At the summit of the hill were a number of exquisitely-carved elephants guarding the shrine, but only two remain today, one partially buried in the mud, the other adorned with local offerings. Two others can be seen on display in the National Museum in Phnom Penh and the Musée Guimet in Paris.

In the centre of the baray is an island temple called **Prasat Preah Thkol** (known by locals as Mebon) that's similar in style to the Western Mebon at Angkor. At the western end of the baray is **Prasat Preah Stung** (known by locals as Prasat Muk Buon or Temple of the Four Faces), perhaps the most memorable temple at Preah Khan. Prasat Preah Stung has all the hallmarks of Jayavarman VII, with the enigmatic faces seen at the Bayon carved into its central tower. The temple is fairly overgrown, but it is possible to clamber around and explore.

It is a further 400m southwest to the walls of Preah Khan itself, which are surrounded by a moat similar to that around the walled city of Angkor Thom. Much of the moat has vanished under weed and the bridges here no longer have naga. Entering through the eastern *gopura* (entrance pavilion) there is a **dharmasala** (rest house). Many of these rest houses were constructed by Jayavarman VII for weary pilgrims across the Angkorian empire. Much of this central area is overgrown by forest, giving it an authentic, abandoned feel, but local authorities are already undertaking a clearing programme.

The central structure, which included libraries and a pond for ablutions, has been devastated by looting in recent years. As recently as the mid-1990s, it was thought to be in reasonable shape, but some time in the second half of the decade, thieves arrived seeking buried statues under each *prang* (temple tower). Assaulted with pneumatic drills and mechanical diggers, the ancient temple never stood a chance and many of the towers simply collapsed in on themselves, leaving the depressing mess we see today. Once again, a temple that had survived so much couldn't stand the onslaught of the 20th century and its all-consuming appetite.

This was not the first looting to strike Preah Khan. Louis Delaporte, in charge of the first official expedition to study Cambodia's temples, carted off tonnes (literally!) of carvings that are now in the Musée Guimet in Paris. Also found at the site was the bust of Jayavarman that's now housed in Phnom Penh's National Museum and widely copied as a souvenir for tourists. The body of the statue was discovered a few years ago by locals who realised the strangely shaped stone must have significance and alerted authorities. The head and body were finally rejoined in 1999.

Most locals refer to this temple as Prasat Bakan; scholars officially refer to is as Bakan Svay Rolay, combining the local name for the temple and the district name. Locals say there are no land mines in the vicinity of Preah Khan, but stick to marked paths just to be on the safe side.

Places to Stay & Eat
To get the most out of a visit to Preah Khan really requires an overnight stay at the nearby village of Ta Seng. Making a day trip from Kompong Thom, Tbeng Meanchey or Siem Reap requires at least eight hours on the road, usually more, and that doesn't leave a whole lot of time for exploring. There is no guesthouse in Ta Seng as yet, but with a hammock and mosquito net, it is possible to sleep either within the **Preah Khan complex** or in a **private house** in the village. Sleeping at the temple may sound romantic, but staying in Ta Seng is more practical, as there is some electricity and basic supplies such as food and water. Expect to pay villagers about 5000r as night for the privilege of sleeping on their floor. Sleeping at the temple also means taking on the kamikaze mosquitoes that come at you from every angle throughout the night. There is always at least one that gets through! Basic noodle dishes such as *nam ben choc* are available in Ta Seng.

Getting There & Away
Unless you particularly like travelling by ox cart, it is extremely difficult to get to

Preah Khan between the months of May and November. The best time to visit is from February to April, as the trails are reasonably dry.

There is no public transport to Preah Khan itself, but there are very infrequent trucks to Ta Seng. However, realistically most visitors are going to get here under their own steam, either by moto, rented motorbike or chartered 4WD. Only *very* experienced bikers should attempt this on rental motorbikes, as conditions are extremely tough from every side. The ox-cart trails snake their way through remote forest in areas that are still mined. Stick only to the trails that have fresh tracks, which requires leaving the original trail from time to time. It may be sensible to take a local moto driver to lead the way, even if you have your own bike; this should cost about US$10 per day plus petrol. Do not attempt to visit in the wet season, as the whole area is prone to serious flooding and there are several rivers to cross.

Getting to Preah Khan is quickest by motorbike from Kompong Thom, although most moto drivers aren't familiar with the route. Take NH6 towards Siem Reap out of Kompong Thom for 5km and then follow NH64 (the right fork that goes to Tbeng Meanchey). After about 70km a small track leads west from the village of Phnom Dek through the forest to Ta Seng and Preah Khan. The trail starts from pretty much opposite the right fork to Rovieng district. The total distance is about 105km from Kompong Thom and the journey should take about four hours in the dry season. There is a large riverbed to cross to the right of the trail a few kilometres before Ta Seng. Don't miss it or you'll end up in the middle of nowhere, literally.

Coming from Tbeng Meanchey, head south on NH64 for 37km before turning right at the Preah Khan 56km sign. This is an unpleasant 56km for motorbikes, as it is deep sand for much of the way, but it's the easiest way for 4WDs in the dry season. This route takes four to five hours and leads to Ta Seng via Prasat Damrei.

Coming from Siem Reap there are several choices. By car it requires a long journey

> ## WARNING
>
> There are countless land mines in the area around Koh Ker. Do not, under any circumstances, stray from previously trodden paths during a visit to this temple, as several locals have been killed or maimed in recent years.

down NH6 to Stoeng, before heading north on a bad dirt road to Ta Seng and Preah Khan. However, only the best Cambodian drivers can make it this way, as the road is dire and the trip realistically requires two days. By motorbike there are two ways. Easiest is to follow NH6 southeast to Kompong Kdei before heading north on a good dirt road to the village of Khvau. From Khvau, it is 30km east to Preah Khan on a miserable ox-cart track. This can just about be done in a 'dawn til dusk' day trip in the dry season. Don't bank on it though.

More adventurous and romantic is to follow the old Angkor road from Beng Mealea east to Preah Khan, which includes about 10 Angkorian bridges dating from the 12th and 13th centuries. For details on how to get to Beng Mealea, see the 'Temples of Angkor' special section earlier in the book. From Beng Mealea, the road vanishes into a rough ox-cart track to nowhere, but some huge bridges in the middle of this empty forest make the gain worth the pain. Spean Ta Ong, a magical place, is 77m long with about 15 arches, and is 7km west of the village of Khvau. This trail is not always easy to follow, as in many places small tracks lead into the forest before rejoining the main route. Take a local moto driver as a guide or carry a compass and stay due east.

KOH KER
កោះកេរ្ដិ៍

Koh Ker, a former 10th-century capital of the Angkorian empire, is one of the most remote and inaccessible temple sites in Cambodia, long abandoned to the forests of northern Cambodia. Also known as Chok Gargyar, it served as the capital of Jayavarman IV (reigned 928–42) who, having seized the

KOH KER

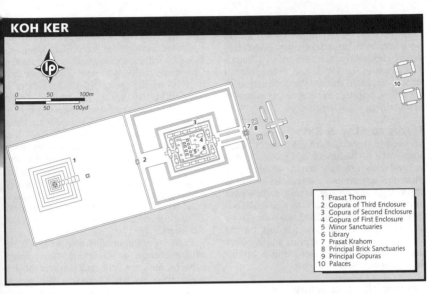

1 Prasat Thom
2 Gopura of Third Enclosure
3 Gopura of Second Enclosure
4 Gopura of First Enclosure
5 Minor Sanctuaries
6 Library
7 Prasat Krahom
8 Principal Brick Sanctuaries
9 Principal Gopuras
10 Palaces

throne from a rival, left Angkor and transferred his capital here, where it remained throughout his reign. His son and successor Harshavarman I moved the capital back to Angkor in 944.

There are a remarkable number of religious buildings in the Koh Ker region, considering the short space of time that it was the capital of the empire. There are more than 30 major structures and experts believe there may have been as many as 100 minor sacred buildings in the region. It was also a prolific period for gigantic sculpture and several of the most impressive pieces in the National Museum in Phnom Penh come from Koh Ker, including a huge *garuda* (half-man, half-bird creature) greeting visitors in the entrance hall and a unique carving depicting a pair of wrestling monkey kings.

The principal monument at Koh Ker is **Prasat Thom**, sometimes referred to as Prasat Kompeng, a 40m-high sandstone-faced pyramid of seven levels. This is now very overgrown with bushes and scrub, but offers some spectacular views across the forest from its summit. Some 40 inscriptions, dating from 932 to 1010, have been found at Prasat Thom, offering an insight

into Cambodian history at this time. Heading northeast, the compound includes the obligatory libraries, as well as a host of smaller brick sanctuaries. Beyond the inner wall and across a naga-flanked causeway lies **Prasat Krahom** (Red Temple), the second-largest structure at Koh Ker. Named after the red bricks from which it is constructed, Prasat Krahom is famous for its carved lions (sadly none of which remain today), similar to those found at Prasat Tao in the Sambor Prei Kuk group of temples near Kompong Thom.

South of this central group is a large baray known as the **Rahal**, fed by Stung Sen, which would have supplied water to irrigate the land in this arid area. There are many other structures in the area, including **Prasat Damrei**, named after its now-vanished elephant statues; **Prasat Chen**, where the wrestling apes were found; and **Prasat Neang Khmau**, with some fine door lintels still in place.

Koh Ker is one of the least-studied temple areas from the Angkorian period. Louis Delaporte visited in 1880 during his extensive investigations into Angkorian temples. It was surveyed in 1921 by the great Henri

Parmentier for an article in the *Bulletin de l'Ecole D'Extreme Orient,* but no restoration work was ever undertaken here. Archaeological surveys were carried out by Cambodian teams in the 1950s and 1960s, but all records vanished during the destruction of the 1970s, helping to preserve this complex as something of an enigma.

Places to Stay & Eat
Nowhere and nothing (to get straight to the point). Bring a hammock and mosquito net, as conditions are very basic, whether you choose to stay around the **temples** or in the tiny **village** of Koh Ker. Locals can prepare some very basic food such as rice and noodles, but carry enough food and water to be self-sufficient in case you get lost on the way. There are more supplies and a better chance of something resembling a bed in Siyong, about 9km southeast.

Getting There & Away
A tiny number of adventurous travellers have made it here, but it is no picnic, involving some of the meanest roads in the country. To really appreciate the temples, it is necessary to spend the night here, as a day trip leaves little time to explore. There are currently three routes here – two from Siem Reap and the most popular one from Tbeng Meanchey – all passing through the strategic village of Siyong. From Siyong to Koh Ker, a moto should cost around US$3 to US$4 including wait time. For now, it is only possible to get here in the dry season by 4WD or motorbike from Siem Reap, as well as moto from Tbeng Meanchey. However, there are plans afoot to redevelop the old Angkor road from Beng Mealea to Koh Ker, which could radically alter accessibility.

Currently the old Angkor road is one of the options from Siem Reap (definitely the worst), which involves first travelling to the village of Beng Mealea. Rather than continue straight on to the village centre and temple, veer left in the direction of Phnom Kulen to a village called Svay Leu. From Svay Leu, the trail turns into a disaster of Congolese proportions for a further 50km, until the village of Siyong. It takes all day

from Siem Reap in the dry season and is impossible by all but ox cart in the wet season.

Considerably easier from Siem Reap, although it's like choosing between Scylla and Charybidis really, is to head 60km southeast on NH6 to Kompong Kdei where there is a beautiful Angkorian-era bridge, Spean Pratpos. From here there is a good dirt road north to the village of Khvau (40km) and then a logging road north to Koh Ker (55km). Once again, this is impossible in the wet season, but can be done in the dry season in as little as six hours, offering the intriguing but unlikely possibility of a day adventure from Siem Reap. Don't count on it, so pack a mossie net and a hammock. This route offers the least-difficult road conditions.

There is regular public transport to Khvau, with a change in Kompong Kdei. From Khvau it can get a little tricky, but in the dry season there are some pick-ups and tractors heading to Siyong. A pick-up all the way from Kompong Kdei to Siyong is 15,000/10,000r inside/on the back. It is possible to rent a 4WD with driver for the trip from Siem Reap, but this is pretty expensive. Highly experienced bikers can also rent trail bikes, but will still need a local moto driver to lead the way. See the Siem Reap chapter for rental details.

The most popular route has been to approach Koh Ker from the west, starting in the provincial capital of Tbeng Meanchey. From here, it can be done as a long day trip for those who don't fancy a night in the malaria-infested forests of remote Cambodia. The trail involves a lot of deep sand, but can be covered in three to four hours via the village of Kulen. The best news about this route is that it can be partly covered by public transport. There are sometimes pick-ups to Kulen (8000/4000r), but it's more likely you'll end up on a moto (15,000r) for the two-hour journey. From Kulen, there are Russian jeeps to Siyong (8000r, two hours). There are often pick-ups (15,000/10,000r) going south from Siyong to Khvau so it could be turned into something of a long loop on the way from Phnom Penh to Siem Reap – dry season only of course. Serious bikers can take on this route, although it's best to take a local moto driver as a guide. The services of a moto the whole way, whether guide or driver, are about US$10 per day plus petrol. This is money well earned on these roads.

CHOAM KSANT
ជាំក្សាន្ត

Choam Ksant, a major trade hub for northern Preah Vihear Province, is little more than a large village serving as a night stop on the long haul to Prasat Preah Vihear. Much of the town engages in petty trade with Thailand, as there is a local border market at Anh Seh, 20km north of town in the Chuor Phnom Dangkrek mountains. The Cambodians ship pigs into Thailand, while the Thais shift a whole host of consumer goods into Cambodia. The border is closed to foreigners and there is nothing of interest to see up there, except some big views.

Choam Ksant has two guesthouses for those hardy enough to make it here, both fairly basic and offering electricity for only a few hours in the evening. **Heng Heng Guesthouse** is the better option, located opposite the new market, offering doubles with fan for 8000r. It also has a couple of rooms with bathroom, including a toilet raised like a throne, that go for 10,000r.

The **Sok San Guesthouse** is really more of a brothel for the military base across the road, but allows tourists to stay in tiny cubicles for 8000r a night.

There are a few basic **food stalls** around the old and new markets, as well as more **street stalls** around the village.

For the deeply disturbing details on how to get here from Tbeng Meanchey, see the Tbeng Meanchey section earlier in this chapter. For more on how to continue the journey northwest to Prasat Preah Vihear, see the following entry.

PRASAT PREAH VIHEAR
ប្រាសាទព្រះវិហារ

The imposing mountain temple of Prasat Preah Vihear has the most dramatic location of all of the Angkorian monuments,

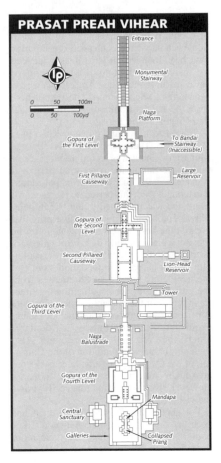

PRASAT PREAH VIHEAR

Entrance

Monumental Stairway

Naga Platform

Gopura of the First Level

To Bandai Stairway (inaccessible)

Large Reservoir

First Pillared Causeway

Gopura of the Second Level

Second Pillared Causeway

Lion-Head Reservoir

Tower

Gopura of the Third Level

Naga Balustrade

Gopura of the Fourth Level

Mandapa

Central Sanctuary

Galleries

Collapsed Prang

perched atop the cliff face of Chuor Phnom Dangkrek, towering 550m above the plains below. The views from this most mountainous of temple mountains are breathtaking: lowland Cambodia stretching as far as the eye can see, and the holy mountain of Phnom Kulen looming in the distance.

Prasat Preah Vihear was built by a succession of seven Khmer monarchs beginning with Yasovarman I (reigned 889–910) and ending with Suryavarman II (reigned 1112–52), builder of Angkor Wat. This progressive construction is easily appreciated once at the temple itself, as there are a series of gopura rising to the summit of the cliff. Some scholars have contended the site may have been founded earlier still, as evidenced by inscriptions linking it to the son of Jayavarman II, the first of Angkor's *devaraja* (god kings), who transported holy stone here from the ancient Cambodian temple of Wat Phu Champasak in Laos.

Prasat Preah Vihear, known as Khao Phra Wiharn by Thais, translates as 'Sacred Monastery' and it was an important place of pilgrimage during the Angkorian period. It was constructed, like other principal mountain temples from this period, to represent Mt Meru and was dedicated to the Hindu deity Shiva. The complex includes five principal gopura, the best preserved of which are the those at a higher level. The central sanctuary is constructed right on the edge of the mountain and in places the foundation stones of the temple are just a few centimetres from the cliff face, further proof of the architectural genius of the ancient Khmers. The site is in reasonable condition and includes many exquisitely carved lintels, particularly around the third, and largest, gopura. Also look out for an early rendition of the Churning of the Ocean of Milk, as later perfected at Angkor Wat, on the southern doorway. However, it is the location that really draws the visitors.

For generations Prasat Preah Vihear has been the subject of tensions between Cambodia and Thailand, which are once more threatening to boil over. Much of this area was occupied by Thailand for several centuries, but was returned to Cambodian sovereignty during the French protectorate under the treaty of 1907. In 1959, the Thai military seized the temple from Cambodia and then Prime Minister Sihanouk took the dispute to the International Court, gaining worldwide recognition for Cambodian sovereignty in a 1962 ruling.

That was that, at least for a few decades, and the only time Prasat Preah Vihear made international news was in 1979 when the Thai military pushed more than 40,000 starving, diseased Cambodian refugees across the border in what was then undoubtedly the worst case of forced repatriation in UN history. The whole area was mined and the refugees stumbled right back into the middle of Armageddon. Many people died from horrific injuries, starvation and disease before the occupying Vietnamese army could cut a safe passage through to the survivors and escort them on the long walk south to Kompong Thom. Many no doubt then ended up imprisoned in Phnom Penh for a time for having fled the country in the first place.

Prasat Preah Vihear hit the headlines again in May 1998, as the Khmer Rouge regrouped there after the fall of Anlong Veng and staged a last stand. Stand turned to surrender and the government proudly flew in a contingent of journalists and diplomats to see their success. Unfortunately, the helicopter was overladen, as the air force had been selling seats to eager correspondents, and in trying to land, its rotor clipped a land mine. No-one was injured, but it was an uncomfortable wait for a rescue and the remains of the helicopter can still be seen today.

With peace came an agreement between the Cambodians and Thais to open the temple to tourism. The Thais built a huge road up the mountain and began to appropriate Cambodian territory along the ill-defined border. Today, there is a large visitors centre and car park built on what was not so long ago Cambodian land. This is not enough, it would seem, and the Thais now claim their territory goes right up to the temple steps and want to close the small Cambodian market that has grown up at the base of the temple. The stand-off resulted in the temple being closed to visitors from the Thai side in December 2001 and it looks like the Cambodians will have the last laugh, as they are bulldozing new roads from Anlong Veng and Tbeng Meanchey direct to the temple. The Thais will be left with a very nice road to nowhere.

For more on the carvings of Prasat Preah Vihear and the temple's history, look out for *Preah Vihear* by Vittorio Roveda, a readable souvenir book accompanied by some attractive photographs.

WARNING

Prasat Preah Vihear was the scene of heaving fighting as recently as 1998 and numerous land mines were used by the Khmer Rouge to defend this strategic location against government forces. Do not stray from marked paths during a visit to this temple, as several locals have been killed or maimed in recent year.

Getting There & Away

The easy way to get to Prasat Preah Vihear is from Thailand, as there are paved roads right up to the back door. Anyone coming from Thailand will no doubt be armed with a copy of Lonely Planet *Thailand,* which contains all the details for this route. However, this is a guidebook about Cambodia and getting here from the Cambodia side is a unique and challenging experience, a hardcore adventure. The struggle outlined here may soon become unnecessary, as the Cambodian government is in the process of building roads here from Anlong Veng and Tbeng Meanchey. This may put Prasat Preah Vihear within four hours of Siem Reap on a good road and consign the Choam Ksant route to the history books – no bad thing perhaps, as those who have done it might agree.

Getting to Prasat Preah Vihear is seriously difficult and shouldn't be attempted by anyone who isn't willing to put up with misery along the way. It can only be done between December and May, as in the wet season roads are impassable in this part of the country. It can just about be done in a round trip of three full days from Phnom Penh, with two overnight stays in Choam Ksant, but this requires a 6am start every day and 12 hours on the road. More realistic is a five-day journey with overnights in Tbeng Meanchey or Kompong Thom on the way to and from Choam Ksant. For the depressing story on how to get to Choam Ksant via Tbeng Meanchey, see the Tbeng Meanchey section earlier in this chapter.

From Choam Ksant to Prasat Preah Vihear is a harsh journey but it can be done in one long day. The sandy ox-cart trails are hard to determine, so take a local moto driver who knows the way. It takes about three hours to get to the base of Chuor Phnom Dangkrek. There is an army post at the bottom, which may be heavily reinforced by now thanks to the ongoing temple tensions between Cambodia and Thailand. From the army post, it is necessary to leave the motorbike and hike up the mountain. This is where the moto driver really earns his money, as much of this area is still heavily mined and it pays to be with someone who knows the safe route. The ascent takes between 1½ and two hours and requires a lot of water. There is plenty of bottled water and other drinks on sale at the temple for the return journey.

Once at the summit of the mountain, you have the satisfaction of knowing that you have undertaken a modern-day pilgrimage that is easily the equal of any undertaken at the height of the Angkorian empire. On the downside, you may also have (if the temple reopens from the Thai side) the deeply disheartening sight of hundreds of package tourists who have steamed up to the temple in air-conditioned coaches along a tarmac superhighway in Thailand – they will never know what you have been through.

All said, the round trip from Choam Ksant takes a whole day and requires as early a start as possible. Try to link-up with a moto driver who has been there before – find a guy called Borit and you'll be in safe hands – and expect to pay around US$10 for the day, plus petrol.

Eastern Cambodia

Eastern Cambodia is a vast area stretching from Laos in the north, down the long frontier of Vietnam in the east. The landscape changes from hilly forests, to dry savannah grasses, to the agricultural lowland plains that are more commonly associated with Cambodia. The Mekong River and its minor tributaries pass through this densely populated agricultural area, which often floods in the wet season. For much of the eastern region the massive Mekong and its tributaries form the main transport routes and are a basis for the livelihood of many people.

In the 1960s Vietnamese communist forces sought sanctuary in eastern Cambodia to escape the fire power of the American army and much of the area was heavily under the influence of the Vietnamese. Prince Sihanouk became increasingly anti-American as the 1960s progressed and cut a deal to tacitly allow this to continue, as well as suppling the Vietnamese communists with weapons from the Chinese, via the port of Sihanoukville. By the end of the decade, as the USA began its bombing raids and incursions, the Vietnamese communists had moved deep into the country. Following the overthrow of Sihanouk, Lon Nol demanded that all Vietnamese communist forces withdraw from Cambodia within 48 hours, an ultimatum they could not possibly accept, and open war erupted. In just a few months, much of the region fell to the Vietnamese communists and their Khmer Rouge allies.

During the rule of the Khmer Rouge, the eastern zones were known to be more moderate than elsewhere in the country and it wasn't until 1977 that Pol Pot and the central government tried to impose their will on the east. Militarily, eastern Cambodia was independent and strong, and the centre's crackdown provoked what amounted to a civil war between Khmer Rouge factions. This tussle lingered until December 1978, when the Vietnamese invasion sent the Khmer Rouge leadership fleeing to the Thai border. It became one of the safest areas of

Highlights

- Sight rare freshwater dolphins in the Mekong River near Kratie.

- Escape to the rolling hills of remote Mondulkiri, home to many of Cambodia's ethnic minorities.

- Plunge into Boeng Yeak Lom, the best swimming pool in the country, with its crystal-clear water and lush jungle surrounds.

- Hitch a ride on an elephant in the northeast, the local form of transport for the hill tribes.

the country during much of the 1980s, as the Khmer Rouge kept well away from areas near the Vietnamese border.

Eastern Cambodia is one of the most inaccessible parts of the country and conditions vary widely between wet and dry seasons. Northeastern Cambodia is the country's wild east, home to many ethnic minority groups known as Khmer Loeu (Upper Khmer) or *chunchiet* (ethnic minorities). Illegal logging is also a major problem in provinces of the northeast, and has replaced rubber as the most important industry in the region.

EASTERN CAMBODIA

THAILAND

LAOS

Choam Ksant

Kulen Prum Tep
Wildlife Sanctuary

PREAH
VIHEAR

Kulen

Tbeng Meanchey   Chaeb

Phnom
Dek   Rovieng

64

Mekong River

Muang Khong   Hat Xai Khun
Nakasong

Dom Kralor

Ko Chheuteal
Thom

Thala Boravit

Stung Treng

Siem Pang

Virachay National Park

Voen Sai   Kachon   Ta Veng

RATANAKIRI
78A

Ban Lung
Boeng Yeak   Bokheo
Lom

78

Lumphat

STUNG
TRENG

Tonlé Kong

Tonlé San

Srepok

KOMPONG
THOM

Kompong Thom

6

Lumphat
Wildlife
Sanctuary

Koh Nhek

7

KRATIE

Sambor
Sandan
Kampi

Kratie

MONDULKIRI

Phnom Prech
Wildlife Sanctuary

Phnom Namlier
Wildlife
Sanctuary

Phulung   Bou Sraa
Waterfall

Sen Monorom
Putang   Dak Dam
Waterfall

Romanear
Waterfall

Tonlé Sap
River

Baray

Kompong
Chhnang

5

Spoe Tbong

Phnom Pros &
Phnom Srei

71

Stung
Trang   Wat
Handchey

Mekong   River

Chhlong

Snuol
Wildlife
Sanctuary

76

Khao Si Ma

Skuon

Prasat Kuk
Yeay Hom

7

KOMPONG
CHAM

73

Snuol

7

Kompong Cham
Suong

Bridge

Chub
Krau   Prey
Nokor

Memot

Udong

Prek
Kdam
Ferry

6

PHNOM
PENH

Takhmau

11

Prey Veng

PREY
VENG

Tay Ninh

VIETNAM

KANDAL

3

2

Neak
Luong
Ferry

Tonlé Bassac

Kompong Suong

Kaam
Samnor

Ba Phnom

SVAY
RIENG

Svay Rieng

Chiphu

Bavet

Moc
Bai
Border
Crossing

Takeo

TAKEO

Tani

Vinh Xuong

Chau Doc

Mekong River

HO CHI MINH CITY
(SAIGON)

0   25   50km
0   15   30mi

Due to its inaccessibility, tourists tend to pass through eastern Cambodia when travelling between Phnom Penh and Ho Chi Minh City (Saigon), but rarely spend much time here. However, much of the east is well worth the effort, with a distinctly different feel from the rest of the country. The provinces of Mondulkiri and Ratanakiri, best visited from November to March, are home to some of Cambodia's most beautiful landscapes, as well as tigers, leopards, elephants and possibly rhinoceroses. *Kouprey* (an extremely rare wild ox; also the country's national symbol) can be found in the region. On the stretch of the Mekong River between Kratie and Stung Treng, live the remaining freshwater Irrawaddy dolphins.

As overland travel opens up in Cambodia, it is possible to reach many of the more remote provinces by a combination of boat and road travel. A round trip from Phnom Penh to Ratanakiri by land can take as little as one week (if you set a fast pace). Mondulkiri is more straightforward and, with good connections, a round trip can be done in five days, but be aware that you can sometimes be stranded in the wet season.

Svay Rieng Province

ខេត្តស្វាយរៀង

This small province occupies a jut of land sticking into Vietnam, an area known as the parrot's beak. During the Vietnam War, this area became an obsession with the American forces, as they believed that this was where the Vietnamese communists' version of the Pentagon was situated. While there were undoubtedly a lot of Vietnamese communists hiding out in Cambodia during much of the war, there was no such thing as a Pentagon. In 1969 the Americans began unauthorised bombing in this area and in 1970 joined forces with South Vietnamese forces and launched a ground assault.

Svay Rieng is considered one of Cambodia's poorest provinces because of the poor quality of its land. Most of the population eke out a subsistence living based on farming and fishing. There is really nothing to attract visitors, but the provincial capital, Svay Rieng, is a typical Cambodian town with some charm. National Hwy 1 (NH1), which passes right through the heart of the province, is being comprehensively rebuilt to smooth the journey between Phnom Penh and Ho Chi Minh City, but elsewhere the roads are poor.

SVAY RIENG
ស្វាយរៀង
☎ 044 • pop 21,000

Svay Rieng is the quiet provincial capital that many travellers zoom through when making the journey between Phnom Penh and Ho Chi Minh City. It is much like Cambodia's other sleepy towns, but if you feel the urge to recharge the batteries, this is the most convenient place to do it. Winding its way through town is Tonlé Wayko, a tributary of the Mekong.

Information
This is another town where cash is king, so come with US dollars or riel. Acleda Bank (☎ 945545), a few blocks west of the Independence Monument, represents Western Union if you need a money transfer.

Places to Stay
At the budget end, there are several guesthouses to choose from with pretty basic rooms for US$4 to US$5 per night. **Santepheap Guesthouse**, **Samaki Guesthouse** and **Guesthouse Sopheak Mongkol** are all clustered around a junction in the centre of town, just a few hundred metres west of the Independence Monument. There is really nothing to choose between them and all have the same small rooms with bathroom.

Khmean Kangval Guesthouse Rooms with fan/air-con & bathroom US$7/10. Located to the right at the fork on the road to Phnom Penh, this guesthouse has clean and comfortable rooms.

There are two fully fledged hotels in town that offer air-con, satellite TV and

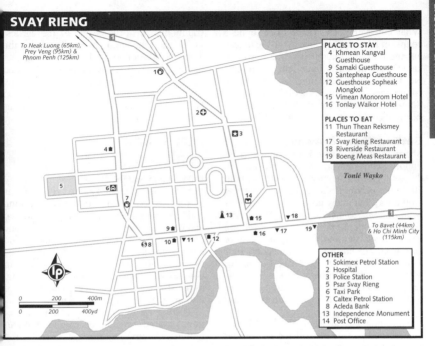

SVAY RIENG

To Neak Luong (65km),
Prey Veng (95km) &
Phnom Penh (125km)

Tonlé Wayko

To Bavet (44km)
& Ho Chi Minh City
(115km)

PLACES TO STAY
4 Khmean Kangval
  Guesthouse
9 Samaki Guesthouse
10 Santepheap Guesthouse
12 Guesthouse Sopheak
  Mongkol
15 Vimean Monorom Hotel
16 Tonlay Waikor Hotel

PLACES TO EAT
11 Thun Thean Reksmey
  Restaurant
17 Svay Rieng Restaurant
18 Riverside Restaurant
19 Boeng Meas Restaurant

OTHER
1 Sokimex Petrol Station
2 Hospital
3 Police Station
5 Psar Svay Rieng
6 Taxi Park
7 Caltex Petrol Station
8 Acleda Bank
13 Independence Monument
14 Post Office

0 200 400m
0 200 400yd

---

bathroom, both overlooking the Independence Monument:

Vimean Monorom Hotel (☎ 945817) Rooms with fan/air-con US$5/10. This place has a touch of the Soviet about its exterior, but the rooms are large and comfortable. This is very much a karaoke love-emporium, however, so don't be surprised to see the lobby full of heavily made-up Vietnamese girls by night.

Tonlay Waikor Hotel (☎ 945718) Singles/doubles with air-con US$15/20. This huge hotel has carpeted rooms with bathroom, but the price seems a little high compared with elsewhere around town. It's owned by the National Police Chief, which may explain why the management are unwilling to discount the rooms, even when the hotel is clearly crying out for customers.

Places to Eat

There are cheap **food stalls** around Psar Svay Rieng (Svay Rieng Market), as well as some

by the river at night. Many of Svay Rieng's restaurants double as karaoke bars by night, so pick your establishment carefully if you want to be able to hold a conversation.

Riverside Restaurant *(NH1)* Mains 3000r. The name is a little misleading, as this restaurant has moved from the riverfront to NH1. There is an English menu and the food is very reasonably priced.

Boeng Meas Restaurant Mains 3000-5000r. Built on stilts near the riverside, this eatery is considered by many Khmers to be the best in town. It is an inexpensive place for breakfast and a coffee recharge.

Svay Rieng Restaurant This is a hole-in-the-wall place that draws a reasonable breakfast and lunch crowd – popular with locals for its soups.

Thun Thean Reksmey Restaurant This place was closed at the time of writing but there were signs that this once very good restaurant would reopen. If it does, check it out for tasty food.

Entertainment

What entertainment? There used to be a couple of Khmer nightclubs in the big hotels, but these have succumbed to the power of karaoke. Both hotels have karaoke rooms, but these seem to be as much about meeting commercial sex workers as singing songs. Some of the riverfront stalls have beer for sale and could be nice for a quiet drink.

Getting There & Away

Share taxis for Svay Rieng leave from Phnom Penh's Chbah Ampeau taxi park in the southeast of the city. The cost is about 7000r per person if you can find one going all the way, but many taxis only go as far as Neak Luong to avoid paying the US$1 charge for the ferry across the Mekong River. It is easier and more comfortable to take an air-con bus from Phnom Penh's Psar Thmei (New Market) to Neak Luong for 4000r, cross the river by ferry as a foot passenger (100r) and arrange a share taxi on to Svay Rieng from the other side for about 4000r a person.

Travelling to Svay Rieng from Bavet (on the Cambodian side of the Moc Bai border crossing) may be more difficult because taxi drivers simply won't believe you want to go there and generally prefer to wait for the more lucrative option of taking foreigners all the way to Phnom Penh. The best plan may be to stuff yourself into a taxi with some other tourists and ask to be dropped off at Svay Rieng (US$1 to US$2). Taxis usually drop people off near Psar Svay Rieng.

Prey Veng Province

ខេត្តព្រៃវែង

Prey Veng means 'Long Forest', but it's a long time since there was any forest in this province. It is a small but heavily populated agricultural province nestled on the east bank of the Mekong. Rubber played a large part in Prey Veng's prewar economy, but most of the plantations are no longer commercially viable. There is little of significance to be seen in the province today, but it may have played a significant role in Cambodian history, as one of the earliest pre-Angkorian kingdoms was located in the area around Ba Phnom. It is a province that has experienced few visitors and the road network does not serve to encourage more. The provincial capital is hidden away on NH11, a broken road that is regularly inundated in the wet season.

PREY VENG

ព្រៃវែង

☎ 043 • pop 55,000

Very few travellers make it to Prey Veng, as it is located on NH11 between Neak Luong and Kompong Cham, not really a road that visitors need ever use. It is undoubtedly one of the sleepiest backwaters in Cambodia and most of the population is tucked up in bed by 9pm. Those who want to get away from other tourists may enjoy a visit to Prey Veng, as it offers an alternative route between Phnom Penh and Kompong Cham.

There are a few decaying colonial structures around town, attesting to a once-important centre. During most of the year a vast lake marks the western edge of town, but from March to August this evaporates and the local farmers cultivate rice.

Information

Come with US dollars or riel as other currencies are not so popular around here. Acleda Bank (☎ 944555) is the representative for Western Union for those needing quick transfers. The main post office is in the centre of town opposite Wat Sam Samay.

Things to See & Do

In short, not a lot. There is a small **museum** in the middle of town, but it's locked up for most of the year. Don't be put off, however, as it is so small that you can see everything it has to offer by peeping through the window.

There are several attractive **wats** around town, each of which boasts a tremendous longboat. Prey Vengers travel to Phnom Penh in November each year to celebrate the Bon Om Tuk water festival.

PREY VENG

PLACES TO STAY & EAT
2 Rorg Damrey Hotel
4 Kessor Hotel
7 Bopha Vimean Suor Hotel
10 Mittapheap Hotel
11 Mittapheap Restaurant
20 Chong Pam Motel

To Kompong Cham (78km)

OTHER
1 Wat Roung Damrey
3 Olympic Stadium
5 Boats to Phnom Penh
6 Psar Prey Veng
8 Tela Petrol Station
9 Police Station
12 Wat Sam Samay
13 Post Office
14 Hospital
15 Wat Sovann Rengsay
16 Acleda Bank
17 Museum
18 Tourism Office
19 Former Governor's Residence (Proposed Hotel)

Submerged During Wet Season (July–February)

To Neak Luong (30km) & Phnom Penh (90km)

0   100   200m
0   100   200yd

Places to Stay & Eat

Most of Prey Veng's hotels double as knocking-shops at night.

Kessor Hotel Rooms with fan/air-con & bathroom US$5/10. This place has basic rooms, some with a waterfront view.

Chong Pam Motel Rooms with bathroom US$5. This hotel has a nice location on the edge of the lake and most of the basic rooms come with a view. However, it could get whiffy when the waters recede.

Mittapheap Hotel Rooms with fan/air-con & bathroom US$5/10. This is one of the best places to stay, with a convenient location and clean rooms. It's on the central crossroads on the road to Kompong Cham.

Bopha Vimean Suor Hotel (☎ 348878) Rooms with fan/air-con US$5/10. This place is in it for the money and not among the best choices in town.

Rorg Damrey Hotel Rooms US$5, with fan/air-con US$10/12. Tucked away in the northeastern corner of town behind the Olympic stadium, this is a clean, comfortable establishment with nice rooms, although watch out for the low doors in some of them.

Apart from the **food stalls** around Psar Prey Veng (Prey Veng Market) and a couple of basic holes-in-the-wall, there is only one real restaurant in town:

Mittapheap Restaurant Dishes 3000-4000r. Across the road from the Mittapheap Hotel, this restaurant is a friendly, fun place with inexpensive Khmer and Vietnamese food.

Getting There & Away

Prey Veng is 90km east of Phnom Penh and 78km south of Kompong Cham. During the floods of 2000 and 2001, the road from Prey Veng to Neak Luong was cut off to all vehicles except motorbikes from August to November, so cars could only come in from Phnom Penh via Kompong Cham. Normally, the easiest way to get here from the capital is to take an air-con Ho Wah Genting bus from Psar Thmei to Neak Luong for 4000r, cross on the ferry as a foot passenger (100r) and arrange a seat in a share taxi to Prey Veng for about 3000r. Minibuses and share taxis operate between Prey Veng and Kompong Cham for about 4000r and 6000r respectively.

Getting here by motorbike is reasonably straightforward in the dry season, but should only be undertaken by experienced riders in the wet season. The road from Neak Luong to Prey Veng is in poor condition, while the road from Prey Veng to Kompong Cham can get pretty messy through the rubber plantations.

During the wet season, fast boats (10,000r, two hours) and slow boats (6000r, four hours) run between Prey Veng and Phnom Penh. Check the departure times the day before, as the schedule changes.

NEAK LUONG
អ្នកលឿង

Neak Luong is the point at which travellers speeding between Phnom Penh and the Vietnamese border have to slow to a stop to cross the mighty Mekong River. The car ferry chugs back and forth giving children ample time to try to sell you strange looking insects and other unidentifiable food on sticks. The first bridge to span the Mekong's girth in Cambodia was recently opened at Kompong Cham. The second is likely to be built here at Neak Luong some time in the second half of the decade.

Neak Luong rates a mention as one of the locations depicted in *The Killing Fields*. In August 1973, American B-52s mistakenly razed it to the ground in an attempt to halt a Khmer Rouge advance on Phnom Penh. The intensive bombardment killed 137 civilians and wounded 268. The US government tried to cover it up by keeping the media out, but Sydney Schanberg, played by Sam Waterstone in the film, managed to travel to the city by river and publicise the true scale of the tragedy. The US ambassador offered compensation of US$100 per family and the navigator of the B-52 was fined US$700, which pretty much summed

up the American attitude to the price of Cambodian lives in this most miserable of sideshows.

The most straightforward way to get here is to take an air-con bus (4000r) from Psar Thmei in Phnom Penh and pay the foot passenger toll (100r) to cross the Mekong on the ferry. From Neak Luong, it is possible to continue east to Svay Rieng (64km), north to Prey Veng (30km) or south to Kaam Samnor and the Mekong Delta – for more on the route between Phnom Penh and Chau Doc see the Getting There & Away chapter earlier in this book.

BA PHNOM
បាភ្នំ

Ba Phnom is one of the earliest religious and cultural sites in the Kingdom of Cambodia, dating back to the 5th century and the time of the mysterious Funan. Some scholars consider it a birthplace of the Cambodian nation, in the same way that Phnom Kulen is revered as the first capital of Angkor. It remained an important place of pilgrimage for kings of the subsequent empires of Chenla and Angkor and continued to be a place of spiritual significance into the 19th century, but its past conceals a darker side of human sacrifice. According to French records, human sacrifices continued into the protectorate and were only finally stamped out in 1872.

Today there is little left to see considering the site's extensive history. At the eastern extremity of the small group of hills lie the kitsch ruins of an 11th-century temple known as **Preah Vihear Chann**. The temple was evidently destroyed by the ravages of time, but has been rebuilt by the local monastery using a few original blocks and a whole lot of cement, all set under a corrugated roof.

There is a modern **wat** at the base of the hill and a series of concrete steps lead up the slope to some small **pagodas** on the summit. It is only really worth the detour for those who have a keen interest in early Cambodian history, as for the casual visitor there is unfortunately little to see.

Getting There & Away

To get to Ba Phnom from Phnom Penh, head east on NH1 and turn north at Kompong Suong, just over 9km east of Neak Luong. Follow this dirt road for 3km before turning right and bearing east along the base of the hill. After another 7km, turn left under a wat-style arch and head to the bottom of the hill. Those without wheels can engage the services of a *moto* (small motorcycle with driver) in Neak Luong for about US$4 for the round trip. It may be cheaper to take two *remorque-moto* (trailers pulled by motorcycles), first from Neak Luong to Kompong Suong, then from there to Ba Phnom. This should cost about 1000r for each sector, making a round-trip total of 4000r, but will require a bit of walking from Ba Phnom village to the foot of the hill, and a lot more time.

Kompong Cham Province

ខេត្តកំពង់ចាម

The most heavily populated province in Cambodia, Kompong Cham has also supplied a steady stream of Cambodia's current political elite including Prime Minister Hun Sen, Senate Head Chea Sim and Phnom Penh mayor Chea Sophara. Most Kompong Cham residents have quieter lives, living off the land or fishing along the Mekong River. Rubber was the major prewar industry and there are huge plantations stretching eastwards from the Mekong. Some of these are being redeveloped for industrial use and there are even encouraging signs of young saplings being planted around Memot. Some of Cambodia's finest silk is also produced in this province and most of the country's *krama* (scarves) originate here.

Kompong Cham Province draws a fair number of visitors thanks to its role as a gateway to the northeast. Attractions include several pre-Angkorian and Angkorian temples, as well as some pleasant riverbank rides for cyclists or bikers. Getting about has became a lot easier thanks to the excellent condition of NH7 as far as the provincial capital. East of the Mekong used to be an almighty mess, but the road is being completely rebuilt and widened. Beyond the main roads, travel is not too bad, as the large population has helped to prioritise tertiary road improvements.

KOMPONG CHAM
កំពង់ចាម

☎ 042 • pop 46,000

Cambodia's third-largest city, little more than a quiet town in fact, is a peaceful provincial capital spread along the banks of the Mekong River. It was an important trading post during the French period, the legacy evident as you wander through the streets of bruised yet beautiful buildings. Kompong Cham is an important travel hub for road and river and acts as a gateway to eastern and northeastern Cambodia. This role is set to expand with the completion of a Japanese-financed bridge across the Mekong, the first in Cambodia to span the river's width. The bridge will form a crucial link in a major highway between Bangkok and Ho Chi Minh City.

Orientation

Kompong Cham may be Cambodia's third-largest city, but that doesn't make it very big. Navigating on foot is pretty straightforward. Arriving from Phnom Penh, all roads east end up at the Mekong River, near many of the guesthouses and hotels. The market is a few blocks west of the river.

Information

Canadia Bank (☎ 941361), located on Preah Monivong Blvd, can cash travellers cheques in various currencies, perform foreign-currency exchange and Moneygram transfers. Acleda Bank (☎ 941703) represents Western Union for quick transfers.

Internet access is now available with ABC Computer (☎ 941477), at 11 Ph Ang Duong, but requires an expensive telephone connection that costs US$6 an hour.

Vannat is a good local guide, and if you sip an evening drink overlooking the Mekong,

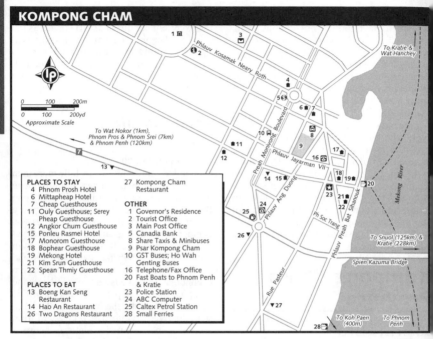

KOMPONG CHAM

PLACES TO STAY
4 Phnom Prosh Hotel
6 Mittapheap Hotel
7 Cheap Guesthouses
11 Ouly Guesthouse; Serey Pheap Guesthouse
12 Angkor Chum Guesthouse
15 Ponleu Rasmei Hotel
17 Monorom Guesthouse
18 Bophear Guesthouse
19 Mekong Hotel
21 Kim Srun Guesthouse
22 Spean Thmiy Guesthouse

PLACES TO EAT
13 Boeng Kan Seng Restaurant
14 Hao An Restaurant
26 Two Dragons Restaurant

27 Kompong Cham Restaurant

OTHER
1 Governor's Residence
2 Tourist Office
3 Main Post Office
5 Canadia Bank
8 Share Taxis & Minibuses
9 Psar Kompong Cham
10 GST Buses; Ho Wah Genting Buses
16 Telephone/Fax Office
20 Fast Boats to Phnom Penh & Kratie
23 Police Station
24 ABC Computer
25 Caltex Petrol Station
28 Small Ferries

he'll likely find you before long. He speaks English and French.

Wat Nokor
វត្តនគរ

Just outside town is an 11th-century Mahayana Buddhist shrine of sandstone and laterite, which today houses an active Theravada wat. It is a kitsch kind of place, as it is really a temple within a temple and many of the older building's archways have been incorporated into the new building as shrines for worship. On weekdays, there are only a few monks in the complex and it is peaceful to wander among the many alcoves and their hidden shrines. There is also a large reclining Buddha.

To get here, head out of town on the road to Phnom Penh, and take the left fork at the large roundabout about 1km from the centre of town. The temple is at the end of this dirt road.

Koh Paen
កោះប៉ែន

Koh Paen is a rural island in the Mekong river, connected to the southern reaches of Kompong Thom town by an elaborate bamboo bridge in the dry season or a local ferry in the wet season. There are plenty of local wats on the island and locals make a living fishing, as well as growing tobacco and sesame. During the dry season, several sandbars appear around the island, the closest thing to a beach in this part of Cambodia. The best way to get around the island is by bicycle, which may be possible to arrange through a guesthouse.

Places to Stay

There are a fair number of cheap rooms to rent in this city, as they were originally let to Cambodian soldiers when Kompong Cham was near the frontline in the war against the Khmer Rouge. In most hotels rates can be negotiable, as few customers come their way.

One street off the market has a whole row of cheap **guesthouses** advertising rooms for 5000r, although most 'guests' seem to pay by the hour, so it could get noisy. Rooms are cells, but if money's too tight to mention, consider taking one for a night.

Most visitors prefer to stay on the riverfront, with a view over the Mekong. There are several guesthouses and a hotel here – the only drawback is the Kratie boat sounding its foghorn at an ungodly hour.

Spean Thmiy Guesthouse *(95 Ph Preah Bat Sihanouk)* Singles/twins with bathroom US$3/5. This place has a bird's-eye view of the new bridge, hardly surprising given the hotel's name means 'New Bridge'. The US$3 rooms with bathroom are good value and there is a nice outdoor veranda.

Kim Srun Guesthouse *(☎ 941507, 81 Ph Preah Bat Sihanouk)* Singles/doubles with bathroom US$3/5. The doubles with TV are better than the cell-like singles at this friendly guesthouse on the Mekong. Definitely no karaoke these days!

Mekong Hotel *(☎ 941536, fax 941565, Ph Preah Bat Sihanouk)* Rooms with fan & bathroom US$5, with air-con & hot water US$10. Farther north along the riverfront is this vast hotel, offering perhaps the best value in town. All rooms come with satellite TV, but remember to ask for a Mekong view. The corridors are so large, they are begging for a five-a-side football match.

Elsewhere in town are a glut of guesthouses and hotels, although for those wanting to spend US$5 and up, the hotels are much better value.

Bophear Guesthouse *(Vithei Pasteur)* Doubles with fan & bathroom US$3. This friendly, clean place, one block off the river, has huge rooms and is the best of the budget places in town.

Monorom Guesthouse *(☎ 941441)* Rooms with fan & bathroom US$5, with air-con & hot water US$10. Don't be put off by the old house at the front, as the guesthouse is in a clean, new wing at the back.

West of the market are some more guesthouses, but they lack the draw of the riverfront.

Angkor Chum Guesthouse *(108 Old NH7)* Singles/doubles with fan, TV & bathroom US$3/4. This is the cheapest of these places, with a friendly French- and English-speaking owner.

Ouly Guesthouse *(138 Old NH7)* Rooms with fan/air-con & bathroom US$5/10. Opposite the Angkor Chum, this place is overpriced when compared with the hotels in town.

Serey Pheap Guesthouse *(136 Old NH7)* Rooms with air-con & bathroom US$8. Next door to the Ouly Guesthouse, this place has slightly better-value rooms and a mini-arcade in the lobby for those who are getting Playstation withdrawal symptoms.

Ponleu Rasmei Hotel *(☎ 941303, Ph Ang Duong)* Rooms with fan/air-con & bathroom US$5/10. South of the market, this hotel used to be popular with nongovernmental organisations (NGOs), but hasn't upgraded to compete with the bigger hotels in town.

Mittapheap Hotel *(☎ 941565, fax 941465)* Rooms with fan, TV & bathroom US$5, with air-con, fridge & hot water US$10. This place has the smartest rooms in town for those not so worried about overlooking the river.

Phnom Prosh Hotel *(☎/fax 941444, Ph Kosamak Neary Roth)* Rooms with fan, TV & bathroom US$5, with air-con and hot water US$10. This hotel is owned by a nephew of Samdech Hun Sen, Cambodia's prime minister. It also has the town's only nightclub, downstairs.

Places to Eat

There are several good restaurants in town and a lot of cheaper hole-in-the-wall places dotted around the market. There are a host of stop-and-dip **food stalls** in the market and a number of **tukalok stalls** (fruit smoothie stalls) near the police station.

Hao An Restaurant *(☎ 941234, Preah Monivong Blvd)* Dishes 6000-10,000r. This is an impressive-looking place with pretty reasonable prices. The service is good and there

EASTERN CAMBODIA

is always a regiment of 'beer girls' to ensure you don't go thirsty.

Kompong Cham Restaurant *(Rue Pasteur)* This place has more than 100 dishes on the menu, including Khmer, Thai and Chinese influences. Prices are reasonable and you'll usually find a number of expats dining here. The curries are particularly good.

Two Dragons Restaurant *(Ph Ang Duong)* Dishes US$2. This is a small, friendly, family-run restaurant with a limited menu of tasty dishes.

Boeng Kan Seng Restaurant *(NH7)* This place offers a nice location near a small lake on the outskirts of town. Some local expats rave about the shrimp in batter with sweet chilli sauce, others more likely the myriad 'beer girls'.

Entertainment

Locals and expats gather on the waterfront outside the Mekong Hotel, where a number of stalls sell cheap drinks and cold beers in the evening.

Leave the platform heels in the capital, as the only nightclub in town is the extremely provincial **Phnom Prosh Nightclub** in the Phnom Prosh Hotel. However, with the demise of nightclubs in many other parts of Cambodia, it makes a good place to shape up on Khmer dancing if your moves are getting a little rusty.

Getting There & Away

Kompong Cham is 120km northeast of Phnom Penh and the road is one of the best in the country. Ho Wah Genting and GST offer regular air-con bus services between Kompong Cham and the capital (7000r, two hours, eight per day in either direction). Overcrowded minibuses also do the run (5000r).

NH7 to Kratie is in pretty miserable condition, but being entirely renovated. Pickups do the run for about 25,000/15,000r inside/on the back. For more details on road routes, see the Snuol and Kratie sections later in this chapter.

Few people use the fast boat to Phnom Penh these days, as the bus service is cheaper. However, the boats heading south from Kratie pass through at 9.30am (10,000r, 2½ hours), while those heading north leave Phnom Penh at 7am. There are several services a day to Kratie (20,000r, three hours) leaving from in front of the Mekong Hotel at about 6.30am, 9.30am and 1pm. There are also slower boats up to Kratie (10,000r, four hours), one of which leaves at 9am. A host of slow boats and ferries make sporadic runs as well. Travel is slow (it takes pretty much all day) and departures infrequent, but it's cheap: to Phnom Penh or Kratie the fare is as little as 5000r.

Between July and January, boats continue up to Stung Treng (fast boats 45,000r, six to seven hours; slow boats 25,000r, two days and one night). If you are intent on getting a slow boat, you're best to board at Kratie to save some time.

Getting Around

Most moto journeys around town are only 500r to 1000r, a little more at night. Bicycles or motorcycles may be arranged through negotiations with your guesthouse or hotel.

AROUND KOMPONG CHAM
Phnom Pros & Phnom Srei
ភ្នំប្រុសភ្នំស្រី

Phnom Pros and Phnom Srei translate as 'Man Hill' and 'Woman Hill' respectively. Local legend has it that two teams, one of men and the other of women, toiled by night to be the first to construct a stupa on the summit of their hill by daybreak. The women built a big fire, which the men took to be the rising sun and gave up work. The women, having won, no longer had to ask for the man's hand in marriage which had previously been the tradition. Phnom Srei has good views of the countryside during the wet season. Phnom Pros is an interesting place for a cold drink, as a band of inquisitive monkeys populate the trees.

The hills are about 7km out of town on the road to Phnom Penh and can be reached by moto for about US$2 (round trip) depending on wait time.

Wat Hanchey
វត្តហានជ័យ

Wat Hanchey is a hilltop pagoda that was an important centre of worship during the Chenla period, and today offers some of the best Mekong views in Cambodia. As well as a large, contemporary wat, there is a brick sanctuary dating from the 8th century and the foundations of several others. During the time of the Chenla empire, this may have been an important transit stop on journeys between the ancient cities of Thala Boravit (Stung Treng) and Angkor Borei (Takeo); and Sambor Prei Kuk (Kompong Thom) and Banteay Prei Nokor (Kompong Cham).

The simplest way to get to Wat Hanchey is to charter an outboard from outside the Mekong Hotel in Kompong Cham. Boats with a 15hp engine cost around 40,000r, while faster boats with a 40hp engine are 50,000r. Solo travellers who want to save money can jump on the fast boat to Kratie at 6.30am and ask to be let off here (5000r, 30 minutes). After sniffing around for a while, walk south to the village and jump on the Kompong Cham fast boat when it passes through from Kratie at around 9am.

Local expats like to cycle up here in the dry season through the pretty riverbank villages. If you can get your hands on a bicycle, this might be a good way to pass a day.

Rubber Plantations
ចំការកៅស៊ូ

Kompong Cham was the heartland of the Cambodian rubber industry and rubber plantations stretch across the province. Many of these are no longer commercially tapped, but tapped by locals for a variety of uses. However, some of the largest plantations remain active and can be visited by interested groups, usually French tourists on a tour of their colonial past. The most commonly visited is **Chup Rubber Plantation** (NH7), a large plantation in Tbong Khmom district, about 15km east of Kompong Cham.

Prasat Kuk Yeay Hom
ប្រាសាទគុកយាយហាម

This is a ruined Angkorian structure (NH7) languishing in the rice paddies of Kompong Cham, forgotten by all but the most slavish of temple devotees. Locals suggest it was damaged during the US bombing campaign of the early 1970s. Not exactly a regional highlight, it is about 7km from Prey Chor between Skuon and Kompong Cham. Local moto drivers can guide visitors after they abandon the bus in Prey Chor.

MEMOT
មេមត់

Pronounced more like may-**moot**, this is a surprisingly large town set amid the rubber plantations of eastern Kompong Cham Province. It sees very few visitors, as there is little of interest here unless you happen to work for Michelin. However, some travellers may find themselves stuck here during the height of the wet season when travelling between Phnom Penh and Mondulkiri or Kratie. There are a couple of very basic **guesthouses** and some good local **restaurants** near the market.

Pick-ups from Memot to Kompong Cham cost 7000/4000r inside/on the back; taxis charge 8000r. From Memot to Snuol is the same price for a much shorter distance, as the road is a horrible mess for now. Many drivers avoid it altogether by heading cross-country to link up with the logging road between Chhlong and Snuol, referred to as Phlau Chen (Chinese Road) by locals.

Kratie Province
ខេត្តក្រចេះ

Kratie is a heavily forested province spanning the Mekong River, whose banks are home to most of the province's population. Beyond the mighty river, it is a remote and wild area that has seen few outsiders. This was one of the first areas to fall to Khmer Rouge control in the civil war, although for

The Eight-Legged Food Routine

Locals in the small Cambodian town of Skuon (otherwise known affectionately as Spiderville) eat eight-legged furry friends for breakfast, lunch and dinner. Most tourists travelling between Siem Reap and Phnom Penh pass through Skuon without ever realising they have been there. This is hardly surprising, as it has nothing much to attract visitors, but it is the centre of one of Cambodia's more exotic culinary delights – the deep-fried spider.

Pick-up trucks usually pause in Spiderville, so take a careful look at the goodies the food sellers are offering. The creatures, decidedly dead, are piled high on platters, but don't get too cocky, there are usually live samples lurking nearby.

The spiders are bred in holes in the ground in villages way north of Skuon and are quite an interesting dining experience. They are best treated like a crab and eaten by cracking the body open and pulling the legs off one by one, bringing the juiciest flesh out with them – a cathartic experience indeed. They taste a bit like…mmm chicken – well doesn't everything new and exotic? Alternatively, for a memorable photo, just bite the thing in half and hope for the best. Watch out for the abdomen, which seems to be filled with some

KATE NOLAN

pretty nasty-tasting brown sludge, which could be anything from eggs to excrement.

No-one seems to know exactly how this micro-industry developed around Skuon, although some have suggested that the population may have developed a taste for these creatures during the years of Khmer Rouge rule, when food was in short supply.

several years it was in fact the Vietnamese communists running the show. The port of Chhlong in southwest Kratie somehow held out against the surrounding communists until 1975, probably a useful way for the Khmer Rouge to acquire arms from the Lon Nol military. It was also one of the first provincial capitals to fall to the liberating Vietnamese forces in the overthrow of the Khmer Rouge on 30 December 1978.

Most visitors focus on the rare freshwater dolphins found 15km north of the provincial capital, and for good reason, as other attractions are thin on the ground. However, the town of Kratie is a charming little place and makes a good base to check out the surrounding countryside. Getting about is generally easier by boat than by road, as most roads in the province are pretty horrible. Currently, the appalling NH7, running right through the centre of Kratie, is being entirely reconstructed; this is very good news for anyone who remembers the old road. The

long haul north to Stung Treng is still not earmarked for overhaul and remains a truly nasty piece of work. The major highway from Chhlong to Snuol and on to Mondulkiri Province is in fairly good condition though.

KRATIE

ក្រចេះ

☎ 072 • pop 79,000

This compact, but populous riverside town, pronounced kra-**cheh**, is well preserved as it was spared war time bombing and was one of the first towns to be 'liberated' by the Khmer Rouge (actually the North Vietnamese, but the Khmer Rouge later claimed the credit) in the summer of 1970. There are some dramatic sunsets over the Mekong and some very old Khmer houses on the northern reaches of Rue Preah Sihanouk. Kratie is the best place in the country to see the rare Irrawaddy dolphins, which inhabit the Mekong River in ever-diminishing numbers. It also

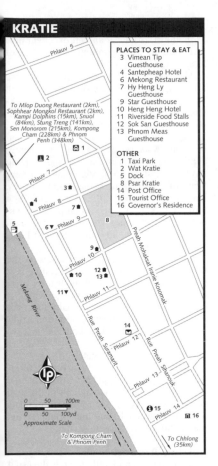

KRATIE

PLACES TO STAY & EAT
3 Vimean Tip
   Guesthouse
4 Santepheap Hotel
6 Mekong Restaurant
7 Hy Heng Ly
   Guesthouse
9 Star Guesthouse
10 Heng Heng Hotel
11 Riverside Food Stalls
12 Sok San Guesthouse
13 Phnom Meas
   Guesthouse

OTHER
1 Taxi Park
2 Wat Kratie
5 Dock
8 Psar Kratie
14 Post Office
15 Tourist Office
16 Governor's Residence

To Mlop Duong Restaurant (2km),
Sophhear Mongkol Restaurant (2km),
Kampi Dolphins (15km), Snuol
(84km), Stung Treng (141km),
Sen Monorom (215km), Kompong
Cham (228km) & Phnom
Penh (348km)

Phlauv 5
Phlauv 7
Phlauv 8
Phlauv 9
Phlauv 10
Phlauv 11
Phlauv 12
Phlauv 13
Phlauv 14

Mekong River

Preah Mohaksat Iranie Kosomak
Rue Preah Suramarit
Rue Preah Sihanouk

0   50   100m
0   50   100yd
Approximate Scale

To Kompong Cham
& Phnom Penh

To Chhlong
(35km)

makes for a handy overnight stop on the land route to Ratanakiri or an alternative stop on the way to or from Mondulkiri Province.

Information

There are no banks in town, so carry cash. Telephone services are available at kiosks around the market, but there is no Internet access as yet.

There is a tourist office by the river in the south of town, but for general information on getting around the province, the Star Guesthouse is hard to beat. For a humorous look at Kratie up close and personal, pick up a copy of *Plumbing the Depths of Kratie – A Wet Season Guide* by Zenia Davies for US$1.

For information on the dolphins, see the 'Dolphin Watching Around Kratie' boxed text later in this chapter.

Places to Stay

The cheapest places to stay in Kratie are the guesthouses along Rue Preah Sihanouk near the market.

Star Guesthouse (☎ 971663) Singles with bathroom from US$2, doubles with bathroom & balcony US$5. Setting the pace in Kratie, this friendly guesthouse has a good selection of rooms at bargain prices. The young staff all speak excellent English and the small restaurant here turns out tasty and inexpensive food. It is hard to countenance the other cheap deals in town unless you particularly want to avoid your fellow travellers.

Sok San Guesthouse Rooms with squat toilet & TV US$4. This place is the best of the rest and is cleaner than the neighbouring Phnom Meas Guesthouse and brighter than Vimean Tip Guesthouse.

Phnom Meas Guesthouse Rooms with/ without TV US$4/3. All rooms here have bathrooms, although there's little to set it apart from the competition.

Vimean Tip Guesthouse Rooms with/ without bathroom 10,000/7000r. This place is dark and gloomy with basic rooms.

Hy Heng Ly Guesthouse Rooms without bathroom 7000r, large rooms with bathroom US$3. Opposite the market, this is another cheapie that might be worth considering if the Star is packed out.

Heng Heng Hotel (☎ 971405) Rooms with fan/air-con, TV & bathroom US$5/12. Formerly a guesthouse, this place has upgraded and now has comfortable riverfront rooms.

Santepheap Hotel (☎ 971537) Rear doubles with fan & bathroom US$5, main-building doubles with air-con, TV & hot water US$15. The most comfortable hotel in town, this is the place to stay if you crave the luxuries of hot water and CNN.

Places to Eat

Aside from the restaurants at **Star Guesthouse** and the **Heng Heng Hotel**, there is not a whole lot of choice in town. Cheap dining can be had on the riverfront during the evening when **food stalls** set up shop overlooking the Mekong. By day, the market has the usual range of cheap food stalls hawking Cambodian, Chinese and Vietnamese dishes for next to nothing.

Mekong Restaurant Dishes 4000r. Arguably the best place in town for a bite, this place has an English menu with a fair range of local food, as well as some good interpretations of *barang* (foreigner) favourites such as french fries.

There are a couple of large garden restaurants on the road down to Phnom Penh, the **Mlop Duong Restaurant** and the **Sophear Mongkol Restaurant**. Local expat consensus is that the service is slow to the point of indifferent and that was certainly our experience with about an hour passing between each dish – perhaps they thought we were French? These places may be worth a look at the weekend, as they fill up with Khmers on family nights out.

Getting There & Away

NH7 puts Kratie 348km northeast of Phnom Penh and 141km south of Stung Treng. The roads linking Kratie to the outside world are in a shameful state, but major work is underway on all sections from Kratie to Snuol and on to Kompong Cham, which is scheduled for completion at the start of 2004. Until this is completed it really makes sense to take the boat to or from Phnom Penh or Kompong Cham and forget the road altogether.

By road from the capital it takes from seven hours to as much as 10 hours and sometimes involves a change in Kompong Cham. Between Kompong Cham and Kratie a pick-up costs 20,000/10,000r inside/on the back. All the way to Phnom Penh is 30,000/15,000r, although get to the taxi park early as it is a long old day. The road is a tragedy in places, particularly the mid-section between Kratie and Snuol and the whole lot between Snuol and Memot. However, one day there will be air-con buses plying this route and people won't know how lucky they are!

There is also a new road under construction to Chhlong, about 35km south of

Kratie, which links up to the logging road to Mondulkiri Province, and an excellent new dirt road to Suong, about 26km east of Kompong Cham on NH7.

There is a better dry-season route for those travelling by motorcycle or willing to shell out for a series of long moto rides and pick-ups. Take the river road north out of Kompong Cham as far as Stung Trang (no, not Stung Treng – that's way north of Kratie) and cross the Mekong on a small ferry before continuing up the east bank of the Mekong through Chhlong to Kratie. This is a very beautiful route through small rural villages, but can take from as little as six hours on a trail bike to up to 10 hours on public transport. Still, anything could be considered preferable to travelling along the old highway from hell.

Infinitely more sensible than roads are the fast boats to Phnom Penh (30,000r, five hours), which are a good deal, as there is no dodgy foreigner price. Boats leave Kratie at 7am and stop at Kompong Cham; there are also slower wooden boats to and from Kompong Cham (10,000r, four hours) that leave later in the morning.

For the lowdown on getting from Kratie to Mondulkiri Province, check out the Mondulkiri Province section later in this chapter.

For full and unpleasant details of the road north to Stung Treng and for details of boats running between Kratie and Stung Treng, see the Stung Treng section later.

Getting Around

A moto ride around Kratie town is the usual 500r to 1000r depending how far into the suburbs you venture. Star Guesthouse rents out motorbikes for US$6 a day with or without driver and should also be able to set visitors up with a bicycle.

AROUND KRATIE
Phnom Sombok
ភ្នំសំបុក

Phnom Sombok is a small hill with an active wat, located on the road from Kratie to Kampi. The hill offers the best views across the Mekong on this stretch of the river and a visit here can easily be combined with a trip to see the dolphins for an extra buck or so.

Sambor
សំបូរ

Sambor was the site of a thriving pre-Angkorian city during the time of Sambor Prei Kuk and the Chenla empire. Not a stone remains in the modern town of Sambor, which is locally famous for the largest **wat** in Cambodia, complete with 108 columns. Constructed on the site of a 19th-century wooden temple, the new one is something of a minor place of pilgrimage for residents of Kratie Province. To get to Sambor, follow the Stung Treng road north to Sandan, before veering left along a reasonable 10km stretch of road.

SNUOL
ស្នួល

This is a real end-of-the-earth town that some travellers find themselves stuck in when travelling upcountry during the wet season. A lot of folk end up having at least one meal here, as it is common to have to change vehicles when journeying between Mondulkiri Province and towns on the Mekong.

Mittapheap Guesthouse, just south of the market, has simple rooms for 10,000r. There are also a few small **restaurants** around town, but you will need some Khmer language skills or some vigorous pointing at the dishes around you if you hope to be fed.

Snuol is about 125km southwest of Mondulkiri Province and 135km east of

---

Dolphin-Watching Around Kratie

The freshwater Irrawaddy dolphin *(trey pisaut)*, is an endangered species throughout Asia, with shrinking numbers inhabiting stretches of the Mekong in Cambodia and Laos, and others found in isolated pockets in Bangladesh and Myanmar.

Before the civil war, locals say, Cambodia was home to as many as 1000 dolphins and their habitat included the Tonlé Sap lake. However, during the Pol Pot regime, many were hunted for their oil and their numbers have plummeted. Dynamite fishing, whereby lazy locals chuck a grenade in the river because they can't be bothered to wait around for a catch, hasn't exactly helped the dolphins' plight either.

Locals and experts alike believe there may be as many as 60 Irrawaddy dolphins left on stretches of the Mekong River north of Kratie. It is possible to see them at a place called Kampi, about 15km north of Kratie, on the road to Stung Treng. There are local motorboats available to shuttle visitors out to the middle of the river to view the dolphins at close quarters. The boat operators try to claim the price has been fixed at US$5 per person, but this is expensive com-

MARTIN HARRIS

pared with boat hire elsewhere in Cambodia; US$5 for the boat plus US$1 per person seems more reasonable. Try to encourage the boat driver to use the engine as little as possible once near the dolphins, as the noise is sure to disturb them.

Locals say the best time of year to see the dolphins is at the height of the wet season; however, with the assistance of an able boat driver, it is just as easy to spot 10 or more in the dry season. There is no particular time of day that's best suited to spotting, although early morning and late afternoon draw the most visitors.

A *moto* (small motorcycle with driver) for the 30km round trip should be around 10,000r depending on how long the driver has to wait.

Kompong Cham. It is only about 15km north of the Vietnamese border, but this crossing is not open to foreigners. Pick-ups to Sen Monorom (20,000/15,000r inside/on the back, four hours) aren't all that regular and are easier to find in the early part of the morning. Pick-ups also go to Chhlong (10,000/6000r, 1½ hours) via the logging road (known locally as Phlau Chen or Chinese Road), where the fast boats between Kompong Cham and Kratie stop. The rough trip to Kompong Cham costs 15,000r in a taxi, or 12,000/8000r in a pick-up and takes around three hours. The dubious privilege of a pick-up journey to Kratie is about 8000/6000r.

Stung Treng Province

ខេត្តស្ទឹងត្រែង

This remote province looks set to become a major commercial crossroads for trade between Cambodia, Laos, Thailand and Vietnam. Currently, it is a forgotten place, but once the roads south are finished, it will once again be plugged into the rest of the country. Much of Stung Treng's traffic travels by water, as several major rivers traverse the province, including Tonlé Kong, Tonlé San, Tonlé Srepok and, of course, the Mekong. However, the roads are improving and NH78 east to Ratanakiri is now in very reasonable shape.

Visitor attractions are extremely limited for now, but as tourism takes off elsewhere in Cambodia, it is possible that boat trips up the Mekong's tributaries will be a different way to see some remote areas. The population of Stung Treng includes several minority groups and the western chunk of massive Virachay National Park, accessible from Siem Pang – two factors that suggest there is some tourism potential as the province's infrastructure develops. Part of its problem is being sandwiched between Ratanakiri, one of Cambodia's most interesting provinces, and southern Laos, an area rich in

attractions – why hang around Stung Treng? Right now, anywhere outside the provincial capital is pretty much the ends of the earth.

STUNG TRENG
ស្ទឹងត្រែង

☎ 074 • pop 24,500

With improved security countrywide, the opening of the Cambodian-Lao border just 50km north of town and a strategic location on the overland route to Ratanakiri, Stung Treng looks set for a surge in visitor numbers. It is an active trading town located on the banks of Tonlé San, which flows into the mighty Mekong on the western outskirts of the city limits. Some locals call Tonlé San Tonlé Kong or Tonlé Sekong as these two rivers merge 10km east of town. *Se* is actually Lao for 'river' so Tonlé Sekong is pretty much 'River River Kong'.

Information

Familiar story, there are no banks in Stung Treng, but US dollars are happily accepted everywhere. For telephone services, try the mobile-phone kiosks sprinkled around the market. Believe it or not, there is now Internet access in Stung Treng at the Sekong Internet Centre (☎ 973909) on Ph 1, but at the crippling price of 1500r a minute (a whopping US$24 an hour). Better to wait until Phnom Penh or Pakse for now.

Tourist information is available at the tourist office (☎ 973967) in the government compound located in the south of town. It is a mini city of portacabins and in and among it all is Mom Rotha, the provincial director of tourism, who speaks some English.

Visitors planning to head to Laos need to visit the provincial police station to arrange a *laissez passer* to exit, costing US$5. Don't use intermediaries, as it costs more.

Thala Boravit
ថ្លាបូរវិត

Thala Boravit was an important Chenla-period trading town on the river route connecting the ancient city of Champasak and the holy site of Wat Phu with the southern

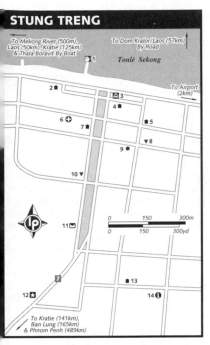

STUNG TRENG

To Mekong River (500m),
Laos, (50km), Kratie (125km)
& Thala Boravit By Boat

To Dom Kralor/Laos (57km)
By Road

Tonlé Sekong

To Airport
(2km)

0   150   300m
0   150   300yd

To Kratie (141km),
Ban Lung (165km)
& Phnom Penh (489km)

STUNG TRENG

PLACES TO STAY & EAT
2   Sekong Hotel; Gaot Soup Restaurant
4   Piphop Thmei Guesthouse
5   Sok Sambath Hotel
7   San Penn Chet Guesthouse;
     Sekong Internet Centre
8   Sophak Mukul Restaurant
10   Arunreas Restaurant
13   Mohasal Hotel & Restaurant

OTHER
1   Boats to Kratie, Thala Boravit & Laos;
     Car Ferry
3   Taxi Park
6   Hospital
9   Royal Phnom Penh Airways
11   Post Office
12   Provincial Police Station
14   Tourist Office

reaches of the Chenla empire, including the ancient cities of Sambor Prei Kuk (Ishanapura) and Angkor Borei. For all its past glories, there is very little to see today. There are the limited remains of several brick towers, but only one is easily identifiable by the lower section that still stands. It is hardly worth the effort for the casual visitor, but temple fiends may feel the urge to tick it off. Thala Boravit is on the west bank of the Mekong River and irregular boats cross from Stung Treng throughout the day. It should be easy enough to wait for locals to fill up the regular boats (1000r), rather than charter an outboard (US$5 or so). It is from here that the jungle road to Kompong Thom or Tbeng Meanchey starts via the village of Chaeb. See the Getting There & Away entry later for more details.

Places to Stay & Eat

When it comes to the cheap guesthouses, they are not all that inspiring, making it

worth the extra couple of dollars to go for a hotel.

Piphop Thmei Guesthouse Rooms with fan & bathroom US$3. This is not the cleanest guesthouse in Cambodia, but it does have a riverfront location.

Sen Penh Chet Guesthouse (☎ 973772) Rooms with fan & bathroom US$3. This clean place offers the best deal among the guesthouses, although that doesn't make it stunning.

Sok Sambath Hotel (☎ 973790) Rooms with fan & bathroom US$7, with air-con & hot water US$15. This is the smartest place in town, offering well-tended rooms with TV and creature comforts for those who are prepared to spend the extra dollars.

Sekong Hotel (☎ 973762) Rooms with fan/air-con, TV & bathroom US$7/15. This kitsch place looks like it came straight out of the communist manual for hotel building. It's poor value when compared to the Sok Sambath, but the US$5 rooms with no TV might be an option for some.

Mohasal Hotel (☎ 973999) Rooms with fan US$5, rooms with air-con, fridge & TV US$10. Tucked away in the deep south of town, this quiet place has flamboyant, cavernous air-con rooms with bathroom that are worth considering. They come complete with ornately carved wooden beds. The fan rooms, however, are not such a steal.

Cheap **food stalls** can be found on the riverfront and around the market. When it comes to real restaurants, there are only a few options.

Sophak Mukul Restaurant This place is very popular with the tiny expat population and serves huge portions of tasty Cambodian food, including lively dishes with ginger.

Arunreas Restaurant This restaurant often looks more closed than open, but is popular at breakfast.

Gaot Soup Restaurant At the Sekong Hotel, this place specialises in goat soup rather than correct spelling, but it does serve more than just goat for those who don't fancy Billy for dinner.

Getting There & Away

There are several flights a week to Stung Treng (US$55/105 one way/return) with Royal Phnom Penh Airways (☎ 973963) at Ph 3 on the south side of the market.

NH7 south to Kratie (141km) is a nasty piece of work for much of its length. It used to be plagued by bandits, and ambushes were common, as it passes through some very remote country. It has been safe for a few years now, but it doesn't hurt to check the latest with locals before heading this way. It is a very smooth dirt road within Stung Treng Province (30km), but thereafter degenerates into a hellish mix of broken bitumen, small rocks and sandy gullies. There is still no funding earmarked to upgrade this stretch so it may be a last reminder of how bad all of Cambodia's roads used to be. It costs 25,000/15,000r inside/on the back by pickup to Kratie; by share taxi it is 30,000r. The journey takes around six hours by pick-up or five hours by taxi in the dry season, and 10 hours or more in the wet season. Take the boat instead.

For details on the journey farther south by either road or boat, see the Kratie and Kompong Cham sections earlier in this chapter.

For the scoop on the much improved road between Stung Treng and Ban Lung in Ratanakiri, see the Ratanakiri section following.

Fast boats run between Kratie and Stung Treng from July through to November (25,000r, three hours), leaving Stung Treng at 7am and Kratie around 12.30pm, later if they are not full. During the rest of the year, slower wooden boats (25,000r, four/six hours down/up) make the trip, as the river becomes perilous with rocks and sandbars appearing everywhere.

For the inside story on the border crossing with Laos, see the Getting There & Away chapter earlier in this book.

There is also a trail that leads across northern Cambodia from Stung Treng to either Tbeng Meanchey or Kompong Thom. It is unwise for the average traveller to take on this route, but for adventure addicts who don't mind a very long and bumpy moto ride it is an option. First, cross the Mekong to Thala Boravit from where a jungle trail leads west to the large village of Chaeb. The route starts as a dusty logging road, but soon whittles down to a remote jungle trail. If trail conditions are bad you may need to overnight in Chaeb in the wat or with some locals. From Chaeb, there is a logging road west that joins with the main road from Kompong Thom to Tbeng Meanchey at a point about 25km south of Tbeng Meanchey.

For Kompong Thom, there is a more direct route southwest passing through the Rovieng district to Phnom Dek, but the road is much worse than the logging road. The last stretch over the mountain to Tbeng Meanchey is pretty rough in places, while the southern stretch to Kompong Thom is in excellent shape. Heading to Stung Treng from the west is easier from Tbeng Meanchey, as moto drivers know short cuts and Kompong Thom drivers just won't have been up this far before, contrary to what they might claim. A moto from Tbeng Meanchey should cost about US$20, as the drivers need to cover the cost of their return. Only highly experienced bikers should undertake this route on their own machine and will need to be seriously alert to huge logging trucks thundering around blind bends. This route should not be attempted in the wet season.

Ratanakiri Province

ខេត្តរតនគីរី

Ethnic minorities, elephants, waterfalls and jungle combine to make this one of the most popular provinces in the northeast of Cambodia. Many of the inhabitants come from minority groups known as Khmer Loeu (Upper Khmer), including Kreung, Tompuon and Jarai. These tribes each have their own distinct language and customs, although today they dress as most other poor Cambodians and lack the colourful clothing seen in Thailand and Vietnam. This may be a blessing in disguise, as it may spare the tourist onslaught seen in northern Thailand. There is also a large Lao population throughout the province and many languages will be heard in villages such as Voen Sai.

The province played its part in Cambodia's contemporary tragedy, serving as a base for the Khmer Rouge leadership during much of the 1960s. Pol Pot and Ieng Sary fled here in 1963 and established headquarters in Ta Veng in the north of the province. A limited guerrilla war was launched in 1968, with little success except among the marginalised minority groups. Sihanouk was too popular and it was only with his overthrow and subsequent support for the communists that the revolution was to take shape. Many of the Khmer Rouge leaders used Khmer Loeu as bodyguards and their families ended up in Thai border camps. Most only returned as recently as 1999, after as much as three decades away.

Rubber used to be a large industry up here, but these days it looks to be gem mining and tourism that form the lifeblood of the province. There is good quality zircon mined in several parts of the province and the prices are low compared to the west. However, in the long run, tourism is the future thanks to the abundant natural attractions the province has been blessed with. Boeng Yeak Lom volcanic lake is outstanding, but in time the massive Virachay National Park may prove popular.

Roads in Ratanakiri are not as impressive as the sights – dry season means dust, wet season means mud, take your pick. Boats are a popular means of transport for scenic trips, but the province is too isolated to make travel into Stung Treng a realistic option.

BAN LUNG

បានលុង

☎ 075 • pop 17,000

Ban Lung is the dusty provincial capital of Ratanakiri Province and the best base from which to explore the natural attractions of the area. The town was originally known as Labansiek before the war, but the district name of Ban Lung has gradually slipped into use among locals. The town itself is far from interesting, but with attractions such as Boeng Yeak Lom just a short distance away, there is room for forgiveness. Many of the minorities from the surrounding villages come to Ban Lung to buy and sell at the market, making it one of the more lively commercial centres in the provinces.

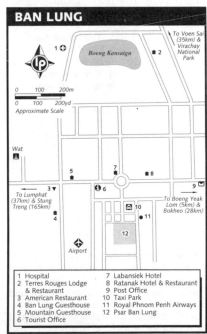

BAN LUNG

To Voen Sai (35km) & Virachay National Park

Boeng Kansaign

0   100   200m
0   100   200yd
Approximate Scale

Wat

To Lumphat (37km) & Stung Treng (165km)

To Boeng Yeak Lom (5km) & Bokheo (28km)

Airport

1 Hospital	7 Labansiek Hotel
2 Terres Rouges Lodge & Restaurant	8 Ratanak Hotel & Restaurant
3 American Restaurant	9 Post Office
4 Ban Lung Guesthouse	10 Taxi Park
5 Mountain Guesthouse	11 Royal Phnom Penh Airways
6 Tourist Office	12 Psar Ban Lung

Information

There are no banks in Ban Lung, but you can change US dollars into riel at jewellers shops in the market. There is a post office on the road to Bokheo that offers international connections, but the mobile-phone kiosks around the market area are cheaper. There is a small provincial tourist office in the centre of town, but visitors may find their guesthouse or hotel to be of more use in the quest for information.

Places to Stay & Eat

There are a limited number of places to stay in Ban Lung, but something to satisfy every budget.

Ratanak Hotel (☎ 974033) Doubles/twins with fan & bathroom US$5/6, rooms with air-con & hot water US$10. Under the enthusiastic management of Mr Leng, this place has improved immeasurably from the old days. The rooms are large and comfortable, tourist information is available and there is a very good restaurant downstairs.

Mountain Guesthouse (☎ 974047) Large singles without bathroom US$3, doubles with bathroom US$5. This place has been around an eternity and Mrs Kim has kept her rooms occupied by ambushing every plane that arrives in town. It is a comfortable-enough guesthouse with a new restaurant under construction.

Ban Lung Guesthouse Rooms with fan/air-con & bathroom US$5/10. This is the nearest accommodation to the airport, but the rooms are rather small and pokey.

Labansiek Hotel (☎ 974035) Small doubles with fan, TV & bathroom US$5, large rooms with air-con, TV, fridge & hot water US$10. This place looks in dire need of facelift from the outside and suffers from a general atmosphere of neglect, but the sprawling air-con rooms are actually a pretty good deal.

Terres Rouges Lodge (☎ 974051) Singles/doubles with fan & without bathroom US$20/25, suite US$30-35. This lavish wooden house sets the standard for style and charm in the wilds of the northeast. All the tasteful rooms are decorated with thoughtful local touches and there is a homely feel throughout. This is definitely worth a splash for those who want to pamper themselves. It is a small place so book ahead at weekends. Prices include breakfast.

The cheapest food in town is to be found in and around **Psar Ban Lung** (Ban Lung Market) and this is also the area to find tukalok and desserts by night.

American Restaurant Near the Mountain Guesthouse, this used to be the only place to eat in town. Various foreign visitors have contributed to the menu, which includes some very local interpretations of hamburgers and a selection of Khmer dishes. The food wasn't up to old standards on our last visit, but we might have just been unlucky.

Ratanak Restaurant The food at this place is very good value. It specialises in *phnom pleung* (beef on volcano) and there is a range of other Asian dishes that help to ensure this is the best place in town to get fed.

Terres Rouges Restaurant Dinner US$6. The restaurant here doesn't quite live up to the sophistication of the rooms, although the food is well presented.

Getting There & Away

President Airlines and Royal Phnom Penh Airways fly to Ban Lung from Phnom Penh (US$55/105 one way/return) several times a week and some flights go via Stung Treng, regardless of the published schedules.

The road between Ban Lung and Stung Treng has been thoroughly overhauled, slashing journey times by more than half (25,000/15,000r inside/on the back of a pick-up). It is now a level, graded dirt road for most of its length with just a few short, sticky patches. In the dry season it takes less than four hours, but in the wet season times could double. These improvements mean it is now possible to make a dry-season overland journey to or from Phnom Penh in just two days. For those in a hurry, there are now direct pick-ups running between Ban Lung and Kratie (40,000/30,000r, eight to 10 hours), although this would be tough in the wet season. Higher prices might be quoted in Ban Lung, as the taxi drivers are more mercenary here.

There is no real road linking Ratanakiri to Mondulkiri, contrary to what older maps may show. There is a road as far as Lumphat, but after crossing Tonle Srepok by ferry, it descends into a series of sandy ox-cart tracks until Koh Nhek in northern Mondulkiri Province. A trickle of hardcore bikers have been using this route over the past few years, but it really isn't for the average traveller – only attempt it if you have years of biking experience or are an extremely hardy soul with an iron backside.

Realistically, it is a two-day journey between Ban Lung and Sen Monorom, with an overnight stay in Koh Nhek. It is almost impossible in the wet season and pretty tough in the dry, but has improved with the return of settlers from refugee areas. Anyone seriously considering this option should link up with a local who knows the route, as there are lots of opportunities to get lost. Cross at the new truck ferry a few kilometres upstream from Lumphat and stick to the trail that's been used the most. A range of motorbike spares, copious amounts of water, old US 1:50,000 military maps of the area and a compass should make for a smoother journey.

Getting Around

Motorbikes, jeeps and pick-ups are available for hire from most of the guesthouses in town. Korean motorbikes from Ratanak Hotel are just US$5 a day and newer Suzukis are US$7. Ratanak Hotel also offers a 4WD pick-up for just US$30 a day with driver, which is a real bargain for small groups. Mountain Guesthouse rents motorbikes for US$7 a day and has a Chinese jeep available at US$40 a day. Terres Rouges Lodge offers old Sanyang motorbikes for US$7 a day, or US$12 with driver, and jeeps for US$50.

You could also hire a moto for the day (US$8) from around the market area and sit back surveying the scenery. There are also pick-ups and jeeps available for charter at the taxi park. Figure on a price of US$30 to US$50 depending on how far you want to go and how far you are willing to negotiate.

AROUND BAN LUNG
Boeng Yeak Lom
បឹងយក្សឡោម

The protected area of Yeak Lom (admission 1000r) includes a circular crater-lake, believed to have been formed 700,000 years ago, situated amid pristine jungle. The indigenous minorities in the area have long considered Yeak Lom a sacred place and their legends talk of mysterious creatures that inhabit the waters of the lake. It is one of the most peaceful, beautiful locations Cambodia has to offer and the water is extremely clear with visibility of up to 5m. It is a great place to take a dip early in the morning or late in the afternoon. There is a small centre nearby that has information on ethnic minorities in the province, local handicrafts for sale and suggested walks around the lake. The area is administered by the local Tompuon minority and proceeds from the entry fee go towards improving life in the nearby villages.

Boeng Yeak Lom is 5km east of Ban Lung. Turn right off the road to Bokheo at the statue of the chunchiet husband and wife. Motos are available for around US$1 return, but expect to pay more if the driver has to wait around.

Waterfalls

There are numerous waterfalls in the province, but many are difficult to reach in the wet season and lacking much water in the dry season. The three most commonly visited are **Chaa Ong**, **Ka Tieng** and **Kinchaan** and these are now signposted from the main road towards Stung Treng, about 5km west of town. The most spectacular of the three is Chaa Ong, as it is set in a jungle gorge and you can clamber behind the waterfall or venture underneath for a power shower.

Tuk Chrouu Bram-pul is a popular waterfall with seven gentle tiers located about 35km southeast of Ban Lung, but the trail to get here is tough at any time and pretty much impossible in the wet season. A visit here can be combined with a visit to the current hot spot for **gem mining** in Chum

Rum Bei. This involves a walk of several kilometres through the forest, as motorbikes cannot make it. Take a local guide for this combination trip, but check in Ban Lung that the mines are still active.

Voen Sai
រំនសៃ

Located on the banks of Tonlé San, Voen Sai is a pleasant little community of Chinese, Lao and Kreung villagers. Originally, the town was located on the north bank of the river and known as Virachay, but these days the main settlement is on the south bank. The north side of the river is the most interesting, with an old Chinese settlement that dates back almost 200 years and several **Lao and chunchiet villages** nearby. It is possible to cross the river for 500r on a small ferry and walk west for a couple of kilometres, passing through a Chinese village, a Lao community and a small chunchiet area, before emerging on a wealthy Chinese village complete with large wooden houses and inhabitants who still speak Chinese.

Voen Sai is also home to Virachay National Park headquarters and the best place to organise a hike into the park with rangers as guides.

Voen Sai is about 35km northwest of Ban Lung on an average-to-poor road. There is an old Soviet bonerattler (2000r, two to three hours) that leaves about 7am from Psar Ban Lung, returning some time around midday. Some pick-ups come this way for 5000/3000r inside/on the back, and it is easy enough to find on a motorbike.

Chunchiet Cemeteries
កន្លែងបញ្ចុះសពពួកជនជាតិ

There are many chunchiet cemeteries scattered throughout the forests of Ratanakiri. **Kachon** is a one-hour boat ride east of Voen Sai and has an impressive **Tompuon cemetery** in the forest beyond the village. Family groups are buried side by side in the forest and there are effigies of the deceased. When a lengthy period of mourning is complete, villagers hold a big celebration and add two

carved wooden likenesses of elephant tusks to the structures. Some of these tombs date back many years and have been abandoned to the jungle. Newer tombs of wealthy individuals have been cast in concrete and show some gaudy influences from China. Sadly, some unscrupulous art collectors and amateur anthropologists from Europe have reportedly been buying up the old effigies from poor villagers, something tantamount to cultural rape. Remember that this is a sacred site for local Tompuon people – touch nothing and act respectfully.

Expect to pay around US$10 for the boat trip to Kachon, including a jaunt to the Chinese and Lao villages opposite Voen Sai. It is also possible to get to Kachon by road – head south out of Voen Sai and turn left at the first major junction. To get to the cemetery, walk through the health centre located at the riverbank and turn right. The cemetery is just a couple of hundred metres from the village.

Ta Veng
តាវែង

Ta Veng is an insignificant village on the southern bank of Tonlé San, but acts as an alternative gateway to Virachay National Park. It was in the Ta Veng district that Pol Pot, Ieng Sary and other leaders of the Khmer Rouge established their guerrilla base in the 1960s. Locals say nothing remains of the remote base today, although in a dismal sign of decline, they point out that both Ta Veng and the Khmer Rouge jungle base had electricity before the war.

Ta Veng is about 57km north of Ban Lung on a rollercoaster road through the mountains that affords some of the province's finest views. There are some very steep climbs in sections and for this reason it wouldn't be much fun in the rain. No scheduled pick-ups run up here so it is necessary to come by motorbike or charter a vehicle. The road passes through several **minority villages**, where it is possible to break the journey.

It is possible to arrange small boats in Ta Veng for gentle river jaunts; try US$5 in the local area or US$40 for the three-hour trip to Voen Sai.

Virachay National Park
ឧទ្យានជាតិវីរៈជ័យ

Virachay National Park is the largest protected area in Cambodia, stretching east to Vietnam, north to Laos and west to Stung Treng Province. The park has never been fully explored and is likely home to a number of larger mammals, including elephants, leopards and tigers. Some wildlife experts speculate that there may even be isolated rhinoceroses or kouprey (wild oxen). Rangers also claim there are **waterfalls**, some as high as 100m, but these are many days' hike from Voen Sai. Facilities are minimal, but if you contact the ranger post in Voen Sai, it is possible to arrange a customised walk in the area.

Lumphat
លុមផាត់

The former provincial capital of Lumphat is something of a ghost town these days thanks to sustained US bombing raids in the early 1970s. However, as the area of Tonlé San around Voen Sai becomes more commercialised, this could become an alternative place for an adventurous boat trip to isolated minority villages. This is also the last gasp of civilisation, if it can even be called that, for hardcore bikers heading south on the tough trails to Mondulkiri Province.

To get here from Ban Lung, take the road to Stung Treng for about 15km before heading south. The 35km journey takes around an hour and pick-ups do a few runs from Ban Lung for 5000r.

Mondulkiri Province
ខេត្តមណ្ឌលគិរី

Mondulkiri means 'Meeting of the Hills', a suitable name for such a hilly province. Nestled against Cambodia's eastern border, Mondulkiri really is another Cambodia, with scenery and a climate quite unlike anywhere else in the country. In the dry season it is a little like Wales with sunshine; in the wet season, like Tasmania with dreadful roads. There are endless grassy hills with the occasional clump of pines huddled together against the winds. At an average elevation of 800m, it can get quite chilly at night, so carry something warm.

Mondulkiri is the most sparsely populated province in the country, with just two people per sq km. Almost half of the 35,000 inhabitants come from the Pnong minority group, other minorities making up much of the rest of the population. The lack of people adds to something of a wild-east atmosphere and there are certainly a lot of wild animals in the remoter parts of the province, including tigers, elephants, bears and leopards.

There has recently been an influx of refugees returning from the Thai border area, which has pushed the province forward a little. Rice farming is picking up, but hunting remains the profession of choice for many minorities. Roads are bad throughout the province, but several have been earmarked for improvement, which could speed up travel in the next couple of years.

SEN MONOROM
សែនមនោរម្យ

☎ 023 • pop 7000

Sen Monorom, the provincial capital of Mondulkiri, is a charming little community set amid rolling hills. The centre of town, a village really, has two lakes, leading some dreamers to call it 'The Switzerland of Cambodia'. The area around Sen Monorom has plenty of minority villages and picturesque waterfalls, making it a pleasant place to pass a few nights. Many of the Pnong people from nearby villages come into Sen Monorom to trade and the distinctive baskets they carry on their back make them easy to distinguish from the immigrant Khmers. High winds billow throughout the year and it can get pretty fresh at night, so bring some warm clothing.

Information
Bring a suitable amount of cash as this is no place for travellers cheques or plastic. Prices

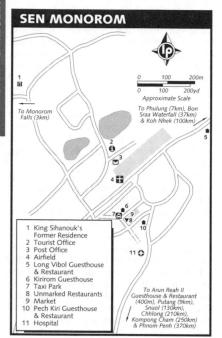

SEN MONOROM

0   100   200m
0   100   200yd
Approximate Scale

To Monorom Falls (3km)

To Phulung (7km), Bon Sraa Waterfall (37km) & Koh Nhek (100km)

1. King Sihanouk's Former Residence
2. Tourist Office
3. Post Office
4. Airfield
5. Long Vibol Guesthouse & Restaurant
6. Kirirom Guesthouse
7. Taxi Park
8. Unmarked Restaurants
9. Market
10. Pech Kiri Guesthouse & Restaurant
11. Hospital

To Arun Reah II Guesthouse & Restaurant (400m), Putang (9km), Snuol (130km), Chhlong (210km), Kompong Cham (250km) & Phnom Penh (370km)

are a little higher than in other parts of the country, as everything has to be shipped in from Phnom Penh or Vietnam, so budget on at least US$15 a day.

There are plenty of mobile phones in Sen Monorom and calls are easy to make.

There is a small tourist office in town run by Sam Chin and Long Vanny, who speak excellent French and good English. Sorn Sarun is the official guide and between them they can arrange elephant treks and overnight stays in minority villages.

Another man who knows the province very well is Long Vibol, an all-round Mr Fixit who works for the Red Cross, runs a guesthouse, is a dentist and wedding photographer and, of more relevance perhaps, an English-speaking tour guide.

Elephant Treks

The villages of Phulung, 7km north of Sen Monorom, and Putang, 9km southwest of town, are the most popular places to arrange an elephant trek. Most of the guesthouses around town, as well as the local tourist office, can arrange day treks for around US$25, including lunch and transport to and from the village. It is also possible to negotiate a longer trek with an overnight stay in a Pnong village. It can get pretty uncomfortable up on top of an elephant after a couple of hours, so carry a pillow or something similar to ease the strain.

Places to Stay & Eat

Sen Monorom has electricity from around 6pm to 10pm only, so a torch is useful for late-night ablutions. Hot water is more important in this part of the country, as the temperature can drop dramatically at night. Places without hot-water showers can usually provide flasks of boiling water for bathing. There is no need for air-con in this neck of the woods.

Pech Kiri Guesthouse (☎ 012-932102) Bungalows with bathroom US$10, singles without bathroom US$3-5, doubles without bathroom US$8. The first and, for many years, only guesthouse in town is still going strong under the lively direction of Madame Deu. There are two main buildings built around a pleasant garden, and several individual bungalows. Her design has influenced a new generation of guesthouses springing up in Sen Monorom. Prices include breakfast.

Arun Reah II Guesthouse (☎ 012-856667) Bungalows US$5, main-house twins US$7. Strategically located to catch the eye of everyone approaching town, this place has some fine views across the hills of Mondulkiri. The bungalows are pretty cute and very good value, including bathroom, TV, free water and a torch. Prices may rise to US$8 when they install hot water. The twins are larger.

Long Vibol Guesthouse (☎ 012-944647) Doubles with bathroom US$10, singles without bathroom US$5. Vibol has long been a guide on the tourist scene and now runs his own guesthouse. It offers clean and comfortable rooms, some of which include hot-water showers. Vibol is one of the best sources of tourist information around Mondulkiri.

He plans to add a dormitory for those on a tight budget.

Kirirom Guesthouse Rooms without bathroom 7000r. This unmarked guesthouse overlooking the taxi park has the cheapest rooms in town, but they are really too close to prison cells for comfort, with little room to manoeuvre.

There are several cheap **food stalls** around the market that are open for lunch. There are a couple of **unmarked restaurants** with San Miguel signs by the entrance to the market, which can knock together some pretty good food. It may be wise to turn up early for dinner, as they don't open late.

Most of the guesthouses have small restaurants.

Long Vibol Restaurant This guesthouse has a popular little restaurant serving Khmer food and it often screens videos about Cambodia.

Arun Reah Restaurant This is a major dining centre by Mondulkiri standards and offers reasonable fare.

Pech Kiri Restaurant This establishment has an attractive menu of delicious local food and offers the best guacamole in Cambodia.

Getting There & Away

The airstrip at Sen Monorom has been closed since mid-2000 and local officials don't expect it to be reopened in the near future. For now, visitors who want to get to this unique region have to come overland, relatively straightforward in the dry season, but rather more 'complicated' in the wet season.

There are three ways to get to Mondulkiri, all of which include the same section of logging road from Snuol to Sen Monorom, and a fourth, harsh trail north to Ratanakiri – see the Ban Lung section earlier for details. This stretch passes through some wild jungle after Khao Si Ma district and is one of the most dramatic roads in Cambodia. At the time of writing, the Cambodian military was overhauling this mountainous route and turning it into some sort of superhighway.

There is usually at least one pick-up a day heading from Phnom Penh to Sen Monorom (50,000/30,000r inside/on the back, 10 hours) in the dry season, leaving from Psar

Thmei soon after 6am, but it's best to arrange a seat the day before, as places are limited.

Coming from Kompong Cham, there are few direct pick-ups to Sen Monorom, so it is usually necessary to first go to Snuol (15,000r by taxi, 12,000/8000r by pick-up, three hours). From Snuol, there are pick-ups to Sen Monorom (20,000/15,000r, four hours). Starting early from Kompong Cham, it should be easy enough to cover this in a day.

From Kratie there are direct pick-ups heading to Sen Monorom (45,000/30,000r, seven hours) very early in the morning. Anyone leaving after 7am will need to change vehicles in Snuol. From Kratie to Snuol is about 8000/6000r.

Approaching from Chhlong in the dry season offers an interesting boat-truck combination. Take one of the Kratie fast boats as far as Chhlong (25,000r, 4½ hours), where the logging road begins. From Chhlong board a pick-up to Snuol (10,000/8000r, 1½ hours). In Snuol, change pick-ups for the journey to Sen Monorom (20,000/15,000r, four hours). It may be better to undertake this journey in a group, as it is possible to charter whole vehicles if there are slim pickings in Chhlong and Snuol later in the day. However, if logging activity stays dormant, the logging company won't upgrade the road and it may deteriorate. Ask around at guesthouses in Kratie or Kompong Cham for the latest or telephone one of the guesthouses in Sen Monorom.

Getting from Mondulkiri Province to any of these destinations is generally easier to accomplish in one day, as most locals are going beyond Snuol and so no change is required.

For experienced bikers, it is a long, dusty ride on NH7 from Kompong Cham to Snuol or a rollercoaster road from Kratie to Snuol. It is also possible to put the motorbike on the fast boat and start out from Chhlong. Travelling by motorbike from Kratie to Chhlong is also possible, as there is a good road along the banks of the Mekong River. It is necessary to cross several rivers by boat, but the village scenery makes it a journey well worth doing for experienced bikers. Kratie to Chhlong can be completed in just 45 minutes and from there to Sen

Monorom, some 210km east, can be done in as little as five hours.

Getting Around

The cheapest place to rent a motorbike is Arun Reah II Guesthouse (US$5 a day). The other guesthouses charge US$10, but this may drop. Russian jeeps and pick-up trucks can be chartered for the day. It costs about US$40 around Sen Monorom in the dry season, around US$80 or more to Bou Sraa, and more again in the wet season.

AROUND SEN MONOROM
Monorom Falls
ទឹកជ្រោះមនោរម្យ

This small waterfall is the closest thing to a public swimming pool for Sen Monorom. It has an attractive location in the forest about 3km northwest of town. Motos can run people out here for about US$2 for the round trip. Walking there, head straight on beyond Sihanouk's abandoned villa and when the trail eventually forks, take the left-hand side.

Bou Sraa Waterfall
ទឹកជ្រោះប៊ូស្រា

This double-drop waterfall is one of the largest in Cambodia and famous throughout the country. It is an unforgiving 37km journey east of Sen Monorom, but the reward is worth the effort. The upper tier of Bou Sraa drops some 10m and the lower tier drops 25m. To get to the bottom of the upper falls, take a left turn just before the river that feeds the falls. To get to the bottom of the lower falls, cross the river and take a left farther down the track; it takes about 20 minutes to get down. A little way on is the Pnong village of Pichinda where there is a tiny **guesthouse** and **restaurant** where basic rooms are available for 10,000r. There are also basic food and drink supplies available in the village.

Getting There & Away The road from Bou Sraa to Sen Monorom has long been appalling – the bastard child of the devil himself! It is one of the worst stretches of road in the country, and there's a lot of

competition. There are two large rivers to cross, three if you include the one at the top of the falls, and several deep gullies. Most vehicles take more than two hours to complete the journey. But all this should soon be a thing of the past, as the road is marked for a complete upgrade by the end of 2002 – hurrah!

To get here, hire a moto driver for the day or charter a Russian jeep in a group. Coming alone by motorcycle is tough with current conditions, but should get easier after the road improvements. Be especially careful if crossing the river above the Bou Sraa Falls, as the riverbed is as slippery as ice. Going over the top of the falls, motorbike and all, is not good for your health.

Other Waterfalls

Other popular waterfalls in Mondulkiri include **Romanear Waterfall**, 18km southeast of Sen Monorom, and **Dak Dam Waterfall**, 25km east of Sen Monorom. Both are very difficult to find without assistance, so its best to take a moto driver or local guide. Romanear is a low, wide waterfall with some convenient swimming holes. There is also a second Romanear Waterfall, known rather originally as Romanear II, which is near the main road between Sen Monorom and Snuol. Dak Dam is similar to the Monorom Falls, albeit with a greater volume of water. The waterfall is several kilometres beyond the Pnong village of Dak Dam and locals in the village are able to lead the way if you can make yourself understood.

KOH NHEK
កោះញែក

This is the final frontier as far as Mondulkiri goes, a remote village in the far north of the province, but a strategic place on the difficult overland route between Sen Monorom and Ratanakiri. There is a **big house** in town with a friendly owner who accepts foreigners for 10,000r and can prepare some basic food. Ask for 'dam svay' or 'mango tree' and most villagers can point the way. There are also basic supplies in the village, including beer – well-earned once you get here.

Language

The Khmer or Cambodian language is spoken by approximately nine million people in Cambodia, and is understood by many in bordering countries. Written Khmer is based on the ancient Brahmi script of southern India. Arguably one of the oldest languages in Southeast Asia, Khmer inscriptions have been dated back to the 7th century AD. Although separate and distinct from its Thai, Lao and Burmese neighbours, Khmer shares with them the common roots of Sanskrit and Pali – a heritage of centuries of linguistic and cultural interaction and of their shared faith in Theravada Buddhism. More recently, many French words entered the Khmer language during the colonial period, especially medical and technical terms.

Unlike the languages of neighbouring countries, Khmer is non tonal, meaning that there are no special intonations of words that alter their meaning. This may be a relief for travellers in the region who have been frustrated in their attempts at tonal languages such as Thai, Vietnamese and Lao. However, the lack of tones is easily offset by the complexity of the Khmer pronunciation. There are 33 consonants, often paired in seemingly bizarre combinations, and some 24 vowels and diphthongs. Further complicating the language is the haphazard transliteration system left over from the days of French rule, which does not reflect accurate pronunciation of Khmer words by English speakers.

On the positive side, Khmer grammar is very simple. There are no verb conjugations or gender inflections, no endings for single or plural, masculine or feminine. Adding a few words changes sentence tense to past, present or future.

In any case, a bit of Khmer will go a long way – no matter how rough it is. The Khmers sincerely appreciate any effort to learn their language and are very supportive of visitors who give it even a half-hearted try. You'll find that as your skill and vocabulary increase, so does your social standing: people go out of their way to complement you, moto fares and prices at markets drop, and you may even win a few friends.

Though English is fast becoming Cambodia's second language, the Khmer still cling to the Francophone pronunciation of the Roman alphabet and most foreign words. This is helpful to remember when spelling Western words and names aloud; thus 'ay-bee-cee' becomes 'ah-bey-sey' and so on. French speakers will definitely have an advantage when addressing the older generation, as most educated Khmers studied French at some point during their schooling. Many household items retain their French names as well, especially those which were introduced to Cambodia by the French, such as *robine* (faucet) and *ampuol* (light bulb).

Recommend reading for those interested in further study of spoken and written Khmer are *Cambodian System of Writing and Beginning Reader*, *Modern Spoken Cambodian* and any other books by Frank Huffman.

Dialects

Although the Khmer language as spoken in Phnom Penh is generally intelligible to Khmers nationwide, there are several distinct dialects in other areas of the country. Most notably, the Khmers of Takeo Province tend to modify or slur hard consonant/vowel combinations, especially those that contain 'r'; thus *bram* (five) becomes *pe-am*, *sraa* (alcohol) becomes *se-aa*, and *baraang* (French/foreigner) becomes *be-ang*. In Siem Reap, sharp-eared travellers will notice a very Lao-sounding lilt to the local speech. Here, certain vowels are modified, such as *poan* (thousand), which becomes *peuan*, and *kh'sia* (pipe), which becomes *kh'seua*.

Transliteration

The transliteration system used in this chapter has been designed for basic communication rather than linguistic perfection.

Several Khmer vowels, however, have no English equivalent, thus they can only be approximated by English spellings. Other words are written as they are pronounced and not necessarily according to the actual vowels used in the words. (Khmer place names in this book will follow their common or standard spellings.)

Pronunciation

The pronunciation guide below covers the trickier parts of the transliteration system used in this chapter. It uses the Roman alphabet to give the closest equivalent to the sounds of the Khmer language. The best way to improve your pronunciation is to listen carefully to native speakers.

Vowels

Vowels and diphthongs with an 'h' at the end should be pronounced hard and aspirated (with a puff of air).

aa	as the 'a' in 'father'
i	as the 'i' in 'kit'
uh	as the 'u' in 'but'
ii	as the 'ee' in 'feet'
ei	a combination of 'uh' and 'ii' above, ie, 'uh-ii'
eu	similar to the French *peuple;* try pronouncing 'oo' while keeping the lips spread flat rather than rounded
euh	as 'eu' above; pronounced short and hard
oh	as the 'o' in 'hose'; pronounced short and hard
ow	as in 'glow'
u	as the 'u' in 'flute'; pronounced short and hard
uu	as the 'oo' in 'zoo'
ua	as the 'ou' in 'tour'
uah	as 'ua' above; pronounced short and hard
aa-œ	a tough one, with no English equivalent; like a combination of 'aa' and 'œ'. When placed between consonants it's often pronounced like 'ao'.
œ	as 'er' in 'her', but more open
eua	combination of 'eu' and 'a'
ia	as 'ee-ya', like 'beer' without the 'r'
e	as the 'a' in 'late'
ai	as the 'i' in 'side'
ae	as the 'a' in 'cat'
ay	as 'ai' above, but slightly more nasal
ey	as in 'prey'
ao	as the 'ow' in 'cow'
av	no English equivalent; like a very nasal 'ao'. The final 'v' is not pronounced.
euv	no English equivalent; like a very nasal 'eu'. The final 'v' is not pronounced.
ohm	as the 'ome' in 'home'
am	as the 'um' in 'glum'
oam	a combination of 'o' and 'am'
a, ah	shorter and harder than 'aa' above
eah	combination of 'e' and 'ah'; pronounced short and hard
ih	as the 'ee' in 'teeth'; pronounced short and hard
eh	as the 'a' in 'date'; pronounced short and hard
awh	as the 'aw' in 'jaw'; pronounced short and hard
oah	a combination of 'o' and 'ah'; pronounced short and hard
aw	as the 'aw' in 'jaw'

Consonants

Khmer uses some consonant combinations that may sound rather bizarre to Westerners' ears and be equally difficult for the Western tongue, eg, 'j-r' in *j'rook* (pig), or 'ch-ng' in *ch'ngain* (delicious). For ease of pronunciation such consonants are separated in this guide with an apostrophe.

k	as the 'g' in 'go'
kh	as the 'k' in 'kind'
ng	as in the final sound of 'sing'; a difficult sound for Westerners to emulate. Practise by saying 'singing-nging-nging-nging' until you can say 'nging' clearly.
j	as in 'jump'
ch	as in 'cheese'
ny	as in the final syllable of 'onion', ie, 'nyun'.
t	a hard, unaspirated 't' sound with no direct equivalent in English. Similar to the 't' in 'stand'.
th	as the 't' in 'two', never as the 'th' in 'thanks'

p	a hard, unaspirated 'p' sound, as the final 'p' in 'puppy'
ph	as the 'p' in 'pond', never as the 'ph' in 'phone'
r	as in 'rum', but hard and rolling, with the tongue flapping against the palate. In rapid conversation it is often omitted entirely.
w	as the 'w' in 'would'. Contrary to the common transliteration system, there is no equivalent to the English 'v' sound in Khmer.

Greetings & Civilities

Hello.
johm riab sua/ ជំរាបសួរ/សួស្ដី
sua s'dei

Goodbye.
lia suhn hao-y លាសិនហើយ

See you later.
juab kh'nia ជួបគ្នាថ្ងៃក្រោយ
th'ngay krao-y

Yes.
baat បាទ
(used by men)
jaa ចាស
(used by women)

No.
te ទេ

Please.
sohm សូម

Thank you.
aw kohn អរគុណ

You're welcome.
awt ei te/ អត់អីទេ/សូមអញ្ជើញ
sohm anjœ-in

Excuse me/I'm sorry.
sohm toh សុំទោស

Pardon? (What did you say?)
niak niyey thaa អ្នកនិយាយថាម៉េច?
mait?

Small Talk

Hi. How are you?
niak sohk sabaay te? អ្នកសុខសប្បាយទេ?

I'm fine.
kh'nyohm sohk sabaay ខ្ញុំសុខសប្បាយ

Where are you going?
niak teuv naa? អ្នកទៅណា?

(NB This is a very common question used when meeting people, even strangers; an exact answer is not necessary.)

What's your name?
niak ch'muah ei? អ្នកឈ្មោះអ្វី?

My name is ...
kh'nyohm ch'muah ... ខ្ញុំឈ្មោះ ...

Where are you from?
niak mao pii prateh naa? អ្នកមកពីប្រទេសណា?

I'm from ...
kh'nyohm mao pii ... ខ្ញុំមកពី ...

I'm staying at ...
kh'nyohm snahk neuv ... ខ្ញុំស្នាក់នៅ ...

May I take your photo?
kh'nyohm aa-it thawt ruup niak baan te? ខ្ញុំអាចថតរូបអ្នកបានទេ?

Forms of Address

The Khmer language reflects the social standing of the speaker and subject through various personal pronouns and 'politeness words'. These range from the simple *baat* for men and *jaa* for women, placed at the end of a sentence, meaning 'yes' or 'I agree', to the very formal and archaic *Reachasahp* or 'Royal language', a separate vocabulary reserved for addressing the King and very high officials. Many of the pronouns are determined on the basis of the subject's age and sex in relation to the speaker. Foreigners are not expected to know all of these forms. The easiest and most general personal pronoun is *niak* (you), which may be used in most situations, with either sex. Men of your age or older may be called *lowk* (mister). Women of your age or older can be called *bawng srei* (older sister) or for more formal situations, *lowk srei* (madam).

Bawng is a good informal, neutral pronoun for men or women who are (or appear to be) older than you. For third person, male or female, singular or plural, the respectful form is *koat* and the common form is *ke*.

Language Difficulties

Does any one here speak English?
tii nih mian niak jeh phiasaa awngle te?
ទីនេះមានអ្នកចេះភាសាអង់គ្លេសទេ?

Do you understand?
niak yuhl te/niak s'dap baan te?
អ្នកយល់ទេ/អ្នកស្តាប់បានទេ?

I understand.
kh'nyohm yuhl/kh'nyohm s'dap baan
ខ្ញុំយល់ /ខ្ញុំស្តាប់បាន

I don't understand.
kh'nyohm muhn yuhl te/kh'nyohm s'dap muhn baan te
ខ្ញុំមិនយល់ទេ/ខ្ញុំស្តាប់មិនបានទេ

How do you say ... in Khmer?
... kh'mai thaa mait?
... ខ្មែរថាម៉េច?

What does this mean?
nih mian nuh-y thaa mait?
នេះមាននៃ្យថាម៉េច?

Please speak slowly.
sohm niyay yeut yeut
សូមនិយាយយឺតៗ

Please write that word down for me.
sohm sawse piak nu ao-y kh'nyohm
សូមសរសេរពាក្យនោះឱ្យខ្ញុំ

Please translate for me.
sohm bawk brai ao-y kh'nyohm
សូមបកប្រែឱ្យខ្ញុំ

What is this called?
nih ke hav thaa mait?
នេះគេហៅថាម៉េច?

Getting Around

Where is the ...?
... neuv ai naa?
... នៅឯណា?

bus station
kuhnlaing laan ch'nual
កន្លែងឡានឈ្នួល

bus stop
jamnawt laan ch'nual
ចំណតឡានឈ្នួល

train station
s'thaanii roht plæng
ស្ថានីយរថភ្លើង

airport
wial yohn hawh
វាលយន្តហោះ

What time does the ... leave?
... jein maong pohnmaan?
... ចេញម៉ោងប៉ុន្មាន?

bus	*laan ch'nual*	ឡានឈ្នួល
train	*roht plæng*	រថភ្លើង
plane	*yohn hawh/*	យន្តហោះ/
	k'pal hawh	កប៉ាល់ហោះ

What time does the last bus leave?
laan ch'nual johng krao-y jein teuv maong pohnmaan?
ឡានឈ្នួល ចុងក្រោយ ចេញទៅម៉ោងប៉ុន្មាន?

How can I get to ...?
phleuv naa teuv ..?
ផ្លូវណាទៅ ...?

Is it far?
wia neuv ch'ngaay te?
វានៅឆ្ងាយទេ?

Is it near?
wia neuv juht te?
វានៅជិតទេ?

Is it near here?
wia neuv juht nih te?
វានៅជិតនេះទេ?

Go straight ahead.
teuv trawng
ទៅត្រង់

Turn left ...
bawt ch'weng បត់ឆ្វេង

Turn right ...
bawt s'dam បត់ស្តាំ

at the corner
neuv kait j'rohng នៅកាច់ជ្រុង

in front of
neuv khaang mohk នៅខាងមុខ

next to
neuv joab នៅជាប់

behind
neuv khaang នៅខាងក្រោយ
krao-y

opposite
neuv tohl mohk នៅទល់មុខ

I want to get off (here)!
kh'nyohm jawng joh (tii nih)!
ខ្ញុំចង់ចុះ (ទីនេះ)!

How much is it to ...?
teuv ... th'lay pohnmaan?
ទៅ ... ថ្លៃប៉ុន្មាន?

That's too much.
th'lay pek
ថ្លៃពេក

Please take me to ...
sohm juun kh'nyohm teuv ...
សូមជូនខ្ញុំទៅ ...

this address
aadreh/aasayathaan nih
អាស័យដ្ឋាននេះ

Here is fine, thank you.
chohp neuv tii nih kaw baan
ឈប់នៅទីនេះក៏បាន

north	*khaang jœng*	ខាងជើង
south	*khaang d'bowng*	ខាងត្បូង
east	*khaang kaot*	ខាងកើត
west	*khaang leit*	ខាងលិច

Around Town

Where is a ...
... neuv ai naa? ... នៅឯណា?

bank	*th'niakia*	ធនាគារ
cinema	*rowng kohn*	រោងកុន
consulate	*kohng sul*	កុងស៊ុល
embassy	*s'thaantuut*	ស្ថានទូត
hospital	*mohntii paet*	មន្ទីរពេទ្យ
market	*p'saa*	ផ្សារ
museum	*saramohntii*	សារមន្ទី
park	*suan*	សួន

post office	*praisuhnii*	ប្រៃសណីយ
temple	*wawt*	វត្ត

police station
poh polih/s'thaanii nohkohbaal
ប៉ុស្តប៉ូលីស/ស្ថានីយនគរបាល

public telephone
turasahp saathiaranah
ទូរស័ព្ទសាធារណៈ

public toilet
bawngkohn saathiaranah
បង្គន់សាធារណៈ

How far is the ...?
... ch'ngaay pohnmaan?
... ឆ្ងាយប៉ុន្មាន?

I want to see the ...
kh'nyohm jawng teuv mœl ...
ខ្ញុំចង់ទៅមើល ...

I'm looking for the ...
kh'nyohm rohk ...
ខ្ញុំរក ...

What time does it open?
wia baok maong pohnmaan?
វាបើកម៉ោងប៉ុន្មាន?

What time does it close?
wia buht maong pohnmaan?
វាបិតម៉ោងប៉ុន្មាន?

Is it still open?
wia neuv baok reu te?
វានៅបើកឬទេ?

What ... is this?
... nih ch'muah ei?
... នេះឈ្មោះអី?

I want to change ...
kh'nyohm jawng dow ...
ខ្ញុំចង់ដូរ ...

US dollars
dolaa amerik
ដុល្លាអាមេរិក

What is the exchange rate for US dollars?
muy dolaa dow baan pohnmaan?
មួយដុល្លាដូរបានប៉ុន្មាន?

Accommodation

Where is a ...?
... neuv ai naa? ... នៅឯណា?
(cheap) hotel
sahnthaakia/ សណ្ឋាគារ/
ohtail thaok អូតែល(ថោក)

I've already found a hotel.
kh'nyohm mian ohtail hao-y
ខ្ញុំមានអូតែលហើយ

I'm staying at ...
kh'nyohm snahk neuv ...
ខ្ញុំស្នាក់នៅ ...

Could you write down the address, please?
sohm sawse aasayathaan ao-y kh'nyohm
សូមសរសេរអាសយដ្ឋានឱ្យខ្ញុំ

I'd like a room ...
kh'nyohm sohm bantohp ...
ខ្ញុំសុំបន្ទប់ ...

for one person
samruhp muy niak
សំរាប់មួយនាក់

for two people
samruhp pii niak
សំរាប់ពីរនាក់

with a bathroom
dail mian bantohp tuhk
ដែលមានបន្ទប់ទឹក

with a fan
dail mian dawnghahl
ដែលមានកង្ហារ

with a window
dail mian bawng-uit
ដែលមានបង្អូច

I'm going to stay for ...
kh'nyohm nuhng snahk tii nih ...
ខ្ញុំនឹងស្នាក់ទីនេះ ...

one day *muy th'ngay* មួយថ្ងៃ
one week *muy aatuht* មួយអាទិត្យ

Do you have a room?
niak mian bantohp tohmne te?
អ្នកមានបន្ទប់ទំនេទេ?

How much is it per day?
damlay muy th'ngay pohnmaan?
តំលៃមួយថ្ងៃប៉ុន្មាន?

Does the price include breakfast?
damlay bantohp khuht teang m'hohp pel pruhk reu?
តំលៃបន្ទប់គិតទាំងម្ហូបពេលព្រឹកឬ?

Can I see the room?
kh'nyohm aa-it mœl bantohp baan te?
ខ្ញុំអាចមើលបន្ទប់បានទេ?

I don't like this room.
kh'nyohm muhn johl juht bantohp nih te
ខ្ញុំមិនចូលចិត្តបន្ទប់នេះទេ

Do you have a better room?
niak mian bantohp l'aw jiang nih te?
អ្នកមានបន្ទប់ល្អជាងនេះទេ?

I'll take this room.
kh'nyohm yohk bantohp nih
ខ្ញុំយកបន្ទប់នេះ

Can I leave my things here until ...?
kh'nyohm aa-it ph'nyaa-œ tohk eiwuhn r'bawh kh'nyohm neuv tii nih dawl ... baan te?
ខ្ញុំអាចផ្ញើអីវ៉ាន់របស់ខ្ញុំនៅទីនេះដល់ ... បានទេ?

this afternoon *l'ngiak nih* ល្ងាចនេះ
this evening *yohp nih* យប់នេះ

Food

Where is a ...
... neuv ai naa? ... នៅឯណា?
cheap restaurant
haang baay/ ហាងបាយថោក
resturaan thaok
restaurant
resturaan/ ភោជនីយដ្ឋាន
phowjuhniiyathaan
food stall
kuhnlaing luak កន្លែងលក់ម្ហូប
m'howp
market
p'saa ផ្សារ

I'm vegetarian. (I can't eat meat.)
kh'nyohm tawm sait
ខ្ញុំតមសាច់
vegetables
buhnlai បន្លែ

Not too spicy please.
sohm kohm twœ huhl pek
សូមកុំធ្វើហឹរពេក

No MSG please.
sohm kohm dahk bii jeng
សូមកុំដាក់ប៊ីចេង

This is delicious.
nih ch'ngain nah
នេះឆ្ងាញ់ណាស់

Meat & Seafood
beef
sait kow សាច់គោ
chicken
sait moan សាច់មាន់
crab
k'daam ក្តាម
fish
trei ត្រី
shrimp
bawngkia ព្រាន
squid
meuk ត្រីមឹក

Condiments
chilli
m'teh huhl ម្ទេស
fish sauce
tuhk trei ទឹកត្រី
pepper
m'ret ម្រេច
salt
ambuhl អំបិល
soy sauce
tuhk sii iw ទឹកសណ្ដែក
sugar
skaw ស្ករ

Fruit
apples
paom ប៉ោម
coconut
downg ដូង
durian
thuuren ធុរេន
jackfruit
kh'nao ខ្នុរ
lemon
krow-it ក្រូចឆ្មា

mangosteen
mangkoht មង្ឃុត
orange
krow-it pow sat ក្រូចពោធិសាត់
pineapple
m'noah ម្នាស់

Drinks
coffee
kaafe កាហ្វេ
boiled water
tuhk ch'uhn ទឹកធ្អុន
milk
tuhk dawh kow ទឹកដោះគោ
tea
tai តែ

Shopping
How much is it?
nih th'lay pohnmaan?
នេះថ្លៃប៉ុន្មាន?

That's too much.
th'lay pek
ថ្លៃពេក

I'll give you ...
kh'nyohm ao-y ...
ខ្ញុំឱ្យ ...

No more than ...
muhn lœh pii ...
មិនលើសពី ...

What's your best price?
niak dait pohnmaan?
អ្នកដាច់ប៉ុន្មាន?

Health
Where is a ...
... neuv ai naa? ... នៅឯណា?
dentist
paet th'mein ពេទ្យធ្មេញ
doctor
kruu paet គ្រូពេទ្យ
hospital
mohntrii paet មន្ទីរពេទ្យ
pharmacy
kuhnlaing luak កន្លែងលក់ថ្នាំ/
th'nam/
ohsawt s'thaan ឱសថស្ថាន

I'm ill.
kh'nyohm cheu ខ្ញុំឈឺ
My ... hurts.
... r'bawh kh'nyohm cheu
... របស់ខ្ញុំឈឺ
I feel nauseous.
kh'nyohm jawng k'uat
ខ្ញុំចង់ក្អួត
I feel weak.
kh'nyohm awh kamlahng
ខ្ញុំអស់កំលាំង
I keep vomiting.
kh'nyohm k'uat j'raa-æn
ខ្ញុំក្អួតច្រើន
I feel dizzy.
kh'nyohm wuhl mohk
ខ្ញុវិលមុខ
I'm having trouble breathing.
kh'nyohm pi baak dawk dawnghaom
ខ្ញុំពិបាកដកដង្ហើម

I'm allergic to ...
kh'nyohm muhn treuv thiat ...
ខ្ញុំមិនត្រូវធាតុ ...
penicillin
penicillin ប៉េនីស៊ីលីន
antibiotics
awntiibiowtik អង់ទីប៊ីយោទិក

I need medicine for ...
kh'nyohm treuv kaa th'nam samruhp ...
ខ្ញុំត្រូវការថ្នាំសំរាប់ ...
diarrhoea
rowk joh riak រោគចុះរាក
dysentery
rowk mual រោគមូល
fever
krohn/ គ្រុន/ក្ដៅខ្លួន
k'dav kh'luan
pain
cheu ឈឺ

antiseptic
th'nam samlahp ថ្នាំសំលាប់មេរោគ
me rowk
aspirin
parasetamol ប៉ារ៉ាសេតាម៉ុល

codeine
codiin ខូឌីន
quinine
kiiniin គីនីន
sleeping pills
th'nam ng'nguy dek ថ្នាំងងុយដេក

condoms
sraom ahnaamai ស្រោមអនាម័យ
medicine
th'nam ថ្នាំ
mosquito repellent
th'nam kaa pia ថ្នាំការពារមូស
muh
razor blade
kambuht kao pohk កាំបិតកោរពុកមាត់
moat
sanitary napkins
samlei ahnaamai សំឡីអនាម័យ
shampoo
sabuu kawk sawk សាប៊ូកក់សក់
shaving cream
kraim samruhp ក្រែមសំរាប់កោរពុកមាត់
kao pohk moat
sunblock cream
kraim kaa pia ក្រែមការពារពន្លឺថ្ងៃ
pohnleu th'ngay
toilet paper
krawdah ahnaamai ក្រដាស់អនាម័យ

Time & Days
What time is it?
eileuv nih maong pohnmaan?
ពេលវេនេះម៉ោងប៉ុន្មាន?

in the morning
pel pruhk ពេលព្រឹក
in the afternoon
pel r'sial ពេលរសៀល
in the evening
pel l'ngiat ពេលល្ងាច
at night
pel yohp ពេលយប់
today
th'ngay nih ថ្ងៃនេះ
tomorrow
th'ngay s'aik ថ្ងៃស្អែក
yesterday
m'suhl mein ម្សិលមិញ

Monday			20	*m'phei*	ម្ភៃ
th'ngay jahn	ថ្ងៃចន្ទ		21	*m'phei muy*	ម្ភៃមួយ
Tuesday			30	*saamsuhp*	សាមសិប
th'ngay ahngkia	ថ្ងៃអង្គារ		40	*saisuhp*	សែសិប
Wednesday			100	*muy roy*	មួយរយ
th'ngay poht	ថ្ងៃពុធ		1000	*muy poan*	មួយពាន់
Thursday					
th'ngay prohoah	ថ្ងៃព្រហស្បតិ៍		one million	*muy lian*	មួយលាន
Friday					
th'ngay sohk	ថ្ងៃសុក្រ		1st	*tii muy*	ទីមួយ
Saturday			2nd	*tii pii*	ទីពីរ
th'ngay sav	ថ្ងៃសៅរ៍		3rd	*tii bei*	ទីបី
Sunday			4th	*tii buan*	ទីបួន
th'ngay aatuht	ថ្ងៃអាទិត្យ		10th	*tii dawp*	ទីដប់

Numbers & Amounts

Khmers count in increments of five. Thus, after reaching the number five *(bram)*, the cycle begins again with the addition of one, ie, 'five-one' *(bram muy)*, 'five-two' *(bram pii)* and so on to 10, which begins a new cycle. This system is a bit awkward at first (for example, 18, which has three parts: 10, five and three) but with practice it can be mastered.

You may be confused by a colloquial form of counting that reverses the word order for numbers between 10 and 20 and separates the two words with *duhn: pii duhn dawp* for 12, *bei duhn dawp* for 13, *bram buan duhn dawp* for 19 and so on. This form is often used in markets, so listen keenly.

1	*muy*	មួយ
2	*pii*	ពីរ
3	*bei*	បី
4	*buan*	បួន
5	*bram*	ប្រាំ
6	*bram muy*	ប្រាំមួយ
7	*bram pii/puhl*	ប្រាំពីរ
8	*bram bei*	ប្រាំបី
9	*bram buan*	ប្រាំបួន
10	*dawp*	ដប់
11	*dawp muy*	ដប់មួយ
12	*dawp pii*	ដប់ពីរ
16	*dawp bram muy*	ដប់ប្រាំមួយ

Emergencies

Help!
juay kh'nyohm phawng!
ជួយខ្ញុំផង!

It's an emergency!
nih jia reuang bawntoan!
នេះជារឿងបន្ទាន់!

Call a doctor!
juay hav kruu paet mao!
ជួយហៅគ្រូពេទ្យមក!

Call the police!
juay hav polih mao!
ជួយហៅប៉ូលីសមក!

Could you help me please?
niak aa-it juay kh'nyohm baan te?
អ្នកអាចជួយខ្ញុំបានទេ?

Could I please use the telephone?
kh'nyohm braa-œ turasahp baan te?
ខ្ញុំប្រើទូរស័ព្ទបានទេ?

I wish to contact my embassy/consulate.
*kh'nyohm jawng hav s'thaantuut/
kohngsuhl r'bawh prawteh kh'nyohm*
ខ្ញុំចង់ហៅស្ថានទូត/កុងស៊ុលរបស់ប្រទេសខ្ញុំ

I've been robbed.
kh'nyohm treuv jao plawn
ខ្ញុំត្រូវចោរប្លន់។

Stop!
chohp!
ឈប់!

Watch out!
prawyaht!
ប្រយ័ត្ន!

Is this path safe to walk on?
phleuv nih mian sohwatthaphiap dai reu te?
ផ្លូវនេះមានសុវត្ថិភាពដែរឬទេ?

Are there any land mines in this area?
neuv m'dohm nih mian miin reu te?
នៅម្តុំនេះមានមីនឬទេ?

toilets
bawngkohn
បង្គន់

Where are the toilets?
bawngkohn neuv ai naa?
បង្គន់នៅឯណា?

Glossary

apsara – heavenly nymph or angelic dancer, often represented in Khmer sculpture
Asean – Association of Southeast Asian Nations
Avalokiteshvara – the Buddha of Compassion and the inspiration for *Jayavarman VII*'s Angkor Thom

barang – foreigner
baray – reservoir
boeng – lake

CCB – Cambodian Commercial Bank
CCC – Cooperation Committee for Cambodia
CFF – Cambodian Freedom Fighters
chunchiet – ethnic minorities
CPP – Cambodian People's Party
cyclo – pedicab; bicycle rickshaw

devaraja – cult of the god king, established by *Jayavarman II*, in which the monarch has universal power

EFEO – École Française d'Extrême Orient
essai – wise man or traditional medicine man
étage zéro – ground floor

Funcinpec – National United Front for an Independent, Neutral, Peaceful and Cooperative Cambodia

garuda – mythical half-man, half-bird creature
gopura – entrance pavilion in traditional Hindu architecture

Hinayana – literally, Small Vehicle; a school of Buddhism also known as *Theravada*
Hun Sen – Cambodia's prime minister (1998–present)

Jayavarman II – the king (reigned 802–50) who established the cult of the god king, kicking off a period of amazing architectural productivity that resulted in the extraordinary temples of Angkor
Jayavarman VII – the king (reigned 1181–1201) who drove the Chams out of Cambodia before embarking on an ambitious construction programme, of which the walled city of Angkor Thom was part

Kampuchea – the name Cambodians use for their country; it is associated with the bloody rule of the Khmer Rouge, which insisted that the outside world use the name Democratic Kampuchea from 1975 to 1979
Khmer – a person of Cambodian descent; the language of Cambodia
Khmer Krom – ethnic Khmers living in Vietnam
Khmer Loeu – Upper Khmer or ethnic minorities in northeastern Cambodia
Khmer Rouge – a revolutionary organisation that seized power in 1975 and implemented a brutal social restructuring, resulting in the suffering and death of millions of Cambodians in the following four years
kouprey – extremely rare wild ox of Southeast Asia
krama – scarf

laissez passer – exit pass
linga – phallic symbol

Mahayana – literally, Great Vehicle; a school of Buddhism (also known as the northern school) that built upon and extended the early Buddhist teachings; see also *Theravada*
moto – small motorcycle with driver; a common form of transport in Cambodia
Mt Meru – the mythical dwelling place of the Hindu god Shiva
MPTC – Cambodian Ministry of Post & Telecommunications

naga – mythical serpent, often multi-headed; a symbol used extensively in Angkorian architecture
nandi – sacred ox

NCDP – National Centre for Disabled Persons

NGO – nongovernmental organisation

NH – national highway

Norodom Ranariddh, Prince – son of King Sihanouk and leader of *Funcinpec*

Norodom Sihanouk, King – king of Cambodia, film director and constant presence in Cambodian politics

Pali – ancient Indian language that, along with Sanskrit, is the root of modern *Khmer*

Party of Democratic Kampuchea – the political party of the *Khmer Rouge*

phlauv – street; abbreviated to Ph

phnom – mountain

Pol Pot – the former leader of the Khmer Rouge who is roundly blamed for the suffering and deaths of millions of Cambodians under a radical social experiment from 1975 to 1979; also known as Saloth Sar

prang – temple tower

prasat – stone or brick hall with religious or royal significance

psar – market

RAC – Royal Air Cambodge

Ramayana – an epic Sanskrit poem composed around 300 BC featuring the mythical Ramachandra, the incarnation of the god Vishnu

RCAF – Royal Cambodian Armed Forces

remorque-kang – trailer pulled by a bicycle

remorque-moto – trailer pulled by a motorcycle

Sangkum Reastr Niyum – People's Socialist Community; a national movement, led by King Sihanouk, that ruled the country during the 1950s and 1960s

Sanskrit – ancient Hindu language that, along with *Pali,* is the root of modern *Khmer* language

SNC – Supreme National Council

soup chhnang dei – cook-your-own soup

stung – river

Suryavarman II – the king (reigned 1112–52) responsible for building Angkor Wat and for expanding and unifying the Khmer empire

Theravada – a school of Buddhism (also known as the southern school or Hinayana) found in Myanmar (Burma), Thailand, Laos and Cambodia; this school confined itself to the early Buddhist teachings rather than the expanded doctrine called *Mahayana*

tonlé – large river

tukalok – like a fruit smoothie, often very sweet and, if an egg is added, frothy

UNDP – United Nations Development Programme

Unesco – United Nations Educational Scientific and Cultural Organization

UNHCR – United Nations High Commissioner for Refugees

Untac – United Nations Transitional Authority in Cambodia

vihara – temple sanctuary

WHO – World Health Organization

Year Zero – 1975, the year the *Khmer Rouge* seized power

Thanks

Many thanks to the travellers who used the last edition and wrote to us with helpful hints, useful advice and interesting anecdotes. Your names follow:

Jan Achten, Philippe Adam, Ben Alcock, Rachel & Jules Allen, Lael Ambrose, Mike Amdur, Dean Anderson, Tina Anderson, Kenny Ang, Sean Ardussi, Luke Arnold, Jacopo Arpesani.

Ilone Baake, Tim Bailey, Chris Bain, Karren Baker, Kim Baldwin Radford, Martin Ball, Eleonora Balsano, Bonnie Baskin, Sue Bazzana, Claire & Mark Beastall, Jacques Beaudry, Ernst Bechthum, James Beffa, Martin Belanger, Volker Belz, Petr Benda, A Bennett, Jean Berger, Mikael Berglof, Linda Bettman, Kees Beukelman, Ferry & Annieke Bezem, Markus Bhnert, Roger Biefer, Gordon Biggar, Heath Black, John Devendra Black, Michelle Blancpain, Udo Blasel, Marc Blehert, Christoph Bohl, Markus Bohnert, Frederique Boismenu, Grazyna Bonati, Jane Bone, Ana Borges, Don Boring, Kees Botschuijver, Anne Marie Boye, Minkin Brain, Philippe Branlant, Francis Brannigan, Greg Brett, Louise Brooks, Richard Buckley, Peter Budd, Ian Butler.

Sophie C, Clare Cameron, Ruth Campbell, Fergy Campbell, Ben Capell, Alice Chan, Jayne Chan, David Chen, Karen Cheung Ka Lam, Marie Chrysander, Ken Chuah, Dave Citra, David Clark, Scott & Chris Coats, Rob Cohen, Hazel Colbert, John Collins, J A Coombs, Christophe Le Cornu, John Joseph S Coronel, Jane Costello, Josie Cowden, Elisabeth Cox, John Cox, Ken Cramer, Robin Crompton, Ian Cruickshank.

Kate Davey, Geoff Davies, Wayne Dawson, Jos De Block, Sallyann Deans, Bregje Deben, Sandy Denize, Andrew Derham, Mona Dienhart, Frederik Divall, Denis Doolan, Eva Doove, Richard Dudley, Chris & Phil Duguid, Jocie Dye, Katarzyna Dziewulska.

Rick Eastman, Ditte Eckstein, Darren Eddy, Caroline Edge, Ted Edmondson, Dee Eltaief, Cati Esteva.

Leo Fagan, Anne Falconnier, Roger Feller, Ann Feng, Poul Fersling, Luci Ferspal, Saskia Fijma, Jeff Fischer, John Flanders, Kellie Anne Foreman, John Forte, Yasmin Fortune, Paul Foster, Jez Frankel, Fabio Friscia, Peter Frith, Tony Fuery, Jens Funk.

Sio Lye Gaik, Carol Gall, Avi Galler, Michael Gardener, Dana Garrison, Mickael Gaupillat, Mathias Gellein, Henk Geurtsen, Andrea Giachetti, Laurie Gibbons, W Giessler, Mary Gillespie, George Girling, Dawn Glenn, Laurensz Goedhart, Edwin Goffin, Keynan Goichman, Eric Goodfield, Kit Goodrick, Ilana Gordon, Gorrit Goslinga, Noni Gove, Matthew Gregory, Paul Gregory, Tanja Greil, Jose Groothuis.

David H Haerry, Robert Haines, Tamara Hale, Jenny Hall, Sue Hall, Caul Haney, Sarah Hanks, Paul Hannon, Joergen S Hansen, Candida Hardenberg, Audrey & Dennis Harper, Tony Harvin, Erin Havers, Frances Hayes, Jonas Heide Munck, Marie Hellberg, Philippe Hellemans, Catherine Henderson, John Hitchcock, Rune Holmstad, H Hood, Marcia Hopper, Anne Horsley, Song I Hsing, Marjolaine Hubault, Brent Huff, Laura Hughes, Karen Hungerford, Catherine Hunter, Scott Hunter.

Christine Ingemorsen, George Ionita.

Emma James, Christ Jan Gehoel, Robert Jan Van Mulst, Gerbert Jansen, Rich Jenulis, Jo Johansen, Daniel Jones, Jeremy Jones, Volkert Jung.

Jay Kane, H Karst, Jeffrey Kaye, Guido Keller, Louise Kelly, Jim Kendall, Kristel & Filip Kennis-Verbeek, Dave King, Martyn King, Jenny Kirby, Jette Kjertum, Christian Kober, Guus Koelman, Chas Koines, Nicola Kolisch, Mihai Kover-Carseli, Sibel Kozak, Mike Krage, Gabriela Kresse, Kai Kroeger, Janice & Helmut Kron, Jasper Kuipers.

Norman Lagerquist, Ryan Laird, Marie Lall, Kam Lam, Ali Lane, Marjorie L Larney, Fredrik Larsen, Jenny Larsson, Winnie Lau, Hind & Lol Laurent, Aid Lavin, Ena-Rebecca Lawless, Damien Le Gal, Deborah Leaver, Jennie Lee, Alida Lehnort, Nancy Lemmon, Emma Lenz, Marie Lesaicherre, Lee Hong Liang, Alvin Lim, Hansan Lim, Harm Linssen, Lorraine Little, Andrew & Gina Livingstone, Dr W K Loftus, Jo Et Loic, Koen Loossens, Donna Lougher, Marc Lucas, Wendy Lucas, Dagmar Lukas, Damian Lyn.

Jan van den Maagdenberg, Bradley Leonard MacDonald, David Mackertich, Madi Maclean,

335

Kaye & Keith Main, Carl Mandabach, Eric Mansfield, Ariel Maor, Andrew Margolin, Dave Marini, Catelijne Markenstein, N Marsh, John Marshall, David Martin, Gina Martin, Jason Mayeroff, A M McCann, Colleen McClure, Gillian McConnell, Paul McHugh, J McKillop, Dr J S McLintock, Sunil S Mehta, Rachelle Meilleur, Bjoern Meiswinkel, David Melhuish, Murray Metherall, Allan Micaud, Ryma Michel, Brooke Middleton, Matt & Debs Miles, Husain Mishal, Guy Missotten, Fiona Moir, Lars Molin, Adrian Mondry, Gavin Mooney, Mr Moose, Krista Moriarity, Joanne Morrison, Steve Morrison, Patty Morrissey, Eugene Mosier, Bob Moulang, Pawel Mroczkowski, Jerry Muller, Sean Mulligan, Mark Murnane, Patrick Murphy, R H Murray-Philipson.

Dain Nastel, Troy Neatte, Steve Needham, Peter Neubauer, Gloria Neumeier, Brad & Rhea Ng, Hugo M Nijhof, Tommer Nir, Jan Noorlander, Ian & Delia Norris, Sally Ann Northcliffe, Andrzej Nowak.

Noel O'Hanrahan, Timo Tapani Ojanen, Kristin Olson, Jodi Olstead, George Onderdelinden, Roger Osborne, Gina Ossanna, Elin Ostbo.

Declan Page, Andrea Panzoni, Joanna & Todd Papaioannou, Olga Parra, Chapman-Pincher Pat, Malcolm Pearch, Sune Pedersen, Renate Pelzl, Phnom Penh, Edward Pennington, John Petrou, Bridget Phelan, Gareth Phillips, Karin Pihlsgard, Lucy Pike, J Plampin, Steven Pontolaeng, Toni Pozo, Robert & Alix Pratt, Robyn Present, Robyn Preston, Daniel & Catherine Price.

Cleo Race, Andrew Rafuse, Jose Ramon, Isabelle Ranchet, Thomas Rau, Tjalling Jan & Christa Raukema, Michael Rayment, Liza & Tom Redston,

Christophe & Man Fung Rentsch, Donna Reynolds, Jeroen Rijbroek, Peter Roberts, Judith Robertson, Eduardo Robinovich, Jared Rod-rigues, Joanne Rogers, Andrea Rogge, Estelle Rolin, H Rose, Georgina Ross, Martin Ruschitzka, Svante Rusck, Angie Russell, Paul Rydon, Ruth Rydon.

Stijn Saelens, Christine Salerno, Damien Sams, Pete Savage, Christian Schmid, Dr Reuven Schossen, Harald Schubert, Esther Schuller, Jeff Scott, Mike Scott, Roy Sharma, Mick Shaw, Cindy Shurtleff, Carloine Simpson, Say Sisakith, Iain Sivers, Steven Smathers, Ageeth Harriet Smid, Emma Smith, Jady Smith, Johnnie Smith, Thomas Soerensen, Sovannsamnang Soksovann, Pierre Soum, Marakani Srikant, Terry Stark, Elliot Steel, Ulrike Steinbrenner, Stine Strandkjaer, Antje Struewing, Dr Peter Stutchbury, Darren Sugrue.

Jason Tanner, Takis Tap, Jesse Tepll, Tamiko Thomas, Eric Timewell, Thomas Tingstrup, N L Tran, Kevin Troy, Deon Tse, Marty Tunney.

Ute Ultsch, K T Upsdale.

Hendrik van Dam, Michael van de Ghinste, Frank van der Sluijs, Mario van Hecke, Ronny van Loon, Richard van Thiel, Wouter van Vliet, Becky Vander Eyk, Koen Vanrumste, Jacques et Gi Veit, Carol Vernal, Gabriel Vital-Durand, Thi A Vorghin.

Carol Wagner, Law Wai Man, Stephanie Walpen, Allison Webb, Anna Weeks, Laurence Weeks, Perry Whalley, Mark Widdifield, Ian Wilkinson, Ed Williams, Jennifer P Wilson, Max Wiman, Joanna Wiseman, Anthony Wong, Michael & Christine Wong, Jane Woolley, C Wrentmore.

Shi Xiaodong, Angela Yik, Michael Yon, Cecilia Yuen, Doerte Zehler, Jane Zhang, Maike Ziesemer, Anat Zverdling, Craig Zwicky.

LONELY PLANET

You already know that Lonely Planet produces more than this one guidebook, but you might not be aware of the other products we have on this region. Here is a selection of titles that you may want to check out as well:

Read This First: Asia & India
ISBN 1 86450 049 2
US$14.95 • UK£8.99

Cycling Vietnam, Laos & Cambodia
ISBN 1 86450 168 5
US$21.99 • UK£13.99

South-East Asia phrasebook
ISBN 0 86442 435 3
US$6.95 • UK£3.99

Lonely Planet Unpacked
ISBN 1 86450 062 X
US$12.95 • UK£6.99

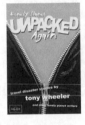 

Lonely Planet Unpacked Again
ISBN 1 86450 319 X
US$12.99 • UK£6.99

Travel Photography: A guide to taking better pictures
ISBN 1 86450 207 X
US$16.99 • UK£9.99

Healthy Travel Asia & India
ISBN 1 86450 051 4
US$5.95 • UK£3.99

Chasing Rickshaws
ISBN 0 86442 640 2
US$34.95 • UK£19.99

South-East Asia on a shoestring
ISBN 1 86450 158 8
US$21.99 • UK£12.99

Buddhist Stupas in Asia: The shape of perfection
ISBN 1 86450 120 0
US$34.99 • UK£29.99

Thailand, Vietnam, Laos & Cambodia Road Atlas
ISBN 1 86450 102 2
US$14.99 • UK£8.99

Available wherever books are sold

 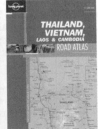

LONELY PLANET

ON THE ROAD

Travel Guides explore cities, regions and countries, and supply information on transport, restaurants and accommodation, covering all budgets. They come with reliable, easy-to-use maps, practical advice, cultural and historical facts and a rundown on attractions both on and off the beaten track. There are over 200 titles in this classic series, covering nearly every country in the world.

 Lonely Planet Upgrades extend the shelf life of existing travel guides by detailing any changes that may affect travel in a region since a book has been published. Upgrades can be downloaded for free from **www.lonelyplanet.com/upgrades**

For travellers with more time than money, **Shoestring** guides offer dependable, first-hand information with hundreds of detailed maps, plus insider tips for stretching money as far as possible. Covering entire continents in most cases, the six-volume shoestring guides are known around the world as 'backpackers bibles'.

For the discerning short-term visitor, **Condensed** guides highlight the best a destination has to offer in a full-colour, pocket-sized format designed for quick access. They include everything from top sights and walking tours to opinionated reviews of where to eat, stay, shop and have fun.

CitySync lets travellers use their Palm™ or Visor™ hand-held computers to guide them through a city with handy tips on transport, history, cultural life, major sights, and shopping and entertainment options. It can also quickly search and sort hundreds of reviews of hotels, restaurants and attractions, and pinpoint their location on scrollable street maps. CitySync can be downloaded from **www.citysync.com**

MAPS & ATLASES

Lonely Planet's **City Maps** feature downtown and metropolitan maps, as well as transit routes and walking tours. The maps come complete with an index of streets, a listing of sights and a plastic coat for extra durability.

Road Atlases are an essential navigation tool for serious travellers. Cross-referenced with the guidebooks, they also feature distance and climate charts and a complete site index.

ESSENTIALS

Read This First books help new travellers to hit the road with confidence. These invaluable predeparture guides give step-by-step advice on preparing for a trip, budgeting, arranging a visa, planning an itinerary and staying safe while still getting off the beaten track.

Healthy Travel pocket guides offer a regional rundown on disease hot spots and practical advice on predeparture health measures, staying well on the road and what to do in emergencies. The guides come with a user-friendly design and helpful diagrams and tables.

Lonely Planet's **Phrasebooks** cover the essential words and phrases travellers need when they're strangers in a strange land. They come in a pocket-sized format with colour tabs for quick reference, extensive vocabulary lists, easy-to-follow pronunciation keys and two-way dictionaries.

Miffed by blurry photos of the Taj Mahal? Tired of the classic 'top of the head cut off' shot? **Travel Photography: A Guide to Taking Better Pictures** will help you turn ordinary holiday snaps into striking images and give you the know-how to capture every scene, from frenetic festivals to peaceful beach sunrises.

Lonely Planet's **Travel Journal** is a lightweight but sturdy travel diary for jotting down all those on-the-road observations and significant travel moments. It comes with a handy time-zone wheel, a world map and useful travel information.

Lonely Planet's eKno is an all-in-one communication service developed especially for travellers. It offers low-cost international calls and free email and voicemail so that you can keep in touch while on the road. Check it out on **www.ekno.lonelyplanet.com**

FOOD & RESTAURANT GUIDES

Lonely Planet's **Out to Eat** guides recommend the brightest and best places to eat and drink in top international cities. These gourmet companions are arranged by neighbourhood, packed with dependable maps, garnished with scene-setting photos and served with quirky features.

For people who live to eat, drink and travel, **World Food** guides explore the culinary culture of each country. Entertaining and adventurous, each guide is packed with detail on staples and specialities, regional cuisine and local markets, as well as sumptuous recipes, comprehensive culinary dictionaries and lavish photos good enough to eat.

LONELY PLANET

OUTDOOR GUIDES

For those who believe the best way to see the world is on foot, Lonely Planet's **Walking Guides** detail everything from family strolls to difficult treks, with 'when to go and how to do it' advice supplemented by reliable maps and essential travel information.

Cycling Guides map a destination's best bike tours, long and short, in day-by-day detail. They contain all the information a cyclist needs, including advice on bike maintenance, places to eat and stay, innovative maps with detailed cues to the rides, and elevation charts.

The **Watching Wildlife** series is perfect for travellers who want authoritative information but don't want to tote a heavy field guide. Packed with advice on where, when and how to view a region's wildlife, each title features photos of over 300 species and contains engaging comments on the local flora and fauna.

With underwater colour photos throughout, **Pisces Books** explore the world's best diving and snorkelling areas. Each book contains listings of diving services and dive resorts, detailed information on depth, visibility and difficulty of dives, and a roundup of the marine life you're likely to see through your mask.

LONELY PLANET

OFF THE ROAD

Journeys, the travel literature series written by renowned travel authors, capture the spirit of a place or illuminate a culture with a journalist's attention to detail and a novelist's flair for words. These are tales to soak up while you're actually on the road or dip into as an at-home armchair indulgence.

The range of lavishly illustrated **Pictorial** books is just the ticket for both travellers and dreamers. Off-beat tales and vivid photographs bring the adventure of travel to your doorstep long before the journey begins and long after it is over.

Lonely Planet **Videos** encourage the same independent, tough-minded approach as the guidebooks. Currently airing throughout the world, this award-winning series features innovative footage and an original soundtrack.

Yes, we know, work is tough, so do a little bit of deskside dreaming with the spiral-bound Lonely Planet **Diary** or a Lonely Planet **Wall Calendar**, filled with great photos from around the world.

TRAVELLERS NETWORK

Lonely Planet Online. Lonely Planet's award-winning Web site has insider information on hundreds of destinations, from Amsterdam to Zimbabwe, complete with interactive maps and relevant links. The site also offers the latest travel news, recent reports from travellers on the road, guidebook upgrades, a travel links site, an online book-buying option and a lively travellers bulletin board. It can be viewed at **www.lonelyplanet.com** or AOL keyword: lp.

Planet Talk is a quarterly print newsletter, full of gossip, advice, anecdotes and author articles. It provides an antidote to the being-at-home blues and lets you plan and dream for the next trip. Contact the nearest Lonely Planet office for your free copy.

Comet, the free Lonely Planet newsletter, comes via email once a month. It's loaded with travel news, advice, dispatches from authors, travel competitions and letters from readers. To subscribe, click on the Comet subscription link on the front page of the Web site.

Lonely Planet Guides by Region

Lonely Planet is known worldwide for publishing practical, reliable and no-nonsense travel information in our guides and on our Web site. The Lonely Planet list covers just about every accessible part of the world. Currently there are 16 series: Travel guides, Shoestring guides, Condensed guides, Phrasebooks, Read This First, Healthy Travel, Walking guides, Cycling guides, Watching Wildlife guides, Pisces Diving & Snorkeling guides, City Maps, Road Atlases, Out to Eat, World Food, Journeys travel literature and Pictorials.

AFRICA Africa on a shoestring • Botswana • Cairo • Cairo City Map • Cape Town • Cape Town City Map • East Africa • Egypt • Egyptian Arabic phrasebook • Ethiopia, Eritrea & Djibouti • Ethiopian Amharic phrasebook • The Gambia & Senegal • Healthy Travel Africa • Kenya • Malawi • Morocco • Moroccan Arabic phrasebook • Mozambique • Namibia • Read This First: Africa • South Africa, Lesotho & Swaziland • Southern Africa • Southern Africa Road Atlas • Swahili phrasebook • Tanzania, Zanzibar & Pemba • Trekking in East Africa • Tunisia • Watching Wildlife East Africa • Watching Wildlife Southern Africa • West Africa • World Food Morocco • Zambia • Zimbabwe, Botswana & Namibia
Travel Literature: Mali Blues: Traveling to an African Beat • The Rainbird: A Central African Journey • Songs to an African Sunset: A Zimbabwean Story

AUSTRALIA & THE PACIFIC Aboriginal Australia & the Torres Strait Islands •Auckland • Australia • Australian phrasebook • Australia Road Atlas • Cycling Australia • Cycling New Zealand • Fiji • Fijian phrasebook • Healthy Travel Australia, NZ & the Pacific • Islands of Australia's Great Barrier Reef • Melbourne • Melbourne City Map • Micronesia • New Caledonia • New South Wales • New Zealand • Northern Territory • Outback Australia • Out to Eat – Melbourne • Out to Eat – Sydney • Papua New Guinea • Pidgin phrasebook • Queensland • Rarotonga & the Cook Islands • Samoa • Solomon Islands • South Australia • South Pacific • South Pacific phrasebook • Sydney • Sydney City Map • Sydney Condensed • Tahiti & French Polynesia • Tasmania • Tonga • Tramping in New Zealand • Vanuatu • Victoria • Walking in Australia • Watching Wildlife Australia • Western Australia
Travel Literature: Islands in the Clouds: Travels in the Highlands of New Guinea • Kiwi Tracks: A New Zealand Journey • Sean & David's Long Drive

CENTRAL AMERICA & THE CARIBBEAN Bahamas, Turks & Caicos • Baja California • Belize, Guatemala & Yucatán • Bermuda • Central America on a shoestring • Costa Rica • Costa Rica Spanish phrasebook • Cuba • Cycling Cuba • Dominican Republic & Haiti • Eastern Caribbean • Guatemala • Havana • Healthy Travel Central & South America • Jamaica • Mexico • Mexico City • Panama • Puerto Rico • Read This First: Central & South America • Virgin Islands • World Food Caribbean • World Food Mexico • Yucatán
Travel Literature: Green Dreams: Travels in Central America

EUROPE Amsterdam • Amsterdam City Map • Amsterdam Condensed • Andalucía • Athens • Austria • Baltic States phrasebook • Barcelona • Barcelona City Map • Belgium & Luxembourg • Berlin • Berlin City Map • Britain • British phrasebook • Brussels, Bruges & Antwerp • Brussels City Map • Budapest • Budapest City Map • Canary Islands • Catalunya & the Costa Brava • Central Europe • Central Europe phrasebook • Copenhagen • Corfu & the Ionians • Corsica • Crete • Crete Condensed • Croatia • Cycling Britain • Cycling France • Cyprus • Czech & Slovak Republics • Czech phrasebook • Denmark • Dublin • Dublin City Map • Dublin Condensed • Eastern Europe • Eastern Europe phrasebook • Edinburgh • Edinburgh City Map • England • Estonia, Latvia & Lithuania • Europe on a shoestring • Europe phrasebook • Finland • Florence • Florence City Map • France • Frankfurt City Map • Frankfurt Condensed • French phrasebook • Georgia, Armenia & Azerbaijan • Germany • German phrasebook • Greece • Greek Islands • Greek phrasebook • Hungary • Iceland, Greenland & the Faroe Islands • Ireland • Italian phrasebook • Italy • Kraków • Lisbon • The Loire • London • London City Map • London Condensed • Madrid • Madrid City Map • Malta • Mediterranean Europe • Milan, Turin & Genoa • Moscow • Munich • Netherlands • Normandy • Norway • Out to Eat – London • Out to Eat – Paris • Paris • Paris City Map • Paris Condensed • Poland • Polish phrasebook • Portugal • Portuguese phrasebook • Prague • Prague City Map • Provence & the Côte d'Azur • Read This First: Europe • Rhodes & the Dodecanese • Romania & Moldova • Rome • Rome City Map • Rome Condensed • Russia, Ukraine & Belarus • Russian phrasebook • Scandinavian & Baltic Europe • Scandinavian phrasebook • Scotland • Sicily • Slovenia • South-West France • Spain • Spanish phrasebook • Stockholm • St Petersburg • St Petersburg City Map • Sweden • Switzerland • Tuscany • Ukrainian phrasebook • Venice • Vienna • Wales • Walking in Britain • Walking in France • Walking in Ireland • Walking in Italy • Walking in Scotland • Walking in Spain • Walking in Switzerland • Western Europe • World Food France • World Food Greece • World Food Ireland • World Food Italy • World Food Spain **Travel Literature:** After Yugoslavia • Love and War in the Apennines • The Olive Grove: Travels in Greece • On the Shores of the Mediterranean • Round Ireland in Low Gear • A Small Place in Italy

Lonely Planet Mail Order

onely Planet products are distributed worldwide. They are also available by mail order from Lonely Planet, so if you have difficulty finding a title please write to us. North and South American residents should write to 150 Linden St, Oakland, CA 94607, USA; European and African residents should write to 10a Spring Place, London NW5 3BH, UK; and residents of other countries to Locked Bag 1, Footscray, Victoria 3011, Australia.

INDIAN SUBCONTINENT & THE INDIAN OCEAN Bangladesh • Bengali phrasebook • Bhutan • Delhi • Goa • Healthy Travel Asia & India • Hindi & Urdu phrasebook • India • India & Bangladesh City Map • Indian Himalaya • Karakoram Highway • Kathmandu City Map • Kerala • Madagascar • Maldives • Mauritius, Réunion & Seychelles • Mumbai (Bombay) • Nepal • Nepali phrasebook • North India • Pakistan • Rajasthan • Read This First: Asia & India • South India • Sri Lanka • Sri Lanka phrasebook • Tibet • Tibetan phrasebook • Trekking in the Indian Himalaya • Trekking in the Karakoram & Hindukush • Trekking in the Nepal Himalaya • World Food India **Travel Literature:** The Age of Kali: Indian Travels and Encounters • Hello Goodnight: A Life of Goa • In Rajasthan • Maverick in Madagascar • A Season in Heaven: True Tales from the Road to Kathmandu • Shopping for Buddhas • A Short Walk in the Hindu Kush • Slowly Down the Ganges

MIDDLE EAST & CENTRAL ASIA Bahrain, Kuwait & Qatar • Central Asia • Central Asia phrasebook • Dubai • Farsi (Persian) phrasebook • Hebrew phrasebook • Iran • Israel & the Palestinian Territories • Istanbul • Istanbul City Map • Istanbul to Cairo • Istanbul to Kathmandu • Jerusalem • Jerusalem City Map • Jordan • Lebanon • Middle East • Oman & the United Arab Emirates • Syria • Turkey • Turkish phrasebook • World Food Turkey • Yemen **Travel Literature:** Black on Black: Iran Revisited • Breaking Ranks: Turbulent Travels in the Promised Land • The Gates of Damascus • Kingdom of the Film Stars: Journey into Jordan

NORTH AMERICA Alaska • Boston • Boston City Map • Boston Condensed • British Columbia • California & Nevada • California Condensed • Canada • Chicago • Chicago City Map • Chicago Condensed • Florida • Georgia & the Carolinas • Great Lakes • Hawaii • Hiking in Alaska • Hiking in the USA • Honolulu & Oahu City Map • Las Vegas • Los Angeles • Los Angeles City Map • Louisiana & the Deep South • Miami • Miami City Map • Montreal • New England • New Orleans • New Orleans City Map • New York City • New York City City Map • New York City Condensed • New York, New Jersey & Pennsylvania • Oahu • Out to Eat – San Francisco • Pacific Northwest • Rocky Mountains • San Diego & Tijuana • San Francisco • San Francisco City Map • Seattle • Seattle City Map • Southwest • Texas • Toronto • USA • USA phrasebook • Vancouver • Vancouver City Map • Virginia & the Capital Region • Washington, DC • Washington, DC City Map • World Food New Orleans **Travel Literature**: Caught Inside: A Surfer's Year on the California Coast • Drive Thru America

NORTH-EAST ASIA Beijing • Beijing City Map • Cantonese phrasebook • China • Hiking in Japan • Hong Kong & Macau • Hong Kong City Map • Hong Kong Condensed • Japan • Japanese phrasebook • Korea • Korean phrasebook • Kyoto • Mandarin phrasebook • Mongolia • Mongolian phrasebook • Seoul • Shanghai • South-West China • Taiwan • Tokyo • Tokyo Condensed • World Food Hong Kong • World Food Japan **Travel Literature:** In Xanadu: A Quest • Lost Japan

SOUTH AMERICA Argentina, Uruguay & Paraguay • Bolivia • Brazil • Brazilian phrasebook • Buenos Aires • Buenos Aires City Map • Chile & Easter Island • Colombia • Ecuador & the Galapagos Islands • Healthy Travel Central & South America • Latin American Spanish phrasebook • Peru • Quechua phrasebook • Read This First: Central & South America • Rio de Janeiro • Rio de Janeiro City Map • Santiago de Chile • South America on a shoestring • Trekking in the Patagonian Andes • Venezuela **Travel Literature**: Full Circle: A South American Journey

SOUTH-EAST ASIA Bali & Lombok • Bangkok • Bangkok City Map • Burmese phrasebook • Cambodia • Cycling Vietnam, Laos & Cambodia • East Timor phrasebook • Hanoi • Healthy Travel Asia & India • Hill Tribes phrasebook • Ho Chi Minh City (Saigon) • Indonesia • Indonesian phrasebook • Indonesia's Eastern Islands • Java • Lao phrasebook • Laos • Malay phrasebook • Malaysia, Singapore & Brunei • Myanmar (Burma) • Philippines • Pilipino (Tagalog) phrasebook • Read This First: Asia & India • Singapore • Singapore City Map • South-East Asia on a shoestring • South-East Asia phrasebook • Thailand • Thailand's Islands & Beaches • Thailand, Vietnam, Laos & Cambodia Road Atlas • Thai phrasebook • Vietnam • Vietnamese phrasebook • World Food Indonesia • World Food Thailand • World Food Vietnam

ALSO AVAILABLE: Antarctica • The Arctic • The Blue Man: Tales of Travel, Love and Coffee • Brief Encounters: Stories of Love, Sex & Travel • Buddhist Stupas in Asia: The Shape of Perfection • Chasing Rickshaws • The Last Grain Race • Lonely Planet … On the Edge: Adventurous Escapades from Around the World • Lonely Planet Unpacked • Lonely Planet Unpacked Again • Not the Only Planet: Science Fiction Travel Stories • Ports of Call: A Journey by Sea • Sacred India • Travel Photography: A Guide to Taking Better Pictures • Travel with Children • Tuvalu: Portrait of an Island Nation

Index

Text

Boxed Text

MAP LEGEND

CITY ROUTES

Freeway .... Freeway
Highway .... Primary Road
Road .... Secondary Road
Street .... Street
Lane .... Lane
.... On/Off Ramp

=== === ===.... Unsealed Road
.... One Way Street
.... Pedestrian Street
.... Stepped Street
=)= ==.... Tunnel
.... Footbridge

REGIONAL ROUTES

.... Tollway, Freeway
.... Primary Road
.... Secondary Road
.... Minor Road

BOUNDARIES

.... International
.... Province
.... Disputed
.... Fortified Wall

HYDROGRAPHY

.... River, Creek
.... Canal
.... Lake

Dry Lake; Salt Lake
.... Spring; Rapids
.... Waterfalls

TRANSPORT ROUTES & STATIONS

.... Train
.... Underground Train
.... Metro
.... Tramway
.... Cable Car, Chairlift

.... Ferry
.... Walking Trail
.... Walking Tour
.... Path
.... Pier or Jetty

AREA FEATURES

.... Building
.... Park, Gardens
.... Market
.... Sports Ground
.... Beach
.... Cemetery
.... Campus
.... Plaza

POPULATION SYMBOLS

○ **CAPITAL** .... National Capital
◉ **CAPITAL** .... Provincial Capital

● **CITY** .... City
● **Town** .... Town

● Village .... Village
.... Urban Area

MAP SYMBOLS

● .... Place to Stay
▼ .... Place to Eat
● .... Point of Interest

⊠ ⊞ ...... Airport, Airfield
⊠ .. Archaeological Site
⊖ .... Bank
⊟ ⊟ ... Bus Stop, Terminal
⌂ .... Cave
⊞ ⊟ ... Cathedral/Church
⊟ ⊟ ..... Cinema, Theatre

⊡ .... Embassy
⊙ .... Golf Course
⊕ .... Hospital
⊡ .... Internet Cafe
⚑ ⚑ Monument, Fountain
⊙ .... Mosque
▲ .... Mountain

⌂ .... Museum
⊡ .... National Park
⊙ .... Petrol
⊞ .... Police Station
⊡ .... Post Office
⊡ .... Pub or Bar
⊠ .... Shopping

⊡ .... Stately Home
⊞ .... Swimming Pool
⊟ .... Taxi
⊟ .... Telephone
▲ .... Temple
⊡ .... Tomb
❶ .. Tourist Information

Note: not all symbols displayed above appear in this book

LONELY PLANET OFFICES

Australia
Locked Bag 1, Footscray, Victoria 3011
☎ 03 8379 8000 fax 03 8379 8111
email: talk2us@lonelyplanet.com.au

USA
150 Linden St, Oakland, CA 94607
☎ 510 893 8555 TOLL FREE: 800 275 8555
fax 510 893 8572
email: info@lonelyplanet.com

UK
10a Spring Place, London NW5 3BH
☎ 020 7428 4800 fax 020 7428 4828
email: go@lonelyplanet.co.uk

France
1 rue du Dahomey, 75011 Paris
☎ 01 55 25 33 00 fax 01 55 25 33 01
email: bip@lonelyplanet.fr
www.lonelyplanet.fr

World Wide Web: www.lonelyplanet.com *or* AOL keyword: lp
Lonely Planet Images: www.lonelyplanetimages.com.au